THE GREAT PHARAOHS

TEXT BY
T.G.H. James

CONTENTS

EDITED BY
Valeria Manferto De Fabianis
Laura Accomazzo

GRAPHIC DESIGN
Patrizia Balocco Lovisetti
Paola Piacco

1
In Tutankhamun's cartouche on the left, the scarab symbolizes the rising sun. The cartouche on the right (Usimara Setepenra) includes the first name of Ramesses II.

2 and 3
Tutankhamun (the mask from his second sarcophagus is on the left) and Ramesses II (his portrait is the head seen on the right) are the most famous pharaohs.

However, that does not signify they are 'known': we are almost ignorant of the life and death of the former.

4
A red precious stone symbolizes the heart of the king in this amulet found on Tutankhamun's mummy.

5
The tip of a ritual staff bearing the king's first name projects from the fist of a colossal statue of Ramesses II.

WHITE STAR PUBLISHERS

White Star Publishers® is a registered trademark property of Edizioni White Star s.r.l.

THE GREAT PHARAOHS
© 2004, 2011 Edizioni White Star s.r.l.
Via M. Germano, 10 - 13100 Vercelli, Italy
www.whitestar.it
Revised edition

ISBN 978-88-544-0630-8
1 2 3 4 5 6   15 14 13 12 11

Printed in China

Taken from:

TUTANKHAMUN
The eternal splendor of the boy pharaoh
© 2000 White Star S.r.l.
ISBN 88-8095-451-2

RAMESSES II
© 2002 White Star S.r.l.
ISBN 88-8095-826-7

PREFACE

Plutarch, the first-century Greek moralist and memorialist, composed a series of Parallel Lives in which he took pairs of famous Greeks and Romans and considered them against each other in what they had achieved, in what they had in common, and in what they differed. He made use of straight history reported stories and gossip. What would he have made of the pairing of Tutankhamun and Ramesses II? Nothing, I suspect. Setting on one side the fact that neither was a Creek or a Roman, I very much doubt whether Plutarch would have thought it even possible to make much from the lives of two so different monarchs. He would certainly not have hoard of Tutankhamun. He might, on the other hand, have known something of Ramesses II, if only as the Rampsinitus of Herodotus; but probably not enough to warrant even a separate biography, like the one he wrote of Artaxerxes Mnemon, the fouth-century Persian king.

The only significant ground on which Tutankhamun and Ramesses II can be compared is that of present-day reputation. It is just possible that if a poll were taken, more people would know Tutankhamun's name than Ramesses; but not among those who have visited Egypt, or have some interest in and knowledge of ancient Egypt. Tutankhamun has been generally known only since 1922 when his tomb was discovered. It was the archaeological sensation of the 1920s, and the extraordinary collection of objects that made up his funerary equipment has subsequently never ceased to astonish. For some people Tutankhamun is invested with a kind of personality in being the son of Akhenaten – a possibility not yet established as fact – and therefore blessed with the aura of Atenism; he is thought by a few to have been murdered, the victim of an ancient plot. His life was short, his reign of little consequence in the long span of Egyptian history. But his face gazes brightly and clearly from his golden mask, recognizable and seemingly sympathetic; he is known and can be seen – probably fallaciously – to be human in ways not available

to most ancient Egyptian kings. In his tomb were things from his childhood, the clothes he had worn, his writing equipment, his precious objects, his weapons, the chariots in which he had travelled, models of the ships in which he progressed on the Nile. It seems possible to get closer to him than to any other royal person of remote antiquity.

Unfortunately, on cool consideration it can be seen that this sentimental assessment of Tutankhamun is based on a kind of mirage created by a haze of uncertainty in a desert of ignorance. In the king-lists of the Nineteenth Dynasty his name is omitted, deliberately, along with those of his putative father, Akhenaten, of that king's successor, Neferuneferuaten (whoever that may have been), and of Tutankhamun's successor, the upstart Ay. So, by family association with' that heretic of Akhetaten' he was expunged from Egyptian history and memory, and ony began to achieve some visibility in the nineteenth century when his name, and more particularly his prenomen, Nebkheperure, were found on occasional monuments and small objects. His name had scarcely lived as he would have wished. Then, his destiny was changed by the discovery of his tomb and its marvellous contents, most of which were inscribed with his name. Tutankhamun now is indeed known, and his name lives and shines brightly.

For Ramesses II the situation could scarcely be more different. Throughout antiquity his memory persisted in history and in legend. From the Biblical narrative of the Jewish exodus from Egypt, his name occurs as that of one of the two store-cities on which the Israeites laboured, and in the description of Egypt as the land of Ramesses, as if Ramesses was by itself enough to identify the country of the oppression. His was one of the first cartouches to be indentified by Champollion, and as soon as this royal name was recognized, his presence was detected throughout Egypt and Nubia as the great builder of temples and erector of colossal statues. No special pleading had to be advanced to make the case for his greatness and importance as a mighty warrior

6 and 7
The goddess Nut (left) appears in one of the wall paintings in
Tutankhamun's tomb. The king himself (right) is greeted by
Osiris, the god who was resurrected and rules over the dead.

8
Two seated colossi flank Ramesses II's pylon in the temple of Luxor. The pharaoh had this new monumental entrance and the courtyard behind built in the temple, which was much smaller than Karnak.

10–11
Tutankhamun hunting with his royal bride Ankesanamun.

12–13
The colossi of Ramesses II north of the entrance at Abu Simbel have been defaced by the 'signatures' of ancient visitors.

Pharaoh, and also as a prodigious begetter of children. His great tomb in the Valley of the Kings had been open in part since antiquity, although huge mounds of debris prevented its clearance and full examination until recent years: it is yielded little more than scraps and hints of the splendid funerary equipment it is thought once to have contained. The supposition to be that this equipment must have been many times more lavish and opulent than that of the short-reigned, unimportant, Tutankhamun, but that could well be wrong. A royal funerary equipment contained what was needed for the successful posthumous existence of the monarch, and the size of a tomb was determined not by the amount of material it was to contain, but the accommodation it provided for the many texts needed to assist the progress and well-being of the deceased in the journey to eternity with the sun-god.

Ramesses II surely took more 'treasure' for his life beyond death than Tutankhamun, but not necessarily much more.

Ramesses II departed this life after a very long reign. The facial features of his mummy (rescued in antiquity from destruction) reveal him, not surprisingly, as a very old man, but still recognizable as the strong, handsome, ruler, so well-known from the many true sculptures which have helped to keep his memory alive. In this respect he is more fortunate than Tutankhamun, whose beauty and even vulnerability, finely delineated in the death-mask and the few remaining stone sculptures (including those usurped by Horemheb), are caricatured by the wretched condition of his mummified head. In death, therefore, Ramesses could balance the relatively successful survival of his body in a state fit for his posthumous existence, against the loss of his funerary equipment, much of which was also needed to secure his full survival. Tutankhamun was not so fortunate. When it comes to a consideration of the lives and reigns of the two kings, there can be no question about the victor. Ramesses wins on most counts. 'And quite rightly so', he would undoubtedly have said.

Everything went Ramesses ' way: that was how his reputation was constructed in his lifetime – a lifetime which was so long that the bombastic claim that he was the great conqueror of Qadesh, put out in the propaganda of his early years, could be established as incontrovertible truth as time went by. Nevertheless, there were in his reign some major triumphs: on the diplomatic front, the Hittite Treaty and his marriages of convenience to foreign princesses, and the consequent peace which so much benefited Egypt; domestically, the settled conditions which resulted from this peace allowed much of the national energies to be channelled into great constructions. It is a tragedy that from this field of activity so little remains of what may have been the great king's greatest achievement, the city of Piramesse, the Delta Residence par excellence, of which he was so proud.

Unlike the vast and impressive temples which were built, increased and embellished in his name, Piramesse was a show-place for all to enjoy, accessible and full of wonders. Sadly, like his tomb, it was, relatively soon after his death, abandoned, and largely dismantled, the great sculptures and obelisks (many of which had been usurped by Ramesses and brought to the Delta from Memphis, Heliopolis and elsewhere) were dispersed to Tanis and Bubastis. Egyptian kings may have maintained a pious deceit of honouring their monuments, or annexing them for their own purposes. Even so, the rulers of the Twenty-first and Twenty-second Dynasties did not bother to remove Ramesses' names from the obelisks and sculptures moved from Piramesse, with the result that for many years Ramesses II could also be credited with the foundation of the great city of Tanis. His reputation did not suffer, and it did not suffer subsequently. His name was always big, and it remains big. Tutankhamun is in a different league. He may never have expected much during his short life, and he left little in the way of visible monuments by which he could be remembered; but an accident of fate preserved his tomb, and secured for him an unexpected, and belated celebrity. He would, I believe, be very surprised to find himself so established on a pinnacle of notoriety. Ramesses II would surely be singularly vexed to have such a close companion in the Egyptian hall of fame.

TUTANKHAMUN

CONTENTS

14–15
A winged uraeus-serpent protects
Tutankhamun's cartouche on the king's
throne.

16–17
The nemes headdress on Tutankhamun's
burial mask is made from gold and blue
glass-paste inserts.

PREFACE

The superlatives applied to Howard Carter and the momentous discovery of the tomb of Tutankhamun, piled up and reiterated over the years since 1922, should have dulled the responses of most people. In fact, interest in the tomb is perhaps greater today than at any time since the early years of the discovery.

When the tomb was found in November 1922, the news broke with unexpected force on a world public which seemed to be only too ready to enjoy the thrill and drama of what was happening in distant Luxor. It was not as if there had been no archaeological discoveries of importance in the few years since the First World War; but nothing could compete with the tantalizing revelation of a tomb entrance, blocked and sealed with the promise of untold treasure beyond. Carter himself was not at all sanguine: he had received disappointments in the past, when expected success turned to naught.

Now to discover a new tomb in the Valley of the Kings was in itself a dramatic achievement; to discover one which was still furnished with a huge quantity of remarkable objects, and an intact coffin and burial, was almost too much to expect.

The representatives of the world press descended on Luxor like vultures on a dying prey. Every stage in the clearance of the tomb was watched with close attention; every day brought new insights into ancient Egyptian life and death.

18–19
Detail from the Golden Throne. The brilliance of the colored inlays heightens the impression of regal elegance.

The atmosphere, already heavily charged with the tension of discovery, was clouded by the inadequacy of the channels of information, controlled by the agreement made by the Earl of Carnarvon with *The Times*. And then, when the opening of the Burial Chamber, and the realization that an intact burial lay within, were followed by the tragic death of Lord Carnarvon, rumor and suspicion took over, and allowed those who find esoteric forces in all Egyptian things to indulge in a welter of fanciful imagination and fertile invention. And so it went on: the progress of the clearance was dogged by drama, tragedy, misunderstanding, and bad temper. Howard Carter was a hero, and he was fêted wherever he went; but he was also a sad, disillusioned man, whose success never quite brought him to the haven of content and happiness which he deserved.

In the last thirty years there has been a remarkable surge of interest in Tutankhamun. International exhibitions have brought selected treasures to the fascinated gaze of millions of people. The huge increase in tourism to Egypt has allowed waves of visitors to swamp the Valley of the Kings, to gaze in wonder at the coffin in the young king's tiny tomb; and in Cairo to view the overwhelming riches in the Egyptian Museum. Books have proliferated; Carter has been honored and vilified; the treasures have been lauded, and occasionally scorned. In this volume, a wider range of material than usual is offered for close examination in a series of outstanding photographs.

Tutankhamun and his times

TUTANKHAMUN AND HIS TIMES
The historical background

When the Earl of Carnarvon and Howard Carter entered the Antechamber of Tutankhamun's tomb on November 27, 1922, they found themselves standing in what looked like a rather superior furniture store, abandoned for three thousand years. It was both thrilling and worrying: as Carter later wrote, 'everywhere the glint of gold'. But what problems faced them! In due course, reinforced with help from specialists loaned by the Metropolitan Museum and the Egyptian Government, Carter set about untangling the jumble of objects which were placed and stacked topsy-turvy in that confined space. Among the pieces which caught his eye on first inspection was the chair standing beneath the great couch with hippopotamus heads. Now often called the Golden Throne, it impressed the excavators with its dazzling splendor and sheer beauty. The panel forming the back of this chair was its most striking part. Carter claimed that it 'was the chief glory of the throne and I have no hesitation in claiming for it that it is the most beautiful thing that has yet been found in Egypt'. What concerns us here, however, is one element in the decoration of the panel which would certainly have been spotted by Carter at first sight. It is the sun disk at the top of the scene, sending down its life-giving rays on the seated king and his wife. Although Carter may not have taken much scholarly interest in the developing historical debate about the Amarna Period and the rise and fall of the deity, the Aten (or Aton), he can scarcely have failed to make a connection with what he had seen in his early days in Egypt.

When he was excavating with Flinders Petrie in the spring of 1892 he would have met this motive of the Aten during the excursions he made with Petrie, visiting the rock-cut inscriptions set up by the king, Akhenaten, to mark the sacred area of his new city. He would remember his drawing of that scene in the tomb of Akhenaten which was used by Petrie to illustrate his report in the *Daily Graphic*; it too contained the Aten motif. He would also recall the short time he spent with Percy Newberry in January 1893 when they began an abortive campaign to copy the scenes and inscriptions in the northern group of

private tombs at El-Amarna. The life-giving rays of the Aten were ubiquitous, and Carter drew several scenes containing them before work in the tombs was brought to a halt. Carter retained an affection for the site, although he did not, it seems, revisit it until March 1918, after his first short season in the Valley of the Kings. At that time Carnarvon was actively looking for a second site at which to work. Carter pressed the case for El-Amarna very strongly: 'For you it is an ideal site, convenient in every way... with a dahabiyeh you would never be more than a mile from the scene of operations, beautiful desert, light and clean digging and one need hardly say with luck the chance of beautiful things'. In the years before the First World War, the Germans had worked there, and found much important sculpture, including the famous head of Nefertiti.

Howard Carter, therefore, was well aware of the significance of that sun disk when he saw it on the back-panel of the Golden Throne, but he may have been puzzled at finding such a potent symbol of recent heresy on such a striking object in the tomb of the king in whose reign normality in Egypt's religious affairs had been re-established. The taint of Atenism was undoubtedly difficult for the Egyptian monarchy to eliminate at this point and in due course it would lead to the removal of Akhenaten, Smenkhkare, Tutankhamun and his successor Ay from the official record of dynastic succession. Only with King Horemheb could the legitimate sequence recommence; he at least seemed to have a paternity unblemished by heresy, although he had served in high office under Tutankhamun. But all these problems and consequences arose from what had developed in the shining reign of Amenophis III.

To understand, in so far as is possible, it is necessary to go back to that glorious time when Egypt's power abroad was at its height, and the splendor of its culture at home was evident in most aspects of life, and especially in the arts of sculpture, relief, painting, in the small crafts of ceramics, metalwork, glass-making, and in the production of small, intimate items which enhanced the private lives of those who could afford them.

24–25
The face of Tutankhamun's Golden Mask: a portrait by a master artist in beaten gold.

26
One of the two lion heads placed on either side of the seat of the Golden Throne; they represent the east and west horizons over which they stand guard.

27
A scene of intimacy between Tutankhamun and Ankhesenamun on the back of the Golden Throne. The queen anoints the king with perfumed ointment from a stemmed vessel.

It was the first half of the fourteenth century BC. After the successful military campaigns of the earlier kings of the Eighteenth Dynasty, in Asia and Nubia, a state of equilibrium had been established in the eastern part of the Egyptian empire. It was not an empire of domination by military might, of the kind so often found subsequently in the ancient world. The Egyptian king maintained his influence by threat of intervention and by the lavish use of subsidies paid to the small rulers whose territories made up the empire. Powerful neighbors to the east were equally restrained from attacking by means of dynastic alliances and again by the dispensation of valuable gifts – in effect subsidies – from the Egyptian king. The parade of power and wealth by Egypt encouraged the expectations of subordinate powers, and also the more powerful neighbors. The King of Mitanni, writing to Amenophis III, expressed what was no doubt the common view in saying that 'gold was like dust in my brother's land'.

The possession of empire affected Egypt in many ways, and among those that are less easy to quantify were those involving religion. Egyptian religion, diverse in its variety of deities and local traditions, was not easy to export to other countries. In this respect the Egyptians were not a proselytizing people. There was, however, always the possibility for additional traditions from elsewhere to be imported and grafted directly or by partial assimilation into the body of Egyptian religious ideas. It seems likely that a need developed which required the acceptance of a conception of divinity of more universal application. The course of change led, almost imperceptibly, to the evolution of parts of the traditional Egyptian cult of the sun into a breakaway sub-cult in which the disk of the sun itself, the Aten (the Egyptian word for sun disk) became the principal, even the sole, object of worship.

The signs of this kind of sun worship can be traced back to at least the reign of Tuthmosis IV (c. 1400–1390 BC); but its growth became more marked in the reign of Amenophis III (c. 1390– 1352 BC), when some important officials included Aten references in hymns which glorified the sun as the creator and sustainer of life. It is possible that this development may have been promoted by the king's chief wife, Queen Tiye, who exercised unusual influence in many areas of life. Amenophis III, who may have suffered long periods of ill-health, seemed content to allow this apparent transfer of power, while he restricted his activities to the domestic sphere. It has often been suggested that he succumbed to luxury and soft living – *la dolce vita* – but it is not easy to prove that this was the case.

28
Portrait-head of King Amenophis III wearing the blue crown. It is made of painted plaster, and was found in the great deposit of sculpture in the Karnak temple.

29
Head of Queen Tiye, found in Sinai. In spite of the very small scale, the sculptor has succeeded in conveying the strong character of this determined lady.

What is certain, however, is that his son and successor, also called Amenophis, readily embraced the growing cult of the Aten, and began its promotion, perhaps even before he became king. His mother, Queen Tiye, who continued to be a powerful political influence after his accession to the throne, may have been an encouraging agent in the move towards Atenism. An even greater supporter was the new king's wife, Nefertiti. Some historians believe that Amenophis III elevated his son to be a co-regent with himself some years before his death, but the evidence is mostly circumstantial. It must be admitted that historical evidence for the whole of the so-called Amarna Period is often inexplicit. Nevertheless, the more acceptable view is that the son became king after the death of his father in about 1352 BC. He retained the name Amenophis 'Amun is content' for the first few years of his reign, and then changed it to Akhenaten 'who is beneficial to the Aten'. In Thebes his father had built on a grand scale in honor of the great imperial god Amon-Re, and it was in Thebes that Amenophis IV, supported by his wife Nefertiti, began his campaign to establish the primacy of the Aten cult. Here he built an entirely new and original temple in honor of the Aten very close to the great temple of Amon-Re at Karnak. In design it was quite unlike the normal Egyptian temple, and in its decoration, in its reliefs and sculptures, it departed from what was conventional both in style and in content. It was a very provocative act, and it brought the royal family into direct opposition with the traditional priestly colleges, and also the established bureaucracy, which itself was closely integrated into the religious establishment.

It is not difficult to imagine the state of tension which built up in Thebes after this revolutionary turn of events. There could be no peaceful co-existence between the old and the new religious regimes.

The formal suppression of the ancient cults followed, but no act of this kind could destroy old beliefs and allegiances; the situation in the capital must have become unbearable for both sides.

30
The exaggerated facial features of this colossus shows Akhenaten in the style of his early reign, almost in caricature but strikingly dramatic. From Karnak.

31
Sculptor's trial or model showing Akhenaten, Nefertiti and two daughters making floral offerings to the Aten. From the royal tomb at El-Amarna.

As far as the king was concerned, nothing but a complete break with the past, religiously, politically and territorially, would do. His own beliefs in the Aten, the divine and sole creator of the universe, had developed in these early years, and, as he claimed himself, the full practice of life under the Aten would have to be continued in a place unsullied by the old religions. And so, in his sixth year, having changed his name to Akhenaten, he moved his capital from Thebes to a place in Middle Egypt, about 350 kilometres to the north. Here the new life could be practiced, purged of all past associations. The chosen place was a virgin plain set in a great bay of rocky hills on the east bank of the Nile. Here the sun daily could be observed to rise in a dip in the hills. It was to be called Akhetaten, 'horizon of the Aten'.

The precinct of the Aten, the area delimited as the domain of the god, was marked by a series of boundary stelae – inscriptions setting out the limits of Akhetaten, and establishing the principles by which life would be lived there by the royal family, and consequently by those who chose to follow the king to the new city. The laying out of Akhetaten was one of the earliest pieces of conscious town-planning in the ancient world. The great Aten temple was the focal point; it was quite unlike the traditional Egyptian temple, an open structure with many altars for offerings to the god.

There were palaces, processional ways, huge administrative buildings, areas given over for fine villas for the high officials. There were districts for servicing the city with food and with industrial products such as pottery and glass. Outlying satellite villages housed workmen who, living apart from the main city and undoubtedly unfamiliar with the nature and rituals of the new religion, practiced their own personal cults in much the way that Egyptians in lowly levels of society had always done.

In Akhetaten the devotees of Atenism could follow the new life without being constantly aware of the disapprobation of those whose traditions were being destroyed. Akhetaten became a kind of cocoon in which the king and his family could promote and serve the Aten, loyally supported by those who ran the new bureaucracy and serviced the city. Every aspect of life was dominated by the Aten, whose worship became, seemingly, the supreme, even the sole, purpose of existence. The great hymns which contain the essence

his mother.... How various are your works!... Sole god, like whom there is none other... You establish every man in his place, making their sustenance... tongues made different in speech... their complexions distinct, for you have differentiated country from country... You make the seasons to allow all that you have created to prosper...'

At the end, Akhenaten's own position in the scheme of things is established: 'There is no one else who knows you except your son, Neferkheperure-Waenre [Akhenaten's prenomen]. You have made him skilled in your ways and in your power.'

In the early years of the twentieth century the publication of significant texts, like that of the great hymn, led scholars to study the nature of the Aten revolution. Historians like James Henry Breasted were so impressed by the Atenist hymns and their similarities to some of the Biblical psalms that they not only proclaimed the monotheistic nature of Atenism, but even saw in it the germs of Christianity. Modern Egyptologists are inclined to make more modest claims. It is now generally accepted that

of the new theology, and usually considered to be the compositions of Akhenaten himself, provide the evidence by which Atenism may be judged. The greatest of these hymns is found in the unused Amarna tomb of Ay, 'master of all the king's horses', who later succeeded Tutankhamun for a few years. Here is the flavor of Atenism:

'You arise beautiful in the horizon of heaven, O living Aten initiator of life when you shine forth in the eastern horizon, filling every land with your beauty... The earth grows bright when you have arisen in the horizon... The whole land performs its work. All cattle are content in their meadows. Trees and pastures flourish... All animals gambol on their feet... The one who makes men's fluid grow in women.... bringing to life the son in the body of

Atenism was monotheistic, perhaps the first religion with a single nature to its deity; but to consider it in any way as a precursor of Christianity presses the evidence beyond possibility. Verbal similarities are very seductive, but establish very little. If the content of the Amarna hymns is examined it can be shown that the phraseology of the praise to the Aten, and the claims made on its behalf, can be found in earlier hymns addressed to other Egyptian gods, especially the sun-god Re. What is special at Amarna is the exclusive focus of worship, and the emphasis placed on Akhenaten as the conduit for the delivery of the divine power of the Aten to the Egyptian people. Atenism was in effect wholly identified with Akhenaten and his family; the impression gained is that the new creed was tailor-made for them.

The rest of the dwellers at Akhetaten and elsewhere in Egypt could participate only through Akhenaten. Atenism placed almost all its emphasis on worship, and not on morality in the Judaeo-Christian sense. You were to order your life in accordance with the Egyptian principle of *ma'et*.

In Amarna terms this meant living by order, by strict balance, by conformity with the proper regularity of life.

It was a kind of reinterpretation of the idea of truth embodied in the goddess named Ma'et, who played an important part in the ordering of conventional Egyptian life, and in the idea of judgement in the after-life.

A new and unusual feature of Atenism and life at Akhetaten was the emphasis placed on the inner circle of the royal family, on Akhenaten, his wife Nefertiti, and the six daughters of their marriage. In almost every scene in which the king is shown, he is accompanied by Nefertiti,

and often by a selection of children. Many surviving scenes represent the king and queen in intimate, affectionate relations, usually with daughters sitting on laps, climbing over them, being held up for embrace, standing beside them. The impression is given that the family was unusually close-knit, and more loving than was common for the period; it undoubtedly formed part of Amarna propaganda that this aspect of royal family life at Akhetaten should be emphasized.

In all probability it was in the wider circle of the extended royal family that Tutankhamun was brought up. He was at first named Tutankhaten, 'living image of the Aten'; this name, with such a positive reference to the Aten, indicates that he must have been fairly closely connected with the principal royal family of Akhenaten and Nefertiti. But his parentage has never been convincingly established.

There is only one reference to him from the time of
the reign of Akhenaten: on a block from one of the
destroyed buildings of Akhetaten he is described as 'king's
son of his body'. Such a statement establishes royal
parentage, but it does not make his mother Nefertiti. It is
very likely that Tutankhamun was fathered by
Akhenaten, but by a secondary wife. The probable
candidate is Kiya, the very existence of whom became
known only in fairly recent years. She is referred to as 'the
greatly beloved wife of the King of Upper and Lower
Egypt... beauteous child of the living Aten who will live
for ever and ever'. It is possible that some of Kiya's
funerary equipment was included among the confused
collection of Amarna material found in tomb 55 in the
Valley of the Kings, which had been discovered by
Theodore Davis in 1907; it lay not very far from the tomb
of Tutankhamun. It is unlikely that the young king's
parentage will ever be determined with certainty unless
good new textual evidence is found. Even scientific
evidence at present can do little more than confirm a
family relationship.

Tutankhaten therefore will have spent his early years in the royal harem at Akhetaten, brought up, presumably, in a culture dominated by the cult of the Aten. He would have had little reasonable expectancy of becoming king; but he may have been seen by some ambitious officials, and even his mother, as having good prospects. In these early years he could have absorbed much of the grace and color of the palace environment in which he lived. In its prime, which lasted for such a short time, Akhetaten was undoubtedly a place of vibrant beauty. The pitiful remnants of the city, which had been utterly devastated after the collapse of Atenism, have been painstakenly retrieved by excavation over the last century, and they show how strikingly the palaces and villas were enlivened with wall decorations in which a new, naturalistic style of painting conveyed much greater freedom and vivacity than in preceding times. The standards of craftsmanship and perfection of design which characterized the art of

in the tradition of Akhenaten's reign. The intimacy suggested in the queen's approach to the king is apparent; the whole is dominated by the Aten, its descending rays ending in little hands, some of which hold the *ankh*, the hieroglyph for 'life'.

It might be thought that life in Akhetaten was idyllic; that, no doubt, was what Akhenaten hoped to achieve. Unfortunately, much as he might have wished it, it was impossible for him, King of Upper and Lower Egypt, to shut himself away from the business of state, or from the problems arising in the Egyptian vassal states in Asia Minor. There is little evidence from the time of how the greater part of Egypt fared during the Amarna years, but it is probable that a fairly tight control was exercised. Some indication of the efficiency of this control is provided by the way in which, at a late stage in the reign, royal agents scoured the country seeking out and destroying in visible inscriptions the names of the

the reign of Amenophis III were still in evidence, but now distinguished by a degree of free expression quite alien to conventional Egyptian art. Innovations were introduced in the early years of Akhenaten's reign, but much of what was then produced had a gauche, unfinished, quality to it. But as the reign advanced, and after the move to Akhetaten, artists came to terms with the changes in style and convention and, still employing the skills they had acquired in their years of apprenticeship under the old regime, began to produce works of surpassing beauty, especially in the field of sculpture. The best of what was new in the Amarna style was not jettisoned when Akheteten was abandoned, and many of the objects found in the tomb of Tutankhamun incorporate the freedom of design and the intimacy in the representation of royalty which distinguished Amarna art. Again we may return to that Golden Throne and its back panel which carries a scene wholly

old gods, and particularly of Amun. Wherever that last hated name occurred it was cut out, even at the tops of obelisks, and the highest point of temples. Such a successful campaign needed remarkable organization, even though a flavor of desperation may be detected in it.

No such attention to detail was applied to foreign affairs. A surprising survival from the subsequent destruction of Akhetaten was part of the state archive consisting of clay tablets containing letters and dispatches from vassal rulers, written mostly in Accadian, the diplomatic *lingua franca* of the period. The subject rulers complain of their neglect by the Egyptian king, and they set out the problems they faced from powerful rulers like the Hittites in the north. The failure of Egypt to maintain its presence in Asia Minor also encouraged the warlike intentions of some of these vassals to renew old antagonisms with their small neighbors.

When Akhenaten died in about 1336 BC he did not leave a united country or a settled empire. A strong hand was needed to keep the ship of state steady, and to re-establish Egypt's authority in the East. An attempt to secure continuity for the Atenist revolution had been made by Akhenaten, who had a co-regent appointed in advance of his death. Paucity of evidence again prevents a certain identification of this co-regent. The name was Neferneferuaten; for long it has been thought that this person was a half-brother of Akhenaten called Smenkhkare; it has more recently been suggested that it was none other than Nefertiti herself, whose prenomen in cartouche was also Neferneferuaten. Nefertiti's disappearance from the Amarna scene towards the end of Akhenaten's reign has otherwise been ascribed either to her death, or to her disgrace for reasons unknown. The matter cannot satisfactorily be solved without further, more explicit evidence. What remains clear, however, is that during the short independent reign of Neferneferuaten the first moves were made to re-establish relations with the old

bureaucracy and the suppressed (but certainly not destroyed) priestly cadres at Thebes and elsewhere. It might be thought surprising if such moves towards reconciliation took place under a ruler who might have been Nefertiti; she had seemingly been so closely associated with Akhenaten in the development of Atenism. However, the interpretation of slim evidence from antiquity is always subject to uncertainty, and can lead to mistakes.

38
Carving on the back of the trial of a head of Nefertiti.
Here a person, even the queen, kneels with arms
raised in adoration. From El-Amarna.

39
Quartzite face of Akhenaten from El-Amarna, made
to fit into a relief of the king with inlays of different
materials. The eyes and brows were separately inlaid.

40–41
Wonderfully stylish head of Nefertiti carved as a trial
for a larger-scale relief for the temple at Karnak.
She wears her characteristic crown with pendent
uraei and flowing ribbons.

After a very short reign Neferneferuaten died in about 1336 BC, to be succeeded by Tutankhaten. He was very young, probably no more than eight years old; but he had royal parentage, and therefore the necessary legitimacy to succeed. His position was strengthened by an early marriage to Ankhesenpaaten, the third daughter of Akhenaten and Nefertiti. She had been born before the move from Thebes to Akhetaten in the sixth year of her father's reign, so it is unlikely that she was much less than fourteen or fifteen when she became the wife of the much younger Tutankhaten. She was, nevertheless, approaching an age when she could have given useful support to her juvenile husband. She would, much later, after his death, display an independence of mind which was wholly in the character of the royal women of the Amarna Period. At the start of the reign, however, there had to be more mature support than that of a wife in her early teens. The position of regent was occupied by Ay, who had been closely associated with the royal family at least since its move to Akhetaten. Under Akhenaten he had been 'master of all the king's horses'; in the new reign he took the title 'god's father' and he is also credited with the secular title 'vizir' on one of the gold fragments found in the deposit which Theodore Davis thought was the tomb of Tutankhamun.

The usual shortage of evidence makes it difficult to chart with any detail the course of events which followed the accession of Tutankhaten. Early in his reign, however, he and his wife, presumably on the advice of their advisers, changed their names to Tutankhamun and Ankhesenamun. With the Aten element replaced by Amun it would be easier to proceed politically to the reconciliation with the representatives of the old regime. There seems to have been a particular problem as far as Thebes was concerned. At Thebes, the old political center, the Atenist revolution had begun; at Thebes were the greatest temples in the land; Thebes was the city of Amun. At Thebes, no doubt, resentment against the heretic regime was strongest; the move to El-Amarna had certainly affected Thebes not only religiously, but also, and perhaps even more so, economically. Thebes, therefore, was not a promising place in which to establish the royal Residence and Court for the new reign. Consequently, in Tutankhamun's second year the move was made to Memphis in the north. This city had always been a place of major importance in Egypt; it had been so since it was founded as the first capital of the united land of Upper and Lower Egypt by King Menes at the beginning of the First Dynasty (c. 3100 BC). Memphis had remained an important commercial city, and during the Eighteenth Dynasty it had become the base of the Lower Egyptian vizir, and the center of a developing administrative and military bureaucracy. From Memphis it was easier to mount expeditions and control military operations in Asia Minor than from Thebes. Memphis was also the cult-center of the great god Ptah, one of the oldest and most influential of Egypt's deities; he seems to have avoided many of the worst indignities suffered by other deities during the Amarna Period. Memphis was a very cosmopolitan city where new influences could be absorbed

without causing resentment. It seems to have taken Atenism in its stride. A temple to the Aten was established there, and also at nearby Heliopolis, the great cult-center of the sun-god Re. The trauma of Thebes was absent from Memphis, and the latter was in most ways the obvious choice for the new royal Residence. Meanwhile, the brilliant city of Akhetaten was abandoned, and over the years its stones were pillaged for buildings elsewhere; its palaces, offices and villas were allowed to crumble; the temples of the hated Aten were laid waste. Blown sand covered the site and kept it hidden for three thousand years. Akhenaten was anathematized as the 'criminal of Akhetaten'.

In spite of the later blotting-out of the memory of the Amarna Pharaohs, something of what was accomplished in Tutankhamun's reign can be discovered. Any initiatives were of course not taken by the young king, but by his advisers. Above all, in seniority at least, was the regent Ay. Probably more important were powerful officials like the Treasurer, Maya, and, particularly, the General, Horemheb. Such men controlled policy and its execution, in the name of the king. Apart from the moves towards reconciliation there were more practical matters like the reconstruction of damaged sanctuaries. The most important evidence of what happened comes from one surviving inscription from Karnak. Its date is not known, and it has survived due to the fact that Horemheb, when he became king after the death of Ay, appropriated the text, inserting his own name wherever that of Tutankhamun occurred. Happily there are enough surviving traces of the young king's name to confirm that the inscription belongs to his reign.

The theme of this inscription is reconciliation. In the semi-circular lunette at the top of the stela Tutankhamun is shown before Amon-Re of Karnak and his divine consort Mut. The god bestows divine power on the king. The representations are carved in the fluid artistic style of the late Amarna Period. In the preamble to the main text the king's full titulary is given, followed by a long series of epithets in which, among other things, he is said to be beloved of Amon-Re, Lord of the Thrones of the Two Lands, of Atum of Heliopolis, of Re-Herakhty, of Ptah and of Thoth; here there is no religious discrimination. The text then goes on to state, 'When his Majesty arose as king, the temples of the gods and goddesses, from Elephantine [in the south] to the marshes of the Delta [in the north] had fallen into decay; their shrines fallen into desolation, overgrown with weeds; their sanctuaries as if they had never existed; their halls had become foot-paths'. In consequence, the king took counsel to see what could be done to please Amun and the other gods. Cult-statues of gold and precious stones were made, temples repaired and rebuilt, endowments of land and people were renewed, so that 'the gods and goddesses who are in this land are joyous in heart; the owners of shrines are glad; lands are in a state of jubilation and festivity; joyfulness exists throughout the country; a happy state has come about'.

43

Red quartzite colossal statue made for Tutankhamun's unfinished and abandoned funerary temple. It was later usurped by Ay and Horemheb and set up in their funerary temple at Medinet Habu.

44–45
By a magical fiction Tutankhamun drives his chariot with prancing horses into the confused mass of his Nubian enemies. With bow and arrow and the help of his dogs and soldiers he smites 'this land of vile Cush'.

45 bottom
On both ends of the painted box from which these details are taken Tutankhamun is shown as a destructive sphinx, wreaking havoc on behalf of Egypt. Here he tramples the Asiatic and the Nubian.

itself, had been executed in the reign of Horemheb. His name could be read everywhere, and then, before the discovery of Tutankhamun's tomb, it could hardly have been conceived that such fine work could have been produced in the reign of a royal nonentity. Subsequently it has become increasingly clear, as a result of scholarly scrutiny of texts, that Horemheb freely appropriated from Tutankhamun, substituting his name for that of his young predecessor. This was not uncommon in ancient Egypt, but in the case of Horemheb and Tutankhamun its extent points very clearly to a conscious attempt by the former to eradicate the latter from the record.

Horemheb himself probably first achieved high office in the reign of Akhenaten, but he did not exercise great authority until Tutankhamun came to the throne. From the many titles, civil and military, which he held, and which are enumerated in the tomb he had constructed as a commoner at Saqqara, it is clear that he had a controlling hand in most spheres of government. He may have throughout his career been based at Memphis, enabling him to keep the regime at Akhetaten at arm's length; but under Tutankhamun he was Chief General, Deputy of the king, High Steward, Overseer of all the works of the king, Overseer of all divine offices. The tomb of Horemheb at Saqqara, high on the desert escarpment close to Memphis, is decorated with reliefs of the finest quality, very much in the style of the Luxor reliefs copied by Howard Carter, but even outdoing them in the representation of individuals and in the grouping of figures. Craftsmen in the Memphite area had always excelled in the carving of fine relief in good quality limestone. Traditional Memphite style had, it seems,

Tutankhamun was not alone in his campaigns. Here an Egyptian foot soldier stabs a Nubian. Note the difference between the Egyptian and Nubian shields, and the rare full-face depiction of one fallen enemy.

Positive evidence of work carried out at Thebes, the heartland of Amon-Re, can be seen in the temple of Luxor, one of the most beautiful of Egyptian temples, founded by Amenophis III. In the great hall containing a massive colonnade, Tutankhamun's agents arranged for a wonderful series of reliefs, possibly started under Amenophis III, to be completed; it was in celebration of the Feast of Opet in which the sacred marriage between Amon-Re and his consort Mut was solemnized annually. These wonderful sunk reliefs depict the processions by land and river of the divine image of Amon-Re from Karnak to Luxor. These were the reliefs which Howard Carter was commissioned to draw for the publication planned by Alan Gardiner, but sadly never completed. At the time – it was during the First World War – it was reasonably thought that these reliefs, like the colonnade

remained largely uninfluenced by the grossest mannerisms of early Amarna art, but it had assimilated the fluid grace of the later period, as is evident in the reliefs in the tombs of Horemheb and his contemporaries at Saqqara.

There is some evidence to suggest that small military operations were conducted in Asia Minor and Nubia during the young king's reign. Here can be detected the initiative of Horemheb, although he may not have supervised the campaigns personally. Much needed to be done to repair the condition of the Egyptian empire, but it is unlikely that any large-scale expeditions could be mounted while the country of Egypt was recovering from the neglect and physical destruction of the reign of Akhenaten. While there is very little direct evidence to demonstrate the steps taken under Tutankhamun to

return the country to a pre-Amarna state of affairs, confirmation that much was successfully achieved is provided by the apparently settled position of the country during the reigns of Horemheb and of his successors, the first kings of the Nineteenth Dynasty.

When Tutankhamun's tomb was discovered in 1922 there were at first some expectations that it might contain papyrus documents which would provide unique historical information about his reign, and perhaps even preceding reigns. The Earl of Carnarvon even wrote to Alan Gardiner immediately after the discovery to say

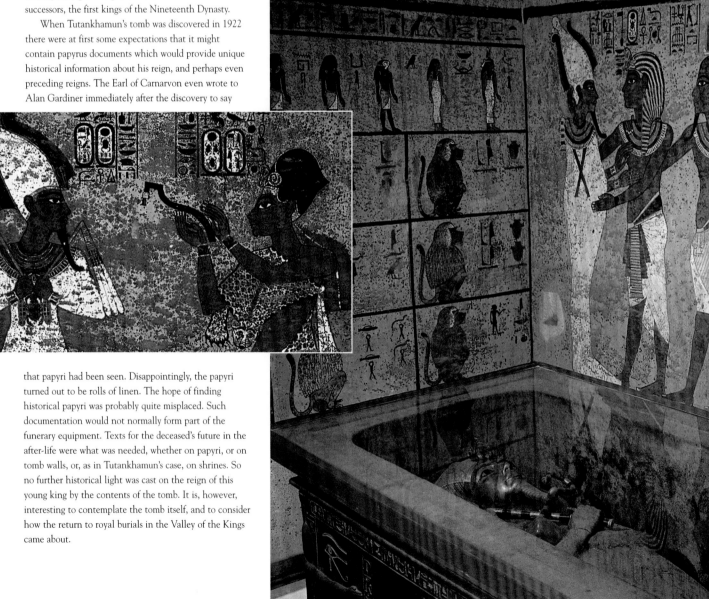

that papyri had been seen. Disappointingly, the papyri turned out to be rolls of linen. The hope of finding historical papyri was probably quite misplaced. Such documentation would not normally form part of the funerary equipment. Texts for the deceased's future in the after-life were what was needed, whether on papyri, or on tomb walls, or, as in Tutankhamun's case, on shrines. So no further historical light was cast on the reign of this young king by the contents of the tomb. It is, however, interesting to contemplate the tomb itself, and to consider how the return to royal burials in the Valley of the Kings came about.

Amenophis III was buried in the West Valley of the Kings in about 1352 BC. Akhenaten had a large tomb prepared for himself and his family in a remote *wadi* to the east of his chosen city of Akhetaten. It should be assumed that he, and possibly his wife Nefertiti (whether or not she succeeded him as Neferneferuaten), were buried there, he in about 1336 BC. Shortly afterwards, Tutankhaten became king, and soon, as Tutankhamun, nominally organized the reconciliation with the ancient gods of Egypt, Amon-Re in particular. Akhetaten was abandoned and the court moved to Memphis. What then should be done in preparation for the future burial of the king? It must be assumed that the event was not thought to be

46 bottom left
The long south wall carries scenes preparing the king for his afterlife. Here he is shown as Osiris, with whom he is identified in death. His successor Ay, with ritual implement, restores his faculties.

46–47
The Burial Chamber of Tutankhamun with scenes painted in tempera. In the center stands the quartzite sarcophagus which still holds the outermost of the royal coffins, containing the king's mummified body.

47 top
On the west wall of the Burial Chamber: above, the solar bark with Khepri, the sun at dawn, with kneeling Osirises; beneath, baboons of two of the twelve hours of the night through which the king must pass.

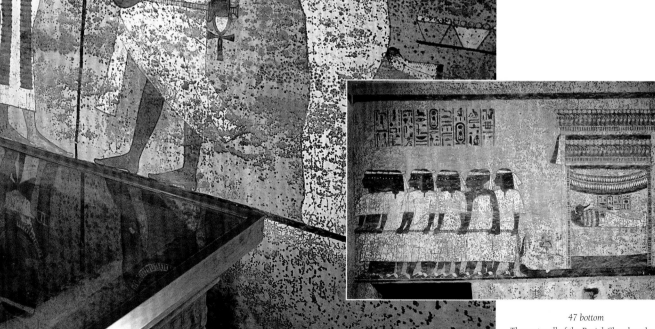

47 bottom
The east wall of the Burial Chamber shows part of the funeral cortege of the king. His mummy, lying in a kiosk is dragged by 'the great officials of the palace', including the two viziers of Egypt (with bald heads). They say: 'Nebkheperure, Come in peace! O God, protector of the land!'

48–49

The burial chamber in the tomb of Ay in the Western Valley of the Kings. In the center stands the king's reconstructed sarcophagus with a domed lid. The tomb may have been intended originally for the burial of Tutankhamun.

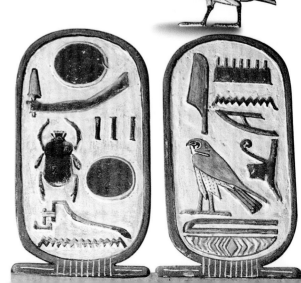

Akhenaten's family, and, uncertain of her future, she turned to the king of the Hittites, Shuppiluliuma, in a letter asking him, 'Had he a son who could marry her and be the next king of Egypt?' A son was sent, but never reached Egypt, presumably assassinated on the way. The way was then clear for Ay to succeed. His reign (c. 1327–1323 BC) made little mark, and in due course he too would be expunged from the record. He was buried in a tomb – possibly one that had originally been planned to receive Tutankhamun – in the West Valley of the Kings. It was then the turn of Horemheb to take up the threads of royalty, to rule with real authority, overcoming his non-royal origins by pragmatic engagement with the problems facing Egypt at home and abroad.

The Amarna Period was over. The idyll of Akhetaten had finished. The great warrior kings of the Nineteenth Dynasty were in the wings, ready to follow Horemheb in restoring Egypt's security and empire.

49 top
The god Anubis greets King Horemheb.
A scene from the Antechamber of the king's
tomb. The blue-grey background of the
painted reliefs is unusual, but very effective.

49 bottom
The falcon-headed Harsiese, 'Horus-son-of-Isis',
wearing the double crown of royalty. From
Horemheb's Theban tomb.

48 bottom left
The goddess Isis, with characteristic
horned disk headdress, receives wine
from Horemheb; from his tomb in the
Valley of the Kings.

48 bottom right
The cartouches of Horemheb from his
Theban tomb. Horemheb's first tomb was
constructed at Saqqara while he was still
a general in the reign of Tutankhamun.
Its secular scenes contrast strongly with
the ritual scenes of his royal sepulchre.

imminent, even though Tutankhamun may not have been a healthy child. He had been brought up as an Atenist, but had renounced his old religious attachments when reconciliation commenced. It is foolish to think that any of these moves were carried through in consultation with, or even with the acceptance of, a child of under ten years of age. But they happened. After the process of reconciliation it was probably considered logical to return to Thebes and the Valley of the Kings as the proper place for the burial. The return to the Valley may first have been tested by the placing of some of the funerary equipment of Amarna royalty in the cache known as KV 55; there was at least one body in a coffin; there was material from the burial of Queen Tiye, consort of Amenophis III and mother of Akhenaten; there may have been parts of the burial of Kiya, Tutankhamun's putative mother. Sealings suggest that this deposit was made in Tutankhamun's reign. The return to the traditional Eighteenth Dynasty royal burial ground had begun.

Then Tutankhamun died. It was probably unexpected. Certainly the tomb in which he was buried had not been cut specially for him.

It has been suggested that it was originally planned for Ay, his regent, but this is not certain. Ay, however, supervised Tutankhamun's burial. Many of the objects included formed part of earlier royal equipment; some objects from earlier reigns, often described as heirlooms, were included. This practise may always have been followed. In any case, the burial cannot be described as inadequate. The splendor and lavishness of its contents speak for themselves.

Who should succeed? A pre-emptive move was made by Queen Ankhesenamun, who was by now about twenty-five years old. She was the last surviving member of

THE DISCOVERY
OF THE TOMB OF
TUTANKHAMUN

50–51
The moment of truth: At last the doors of the four shrines in the Burial Chamber have been unsealed and opened. Howard Carter, kneeling in front, points towards the sealed quartzite sarcophagus, not knowing what to expect next. Behind him stand his assistant Arthur Callender and an Egyptian workman.

I n his work diary for his new season of excavation in November 1922, Howard Carter lists as the first discovered object 'Item 433', continuing the numbering series of finds which he had begun in February 1915. This last was the date when he took up the concession for excavation in the Valley of the Kings on behalf of his employer, the 5th Earl of Carnarvon; the first object, 'Item 1' was a fragment of a *shabti* figure of Queen Tiye found near the entrance to the tomb of king Amenophis (Amenhotep) III. From February 1915 until November 1922, with a long period of inactivity during the First World War, the harvest of objects, therefore, was a very modest 432. The laconic entry for Item 433 was 'Entrance of tomb of', and on the opposite page Carter wrote: 'in bed rock floor of water course (below entrance of R VI). Discovered 4th Nov. 1922.' After the clearance of the steps leading down to the blocked entrance of the tomb, Carter telegraphed Lord Carnarvon: 'At last have made wonderful discovery in the Valley. A magnificent tomb with seals intact. Re-covered same for your arrival. Congratulations. Carter.'

There is no mention of Tutankhamun, and the identity of the owner of the newly discovered tomb was not revealed until his name was read in some of the seal impressions on the lower part of the blocked entrance, when the excavation was resumed after Carnarvon's arrival in Luxor later in November. Carter was at first not able to make an identification, but he may have suspected, even hoped, that Tutankhamun was the king in question. He quite probably had earlier suggested to Carnarvon that Tutankhamun's tomb was a likely candidate for discovery. How else can one explain the question put to Alan Gardiner, the great British grammarian of the ancient Egyptian language, by Carnarvon on the day after the telegram had arrived: 'Carnarvon asked me whether it could possibly be the tomb of Tutankhamun. I replied that I was not well up in the history of the Valley and that we should have to wait and see.'

Carter's belief in the identification of the tomb owner will be examined a little later. But now let us consider how the Amarna Period, the time of heresy, of which Tutankhamun's reign marked the turning point back to what for most ancient Egyptians was normality, in strange ways impinged on the career of Howard Carter from its very beginnings.

Samuel John Carter, a very good naturalistic artist in the Victorian tradition, taught all his many children to draw and paint. Howard, his youngest son, was brought up to think of no other career than that of an artist, not perhaps a successful painter of portraits (like his older brother William), or genre paintings (like his father),

52
Carnarvon arrives in Luxor. The first steps
to the tomb were found on November 4,
1922, and Carter immediately telegraphed
the good news to his patron in England.
With all haste Carnarvon left for Egypt
accompanied by his daughter Lady Evelyn
Herbert. In those leisurely times it took
many days for them to arrive in Egypt,
and a few more before they reached Luxor.
Here they are met outside Luxor station by
Carter and the Governor of Qena
province. Carnarvon, not in good health, is
warmly dressed for Egypt in November.

53 top
Lord Carnarvon photographed at ease on
the porch of Carter's house in Western
Thebes. In Egypt he preferred to live in
luxury in a good hotel, in Luxor at the
Winter Palace. Carter's house served as a
comfortable haven away from the
newspaper reporters and importunate
tourists, where he could retire from time
to time for peace and quiet.

53 center
Detail from the 1924 painting of Howard
Carter by his brother William, a most
accomplished portrait painter. The bow tie
was one of Carter's characteristic articles
of dress. Here he may seem to be at ease,
but his eyes suggest a certain deep-set
anxiety. It was a difficult time for him.

53 bottom
The entry in Howard Carter's work diary
for November 24, 1922. The Carnarvon
party had reached Luxor and Carter's
workmen, supervised by Arthur Callender,
had begun to clear completely the stairway
down to the first blocked entrance to the
tomb. At last the whole plastered wall was
visible and the prenomen cartouche of
Tutankhamun could clearly be read.

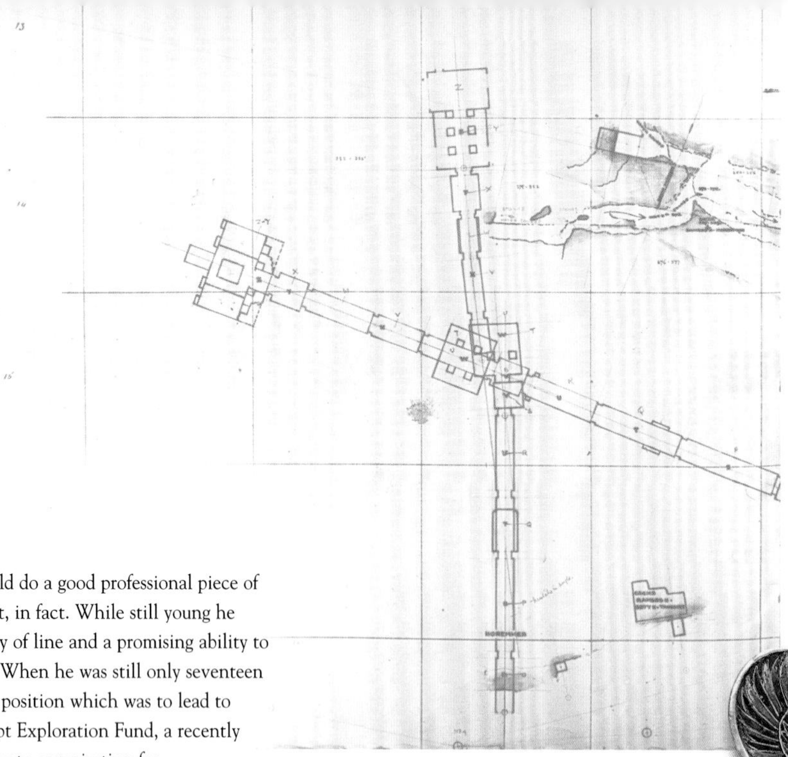

54

Parts of the detailed map of the Valley of the Kings made by Howard Carter. The two sections shown here are adjacent to each other. In the upper section the main features are the tombs or Horemheb and Ramesses VI, the line of the former running beneath the latter. It demonstrates how carefully the ancient tomb-cutters had to work. In following the line of the best limestone they were constrained by the existence of earlier tombs. In this case the tomb of Ramesses VI was cut at a higher level. In the lower section the remains of the workmen's huts built over Tutankhamun's tomb can be seen at the lower left. On the right in the middle is Tomb 55, the so-called Amarna cache, near the entrance to the tomb of Ramesses IX.

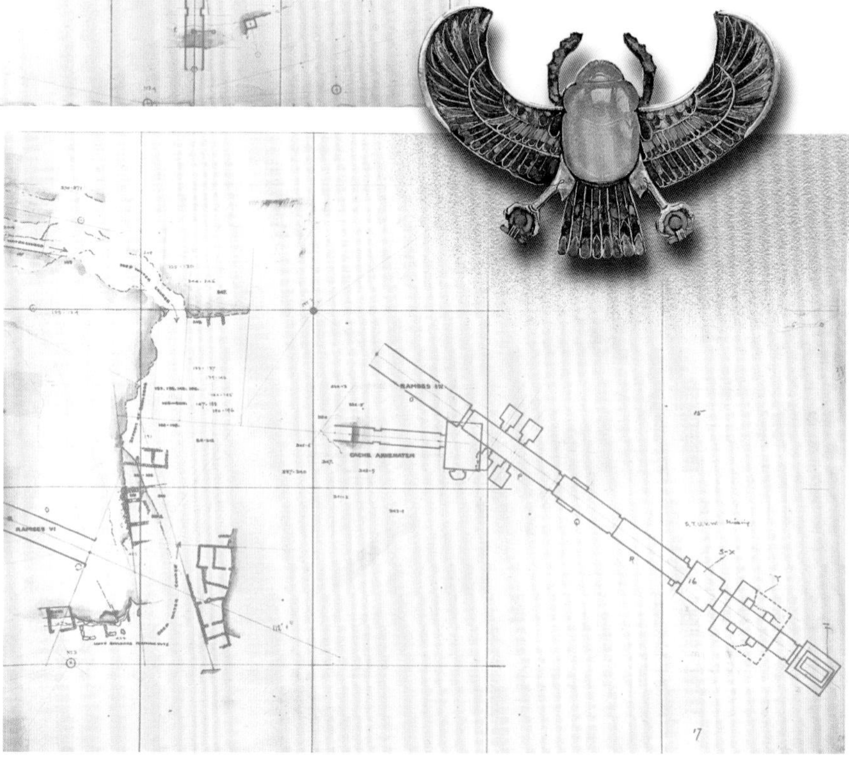

but someone who could do a good professional piece of work – a jobbing artist, in fact. While still young he showed a good mastery of line and a promising ability to paint in water-colors. When he was still only seventeen he obtained a modest position which was to lead to great things. The Egypt Exploration Fund, a recently established British private organization for archaeological works in Egypt, needed an artist to help record the scenes and inscriptions in tombs at Beni Hasan and El-Bersha in Middle Egypt. Carter already had some knowledge of Egyptian antiquities from being allowed to draw in the collection of William Amhurst Tyssen-Amherst (later Lord Amherst), a rich landowner in Norfolk. He had, however, never been to Egypt, had indeed scarcely travelled beyond London and Norfolk, when he was sent to Egypt in the Autumn of 1891. Within a few weeks he was sent to assist in the excavations at El-Amarna conducted by Flinders Petrie, who was to become the most famous field-worker in Egypt in the early twentieth century.

El-Amarna had already been identified as the site of the ancient town of Akhetaten, founded by King Akhenaten (c. 1352–1336 BC), whose history was outlined in the previous chapter. In 1892 very little was known of the period and its religion, but interesting objects of unusual style had been found in the area, and Petrie was the first serious archaeologist to excavate there. Carter spent over four months with Petrie and they were momentous months in the early career of one whom Petrie first described as 'a good-natured lad, whose interest is entirely in painting and natural history.... it is of no use to me to work him up as an excavator'. This was perhaps rather a premature judgement by an experienced thirty-eight-year-old on an immature, inexperienced seventeen-year-old. At El-Amarna Carter first learned about Akhenaten and the Amarna Period, and was bitten by the bug of excavation. In his methods of work, and of life generally, Petrie was uncompromising, severe and methodical. He was also dogmatic and eccentric, and the young Carter did not appreciate many of his peculiar economies. Nevertheless, he watched the older man, listened to what he said, and understood the reasons for some of his oddities. It was indeed an acknowledgement that his 'pupil' of thirty years earlier was doing well (in the Petrie sense) that he could comment in 1923: 'We may only say how lucky it is all in the hands of Carter and Lucas'. And that was but two months after the discovery of Tutankhamun's tomb.

It was in this season with Petrie that Carter was introduced to his first royal tomb, that of Akhenaten himself, possibly the father of Tutankhamun. So the circle of interest started, although it would be foolish to claim that this early experience established the path that was to lead to the great discovery of 1922. Rumors of the finding of the Akhenaten tomb had been circulating for several months in 1891, and it was in December that the Egyptian Antiquities Service announced the event. In February 1892 Petrie took Carter to see it. They walked for many miles, mostly up a rocky *wadi* or valley, and what was to be seen did not excite the young man. He wrote to his mentor Percy Newberry: 'The tomb... is a great sell [anti-climax], is very rough and unfinished... I have made some drawings for Mr. Petrie of the Valley and the Tomb.' Indeed the tomb at first sight is not very impressive, and not nearly as spectacular as the private tombs Carter had been working on at Beni Hasan. It was dark, and the few reliefs not easy to make out. The drawings Carter made were published with an article

55

View of the entrance to Tutankhamun's tomb taken some time after its discovery. The large tomb entrance in the middle of the picture marks the tomb of Ramesses VI, in front of which ran the regular tourist path into the Valley which inhibited excavation in the area. A newly built low wall surrounds the small area leading down to the tomb of Tutankhamun. The boxes and timber lying to the right are part of the excavator's equipment. The path on the left runs up to the tomb of Amenophis II which was robbed while Carter was Chief Inspector in Thebes. At the point where another path turns off to the left is the deep entrance to the tomb of Horemheb which runs into the cliff beneath the line of Ramesses VI's tomb. Holes just above the tent mark other Carter investigations. His searchings were very thorough, but accompanied by little success until the end.

Petrie wrote for a London newspaper, the *Daily Graphic*, on the March 23 – the very first published drawings by the budding archaeologist. One of them shows Akhenaten and his wife Nefertiti mourning their dead daughter Meketaten. Above the king the divine sun-disk, the Aten, pours down its life-giving rays, an idea Carter would meet again, most notably on the back of the Golden Throne found in the Antechamber of Tutankhamun's tomb. In spite of the lack of light in the tomb, Carter's drawing is remarkably accurate for a quick sketch by someone who had scarcely served his apprenticeship as an archaeological artist. Carter completed his work with Petrie at the end of May 1892. His taste for excavation was established; he had worked with the best of instructors and survived. By the end Petrie would discuss objects with him, and even sometimes seemed to respect his opinion. Carter would never forget those months at El-Amarna, and he would, if only subconsciously, carry in his mind the experience of working in the area of the Great Temple of the Aten in Akhenaten's city, where Tutankhamun passed his childhood. And there he first met Amarna art, finding many examples of Amarna sculpture, all sadly damaged, but still showing the craftsmanship and exquisite lines of the finest art of the period.

The next step on the road which would lead him in the direction of his ultimate triumph came in late 1899, when Carter was appointed Chief Inspector of Antiquities for Upper Egypt with his base in Thebes. It was an unexpected promotion for him, and not welcomed by many of his British colleagues. This was not surprising. Carter had not readily been accepted into the British archaeological community for several reasons. He was poorly educated, and had few apparent talents apart from an outstanding ability to draw. Unlike most of his contemporaries he had not attended a good school and been to one of the older universities; he had not, as it seemed, made noticeable efforts to learn systematically about ancient Egypt. He was also less well mannered than those with whom he came into contact professionally and socially in Egypt. By temperament he did not make friends easily among his Egyptological colleagues, and sought rather the company of artists and foreign visitors to Egypt who might not expose his Egyptological uncertainties. But he had proved his worth

as a practical worker in the field, especially during the six years he spent at Deir el-Bahri as principal artist, and as virtual deputy to Edouard Naville, director of the excavation and reconstruction of the great temple of Queen Hatshepsut. In all practical matters he worked successfully for Naville, and it was probably Naville who recommended Carter to Gaston Maspero, Director-General of the Antiquities Service of Egypt.

Although Howard Carter was not book trained, he was an observant and pragmatic person who clearly learned lessons quickly from the knowledge and practices of others. He may never have learned the intricacies of the ancient Egyptian language, but he was a brilliant copier of hieroglyphic texts. Naville once wrote about the work done by Carter and his assistant Percy Brown on one series of reliefs at Deir el-Bahri: 'Most of the inscriptions copied had been erased (in antiquity), and were difficult to read, but owing to the familiarity which the artists had acquired with hieroglyphs at Deir el-Bahari, and to their skill in recognizing a sign from a few broken lines or a small colored fragment, it has been possible not only to correct the former publications of Mariette and Duemichen, but here and there to add materially to what had been deciphered previously by those scholars'.

So far in his career in Egypt Carter had mostly been an employee of the Egypt Exploration Fund, carrying out tasks assigned to him, and only occasionally having the freedom to act independently. But his independence had always been circumscribed. Now at last, from December 1899, he was virtually his own master, operating far from Cairo, and capable of setting his own priorities, except in matters involving the substantial expenditure of money. Shortage of funds was a constant problem. Excavation was the activity that attracted Carter most. At Thebes, after many decades of inactivity, work had been resumed in the Valley of the Kings in 1898 by Victor Loret, Maspero's predecessor as Director-General. His most important find was the tomb of King Amenophis II (c. 1427–1400 BC), which turned out to be a cache containing a group of very important royal burials.

In January 1900, as one of his first official tasks, Carter supervised the removal of the royal mummies to Cairo, leaving in the tomb only that of Amenophis II in his sarcophagus.

The entrance to the Annexe lay behind the hippopotamus-headed couch. Its floor was much lower than that of the Antechamber, and it contained an even more confused mass of material, deposited in a haphazard manner which cannot wholly be attributed to tomb-robbers. Here there were remarkable pieces like the so-called Ecclesiastical Throne, other fine furniture, weaponry, boats, chests of shabti-figures, and many more containers of food and the king's 'cellar' of wine for the afterlife.

The extraordinary assembly of shrines and coffins in the Burial Chamber is described on the next page. This room was alone in having wall paintings of ritual purpose. It also contained items of special funerary significance, and, in each wall, a magical brick.

Out of the Burial Chamber opened the Treasury, so called because of its precious contents, chief of which was the Canopic Shrine protecting the king's embalmed entrails. There were also many chests containing divine and royal figures, boxes of shabti-figures, a fleet of boats sailing to the West, more chests of linen and jewelry. And over all brooded the impressive Anubis jackal on a shrine-shaped pedestal.

59–62

Howard Carter assigned names to the four chambers in the royal tomb, which through usage have become established, although they do not all properly reflect the functions of the rooms.

The first room, the Antechamber, was not just the room of approach to what Carnarvon called the 'Holy of Holies', but a storeroom of miscellaneous material. Facing the entrance were the three great ritual couches with dramatic animal heads. Above and beneath them were items of furniture, the Golden Throne, fine chairs and stools, smaller beds, boxes filled with linen and items of clothes, calcite jars of unguents, white-painted, egg-shaped containers for food to sustain the dead king. To the right, by the blocked entrance to the Burial Chamber, stood the guardian statues and on the floor, the painted box, one of the greatest treasures in the tomb. The other end of the room was mostly filled with parts of chariots, dismantled at the time of the funeral.

Sketch-plan of the tomb of Tutankhamun:
a – the stairway down;
b – the descending corridor;
c – the Antechamber;
d – the Annexe;
e – the Burial Chamber with
f – the Sarcophagus;
g – the Treasury.

The section passes through the stairs, the descending corridor, the Antechamber and the Annexe, the floor of which is lower than that of the Antechamber.

FIRST GILDED SHRINE

SECOND GILDED
SHRINE WITH
WOODEN FRAME
AND LINEN PALL

SECOND
GILDED
SHRINE

THIRD
GILDED
SHRINE

FOURTH
GILDED
SHRINE

THE QUARTZITE
SARCOPHAGUS

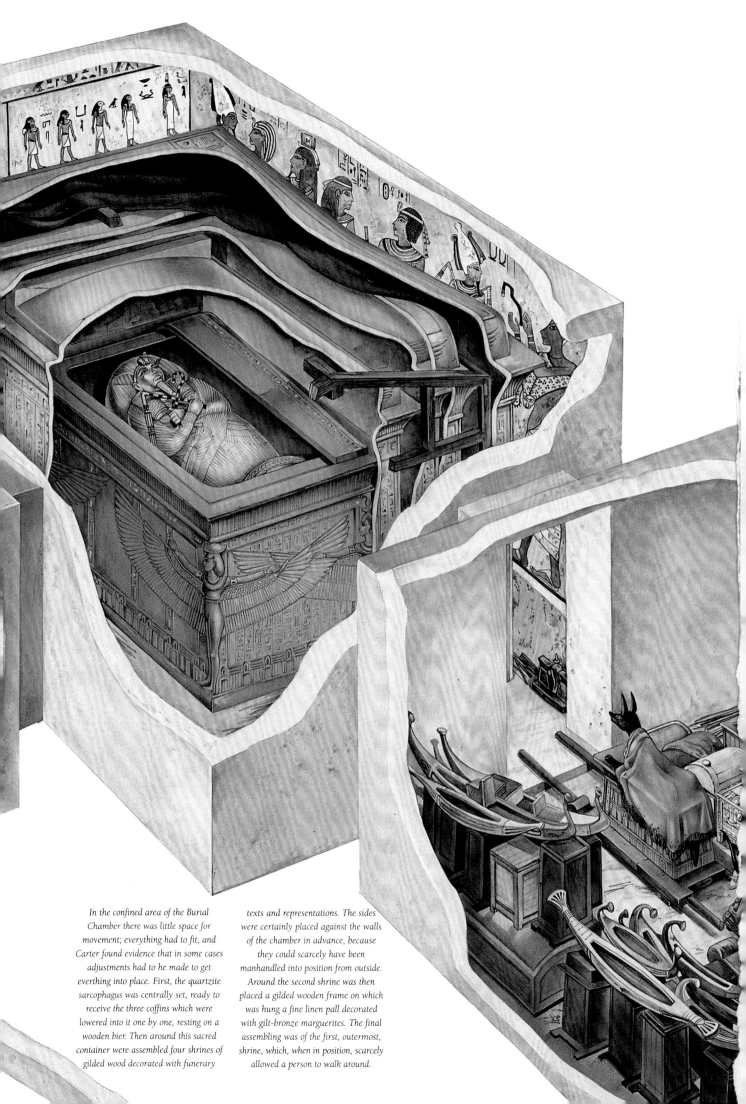

In the confined area of the Burial Chamber there was little space for movement; everything had to fit, and Carter found evidence that in some cases adjustments had to he made to get everthing into place. First, the quartzite sarcophagus was centrally set, ready to receive the three coffins which were lowered into it one by one, resting on a wooden bier. Then around this sacred container were assembled four shrines of gilded wood decorated with funerary texts and representations. The sides were certainly placed against the walls of the chamber in advance, because they could scarcely have been manhandled into position from outside. Around the second shrine was then placed a gilded wooden frame on which was hung a fine linen pall decorated with gilt-bronze marguerites. The final assembling was of the first, outermost, shrine, which, when in position, scarcely allowed a person to walk around.

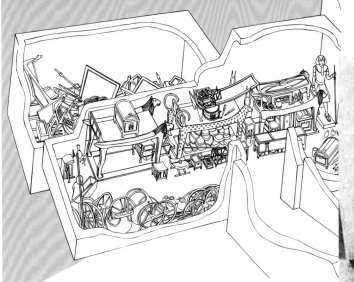

This was Carter's first involvement in the Valley of the Kings, and for the rest of his career the Valley was to occupy a central position in his thoughts, if not in his day-to-day activity. Its pull took time to develop, but by chance and design the Valley fixed itself in his mind, and cast its spell on this young, scarcely formed archaeologist. There was, it seems, a strong romantic element in this fascination, which was over the years to develop into an obsession. For no good reason, and with unrealistic expectation, Carter came to believe that there was – there must be – one undiscovered tomb, unplundered, he hoped, which dogged determination would in the end yield to his passion. To begin with it is unlikely that a special burial occupied his thoughts. In fact any burial would do. Could he ever have the chance to make that discovery? Would someone else get there first?

In his few years as Chief Inspector in Upper Egypt, some opportunities came his way. His first independent excavation was not in the Valley of the Kings, but in the plain before Deir el-Bahri where Maspero allowed him to investigate a hole in which his horse had tripped a year or two earlier. This 'Tomb of the Horse', as it came to be known, turned out to be in some way connected with the temple of Nebhepetre Mentuhotpe II (c. 2055–2004 BC), also in Deir el-Bahri just to the south of Hatshepsut's more famous temple. It did not turn out to be the unviolated tomb Carter hoped it might be, and its one significant object, a remarkable life-size seated statue of the king dressed for the *sed* or jubilee festival, was no consolation for the general disappointment of a practically empty sepulchre. But it was his first royal tomb, or perhaps cenotaph.

His next involvement with a royal tomb brought him back to the Valley of the Kings, and in even less happy circumstances. On the evening of November 24, 1901, while Carter was away from Thebes on a tour of inspection, robbers broke into the tomb of Amenophis II, only recently discovered. Local rumor had it that the tomb still contained precious objects, and the mummy of the king, still lying in its sarcophagus, was carefully cut open in a search for gold jewelry. Although there was good forensic evidence pointing to the guilt of members of a well-known local Qurnawi family, with a fully justified reputation for tomb-robbing, no successful prosecution followed. Carter was in no way to blame, but the episode left a stain on his reputation which could subsequently be used by those who resented his presence in Luxor.

Victor Loret's work in the Valley of the Kings had shown that there were royal tombs still to be found. Although Carter had no further funds for excavation himself, he carried out much needed work in the Valley, clearing tombs, fitting steel doors, and installing electric light. He had the best of opportunities to get to know the place in detail, and to observe likely places where more tombs might be found. It was a chance to survey and to reconnoitre – the best of preparations for serious work; this might be considered the period when the seeds of his final harvest with the Earl of Carnarvon were sown. There was a way, however, by which even then he could involve himself in excavation. With Maspero's encouragement he sought out a wealthy sponsor who could finance excavations in the Valley, to be conducted on his behalf by Howard Carter. It was not at all difficult to persuade the rich American businessman Theodore Davis to be that sponsor, and in 1902 there began the Davis excavations in the Valley which were to continue until 1915. Carter remained in charge of the work until he left Thebes for Cairo at the end of 1904. In that time he demonstrated that there were more tombs to be discovered and, perhaps more importantly for his own archaeological development, that he was an excavator ideally suited in skills and temperament for this kind of work.

Carter's best success with Davis came in January 1903 when he found his first royal tomb in the Valley. It had been prepared for King Tuthmosis IV of the Eighteenth Dynasty (c. 1400–1390 BC), and had, one

64 bottom left
One of the two life-size guardian or ka-statues placed on either side of the blocked entrance to the Burial Chamber. When discovered they were partly covered with linen sheets, as were many other objects in the tomb. The black-painted wooden figures with gilded headdresses, kilts and staves made a dramatic effect.

64–65 and 65 top
As my eyes grew accustomed to the light, details of the room within emerged slowly from the mist, strange animals, statues, and gold – everywhere the glint of gold'. So wrote Carter of his first impressions. 'A roomful – a whole museumful it seemed – of objects.' To the left was a tangled mass of chariot parts; to the front were three huge ritual beds with monstrous heads and beneath them chests of personal possessions, egg-shaped boxes for food offerings, and pieces of furniture, some quite simple in design, others grand beyond imagination.

65 bottom
To the right the excavators could see the unmistakeable signs of a blocked entrance, flanked by the two guardian figures. On the floor was the magnificent painted box, then even more brilliant in its colors which after essential conservation became darkened. And, against the wall a round basket concealing a hole into the Burial Chamber, through which Carter, Carnarvon and Evelyn Herbert would later squeeze to view the 'Holy of Holies'.

may say inevitably, been ransacked in antiquity. Nevertheless, considerable remains of impressive painted wall reliefs still remained, and there were large quantities of fine, but mostly damaged, antiquities. Carter carefully stage-managed the official opening, having himself made in advance preparations to ensure a relatively comfortable experience for the distinguished visitors, and as little damage as possible to the tomb and its contents. Electric light, an almost unheard of luxury in a newly excavated tomb, had been installed. Mrs. Emma Andrews, close companion and relative of Davis and the social chronicler of their annual trips on the Nile, described what happened on the February 3. The whole event must have been difficult, dangerous, thrilling and at times hilarious. She went in with Gaston Maspero, Director-General. There were two long inclines: 'Maspero being so stout had actually to lie down, with his feet sometimes on Carter's shoulders'. They crossed the deep well – a characteristic feature of Eighteenth Dynasty tombs – by a precarious suspension bridge. The great burial hall 'was strewn with a mass of beautiful debris... Carter placed boards along which we walked and were requested not to step off them'. Getting out was even more difficult. After a late lunch they returned to Davis's house-boat: 'We were glad enough to have tea'.

Changes in the appointments of Chief Inspectors were, however, to bring Carter's work with Davis to an

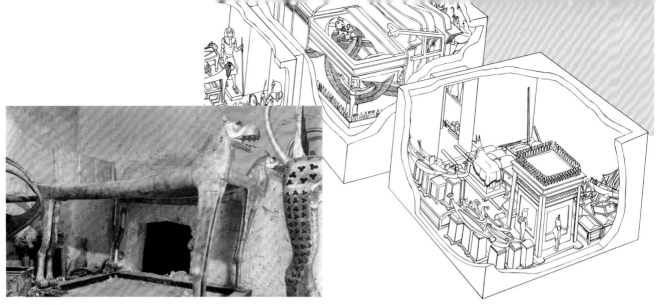

66 top left
After the clearance of smaller items from the Antechamber, in the wall behind the great hippopotamus couch, it could be seen there was a low square entrance to another room. This small storeroom, the Annexe, lay at a level lower than the Antechamber and it was so full of objects that it could not be entered at that point.

66 bottom left
The first object to be seen in the Treasury was the great Anubis shrine, the recumbent jackal figure of the god on duty for eternity, protecting the most precious Canopic Shrine and embalmed internal organs of the king. The finely modeled head of the god, with gilded eyes and ears, made a profound impression on the first modern visitors to the tomb.

end. It had been Maspero's intention to switch the Lower and Upper Egyptian Inspectors after four or five years, and he decided to make the change in 1904. It could not have pleased Carter, although no adverse comment by him has survived. He was now a government official and had to do what he was told. But for ten years Thebes had been the center of his life in Egypt, and for recent years the focus of his professional interest had been the Valley of the Kings. Royal tombs were what he enjoyed discovering, and there would be none in the North where pyramid investigation was quite another thing, and not on offer in any case. If he had at that time a particular tomb in mind it was that of King Amenophis I (c. 1525–1504 BC), which, according to indications in ancient Egyptian papyrus records, lay outside the Valley of the Kings. He could therefore conduct a search for it as Chief Inspector without compromising Theodore Davis's concession in the Valley. For funds Carter approached his old patron Lord Amherst: 'I can do it this summer before I leave for Lower Egypt'. In the event he could do little more than scratch around on the heights of Dra Abu'l Naga, a hill overlooking the plain running east from Deir el-Bahri, and the known site of small royal tombs of the Seventeenth Dynasty. To find the tomb of Amenophis I became something of an *idée fixe* with Carter; it was something he could later interest the Earl of Carnarvon in, while they waited for the Valley concession.

66 right
This black-painted shrine in the Treasury
held four statues shrouded in linen,
three being gilded. Two show
Tutankhamun in a papyrus skiff, hunting
the hippopotamus with harpoon; in front
is a standing figure of the king holding
a flail and a long curved staff. A fourth
figure, painted black, probably
represented the god Ihy.

The move north in late 1904, accepted if not welcomed by Carter, soon brought calamity. He was still only thirty years old, mature in experience but not easy in his ways. Maspero described him as 'entêté', obstinate. Called to intervene in a dispute between Antiquities Service guards and a group of visitors to Saqqara, Carter failed to resolve the matter before a brawl occurred and blood was drawn. The outcome, greatly exacerbated by his unwillingness to compromise, led to his being moved to Tanta in the Delta. He was not happy, and in the autumn of 1905 he resigned from the Antiquities Service.

For three years he became an outcast from the archaeological community. He scraped a living by selling his water-colors to European and American visitors, many of whom were wealthy, and pleased to employ him as a guide to the ancient sites, with very special

professional knowledge. He returned to Thebes, living, it has been suggested, sometimes on the charity of his former Egyptian employees. He was helped a little by some of his old associates like Theodore Davis, who had made his best discovery in the Valley in February 1905, only a few months after Carter had left Thebes. The tomb of Yuia and Tjuiu, parents of Queen Tiye, favourite wife of Amenophis III, contained the largest quantity of well preserved funerary furniture, including their intact coffins, ever found in the Valley. Davis in due course asked Carter to make water-colors of some of the most spectacular objects in the tomb, and they were used to illustrate the subsequent publication. Undoubtedly it was all very galling for Carter, and Davis's commission was small compensation for what might have been his own success. Had he stayed in Thebes for another three months he might have made that discovery. But the success fell to his colleague James Quibell, with whom he had exchanged Inspectorships.

For the time being, therefore, all Carter could do was to stay in Thebes picking up small pieces of work, and observing the not infrequent triumphs over the hill in the Valley of the Kings. Each royal discovery by the Davis team meant one less discovery to be made in the future. And would Carter ever have the chance to work there again? Triumph followed triumph for Davis. In late 1905, no doubt on the advice of his newly engaged full-time excavator, Edward Ayrton, Davis had decided to systematize his operations in the Valley, 'exhausting every mountain and foot-hill' – a pattern of work which would be carried through more thoroughly by Carter himself after 1917. Ayrton was eight years younger than Carter and less experienced; but he joined Davis before Carter had resigned. It is piquant to think that Carter might have received the Davis appointment if he had known about it at the time when he was feeling so dissatisfied with his life in Tanta. In late 1905 the tomb of King Siptah (c. 1194–1188 BC) was discovered, but not fully cleared until some years later. In January 1907 a tomb used or reused as a cache for funerary furniture and equipment was opened. This controversial deposit, famously known by its Valley of the Kings number, KV 55, contained material belonging to royal individuals closely connected to Akhenaten and the Amarna court. In February 1908 Ayrton discovered the spectacularly decorated tomb of Horemheb, last king of the Eighteenth Dynasty (c. 1323–1295 BC). One by one the tombs of the kings of the New Kingdom were being found; but the lure of the Valley did not diminish for Howard Carter. It

66–67
In the Treasury, in front of the Canopic shrine, stood a gilded cow's head; the goddess Hathor emerging from the West; three lidded tazze on tall stands contained natron used in mummification. The chests on the left for jewelry and personal possessions had all been opened and rifled.

67 bottom
In the Antechamber between the first and second of the great ritual couches, there stood, stacked against the back wall of the room, a clutch of what Carter called 'perfume vases'. But what perfume vases! In this group there were five of the most elaborate kind, mostly with decorative elements incorporating stems and flowers of lilies and papyrus plants, representing the union of Upper and Lower Egypt. Because of their awkward position, tucked behind other material, they were ignored by the tomb robbers, and retain their lids and much of their contents, reduced sadly to unromantic residues. All these vases are made from calcite, often called alabaster in the Egyptian context.

is unlikely that he lay in bed at night counting on his fingers the missing sepulchres. It would be some years before he made researches into the history of the Valley, investigating the possibilities of further discoveries. But it would not have escaped him that there could be other non-royal tombs like that of Yuia and Tjuiu, unexpectedly located in the Valley and still unplundered.

In January 1909 Howard Carter wrote to Mrs. Kingsmill Marrs of Boston, one of his wealthy American clients: 'At the Tombs of the Kings Mr. Davis found a small tomb pit but nothing of great interest in it beyond some gold foil'. In the light of later events, Carter should perhaps have taken greater interest in what had been found. It is of course likely

that he had not seen the discovery when he wrote the letter. Some of the gold fragments bore the name of Tutankhamun, and others the name of Ay, his short-reigned successor (c. 1327–1323 BC), and Davis and his new excavator Harold Jones, identified this very modest tomb pit as the actual burial place of Tutankhamun. It was later published as such, but the evidence did not support the identification, and it was not generally accepted. At the very least, however, it brought forward the name of Tutankhamun. For Carter's immediate future, however, what he later said to Mrs. Marrs in the same letter was of particular significance: 'I have just been offered an enormous fee by Lord Carnarvon to undertake a month's excavation (February) at Drah abou'l Neggeh a site no doubt you will remember

between Deir el-Bahari and the mouth of the valley of the Tombs of the Kings – to try to find the Tombs of Amenhotep I and Aahmes Nefertari (the founders of the 18th Dynasty) which the Abbot Papyrus mentions to be in the neighbourhood – the circumstances being so good and such an interesting rest for a short time from ones work I have accepted and shall try and do my best'.

So, with apparent reluctance Carter showed himself ready to return to excavation, and to take up the project which he had proposed to Lord Amherst five years earlier. He must have been thrilled at the prospect of excavating again in the Theban Necropolis, although he might have had some misgivings arising from his unhappy experiences in the past as a government official. Furthermore he seems to have enjoyed his time as an artist and high-class dragoman; he was very much his own master, and he had gained much social confidence through mixing with rather grand clients. No longer was he the gauche, awkwardly mannered, young man; he could more than pass as a gentleman. As such he would fit reasonably well into the kind of life enjoyed by the Earl of Carnarvon, who did not expect to live in discomfort or enjoy pointless economies like Petrie. Further, there was the attraction of 'an enormous fee'. In a letter to Percy Newberry in 1911, Carnarvon mentioned that he paid Carter £200 'per mensem'; it is unlikely that he was paying much less in 1909.

68–69
On February 17, 1923, Howard Carter and Arthur Mace, in the presence of distinguished guests and officials, breached the sealed blocking between the Antechamber and the Burial Chamber. When this picture was taken, most of the blocking had been removed and the visitors were faced with the wall of the great outermost shrine with an open-work pattern of djed and tyet amuletic hieroglyphs, signifying endurance and life. The background is made of blue faience of a wonderful purity of color.

69 top and 69 right
These two pictures illustrate the care with which the objects in the tomb were prepared for the short journey to the tomb of Sethos II where conservation took place. But this journey involved the negotiating of the exit from the tomb, and Carter took no chance in ensuring that adequate packing material and carrying trays were available. Here the guardian statues are prepared by Carter and Callender.

Carter came to work with Carnarvon with the blessing of Gaston Maspero. He had been very disappointed when Carter resigned in 1905, and had done his best to persuade him to stay. So, when Carnarvon came to him in 1908 and asked him to find a 'learned man' to help him with his excavations, it gave Maspero a wonderful chance to effect Carter's rehabilitation as an archaeologist. Carnarvon had been conducting modest excavations in the Theban Necropolis since 1907. He supervised his workmen himself, but overall control was exercised by Arthur Weigall, the current Chief Inspector for Upper Egypt. Weigall was a clever man and a good Egyptologist who did not suffer fools or incompetents gladly. He was not sympathetic to Carnarvon and did little to help him work in places where he might find something. He confessed to Francis Llewellyn Griffith, the leading British Egyptologist of the day: 'I placed him on the rubbish mounds of Shekh abd'el Gurneh, where of course he worked for the season without finding anything, though I had hoped that he might find a good painted tomb which would have been a useful find, without much to damage in it'. In his second season in early 1908 Carnarvon had greater success. He had negotiated, without the unhelpful advice of Weigall, a much more promising area for excavation; he found a number of interesting antiquities and several tombs, including one dating to the early Eighteenth Dynasty, made for a mayor of Thebes, Tetiky. His success annoyed Weigall, who had been to some extent side-lined. He complained to Griffith: 'Lord Carnarvon does his best, and sits over his work conscientiously; but that is not enough… He is a good sort, but perfectly irresponsible.' Weigall had a good point to make. Rich men do not necessarily make good excavators. Carnarvon himself had his doubts. He could see that he was wholly unequipped technically to conduct successful excavations, and without proper support from the representative of the Antiquities Service he had to find his own man. Carter it would be.

In this way began an association which would last for fourteen years, culminating in the greatest discovery in the history of Egyptian archaeology. Carter turned out to be just the right man. He and Carnarvon came from very different strata of society, but Carter had the abilities and

personal qualities which Carnarvon appreciated. And, in addition to being an accomplished excavator, Carter was an unusually skilled handler of antiquities and a fine artist; he was totally at home in the Theban Necropolis. He knew the Qurnawis well, and understood their strengths, comprehended their weaknesses, and was trusted by them sufficiently for them to bring him advanced knowledge of good illicit finds. So he was often able to acquire for Carnarvon's growing collection objects of exceptional quality before they were passed into the general antiquities market. But Carter was not, as he had hoped, to work on finding the tombs of Amenophis I (Amenhotep) and his mother Queen Ahmes Nefertari.

Carnarvon's concession in the Theban Necropolis had begun to yield very interesting material, and there was every reason to continue work in the same area. For the next six years Carter worked steadily to the east of the Deir el-Bahri temples. Work was on a large scale, but tight control was exercised; excellent procedures in the technical operation of the excavation were developed. At last Carter was gaining the experience of serious excavation which he had not been able to acquire in his early years of clearance in the Valley. In 1912 a fine volume describing the results for the years 1907–1911 was published. It was issued under the joint authorship

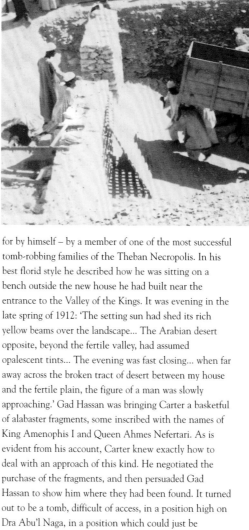

of Carnarvon and Carter, but it is certain that it was master-minded by the latter. By 1912 a certain repetitive quality to the finds began to persuade Carnarvon that a change was necessary. He considered sites in other parts of Egypt. Carter kept his eye on the Valley of the Kings, where Theodore Davis still retained the concession. Davis was now well into his seventies and not in the best of health. He could scarcely continue his annual visits to Egypt much longer. Discoveries in the Valley had been trivial in recent years; yet he hung on to his concession as if he too believed that one great discovery was there to be made.

In 1912, as a diversion, Carter dug a short season at Sakha in the central Delta, site of the ancient city of Xois. In 1913 he investigated Tell el-Balamun, a vast mound in the northern Delta. Neither place proved very profitable, and neither was further investigated by Carter. A certain aimlessness seemed to overcome the Carnarvon-Carter enterprise. Other sites, very desirable, could not be obtained. Carter was the professional, and for the sake of his own future he had to pay attention to his employer's wishes. Then chance intervened, reviving the possibility of the discovery of the tomb of King Amenophis I. In an essay Carter wrote in the 1930s he told the story of how he was put on to the exact location of the tomb – long sought

for by himself – by a member of one of the most successful tomb-robbing families of the Theban Necropolis. In his best florid style he described how he was sitting on a bench outside the new house he had built near the entrance to the Valley of the Kings. It was evening in the late spring of 1912: 'The setting sun had shed its rich yellow beams over the landscape... The Arabian desert opposite, beyond the fertile valley, had assumed opalescent tints... The evening was fast closing... when far away across the broken tract of desert between my house and the fertile plain, the figure of a man was slowly approaching.' Gad Hassan was bringing Carter a basketful of alabaster fragments, some inscribed with the names of King Amenophis I and Queen Ahmes Nefertari. As is evident from his account, Carter knew exactly how to deal with an approach of this kind. He negotiated the purchase of the fragments, and then persuaded Gad Hassan to show him where they had been found. It turned out to be a tomb, difficult of access, in a position high on Dra Abu'l Naga, in a position which could just be reconciled with the ancient description given in the Abbott Papyrus in the British Museum.

The tomb was in a wretched condition: 'Every remnant of the old grandeur and divinity had gone...

72 top and 72 left
The clearance of the tomb continues. Howard Carter and Arthur Callender work together in moving objects to the conservation tomb. The two made a good team. Carter, undisputed director, experienced in all aspects of field activities; Callender, by training and profession an engineer, a good practical assistant, wholly reliable. Carter did not mind getting his hands dirty, and when it was necessary to move an object with particular care he would be there to do it himself. Here he and Callender gently lower one side of the great Hathor (cow) couch into a prepared tray; and again the two themselves carry a chest to Sethos II's tomb.

72–73
An open crate of objects is manhandled from the tomb. Such movements took place at fairly regular intervals throughout the day while work on the clearance in the tomb continued. They provided moments of excitement for the perpetual crowds of visitors who gathered around the perimetre of the tomb in the expectation of seeing some particular treasure, or even Carter and Carnarvon. Rarely would they be disappointed.

73 bottom left
Carter helps to manuever a large tray with an object up the stairs of the tomb into the open and relative safety. It was vitally important to have every piece securely fastened on its tray so that it could not slip about during this awkward point in its removal. The slightest shock or movement on the tray could lead to the damage of the fragile gilded gesso-plaster which covered many of the objects. They had survived more than 3000 years with little damage. It would not be proper to damage them in transit.

73 bottom right
From time to time a consignment of antiquities was sent down-river to Cairo. Carter worried about their treatment on the journey north, and after their reception in the Cairo Museum. But at the Luxor end he did his best to see that their passage to the river bank would be trouble free and fully supervised. He borrowed a Decauville light railway, much used in excavation and for the transport of materials, to move his precious cargo from the Valley of the Kings to the Nile.

The walls were sullen and black from the fires lit by its dynastic desecrators. The charred remains of its equipment were but evidence of base minds that had wrought revenge upon the illustrious dead.' It was, however, still worth careful examination, and in due course, at what seemed to be the right moment, Carter proposed its clearance to Carnarvon. In the event, it was the last piece of work to be undertaken by Carnarvon and Carter before the outbreak of the First World War. A short season began in late February 1914; it was not promising and the results were disappointing – mostly more fragments of stone vessels and *shabti* figures; identification was not certain, but Carter himself was convinced that it had been the burial place of Amenophis I and his mother.

After the completion of that piece of work, Carnarvon gave up his concession in the Theban Necropolis, and planned to move operations to Hawara, at the entrance to the Faiyum depression much further north. But at the same time, almost precisely, Theodore Davis surrendered his licence for the Valley of the Kings. He was seventy-seven; recent results had been negligible. In 1912 he had written 'I fear that the Valley of the Tombs is now exhausted'. He was echoing what Giovanni Battista Belzoni had written nearly a century earlier: 'It is my firm opinion that in the valley of Beban el Mulook there are no more tombs than are now known in consequence of my late discoveries'. Maspero also considered the Valley completely worked out. How could Howard Carter expect any further success? Well, he could have argued, Belzoni was wrong, why not Davis and Maspero also? Carnarvon was persuaded to apply for the licence, and it was granted to him in June 1914.

It may be imagined – for there is no contemporary evidence to show to the contrary – that Carter was both delighted and disconcerted by this development. What should his strategy be in tackling this difficult area? Where should he begin? Had he a precise objective? As it happened, no immediate decisions had to be made, for war broke out in the summer, and it became clear that nothing systematic could be started while hostilities continued. The Earl of Carnarvon would not be returning to Egypt for the time being. Carter, still retained, at least nominally, by Carnarvon, and comfortably equipped with his own house, decided to remain in the country, offering himself for whatever war-work might become available, and making only rare visits to Britain. It seemed proper, however, in order to clinch the concession, to carry out one small task in the tomb of Amenophis III, which lay not in the main Valley of the Kings, but in the side *wadi* known as the West Valley. In 1912 Davis's men had done some work near the entrance to this tomb, which had been known since the time of the Napoleonic Expedition to Egypt in 1799. Nothing much had been found by Davis, but Carter subsequently purchased in Luxor for Lord Carnarvon

74 left
*After the removal of the sealed wall, the
remainder of the wall on either side had
to be taken down to make room for the
shrines to be dismantled and removed
without damage. In this picture it is
clear that the shrines were protected
with planks while the wall was taken
down. Carter here works with his
Egyptians and Callender.*

74 right
*The removal of the sealed blocking in the
Antechamber was a tricky operation,
requiring great care to avoid damage to
the shrines, and also to ensure that the
archaeological evidence of the blocking
should be properly recorded. In this
view Carnarvon himself can be seen
participating, helping Carter to remove
parts of the sealed area.*

that the buckles came from this tomb, stolen by Davis's workmen.

For nearly three years Carter was unable to resume work for Lord Carnarvon. He was not, however, entirely idle from the archaeological point of view. Whenever he came south to Thebes from Cairo, where he was engaged in work for Military Intelligence, he had time on his hands. 'Glad to say well occupied with drawing and painting.' Some of his drawing resulted from a commission he received to copy the very interesting, and artistically very fine, reliefs in the colonnade of the Temple of Luxor. Alan Gardiner planned a *de luxe* volume, the core of which would be Carter's drawings. Carter entered whole-heartedly into the work. The scenes, although always referred to by Gardiner as Horemheb's, had in fact been started in the reign of Amenophis III, and were completed under Tutankhamun. So, by coincidence, if not by planning, Carter found himself involved in material produced during the young king's reign. The project, sadly, was never completed because of the resumption of his work for Lord Carnarvon in late 1917. The drawings were among the finest he had ever made.

While he was staying in his house in Thebes, he was able to keep an eye on the activities of the local antiquities-hunters. Lax control during the war years offered rare opportunities for substantial initiatives in

three fine openwork plaques or buckles: 'They are two of carnelian and one agate cameos of Amenhotep III. I should say without a doubt from his tomb in the second Valley of the Kings (which as you know has never been properly cleared neither inside or out)...' So he reported to Carnarvon, and in February 1915 he followed up his hunch with a month's season in this tomb. The work carried out was perhaps a little perfunctory. He cleared some parts of the tomb, but not all of it as he subsequently claimed; but he did find foundation deposits in front of the entrance to the tomb, and also, most interestingly, part of a fourth buckle.

The month's work, although disappointing in general, provided a good example of Carter's shrewd interpretation of what may have happened when Davis's excavators had been at work; there can be little doubt, as Carter surmised,

clandestine archaeology. Carter exploited his local knowledge and his acquaintance with the Qurnawi, and was able to salvage much useful archaeological information from the confusion caused by illicit tomb-robbing.

He also, more unusually, began a piece of serious research, probably the first in his lifetime, compiling a comprehensive dossier on the history of the Valley of the Kings and its exploration. In Cairo he had access to good libraries, and he engaged the help of specialists to deal with evidence beyond his capabilities. Thus, he sought permission from the Metropolitan Museum Egyptian Expedition to ask their classical archaeologist, Hugh Evelyn-White, 'to help me later on the Classical stuff re Valley of the Kings. Among other reports of our work there which I trust will be exhaustive to the end – or as

Carter, when Chief Inspector, first introduced electric light to the Valley. As soon as Tutankhamun's tomb was opened, he and Callender installed it in the new tomb and found it essential for the efficient inspection and clearance of the objects. Here he is shown with a blaze of light looking through the doors of the second shrine, clearly dazzled by the brilliance of the golden third shrine within.

far as we can go – I aim... to publish in parts a kind of *Record of the Royal Theban Necropolis.*'

It is quite impressive to observe how Carter was preparing himself scientifically for the resumption of work in the Valley. It is now probably the right moment to consider whether Carter had at this time – the war years – seriously considered Tutankhamun's tomb to be a possible candidate for discovery. In his general book on the first season when he discovered that tomb, he states: 'at the risk of being accused of *post factum* prescience, I will state that we had definite hopes of finding the tomb of one particular king, and that king Tut.ankh.Amen'. He then goes on to justify this claim by setting out the archaeological evidence available at the time. All the relevant discoveries had been made by Theodore Davis. In the season of 1905–6 Ayrton found a small blue faience cup bearing the name of Tutankhamun; it lay 'at a depth of twelve feet from the surface' at a point about half way between the tomb of Ramesses VI and that of Amenophis II. It was an isolated find at the time. On December 21, 1907 Ayrton opened a small pit in the hill above the tomb of Sethos I. It contained what seemed to be a collection of ancient refuse – pottery jars, bags of natron, floral collars, mud trays with the remains of food, seal impressions, fragments of linen. Davis showed no interest in these rather dreary objects (although some of the jars were of fine shape), and he subsequently allowed

Herbert Winlock, a senior member of the Metropolitan Museum Egyptian Expedition, to carry the whole collection off to New York. In due course Winlock published a study of this material, concluding that it was indeed a mass of ancient refuse, but refuse deriving from the burial processes of the Tutankhamun inhumation. His name occurred on many objects, and much of the material, especially the natron, was undoubtedly waste from the embalming of the king. The traces of food were remnants of the final royal funerary feast. Winlock believed that the deposit was made some distance from the actual tomb so as not to contaminate the latter. The third piece of evidence pointing towards a tomb for Tutankhamun in the Valley was the cache of objects, including gold foil, about which Carter wrote to Mrs. Kingsmill Marrs in 1909, and which Davis had mistakenly published as the tomb of Tutankhamun.

therefore, were as good evidence for the existence of his tomb as the blue faience cup and the inscribed gold fragments. His own studies of the history of the Valley of the Kings could also have revealed Tutankhamun as being a prime candidate for an undiscovered tomb. But he was a rather insignificant king. James Henry Breasted, the great American historian of ancient Egypt, had found scarcely anything to say about him in his *History of Egypt* (1905, new edition 1909). If his tomb were to be found, could it possibly be in the same class as those of his predecessors of the Eighteenth Dynasty? And could it possibly be intact? There is plenty of room for speculation about Howard Carter's thinking way back in 1914, or even 1917 when he was seriously to start his search. But it scarcely amounts to much when the final triumph of his discovery is considered.

76 left
Three views of the shrines in the process of dismantling. The top picture looks over the cornice of the outermost shrine on to the linen pall with gilt-bronze marguerites. The removal of this pall involved rolling it onto a specially made wooden roller. When it was removed to the tomb of Sethos II, it was laid out for conservation in front of the tomb, and there it suffered damage at the time when Carter was locked out of the tomb in 1924. In the center, a view of the top of the quartzite sarcophagus lying within the innermost shrine, the walls of which are carefully protected with padding.

All these pieces of evidence indicated that there was a tomb for Tutankhamun in the Valley. But can it be believed that Carter had made the right connections as early as his first survey of the Valley with the Earl of Carnarvon after the licence to dig there had passed to them? As far as the burial refuse is concerned Winlock, in his study of 1941, states that he did not fully appreciate what the objects truly signified until the early 1920s. 'Eventually I gave Howard Carter further information about the find and he used it in *The Tomb of Tut.ankh.Amen...*' It is quite possible that Carter was being less than accurate in claiming that he knew about Winlock's findings earlier than seems likely, but it is not unreasonable to believe that he knew that some of the objects carried Tutankhamun's name, and they,

He opened his first campaign on the first of December 1917: 'Beginning in the small lateral valley situated between the tomb of Ramses II and Ramses VI, and running approximately N.W.–S.E.' It was not far from the entrance to that part of the main Valley which was occupied by the royal tombs. Opposite the opening to this 'small lateral valley' was KV 55, which had contained the extraordinary and enigmatic cache of Amarna Period funerary material found by Davis in 1907. The site was cut on its south side by the regular tourist path into the Valley on account of which excavation there had been strictly limited to avoid inconvenience to visitors. Here Carter first began to put into action his plan to clear down to bed-rock, the only certain way, he reckoned, by which he could be

76 right
Working in the confined space of the tomb to remove objects which were not in first-class condition required great delicacy and patience – virtues which Carter had in abundance. The removal of the top of the first shrine was particularly difficult. It was 5 metres long and over 3 metres wide, but was made up of three sections; there was little head-room for manuever. Here Carter and Callender supervise the operation. The original task of assembly after the funeral must have been equally difficult, although the timbers were not then warped.

sure that no tomb entrance was missed. And here in a small triangular area below the entrance to the tomb of Ramesses VI he uncovered the remains of a group of stone structures, workmen's huts connected undoubtedly with the cutting of the adjacent royal tomb. At this point he did not clear down to bed-rock, being anxious to complete his season's work without further inconveniencing visitors to the Valley. He would not return to those huts until November 1922. Generally, the season had not been encouraging; few objects had been found, and Carter's worries were compounded by disturbing news of Lord Carnarvon. Later, in a letter to Albert Lythgoe of the Metropolitan Museum, Carter wrote, 'Poor Lord Carnarvon, as no doubt you have heard, has had a very poor time. He nearly died this spring – saved only by an immediate operation for septic appendix.'

It is as well to bear in mind this crisis in the health of Lord Carnarvon, and to recall it when his mortal illness overtook him in 1923. He had first come to Egypt to recuperate from illness in 1903, and he always needed to watch his health. He was frequently accompanied by his personal physician when he came to Egypt. Yet illness did not prevent him from taking a strong interest in Carter's work. The War was not yet over, but the signs of final victory were beginning to appear as 1918 advanced. Carnarvon still wanted to excavate somewhere other than Thebes, and while the War continued he applied for and received a concession to work at Meir in Middle Egypt. Here there were rock-cut tombs of the Old and Middle Kingdoms, and it was worth giving the place a try. Carter proposed to carry out a limited, economical excavation for a few weeks – a

trial dig. In late November 1918 he began work at Meir with a small body of workmen, and he continued until mid-January. The results were not encouraging, and Carter was happy to return to Thebes. He opened work again in Carnarvon's principal concession on February 19, but continued for one week only, clearing an area deep in the Valley, below the tomb of Tuthmosis III. The shortness of the season appears to have been not the paucity of finds, but the eruption of civil disturbances throughout Egypt. Carter was recruited to act as a political officer for the Nag Hamadi district to the north of Luxor.

The troubles calmed down after a few weeks, and Carter was able to return to England on leave, his first visit home for three years. Returning to Thebes in the autumn he renewed the work in the Valley on the January 5, 1920. Apart from a brief investigation in the 'canyon' (as Carter called it) above the tomb of Tuthmosis III, at the far end of the Valley, in which he detected traces of what he considered to be debris from the cutting of a tomb, and needing further exploration, the work during this ten-week season was concentrated near the entrance to the Valley. Here, between the tombs of Ramesses II and Ramesses IV there were huge deposits of debris, dumped there from earlier excavations. A very large team of workmen was needed, assisted by a length of Decauville rail with trucks to move the spoil well away from the parts to be investigated. Carter had first encountered such a light railway when he assisted Naville in the clearance of the Deir el-Bahri temple of Queen Hatshepsut. The experience he then gained in shifting vast quantities of deposit with the help of large numbers of men proved to be of considerable value in his work in the Valley. He had to vary the pace of the work between large-scale clearance and the careful examination of promising places when the bed-rock had been reached. But by his strategy he found intact foundation deposits of Ramesses IV, and, as in most areas, numbers of inscribed and sketched *ostraca* – fragments of limestone used for casual sketches, memoranda, etc.

78 top and 79
Successive stages in the revealing of the third gold coffin. A reddish colored shroud covered it. The gold face was uncovered; arranged around the nemes-headdress was what Carter described as a linen napkin. An elaborate collar of beads and real flowers covered the neck and chest. When these had been removed, the lid of the gold coffin could be seen, disfigured by solidified unguents, but promising wonderful decoration when cleaned.

In mid-February Carnarvon, in much better health, joined Carter, staying, surprisingly, in Carter's house, while Lady Carnarvon and their daughter Evelyn Herbert stayed in the Winter Palace Hotel. Carter then shifted the focus of work to the area in front of the tomb of King Merenptah of the Nineteenth Dynasty, where again there were ancient, untouched, deposits. Here, in the presence of the Carnarvon family, he made what he described as 'the nearest approach to a real find that we had yet made in the Valley'. It was a collection of thirteen large alabaster vessels inscribed in ink with texts naming Merenptah and his father Ramesses II. They had held sacred oils used in the funerary ceremonies of Merenptah. 'We were naturally excited, and Lady Carnarvon, I remember, insisted on digging out these jars – beautiful specimens they were – with her own hands.' It is not surprising that Carter did not greatly welcome their presence on the dig; eager but untrained hands could easily cause damage.

Part of his plan for this season was to commence the clearance of the workmen's huts below the entrance to the tomb of Ramesses VI. But time ran out, and he decided to leave the huts until the next season, which he proposed to start in the autumn of 1920. Work began at the beginning of December. Once again he continued bed-rock clearance in the lateral valley between the tombs of Ramesses II and Ramesses VI, and he began work on the triangular site containing the huts. Fate was not on his side.

In his excavation diary entry for January 2, 1921 he notes: 'As one is unable to cut away the path in front of T9 (RVI) [i.e. the tomb of Ramesses VI] during the tourist season and the coming visit of the Sultan [I] have removed men for the time being to another portion of the valley'. He had, in spite of good intentions, started his season too late, and VIP visits would at that time always take precedence over ordinary archaeology, as he was to find to his cost after he had made his great discovery, and was overwhelmed by grand visitors. Most of the rest of the season, which ended on March 3, 1921, was spent working a number of sites at the far end of the Valley, near the tomb of Tuthmosis III. This area exercised a notable attraction on Carter, who returned to it again and again, but always with negligible results.

His intention once again to start early in the autumn of 1921, to anticipate the arrival of tourists, was sadly frustrated by his own poor health. In October he wrote to Frederic Whiting, Director of the Cleveland Museum of Art, for whom he was acting as an antiquities adviser: 'unfortunately I have been indisposed for this last few weeks and I am now obliged to undergo a serious abdominal operation'. It would be the removal of his gall bladder, carried out by the same surgeon who had dealt with Lord Carnarvon's appendix in 1918. Carnarvon had become very much Carter's role-model in most things

78 bottom
After the lid of the third coffin was raised, the mummy of Tutankhamun was visible – the first royal body from Egypt to be so discovered, undamaged by tomb robbers. Here it lay, protected at every level by sacred objects. The body, below the crossed arms, was strapped by bands of inscribed gold and straps of inlaid plaques, arranged over the body like restraining bandages. Beneath the golden bands was the ba-bird with outstretched wings, the form of the spirit that could move in and out of the tomb, enabling the deceased to exercise free mobility. Carter with his unfailing desire to keep a proper record of what was discovered, made drawings of what could be seen at each stage in the unwrapping of the mummy. Here is his drawing of the trappings on the body, made not just with care, but with great style. He was a consummate draughtsman, and his drawings form a most important part of his documentary record of the excavation and clearance of the tomb. Even under stress his professionalism enabled him to record to the highest standard.

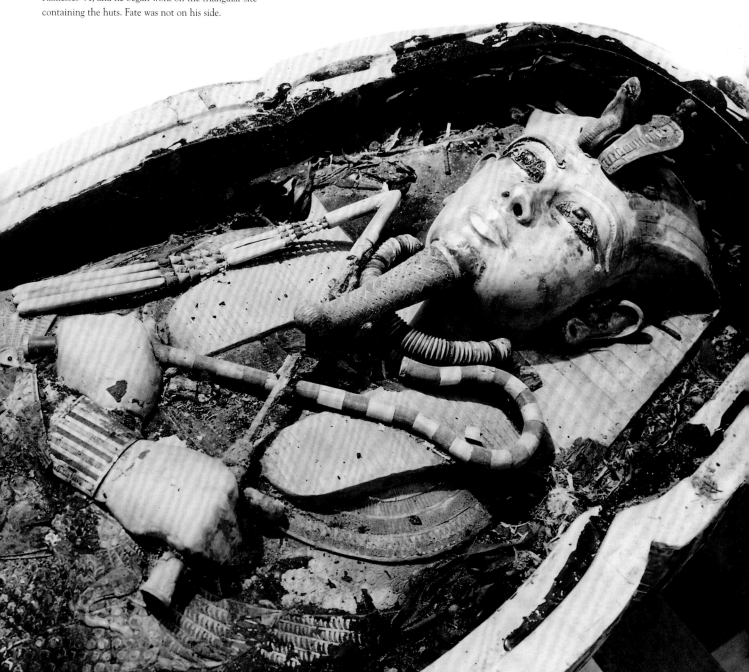

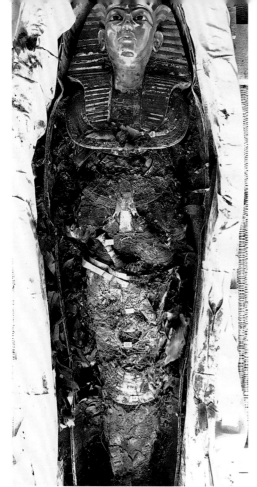

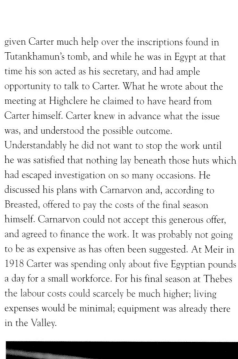

given Carter much help over the inscriptions found in Tutankhamun's tomb, and while he was in Egypt at that time his son acted as his secretary, and had ample opportunity to talk to Carter. What he wrote about the meeting at Highclere he claimed to have heard from Carter himself. Carter knew in advance what the issue was, and understood the possible outcome. Understandably he did not want to stop the work until he was satisfied that nothing lay beneath those huts which had escaped investigation on so many occasions. He discussed his plans with Carnarvon and, according to Breasted, offered to pay the costs of the final season himself. Carnarvon could not accept this generous offer, and agreed to finance the work. It was probably not going to be as expensive as has often been suggested. At Meir in 1918 Carter was spending only about five Egyptian pounds a day for a small workforce. For his final season at Thebes the labour costs could scarcely be much higher; living expenses would be minimal; equipment was already there in the Valley.

non-archaeological! He spent six weeks in hospital and six weeks convalescing before he could return to Egypt on January 25, 1922. Work started on February 8, the day after Lord Carnarvon had joined him. It was much too late for those tiresome but tantalizing workmen's huts, so Carter directed his men further into the Valley to the 'east side of the foot hill containing the tomb of Siptah'. Here Theodore Davis had worked in 1905, and Carter noted: 'The greater part of this spot was covered with large mounds of rubbish thrown out during the excavation of Siptah's tomb'. Carter also noted: 'Its removal took 10 days with 40 men and 120 boys'. The season ended in early March – Carter was still recovering from his gall bladder operation – and the results were minimal and again disappointing. Carnarvon, who had stayed on in Luxor for two weeks, while Carter visited Cairo, had time to reflect, and brood, on the way his excavation was going. It was not at all encouraging.

Later in the year, back in England, Carnarvon had further time for reflexion. Carter had been working in the Valley since late 1917 – over five years. It had not been such an intensive campaign as has sometimes been suggested, in total just about eight months on the ground. Nevertheless, work had at times been very concentrated, large numbers of men were employed, and the expense had been considerable. Carnarvon himself was not old, just fifty-six in June 1922; but his health was not good, and his finances, after the difficult years of the First World War, were not in the best of condition. The yield of fine objects from these recent years had been considerably less than the harvest from the years of work in the lower slopes of Dra Abu'l Naga before the War. It was time to call a halt. Carter was summoned to Highclere Castle. The only evidence of this crucial meeting in the summer of 1922 is contained in Charles Breasted's biography of his father, James Henry Breasted, *Pioneer of the Past*, written in 1948. Breasted senior had

Working in the limited space of a small tomb without adequate ventilation was a constant physical strain on Howard Carter and his associates. Nevertheless, it is strange to see Carter here working in his shirt-sleeves, without a suit or a hat. But Carter was a professional in all he did as far as the tomb was concerned, and he was ever ready to strip down and join in the work whenever he could. He was very much a 'hands-on' archaeologist; he was also endowed with infinite patience. He would never be rushed, and always took care at every point to ensure that everything moved smoothly. Here he is working on the face of the second coffin, dusting it carefully with a soft brush. With such objects there was always the risk that fragments might be lost, especially of glass inlay. The lightest of touches was needed. He worked with the delicacy of a surgeon.

On October 11, Carter arrived in Egypt, and spent two weeks trawling the antiquities shops of Cairo on Carnarvon's and his own behalf. So much for urgency! On October 27 he reached Luxor, and on the November 1 opened his season in front of the tomb of Ramesses VI – the fateful untouched triangle of land. First came the planning and then the removal of those workmen's huts, completed by the evening of November 3. Carter could trust his experienced local workmen to carry out the next stage without initial supervision. Under their foreman, Ahmed Gerigar, they began on the next day to remove the debris beneath the huts, working down to the bed-rock. By the time Carter joined the dig a frisson of expectation indicated that something had happened. The first step down to the tomb had been uncovered. With his knowledge of the arrangements of the entrances to tombs in the Valley, he had to be excited. In the course of the day enough steps had been uncovered to reveal the top of the plastered blocking, which without question indicated the entrance to a tomb. At that point Carter could not make out any royal names in the great seal impressions stamped on the mud plaster, but he could recognize the jackal and nine bound prisoners of the Royal Necropolis seal. Here at last was something to reward him for his persistence and faith, and Carnarvon for his support. Now he must contain his curiosity; and so, filling in the stairs, he crossed the river to Luxor, and sent off the fateful telegram quoted at the beginning of this chapter.

The Earl of Carnarvon and his daughter, Evelyn Herbert, reached Luxor on November 23. Carter and his new assistant, Arthur Callender, had everything ready to resume the clearance. By the afternoon of the 24th the whole blocked entrance was visible, and seal impressions towards the bottom clearly gave Tutankhamun's name. The removal of the blocking revealed a corridor leading down quite steeply and filled with rubble. There was disturbing evidence that this filling had been burrowed through on at least two occasions, and as the excavators removed the rubble, fragments of antiquities were found.

Some of these carried royal names, which suggested that whatever lay beyond had been robbed, and that the contents might have been material from more than one royal burial – possibly another cache. After about eight metres a further mud-plastered blocking with seal impressions was reached. It was November 27. Carter wrote:

'The decisive moment had arrived. With trembling hands I made a tiny breach in the upper left hand corner. Darkness and blank space, as far as an iron testing rod could reach, showed that whatever lay beyond was empty... Candle tests were applied as a precaution against foul gases and then, widening the hole a little, I inserted the candle and peered in... At first I could see nothing... but presently, as my eyes grew accustomed to the light, details of the room within emerged slowly from the mist, strange animals, statues and gold – everywhere the glint of gold.

For the moment... I was struck dumb with amazement, and when Lord Carnarvon, unable to stand the suspense any longer, inquired anxiously. 'Can you see anything?' it was all I could do to get out the words, 'Yes, wonderful things'.

Now the great work of investigation and clearance could begin.

A TREASURE ABOVE ALL TREASURES

82–83

A pectoral from a jewel box in the Treasury. Its main form of a winged scarab incorporates the prenomen of Tutankhamun. The cloisonné inlays are of semiprecious stones and coloured glass, the scarab itself being a fine single piece of lapis-lazuli.

84

A calcite stopper from the Canopic chest. It is a royal head which is surely not that of Tutankhamun; it was possibly prepared originally for the burial of his predecessor Neferneferuaten.

85

A carnelian bird, a swallow or a swift, with a sun-disk on its back. It is mounted on a gold bangle placed within the king's mummy wrappings. The bird may represent a transformation of the sun-god.

When Howard Carter was asked by Lord Carnarvon what he could see through the hole he had made in the blocked entrance to the tomb, he claims to have said 'wonderful things'. These may not have been his precise words at the time, but they have come to represent what he could have said, words which were in any case very appropriate for the discovery. The tomb was not in the state it would have been at the time of the king's funeral, and for Carter and Carnarvon that implied that it was not intact. According to the terms of his licence to excavate, Carnarvon could expect a substantial share of the tomb's contents, and there can be little doubt that he ever thought otherwise. Carter from the first had felt that the whole tomb equipment should go to the Cairo Museum, but he was Carnarvon's man, and he could advise but not decide.

His examination of the many boxes in the Antechamber which had been broken into, rifled, and repacked carelessly by the Necropolis guards convinced him that a very large number of fine and precious objects had been stolen. His view was reinforced when he came to examine the Treasury. Here again there was scarcely a box that had not had its seal broken and been ransaked. In the tomb only the innermost shrines, the sarcophagus and coffins, the royal mummy itself and the Canopic shrine were in the positions and condition in which they had been left on the day of burial.

So, Carter concluded, the majority of fine objects, including most of the best jewellery, had gone, and he was left to deal with the residue. What a residue! Carter never complained about the 'meagre' material with which he and his co-workers had to deal. A residue indeed, but still what riches! It took ten years to clear, clean, conserve and document the objects, with many lost months when official difficulties prevented work at Thebes. It is doubtful whether any other archaeologist of the time would have had the pertinacity and patience to keep the process going for so long: certainly not Sir Flinders Petrie, brilliant but impatient; not even George Reisner of Harvard and Boston, meticulous but restless.

One side of the palm of the ostrich-hunt fan found in the Burial Chamber. Here Tutankhamun is depicted in heroic form. He stands alone in his chariot, driving his team of horses at full speed in the chase after ostriches in the Eastern Desert. Two birds have been shot with the king's arrows, and his hound bounds forward to retrieve them. A fine symbolic touch in the design is the ostrich fan carried behind the chariot by a personified ankh-sign.

Carter, the artist, skilled with pencil and dextrous in handling delicate material, the close observer who spotted the smallest detail and noted it down, was a sticker, and he saw the task through to the end. From the outset he gathered an unparallelled team of helpers who were only too ready to participate in this most wonderful of discoveries. The important ones stuck with him as long as they could, enduring his moods but never doubting his competence and integrity: in particular Arthur Mace and Harry Burton, archaeologist and photographer, loaned by the Metropolitan Museum of Art, New York; and Alfred Lucas, retired forensic chemist, but working for the Egyptian government. These were all at the sharp end of the work, and it is largely due to them that the objects from the tomb were so wonderfully retrieved, documented, examined scientifically and photographed. But Carter was the key and constant presence.

The archaeological and artistic rewards from the tomb have been inestimable. Objects of kinds never previously discovered, or only known from tomb and temple scenes were there – the great shrines, the coffins and the mummy, the Canopic shrine and its precious contents, the ritual couches, the gilded divine figures and the images of Tutankhamun himself. The mummy in particular provided an exercise in excavation in itself. Texts of burial practice, including parts of the Book of the Dead, give many indications of what amulets and other protective objects should be placed on a body; representations of elaborate collars and other items shown in the object friezes on the great wooden coffin of the Middle Kingdom suggested the proper furnishings for a fully equipped mummy.

As Howard Carter removed the bandages from the royal corpse, he uncovered layer after layer of protective objects – representations charged with divine power, amuletic objects invested with magical forces by appropriate texts. Here for the first time was a practical demonstration of what the texts had indicated. Even now the full implications of the mummy accoutrements have not been adequately appreciated or studied.

In many respects the contents of the tomb gave the impression of being a haphazard collection of objects from the palace and the royal storerooms. Did a royal burial provide an opportunity to dispose of royal objects which were no longer of any use, but could not just be thrown away? Why, for example, was a wine jar included which dated back to the reign of Amenophis III? Was it full of wine when deposited in the tomb? Could the wine have been drinkable? Was it just an opportunity to dispose of a jar of royal wine well past its consumable date?

The questions are manifold, and there remains much scope for the analysis and examination of the tomb's contents. What cannot be denied, however, is that the range and excellent condition of so many objects, made by the best craftsmen, using the best materials, provide huge opportunities for the elucidation of technical processes, and the study of styles and even of taste. Let us consider the remarkable calcite vessels used to hold unguents and perfumed oils. For years these extraordinary containers were singled out as examples of bad taste. They were florid, over-decorated, intricate beyond the requirements of utility: in short, they demonstrated the decadence of artistic appreciation at the end of the Eighteenth Dynasty. They lacked the purity of form which seemed so characteristic of Egyptian design in the Middle Kingdom and in the earlier years of the Eighteenth Dynasty. Nowadays it is easier to consider such objects as being creations of their time, made for their particular function according to the principles of contemporary appreciation. Why should our good taste be the same as the good taste of the ancient Egyptians? Some people may not like them, but they are what they are, the remarkable products of remarkable craftsmen who understood the capabilities of their materials and exploited them to the best of their abilities.

The tomb's contents are infinite in their ability to teach, to surprise, to enthral. They make up a cornucopia of treasure, sacred and profane. They are indeed wonderful things.

88

The shape of the pomegranate was a favourite of Egyptian vessel makers of the New Kingdom, examples occurring in glass, calcite and ivory. This little vase, made of silver with a substantial proportion of gold, is one of two such vases in the tomb, the other being made of ivory. It bears bands of chased decoration incorporating cornflowers and vine leaves.

89

A gilded wooden standard of the divine falcon named Gemehsu. It was stored with the standard of Sopdu in one of the black-painted wooden chests in the Treasury. The Gemehsu falcon, shown in mummified form with a royal flail protruding from its back, may represent in form one of several Egyptian divinities so transformed. The details are made of glass inlay.

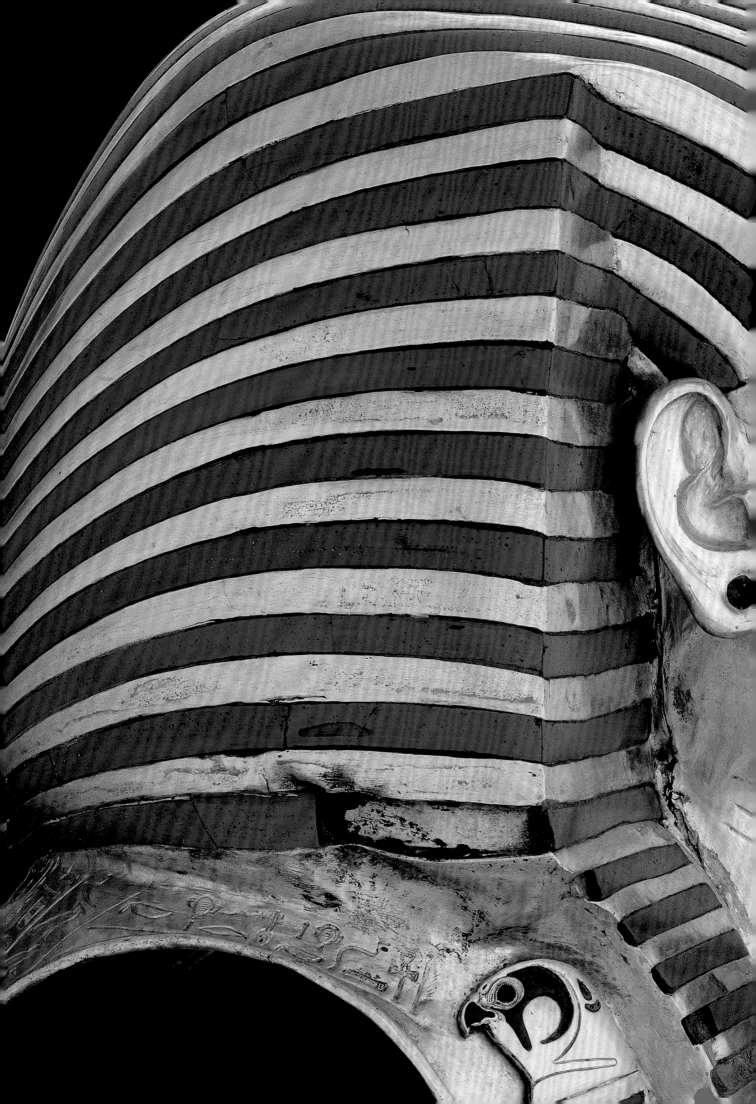

PERSONAL FUNERARY EQUIPMENT

The most important object in a tomb was the mummy of the deceased. The most important purpose of the burial was to ensure the preservation of the mummy so that the dead person could pass to and be equipped for the after-life. The greatest care was therefore taken to protect the mummy.

In the tomb of Tutankhamun was found the most complete set of protective measures discovered in any burial. The mummy was contained within three coffins, all placed in a stone sarcophagus, which in turn was enclosed within four shrines.
A hint of such an arrangement had been found by Carter and Alan Gardiner in a tomb plan on a papyrus in the Turin Museum which they had published in 1917. In this plan the sarcophagus is surrounded by six rectangles, which they had tentatively thought to be steps. In retrospect they could see an arrangement of sarcophagus and shrines like those provided for Tutankhamun.

Tutankhamun's ensemble fitted so neatly into his small burial chamber that it must be concluded that the shrines were almost certainly made after the king's death, when the layout was known.

A secondary part of the personal funerary equipment concerned the mummified internal organs of the deceased. These were usually placed in four vessels called Canopic jars. In Tutankhamun's case the organs were placed in four miniature coffins put in a calcite chest. A gilded wooden shrine covered the chest, and the shrine was protected by an open canopy with an elaborate cornice.
The whole shrine was placed under the protection of four gilded figures of the protective goddesses Isis, Nephthys, Selkis and Neith – among the most enchanting and seductive figures to have been found in Egypt, or any other ancient culture.

The Canopic shrine, because of the lack of space in the Burial Chamber, was placed in the adjacent room, which Carter called the Treasury.

90
A side view of the great golden mask of Tutankhamun; it reveals the extraordinary sensitivity of the royal portrait, produced by a master craftsman.

THE FIRST
GILDED SHRINE

(CARTER 207, J.D'E. 60664; LENGTH 508 CM,
WIDTH 328 CM, HEIGHT 275 CM)

When Howard Carter began to
take down the blocking between
the Antechamber and the Burial
Chamber, the observers gathered
in the tomb were dazzled by the
gradual revelation of this shrine,
a spectacular gold wall with
openwork decoration consisting
of the amuletic signs *djed* and *tyet*,
'endurance and life', with a
background of bright blue glazed
faience. The great shrine
subsequently revealed had a roof
with two humps, somewhat
resembling the sign for the
horizon. As a whole the shrine

also resembles the pavilion used
during the *sed* or jubilee festival
of the king, composed of two
chapels placed back to back. Its
walls are inscribed on the inside
and on the doors with texts from
the Book of the Dead and
passages from a composition for
royal burials known as the Book
of the Divine Cow. Nine
vultures with outstretched wings
decorate the ceiling. Within this
shrine, and embracing the
second shrine was the frame
supporting the linen pall with
gilt-bronze marguerites.

THE SECOND GILDED SHRINE

(CARTER 237, J.D'E. 60660; LENGTH 374 CM, WIDTH 235 CM, HEIGHT 225 CM)

Between the first, outermost, shrine and this second shrine was the linen pall with gilded bronze daisies draped over a wooden frame. The form of the shrine itself, with sloping roof, is that of the *per-wer*, traditionally the Upper Egyptian shrine. The wooden structure is covered with gesso-plaster, carved with fine relief representations and inscriptions, and then gilded. The texts on the inside and the outside are taken from traditional royal compositions like the Pyramid Texts of the Old Kingdom, and also from the more recent compilations, like the Book of the Dead. There are also texts written in hieroglyphs used enigmatically, where incomprehensible switchings of signs are used, presumably to confuse the hostile forces which the king might meet in his journeys after death. Carter detected changes in cartouches which to him suggested re-use from the Amarna Period. The representations, however, are not in the Amarna style.

3

4

THE THIRD GILDED SHRINE

(CARTER 238, J.D'E. 60667; LENGTH 340 CM, WIDTH 192 CM, HEIGHT 215 CM)

Like the second shrine, this one is also in the form of the Upper Egyptian palace shrine, the *per-wer*. In the usual royal tomb of the Eighteenth Dynasty, the walls of the various rooms and corridors were decorated and inscribed with scenes and texts from the newly devised royal compositions to enable the dead king to pass through the Underworld by night, to achieve union with the sun god at dawn. The tomb of Tutankhamun, a makeshift refuge for a king prematurely dead, it seems, was cramped, and the only room to be decorated was the Burial Chamber. In consequence, some of the important texts of divine passage were inscribed on the great shrines. On the outer walls of this third shrine are shortened versions of two of the sections of the composition 'What is in the Underworld', a small part of which is painted on the west wall of the Burial Chamber. There is also an utterance from the Book of the Dead for providing sustenance to the *ka* of the deceased in the underworld.

THE FOURTH GILDED SHRINE

(CARTER 239, J.D'E. 60668; LENGTH 290 CM, WIDTH 148 CM, HEIGHT 190 CM)

This shrine has a vaulted roof, taking the form of the pre-dynastic Lower Egyptian palace shrine, the *per-nu*. When it was erected in the tomb it made a tight fit around the sarcophagus, which had not been positioned with precision; parts of it therefore had to be trimmed to permit its erection. The walls of the shrine have reliefs containing deities closely associated with the protection of the king after death, and the care of his separately mummified internal organs.

All the Canopic deities are shown: Isis, Nephthys, Selkis and Neith; and the genii of the entrails: Amsety, Duamutef, Hapy and Qebhsenuef; also those deities found on the sides of royal sarcophagi: Thoth in two forms, Geb, Anubis and Horus. The main text is Utterance 17 of the Book of the Dead, a long rambling composition concerning the sun god and his doctrinal significance, with many comments on the god and on the deceased.

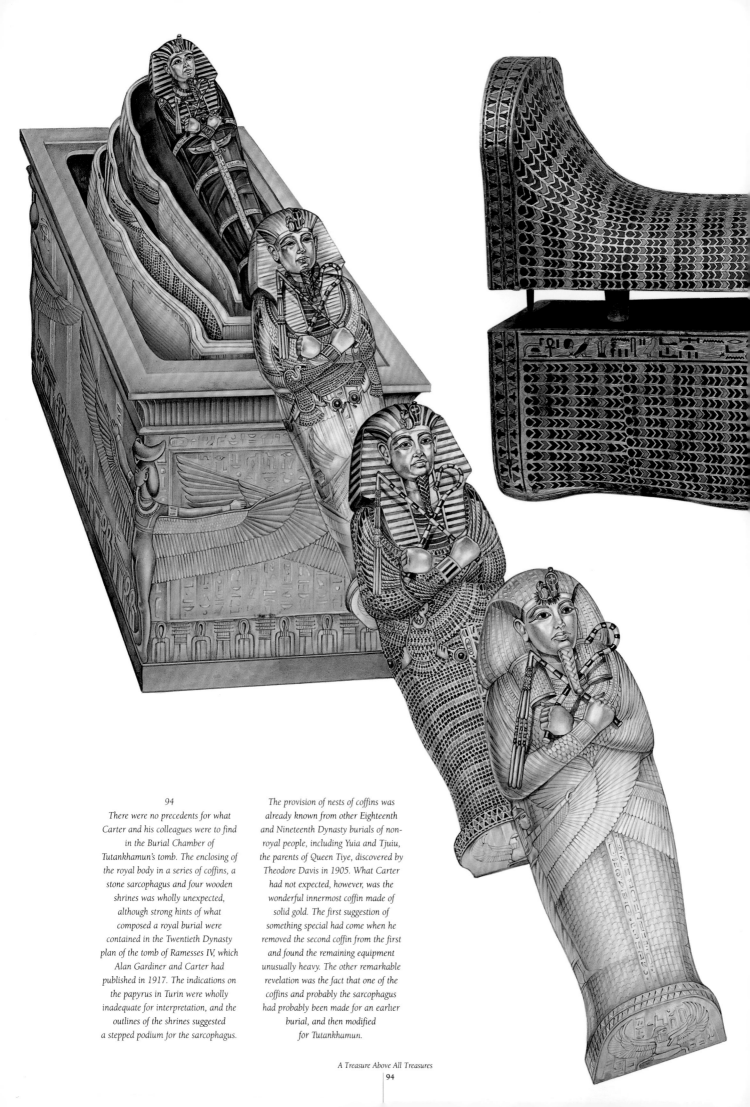

94

There were no precedents for what Carter and his colleagues were to find in the Burial Chamber of Tutankhamun's tomb. The enclosing of the royal body in a series of coffins, a stone sarcophagus and four wooden shrines was wholly unexpected, although strong hints of what composed a royal burial were contained in the Twentieth Dynasty plan of the tomb of Ramesses IV, which Alan Gardiner and Carter had published in 1917. The indications on the papyrus in Turin were wholly inadequate for interpretation, and the outlines of the shrines suggested a stepped podium for the sarcophagus.

The provision of nests of coffins was already known from other Eighteenth and Nineteenth Dynasty burials of non-royal people, including Yuia and Tjuiu, the parents of Queen Tiye, discovered by Theodore Davis in 1905. What Carter had not expected, however, was the wonderful innermost coffin made of solid gold. The first suggestion of something special had come when he removed the second coffin from the first and found the remaining equipment unusually heavy. The other remarkable revelation was the fact that one of the coffins and probably the sarcophagus had probably been made for an earlier burial, and then modified for Tutankhamun.

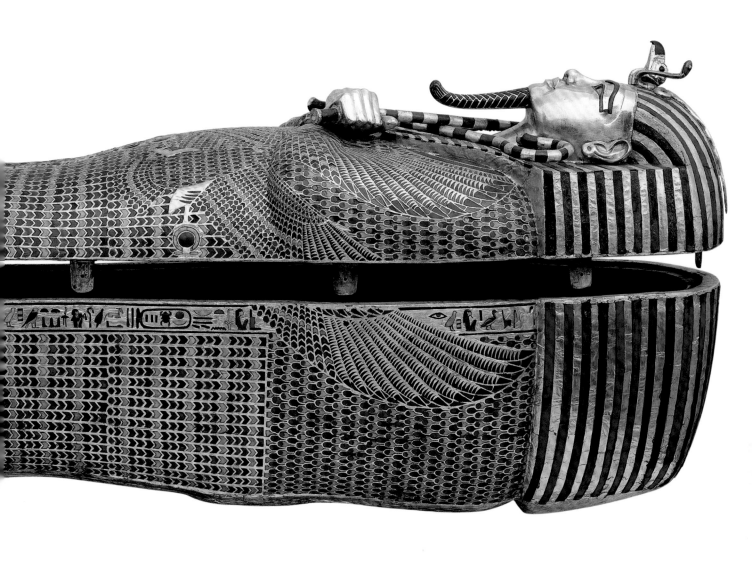

THE MIDDLE COFFIN

(CARTER 254, J.D'E. 60670; LENGTH 204 CM,
MAX. HEIGHT 78.5 CM; MAX. WIDTH 68 CM)

The fine outer coffin of Tutankhamun, of gilded and inlaid wood, now lies in the sarcophagus in the king's tomb in the Valley; it contains the royal mummy.

When Carter returned to Thebes in the autumn of 1925, his first task was to open up the coffin to retrieve and examine the mummy. What he did not appreciate was that there would be three coffins nesting each within another. When the lid of the outermost coffin was raised, he found the middle coffin covered with a linen shroud and garlands of flowers – olives, lotus, cornflowers – attached to strips of papyrus. After removal and cleaning, the coffin presented a magnificent sight.

It is made of wood and covered with sheet gold. The decoration of the body is carried out in a cloisonné technique, which involved the inlaying of pieces of coloured glass and semiprecious stones in cells or cloisons made by soldering thin strips of gold to the main body of the coffin. The inlays

are individually cut to fit the cloisons. Dark blue glass, light blue glass and red glass represent lapis-lazuli, turquoise and red jasper or carnelian. The principal decorative motif is a feather design, called *rishi*, which here looks like chevrons. On the upper part of the coffin inlaid figures of the cobra and vulture deities with outstretched wings protect the body within.

On the lid of the coffin, the king is shown with royal accoutrements, and the headdress known as *nemes*, in reality probably made of folded cloth. On his brow are the two royal protective deities, cobra and vulture heads. The plaited beard with turned up tip is closely associated with Osiris, god of the dead.

The features of the king here are markedly different from those on the outer and innermost coffins, which suggests that this coffin may not have been made originally for Tutankhamun.

THE INNERMOST COFFIN

(CARTER 255, J.D'E. 60671; LENGTH 187 CM,
HEIGHT 51 CM, WIDTH 51.3 CM, WEIGHT 110.4 KG)

The excavators were much puzzled by the great weight of the coffins when they were removed from the sarcophagus. The mystery was solved when the lid of the middle coffin was raised and they found a third coffin made of solid gold. After the removal of its contents and cleaning, it was found to weigh 110.4 kg. It is quite the most impressive coffin ever found, but apart from its bullion value it is an outstanding piece of craftsmanship; the head is particularly well done, the features being distinctly those of the young king. Again he is shown with the *uraeus* and vulture on his brow, and holding the crook and flail, symbols of royalty. Around the neck, separately added, are necklaces of disk beads of gold and coloured glass; on his chest is an elaborate collar made up to represent eleven rows of tubular beads of coloured glass.

When this coffin was placed in the middle coffin, large quantities of bituminous resin were poured over it, which in time fixed it firmly

in place. It took Carter and his assistants much time to soften and chip away this material, in order to separate the two coffins. The hot bitumen had damaged some of the inlays, and caused deterioration in some elements of decoration, including the calcite whites of the eyes.

The decoration of the main body of the coffin is again *rishi*-work, but here in the form of chasing rather than inlay. Splendid figures of the cobra Wadjyt and the vulture Nekhbet with outstretched protective wings are shown on the chest, and further down on the sides of the legs are delicate relief figures of Isis and Nephthys, traditional guardians and mourners of the dead, also with protecting wings. On the foot of the coffin is another figure of the goddess Isis with outstretched wings, beautifully designed to fit the available space. She is shown kneeling on the sign for 'gold', and is described as 'Great Isis, mother of the god'.

98–103
*Two of the Canopic lids
representing Tutankhamun,
but probably portraits of his
predecessor Neferneferuaten.*

THE CANOPIC SHRINE

(CARTER 266, J.D'E. 60686;
HEIGHT 198 CM, LENGTH 153 CM, WIDTH 122 CM)

The purpose of this shrine was to protect the embalmed internal organs of the dead king. The shrine itself is placed under an open canopy on a sledge. All components are made of wood and gilded. The corner posts of the canopy are inscribed inside and out with Tutankhamun's full titulary. The posts support a heavy cornice with a dramatic frieze of *uraei* with sun-disks, inlaid with blue, red and green glass; the effect is spectacular.

Between the posts on each side is a figure of one of the goddesses charged with protecting the containers of the entrails: Isis is identified by a seat on her head, Nephthys by a basket on an enclosure, Selkis by a scorpion and Neith by two bows. The figures are among the most appealing of Egyptian sculptures. Each goddess is shown with a slender, slightly elongated body, designed in accordance with the proportions associated with the art of the Amarna Period. Each is shown wearing a tight-fitting pleated garment with short sleeves; her head is covered by a cloth; her hair, which hangs down the back, being drawn together just below her neck. Most exceptionally, each head is turned to the left in an attractive but quite un-Egyptian manner. Eyes and eyebrows are dramatically marked in black.

The shrine itself also has a cornice and frieze of *uraei*. Each side shows a scene of a god or goddess stretching out a hand towards one of the Canopic deities or genii, identified with the various organs: Isis to Amsety, Geb (the earth god) to Duamutef, Ptah-Sokar-Osiris to Qebhsenuef, and Nephthys to Hapy. The effect of Amarna-style conventions can again be observed in these divine figures; it is particularly noticeable that their heads are exaggerated in size.

110

The arrangement of coffins and shrines, provided for the protection of the mummy of the dead king, has been compared with the idea of 'Chinese boxes' or 'Russian dolls' – a diminishing series of containers, one within another. A similar, but less complicated, arrangement was prepared for the protection of those parts of the royal body which could not be included in the coffins. The diagrammatic illustration here shows clearly the sequence of the protective elements. An open canopy surrounds the shrine proper, which is supported by the four Canopic goddesses, charmingly and sensitively posed. Within the shrine was the Canopic chest with lid, made from two pieces of finely zoned calcite. On the removal of the lid four royal heads become visible. These form the stoppers of four cylindrical depressions cut into the calcite of the chest, each depression containing a solid gold miniature coffin decorated in the cloissonné technique, and containing the mummified internal organs of the king.

THE CANOPIC CHEST

(CARTER 266B, J.D'E. 60687; TOTAL HEIGHT 85.5 CM,
WIDTH OF EACH SIDE OF THE BASE 54 CM)

The very earliest known Canopic chest was made for Queen Hetepheres, mother of Cheops the builder of the Great Pyramid, who lived more than a thousand years before Tutankhamun. It was made of calcite and of very simple design. Tutankhamun's chest is also made of calcite, but more elaborate in design. It was found inside the Canopic shrine, covered with a linen cloth.

In the Eighteenth Dynasty most Canopic chests had compartments containing jars for the internal organs, each with a human head stopper. This royal chest has four cylindrical depressions cut into its mass to receive the Canopic coffins, and each is topped by a stopper in the form of a royal head, finely carved with a few details picked out in black paint, and the lips rouged. The heads seem to be portraits. But of whom? There is good reason to believe that they do not show Tutankhamun, but perhaps his predecessor. This question is discussed further in connection with the Canopic coffins.

The chest is carved from a finely veined block of calcite in the form of a shrine; it has a sloping lid which was fastened to the chest by cords passed through staples and sealed. The chest stands on a gilded wooden sledge, and its lower part is carved with a gilded dado made up of the amuletic *djed* and *tyet* signs connected with Osiris and Isis. At the corners of the chest figures of the four protective goddeses are carved in high relief: Isis, Nephthys, Neith and Selkis. Each figure is quite unusual in that it is folded around its corner with one arm stretched on the two adjacent sides of the chest. Each is shown apparently nude, with very slender elongated limbs, but without the usual protecting wings. The inscriptions carved on the sides of the chest are filled with blue pigment which contrasts sharply with the waxy-yellow colour of the calcite. The texts invoke the protection of the four deities.

114 and 115 The two sides of the Canopic chest shown here carry statements by Canopic goddesses. The left-hand picture shows the back of the chest, and the statements are addressed by Neith (left) and Selkis (right) to Tutankhamun, whose names are in the cartouches. The figures of the appropriate goddesses are carved on the corners of the chest.

The principal picture shows one side of the chest with invocations by Neith (right) and Isis (left) to their Canopic genii, Qebhsenuef and Amsety respectively. Above is the sloping lid of the chest.

CANOPIC COFFINS

(CARTER 266, J.D'E. 60690, 60689;
HEIGHT 39 CM, WIDTH 11 CM, DEPTH 12 CM)

The term Canopic jar is strictly incorrect. Early scholars saw in these human-headed jars confirmation of the ancient story of Canopus, pilot of Menelaus, who was buried at Canopus and worshipped locally in the form of a jar with a human head. Jars were not, however, used for Tutankhamun's internal organs, but miniature coffins. Those illustrated here, protected by Nephthys and Neith, held the king's lungs, identified with the genius Hapy, and his stomach, identified with the genius Duamutef.

Each small coffin is a remarkable example of the Egyptian goldsmith's skills. Made of solid gold, most of the body is covered with the feathered *rishi*-pattern, carried out in the cloisonné technique, with tiny cloisons inlaid with individually cut pieces of coloured glass. The upper part of the body is shown to be enveloped by the wings of two vultures, one with the head of Nekhbet, the other with the *uraeus* head of Wadjyt. A line of text on the lid contains a statement by the appropriate deity: 'I embrace with my arms what is within me; I protect Hapy (or Duamutef) who is in me, Hapy (or Duamutef) of the Osiris King Nebkheperure [prenomen of Tutankhamun], justified before the great god'. The inside of the lid has a figure of the appropriate deity in protective attitude; the body of the coffin contains a long magical text on behalf of the king.

Careful examination shows that changes have been made to the cartouches inside the coffins. Traces indicate clearly that the name in the prenomen cartouche was first Ankh-kheperure, prenomen of Neferneferuaten, predecessor of Tutankhamun. The chest and miniature coffins were clearly made originally for this predecessor; they were either never used or recycled for the young king. The physiognomy of the human-headed stoppers and of the little coffins, so distinctly different from that of Tutankhamun, as shown by his innermost and outermost coffins and many other images in the tomb, provides strong confirmation of this re-use.

SERVANT FIGURES

The burial of every Egyptian of means would include a figure in mummiform which was magically to assist the deceased in carrying out certain manual duties in the afterworld. In the Eighteenth Dynasty many burials were provided with fine *shabtis* in various materials, and later in the dynasty they begin to be called *shawabtis*. They are usually shown carrying hoes, mattocks and baskets – the tools of their trade.

The few surviving *shabtis* of kings of the Eighteenth Dynasty had shown that fine examples were made; but these could in no way have prepared the excavators for the great numbers found in Tutankhamun's tomb: in total 413, mostly stored in black painted boxes, eleven in the Treasury (with 176 figures) and fourteen in the Annexe (236); one which had 'escaped' from the Annexe was found in the Antechamber. Where a figure is named, it is called *shabti*. A common analysis of the 413 establishes 365 as being for single-day duty, thirty-six for duties overseeing groups of more than ten, and twelve as monthly overseers. It is not easy, however, to apply this distribution to the figures themselves. There is a huge diversity in material, size, iconography and inscription. Some are plain wood with a few details emphasized in black paint; gold leaf used sparingly enhances others; some are of wood, wholly gilded. There are many faience examples with different coloured glazes; some are carved of stone – calcite, limestone, granite etc. There are many headdresses, all the principal royal crowns being represented. Some hold royal insignia, but not usually working tools. But large numbers of model hoes, mattocks, yokes and baskets in metal, faience and wood were also found in the Treasury and the Annexe.

The finest figures are of carved wood, large, and presented for the king's burial by the general and royal scribe Nakhtmin, or Minnakhte (five), and the treasurer Maya (one): tokens of devotion in life and beyond the grave.

118 left
Plain wooden shabti with a broad collar and armlets of gold foil, wearing a Nubian wig with bronze uraeus and vulture heads.

118 right
Gilded wooden shabti wearing the white crown of Upper Egypt and holding a bronze crook. Bodily features suggest that this figure was made for a woman.

119
Turquoise glazed shabti with details picked out in black. This is an overseer or reis figure, and it holds the characteristic flail and folded cloth.

SHABTI WITH BLUE CROWN

(CARTER 318A, J.D'E. 60830;
HEIGHT 48 CM)

There is nothing ordinary about this *shabti*-figure. It is a fine small sculpture in its own right, made from a close-grained wood, mostly left plain, but highlighted with a discreet use of gold leaf on the broad collar, head band, *uraeus* and flail. The figure is mummiform, and the king is shown wearing the blue crown, the *khepresh*. The eyes and eye-brows are marked in black and the pupils of the eyes marked with white paint. He holds the crook and the flail, symbols of royal power, in his hands. Two lines of text running down the body contain just part of the common *shabti*-text, in which the figure is charged by the deceased to answer for him if he is conscripted for field-work in the after-life. Of particular interest is the short text underneath the feet: 'Made by the servant, loved of his lord, the general Minnakhte, justified'. It is one of five *shabtis* similarly inscribed, indicating that they were made for Tutankhamun's burial as tokens of respect by Minnakhte, and this accounts for the fine quality of the carving.

SHABTI WITH NUBIAN WIG

(CARTER 326A-F, J.D'E. 60835;
HEIGHT 54 CM)

In some respects the *shabtis* from the tomb made just of wood, or of wood with some gilding, are much more attractive artistically than those heavily gilded. This example is particularly fine, conveying an extraordinary feeling of dignity. It is a simple wooden mummiform figure, beautifully carved, with just enough gilding to enhance the overall effect. There is a thin gold head band, a collar of quite substantial gold foil, and one gold bracelet. The headdress is interesting. It is a kind of wig sometimes called 'Nubian', with some royal connotations, worn both by men and women. Tutankhamun, for example, wears it in scenes on the golden shrine, in activities some of which could be described as informal, such as the king with his queen shooting birds in the papyrus swamp. In tomb 55 in the Valley, often called the Amarna cache, a set of Canopic jars has stoppers with this wig; they may belong to a woman. The coffin in that cache also wears it. It is something of a puzzle. On the brow of this *shabti* there is not just the *uraeus*, but the double insignia of vulture and *uraeus*. A fairly full *shabti*-text occupies four lines which run the full length of the figure.

SHABTI WITH TWO FLAILS

(CARTER 325A, J.D'E. 60838;
HEIGHT 52 CM)

This plain wooden *shabti* with some gilding differs from some of its comparable fellows in a number of respects. To begin with, it shows both hands holding gilded bronze flails. It is impossible to determine whether it was placed in the tomb so equipped, for at the very least it might have been expected that one of the flails should have been replaced by a bronze crook. The figure would then have been truly furnished with the insignia of royalty. And yet the Nubian wig, which fits the head, lacks any royal mark – the *uraeus* or the vulture head and *uraeus* which occur together on many of the larger Tutankhamun *shabtis*. Apart from the gilded flails, gold is used for the multiple bead collar on the chest and the bracelets on the wrists. A thin gold band separates the wig from the brow. Like some other of the large wooden *shabtis*, this figure carries four vertical columns of text containing a fairly full Eighteenth Dynasty *shabti* text, invoking the figure to work on behalf of the dead king if his name is called in the corvée.

A Treasure Above All Treasures

SHABTI PRESENTED BY MINNAKHTE

(CARTER 230J, J.D'E. 60828; HEIGHT 52 CM)

This *shabti* is another of the group of five which the general Minnakhte presented for the king's funeral. Such presentation pieces could be regarded as indications of true loyalty and affectionate piety, directed at a young king who had not lived long enough to gather enemies against him. Like the other presentation *shabtis* it is made simply of wood with just a trifling use of gold: here a thin head band and a gilded bronze *uraeus*. Of the two royal emblems he carries, the crook is of bronze only, while the flail is of gilded bronze. The carver of this piece was a true sculptor, and the royal features are so well and sensitively delineated that there is good reason to think that the ancient craftsman was aiming to show not just a royal head but a portrait of Tutankhamun. He is shown wearing the *nemes* headdress with blue stripes. Over his chest is a multiple broad collar, lightly incised, and below, obscured partially by his folded arms, is a *ba*-bird with outstretched wings – the form of spirit which could move in and out of the tomb after burial. A full *shabti*-text occupies six vertical lines on the body.

SHABTI FROM THE ANTECHAMBER

(CARTER 110, J.D'E. 60825, HEIGHT 51.6 CM)

The large number of *shabti*-figures found in the tomb of Tutankhamun were deposited in two rooms, the Treasury and the Annexe, mostly placed in groups stored in black-painted shrine-shaped boxes. One, however, was found loose in the Antechamber where it had migrated probably from the boxes in the Annexe, not taken by the ancient tomb robbers presumably because it carried little of value on it. Nevertheless, it is a fine wooden example with some effective gilding. The *nemes* headdress which was the most common type of semi-crown worn by kings throughout the Pharaonic Period, is here gilded, but the vulture and *uraeus* heads on the brow are of ungilded bronze. Normally the Egyptian king wore only the *uraeus* on his brow, the embodiment of Wadjyt, the protective deity of Lower Egypt. It was not uncommon, however, for Tutankhamun to be shown with the vulture head also, Nekhbet the protective goddess of Upper Egypt. A carefully detailed gilded flail is held in the right fist; if there was originally a crook, it has not survived. Four lines of incised, yellow-painted text running the length of the body, contain the *shabti*-text in a fairly full form.

GILDED *SHABTI* WITH NUBIAN WIG

(CARTER 330H, J.D'E. 60833; HEIGHT 54 CM)

One of fifteen *shabtis* of different styles found in a white-painted chest in the Treasury, this example represents a group which carries a full version of the *shabti*-text, Utterance 6 of the Book of the Dead. The figure itself is made of wood in mummiform, and it is completely gilded except for those parts of the body which in this form are shown to be not covered by bandages, namely the face, neck and hands. The face is sensitively carved with eye details marked in black, and the whites are painted white; the lips are lightly rouged. It wears a tight short Nubian wig of ebony, with the tight curls clearly marked; a gold band encircles the top. The band on the brow is also gold. A broad collar is marked on the chest and shoulders, and a slightly incongruous, rather ordinary, bronze crook is placed in the left hand. There is no flail, but in the tomb were placed many loose crooks and flails, some of which belonged to *shabtis* like this one. There are four lines of text with the *shabti*-formula.

SHABTI WITH RED CROWN

(CARTER 330C, J.D'E. 60823; HEIGHT 63 CM)

Also found in the chest in the Treasury which housed the last *shabti*, this figure is one of the representative regal examples from the tomb. Here Tutankhamun is king even in death; he is shown wearing the so-called red crown, one of Egypt's oldest royal crowns. It is generally thought to have been made of thin copper, which, having a ruddy colour, could be termed 'red'. It is generally shown with a thin extension and curled end, rising forward from the bottom of the rear vertical projection; but it is often omitted from three-dimensional representations in stone because of the difficulty of carving it. In wooden examples it could be added in metal; but not here. Its absence does not seem to have been a problem. There is here an *uraeus* on the brow. The royal features are picked out in black and the lips are rouged. He carries a gilded bronze flail in his right hand, and a bronze crook in the left. The whole figure is gilded, apart from the face and hands. Two lines of text running down the body contain an abbreviated version of the *shabti*-text.

SHABTI WITH WHITE CROWN

(CARTER 330E, J.D'E. 60824A; HEIGHT 61.5 CM)

This is a fine *shabti*-figure of a very youthful Tutankhamun wearing a white crown, almost a companion piece to the last, from the same chest in the Treasury. There is, however, a significant difference between the two: whereas the last carries just an *uraeus* on the brow, here there are *uraeus* and vulture head in bronze. It has not been possible to discover if there is a significant distinction to be made between royal figures with the single and those with the double form of protective deities. It seems unlikely that a matter of this kind would be left to the whim of the craftsman making the piece, but no other explanation has been put forward.

As in other *shabtis* from the same chest, the whole of the body is gilded apart from the face and hands, which are left in the natural wood. An unusual feature is the raised eyebrow on the figure's right side, giving the face a somewhat quizzical look. Of the royal insignia only the crook has survived. There are four lines containing the *shabti*-text.

SHABTI OF TRADITIONAL FORM

(CARTER 608B, J.D'E. 60795, HEIGHT 26 CM)

Twenty-two gilded wooden *shabtis* were found in one of the black-painted chests in the Annexe. This example is very much of the common shape of Eighteenth Dynasty *shabtis* in which the body is mummiform, and the head equipped with what in Egyptian archaeology is termed the tripartite wig: this form has two parts with heavy tresses hanging on either side of the face down to the upper chest, while the third part hangs down the back. It is much used in funerary contexts, and is regularly shown as the headdress on coffins. The whole figure including face and hands is gilded and some details on the face are added in black. So also is the beard which is unusually long. The hands are shown holding hoes and baskets, to be used in the agricultural works for which it might be conscripted; this would be a working *shabti*. There is no *shabti*-text inscribed, but just a single line in which the king is 'bodily son of Re' and 'beloved of Anubis who is in the place of embalming'.

REIS SHABTI WITH NUBIAN WIG

(CARTER 496B, J.D'E. 60765, HEIGHT 32 CM)

Here is one of the more important *shabtis* in the hierarchy of funerary figures. He is a *reis* or foreman *shabti*, whose task it was to oversee the labouring activities of the ordinary *shabtis*. In later times, when it was regular to have large numbers of *shabtis* even in private burials, the *reis* figure was shown carrying a whip. In the present case, and with other *reises* from the tomb, the implement of control is the flagellum or flail, here carefully marked with its various strands. In the other hand he carries a folded cloth, the purpose of which is not certain – possibly so that the *reis* could wipe his hands if by chance he happened to get them dirty! The figure wears the Nubian wig in its more normal form, and there is an *uraeus* on the brow. A broad bead collar is marked out on the chest. Down the body runs a single line of text giving a simple royal titulary: 'the good god, lord of the two lands, Nebkheperure, son of Re, lord of diadems, Tutankhamun, ruler in southern Heliopolis, given life like Re'.

SHABTI WITH ROYAL BEARD

(CARTER 512C, J.D'E. 60800; HEIGHT 25 CM)

In its usual form the *shabti* is a mummy; it is the deceased as Osiris, and as such it is generally shown either with no beard, or with the long plaited beard with turned-up tip, the characteristic Osirian beard. This *shabti*, which is not otherwise particularly distinctive, is given a straight beard with cross-markings of the kind usually worn by the king. Such beards are not uncommon with *shabtis* of Tutankhamun, and one must concede that some confusion over beards is allowable. This is a working *shabti* made of wood and gilded all over, with some markings in black paint: the striations on the tripartite wig, the eyes and eyebrows, and the cross-markings on the beard. The indications of detail on the body are very lightly marked, but it can be seen that there is a broad collar and that both hands hold hoes; there are no baskets. A single line of text runs down the body contained within an incised frame with a sign for 'heaven' at the top: 'the good god, lord of the two lands, Nebkheperure, son of Re, Tutankhamun, ruler in southern Heliopolis, given life'.

GILDED REIS SHABTI

(CARTER 496B, J.D'E. 60758, HEIGHT 32 CM)

Another *reis* or overseer *shabti*, made of wood and fairly heavily gilded. Here he is shown as king, wearing the *uraeus* on his brow, attached to another headdress, the *khat*, which seems to be exclusively royal. In form it is not a crown in the strictest sense, but some kind of head cloth fitted closely perhaps over a special wig. It is not known whether it was made of cloth. It is neat and brings distinction of appearance, but it is not an obvious symbol of authority. The detail of the face is to some extent suppressed by the gilding, but even so it conveys an impression of great calm. There is no beard. Around the neck is a broad collar of beads, and in the hands are held the folded cloth and flail or flagellum, the characteristic symbols of authority held by the overseer *shabtis* of Tutankhamun. He is named in a single line of text as 'the good god, lord of the two lands' and 'the son of Re'; he is 'given life like Re'.

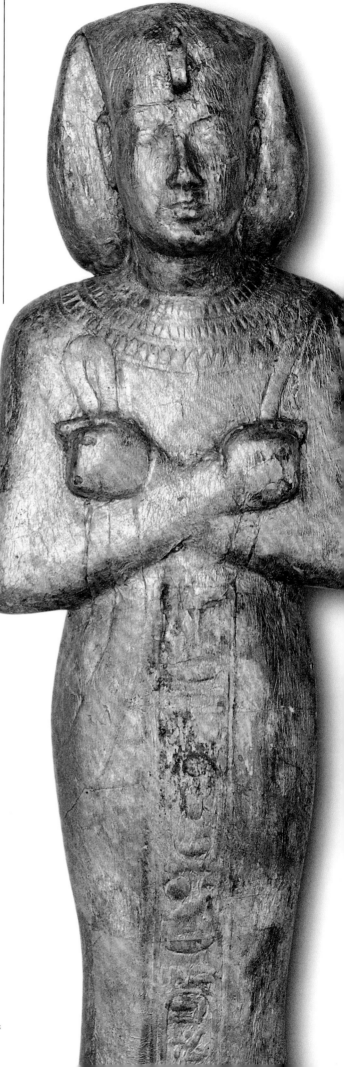

SHABTI WITH BLUE WIG

(CARTER 323N, J.D'E. 60851; HEIGHT 23 CM)

Among the grand, well carved *shabtis* found in the Treasury, there were many much simpler examples, making up the body of workers who would, when called on, carry out the tasks required of the deceased. Even the king, it seems, was unable to avoid these posthumous chores. This *shabti* comes from a group of twenty-three stored in a chest in the Treasury. It is made of wood and very modestly decorated: the tripartite wig is painted blue with the ends of the front lappets painted white; the long spade-shaped beard of the kind worn by the living king is black, as are the eye markings. A broad collar is superficially indicated in white paint with no detailing. The areas of white paint on wig and collar clearly would have been gilded on superior examples. The single line of text describes the king as 'good god, lord of diadems' and 'beloved of Sokar-Osiris'. Sokar is a necropolis deity of the Memphite region.

SHABTI WITH GREEN WIG

(CARTER 319J, J.D'E. 60941; HEIGHT 22 CM)

This *shabti*, found in a troop of fifteen in one of the black-painted chests in the Treasury, is a simple worker figure. It is made of wood of a fairly ordinary kind, and painted. It was first given a wash of white paint on which details and text were then added in other colours. The head is covered by a tripartite wig painted a light green, with striations in dark green. Facial features are in black paint, as is the exceptionally long royal beard.

Details of the *shabti*'s adornments and implements are added in red paint: on the chest a multiple collar with drop-beads forming the outside row; a bangle or bracelet is marked on the wrist; the hands hold hoes and baskets, ready for menial tasks. Down the front of the body is a single line of text written within a frame topped by the heaven-sign: 'the good god, Nebkheperure, beloved of Anubis who is in the embalming chamber'.

SHABTI WITH NO IMPLEMENTS

(CARTER 323P, J.D'E. 60897; HEIGHT 22 CM)

This wooden *shabti*-figure is of ordinary form with a minimal amount of painting. The tripartite wig is not itself painted as in other simple examples: just the striations are delineated in blue on the bare wood. The eyes and brows, and the beard with its side straps, are painted in black. The vertical text is also painted straight on the wood in blue, a fairly standard statement set between framing lines topped by the heaven-sign. It reads: 'the good god, lord of the two lands, Nebkheperure, given life like Re for ever'. No implements are painted in the hands, but this *shabti*, and many others in the tomb without implements, would not go unequipped to clear ditches and move sand in the after-life. In the *shabti*-boxes in the Treasury and the Annexe, and also lying loose in the tomb, the excavators found 1866 miniature implements for them – hoes, mattocks or picks, baskets with yokes to carry them, made of bronze, faience and wood. There were 793 in the Treasury and 1073 in the Annexe.

SHABTI WITH GILDED WIG

(CARTER 323E, J.D'E. 60802; HEIGHT 26.2 CM)

Some of the simple workman *shabtis* are distinguished by certain details and features in their carving. This example, which is from the Treasury, demonstrates the interest that can be derived from a relatively ordinary object. It is of wood, with paint used to highlight some features. The face, to begin with, is remarkably strong; it is only remotely a likeness of Tutankhamun, with eye details marked in black; the beard is long and of the royal kind, with its end painted white. The wig is tripartite and gilded, with the lines of the striations painted in black. There is no broad collar. Both hands hold hoes and baskets which are painted black; they are quite specially delineated, the baskets in particular showing their structure, their handles strung over the wrists. The white painted text in a single column with no framing lines reads 'son of Re, Tutankhamun, ruler in southern Heliopolis, given life like Re for ever'.

SHABTI WITH MINIMAL DECORATION

(CARTER 418F, J.D'E. 60868; HEIGHT 23.4 CM)

The simplicity of plain wood often provides greater aesthetic satisfaction than gilded extravagance. This superficially plain piece is in fact a fine example of wood carving in which just enough basic detail has been added to give it life. It was found in a chest in the Annexe with nineteen other wooden *shabtis*. The tripartite wig on the head is without paint or detail; the face has eyes and brows marked in black, and the beard side straps which hold in place the long black spade beard of living royalty. A fine red painted line is used for the bracelet on one wrist, and for the hoes and baskets held in the hands. The single line of text, in blue paint running down the front of the body, has framing lines and the heaven-sign at the top. Both of Tutankhamun's cartouches are written, and he is 'the good god, lord of the two lands, possessor of joy'; he is 'son of Re' and is 'given life'. The chest containing this *shabti* also held a hundred miniature implements to equip those figures without any tools.

GRANITE *SHABTI* WITH GILDED HEAD

(CARTER 605F, J.D'E. 61040; HEIGHT 15.5 CM)

The majority of the *shabtis* found in Tutankhamun's tomb were made of wood, some entirely gilded, some in part. Stone figures are not common, and among these this black granite example is unusual. It is more solidly proportioned than the wooden *shabtis*, and its bodily details are more suggested than clearly carved, due no doubt to the hardness of the stone. The head is shown with the *khat* cloth headdress, which is gilded, with a bronze *uraeus* attached to the brow, inlaid with blue and red. Eyes and brows are outlined in blue paint with internal details in white and black. The simple royal designation is lightly carved on the front of the piece. It is interesting to consider the materials used for royal *shabtis* at this time: many of those made for Amenophis III were of serpentine; for Akhenaten, from whose tomb many broken examples were recovered, many different stones were used. Tutankhamun's sudden death probably required unexpectedly rapid manufacture, and *shabtis* of wood could be made more quickly.

LIMESTONE *SHABTI* WITH WHITE CROWN

(CARTER 605A, J.D'E. 61043, HEIGHT 20.7 CM)

A hard, close-grained yellowish limestone was used for this *shabti*, one of two found in a box in the Annexe along with twelve other *shabtis* and twenty-seven copper or bronze miniature tools. All the figures were made of stone, of five different kinds, from soft limestone to hard granite. Yellow limestone is found in both the Eastern and the Western Deserts of Egypt, but not in such deposits as could be used for building. This rather austere figure shows the mummiform king with his hands just appearing from his wrappings, with no royal regalia. On his head is the white crown of Upper Egypt, appropriately painted white; the *uraeus* on the brow shows the most adventurous markings: the details of the cobra's hood have small depressions filled with blue and red paint. Eyes and brows are marked in black, and there are traces of red colouring on the lips. The very simple text, in black, reads: 'the good god, lord of the two lands, Tutankhamun, ruler in southern Heliopolis, given life'.

LIMESTONE *SHABTI* WITH BLUE CROWN

(CARTER 605B, J.D'E. 61044; HEIGHT 22.5 CM)

Yellow limestone is used for this *shabti*; like the previous example it was found in a chest in the Annexe. Here the king wears the *khepresh*, or blue crown, a fairly recent addition to the repertoire of royal headgear in the New Kingdom. In its developed form, as seen worn by Tutankhamun in scenes on the painted box and the golden shrine, it is ornamented with little circles, possibly of metal, attached to the body of the crown, made possibly of leather. It is commonly shown as blue, hence its general designation. It is also called the war crown because the king wears it in battle. On this *shabti* it is painted black, as are the facial details. The *uraeus* on the blue crown is usually shown with the coils of the body arranged in circles behind the hood of the cobra, with the tail running up the front of the crown. Here the hood is inlaid with blue and red colour. The simple text gives the king's prenomen, and his titles 'The Good God, Lord of the Two Lands'.

LIMESTONE *SHABTI*

(CARTER 330M, J.D'E. 61050; HEIGHT 28 CM)

The chest that contained this piece had a short hieratic text written on the lid: 'What is in it: smooth gold and *mry*-wood *shawabtis*'. In the box were found fifteen *shabtis*, eight of gilded wood, three of plain wood, four of stone, and seventy-five model tools. It is interesting that in this cursive text the figures are called *shawabtis*, a form which supercedes the older form *shabti*, the word used commonly on Tutankhamun's figures themselves. The hieratic scribe here was being rather up-to-date. This fine figure is shown wearing the tripartite wig, with an *uraeus* on the brow. He holds the crook and the flail in his hands, carved in high relief. Details are sparingly supplied in black paint: the coils and hood markings on the *uraeus*, the eyes, brows and ears, the lines of the head band. The mouth is lightly rouged, and the beard and beard straps are black.

In the simple inscription the king's prenomen and usual preliminary titles are given; he is described as 'beloved of Osiris, the great god'.

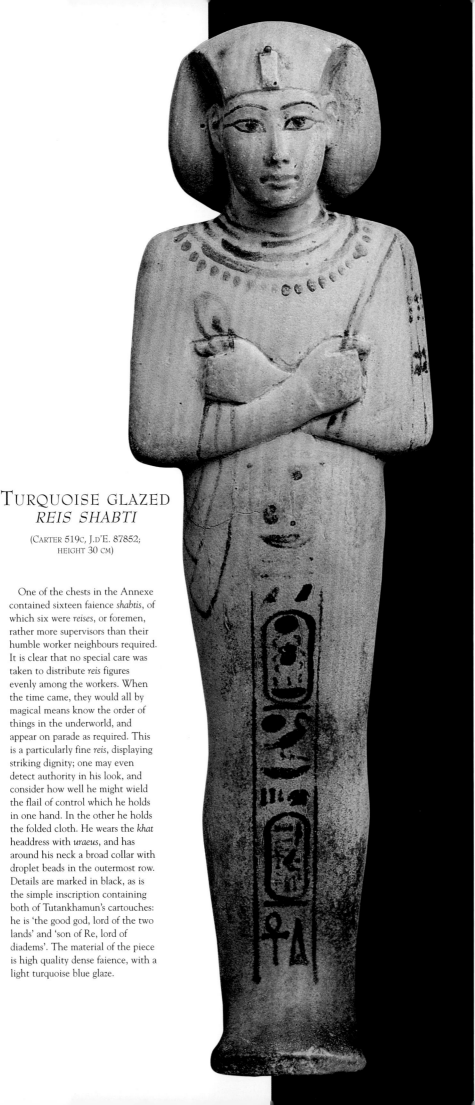

LIGHT BLUE FAIENCE *SHABTI*

(CARTER 519F, J.D'E. 61168; HEIGHT 17 CM)

Faience, a material which should more correctly be called glazed quartz frit, was used by the ancient Egyptians from the earliest historical times. Small moulded objects were ideally suited for this kind of manufacture, and *shabti*-figures were among the objects produced from the Eighteenth Dynasty onwards. In the later periods most *shabtis* were made of faience, often with a glaze very like that used for this example and a number of others in the tomb of Tutankhamun. During the reigns of Amenophis III and Akhenaten the production of fine quality glass and glazed objects reached a peak of quality, with a wide range of colours being developed. The colour of this *shabti* is not very special, but it is still a good example of the discreet use of glazing. The figure is shown wearing a tripartite wig with details marked out in black. The beard is long and royal; no implements are shown in his hands. The text gives the simple royal designation and prenomen, 'given life for ever'.

TURQUOISE GLAZED *REIS SHABTI*

(CARTER 519C, J.D'E. 87852; HEIGHT 30 CM)

One of the chests in the Annexe contained sixteen faience *shabtis*, of which six were *reises*, or foremen, rather more supervisors than their humble worker neighbours required. It is clear that no special care was taken to distribute *reis* figures evenly among the workers. When the time came, they would all by magical means know the order of things in the underworld, and appear on parade as required. This is a particularly fine *reis*, displaying striking dignity; one may even detect authority in his look, and consider how well he might wield the flail of control which he holds in one hand. In the other he holds the folded cloth. He wears the *khat* headdress with *uraeus*, and has around his neck a broad collar with droplet beads in the outermost row. Details are marked in black, as is the simple inscription containing both of Tutankhamun's cartouches: he is 'the good god, lord of the two lands' and 'son of Re, lord of diadems'. The material of the piece is high quality dense faience, with a light turquoise blue glaze.

A NON-ROYAL *SHABTI*

(CARTER 496D, J.D'E. 61108; HEIGHT 17.5 CM)

In the regular text inscribed on these *shabti*-figures, an identification is made between the figure and the named deceased person. Whoever is named is the one for whom the *shabti* will shout out 'Here I am' when the roll of the corvée is called. What then can one make of an anonymous *shabti*? Six such figures were found in Tutankhamun's tomb, three in the Treasury and three in the Annexe. All are similar to this example, light blue glazed, wearing the tripartite wig, with no tools, and a full *shabti*-text written in black in eight or nine horizontal lines. No identifying deceased person is named. The features of these figures are well modelled, but they do not appear to be in the style of the late Amarna Period, or of the reign of Tutankhamun.

It seems possible that they were made either early in the Amarna Period or even in the reign of Amenophis III, as stock figures to be used in an emergency. But why were they used for Tutankhamun when several hundreds could be made for his burial? Who can tell?

REIS SHABTI
WITH NUBIAN WIG

(CARTER 519A, J.D'E. 61054; HEIGHT 30 CM)

Two shades of blue glaze are used on this *reis* figure, with black employed for detail. It is one of the foremen *shabtis* found in the same box in the Annexe as the turquoise glazed piece. It is no duplicate, although they have much in common. This figure wears the Nubian wig, which here is carefully marked with its rows of tight curls. There is an *uraeus* on the brow. A collar, with five rows of beads, is marked on the chest, and in his hands are indicated the signs of office, the flail and folded cloth. These two instruments are marked rather superficially, although the hands emerging from the mummy wrappings and the arms are carefully modelled. The single line of text in lighter blue glaze contains an inscription similar to that on its fellow *reis*. Like so many *shabtis* from this tomb, the text is very simple, and includes no invocation that the *shabti* perform the necessary tasks in the underworld.

SHABTI WITH
A TEXTUAL ERROR

(CARTER 602F, J.D'E. 87853;
HEIGHT 15.5 CM)

One of the boxes in the
Annexe contained eight wooden
reis figures, some with gilding,
and thirty-one faience *shabtis* of
worker status, with violet glaze,
along with thirty-two miniature
copper tools. This example is
characteristic of the group, but
has some features which are
unusual. The striations on the
tripartite wig are made in light
blue glaze, and the same colour is
used for the text, which is of the
shortest kind found on the
Tutankhamun *shabtis*. It contains
his prenomen, the title 'good god,
lord of the two lands', qualified
with 'given life'. There is an error
in the writing of the prenomen in
the cartouche. The signs should
be, from top to bottom, a sun-
disk, a scarab beetle with three
strokes indicating plurality, and a
basket at the bottom. Here the
three strokes of plurality have
been omitted, subtly changing
the meaning of the name from
'master of forms (or possessor of
forms) is Re' to 'master of form is
Re', a subtle theological
distinction which could give rise
to argument in the after-life.

SHABTI WITH
ANKH SIGNS

(CARTER 327MM, J.D'E. 61120,
HEIGHT 16.4 CM)

Royal *shabtis* do not necessarily
follow the simple rules of the *shabti*
tradition either in iconography or in
inscription. Those made for
Akhenaten had very short texts,
and there is no example known
which carries anything like the
conventional *shabti*-text from the
Book of the Dead. It is not
surprising that Akhenaten avoided
the Osirian aspects of the *shabti*
idea; it is surprising that he even
contemplated the use of *shabtis*,
unless their function was to be

diverted towards a solar purpose.
With Tutankhamun the *shabti*
reverted to its subterrestrial
function; Osiris was no longer
abhorred. This modest violet
glazed *shabti* with a simple text
might be thought to be in the
Akhenaten tradition, an idea
strengthened by the presence of
ankh-signs in the clenched hands.
This feature is found on many
Akhenaten *shabtis*. Could this have
been noted by the priests of
Amon-Re in Thebes?

PERSONAL RITUAL OBJECTS

The extraordinary mixture of objects placed in the tomb of Tutankhamun defies simple analysis. Many pieces seem to possess little relevance to the main purpose of the burial of a royal and divine person; some seem to have been included almost as if to enlarge the size of what might otherwise have seemed to be a meager funerary equipment. Why so much furniture, so many beds of ordinary kinds, so many boxes filled with linen, clothes, jewels? It is as if the moving men had been told to clear all unwanted things from the palace storerooms. Was it the practice to include all things bearing the deceased's name? Unfortunately, just not enough is known about

Egyptian funerary procedure in this respect.

Other items in the burial, however, must have had great personal significance for the dead king; some may even have had ritual meanings which can not now be comprehended. Such is the nest of coffins; among other things it contained a tiny coffin bearing the name of Queen Tiye, mother of Akhenaten, which held a lock of hair. Was this just a keepsake or an heirloom, or did it have greater significance? Questions of similar kind apply to the other objects illustrated below.

Other objects not illustrated here invoke the word 'Why?' Is ritual involved, or personal piety? What, for example, is to be made of two further sets of miniature coffins, placed in a plain wooden box in the Treasury? They contained two mummified foetuses, both female and prematurely born. These pitiful little bodies had not been fully mummified, but had been carefully and piously prepared for burial. It is generally thought that they were the children of Tutankhamun and Ankhesenamun, but the parentage is not yet satisfactorily established. The connection must have been intimate, and would have justified the inclusion of the bodies in the most sacred and ritually important part of the tomb. How many more pieces in this remarkable tomb possess hidden significance!

136–137
Tutankhamun lies on his funeral bier, a mummy protected by the wings of a falcon and of his ba*-bird – his spirit of movement after death. The wood-carver who made this piece exploited most cleverly the natural grain of the wood.*

SQUATTING GOLD FIGURE OF THE KING

(CARTER 320c, J.D'E. 60702;
HEIGHT 5.4 CM, LENGTH OF CHAIN 54 CM)

This charming small royal figure was found in the miniature coffin illustrated later. It represents a squatting figure of a king cast in solid gold. He wears the *khepresh* or blue crown, and holds the royal insignia, flail and crook, in one hand. There is no lock of youth and it is difficult, therefore, not to see this piece as a person in some maturity. There is unfortunately no inscription to identify which king is represented. Because it was found with a lock of Queen Tiye's hair, Carter took the view that it was Amenophis III, and that both figure and lock of hair were in the tomb as 'heirlooms'. There is little evidence to support this view as far as this statuette is concerned, and it has been pointed out that the ears are pierced for earrings, a feature not found in royal ears before the reign of Akhenaten. It was designed to be worn as a pendant, and a ring on the back takes the gold chain used for suspension; the ends of the chain do not have a clasp, but are provided with tasselled linen cords for tying. Around the neck of the figure was a tiny necklace of glass beads. There seems no reason to believe that anyone other than Tutankhamun is represented; but the significance of the piece, apart from being decorative, is not easily determined.

BLUE GLASS FIGURE OF THE KING

(CARTER 54FF, J.D'E. 60718;
HEIGHT 5.8 CM)

A box of objects found in the
Antechamber contained, among
other things, parts of Tutankhamun's
corselet, and this small figure. Like
so many other pieces in the tomb it
seems to have no obvious place
among the tomb equipment. It
shows a royal figure, squatting like
the gold statuette shown to the left,
wearing the *khepresh* or blue crown.
He holds his right finger to his
mouth in an attitude commonly
associated in ancient Egypt with the
young, and specifically with the
young Horus, the god with whom
the Egyptian king was identified in
life. This then could be a figure of
the child Horus (called Harpocrates
in later times), or of the king as a
child; presumably Tutankhamun,
although Carter thought it might be
Akhenaten. It is a rare case of glass
sculpture from the Eighteenth
Dynasty, a figure in the round,
almost certainly molded, and then
finished by working with abrasive
materials. The glass itself is
translucent, but not transparent,
which suggests a different
composition from the glass of the
many inlays, beads, amulets etc. from
this tomb, which are almost
exclusively of opaque glass. The
color of Egyptian blue glass was
mostly obtained by the use of a
copper compound, but some
examples show traces of cobalt as the
coloring agent.

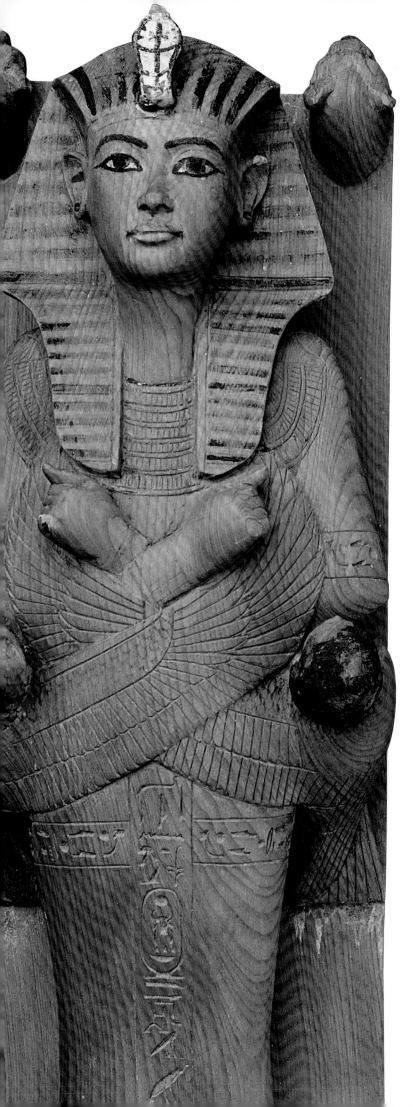

THE KING ON A BIER

(CARTER 331A, J.D'E. 60720; LENGTH 42.2 CM, WIDTH 12 CM, HEIGHT OF BIER 4.3 CM)

Carved in the style of, and with the same artistry as, the best of the wooden *shabtis* of Tutankhamun, this figure was found packed into a small wooden chest in the Treasury, padded around with linen. It shows the king as a mummy lying on his funeral bed, the shape of which incorporates two elongated lions whose heads rise beside that of the king. He is mummiform, wearing the *nemes* headdress, the striations of which are marked in black, and with a gilded *uraeus*. This is the sole piece of gilding on the figure, and it therefore makes a striking effect. The body is lightly marked with a broad bead collar, and it is seen to be wrapped around protectively by the wings of a falcon and of a human-headed *ba*-bird, spirit of movement; bands of text, following the lines of mummy straps, carry a long traditional address by the sky-goddess Nut, and short statements in which the king is said to be 'revered by' the four Canopic genii, with Anubis, Osiris and Horus. Texts on the sides of the bier state that this figure was made for the king by Maia, the royal treasurer, whose own tomb was at Saqqara. He also presented a fine wooden *shabti*-figure to the burial equipment.

THE HEAD
ON THE LOTUS

(CARTER 8, J.d'E. 60723; HEIGHT 30 CM)

One of the most appealing images from Tutankhamun's tomb, this head is a masterpiece of wood sculpture, simple in its conception, complicated perhaps in its religious significance, but wholly engaging as a work of art. What function it served in the tomb is not known; where it was placed is not known. It was found by the excavators in the passage into the tomb, beneath the rubble, but discarded presumably by the ancient robbers, who could see no value in it. It is not thought that there was an illicit trade in works of art in ancient Egypt. The piece consists of a child's head emerging from an open lotus flower, and it is generally thought to represent the birth of the young sun-god at the beginning of time; then the lotus sprang up from the high mound rising from the watery chaos called Nun. It harks back therefore to distant times when earth came into being and the sun-god was born. In this subtle representation the sun-god is given the features of Tutankhamun, modeled very much in the Amarna tradition, with the elongated skull characteristic of the children of Akhenaten and Nefertiti. The carved wood is covered with a thin layer of gesso-plaster painted brown; the eye-brows and the surrounds of the eyes are blue.

MINIATURE COFFIN AND MINIATURE COFFIN LID

(Carter 320, J.d'E. 60698; length 78 cm, width 26.5 cm)
(Carter 320a, J.d'E. 60698; length 74 cm)

A nest of miniature coffins was found in the Treasury, providing one of the great mysteries concerning the funerary equipment of Tutankhamun. The outer coffin was black painted with inscribed gold bands and other gilded parts. It is described below, along with the puzzles raised by its contents. The second coffin was firmly fixed in the outer coffin by solidified unguents, and is inextricably stuck. The lid, however, can be removed, and is illustrated here. It is very reminiscent of the solid gold coffin which contained Tutankhamun's mummy, but lacks the detail and splendor which its full-size counterpart displays. The king is shown mummiform, wearing the *nemes* headdress, but with no *uraeus* on the brow. The piece is of wood, gilded on gesso-plaster, the color of the gold relieved only by the black outlines of the eyes and eyebrows. The body is shown to be wrapped around with the protective wings of two vultures, here probably representing the two mourning goddesses, Isis and Nephthys. As on a full-size coffin, the text down the body is an address by the king: 'O my mother Nut! Spread yourself over me, place me among the imperishable stars which are in you, that I may not die again.'

The miniature coffin, partly described above, takes the form of a standard Eighteenth Dynasty coffin, not necessarily of a royal person. It has an elaborate broad collar around the neck, and a vulture with outstretched wings beneath the arms. Part of the conventional address to Nut runs down the front of the body. The greatest interest in this nest of coffins rests on what was found within. Firstly there was a linen bundle containing the solid gold figure of a king, probably Tutankhamun, described above. Secondly there was a third small plain wooden coffin which contained yet a fourth tiny wooden coffin, wrapped in linen and doused with unguents. This last coffin contained a lock of hair – of auburn hair as Carter romantically described it. This tiny coffin, about 12.5 cm long, carried texts naming 'the great royal wife Tiye', her name in cartouche, and requesting all benefits of food, drink etc from the multiple funerary deity Ptah-Sokar-Osiris. It is more than reasonable to conclude that the hair belonged to Tiye, and had been included in Tutankhamun's burial for reasons of piety, but is not necessarily an indication that Tiye was his mother. The question is too intriguing!

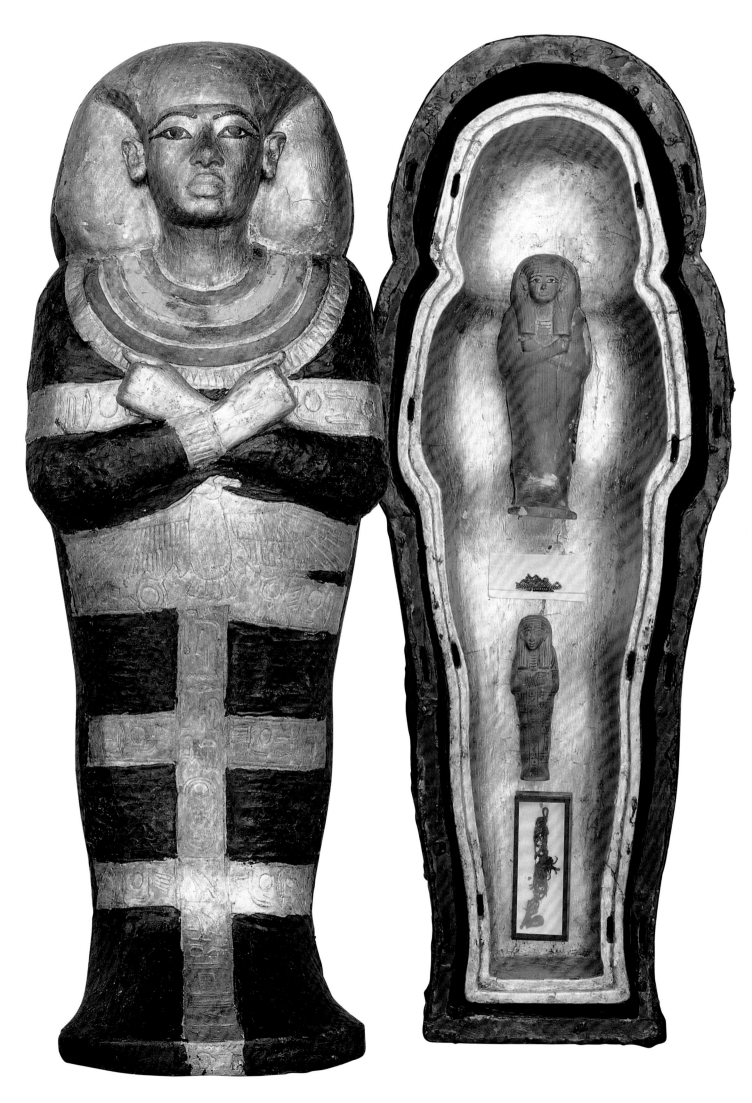

RITUAL FURNITURE AND OBJECTS

144
One of the lion heads from the ritual couch of Meht-weret. The wooden base is covered with gilded gesso, and the blue details of nose and tears are made of blue glass. The eyes are wonderfully rendered in translucent quartz.

145
One of the two hippopotamus heads from the ritual couch of Ammut, the 'gobbler of the dead'. The teeth are made of ivory, and the tongue of pink-stained ivory. The eyes are of translucent quartz and black glass.

The impression of confusion which faced Carter on entering the tomb was caused chiefly by the untidiness left by the ancient intruders. Not all the confusion was due to robbers; it seems unlikely that when the tomb was sealed after the burial the rooms were left in a tidy well-ordered state. But among the tumble of boxes, furniture and chariots stood three great gilded wooden couches, apparently unmoved and undamaged.

These great couches stand high off the ground, held rigid by solid rectangular bases. They are gilded and could not have been used as real beds without suffering damage. Similar couches can be seen on the walls of other tombs in the Valley, and fragments have been found in the debris of robbed tombs. They surely played an important role in the posthumous activities of the king, possibly as means by which the royal mummy might travel to its heavenly destination. Each couch is inscribed simply with the words 'the Osiris Nebkheperure', a designation which

confirms that they were made for the use of the dead king, not in his life.

Two strange, but distinctly ritual, objects were found in the Burial Chamber. In early times they were associated with a funerary deity Imyut, 'he who is within bandages', but later, as here, with Anubis, the divine supervisor of mummification. They clearly possessed great magical power.

Other important and probably obligatory items found in the tomb included a set of magical bricks and an Osiris bed. The unbaked mud bricks, inscribed with magical spells, were placed in niches hidden in the four walls of the Burial Chamber. Each had a specified amulet fixed in it. The Osiris bed in the Treasury awaited the royal resurrection; it consisted of a frame almost two metres long, in the shape of Osiris, filled with Nile mud and planted with grain; the germination of the seed would mark the resurrection of the king as Osiris.

RITUAL COUCH OF ISIS-MEHTET

(CARTER 73, J.D'E. 62013;
HEIGHT 188 CM, LENGTH 208 CM, WIDTH 128 CM)

Two elongated cow figures form the two sides of this magnificent couch. The legs, back and front fit into holes in the plain, black-painted base. Between the bodies is fixed the mattress of the couch by hooks which fit into bronze staples on the inner flanks of the animal bodies. The cows carry on their heads horns and disks which closely resemble the regular headdress of the goddess Isis. The paneled footboard at the tail end carries amuletic protection in the form of *djed* and *tyet* signs for endurance and life. The animal tails swing round in almost complete circles. Apart from the base, the whole couch is covered with gesso-plaster and gilded. The trefoil decoration on the bodies is made of dark blue paste; the eyes are made of translucent quartz with painted details, and are outlined in blue glass. An inscription on the cross board of the mattress, contained within an elongated cartouche, purports to identify the deity represented by these cows. It reads: 'May the good god live, may he exist for ever, Lord of the Two Lands, who effects the kingship of Re the Osiris, King of Upper Egypt, Nebkheper(u)re, beloved of Isis-Mehtet, justified'. Here there is some confusion. This divine name

properly belongs to a lion-goddess, whereas there is a cow-deity called Mehturt often linked with Isis. The name Isis-Mehtet in the text, however, is determined by a hieroglyph showing a seated deity with cow-head. One may possibly ascribe some confusion to the ancient scribe who prepared the inscriptions. But it seems certain that a cow, not a lion, deity was intended.

RITUAL COUCH
OF AMMUT

(CARTER 137, J.d'E. 62012;
LENGTH 236 CM, WIDTH 126 CM,
HEIGHT 134 CM)

Among the objects which specially caught the eyes of Carter and Carnarvon when they entered the Antechamber of Tutankhamun's tomb were the three great gilded couches with animal heads, lined up head to tail against the wall opposite the entrance. They were the first complete examples to be found of a kind that was known only from representations in scenes in the tomb of Sethos II, and from fragments found in earlier excavated royal tombs. Their function puzzled the excavators, and has continued to puzzle scholars. They were undoubtedly ritual beds, and it is possible that they were to assist and protect the dead king in his journeys through the underworld. The deity for this couch is Ammut, the 'gobbler of the dead', as the inscription on the rail between the heads states; the king is 'beloved of Ammut'. The 'gobbler' is usually shown in scenes of judgement in the Book of the Dead, waiting to eat the hearts of those who fail to qualify for the realm of Osiris. In vignettes she usually has a crocodile head, lion forequarters, and hippopotamus rear. Here the heads are hippopotamus, the bodies crocodile, and the back legs lion.

RITUAL COUCH OF MEHT-WERET

(CARTER 35, J.D'E. 62911;
LENGTH 181 CM, WIDTH 91 CM,
HEIGHT 156 CM)

The three ritual couches can be dismantled into four pieces: two sides in the form of elongated animals with long legs, which slot into a plain base, and a top, a curved 'mattress' with footboard, which is attached to the animal sides with hooks and staples. Apart from the bases they are all made of gessoed and gilded wood. This lion-goddess is identified from the text on the cross rail as Meht-weret, who was a cow-goddess in the Egyptian pantheon. There may therefore have been some confusion between the couches when the texts were added, because the goddess named on the cow couch is Isis-Mehtet, usually a lion-deity. Consequently it is likely that this lion couch should be in theory assigned the text on the cow-couch, and the protective deity here should be Isis-Mehtet. Putting on one side this matter of identification, one should consider rather the heads of the goddess – two magnificent lioness-heads, wonderfully lifelike. The details are in glass: blue for the nose and the 'tears' under the eyes, black for the surrounds of the eyes; the eyes are transparent quartz with painted detail on their reverses.

JAR LID WITH FLEDGLING AND EGGS

(Carter 620(1), J.d'E. 62072; width 13.4 cm)

A charming piece like this jar lid needs perhaps little explanation. It was found in the Annexe and probably belonged to one of the perfume vases found there or in the Antechamber, where fragments of the saucer were found. It consists of the flat jar lid with a saucer which here represents the nest. They are made of calcite, as are the four eggs in the nest. The little fledgling, however, is made of wood, painted

in a light creamy brown color with details in black, including the chick's feathers. Its tongue is made of pink-stained ivory. The fledgling has just emerged from its egg and stretches itself, trying out its useless wings. Is there here a reference to Amarna sentiments about nature as expressed in the great Aten hymn:

'The chick in the egg speaks in the shell; you give it air in it to make it live; you have brought it to completion so that it can break it – the egg; and it comes out of the shell to speak of its completion; and it walks on its two feet when it comes out of it'?

It is an indication of the

fascination which scholars and members of the public have with the religious revolution of Akhenaten and its place in the history of monotheism, that connections and suggestions are sought in objects which may only be simple representations of charming subjects. So with this chick!

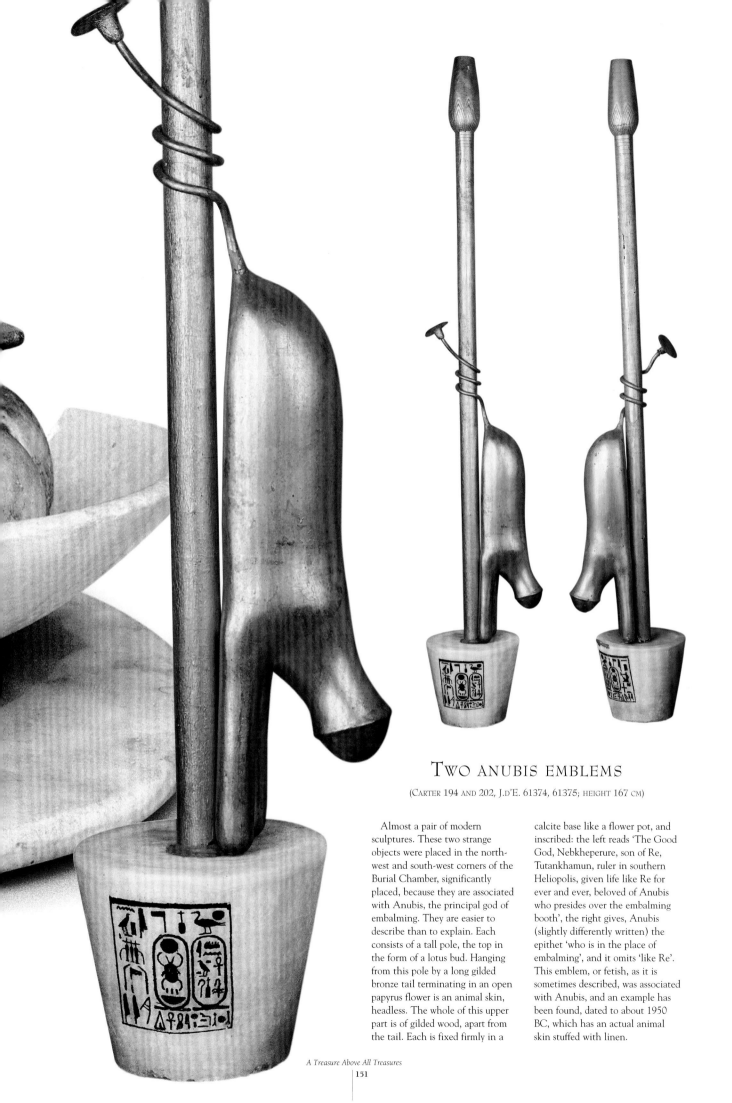

Two anubis emblems

(Carter 194 and 202, J.d'E. 61374, 61375; height 167 cm)

Almost a pair of modern sculptures. These two strange objects were placed in the north-west and south-west corners of the Burial Chamber, significantly placed, because they are associated with Anubis, the principal god of embalming. They are easier to describe than to explain. Each consists of a tall pole, the top in the form of a lotus bud. Hanging from this pole by a long gilded bronze tail terminating in an open papyrus flower is an animal skin, headless. The whole of this upper part is of gilded wood, apart from the tail. Each is fixed firmly in a

calcite base like a flower pot, and inscribed: the left reads 'The Good God, Nebkheperure, son of Re, Tutankhamun, ruler in southern Heliopolis, given life like Re for ever and ever, beloved of Anubis who presides over the embalming booth', the right gives, Anubis (slightly differently written) the epithet 'who is in the place of embalming', and it omits 'like Re'. This emblem, or fetish, as it is sometimes described, was associated with Anubis, and an example has been found, dated to about 1950 BC, which has an actual animal skin stuffed with linen.

FIGURES OF ANTHROPOMORPHIC DEITIES

The Treasury contained many pieces of magical and ritual significance which have not been satisfactorily explained by scholars. Why were they placed in this room and not elsewhere? The explanation might simply be that this material had to be deposited somewhere, and room was not very plentiful in this tomb. It has always to be asked why, but often no profitable answer can be found.

There were in the Treasury twenty-two shrine-shaped black boxes with double doors, sealed when discovered. They contained figures of the king, of deities with animal attributes, and deities in human form. All the figures are made of wood; most are covered with gesso plaster and gilded; all were wrapped with marked and dated pieces of linen. Such markings were common in ancient Egypt, arranged no doubt by the royal housekeeper, just as in a great house of the nineteenth century. Some of the dates go back to the early years of Akhenaten's reign, but this need not necessarily imply that the figures so covered had been made and draped at that time.

The figures with human form make up a strange company. Some are of deities closely associated with the dead king and his protection: such are Isis and Nephthys, the divine mourners for the deceased. There are cosmic gods like Atum and Ptah; and Amsety, the Canopic genius identified with the deceased's liver. All these seem suitable for inclusion in the tomb. But there are others, like Menkaret, who holds a seated figure of the king on her head, and Mamu; such are little known, and probably unimportant, members of the vast company of Egyptian gods. Also puzzling is the presence of two black-painted figures of a young man holding a sistrum, thought possibly to be Ihy, a child of Hathor.

152
Upper part of a figure of the little-known deity Mamu: one of the pieces found in the Treasury. The god is shown mummiform with the Osirian beard. The sensitive face is post-Amarna in style.

153
The great creator god Ptah, the thinking deity, whose principal cult-center was in Memphis, pre-eminent among Egyptian cities. His skull cap here is made of blue faience, and he holds a bronze staff inlaid with gold.

Figure of ihy

(Carter 275a, j.d'e. 60732; height 63.5 cm)

This dramatic, black-painted figure was stored in the Treasury in a shrine-shaped box containing in addition two gilded figures of the king wearing the red crown, and the two figures of the king in a reed boat, harpooning. By association it might seem that the king is again shown in this figure, which unfortunately is not identified by inscription. It has been thought to be the king as a boy, wearing the lock of youth; but more generally it is seen to be Ihy, the child of Hathor of Dendera and Horus of Edfu. Ihy is usually shown carrying a *menat*-necklace and a sistrum, and it is a sistrum, here distinctively gilded, that he holds in his right hand. The sistrum is particularly associated with Hathor, and her distinctive head can be seen on the sistrum held by the young god; it is topped by a shrine-shaped section which in real examples held the metal rods and discs which produced the rather tuneless clattering noise of the shaken instrument. Ihy played a subordinate role in the ceremonies concerning the birth of the king as a royal and divine child. The eyes and brows of this figure are inlaid with gold.

Figure of shu

(Carter 282a, j.d'e. 62735; height 74 cm)

There is a small question of identification with this fine divine figure. In most of the other divine figures found in the Treasury of the tomb the texts on the bases describe Tutankhamun as being 'beloved of' the deities represented. In the case of this figure the text reads: 'Shu, Horus-strong-of-arm'. The king himself is often described as Horus-strong-of-arm, but here it appears that there is a linking of Shu with this form of Horus. It remains an unsolved problem. It seems to be Shu who is principally shown here. He was one of the most distinguished primeval gods of ancient Egypt, a member of the Ennead (company of nine gods) of Heliopolis, the son of Atum and consort of Tefnut. He is the god of air, and his function was to keep apart earth and sky. In this gilded wooden figure he is shown as a mummiform man with a headdress of two double feathers. He has an Osirian beard which, like the eyes and brows, is painted black.

Figure of ta-ta

(Carter 303a, j.d'e. 60741; height 65 cm)

Like some other divine figures from the chests in the Burial Chamber, this figure poses a problem. It is a question of identification. A nice clear inscription in yellow paint on the base names the king: 'the good god, Nebkheperure, justified, beloved of Ta-Ta'. So was the god identified by Carter, presumably with the Egyptological backing of Alan Gardiner or James Henry Breasted, his textual advisers. Ta-Ta is written as if it were a god's name and, on the pattern of other similar texts on these divine figures, the king is 'beloved of' him. No easily identifiable god in the huge Egyptian pantheon carries such a name, and it must be suspected that Ta-Ta is the divine personification of the Two Lands, for *ta* is land in Egyptian, and the Two Lands are the South and the North. It would also explain why the figure wears the white crown of Upper Egypt. If this suggestion is correct then the god should be called Tawy, more correctly the Egyptian for Two Lands.

FIGURE OF PTAH

(CARTER 291A, J.D'E. 60739;
HEIGHT 60.2 CM)

Gods from the Memphis area were well represented among the gilded divine figures found in the Treasury. Here is Ptah, the most important Memphite god throughout the Dynastic Period. He was like Tatjenen, his predecessor and ostensible begetter, a creator god, and considered the patron deity of craftsmen. He is identified on the sloping end of his base as Ptah 'Lord of Truth'; the base itself takes the form of the hieroglyph for 'truth'. The base text also names Tutankhamun. This god is usually shown as a mummiform figure with no headdress, but a tightly fitting cap. Here the body is mummiform, but marked as if it were covered by a feathered garment. He also wears a broad bead collar. The figure is of gilded wood, the gold being of the purplish red kind, except on the face. The cap on the head is made of blue faience, and the eyes marked in blue glass. The straight beard is of gilded bronze. He holds a bronze *was*-scepter of authority incorporating the *ankh*-sign of life and *djed*-sign of endurance. In the Egyptian pantheon Ptah occupied a place among the handful of first-rank deities. He was specially venerated as a god of intellectual integrity, whose reputation never diminished over 3000 years.

Associated with his temple in Memphis was the ancient cult of the Apis bull, the living manifestation of the deity, which flourished especially in the last centuries of the Pharaonic Period.

FIGURE OF ATUM

(CARTER 290A, J.D'E. 60734;
HEIGHT 63 CM)

An inscription in yellow paint on the base of this divine figure identifies the deity as 'Atum, the living god'. It is one of the gilded wooden divine statuettes placed in black-painted chests in the Treasury. Atum was a real heavyweight within the Egyptian pantheon. Here he is shown in a very simple form, unidentifiable by any external mark – crown or headdress, or particular items of divine regalia. He is shown mummiform, with a many-rowed broad bead collar; he has no beard. His eyes are emphasized with black paint. His name, Atum, might mean 'he who does not exist' or 'he who is complete'. The most acceptable – if indeterminate – rendering of the name is 'the undifferentiated one'. But the truth is that Atum was by no means an uncertain deity, but one who always occupied a primary place in the hierarchy of Egyptian gods. In a very late text in the temple of Edfu, Horus is addressed, 'You are Atum, the figure beautiful of face, who fashioned the body of the Ennead'. Atum was indeed the first of the company of nine gods of Heliopolis, the so-called Ennead. He, by himself, created Shu (air) and Tefnut (moisture), who in turn produced Geb (earth) and Nut (sky). This last pair then completed the company by producing Osiris and Isis, Seth and Nephthys. Atum, especially associated with the sun-god as Atum-Re, remained a supreme deity.

FIGURES OF ANIMAL DEITIES

The idea that the ancient Egyptians worshipped animal gods is one of those well-established myths which it may be impossible to dispel. It is true that many Egyptian gods were represented with animal forms, or with animal heads, and it is true that the existence of many mummified animals, particularly cats, baboons and dogs, but also bulls, falcons, snakes, small mammals, even insects, suggests a devotion to the creatures in question. Many gods were manifested as animals, or in some aspects shown in animal form. Even the great sun god at his daily birth at sunrise was shown as Khepri, the scarab beetle. The god Amun might be seen as a goose or a ram; Thoth, the scribe of the gods, could appear as an ibis or a baboon. The rationality behind these theophanies is hard to determine; in most cases, probably, the associations with animals go back to very early times, and their significance may even have been lost for the Egyptians by the Eighteenth Dynasty.

Some of the black-painted boxes in the Treasury contained figures of animal deities; the presence of some is hard to explain. Those of the Canopic genii are properly qualified. Sakhmet, the lioness-headed deity, is not particularly funerary, but may have been included as consort of Ptah, the great creator god. They were not, however, placed conjugally in the same box. The impressive Anubis jackal on a shrine, god of embalming, very properly guarded the Canopic shrine in the Treasury. Nearby was a gilded cow-head of Hathor, appearing from the West, as in some religious papyri – the West to which the deceased was to go. Others are less easily explained, just as the absence of some better known deities with funerary associations is strange. Why the black-painted goose of Amun in the Burial Chamber, or two serpent standards of the Xth Upper Egyptian nome (province) of Aphroditopolis in the Antechamber? One is drawn to the conclusion that much that was put into the tomb was there more by chance than by plan.

158
The elegant, but threatening, jackal of Anubis, the god of embalming, placed to guard the intimate contents of the Canopic shrine in the Treasury.

159
The goose of Amun, a striking black-painted image with gilded beak; one of the sacred creatures placed in the Treasury, a mark of the rehabilitation of the pre-Amarna cults of Thebes.

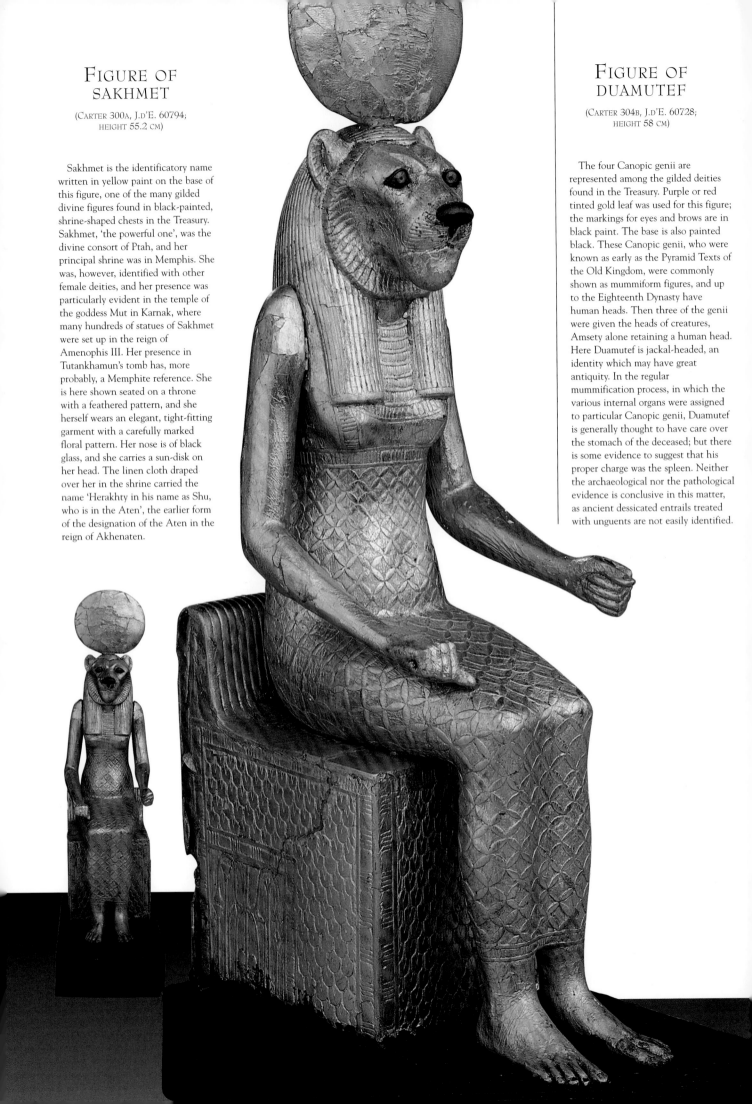

FIGURE OF SAKHMET

(Carter 300a, J.d'E. 60794;
height 55.2 cm)

Sakhmet is the identificatory name
written in yellow paint on the base of
this figure, one of the many gilded
divine figures found in black-painted,
shrine-shaped chests in the Treasury.
Sakhmet, 'the powerful one', was the
divine consort of Ptah, and her
principal shrine was in Memphis. She
was, however, identified with other
female deities, and her presence was
particularly evident in the temple of
the goddess Mut in Karnak, where
many hundreds of statues of Sakhmet
were set up in the reign of
Amenophis III. Her presence in
Tutankhamun's tomb has, more
probably, a Memphite reference. She
is here shown seated on a throne
with a feathered pattern, and she
herself wears an elegant, tight-fitting
garment with a carefully marked
floral pattern. Her nose is of black
glass, and she carries a sun-disk on
her head. The linen cloth draped
over her in the shrine carried the
name 'Herakhty in his name as Shu,
who is in the Aten', the earlier form
of the designation of the Aten in the
reign of Akhenaten.

FIGURE OF DUAMUTEF

(Carter 304b, J.d'E. 60728;
height 58 cm)

The four Canopic genii are
represented among the gilded deities
found in the Treasury. Purple or red
tinted gold leaf was used for this figure;
the markings for eyes and brows are in
black paint. The base is also painted
black. These Canopic genii, who were
known as early as the Pyramid Texts of
the Old Kingdom, were commonly
shown as mummiform figures, and up
to the Eighteenth Dynasty have
human heads. Then three of the genii
were given the heads of creatures,
Amsety alone retaining a human head.
Here Duamutef is jackal-headed, an
identity which may have great
antiquity. In the regular
mummification process, in which the
various internal organs were assigned
to particular Canopic genii, Duamutef
is generally thought to have care over
the stomach of the deceased; but there
is some evidence to suggest that his
proper charge was the spleen. Neither
the archaeological nor the pathological
evidence is conclusive in this matter,
as ancient dessicated entrails treated
with unguents are not easily identified.

FIGURE OF QEBHSENUEF

(CARTER 304A, J.D'E. 60730;
HEIGHT 55.5 CM)

The black-painted base of this figure is uninscribed, but there is no doubt about its identification as the son of Horus, the Canopic genius Qebhsenuef. Here he is shown as a mummiform human body with a falcon head wearing a tripartite wig. It is remarkable how skillfully the Egyptian artist cobbled together such disparate parts to make a figure which seems perfectly natural, once you have come to terms with the idea of a bird-headed human body. The falcon-head has a black-painted top, a black glass beak, and elaborate eye markings in blue glass. Most of the evidence, textual and scientific, seems to agree that Qebhsenuef guarded the intestines, called *mekhtu* by the Egyptians, apparently a corruption of *imy-khet*, 'what is in the body'. In the hierarchy of divine personages in charge of the Canopic equipment of the dead, the goddess who took charge of Qebhsenuef was Selkis, the scorpion, and they are paired on the appropriate Canopic coffinette.

A PAIR OF NOME STANDARDS

(CARTER 37A, 38B, J.D'E. 60751, 60752; HEIGHT 81 CM, 68 CM)

Why would a king want a nome standard in his tomb? A nome was a province of ancient Egypt, 20 in the north and 22 in the south. Why two of the same nome? Certainly there would not have been room for the 42 standards in this small tomb. If, however, these standards should be taken as representatives for the whole series of nomes, why choose the Xth Upper Egyptian nome, called Wadjyt or Edjo, the Greek name of its capital being Aphroditopolis? These questions cannot reasonably be answered, and one is drawn to the conclusion that the standards were in the royal storerooms, and could be used to swell out the royal funerary equipment. But their existence in the tomb is still peculiar. Both take the form of a serpent curved over a typical standard support, with a feather attached to the curve of the snake. They are of gilded wood, beautifully and simply formed. The Aphroditopolite nome is in Middle Egypt, south of Asyut and north of Akhmim.

FIGURE OF NETJER-ANKH

(CARTER 283A, J.D'E. 60754; HEIGHT 56.5 CM)

This fine figure of an erect cobra was stored in the Treasury in a wooden shrine also containing the figures of two falcon deities, Sopdu (see next) and Gemehsu. It is very stylishly carved, with the detailed markings on the body delicately delineated. The cobra-figure itself is of wood, gilded, with just the eyes separately made: the surrounds are of bronze and the eyes of transparent quartz with details painted on the back. At the front top edge of the base is a short text in yellow paint: 'The Osiris, Nebkheperure, beloved of Netjer-ankh'. The divine serpent Netjer-ankh is not a well-known member of the Egyptian pantheon. It is found on some coffins of the Middle Kingdom dating to the Twelfth Dynasty, and a serpent so named can be seen in a part of the Book of what is in the Underworld in royal tombs in the Valley of the Kings. In this later context Netjer-ankh appears as a guardian of the entrance to one of the sections of the Underworld through which the dead king must pass.

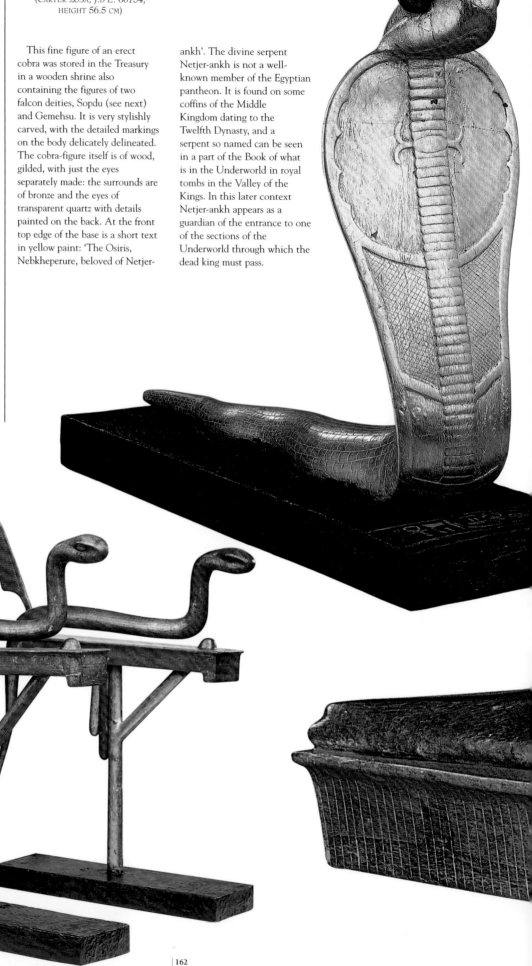

STANDARD WITH SOPDU

(Carter 283b, j.d'E. 60747; height 65.5 cm)

'Lord of the foreign countries' was an epithet given to the god Sopdu as early as the Old Kingdom, and throughout the dynastic period he was seen as exercising authority over desert areas beyond Egyptian frontiers. This image of a falcon with a feathered headdress could be considered a form of Horus of Nekhen (Hierakonpolis), the old Upper Egyptian capital; but here it is undoubtedly the Lower Egyptian deity of Saft el-Henna in the eastern Delta, for the text on the base gives the prenomen of Tutankhamun who is 'beloved of Sopdu'. This excellent representation of Sopdu, 'the sharp one', is of gilded wood with blue glass markings for the eyes and a black glass beak. The gilding has the ruddy tint of purple or red gold. This piece could be seen as another district sign, like those of Aphroditopolis described above, but it is more likely to be just a divine standard of a god protecting the king's interests in the East, and sporting the royal flail from its back.

THE ANUBIS SHRINE

(CARTER 261, J.D'E. 61444;
TOTAL HEIGHT 118 CM, TOTAL LENGTH 270 CM,
WIDTH 52 CM)

The first impressive object to be seen when the Treasury was entered on February 16, 1923 was the jackal-god Anubis, with threatening head, ears pricked high, body swathed in linen, paws outstretched on a gilded shrine, with four long carrying poles. It stood there as if it had just been set down by priestly bearers at the time of the funeral. Everyone who saw it was impressed. The Canopic shrine, with its exquisite figures, was seductive, but the Anubis was haunting. It is not possible to say whether it was so placed as guardian of all the precious and sacred things stored in the Treasury, but it certainly served that purpose. One can imagine the awe, even terror, felt by those ancient intruders who penetrated so far into the tomb. The sight of that head, black and threatening, illuminated by flickering rush-lights, may have deterred the robbers. Many of the boxes there remained sealed.

The black-painted figure of the jackal, noble in its attitude, is made more dramatic by the gilding on the ears and on the collar and scarf around its neck. Its eyes, of calcite and obsidian, are outlined in gold, and – a last subtle touch – its claws are made of silver, a rare metal in the tomb. A point of interest is that one of the linen items draped around the neck was dated to the seventh year of Akhenaten, just about when Tutankhamun was born.

The pylon-shaped shrine is of wood, plastered and gilded, its principal decorative motif consisting of pairs of *djed* and *tyet* signs, powerful amuletic symbols of endurance and life associated with the cult of Osiris. Several compartments in the body of the shrine held amuletic figures and pieces of jewelry, and a number of strange practical items possibly connected with the process of mummification. A scribe's palette inscribed for Meritaten, Tutankhamun's sister-in-law, was placed between the jackal's paws on the top of the shrine.

AMULETS

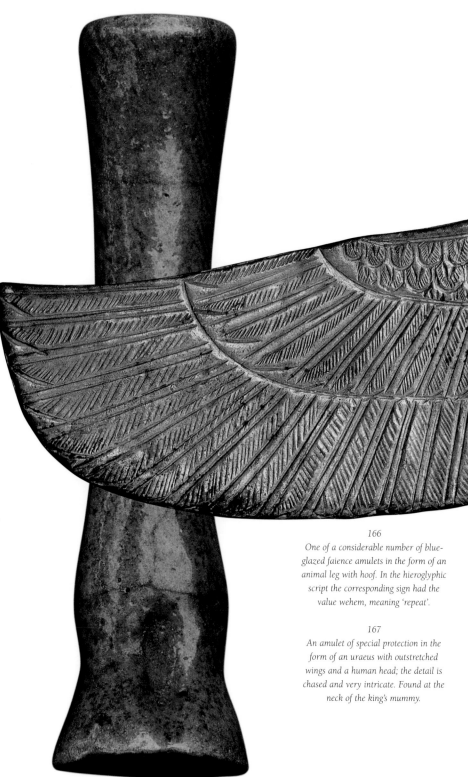

Ancient Egyptian religion was rich in symbolism, and the hieroglyphic script contained many signs with magical and amuletic power. It was not difficult therefore for the composers of texts and the makers of personal objects for life and for death to introduce elements charged with amuletic significance into what they wrote or what they designed. Amuletic forms were in consequence pervasive throughout Egyptian life and death.

Most of the pieces of jewelry found in Tutankhamun's tomb were designed to include the royal names and many amuletic emblems. There were also many single pieces of particular forms with religious meaning, and to these the term 'amulet' is generally assigned. They may represent a particular deity, an object connected with a particular deity, or one of more universal meaning. One sign that is usually thought to be amuletic is the *ankh*, the sign of life, but it is rarely found as an amulet on its own.

The most important amulets found in the tomb were those placed within the bandages of the king's mummy. Of the 150 objects recovered from the mummy, about twenty-five may be classified as amulets. Nearly all were placed around the neck, a part of the body clearly seen to be very vulnerable; here were very potent amulets – the *uraeus* serpent and the vulture, the two protective deities for the king; there were *djed*-pillars for stability, and *wadj*-scepters for renewal; there was a Thoth for wisdom and an Anubis for funerary protection. At the back of the head, very appropriately, was a small head-rest amulet, designed to support and protect the royal head. It was made of pure iron, a very rare material.

About thirty further amulets were found elsewhere in the tomb; their presence was scarcely needed, so well was the king protected otherwise.

166
One of a considerable number of blue-glazed faience amulets in the form of an animal leg with hoof. In the hieroglyphic script the corresponding sign had the value wehem, meaning 'repeat'.

167
An amulet of special protection in the form of an uraeus with outstretched wings and a human head; the detail is chased and very intricate. Found at the neck of the king's mummy.

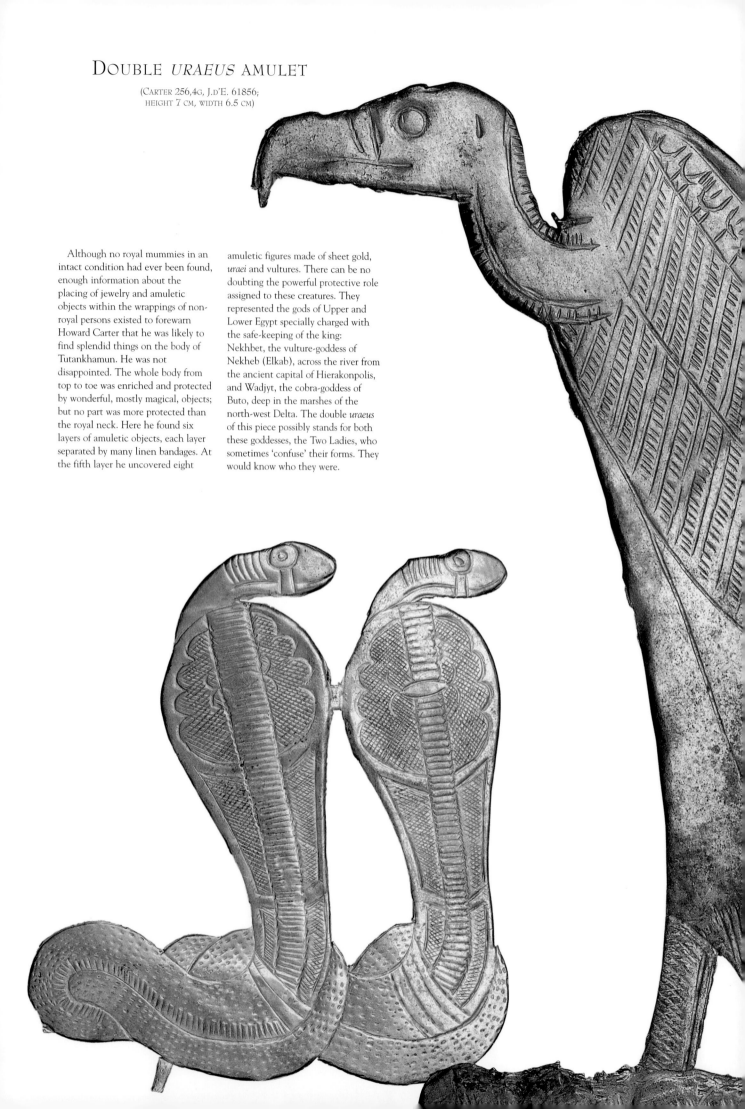

DOUBLE *URAEUS* AMULET

(CARTER 256,4G, J.D'E. 61856;
HEIGHT 7 CM, WIDTH 6.5 CM)

Although no royal mummies in an intact condition had ever been found, enough information about the placing of jewelry and amuletic objects within the wrappings of non-royal persons existed to forewarn Howard Carter that he was likely to find splendid things on the body of Tutankhamun. He was not disappointed. The whole body from top to toe was enriched and protected by wonderful, mostly magical, objects; but no part was more protected than the royal neck. Here he found six layers of amuletic objects, each layer separated by many linen bandages. At the fifth layer he uncovered eight amuletic figures made of sheet gold, *uraei* and vultures. There can be no doubting the powerful protective role assigned to these creatures. They represented the gods of Upper and Lower Egypt specially charged with the safe-keeping of the king: Nekhbet, the vulture-goddess of Nekheb (Elkab), across the river from the ancient capital of Hierakonpolis, and Wadjyt, the cobra-goddess of Buto, deep in the marshes of the north-west Delta. The double *uraeus* of this piece possibly stands for both these goddesses, the Two Ladies, who sometimes 'confuse' their forms. They would know who they were.

Two vulture
AMULETS

(CARTER 256,4J, 256,4H,
J.D'E. 61846, 61847;
HEIGHT 6.6 CM, WIDTH 6.2 CM)

Two of the five sheet-gold vulture
amulets found at the neck of the
king. Like all eight similar pieces
found in this position, they are
made from thin gold sheet,
decorated by chasing, not engraving.
Chasing involved pressing a suitably
pointed tool into the gold;
engraving was a technique in which
a sharp tool cut fine channels in the
gold. Engraving was not used in
ancient Egypt. Carter, who was
proud of his ornithological learning,
believed he could distinguish
between the different kinds of
vulture represented. Two he
recognized as the griffin vulture
(*gyps fulvus*), which was the origin
of the goddess Mut. Three he saw as
the vulture of Nekhbet, the Upper
Egyptian vulture (*vultur auricularis*,
Daud.). The two shown here were
for Carter Nekhbet vultures, and
therefore particularly suitable as
protective creatures for the king in
death. The Egyptians were very
good at representing birds and
animals in a convincing way, but
their accuracy in detail has often
been questioned by naturalists. The
backs of these amulets have eyelets
for strings to pass through for
attachment.

FIGURE OF WERET-HEKAU

(CARTER 108C, J.D'E. 61952; HEIGHT OF FIGURE 14 CM)

The wonderful golden shrine found in the Antechamber contained a stand for a small figure, parts of the ceremonial corselet, and a linen package containing this figure. It may not be precisely an amulet, but it was undoubtedly charged with magical force. Here is illustrated a well-known episode from mythology: the king is suckled by the goddess Isis; and here Isis appears in a transformation, a snake with human head, breasts and arms; she is Weret-hekau 'the great one of magic'. It is again extraordinary how acceptable the Egyptian artist has made an incident that should normally induce loathing. Weret-hekau has become a caring, nursing serpent with a female head wearing a queen's vulture headdress and a double feathered crown with horns. Tutankhamun is shown with distinctly Amarna-style physical characteristics, but not as a child; rather a grown king with the blue crown and a kilt with flowing streamers. The goddess has one arm around the king, and with her other hand she directs her breast to his mouth. The main figure is made of gilded wood strung on a necklace of simple beads of gold, carnelian, felspar and glass. Further strings of tiny beads surround the necks of the goddess and the king, and the feet of the king. The text on the base describes Tutankhamun as 'beloved of Weret-hekau'.

FAIENCE FIGURE OF THOTH

(CARTER 261G(2), J.D'E. 60743; HEIGHT 8 CM)

Compartments in the great Anubis shrine which guarded the entrance to the Treasury contained a very strange assortment of material. There were the important collection of pectoral jewels, pieces of cloth and clothing, a few *shabti*-figures, odds and ends tied up in small linen bundles, and some amulets and small divine figures – the forgotten contents of a drawer in a bureau. Among the amulets and divine figures was this little faience figure of the god Thoth in bright blue glaze with a few markings in manganese of wig striations and head details. The god is shown as a human figure with the head of the ibis, the most common animal form of this important deity. Thoth, the god of Hermopolis (Khmunu) in Middle Egypt, was a regular member of the great company of the gods, whose importance never waned. He can be considered the Head of the Divine Civil Service. He was the scribe of the gods and the patron deity of scribes. He also occurs among the gods and genii represented on coffins and Canopic equipment. His presence in the Anubis shrine cannot be explained, but perhaps no explanation is necessary. As a small sculpture it has merit in its simplicity, and in the fineness of the glaze.

KNOT AMULET

(CARTER 256KKK, J.D'E. 61841; LENGTH 16 CM)

Covering the thorax of Tutankhamun's mummy was a bewildering series of objects separated by much bandaging: Carter identified thirteen layers. In the seventh, among a number of other objects, were two strange pieces of solid gold, shaped as ties or knots. They were placed to the right and the left of the thorax, running parallel to the arms. Carter could offer no explanation; for him they were 'of unknown meaning', the judgement on many objects which are thought to be amulets. Sometimes they cannot be explained physically – what exactly was the *djed*-pillar, or the equally common *tyet*? In some cases meanings can be assigned through the use of the object in the hieroglyphic script in meaningful contexts. Sometimes an amulet has a form which is quite recognizable, but without identifiable meaning. This knot amulet falls into this last category. A slightly different knot-hieroglyph has the sound *tjes*, a root which can mean 'join, tie', and as a noun 'vertebra'. The amuletic possibilities of *tjes* immediately become apparent. An utterance in the Pyramid Texts declares of the king: 'the gods have fastened together your face for you, and Horus has given you his eye'.

Partly gilded
DJED-AMULET

(Carter 620(21), J.d'E. 61780;
height 8 cm)

Most of the conventional
amulets found in Tutankhamun's
tomb, apart from those concealed
in the mummy wrappings, were
retrieved from the Annexe, a kind
of glorious junk-room into which a
huge amount of material of all
kinds was stuffed – much of it
before the great pieces were placed
in the Antechamber, otherwise it
would have been inaccessible.
There were boxes with fine objects,
kiosks containing *shabti*-figures,
boxes of food, jars of wine, boats,
furniture and a great many odds
and ends. There were some fine
amulets, including this *djed*.
It is made of blue glazed quartz frit,
commonly called faience, and the
terminal parts, top and bottom, and
of the four horizontal bars, are
embellished with gold foil. There
are markings in manganese,
including a cartouche containing
the prenomen of the king,
Nebkheperure. Stability or
endurance can be granted to the
deceased by or through the *djed*-
pillar – the stability of a living
person provided by the backbone,
or in nature by the trunk of a tree.
The origins of the *djed* go back to
the earliest times, when Egyptian
religion was concerned with many
natural objects and phenomena.
When it was incorporated in the
Osiris cult, it was not explained.

GOLD
DJED-AMULET

(CARTER 256KK, J.D'E. 61778;
HEIGHT 9 CM)

It is not often that one finds an object placed precisely where it ought to be, especially an amulet. This gold *djed* is one of two which were found at the neck of Tutankhamun's mummy. Spell 155 of the Book of the Dead contains a comment on the short chapter (mentioned below): 'To be said over a gold *djed* embellished with sycomore bark, to be set on the neck of the deceased on the day of burial. He, on whose neck this amulet is set, will be a worthy spirit who will be in the kingdom of the dead on New Year's Day, like those in the following of Osiris. A thing a million times true.' So was Tutankhamun equipped, and this *djed*, symbol of endurance, is inscribed with words from Spell 155: 'Spoken (by) your limbs, to you, weary of heart [that is, dead]. Put yourself on your side that I may put water under you and bring to you a *djed* of gold, and that you may rejoice in it.' And so it was done. The so-called *djed*-pillar, shown being raised to an upright position in ritual scenes, was closely associated with the Osiris cult, and has sometimes been interpreted as a formalized representation of the god's backbone.

GOLDEN PAPYRUS COLUMN

(CARTER 620(72), J.D'E. 61857; HEIGHT 5.9 CM)

The papyrus column in the hieroglyphic script means 'be green, be fresh, be healthy'. It is therefore a very appropriate sign to be used as an amulet. In view of its meaning, the ideal color for it is green, as will be explained in the next entry. This example, however, is of gold; it is carefully marked with the details of the flower head, and of the leaves at the base of the stem. It carries the simple inscription 'the good god, Nebkheperure'. At the top there is a suspension ring. It was found among the miscellaneous objects in the Annexe. Spell 160 of the Book of the Dead concerns the 'giving of a papyrus column of green felspar'. It states: 'I possess a papyrus-column of green felspar which is not flawed, which the hand of Thoth supports, for he abhors imperfection. If it is intact then I shall be healthy; if it is undamaged then shall I be undamaged; if it is not hit, then shall I not be hit. It is what Thoth has said that joins your spine together.'

FAIENCE PAPYRUS COLUMN

(CARTER 261F(6), J.D'E. 61788; HEIGHT 8.5 CM)

The correct place for the papyrus column to be set was on the throat of the deceased person, and it should be made of green felspar. Spell 159 of the Book of the Dead is to be spoken over such a papyrus column 'with this spell written on it; it is to be placed on the neck of the dead person'. The spell itself is somewhat elusive: 'You who have come out of the god's house today; she whose voice is loud, goes around from the door of the Two Houses; she has taken the power of her father, who is advanced as Bull of the nursing goddess, and she accepts those followers of hers who perform great things for her'. A gold papyrus column inlaid with green felspar was found between two *djed*-columns on Tutankhamun's neck. This example, much more modest, is not made of green felspar, but of blue faience; the glaze could have been green, as that was possible in the Eighteenth Dynasty. The markings are carried out in manganese. It was found in the great Anubis shrine in the Treasury.

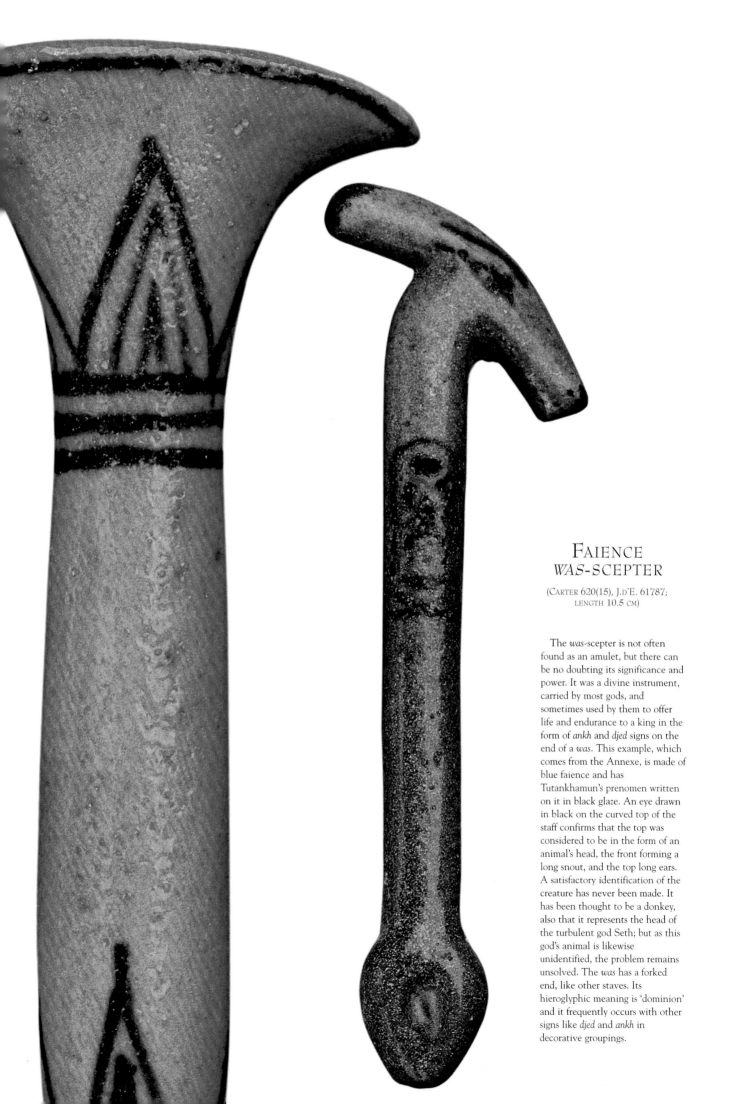

FAIENCE
WAS-SCEPTER

(CARTER 620(15), J.D'E. 61787;
LENGTH 10.5 CM)

The *was*-scepter is not often
found as an amulet, but there can
be no doubting its significance and
power. It was a divine instrument,
carried by most gods, and
sometimes used by them to offer
life and endurance to a king in the
form of *ankh* and *djed* signs on the
end of a *was*. This example, which
comes from the Annexe, is made of
blue faience and has
Tutankhamun's prenomen written
on it in black glaze. An eye drawn
in black on the curved top of the
staff confirms that the top was
considered to be in the form of an
animal's head, the front forming a
long snout, and the top long ears.
A satisfactory identification of the
creature has never been made. It
has been thought to be a donkey,
also that it represents the head of
the turbulent god Seth; but as this
god's animal is likewise
unidentified, the problem remains
unsolved. The *was* has a forked
end, like other staves. Its
hieroglyphic meaning is 'dominion'
and it frequently occurs with other
signs like *djed* and *ankh* in
decorative groupings.

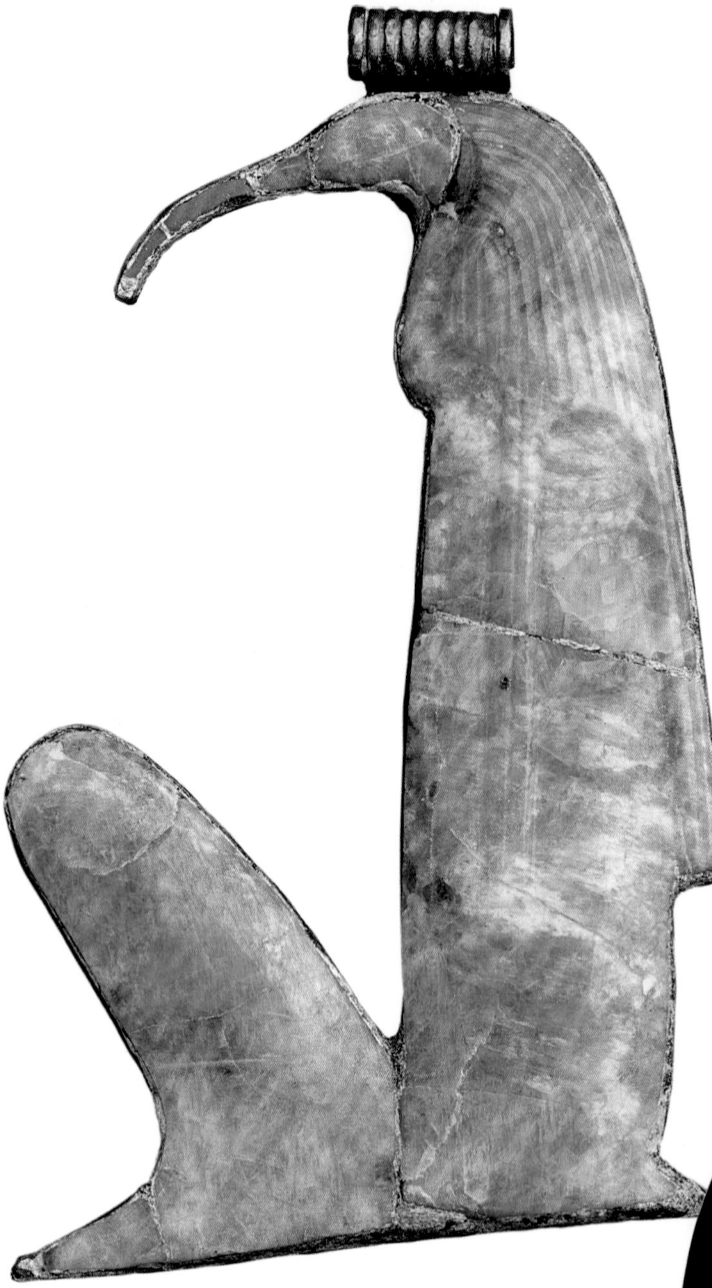

RESIN SCARAB WITH HERON

(CARTER 256Q, J.D'E. 61977; LENGTH 4.8 CM)

This unusual piece was found within Tutankhamun's mummy wrappings at about the level of his navel. It is a scarab made of resin, inlaid with a figure of a heron made up of lapis-lazuli and different colored glass. It is mounted on a gold plate inscribed with a text derived from Spell 29B of the Book of the Dead, which is for 'a heart amulet made of *sehret* stone'. This piece, however, is not a heart amulet, and it is certainly not made of *sehret* stone, which is thought to be hard and dark green. Such stones were commonly used for heart scarabs like the one mounted in the pectoral of a winged scarab with Isis and Nephthys (J. d'E. 61948).

The bird shown here is called *benu* in Egyptian, often translated as 'phoenix'. The *benu* is one of the forms in which the deceased can leave the tomb. Spell 13 of the Book of the Dead is one 'for going in and out of the West', and it includes the words 'I went in as a falcon, but I have come out as the *benu*'. In the spell on this base plate the king states: 'I am the *benu*, the *ba*-spirit of Re who guides the *bas* to the Underworld'.

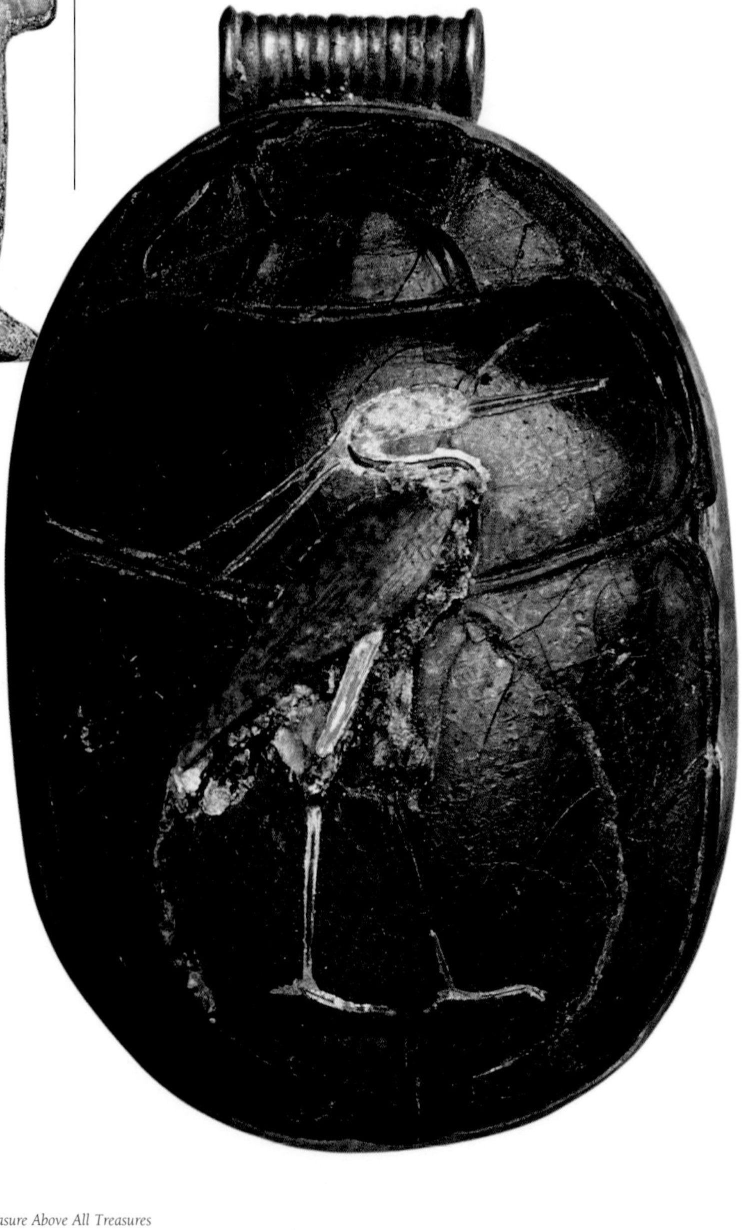

FELSPAR THOTH AMULET

(CARTER 256,4A, J.D'E. 61863; HEIGHT 5.5 CM)

The fourth layer of objects around the neck of Tutankhamun's mummy contained, along with other amuletic objects, this figure of the god Thoth. It is the ibis-headed form of the god, shown with human body in squatting pose. It is backed by a gold plate to which it is cemented as thin pieces of green felspar. Felspar is a crystalline stone with a tendency to fracture, and it is clear that the craftsman who fitted in the pieces had some difficulty in achieving perfect joins. Nevertheless, the felspar shows some moulding of form, and details have been lightly incised. Thoth was very much a diplomatic deity, effecting reconciliation and acting as a go-between either in person or as a letter-writer. In the discussion of the papyrus column amulets above it was seen that he is mentioned in one of the appropriate spells of the Book of the Dead as being one who abhors imperfection. Felspar was the specified material for the papyrus column amulet.

GILDED HEART
WITH HERON

(CARTER 620(67), J.D'E. 61866;
LENGTH 5.8 CM)

This is a true heart amulet; it is shaped like a heart and it is properly associated with the *benu* bird. It comes from the miscellaneous material in the Annexe, and is made of gilded wood. One side is inscribed with the prenomen of Tutankhamun, the cartouche flanked by *heqa*-scepters of royal power and the feather of truth. The other side is inlaid with colored faience forming a figure of the *benu*. This bird is often considered the forerunner of the phoenix in classical mythology.

In some forms of the Egyptian creation myth, the sun-god appears as the *benu*, perched on a reed growing out of the primordial mound. The classical phoenix was the fabulous bird rising from the ashes, promising a form of resurrection. The idea of rebirth is common to both myths, but it is misleading to think of the *benu* as the mythical ancestor of the classical phoenix.

RED GLASS *TYET* AMULET

(CARTER 46Y, J.D'E. 61833;
LENGTH 6.5 CM)

In the confused mass of objects left by the tomb robbers in the Antechamber, among a quantity of linen, was this amulet, called *tyet*. It incorporates an old magical idea connected with the goddess Isis, and there has been much debate about what it represents. Sometimes the ideas behind Egyptian signs wander or migrate over the centuries, and it is probable that any interpretation based on New Kingdom texts will be some way from the origins. This sign and its associated ideas are very old, and in its early form it looks not unlike the *ankh*, but with drooping side arms. It is generally thought to represent a folded cloth, but it has even been considered a form of the female genital organs. It is 'the knot of Isis' or the 'blood of Isis'; the former is more likely. According to the Book of the Dead it should be made of red jasper, and most examples are made of this stone or other red materials. This one is of red glass and it is inscribed 'the good god, Nebkheperure'.

Faience *ANKH*

(Carter 99a, J.d'E. 61790;
height 10.8 cm)

This sharply molded figure of the *ankh* was found along with some cloth and a lump of bread in the Antechamber. It is made of bright blue faience with markings in manganese. The prenomen of Tutankhamun is written down the stem of the piece. *Ankh* was the Egyptian word for 'life', and gods are often shown carrying it, frequently offering it to the king. The *ankh* was an important element in the cult of the Aten during the reign of Akhenaten, being shown extended to the king and other members of the royal family by the rays decending from the divine sun-disk. Although *ankh* was of vital importance for the well-being of everyone, it is surprising to find how few actual *ankh* amulets can be seen in collections of amulets, compared with the large numbers of *djed*-pillars, papyrus columns, eyes of Horus and other magical signs. In a sense, non-royal persons received 'life' through the king; it was the king who was charged with 'life' directly by the gods.

Faience *TYET* AMULET

(Carter 620(18), J.d'E. 61828;
length 8.5 cm)

The markings on this *tyet* amulet show very clearly why it is thought to represent a folded cloth, tied beneath the loop at the top. It is not made of a red material but of blue faience with markings in manganese, including the prenomen of Tutankhamun. Spell 156 of the Book of the Dead applies to the *tyet*: 'You possess your blood, Isis; you possess your power, Isis; you possess your magic, Isis. The amulet is a protection for this Great One, which will drive off anyone who would perform a criminal act against him.' The text comments further that this spell should be spoken over the *tyet* amulet and placed on the neck of the dead person on the day of burial: 'For the one for whom this is done, the power of Isis will be the protection of his body, and Horus, the son of Isis, will rejoice over him when he sees him'. There was a *tyet* of red jasper placed on Tutankhamun's neck.

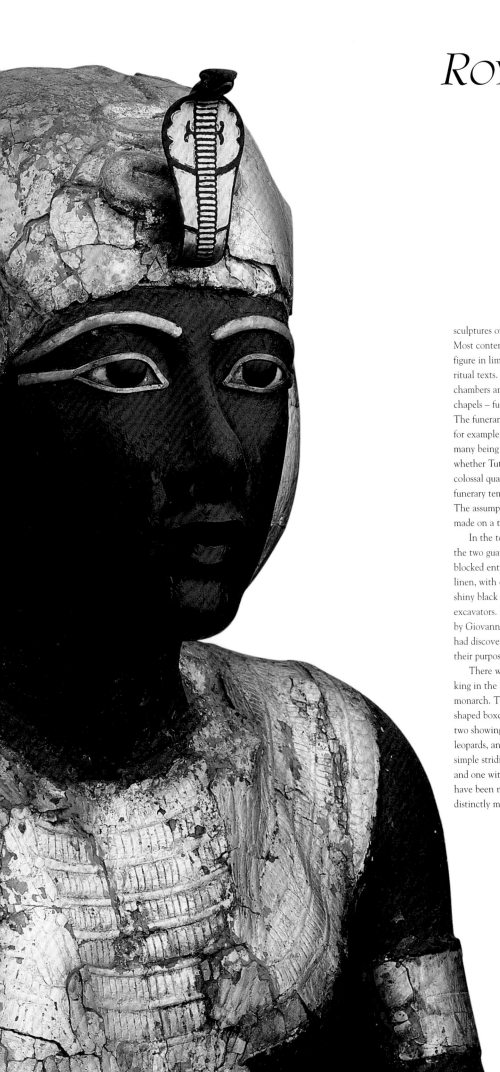

ROYAL FIGURES

I t is perhaps surprising that no stone sculptures of the king were found in Tutankhamun's tomb. Most contemporary private burials would include a votive figure in limestone, granite or quartzite, covered with ritual texts. Private tombs, however, incorporated burial chambers and offering chapels. Royal tombs had their chapels – funerary temples – far away from the Valley. The funerary temples of Amenophis III and Ramesses II, for example, were well populated with stone sculptures, many being colossal. It is not known with certainty whether Tutankhamun had a funerary temple, but two colossal quartzite statues of the king were found in the funerary temple of Ay and Horemheb at Medinet Habu. The assumption must be that a beginning at least was made on a temple.

In the tomb itself the principal images of the king were the two guardian figures in the Antechamber by the blocked entrance to the Burial Chamber. Partly draped in linen, with eyes dramatically outlined in gilded bronze and shiny black faces, they presented an awesome sight to the excavators. Similar figures, but ungilded, had been found by Giovanni Battista Belzoni in badly plundered tombs he had discovered in the Valley one hundred years earlier; their purpose had never been explained.

There were seven other gilded wooden figures of the king in the tomb, not all with the features of the young monarch. They were found in the black-painted shrine-shaped boxes in the Treasury. Four are quite remarkable, two showing statuettes of the king on the backs of leopards, and two showing the king in a papyrus skiff. Two simple striding figures show him wearing the red crown, and one with the white crown. Not all these figures may have been made as images of Tutankhamun, and some are distinctly modeled in the Amarna style.

180 and 181
The heads of the two guardian statues of
Tutankhamun which stood on either side
of the entrance to the Burial Chamber.
They represent the king himself and his
ka-spirit, his constant companion and
double from the time of his birth. The
ka is on the right. The color black
implies regeneration.

GUARDIAN STATUE WITH *NEMES*

(CARTER 22, J.D'E. 60707;
HEIGHT 190 CM, WIDTH 56 CM)

Life-size wooden statues of kings
had been found by Giovanni
Battista Belzoni in tombs in the
Valley of the Kings which he had
opened in the early years of the
nineteenth century. Their function
was never made clear until
Tutankhamun's tomb was
discovered, and the excavators on
entering were confronted by the
two dramatic figures placed on
either side of the sealed entrance
to the Burial Chamber. They are
very similar, but not identical.
Both are made of wood,
constructed of a number of pieces,
plastered over and painted with
thick black paint – here and
elsewhere in the tomb black being
the color of regeneration. They are
gilded over the non-fleshy parts –
headdress, collar and pectoral, arm-
bands, bracelets, staff and mace;
the sandals are of gilded bronze, as
is the *uraeus* fixed to the brow. The
eyes are also outlined in gilded
bronze, and are inlaid with
crystalline limestone and obsidian.
This figure represents the king
himself, wearing the *nemes* head
cloth; the text running down the
middle of the kilt reads: 'the good
god to whom one bows, the
sovereign, of whom one boasts,
Nebkheperure, son of Re, lord of
diadems, Tutankhamun, ruler in
southern Heliopolis, living for
ever, like Re, every day'.

GUARDIAN STATUE WITH *AFNET*

(CARTER 29, J.D'E. 60708; HEIGHT 190 CM, WIDTH 54 CM)

The text on the kilt of this pair to the preceding figure reads: 'the good god, to whom one bows, the sovereign of whom one boasts, the *ka* of Herakhty, the Osiris, King, Lord of the Two Lands, Nebkheperure, justified'. This, then, represents the *ka*-spirit of Tutankhamun, his ever-present companion and counterpart from birth. Here the *ka* joins the king himself in sharing the duties of guarding the Burial Chamber and its precious contents. The figure wears the *afnet* head cloth, but is otherwise scarcely to be distinguished from the other. They are noble pieces, sensitively carved, showing some influence of the art of the time of Akhenaten. The features are those of the young king. Some details of the decoration of the gilded parts are of great interest: they were first overlaid with linen, then layered with gesso-plaster before being gilded, the decoration first being carved on the plaster. The pendant hanging below the broad collar shows a winged scarab, a common theme on royal pectorals, representing rebirth. On the broad front of the kilt, an apron or long sporran-like piece is shown; it carries the text, and is flanked by chevron patterns and cobras hanging down on each side, with sun-disks on their heads. With staff and mace, this *ka*-figure and its fellow of the king himself stand ready to meet intruders.

ROYAL FIGURE WITH WHITE CROWN

(CARTER 296B, J.D'E. 62360; HEIGHT 75.3 CM)

An inscription on the base in yellow paint identifies this statue as 'The Good God, Nebkheperure, justified', that is Tutankhamun. But there is no doubt that it does not look very much like him, and the bodily details are very distinctly in the Amarna style. It may well therefore have been made for Neferneferuaten, Tutankhamun's ephemeral predecessor, or even some other Amarna royal person, even Akhenaten himself. It was in one of the Treasury shrines along with one other piece, a remarkable figure of the little-known deity Menkaret, carrying a small figure of the king on her head. The present piece is more conventional in form. The king is shown stepping forward; he wears the white crown of Upper Egypt with gilded *uraeus*; the eyes are inlaid with crystalline limestone and obsidian, and surrounded with bronze outlines and eye-brows. A conventional broad collar lies on his chest and he wears a pleated kilt which dips down towards the back in a manner characteristic of the Amarna Period. In his right hand he holds the royal flail, and in his left a staff with a curved top, called an *awt*; it is in hieroglyphic writing sometimes replaced by the more familiar *heqa*-scepter, but it seems to be distinctive in its own right, even if its precise significance is not known.

ROYAL FIGURE WITH RED CROWN

(CARTER 275D, J.D'E. 60713; HEIGHT 59 CM)

The various figures of the king stored in black-painted shrine-shaped chests in the Treasury struck Howard Carter, with good reason, as showing Amarna influence. Although they represented traditional types of sculpture, they possessed 'a direct and spontaneous feeling for nature'; further, 'they show both energy and grace, in fact the divine and the human have been brought in familiar touch with one another'. Here speaks the artist in Carter. Some of the gilded royal statues are thought to have been made for Neferneferuaten, Tutankhamun's predecessor.

This piece seems less likely to be a recycled image, although the body shows Amarna characteristics, such as the sagging belly, the forward-thrust head and a general softness of form. In other respects it displays the well-established features of Tutankhamun. It is one of five pieces, including two of the king harpooning, which were found together in one shrine, all swathed in linen shrouds. The king here is shown in a familiar pose, with his left foot set forward, although not at full stride, as might be expected. He wears the red crown with a gilded bronze *uraeus* fitted to the brow. The eyes and eye-brows are inlaid with copper and the eyes themselves are of glass. The king stands with a plain long staff in his left hand, and the royal flail in the right.

THE KING ON
A LEOPARD

(CARTER 289A, J.D'E. 60715;
FULL HEIGHT 85.6 CM)

The two groups of king on leopard differ in one small and one major respect. The former lies in the staff carried by the king: in the illustrated example there is no handrest; in the other there is a papyrus umbel handrest, as in the case of the guardian figures. The second difference will be mentioned later.

In this group the leopard is shown carrying a figure of the king, not the king himself, on its back. Two-dimensional similar figures are depicted on the walls of other royal tombs, but the significance, which must be mythical, is not clear. The whole of the group is made of wood, the royal figure being covered with gesso-plaster and gilded. The flail, the staff, the *uraeus* on the brow, and the sandals are all made of gilded bronze. The eyes and their outlines are in colored glass. The base of the statue is painted black, as is the leopard, which offers a sinister contrast to the gilded figure. The effect is emphasized by the gilded details on the leopard's face and ears. There is a litheness and strength in the animal's figure, demonstrating the Egyptian artist's remarkable ability to capture its essential characteristics.

The major difference between the two royal figures mentioned above is that the two are designed according to different schemes of proportion. The illustrated example uses the common canon used since the Old Kingdom, while the other uses the modified canon introduced during the Amarna Period. The latter appears more elongated than the former; it has fairly prominent breasts and low, broad hips; the effect is more feminine than masculine. It has been suggested that the second figure may represent Nefertiti or Neferneferuaten, rather than Tutankhamun. Both figures were surely made during the Amarna Period, but their identity in the tomb, and for the Egyptians – if not for sceptical historians – was fixed by the inscriptions on their bases; they name Tutankhamun.eft hand, and the royal flail in the right.

THE KING AS HARPOONER

(CARTER 275C, J.D'E. 60709;
HEIGHT 69.5 CM)

One of two similar pieces found with three other royal figures in one of the chests in the Treasury, this remarkable group is undoubtedly among the most sensitive, lively and aesthetically satisfying sculptures to have survived from ancient Egypt. It has a fluidity, grace and subtlety of carving which characterizes the best carvings in wood, as opposed to the more intractable stone. Unfortunately, wooden figures are subject to rot, termites and fire. One of the wonders of Tutankhamun's tomb is that its contents were spared such ravages, and most of the wooden pieces survived in a remarkable state of preservation. Carvings like this harpooner brilliantly demonstrate the supreme and subtle craftsmanship of the Egyptian woodcarvers.

The group shows the king in the act of throwing a harpoon. He wears the red crown of Lower Egypt, a beaded broad collar, a pleated kilt and apron, and sandals. He is shown poised at the point of delivery, his right leg slightly raised, elegantly balanced on a skiff, a light craft made of papyrus stems. The wooden figure of the king is lightly plastered to receive its gold-leaf finish. The harpoon, the *uraeus* on the royal brow, and the sandals are made of gilded bronze; the eyes, set in bronze sockets, are of glass and obsidian. In the left hand is a coil of rope made of bronze, which in reality should be attached to the harpoon. The skiff and its stand are of black painted wood, with gilded terminals.

An incident in the interminable struggle between the gods Horus and Seth for the inheritance of their father Osiris is depicted here. This myth in various forms can be traced back to the earliest historical times, when kings and even high officials are shown hunting the male hippopotamus, the embodiment of Seth, seen as the evil deity. Here the king is Horus; the hippopotamus must be imagined. The outcome is predictably a victory for Horus, although the power of Seth was not completely defeated thereby.

ROYAL REGALIA

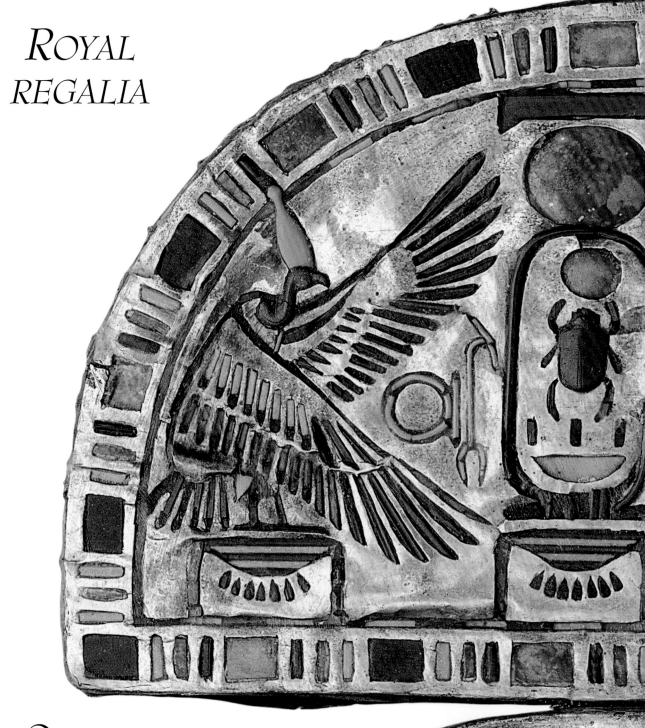

One of the most common, and for Egyptologists annoying, errors perpetrated by stage designers and film-makers involved with ancient Egyptian productions is to dress their casts in clothes which are specifically royal. The headdress with lappets (*nemes*) is a particular candidate for misuse. Designers may be after authenticity, but what they produce is gross inaccuracy.

It would have been very convenient if the tomb of Tutankhamun had contained a set of royal crowns and headdresses. Then some ideas of what they were made of, and how they were made, could have been formed. Unfortunately none was found, apart from a fine linen cap with gold headband on the mummy: it might have been the *afnet*, or bag-wig, such as is shown on one of the guardian statues. The other statue wears the *nemes*, the most common royal headdress, often thought to have been made of pleated linen.

Actual examples would have shown material and

manufacture. So would the red and white crowns
of Lower and Upper Egypt, and the blue crown,
the so-called war crown.

Two examples of the royal ceremonial tail were
found under the mummy. They were made of
beadwork on linen, but were deeply embedded in
the solidified resinous material at the bottom of the
coffin; they have never been satisfactorily restored.

A fine royal diadem was found on the mummy
beneath the mask; but the crook and flail held in
golden hands on the mummy's chest were rotted
away. Happily there were several sets of crook and
flail found elsewhere in the tomb – the first
examples ever found. The same is true of the
ceremonial scepter found in the Annexe.

The fans also included in this chapter were
used for the king, if not by the king, some on
ceremonial occasions.

THE DIADEM

(CARTER 256,4O, J.D'E. 60684;
DIAMETER 19 CM)

This beautiful and ingeniously designed piece was found on Tutankhamun's head, beneath the Golden Mask. At the time of assembling the burial, the vulture and *uraeus* heads were detached and placed on the thighs of the mummy.

The principal element of the diadem is a gold fillet fastened at the back by a bow in the form of lotus flowers. Some rigidity is provided by the snaking body of the *uraeus*, which arches from front to back. Two long gold ribbons and two substantial *uraei* hang down from the back. Diadems formed part of Egyptian royal insignia from early times, and less elaborate but beautifully crafted examples have been found in minor royal burials of the Middle Kingdom.

The principal decorative motif consists of circular pieces of carnelian set in gold with gold central 'buttons'; these are found on the main circlet and also on the pendent ribbons and *uraei*. In all places they are framed by block borders of carnelian and blue glass. The raised heads of the pendent *uraei* are similarly inlaid. The ribbons and pendent *uraei* are attached to the circlet by hinges, so that, as Carter pointed out, they could move to fit over wigs of different sizes.

Other parts of this versatile diadem are adaptable. The vulture and *uraeus* heads are removeable, as already noted; they have grooves on their backs which fit tongues on the diadem. So designed, they could be fitted onto other diadems, crowns or headdresses – an unusually economical arrangement. Carter was particularly struck by the workmanship of the vulture head, noting the obsidian eyes and the details of the wrinkling and feathering. He confidently asserted that it represented a form of the bird known as 'the sociable vulture'. The *uraeus* is equally well worked, with finely fitted inlays, including a blue glass tip to the head.

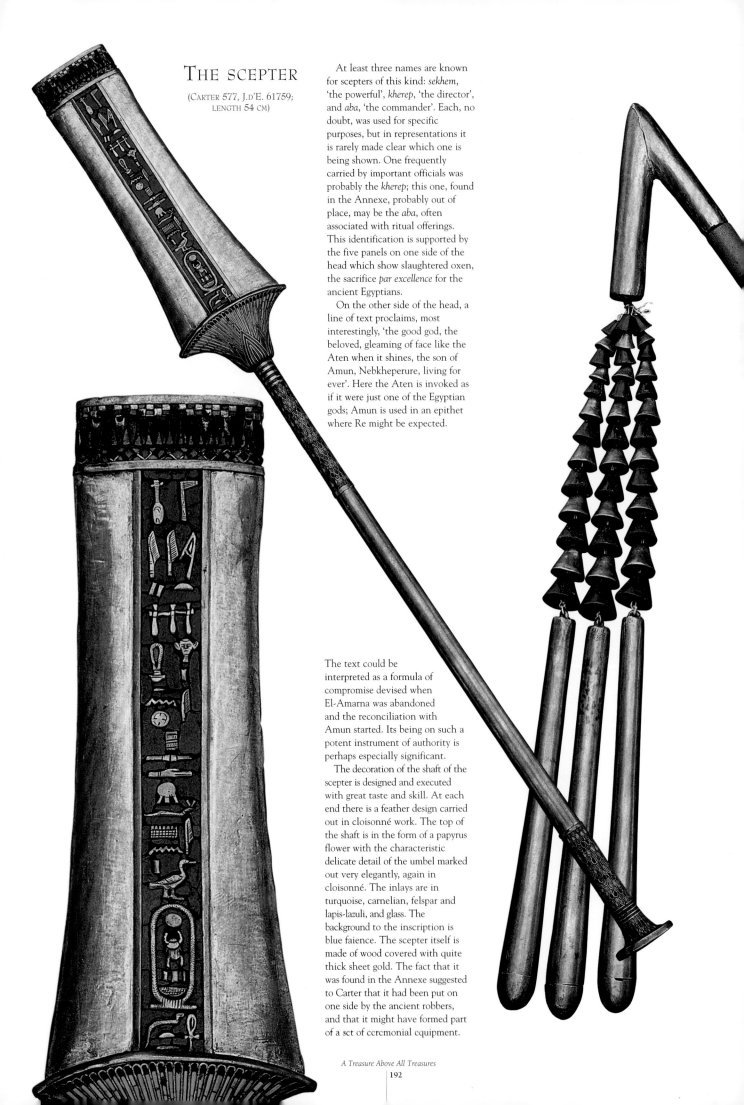

THE SCEPTER

(CARTER 577, J.D'E. 61759;
LENGTH 54 CM)

At least three names are known for scepters of this kind: *sekhem*, 'the powerful', *kherep*, 'the director', and *aba*, 'the commander'. Each, no doubt, was used for specific purposes, but in representations it is rarely made clear which one is being shown. One frequently carried by important officials was probably the *kherep*; this one, found in the Annexe, probably out of place, may be the *aba*, often associated with ritual offerings. This identification is supported by the five panels on one side of the head which show slaughtered oxen, the sacrifice *par excellence* for the ancient Egyptians.

On the other side of the head, a line of text proclaims, most interestingly, 'the good god, the beloved, gleaming of face like the Aten when it shines, the son of Amun, Nebkheperure, living for ever'. Here the Aten is invoked as if it were just one of the Egyptian gods; Amun is used in an epithet where Re might be expected.

The text could be interpreted as a formula of compromise devised when El-Amarna was abandoned and the reconciliation with Amun started. Its being on such a potent instrument of authority is perhaps especially significant.

The decoration of the shaft of the scepter is designed and executed with great taste and skill. At each end there is a feather design carried out in cloisonné work. The top of the shaft is in the form of a papyrus flower with the characteristic delicate detail of the umbel marked out very elegantly, again in cloisonné. The inlays are in turquoise, carnelian, felspar and lapis-lazuli, and glass. The background to the inscription is blue faience. The scepter itself is made of wood covered with quite thick sheet gold. The fact that it was found in the Annexe suggested to Carter that it had been put on one side by the ancient robbers, and that it might have formed part of a set of ceremonial equipment.

Flail and crook

(Carter 269e, 44u,
J.d'E. 61760, 61762;
length of each 33.5 cm)

These two instruments of royal authority are of great antiquity. They are chracteristically shown in later times as part of the regalia carried by Osiris, the god of the afterlife. It is wrong, however, to consider them as Osirian and carried by the living king in expectation of posthumous royalty. Osiris carries the crook and flail because he is a king, a divine king. He carries them because the Egyptian king carries them. The king carries them at the time of his coronation and at the occasions of renewal of royal power in the *sed*-festival. The flail and crook shown here seem to form a pair, not only by general similarity of form and construction, but also because they are of the same length, and would sit well together in the hands of the ruler. They were not, however, found together in the tomb; the flail was in the cartouche-shaped chest in the Treasury, which was intended for jewelry mostly; the crook was stored in a chest in the Antechamber. It is hard to believe that they do not belong together. It is also hard to avoid the conclusion that they may even have been held by Tutankhamun during his coronation in El-Amarna.

This idea is based on the inscription on the base of the flail. It contains the two cartouches of the king, but the nomen is given as Tutankhaten – not Tutankhamun – his name before the move from El-Amarna and the reconciliation with the traditional cults of Egypt.

The handles of both instruments are made of cylinders of blue glass and of metal overlaid with gold, threaded alternately on bronze rods. The three strands of the flail have blue glass elements and gilded wood elements and terminals.

There has been much debate about the origins and purposes of these two objects. The crook, called a *heqat* in Egyptian, has been compared with the shepherd's crook, although there is no evidence that Egyptian shepherds carried crooked staves to manage their flocks. Nevertheless, the idea is persuasive; the fact that in hieroglyphic writing the crook sign is used for the word 'to rule' supports this idea. The flail (*nekhakha* in Egyptian) is more puzzling. It is most probably in origin an instrument of control also, although it has been suggested that it may have been used by shepherds to collect ladanum for the preparation of unguents.

THE OSTRICH HUNT FAN

(CARTER 242, J.D'E. 62001;
LENGTH 105.5 CM,
WIDTH OF PALM 18.5 CM)

Fan-bearing was an important official function in ancient times, particularly in Egypt, where large fans were used also as sun shades. They were further marks of position and status. This fan, most splendid in appearance, is also, from its texts and scenes on the head or palm, very informative. It was found in the Burial Chamber, between the two innermost shrines; from the remains of its feathers it was clear that it had originally been fitted with thirty ostrich feathers, white and brown, alternately set.

What the fan shows in itself, the texts on the handle and the scenes on the palm confirm. The text on the handle states that the feathers were obtained by the king while hunting in the Eastern Desert of Heliopolis, that is not far from Memphis. The scenes illustrate the hunt. One side shows the king in his chariot at full gallop in the heat of the hunt. The two horses with feathered plumes and elaborate trappings pursue a pair of ostriches on the point of being brought down by the king's arrows. The royal hunting hound closes in on the stricken birds. The text on the other side describes the king as hunting as fiercely as Bastet (the cat deity of Bubastis), his horses being like bulls (in their strength). The scene on this side shows the aftermath of the chase: the king rides sedately in his chariot, holding back his horses, which seem to be straining at the bit. In front march two attendants weighed down with the bodies of the two dead ostriches.

The handle and the palm of the fan are made of wood covered with thin gold plate. The top of the handle is in the form of a lotus flower with down-turned petals. The scenes and texts are chased into the gold, with much of the detail produced by delicate punching.

DRESS AND COSMETIC OBJECTS

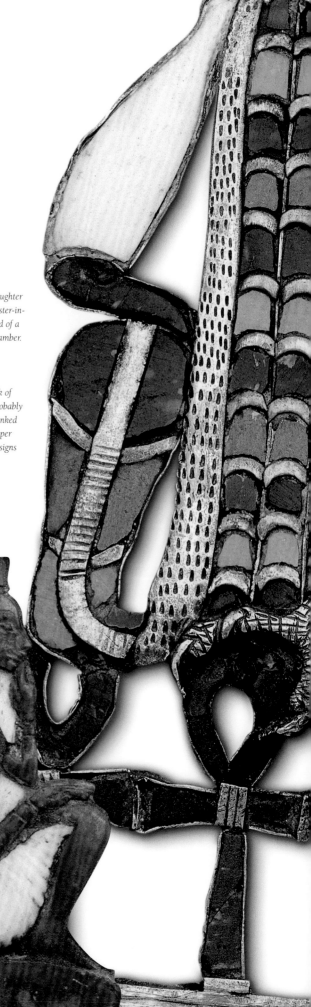

Bed linen, frequently found in unplundered non-royal burials, was unexpectedly lacking from Tutankhamun's tomb. Carter concluded that, being of fine quality and very useable, it was carried away by the ancient robbers. Dress was a very different case. Royal garments, elaborately worked and tailor-made, were not so useable; consequently many garments were found, especially in boxes in the Antechamber. Unfortunately, most had been hastily repacked after the ancient thefts, had been affected by damp, and were very difficult to handle. Skills in dealing with ancient textiles had not been very well developed at the time of the discovery, and many pieces could not be rescued from their wretched state.

Nevertheless, the skilful fingers of Carter, Arthur Mace and Alfred Lucas had much success in recovering many recognizable pieces of clothing, mostly made of fine linen and embellished with delicate embroidery, elaborate beadwork and gold sequins. Tunics, loincloths, shirts, kilts, underclothes and caps, made up the bulk of what could be identified; there were two large garments, heavily embroidered, which Carter compared with the robe called a dalmatic, worn by priests on ceremonial occasions and kings at the time of their coronations. There were sashes and scarves, large numbers of gloves, and many pairs of sandals. The gloves and sandals were made of many materials, and often richly decorated; some were simple and 'everyday'. In total the tomb held a full wardrobe for life in the underworld, formal and casual.

The Egyptians had a huge repertoire of cosmetic containers, often finely designed. Those for a king were special, and many must have been plundered from the tomb, being of exquisite quality. Mirrors of precious metal have gone, but their elaborate cases were left. Several small quantities of galena and malachite for eye-paint were found, but only a few eye-paint containers; there were no combs, and the king's shaving equipment seems scanty; cosmetic spoons were unexpectedly lacking. Undoubtedly most of the missing cosmetic pieces were made of precious materials, and were prime targets for the ancient robbers.

196
A figure of Neferneferure, fifth daughter of Akhenaten and Nefertiti, and sister-in-law of Tutankhamun; from the lid of a cosmetic box found in the Antechamber. The inlays are of faience.

197
The central element of the back of the corselet of the king. A bird (probably a falcon) with scarab body, is flanked by uraei with the crowns of Upper and Lower Egypt. It holds ankh signs in its claws.

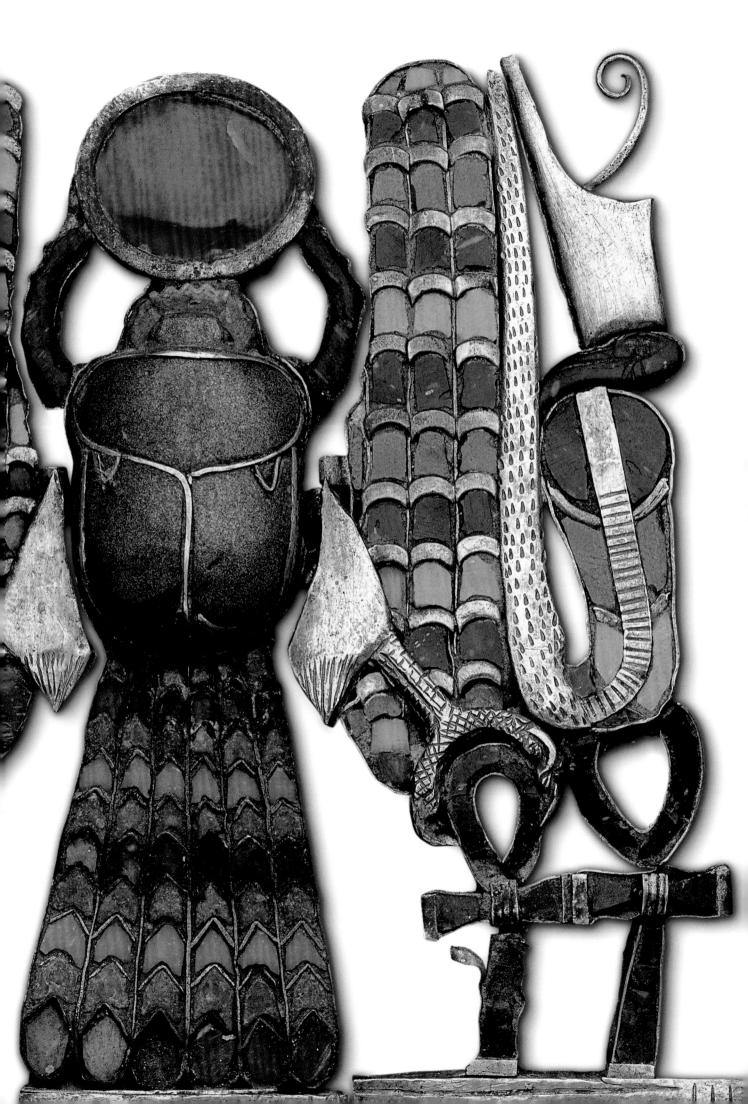

TUTANKHAMUN'S MANNEQUIN

(CARTER 116, J.D'E. 60722;
HEIGHT 73.5 CM)

Close to the golden shrine,
tucked under the great ritual
couches in the Antechamber, the
excavators could see a most realistic
face peering out from among the
parts of chariots and boxes. It was
this armless and legless figure, a
torso painted white with a head
painted brown, and with a gilded
crown. Carter himself suggested
that it was something upon which
royal garments could be tried out,

MIRROR CASE IN
THE FORM OF *ANKH*

(CARTER 269B, J.D'E. 62349;
HEIGHT 27 CM)

This highly decorated and
inscribed gilded wooden case was
made for a mirror. One ancient
Egyptian name for mirror was
ankh, the word used for 'life', and
this case has been made in the
form of the *ankh*. The mirror
which it originally contained
would probably have been pear-
shaped, a form of mirror first used
in the New Kingdom. Mirrors
played a part in funerary
symbolism, and many early tomb
stelae, especially of women, show
mirrors in cases beneath the chair
of the deceased.
This case was surely made for
Tutankhamun's burial, and it may
be assumed that the mirror it
contained would have been made
of silver or gold; the container

itself is lined with thin sheet
silver. Robbers clearly took
the mirror in antiquity.
Most surviving mirrors from
ancient Egypt were made of
bronze, which when well
polished would have a good
reflective surface. The lid of this
truly royal piece has in its central
depression a form of
Tutankhamun's prenomen on top
of a lotus flower, and flanked by
uraei with sun-disks. The inlays
are of glass, apart from the sun-
disks, which are carnelian. Long
texts on the loop and handle of
the case, on both sides, apply
many epithets to the king.
Among other things, he is
'image of Re' and 'pure egg
of Khepri'.

or fitted, a kind of tailor's dummy
or mannequin. Nothing of the kind
has otherwise ever been found from
ancient Egypt. A scrutiny of the
kinds of clothes worn by important
people, as shown in paintings,
reliefs and sculptures, makes it clear
that many items were very carefully
tailored, to fit not just well, but
closely and neatly. The tomb of
Tutankhamun itself produced an
extraordinary amount of clothing of
all kinds, much of which, sadly, was
in a poor condition; but there was
enough material in a reasonable
state to demonstrate the range of
items made for a king, and also the
excellence of workmanship, not
only in the making of garments,
but in embroidering them in many
different techniques.

THE ROYAL CORSELET

(CARTER 54K, J.D'E. 62627;
HEIGHT 40 CM, LENGTH 85 CM)

This rare object, of a kind known from representations on monuments, would have been worn by the king on ceremonial occasions. It was found in fragments in various parts of the Antechamber, including the gilded shrine, but enough has survived to give a fair idea of its original form. Carter's first reconstruction was, however, different from that shown here.

As now shown, there is a broad collar front and back, made up of rows of beads in glass made to look like tubular beads, the outermost row in each case having flower-shaped pendants of cloisonné work inlaid with semiprecious stones set in gold.

A pendent ornament shows Amon-Re presenting life and a long reign to Tutankhamun, who is supported by the god Atum and his divine consort Lusaas. Again the figures are made of cloisonné inlay of semiprecious stones and colored glass, including rare opaque white glass. The counterpoise ornament for the back is in the form of a rhomboidal pendant; in the center is a winged scarab with sun-disk, supported on each side by *uraei* wearing the crowns of Upper and Lower Egypt; from the coils of the *uraei* two *ankh*-signs of life hang. Eleven short strings of beads with floral terminals hang down from the base of this counterpoise.

The main part of the corselet, back and front, is made to represent the *rishi,* or feather decoration, found particularly on coffins. The individual elements are again inlaid with colored glass. In the present restoration, gold slide fasteners are placed along the edges of the body sections. It is altogether an extraordinary *de luxe* piece of armour, carried out spectacularly in gold and cloisonné work.

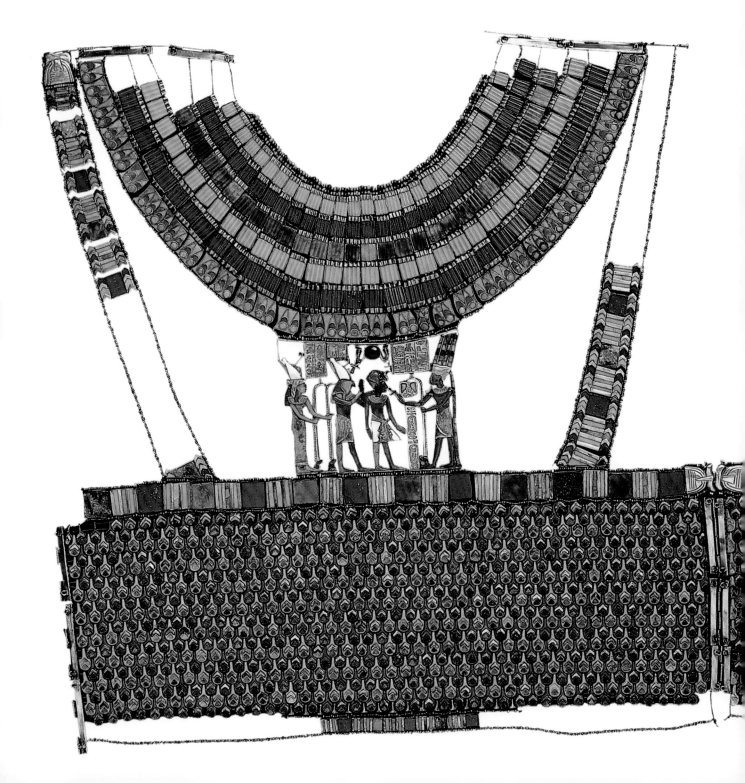

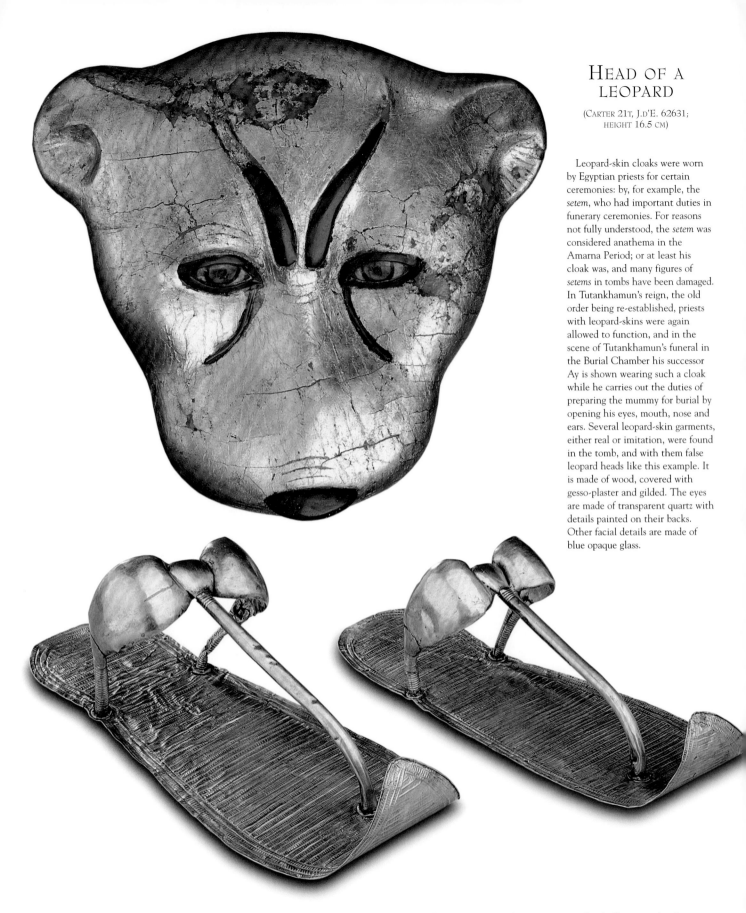

HEAD OF A LEOPARD

(CARTER 21T, J.D'E. 62631;
HEIGHT 16.5 CM)

Leopard-skin cloaks were worn by Egyptian priests for certain ceremonies: by, for example, the *setem*, who had important duties in funerary ceremonies. For reasons not fully understood, the *setem* was considered anathema in the Amarna Period; or at least his cloak was, and many figures of *setems* in tombs have been damaged. In Tutankhamun's reign, the old order being re-established, priests with leopard-skins were again allowed to function, and in the scene of Tutankhamun's funeral in the Burial Chamber his successor Ay is shown wearing such a cloak while he carries out the duties of preparing the mummy for burial by opening his eyes, mouth, nose and ears. Several leopard-skin garments, either real or imitation, were found in the tomb, and with them false leopard heads like this example. It is made of wood, covered with gesso-plaster and gilded. The eyes are made of transparent quartz with details painted on their backs. Other facial details are made of blue opaque glass.

PAIR OF GOLD SANDALS

(CARTER 256LL, J.D'E. 60680;
LENGTH 29.5 CM)

Of the many pairs of sandals found in the tomb of Tutankhamun, this pair is probably the only one which was never used in the king's lifetime. The two soles of the sandals are made of sheet gold, with the straps around the ankles and the 'thongs' passing between the big toes and second toes, also of gold. The soles turn up at the front, a feature still common in casual footwear in the Near East. The surfaces of the soles are striated to represent the weave of the material of which simple Egyptian sandals were made, usually papyrus leaves or rushes. The feet of the mummy were fully equipped with the gold that would help in the king's posthumous regeneration. Each toe was individually wrapped in linen before gold sheaths were fitted, each one marked with nails and toe-joints. Some linen bandages were then applied before the sandals were fitted, the gold thongs adjusted, and finally the feet fully bandaged. In form, these sandals are very similar to those on the feet of the guardian statues.

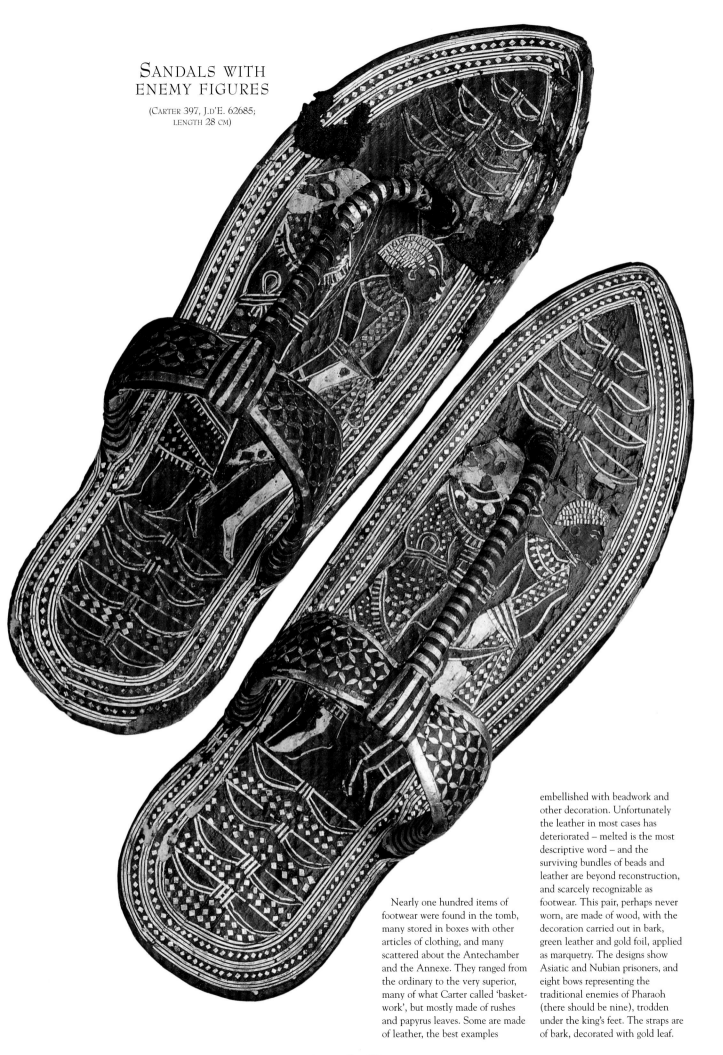

SANDALS WITH ENEMY FIGURES

(CARTER 397, J.D'E. 62685;
LENGTH 28 CM)

Nearly one hundred items of footwear were found in the tomb, many stored in boxes with other articles of clothing, and many scattered about the Antechamber and the Annexe. They ranged from the ordinary to the very superior, many of what Carter called 'basket-work', but mostly made of rushes and papyrus leaves. Some are made of leather, the best examples embellished with beadwork and other decoration. Unfortunately the leather in most cases has deteriorated – melted is the most descriptive word – and the surviving bundles of beads and leather are beyond reconstruction, and scarcely recognizable as footwear. This pair, perhaps never worn, are made of wood, with the decoration carried out in bark, green leather and gold foil, applied as marquetry. The designs show Asiatic and Nubian prisoners, and eight bows representing the traditional enemies of Pharaoh (there should be nine), trodden under the king's feet. The straps are of bark, decorated with gold leaf.

IVORY JEWEL BOX

(CARTER 54DDD, J.D'E. 61449;
HEIGHT 13.97 CM, WIDTH 16.8 CM)

Shape was often of greater importance to the Egyptian artist-craftsman than material. To put it another way, inspiration for a particular form would lead to the making of things in a material for which the form was not really suitable. In architecture it was common. In the case of this small box it turned out to be a success. It was found in the Antechamber in a large chest containing a miscellany of objects, made to the design of wooden boxes but here carried out most skillfully in ivory. The main panels of the top, sides and bottom are single pieces, which must have been difficult to obtain and cut, considering the structure of an elephant's tusk. The ivory is plain, the various sections being cemented together. Remarkably, it still opens and shuts well, without signs of warping. The knobs for closing, the caps on the feet, and the little hinges are made of gold, the hinges in particular being most precisely made. A panel under the front knob contains Tutankhamun's two cartouches and his Horus name, 'strong bull, Tut-mesut'. A hieratic docket on the lid describes its original contents: 'gold, rings for the funeral procession'. It was, as Carter described it, a jewel box. The back panel is decorated with an applied lotus capital column.

MIRROR CASE WITH KNEELING GOD

(CARTER 271C, D, J.D'E. 62348;
HEIGHT 26.8 CM, WIDTH 14.2 CM)

This mirror case is iconographically more interesting than the case in the form of an *ankh* described above. Both are fine examples of the woodworker's craft. This piece was found in a box of mixed material in the Treasury which, according to Carter, had lost most of its original contents and been repacked indiscriminately by the Necropolis guards who attempted to clear up the mess made by the tomb robbers. The mirror itself had been taken from the case; it was undoubtedly made of a precious metal, silver or gold, probably gold because the inner surfaces of the box are gilded. The mirror would have been pear-shaped. The principal feature of this case is the kneeling figure of the god Heh, whose duty it was to promote the long reign of the ruling king. His name means 'million', and he is here shown typically holding two notched palm branches terminating at their bases with tadpoles (which stand for a hundred thousand) over *shen*-signs of 'dominion'. Tutankhamun's cartouches are placed on each side of the god's head, and the upper part of the case has a formalized version of the king's prenomen, incorporating the figure of a flamboyant winged scarab. The gold leaf covering the box is of the purplish-red variety, except for the palm branches, tadpoles and *shen*-signs which are of bright, purer gold.

COSMETIC BOX

(CARTER 240BIS, J.D'E. 61496;
HEIGHT 16 CM, WIDTH 8.8 CM, DEPTH 4.3 CM)

An evil-smelling brown powder found in this box confirmed paradoxically that it was made to contain a scented cosmetic ointment. Carter states that its was found in the bottom of the great sarcophagus, but there is some evidence to suggest that it was placed between the two outermost shrines.

It is a spectacular example of the jeweler's art, its decoration full of symbolism. To begin with, it is by no means clear whether it was made for life or for death. The representations of the king in the cartouches on the front of the box show him as a child, with the side-lock of youth, the *uraeus* on the brow indicating that he was already king. The conclusion ought to be that the piece was made early in his reign; but it is also possible to see

the child not as the young king, but the king as the young Horus. Other interpretations seem possible.

The box is in the form of a double, two-sided, cartouche, its lids topped with double plumes with sun-disk. It is usually accepted that the figures and hieroglyphs in the four cartouches represent cryptic writings of the king's prenomen, Nebkheperure; some scholars, however, take the

contents of the cartouches to be simply figures of the king squatting on a sign for 'festival', and, above, sun-disks with pendent *uraei*. On the other hand, cartouches are for royal names, and this is a royal piece.

The cartouches on the other side of the box show similar figures of the king without side-lock, wearing the blue crown; the face of one is black, which here may be a reference to regeneration. The inlays are of carnelian and colored

glass. Simpler chased designs on the sides of the box show the god of eternity squatting on a festival sign and holding palm branches notched with the promised years of Tutankhamun's reign. The king's names are shown in cartouche with some flamboyance.

The silver base of the box has on its underside a chased design of papyrus and poppy clumps with flying ducks, in form and detail reminiscent of palace paintings at El-Amarna.

JEWELRY

In spite of the great number of pieces of jewelry found in Tutankhamun's tomb, it is thought that what has survived gives an inadequate impression of what was available to a royal person in the Eighteenth Dynasty. All the items found on the mummy, and many of those found in the various boxes in the Antechamber and Treasury, including the great Anubis shrine, were funerary or religious. As for Tutankhamun's personal jewelry, the ancient robbers would surely have chosen to remove such pieces before considering the funerary jewels. One may be sure that his personal jewelry would have been miraculously designed, and made of the finest materials.

If the best has gone, what is one to say of the remainder? 'Not bad!' There are scarcely two pieces that are the same, and as a group they display a remarkable range of metal-working techniques, some of which were not rediscovered after post-classical times until the Renaissance. These ancient craftsmen could beat gold, make gold leaf of the finest quality, build up cloisons for

the reception of inlays, make gold wire, use solder, apply granulation. They could make scenes and designs by repoussé-work and by chasing, but not by engraving. The evidence that they could make cloisonné enamel is very slight, but their skills at inlaying glass were so good that in some cases enamelling has been surmised.

Technically some of the pieces are not of the highest quality of which the Egyptian craftsman was capable, in comparison, for example, with royal pieces of the Middle Kingdom. In design, however, one must marvel at the remarkable invention shown by the jewelry-makers. The pectorals present a range of pattern and use of divine symbolism which suggest that there were master jewelers at work in the ateliers of the royal establishments. Who designed? Who determined the designs? Who chose what was to be made? Who, again, supervised the craftsmen, workmen who had little status in the order of society? Yet even these lowly individuals must have derived much satisfaction from the production of such wonderful pieces.

208–209
Pectoral ornament in the form of a falcon with sun-disk, outstretched wings and holding ankh and shen signs in its claws. The cloisonné inlays are of glass and semi-precious stones.

COLLARS

COLLAR OF THE TWO LADIES

(Carter 256nnn, j.d'e. 61875;
width 48.7 cm)

This most elaborate collar was
one of three found within the
wrappings of the king's mummy,
lying on the breast. From paintings
of collars on wooden coffins of the
Middle Kingdom, this piece should
be called 'the collar of the two
ladies (the *Nebti* in Egyptian)'. The
two ladies are the *uraeus* and the
vulture, goddesses who protect the
king as ruler of Lower and Upper
Egypt – Wadjyt the cobra and
Nekhbet the vulture. Here they are
shown together with a single pair of
outstretched wings; the vulture
shows only one leg.

Technically this piece is a *tour de
force*. Apart from the central figures
of the two goddesses, it is composed
of 171 separate gold plaques, strung
together by threads which pass
through tiny eyelets at the top and
bottom of each plaque. The backs of
the plaques are chased with
feathering detail, and the fronts are
inlaid in cloisons with tiny pieces of
colored glass. Each piece of glass
was individually cut to fit its
appropriate cloison. Towards the
tips of the wings there is less inlay
and more gold. The whole collar is
very flexible and lies easily over a
surface which is not even.

The figures of the two goddesses
are particularly well ornamented
with colored inlays, red glass
imitating carnelian, used to subtle
effect. The vulture head is very
carefully modeled with chased
detail, the beak and the eye being
made of obsidian, naturally
occurring black glass. The folds
of the cobra are strikingly inlaid
with a checker pattern of gold and
colored glass.

All properly designed collars and
heavy necklaces are provided with a
counterpoise, designed to hang
down the back and hold the collar
in position. In Egyptian it was
called *menkhet*. The counterpoise of
this collar is of a simple bell-shape
with panels of colored glass. Gold
wire attached it to the collar.

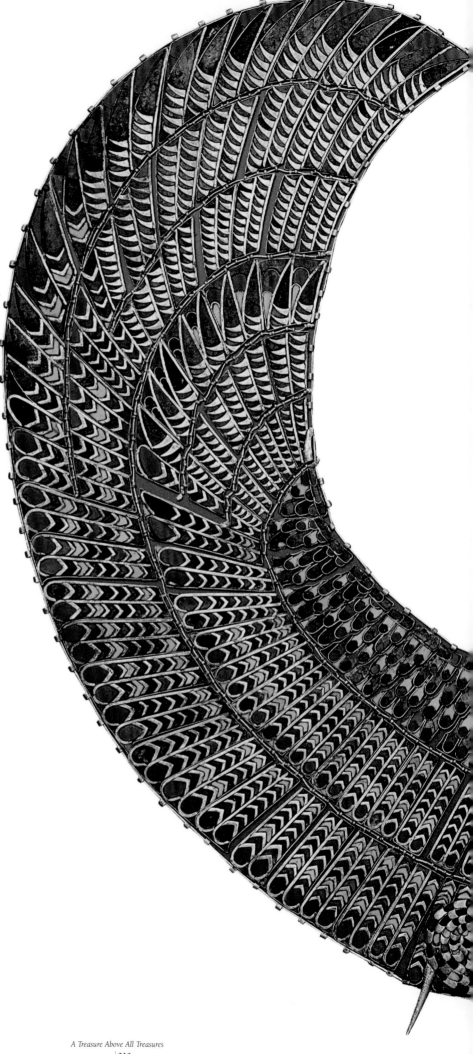

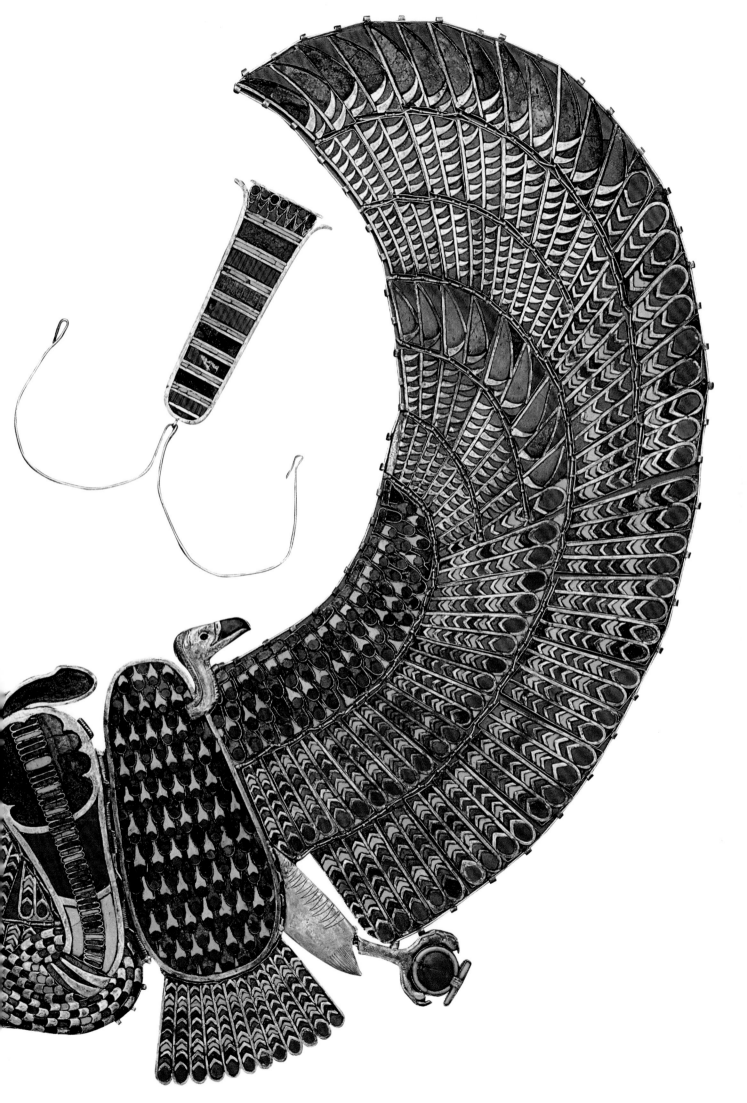

Sheet Gold Collar

(Carter 236g, J.d'E 61917; width 33 cm)

More than one hundred items which can be called 'ornaments' were found on Tutankhamun's body. Not all of these can be described as jewels, but that term can be applied to many that fall into the common categories of jewels: collars, necklaces, bracelets, bangles, rings, circlets, pectorals. Others can more properly be classified as amulets – divine figures or objects associated with gods. Seventeen were placed in the area of the neck and upper thorax, and some of these have already been illustrated as amulets, among them some sheet gold figures of deities.

This piece, which represents a winged form of Wadjyt, the cobra goddess of the ancient northern capital of Buto, is not unlike some of these sheet gold amulets. What distinguishes it as a collar is the presence of a counterpoise attached to the points of the wings by gold wire. It also lay lower down than the neck, on the body's thorax. It was not robust enough for daily use.

The collar was cut to shape from a sheet of gold beaten to less than a millimeter thick. Ancient Egyptian goldsmiths learned in a very early period how to beat gold into thin sheets from small nuggets. There are several scenes in tombs of the Old Kingdom showing the beating of gold on an anvil with what appears to be a rounded stone. Gold sheet and foil were much employed to embellish furniture and funerary objects, and gold leaf was used to gild wood on a base of gesso plaster. Gold leaf was made to a thinness almost equal to modern gold leaf, but one gains the impression that gold foil and sheeting were preferred, because they were more opulent. The detail on this collar and counterpoise were marked out by chasing; the markings on the serpent figure itself are particularly well made.

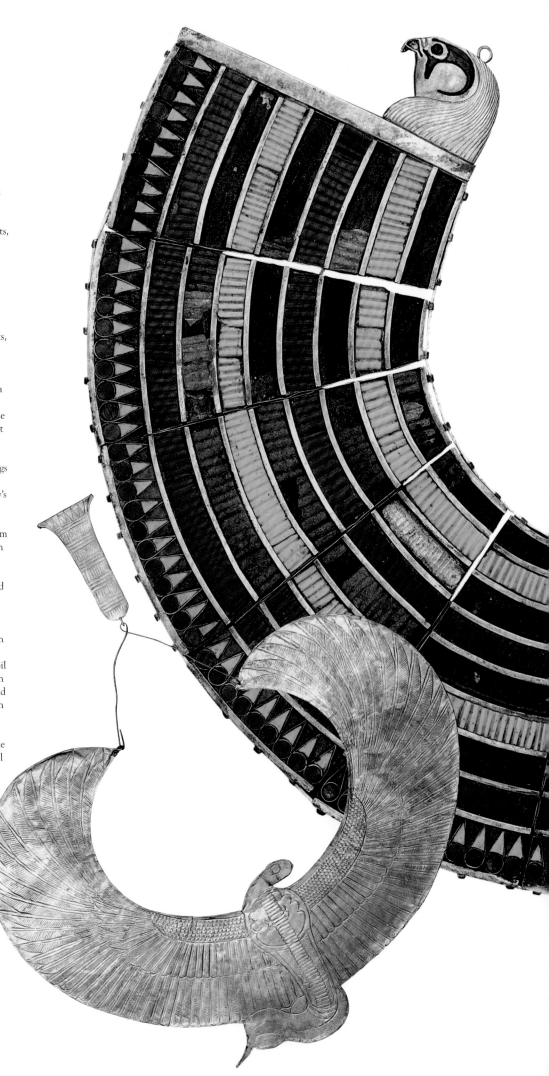

Falcon-Headed Broad Collar

(Carter 256 aa(1), j.d'e. 61880;
width 36 cm)

Four collars of this kind were found among the wrappings of the king's mummy, in the region of the legs, all folded and crushed. It seemed a very casual way to treat objects charged with magical power, and presumably put on the body for good funerary reasons. Fortunately, their method of construction allowed them to be folded without difficulty, and it was not too difficult for the excavators to restore them to their proper shapes.

This kind of collar, the *usekh* or broad collar, is regularly shown being worn by important officials and royalty, and in everyday life it was commonly made up of rows of small cylindrical beads of faience; the outermost row might have beads shaped like petals, as in the case of the example illustrated here. The terminals of such collars are in the form of falcon's heads; consequently, on early coffins this type is called 'collar of the falcon'.

The falcon here presumably represents Horus, god of the living king; but as such collars have been found in non-royal burials, a specific royal association may not be appropriate.

There is a strange mixture of simplicity and ostentation in the design and construction of this collar. It consists of eleven wedge-shaped sections made of sheet gold; the nine concentric rows of beads are reproduced by sections of colored glass, in red, pale blue and dark blue, to represent carnelian, turquoise and lapis-lazuli; the inlays are ribbed to give them the appearance of cylindrical beads. The outermost row imitates drop beads in the form of poppy petals. The falcon head terminals, or shoulder pieces, are made of gold with facial markings in dark blue glass. The *menkhet*, or counterpoise, is also of gold inlaid with rows of ribbed glass 'cylindrical beads'.

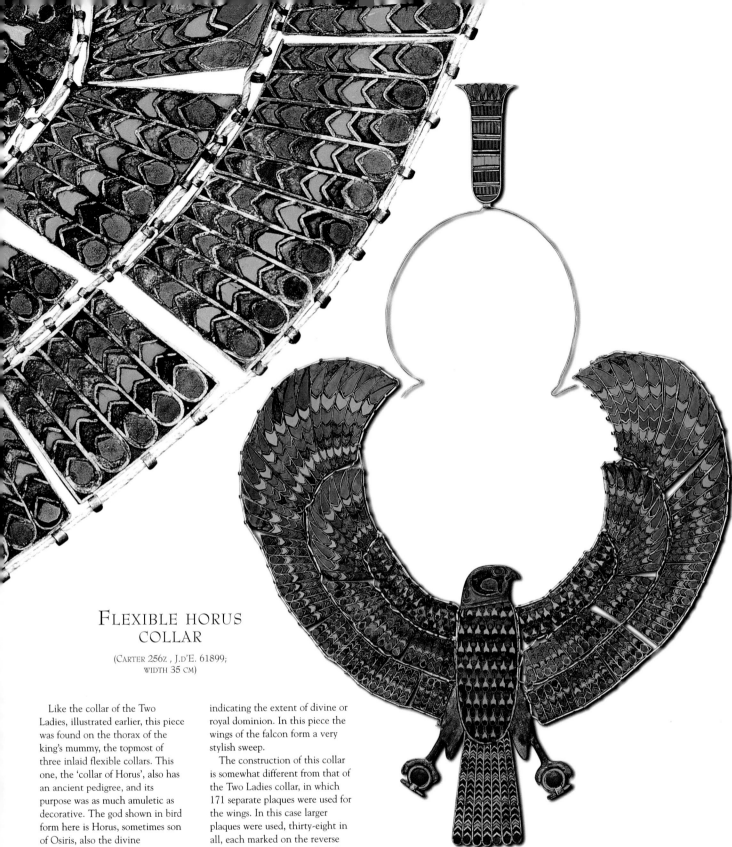

FLEXIBLE HORUS
COLLAR

(CARTER 256z , J.D'E. 61899;
WIDTH 35 CM)

Like the collar of the Two
Ladies, illustrated earlier, this piece
was found on the thorax of the
king's mummy, the topmost of
three inlaid flexible collars. This
one, the 'collar of Horus', also has
an ancient pedigree, and its
purpose was as much amuletic as
decorative. The god shown in bird
form here is Horus, sometimes son
of Osiris, also the divine
representative of royalty of whom
the king was the embodiment in
life. Here the falcon is displayed
frontally with its head turned to
one side in the usual Egyptian
manner; the legs are splayed out
and the claws hold *shen*-signs,
which are like circular cartouches.
The *shen* and the cartouche in
detailed representations are shown
as made of cord or rope, with a tie
at the bottom. Its meaning is not
absolutely established, but it is
generally thought to represent all
that the sun encompasses,

indicating the extent of divine or
royal dominion. In this piece the
wings of the falcon form a very
stylish sweep.

The construction of this collar
is somewhat different from that of
the Two Ladies collar, in which
171 separate plaques were used for
the wings. In this case larger
plaques were used, thirty-eight in
all, each marked on the reverse
for correct assembling and made
up in groups to form the 'districts'
of the wings. Throughout his life
Howard Carter was an eager and
careful student of birds – he
painted them with immense care
and skill – and he was always
punctilious in using the correct
ornithological terms when
describing birds. For this collar he
noted that the ancient craftsman
had distinguished the 'districts' of
the wings in order to reproduce
the different types of feather; he
specifies 'the primaries,

secondaries, coverts, lesser coverts
and so-called bastard wing'.

The glass inlays, individually cut
to fit the cloisons on the plaques,
stand for turquoise, red jasper or
carnelian and lapis-lazuli. The
feather pattern on the falcon's body
and the chevrons on the tail
produce a spectacular effect.
The *menkhet* counterpoise has
ribbed inlays of glass reproducing
cylinder beads.

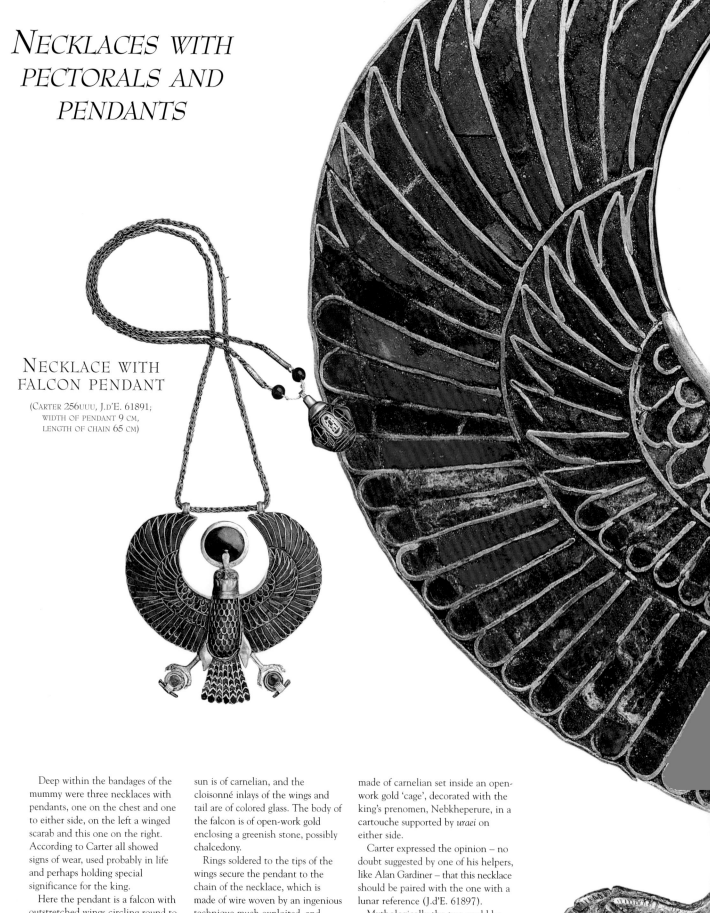

NECKLACES WITH PECTORALS AND PENDANTS

NECKLACE WITH FALCON PENDANT

(CARTER 256UUU, J.D'E. 61891;
WIDTH OF PENDANT 9 CM,
LENGTH OF CHAIN 65 CM)

Deep within the bandages of the mummy were three necklaces with pendants, one on the chest and one to either side, on the left a winged scarab and this one on the right. According to Carter all showed signs of wear, used probably in life and perhaps holding special significance for the king.

Here the pendant is a falcon with outstretched wings circling round to enclose the head with sun-disk and *uraeus* above it. It is Re-Herakhty, the great risen sun. The head looks directly forward, which is unusual; this modest change from the usual iconography gives the piece a dramatic impact. The disk of the

sun is of carnelian, and the cloisonné inlays of the wings and tail are of colored glass. The body of the falcon is of open-work gold enclosing a greenish stone, possibly chalcedony.

Rings soldered to the tips of the wings secure the pendant to the chain of the necklace, which is made of wire woven by an ingenious technique much exploited, and possibly invented, by Egyptian jewelers. The two ends of the chain terminate with round carnelian beads which connect with the small counterpoise. This final element is another *tour de force* of the Egyptian craftsman: it is heart-shaped and

made of carnelian set inside an open-work gold 'cage', decorated with the king's prenomen, Nebkheperure, in a cartouche supported by *uraei* on either side.

Carter expressed the opinion – no doubt suggested by one of his helpers, like Alan Gardiner – that this necklace should be paired with the one with a lunar reference (J.d'E. 61897).

Mythologically the two could be linked to the two eyes – one the sun, one the moon – an idea with associations to Osiris and to Re: 'His right eye is the sun, his left is the moon', one necklace perhaps to be used in the morning, the other in the evening.

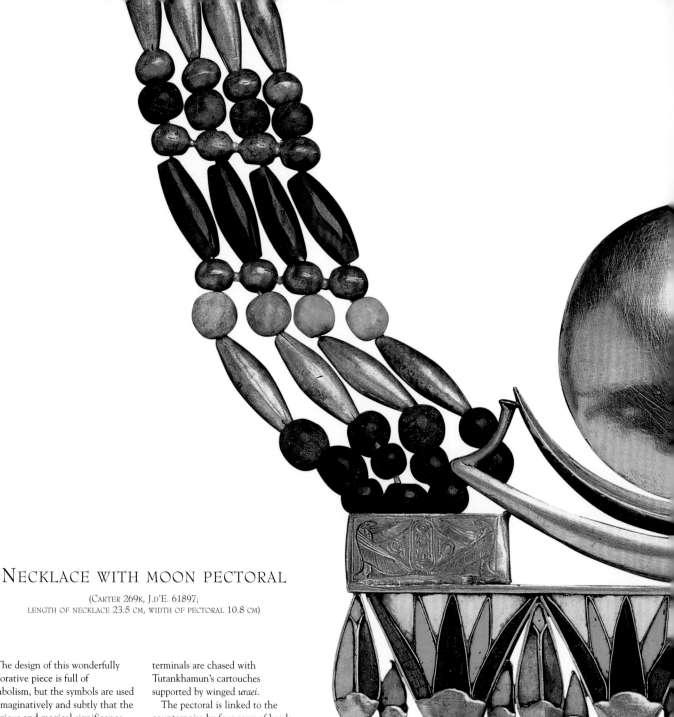

NECKLACE WITH MOON PECTORAL

(CARTER 269K, J.D'E. 61897;
LENGTH OF NECKLACE 23.5 CM, WIDTH OF PECTORAL 10.8 CM)

The design of this wonderfully decorative piece is full of symbolism, but the symbols are used so imaginatively and subtly that the religious and magical significance becomes secondary to the overall appearance. It was found in the cartouche-shaped box in the Treasury, and like others found with it shows signs of wear during the king's lifetime.

The pectoral's central element is the moon, shown as disk and crescent, in the night bark on its nocturnal journey. The bark sits above a grove of lotus flowers and buds growing out of a longitudinal element inlaid with lapis-lazuli, and representing the sky, from which droplets of moisture hang down, inlaid with felspar and lapis. The moon itself is made of electrum (a mixture of gold and silver) to distinguish it from the sun, which in most of this tomb's jewels is made of pure gold, or of inlaid carnelian. To the left and right of the bark are rectangular terminals for the bead strings of the necklace. These

terminals are chased with Tutankhamun's cartouches supported by winged *uraei*.

The pectoral is linked to the counterpoise by four rows of beads, round and barrel-shaped, and made of gold, lapis-lazuli, felspar, glass and a dark colored resin. Some of the gold spherical beads are soldered together to make spacers which hold the four rows together. Design again distinguishes the counterpoise, the main component of which is an open lotus flower, flanked by lotus buds, at the bases of which are poppies and two rosettes. Felspar and lapis-lazuli are used for the lotus inlays, with an imaginative touch of white calcite used for the tips of the buds. The poppies and rosettes are inlaid with carnelian. From a bar beneath the pendant lotus flower and buds hang nineteen tassels of gold and glass beads, joined in pairs at the ends with bell-shaped floral terminals. A clasp on the right side of the counterpoise is held in position by a retractable pin.

NECKLACE WITH PECTORAL OF TUTANKHAMUN WITH THE GODS OF MEMPHIS

(CARTER 267Q, J.D'E. 61941;
PECTORAL: HEIGHT 11.5 CM, WIDTH 14.1 CM;
COUNTERPOISE: HEIGHT 8.4 CM, WIDTH 7.8 CM;
LENGTH OF STRAPS 34.3 CM)

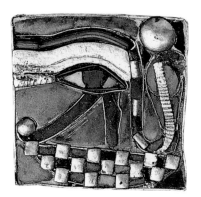

Among the pieces of jewelry found in the tomb, this piece is unusual in that both the pectoral and the counterpoise contain scenes showing the king with gods. It was found in pieces in the Treasury, the main pectoral in the ivory and ebony veneered chest, and the counterpoise and chains in the cartouche-shaped box.

It has been suggested that it was made either for, or to commemorate, the king's coronation. This important event would have been celebrated in Memphis, where the Court had moved from El-Amarna. In the pectoral scene Tutankhamun stands between the mummiform Ptah and lioness-headed Sakhmet, his divine consort, whose principal sanctuaries were in Memphis. The whole conception of the piece is spectacular and dramatic, and yet there are signs of indifferent craftsmanship in some details; also the gold is not of the finest quality.

The theme of the necklace is the king's reign and its infinite duration – a pathetic hope! In the pectoral scene the king holds his instruments of royalty, the crook and flail, and wears the blue crown and a short garment associated with coronation. His face and the crown are made of black glass, the color of regeneration. Ptah offers the king life, Sakhmet presents long reign. Behind Sakhmet stands the king's *ka*, or spirit figure, and behind Ptah kneels Heh, the god of eternity. In the border below is repeated the word for 'eternity'.

In the counterpoise scene, the king, no longer in coronation dress, is seated, receiving life from a winged figure of Ma'at, goddess of truth and order. Gold fishes of uncertain meaning and bell-shaped beads terminate the fourteen strings of beads hanging from the counterpoise. The straps of the necklace are composed of elaborately inlaid gold plaques containing the king's names, good wishes, protective amuletic signs and the motif of royal jubilee. The inlays and beads are mostly of variously colored glass, with a few elements in translucent quartz and calcite.

NECKLACE OF THE SUN RISING ON THE HORIZON

(CARTER 267G, J.D'E. 61896;
LENGTH OF STRAPS 50 CM,
WIDTH OF PECTORAL 11.8 CM)

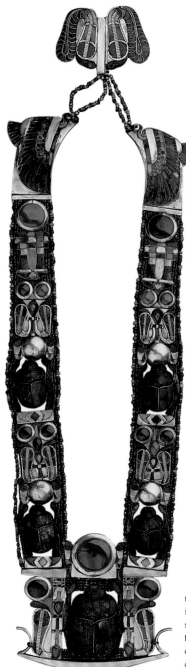

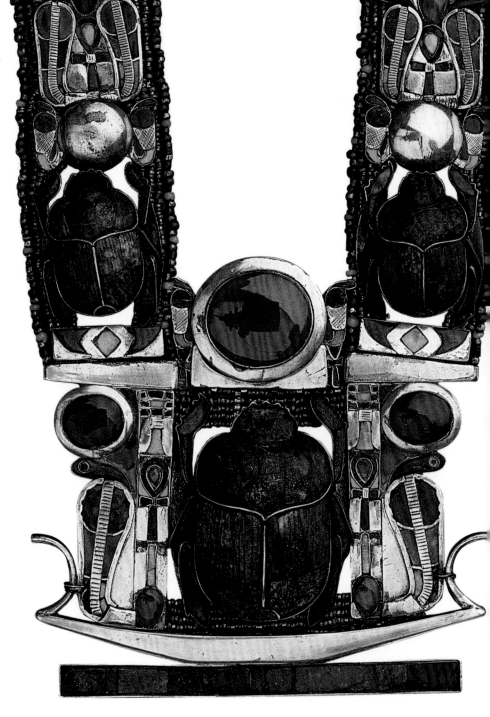

Symbolism in the details of this necklace concentrates on the sun in the early morning, rising as the scarab beetle, Khepri, pushing in front of it the sun, seen as the divine equivalent of the ball of dung pushed by the beetle in nature. The sun here sits in a dip in the hills – the horizon in the Eastern Desert. This is the central element of the pendant of this striking piece; it sits in the morning bark, supported by *uraei* and potent amulets.

The craftsmanship displayed in the making of this necklace is matched by the superior quality of the inlays: lapis-lazuli from distant Afghanistan, carnelian, felspar and turquoise from the Eastern Desert and Sinai. Some of the beads which edge the elaborate straps are of colored glass, but this use of a less splendid material was dictated by practical considerations.

The decorated gold plaques which make up the straps continue the main theme of the pectoral: pairs of scarabs with golden suns flanked by *uraei*, pairs of *uraei* with carnelian suns, and double pairs of the *djed*-symbol for 'endurance', again topped by carnelian suns set in gold. The straps terminate with curved gold elements carrying cloisonné vultures, the embodiment of Nekhbet, protective goddess of the king as ruler of Upper Egypt.

Four short strings of gold and glass beads connect the main straps to the clasp of the necklace, which acts as a counterpoise, although one may doubt its efficacy as such in view of the great weight of the main piece. The clasp is of gold, formed in the shape of two *uraei*, inlaid with semiprecious stones and separated by a gold slide with which the piece can be opened.

The overall heaviness of the necklace is relieved remarkably by the ingenuity of the design and the clever use of color in the inlays. It is an opulent piece.

It was found in the Treasury, in the box veneered with ivory and ebony.

NECKLACE WITH THREE SCARAB PECTORAL

(CARTER 256000, J.D'E. 61900; WIDTH OF PECTORAL 9 CM, WIDTH OF CONTERPOISE 5.3 CM, LENGTH OF STRAPS 18.5 CM)

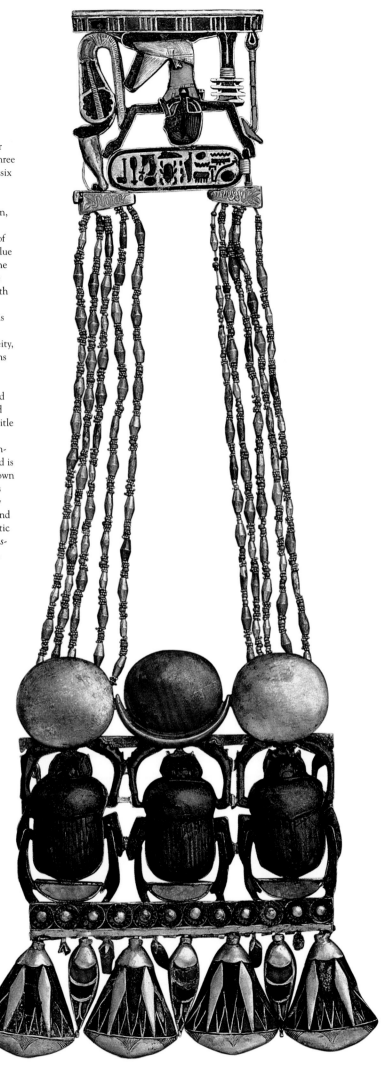

Placed around the neck of the king, this necklace occupied a prime position within the mummy wrappings. Iconographically it is one of the simplest of the many necklaces and pendants, most of which seem almost overloaded with symbolism. Here is restraint.

The principal elements in the design of the pectoral are three lapis-lazuli scarabs set in gold and surmounted by disks, the two outer ones being of gold and representing the sun. The central one is made of electrum and is therefore duller in color; it incorporates a crescent, and is the moon. Beneath each scarab is a basket-shaped sign inlaid with green felspar. There is in the grouping here something of the suggestion of the prenomen of Tutankhamun, which is usually written as a disk above a scarab, below which should be three small strokes indicating plurality and the basket-sign. Here the strokes are missing, but the idea of plurality is suggested by the tripling of the other elements. The bar towards the bottom of the pectoral is ornamented with twelve daisy flowers made of blue glass with gold

centers. From this bar hang four lotus flowers interspersed with three large lotus buds and, originally, six small buds, of which only three now remain. The inlays of the flowers and buds are of carnelian, felspar and blue glass.

Five strings of beads, mostly of gold but with a few spacers of blue glass, connect the pectoral to the counterpoise, to which they are attached by fasteners chased with figures of winged *uraei*. The openwork golden counterpoise is enlivened by a few glass inlays. The design shows a kneeling deity, possibly Heh, the god of millions of years, or Shu, god of the atmosphere, often shown supporting the sky. Here the god supports a long cartouche inlaid with the king's prenomen and title and epithet: 'The good god, Nebkheperure, chosen of Amon-Re'. In front of the kneeling god is an *uraeus* wearing the white crown of Upper Egypt, which here has the curled extension commonly found with the red crown; behind the god are the powerful amuletic signs, the *djed*-pillar and the *was*-scepter – endurance and power.

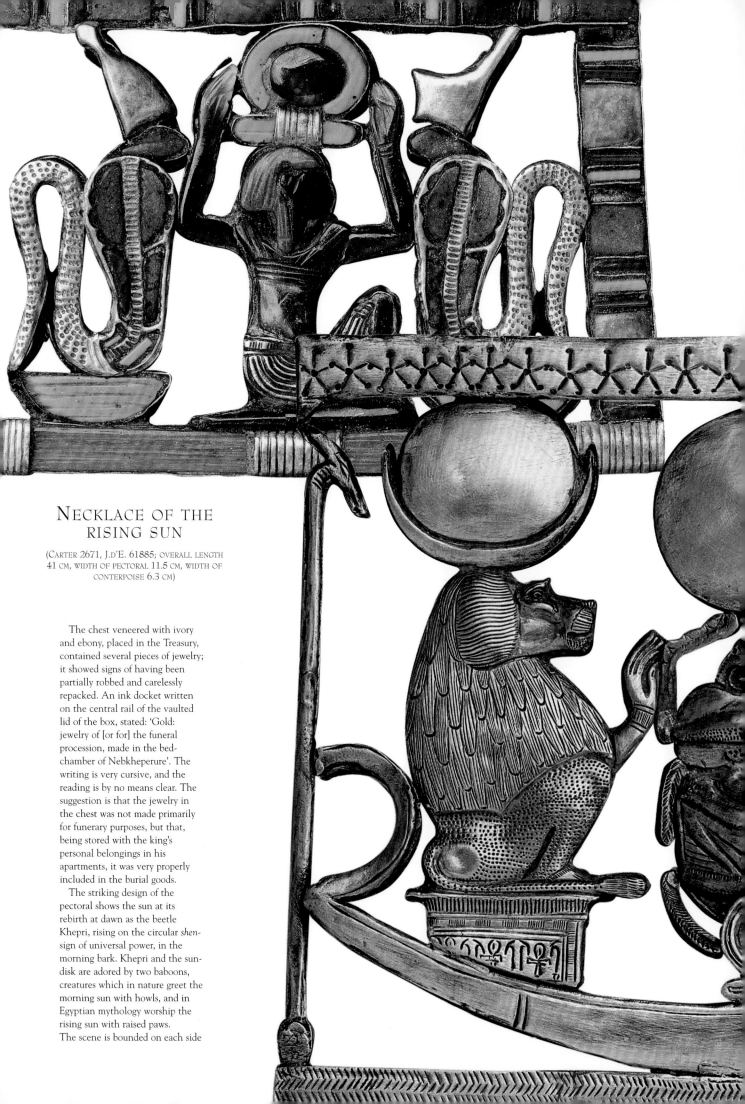

NECKLACE OF THE RISING SUN

(CARTER 2671, J.d'E. 61885; OVERALL LENGTH 41 CM, WIDTH OF PECTORAL 11.5 CM, WIDTH OF CONTERPOISE 6.3 CM)

The chest veneered with ivory and ebony, placed in the Treasury, contained several pieces of jewelry; it showed signs of having been partially robbed and carelessly repacked. An ink docket written on the central rail of the vaulted lid of the box, stated: 'Gold: jewelry of [or for] the funeral procession, made in the bed-chamber of Nebkheperure'. The writing is very cursive, and the reading is by no means clear. The suggestion is that the jewelry in the chest was not made primarily for funerary purposes, but that, being stored with the king's personal belongings in his apartments, it was very properly included in the burial goods.

The striking design of the pectoral shows the sun at its rebirth at dawn as the beetle Khepri, rising on the circular *shen*-sign of universal power, in the morning bark. Khepri and the sun-disk are adored by two baboons, creatures which in nature greet the morning sun with howls, and in Egyptian mythology worship the rising sun with raised paws. The scene is bounded on each side by *was*-scepters of power, below by the waters of the Underworld, and above by the sky studded with stars. All the inlays are of semiprecious stones, set on a solid gold base which is worked with intricate detail on its reverse side. The little shrines on which the baboons sit carry repeated *ankh*-signs of life, supported by *was*-signs. The modeling of the baboons and the feathered markings of their 'capes' are exceptionally well worked.

The straps which connect the pectoral to the counterpoise are made up of eleven plaques on each side. The theme of decoration is long reign and jubilees. The workmanship is not as fine as on the pectoral, but the overall effect is good. The work on the counterpoise is also less precise and finished than that of the pectoral. A shrine shape contains a kneeling figure of the god of millions of years, Heh, supporting the *shen*-sign, and flanked by *uraei* wearing the crowns of Upper (left) and Lower (right) Egypt.

NECKLACE WITH WINGED SCARAB PECTORAL

(CARTER 256QQQ, J.D'E. 61887;
WIDTH OF PECTORAL 9.5 CM,
LENGTH OF CHAIN 42 CM)

Elegant and stylish are words which suitably describe this necklace. Some wear on it suggests that it was worn by the king in his lifetime, and one presumes that it was specially chosen to be worn by him in death. But how can one ever discover whether personal choice entered into the selection of jewels and other objects buried with a king in his mummy wrappings? It was the companion piece to the falcon pendant necklace found on the chest of the mummy (J.d'E. 61891), falcon to the right, scarab to the left: 'His right eye is the sun, his left is the moon'.

The motif of the pendant is Tutankhamun's prenomen, but with a lunar connotation. In simple hieroglyphs the prenomen is made up of sun-disk, scarab, three strokes and a basket. Here the moon-disk

with crescent replaces the sun, and, as is usual with this tomb's jewels, the disk is made of electrum, although the crescent is of gold. The scarab is provided with fine wings which sweep round to touch the horns of the moon's crescent. Lapis-lazuli inlays make up the body of the scarab, and the same stone with carnelian and pale green glass fill the cloisons of the wings. Three gold strokes for plurality separate the scarab from the basket, which is marked out with a central gold diamond and inlaid chevrons on each side. In the hieroglyphic script this kind of basket stands for 'festival'; a plain basket, or one with lines or a checkered design, is expected in the prenomen.

The gold chain which links the pectoral to the counterpoise probably replaces original straps

consisting of five rows of beads, the points of fastening for which are very evident. Two carnelian beads separate the inlaid lotus terminals from the heart-shaped counterpoise, which consists of a carnelian core enclosed in a gold openwork cage which incorporates the royal prenomen supported by *uraei*.

NECKLACE WITH VULTURE PECTORAL

(Carter 256ppp, J.d'E. 61892;
WIDTH OF VULTURE 11 CM,
LENGTH OF STRAPS 25.5 CM)

This necklace is, from a technical point of view, one of the most interesting jewels from the tomb. It was found on the mummy, suspended from the neck; its principal element, the pectoral pendant, is in the form of the vulture, the goddess Nekhbet, tutelary deity of Tutankhamun as King of Upper Egypt.

The design is simple: the vulture is shown with head turned to the left, and its spread wings turned down like a cloak in protective fashion; its legs are splayed out, and the talons hold *shen*-signs of universal power. The head of the bird is separately modeled and soldered to the body; its markings are delicately chased, the eye is of obsidian and the beak of lapis-lazuli. The point of special technical interest concerns the glass inlays of the body, the tail and some parts of the wings. The glass inlays on these parts show little depressions which may have been produced by air bubbles during the process of manufacture. If this is truly the case, these bubbles offer proof of the practice of real enamelling which has not otherwise been found in ancient Egypt. In many of the pieces of jewelry from Tutankhamun's tomb a cloisonné technique with glass inlays has been observed. True cloisonné enamelling consists in filling the cloisons with powdered glass which is then fired in position; this results in inlays which completely fill, and are closely fixed in, their little gold enclosures. It has yet to be confirmed by close scientific examination that the technique was used in this case.

The back of the vulture, which is of solid gold, is carefully worked with chasing, and a pendant is shown hanging from the neck; it contains the royal prenomen.

The straps are made up of plaques of gold and lapis-lazuli, in the center of each of which is a circle of colored glass. The straps connect to the clasp, which is in the form of two resting falcons with heads lying on their backs; they are of gold inlaid with lapis, felspar, onyx, carnelian and green glass. A sliding fastener holds the two together.

NECKLACE WITH SCARAB COUNTERPOISE

(CARTER 101W, J.D'E. 61950;
WIDTH OF PECTORAL 8.5 CM,
LENGTH OF STRAPS 43 CM)

Much of the material found in the various storage boxes in the Antechamber consisted of jewels, the stringing of which had perished. Retrieving and restringing took a great deal of time, mostly carried out by Arthur Mace, a most meticulous archaeologist. This necklace Carter speaks of with some relief. It was found in its box lying flat upon the bottom, so that its shape and order could easily be determined: 'we were able to remove it bead by bead, and re-string it on the spot in its exact original order.' The beads are in three strands of blue glass and gold in droplet form, held in place by sets of three ball beads of gold fused to form spacers. The shrine-shaped pectoral is simple, made of gilded wood inlaid with a block border and a central inscription in glass. There are three lines of text beneath an extended heaven-sign: 'Good god, lord of the two lands, Nebkheperure, beloved of Osiris'. The scarab counterpoise also carries on its base Tutankhamun's prenomen flanked by the *heqat*-scepter of royal authority and the feather of truth and order.

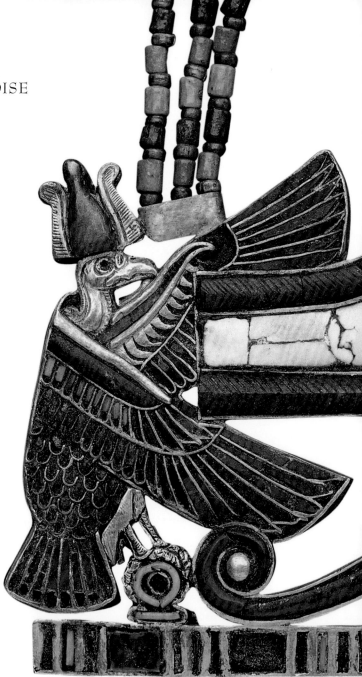

NECKLACE WITH INLAID *WEDJAT*

(CARTER 256VVV, J.D'E. 61901;
PENDANT: HEIGHT 5.7 CM, WIDTH 9.5 CM,
LENGTH OF CHAIN 33 CM)

Like some other of the jewels found on the royal body, this necklace shows signs of wear, and Carter considered it a piece worn by the king in his lifetime. The pendant is particularly handsome, a triumph of design and craftsmanship. It is of solid gold with much cloisonné inlay. The eye itself is inlaid with crystalline limestone and lapis-lazuli. It is flanked by the two royal protective goddesses, Edjo, the serpent of Buto in the Delta, and Nekhbet, the vulture of Elkab in Upper Egypt. Edjo here wears the red crown, and Nekhbet the *atef*, in its form as white crown with side feathers. The inlays are of colored glass, carnelian and lapis-lazuli, and the *shen*-sign in the vulture's claws has a green stone which Carter compared with peridot, rarely used by the Egyptians. Three strings of small beads link the pendant to its counterpoise or *menkhet*, The beads are of variously colored glass with occasional thin gold spacers. The counterpoise consists of two *djed*-signs and one *tyet*-sign, all inlaid with glass, carnelian and lapis.

NECKLACE WITH FAIENCE *WEDJAT*

(CARTER 256RRR, J.D'E. 61951;
PENDANT: HEIGHT 6 CM, WIDTH 8.8 CM,
LENGTH OF CHAIN 29 CM)

One of the most powerful of the protective amulets used by the ancient Egyptians was the *wedjat*, the eye of Horus, stolen by Seth but restored by Thoth. There were several *wedjats* incorporated into the jewelry placed on Tutankhamun's mummy. This piece may seem strangely modest among the many gold jewels with which the deceased was loaded. The pendant itself is a *wedjat* made of blue faience; it incorporates the *uraeus*-serpent, royal protective symbol, and beneath the eye the *sa*-sign, also of protection. The text on the eye reads: 'Khepri, who is within his

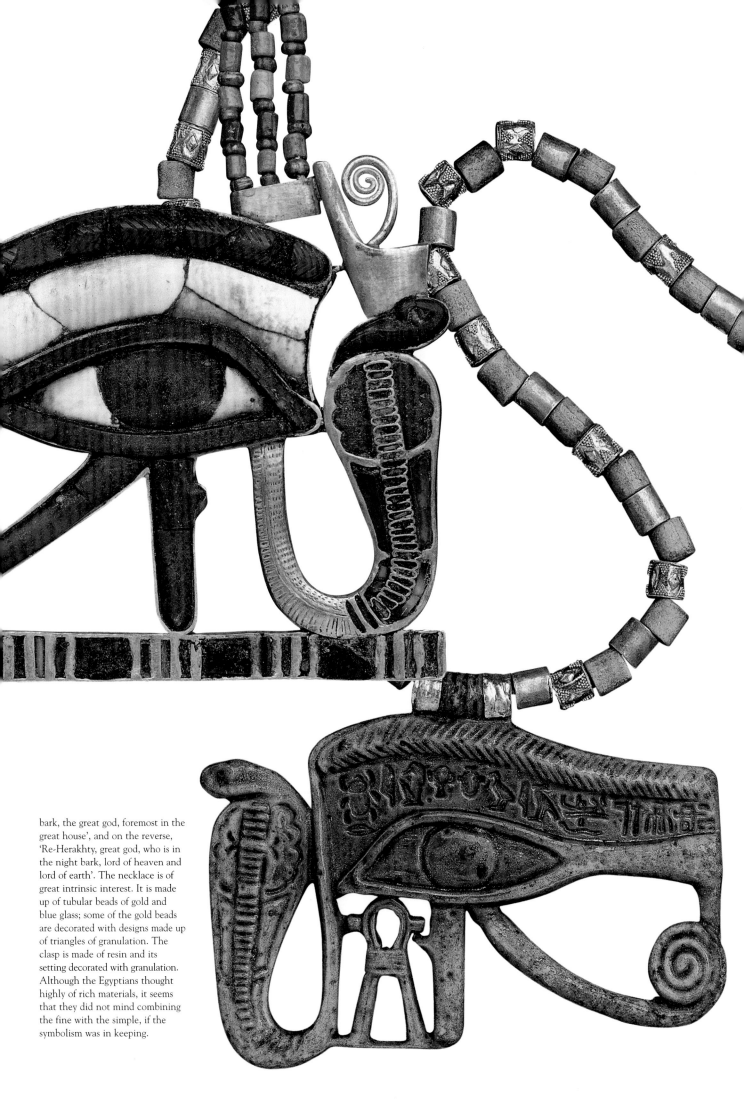

bark, the great god, foremost in the great house', and on the reverse, 'Re-Herakhty, great god, who is in the night bark, lord of heaven and lord of earth'. The necklace is of great intrinsic interest. It is made up of tubular beads of gold and blue glass; some of the gold beads are decorated with designs made up of triangles of granulation. The clasp is made of resin and its setting decorated with granulation. Although the Egyptians thought highly of rich materials, it seems that they did not mind combining the fine with the simple, if the symbolism was in keeping.

PENDANTS

PECTORAL OF ISIS AND NEPHTHYS

(CARTER 261I, J.D'E. 61945;
HEIGHT 12 CM, WIDTH 16.3 CM)

It surprised Carter and his colleagues to find compartments, little cupboards, in the great gilded pylon-shaped shrine on which rested the black-painted figure of the Anubis jackal, just inside the Treasury. The largest of these compartments contained eight pieces of jewelry, all pectorals, with no accompanying necklaces or counterpoises. It is difficult to understand what their purpose was, and why they were placed in this shrine. There were signs that the compartment had been disturbed, so its original contents may have been different from, or more numerous than, what was found. Carter took the view that all the pieces were funerary, and not for everyday use. Their designs all contain much symbolism, and they suggest a posthumous use for the rebirth or regeneration of the king. They vary greatly in workmanship and design, and in the preciousness of the materials used.

This kiosk-shaped pectoral is made of low quality gold, but its design is neat and effective. The main scene consists of a central *djed*-pillar of endurance, surmounted by the sun-disk and flanked by the goddesses Nephthys (left) and Isis (right) with outstretched protective wings. These goddesses have many functions in relation to the dead king; they are among the Canopic deities, they have a more general protective role, and as principal mourners they are often shown as kites, the common scavenger birds of Egypt. In front of the goddesses are two cartouches containing Tutankhamun's names, from each of which hangs down an *uraeus* wearing a crown, the red on the left and the white (shown blue) on the right.

The top of the pectoral is in the form of a cornice, with a design representing palm fronds; beneath it is a frieze of flowers, hanging down. At the very top, at the right and left, are fittings to which the straps of a necklace could have been attached. There would have been four strings of beads on each side. These fittings are chased with winged *uraei*.

Apart from a little quartz, all the inlays are of colored glass.

PECTORAL OF A WINGED SCARAB WITH ISIS AND NEPHTHYS

(Carter 261m, J.d'E. 61948;
height 16.5 cm, width 24.4 cm)

Several features of this interesting piece point to the confused nature of this burial and its contents, and to the problems resulting from the further confusion created by the robbers, and by the necropolis guards in their attempts to tidy up the confusion.

When it was found in the Anubis shrine, this pectoral lacked the large stone scarab which now occupies the central position in the design.

It was later found in the cartouche-shaped chest, also in the Treasury. That the scarab and pectoral belong together is confirmed by the texts on both parts. The scarab, made of a hard green stone, is inscribed on its underside with Spell 30B of the Book of the Dead, in which the heart of the king is exhorted to act as a witness on behalf of the dead Tutankhamun before the divine conclave. It is what is called a heart scarab, found in royal and non-royal burials, and most usually placed on the mummy of the deceased close to the heart, which itself was left in the embalmed body. There were many scarabs among the jewels found on the king's mummy, but none bore this important heart text. Why, it may be asked, was this so?

Could this pectoral have been intended for the mummy and been overlooked? At least it was finally included in the tomb equipment, and placed not far from the Canopic chest containing the mummified remains of the other royal internal organs.

Set in the pectoral, the scarab is winged and supported by kneeling figures of Isis and Nephthys, who, in their texts, invoke Re on behalf of the heart. The top of the pectoral is in the shape of a winged sun-disk flanked by elaborately arranged *uraeus* serpents with sun-disks disposed among the coils. The fittings at the top suggest that the piece was made to have quadruple strings of beads as lateral chains.

All the cloisonné inlays are of colored glass, carefully cut and fitted. Particularly finely done are the inlaid dresses of the two goddesses, reproducing a very characteristic net pattern.

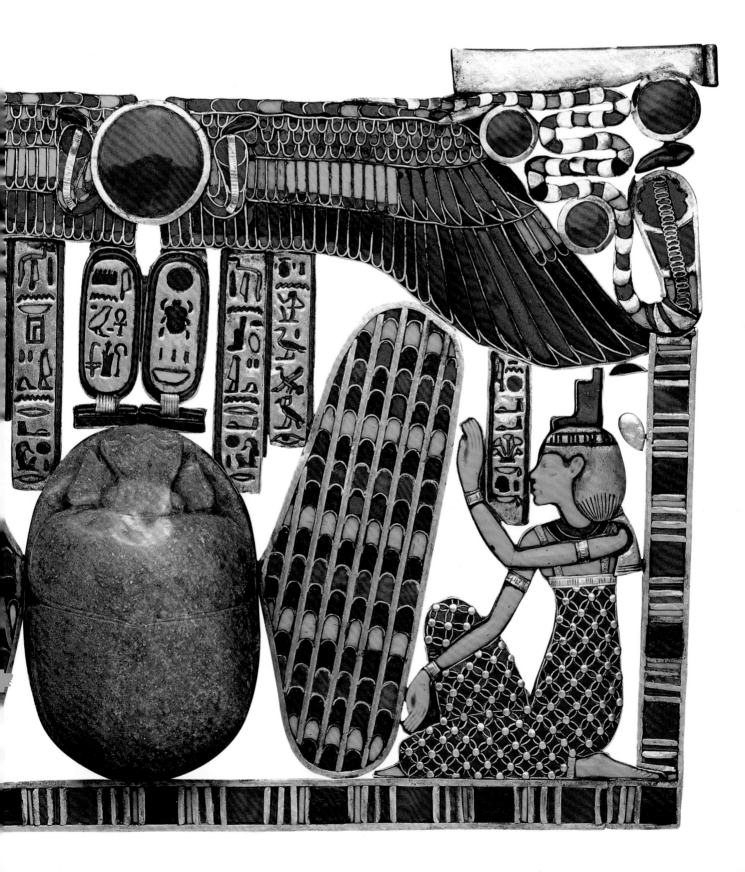

PECTORAL OF THE GODDESS NUT

(CARTER 261P1, J.D'E. 61944;
HEIGHT 12.6 CM, WIDTH 14.3 CM)

This unusual piece, which may not be a pectoral in the strictest sense, was also found in the Anubis shrine. It is itself shrine-shaped, but contrary to the common design of such pieces its suspension fittings are at the sides and not the top. This arrangement suggests that it may have been centrally placed in a belt or girdle which would have encircled the royal body.

A palm-frond cornice forms the top of the piece, and a block border runs around all four sides. The inlays here and elsewhere are of carnelian and colored glass. A solid gold plaque is the basis of this jewel, unlike most of the pectorals and other jewels from the tomb, which are of openwork. The result is to give it greater solidity, and the background is able to hold a substantial religious text. The central figure is the goddess Nut, the sky deity, described as 'great of power'. She stands with outstretched arms and wings which turn up at the tips to enclose

cartouches containing the names of Tutankhamun. In the main text of eight lines Nut declares that she opens her arms over 'her son, the king Nebkheperure', and spreads her wings over 'all the beauty of Tutankhamun, ruler of Southern Heliopolis'. She does this, as Re does, 'in protection of these your limbs'.

The inscriptions are not without errors, some of which may be due to ancient alterations. It has been suggested that the names in the cartouches have been changed from those of Akhenaten, although the surviving traces are not very convincing. If this supposition is correct, it would follow that the piece was made early in Akhenaten's reign, when Nut and her text would not have been considered unsuitable. It would then also follow that it had been stored away in Thebes, waiting for better times, and was then recycled for Akhenaten's young successor.

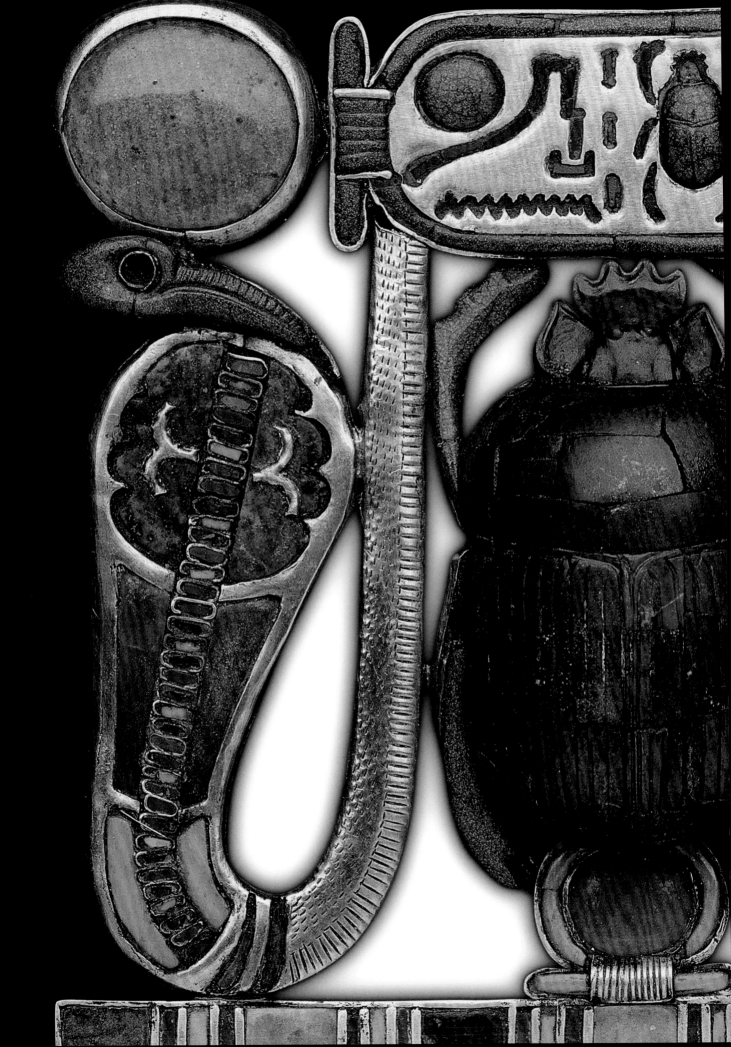

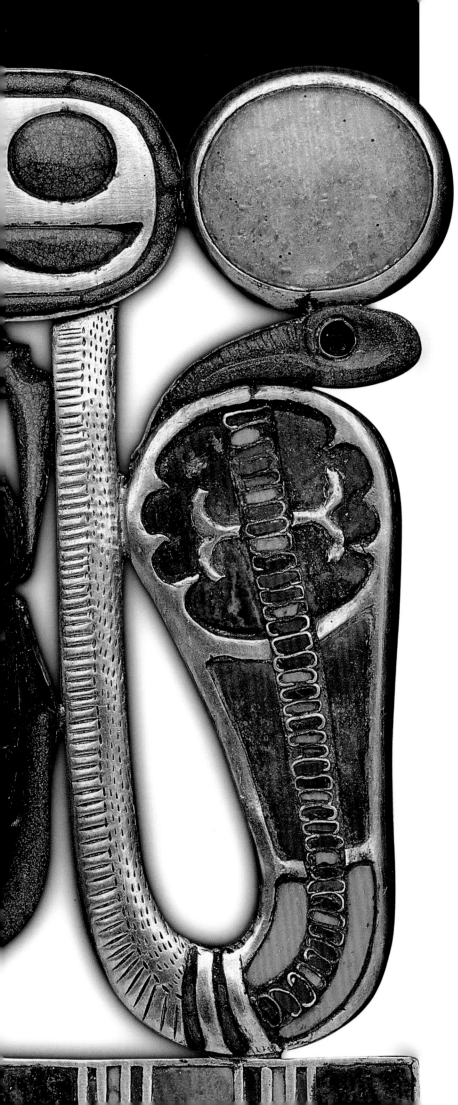

PECTORAL WITH SCARAB SUPPORTED BY *URAEI*

(CARTER 267K, J.D'E. 61899;
HEIGHT 7.8 CM, WIDTH 8.7 CM)

This pectoral ornament, found in the veneered jewel box in the Treasury, is of exceptional quality in terms of design, workmanship and the use of materials. Its basis is good quality gold.

The central element, as often, is the scarab, to be identified with Khepri, the sun at dawn. Here it is carefully carved in the round in lapis-lazuli, with detailed head markings and wing striations. It supports not the sun but a cartouche, carefully formed and inlaid with the prenomen of the king, Nebkheperure, with the added epithet 'Setep-en-Re', 'Chosen of Re'. Between its back legs the beetle holds the *shen*-sign, inlaid with carnelian, the symbol of universal power.

On either side of the scarab, *uraeus* serpents hang down from the cartouche. The bodies are in gold, finely chased with linear markings; but attention in both cases is drawn to the head and the hood of the cobra. Here there is craftsmanship of superb quality on a very small scale: the heads are in lapis-lazuli, carved in high relief; the markings on the hood, although stylized, are exceptionally effective, the larger inlays being in lapis and carnelian, the rest in red, blue and greenish-blue glass. The sun-disks are made of carnelian in gold settings. At the bottom of the pectoral is a block border with glass and calcite inlays, made with unusual precision.

The reverse of this piece also warrants careful attention. It is the solid gold base of the pectoral, but it carries in molding and chasing the same design as the front. The back of the scarab is, in Carter's words, 'richly worked… showing complete articulation of its legs and underparts'. The prenomen in the reverse cartouche is followed by two different epithets: 'ruler of Truth, image of Re'. On the back of the two sun-disks are suspension fastenings, each with three holes, in which pieces of thread were found at the time of discovery.

PECTORAL WITH SOLAR AND LUNAR EMBLEMS

(CARTER 267D, J.D'E. 61884;
HEIGHT CM 14.9; WIDTH CM 14.5)

Ancient Egyptian religion embraced a variety of ideas, developed over thousands of years; it was rich in symbolism, and the hieroglyphic script contained many signs which not only expressed concepts but also served as amuletic forms. The ingenuity of the Egyptian jewelry designer in exploiting this variety in the making of excellent products is fully exemplified by this colorful piece which is saturated with hidden and not-so-hidden meaning. It is the most spectacular of the jewels found in the chest in the Treasury which had been rifled and repacked. Why was a wonderful piece like this not stolen?

The central element, as so often, is a winged scarab, the body of which is formed from an unblemished, translucent chalcedony. It is in itself a solar symbol, the sun-god at dawn, Khepri, who is usually shown rolling the sun-disk in its front legs. Here there is a variation. The front legs support a golden bark, partly inlaid with turquoise, in which rides the left eye of Horus – the moon – flanked by *uraei* with sun-disks on their heads. Most striking is the disk of the moon with its crescent: the crescent is gold, but the disk is silver, and on it are soldered three tiny gold figures of the king flanked by ibis-headed Thoth and falcon-headed Re-Herakhty. Thoth and the king wear lunar disks and Re-Herakhty a sun-disk.

A little less overt symbolism can be found in the lower part of this pectoral. The back legs of the scarab are metamorphosed into vulture legs which characteristically hold *shen*-signs of authority, and also flowers: in the left an open lily, and in the right, a lotus and buds, both plants heraldically representing Upper Egypt. On each side the solar theme is resumed by erect *uraei*. At the bottom is a garland, serving as a kind of fringe, consisting of cornflowers, lotus and poppies.
On the edge of the wings of the

scarab on each side are six small loops, intended presumably to receive the cords of six strands of beads for suspension.

In addition to the materials already mentioned, the inlays are of lapis-lazuli, carnelian, calcite, obsidian and colored glass.

PENDANT WITH TUTANKHAMUN'S PRENOMEN

(CARTER 267A, J.D'E. 61886; HEIGHT 9 CM, WIDTH 10.5 CM)

Some of the most interesting, and less mythological, jewels found in Tutankhamun's tomb were discovered in the domed chest embellished with ivory and ebony veneers, and panels composed of many thousands of pieces of marquetry. It is a splendid box, which, according to its hieratic inscription, was filled with jewelry for the funeral, but from the king's apartments. The contents had been seriously disturbed by robbers who had penetrated as far as the Treasury. What they must have taken must have been exceptionally fine, or at least made of very valuable materials; for what was left behind made by itself a notable collection.

No two pieces of large-scale jewelry in the tomb were made to the same pattern, and even where motifs are repeated the details are varied, and the materials and execution often different. This pendant is a good example of fine design making much of a simple idea. The essence of the whole is Tutankhamun's prenomen, Nebkheperure, which makes up

the central element: the scarab (*kheper*) is made of a fine piece lapis-lazuli, and the three gold strokes below it indicate plurality (making *kheper* into *kheperu*). Between the forelegs of the beetle is the risen sun, a carnelian disk set in gold (*Re*), which in nature was the ball of mud and dung rolled forward by the beetle as food and protection for its eggs. Beneath the plural strokes is a basket shape inlaid with turquoise (*neb*).

What dramatizes this piece are the wings which are often added iconographically to the beetle form of Re (Khepri). Here they sweep around to form almost a complete circle, enveloping the royal name and offering it divine protection. The detailed decoration of the wings is carried out in cloisons filled with colored glass, lapis and carnelian inlays. The whole design has a gold backing with chased details of the front design on the reverse. Behind the sun-disk there is a tubular fitting through which could be threaded a gold chain or cord for suspension.

BA-BIRD PECTORAL

(CARTER 256B(2), J.D'E, 61903; WIDTH 33 CM)

Among the various trappings found on the outer surface of Tutankhamun's mummy was this pectoral in the form of a human-headed bird. It had been, like the whole of the surface, heavily anointed with resinous unguents which had solidified as a kind of carapace. Dextrously cleaned under the guidance of Arthur Lucas, Carter's invaluable chemical and conservation colleague, the various items were removed from the mummy; some had been seriously damaged by the unguents; on this bird the damage was limited to some of the inlays.

Here is a representation of the king's *ba*, a form of his spirit. The Egyptians conceived of the human spirit in two ways, which became active after death. There was the *ka*, sometimes erroneously called the 'double', which was associated with sustenance and potency. In the case of the king it was thought to have been formed at the same time as the royal person itself, and it remained in attendance on him throughout life and in the afterlife. The two great wooden guardian statues of

Tutankhamun which stood at the entrance to the Burial Chamber are often called *ka*-statues, because the royal *ka* is referred to in their inscriptions. The *ba*, on the other hand, was a mobile spirit, acting after the death of the person, enabling the deceased to move about and even to take different forms, and to leave and to enter the tomb. The presence of this pectoral figure on the royal body, unrestricted by the mummy bandages, provided the king with mobility – the ability to move as he willed as the *ba*.

The *ba* is shown as a human-headed falcon, and in this piece the wings, body and legs are those of a falcon. The head, turned to the left, is of gold with a wig of blue glass, somewhat discolored. A gold circlet with ribbons and a *uraeus* on the brow sits on the head. The face is remarkably sensitive; it has a short beard, quite different from the long, plaited, turned-up beard associated with Osiris. The inlays of the body and wings are all of glass, but only those in blue have remained in relatively good condition.

VULTURE PENDANT

(Carter 2671, J.d'E. 61894; height 14.1 cm, width 16.4 cm)

The form and position of the head of the vulture which forms the subject of this pectoral pendant are unusual. In most cases where the vulture is shown its head is turned to one side, following the general principle of confrontation in Egyptian art. Here, however, the head, which has been made separately of gold and soldered to the body of the bird, is modeled in the round; it is so positioned that when the piece lies on the chest, the face of the bird looks up towards the face of the wearer, in this case Tutankhamun. This attitude is quite appropriate, for this vulture is the goddess Nekhbet, Upper Egyptian tutelary deity of the king.

Nekhbet here wears a crown called an *atef*. In this case it takes the form of the Upper Egyptian white crown, the usual crown for Nekhbet, but with added ostrich feathers on the sides. The *atef* is particularly associated with Osiris, and with the dead king when he has posthumously become Osiris. On the walls of the Burial Chamber, in the scene in which Ay, Tutankhamun's successor, is shown opening the mouth of the mummified king, Tutankhamun wears this crown. In

another of the pectorals from the tomb (J.d'E. 61946) Nekhbet is again shown with the *atef*-crown; but Osiris in the same piece wears another form of the *atef*.

This pendant is made of gold and decorated as usual with cloisonné work. The vulture's head, as mentioned, is apparently cast gold, but the *atef*-crown is of lower grade electrum, with its side feathers inlaid with glass. The body and wings of the vulture are inlaid with lapis-lazuli, carnelian, and red and blue glass; the *shen*-signs in the bird's talons are inlaid with carnelian and pale blue glass. The reverse side of the piece is chased with details of the vulture's body and wings, and there are four rings for a suspension chain.

The pendant was found in the 'jewel' box in the Treasury.

Pectoral with royal prenomen and lotus fringe

(Carter 267n, j.d'E. 61890; height 12.5 cm, width 13 cm)

Some of the jewels found in Tutankhamun's tomb seem to have been made with particular religious or funerary ideas in mind. Some are essentially decorative, while still incorporating religious symbolism. Some were clearly made for burial purposes, to be included in the mummy wrappings; some showed signs of use before burial. Most display great inventiveness in the disposition of the various decorative and religious elements used in the designs. Some seem to have been designed when the jeweler-craftsman had perhaps temporarily lost his inspiration.

This pectoral may be considered less successful than many others from the tomb. First impressions are good: it is large, and colorful in its display of semiprecious stones and colored glass; it contains enough amuletic references to keep the reflective mind busy. It is dramatic. But there are criticisms: the gold used for its basic form is of low quality; the workmanship of the inlays is not of the best, as can be seen in so many pieces. In the design itself, the artist seems to have crammed in the *ankh*-signs and the eyes of Horus unnecessarily tightly, while the lateral *uraei* seem too big, dominating the central feature, which is the king's prenomen. In this royal name the central scarab, made of lapis-lazuli, with legs inlaid with the same stone, is provided with falcon wings inlaid with the same stone, and with carnelian and glass.
These wings sweep round to touch the horns of the crescent moon, within which sits the lunar disk, made of pale electrum. The theme of the transfiguration of the king, shown in the form of his name flying up to heaven, is strangely, but not uniquely, modified by the use of the moon instead of the sun; and the name itself is further diminished by the small plural strokes and basket which complete the prenomen.

At the bottom of the pectoral is a border or fringe of lotus flowers, interspersed with cornflowers and roundels, all inlaid with lapis-lazuli, carnelian and colored glass.

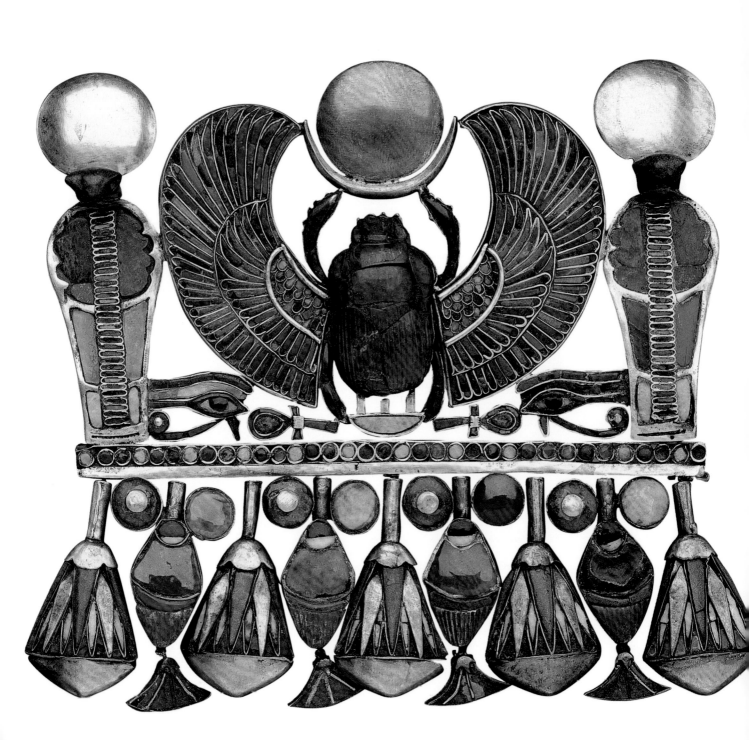

Counterpoise with
a Figure of Eternity

(Carter 267e, J.d'E. 61898; height 6.9 cm, width 8.2 cm)

The veneered jewel box in the Treasury contained four counterpoises which cannot easily be matched with any pendant to make up a complete necklace. There are two terminal bars on the top edge of this piece, one made to slide into a corresponding terminal on one side of a connecting necklace, the other with six perforations to take the threads of six strings of beads. None of the single pectorals found in the tomb has holes for six strings.

A figure of Heh, god of eternity or of millions of years, occupies the centre of the counterpoise. The attitude, with raised arms, is characteristic; the god is commonly shown with a sign for 'year' on his head. Here there is a large eye of Horus, the *wedjat*, a symbol of

wholeness and a strong protective amulet. The bare areas of Heh's body are inlaid with translucent calcite, set in a reddish paste which shows through the stone as a flesh-color. The wig is of blue faience, except for a small part showing beneath the right arm, which has been inlaid with calcite. Closely associated with Heh are the two side elements of the counterpoise; these are formalized palm fronds, notched to mark the years of the king's reign, and at their bottoms are small tadpole figures (*hefen*) on *shen*-signs. The tadpole in Egyptian numbering stood for one hundred thousand. Heh is often shown holding palm fronds similarly terminated. The theme here is clearly the everlasting reign of the Pharaoh.

The two great *uraei* which flank

Heh are rather crudely made, apart from their solid glass heads, which are carefully modeled. The inlays of the sun-disks are carnelian, and those on the hoods of the cobras are glass and calcite. Behind Heh, inserted as if to fill up the space, is a *tyet*-sign, a powerful amulet often used decoratively, alternating with the *djed*-pillar; it is the Isis knot, often interpreted as the 'blood of Isis' and ideally made of red jasper when used as an amulet. Here it is inlaid with blue glass and calcite. The *tyet* offered protection and life.

A hinged lateral fitting of gold at the bottom is pierced to receive eighteen short strings of beads, some ending in fishes made of red and yellow gold, as in another counterpoise. These strings have never been restored.

PECTORAL OF THE WINGED VULTURE OF NUT

(CARTER 261P3, J.D'E. 61943;
HEIGHT 12.1 CM, WIDTH 17.2 CM)

A question can be raised about the king for whom this highly colorful and attractively designed pectoral was first made. The problem lies in the two cartouches containing the prenomen and name of Tutankhamun; both are written in reverse direction, and are wrongly placed according to the titles which go with them; the prenomen should be on the right, with the titles 'good ruler, lord of the two lands', and the name on the left with the title 'son of Re'. In the name cartouche, a sign has been omitted in the epithet '[ruler] in Southern Heliopolis'. It is likely, therefore, that the cartouches have been altered, and the job of replacement has been somewhat botched. It is

thought that the original names in the cartouches were those of Akhenaten. If this were so, then such a piece would have been made early in that king's reign, when a depiction of the goddess Nut would have been acceptable. It may never have left Thebes, being recycled for Tutankhamun, his names inserted in the cartouches in place of those of Akhenaten. The pectoral was found in the Anubis pylon shrine in the Treasury.

Although the divine bird here shown, splendidly enriched with inlays of colored glass and carnelian in the *shen*-signs in her talons, is the vulture commonly recognized as the upper Egyptian royal protective goddess Nekhbet,

the hieroglyphic signs above her humped back identify her as Nut, the sky goddess. She it is who traditionally envelops the dead king with her protective wings. This divine image therefore serves as a good example of how Egyptian iconography is to be understood not just by the forms shown, but also by the accompanying texts. Here it is specified that the vulture is Nut, not Nekhbet.

The shrine shape of the pectoral is framed on the sides and bottom by carefully inlaid block borders of colored glass; at the top is a formal cornice of palm fronds, and below it a frieze of pendent flowers. The fittings at each end at the top are perforated with three holes each to take strings of beads.

PECTORAL OF OSIRIS, ISIS AND NEPHTHYS

(CARTER 261o, J.D'E. 61946; HEIGHT 15.5 CM, WIDTH 20 CM)

The possibilities of iconographic confusion are well shown in this pectoral, which is made of low quality gold. It was found in the Anubis shrine in the Treasury. It is shrine-shaped with an inlaid cornice at the top and a frieze of pendent flowers. *Uraei* with carnelian sun-disks descend from the two sides of the cornice. Block borders of glass inlay form the two sides and the bottom.

The scene in the centre shows a small mummiform figure with the accoutrements of royalty, flanked by a winged serpent and a vulture. Both rest on baskets with a checker design representing the weave of baskets; both have their wings outstretched to protect the mummiform figure. If there were no inscriptions, the two goddesses would be identified as Wadjyt, the cobra deity, and Nekhbet, the vulture deity. These identifications are strengthened by the red crown worn by the cobra, and the white crown with feathers, worn by the vulture. In the description of

Nekhbet in another pectoral, where the same crown is worn, it is usually called the *atef*.

In this pectoral, the small mummiform figure is shown wearing a rather different form of the *atef*, one which is much more commonly associated with Osiris. Its white-crown form splays out at the top and it carries a sun-disk; furthermore, the crown in this form incorporates curled ram's horns which support the ostrich feathers on each side. From its detailed markings this *atef* seems to be made in reality of some kind of wickerwork, tied near the top. It is very different from the simple *atef* worn by the vulture. This mummiform figure is described as 'lord of eternity, ruler of everlasting, the good god, lord of the holy land'. It could be Osiris, but it could also be the king transformed into Osiris after death. And this second interpretation seems more likely, as the two winged deities are by inscription identified as Isis and Nephthys. Isis (the vulture) 'gives protection and life behind him like Re', while Nephthys (the cobra) 'gives protection and life'.

EARRINGS

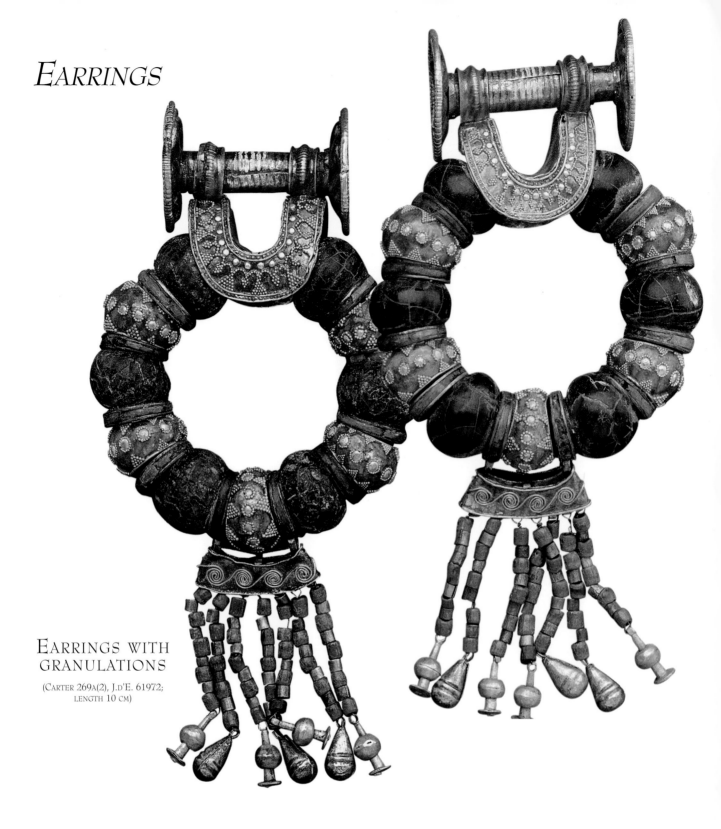

EARRINGS WITH GRANULATIONS

(CARTER 269A(2), J.D'E. 61972;
LENGTH 10 CM)

In this pair of earrings the daintiness and glowing colors of the following pair give way to a chunky, somber appearance which Carter found to be 'barbaric, but not unpleasing'.

The fastenings here are similar to those of the other sets of earrings and studs. A screw bar which passed through the pierced ear lobe fitted into a corresponding hollow tube. Both ends are covered by disk studs, here decorated with applied gold rosettes of gold wire and gold foil petals. All the main parts of the pieces are made of what is termed red, or purple, gold, the dramatic

color achieved by the addition of small quantities of iron, in the form probably of iron pyrites, known as fool's gold.

These earrings are also notable technically for the lavish use of gold granulation, a jeweler's process used throughout Egyptian history. The precise method by which the granules were made is not known, and it is possible that they were just selected from the gold dust supplied to jewelers. They were fixed to the decorated surface by a process of colloidal hard-soldering, but it has not been possible to discover precisely what

materials and technical method may have been used by the Egyptian craftsman to produce the result.

From the fastenings hang down gold hoops to which the main circlet of beads is linked. The hoops are decorated with formalized lotus flowers and buds linked by stems, all carried out in granulation. The beads are made of gold and resin, separated by disks of resin sandwiched between thin gold plates. The gold beads are embellished with granular designs of triangles and tiny gold bosses encircled by granulation. All the

beads are cleverly graduated in thickness from inside to outside so that they sit neatly and tightly in a circle. Beneath the bead circles are wide bar beads decorated with wire scrolls, applied by the same process used for the granulation. The gold used for the scrolls and the granulation is not colored red. Seven strings of gold and glass beads complete these earrings, and they terminate in lotus seed heads in plain gold, and drop beads in red gold.

These earrings may not be 'barbaric', but they may show a foreign influence.

EARRINGS WITH DUCK HEADS

(CARTER 269A(1), J.D'E. 61969; LENGTH 10.9 CM)

Four pairs of earrings and a pair of ear-studs were found in the cartouche-shaped box which was stored in the Treasury. It is probable that all these jewels were used in Tutankhamun's early life, and had been put aside after he achieved puberty, or some other significant point in growing up. They were not, however, discarded completely, but stored to form part of his burial equipment.

This pair is the best designed of all the four, and it is distinguished not only by a superb use of the cloisonné technique, but also by some other technical aspects. The method for fastening the rings to the lobes of the ears was the same for all four pairs, and has been described above. In this case an additional subtle detail has been included. Disks of transparent quartz are fitted on both sides of the fasteners, and on the insides of the outer quartz disks are painted tiny portraits of the king. These are flanked by the pendent *uraei*

visible in the illustration.

The main element in the design takes the form of a bird with wonderfully formed and inlaid wings which sweep round to make a circle. The tiny cloisons are filled with intricately cut inlays of quartz, calcite, colored faience and glass. The head of the bird set in the middle of the wing's circle is anomalous. From the form of the wings, a falcon head is expected; the actual head is of a duck, and it is made, most rarely, of translucent blue glass. The tail of the bird, equally finely inlaid with colored glass, is fringed at its bottom by a minutely worked gold frieze of tiny disks and a block border from which hangs a gold frame mounted with gold and blue glass beads arranged in a chevron pattern, and giving the appearance of pendent strings of beads. From these hang five *uraeus* heads.

In their balance, color, technical perfection and overall appearance, these earrings are among the most satisfying of surviving jewelry from ancient Egypt.

EARRINGS WITH PENDENT *URAEI*

(CARTER 269A(5), J.D'E. 61968; LENGTH 7 CM)

A less ponderous fastening was used for this set of earrings. A circular fitment at the back was pushed through the pierced ear lobe and held in place by a cap. It is a less unwieldy arrangement than that of the ribbed tube, and probably more comfortable for a younger person to wear. There is no evidence to suggest that Tutankhamun wore earrings after childhood and early youth; but his ear lobes would have remained pierced, and it is not impossible that on certain grand occasions earrings were worn. The great Gold Mask found covering the head of the royal mummy shows pierced ears, but when it was first found these perforations were sealed with small covers of gold foil. The only supporting evidence for the wearing of such jewels by the mature king seems to be the representation of pierced ears on statues. Why would a great king like Ramesses II have himself shown with these perforations if they had no function after puberty?

This pair of earrings, perhaps more correctly called ear-studs, are formed of circular gold plates set with carnelian bosses surrounded by four rings of inlay, each designed separately to represent different kinds of bead and decorative device. The materials are carnelian, calcite and light and dark blue glass. The gold is of the red variety used so spectacularly on one of the other pairs of earrings. The inlays are set in colored cement. The outer ring represents ribbed beads; the next ring has unidentified floral forms; the third is of simple glass and gold beads set alternately; the final, innermost, ring reproduces round gold beads. From this main circular element, in each case two rather large *uraei* hang down; they are of gold, with glass inlays, and heads in dark blue glass modeled in the round. Each *uraeus* is topped by a carnelian sun-disk set in gold.

EARRINGS WITH FIGURES OF THE KING

(CARTER 268A(3), J.D'E. 61971; LENGTH 11.8 CM)

The use of somewhat inferior gold rather diminishes the spectacular effect undoubtedly intended for these earrings. The usual ribbed or screw tube fastenings are embellished with terminal bosses of gold inlaid with colored glass and carnelian, and also *uraei*; the inner *uraeus* of one earring is missing, and its companion on the other has a vulture head. Possibly each boss was originally fitted with two *uraei*, one with a vulture head.

The main element of the earring in each case is connected to the fastening by a falcon figure with outstretched wings made of gold inlaid with translucent quartz, through which can be seen details of the bird painted on the gold. The main ring is flanged and of gold with an outer edge marked as if granulated. The whole is surrounded by a ring of lenticular beads in gold, carnelian and blue glass.

The centre of each ring has a figure of Tutankhamun, flanked by two great *uraei* with sun-disks; this group stands on a *heb* or festival sign inlaid, like the *uraei*, with quartz and blue glass. The royal figure is carnelian; the king is shown wearing the blue crown, and he holds a crook of gold wire in his hand; there is a tiny gold *uraeus* on his brow.

From six of the gold lenticular beads hang strings of beads of carnelian and light and dark blue glass. Each pair of beads is separated from the next by four thin beads formed of tiny granules of gold fused together. Drop beads of gold, carnelian and light and dark blue glass serve as terminals for these strings.

While these pieces exhibit some weaknesses, such as the crude blocking out of the king's figure and the poor fitting of some of the inlays, special note must be made of the painting of the falcon details beneath the quartz inlays. Like the tiny royal portraits on the studs of the earrings with duck heads, such details are scarcely to be seen, and could hardly have been noticed when the earrings were being worn in life.

A Treasure Above All Treasures

BANGLES AND BRACELETS

BRACELET WITH SCARAB CLASP

(CARTER 269G, J.D'E. 62374;
LENGTH 15.8 CM,
HEIGHT OF SCARAB 6.6 CM)

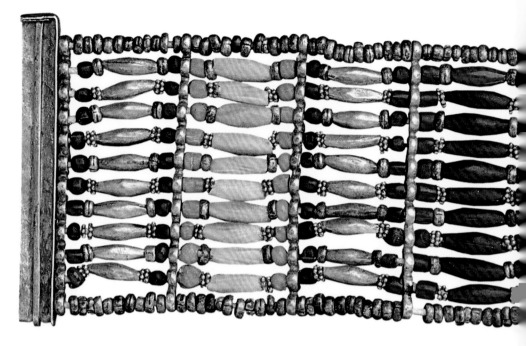

Two types of bracelet were found in Tutankhamun's tomb: the solid hoop-shaped kind with hinges and a pin fastening, and what Carter called the 'wrist-band' kind, composed of rows of beads separated and kept rigid at intervals by spacer beads, and with a large ornamental element at one end which, when the bracelet was worn, would appear as the centre-ornament.

Three bracelets were found in the cartouche-shaped box in the Treasury, which contained several other items of jewelry, like the earrings. All were thought to have been used by the king in his lifetime, and Carter was disappointed at not finding more in this box; it seems to have been used for many of the king's personal jewels. He supposed that the best pieces had been stolen in antiquity. Of the three bracelets, one was of the solid hoop form, and two of the wrist-band type, the one shown here and the other with a fine amethyst as the centre-ornament.

The principal feature of the centre-ornament of this bracelet is a scarab of lapis-lazuli. It is not carved from a single piece of stone but made up of a number of pieces fitted most carefully into gold cloisons fixed to a gold plate; the legs are also inlaid with the same stone. Between the back legs is held a basket shape inlaid with pale blue glass. The constituent parts of this centre-ornament look as if they

were intended to spell out the king's prenomen, Nebkheperure; but instead of the expected sun-disk between the front legs, there is a gold cartouche which contains the signs of the prenomen; the background of the cartouche is inlaid with blue glass.

Apart from the centre-ornament, the bracelet consists of ten rows of beads, the principal ones being barrel-shaped and made of gold,

electrum, blue glass, lapis-lazuli and calcite. Eight gold spacer beads give it rigidity, and there are small beads of blue glass and carnelian, and little granular beads in the form of rings. The bracelet is edged with gold beads, and finished with a fastening in gold which slides into a corresponding fitting on the side of the scarab – a simple but ingenious method of securing the bracelet when worn.

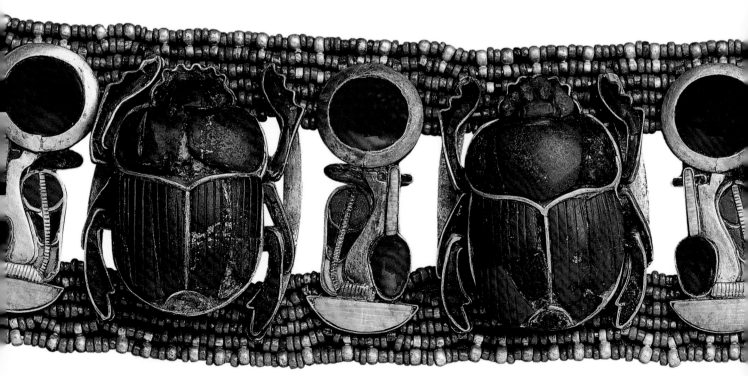

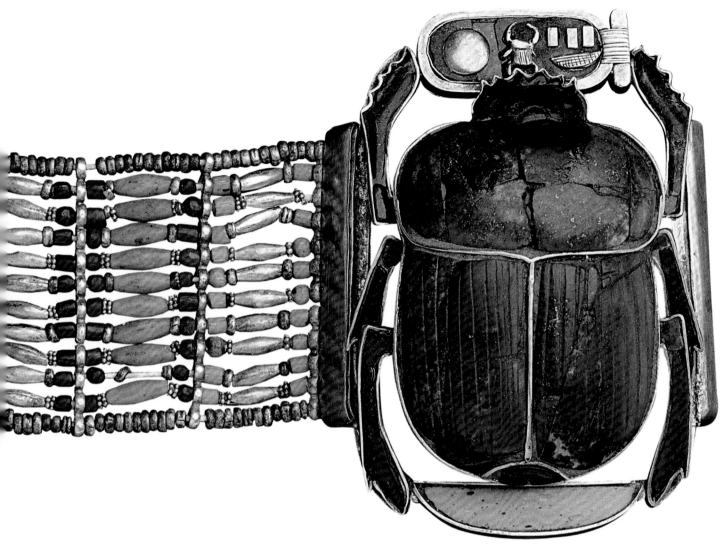

BRACELET WITH THREE SCARABS

(Carter 256yy j.d'E. 62362;
lenght 17.6 cm, height 4.3 cm)

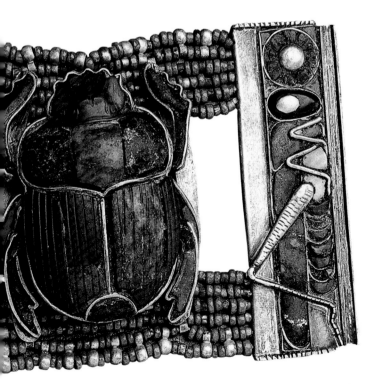

Tutankhamun appears to have had a predilection for bracelets. Apart from those found in boxes, there were numerous examples found within the mummy wrappings. The largest number, not surprisingly, were found on his two arms, seven on the right and six on the left, in each case filling the space between wrist and elbow. Although many of these bracelets incorporated in their designs religious or amuletic signs, like the *wedjat* or sacred eye of Horus, the *uraeus*, scarab and vulture, they were not, it seems, designed specifically for funerary use. Carter believed, with much good reason, that they were all used by Tutankhamun in his lifetime. From their crammed disposition on his arms, he was clearly determined to have as many as possible with him for use in his after-life.

This bracelet, which was on the king's left arm, combines in its design balance, amuletic protection, a wonderful use of color, and an imaginative touch in the clasp which held it closed.

There is here no centre-ornament as such; the whole length of the piece is embellished

with decorative elements, spaced out in pairs. Firstly there are three scarabs in lapis-lazuli, the parts set in cloisons of gold, the scarab being not only the embodiment of the sun-god at dawn, Khepri, but also a symbol of general regeneration. Between the scarabs are very decorative groups of signs: at the bottom of the basket is the hieroglyph often used for simple graphic purposes, but also meaning 'lord' or 'all' – as it may do here; it is inlaid with pale blue glass. On each basket stand the *nefer*-sign and an *uraeus*, the former meaning 'goodness' or 'beauty', the latter being a powerful royal protective symbol. At the top of each group is a sun-disk set in gold; the inlays are of carnelian and colored glass. This decorative group admirably exemplifies the capacity of Egyptian symbolism and the hieroglyphic script to be used graphically, with elegance and meaning.

Six rows of tiny gold and glass beads form the upper and lower borders of the bracelet. The sliding clasp is unusually decorated with the figure of a grasshopper or locust and a rosette.

BRACELET WITH LAPIS-LAZULI CENTRE-PIECE

(CARTER 256DDD, J.D'E. 62370;
LENGTH 16 CM, HEIGHT 4.2 CM)

Of the thirteen bracelets found on Tutankhamun's arms beneath the mummy wrappings, most included religious or magical amuletic signs, but a few seem devoid of meaningful decoration. Most of the bracelets showed signs of having been worn in the king's lifetime. This bracelet is one of those decorative pieces, and as such it is rare not only in the context of this royal burial, but also in Egyptian jewelry generally. The Egyptians liked to have their jewels invested with magical power. The central element of this jewel is a disk of lapis-lazuli flecked, as is so often the case, with brown markings. The setting is gold and decorated with two principal circular bands of design carried out in fine granulation. The outer band has triangular arrangements of granules while the inner has granules arranged around central bosses. The same decoration occurs on the side bars, to which ten strings of beads are attached. The beads are of gold, barrel-shaped and separated by little disks. It is a very flexible bracelet, and was held in place by a sliding bar.

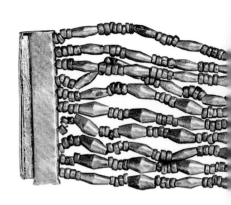

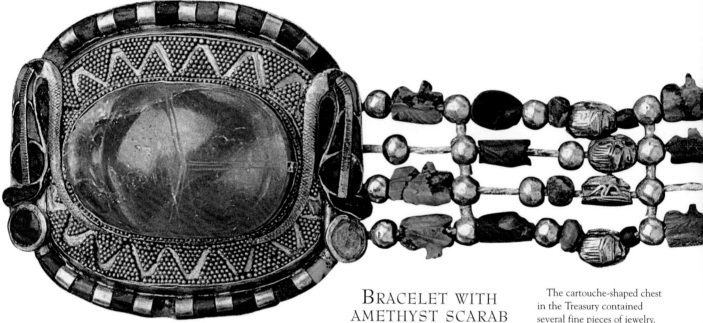

BRACELET WITH AMETHYST SCARAB

(CARTER 269M, J.D'E. 62380;
LENGTH 18 CM, HEIGHT 3.5 CM)

The cartouche-shaped chest in the Treasury contained several fine pieces of jewelry. This piece, in its general design being rather similar to some of the bracelets found on Tutankhamun's arms, was included in this chest. It bears signs of having been worn in the king's lifetime. The main element in the design is the

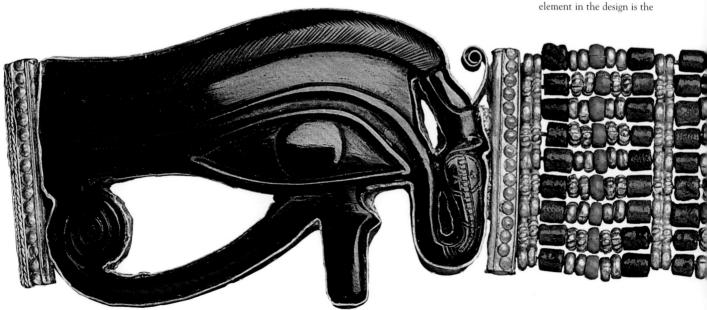

amethyst scarab, lightly marked with detail, as is common with scarabs of this hard stone. It is placed in an oval setting decorated with gold granules arranged in a pattern of little triangles. The outer rim is bordered by gold and hard stone ring beads, and each end has an erect *uraeus* with carnelian sun-disks. The back plate of this centre-piece is chased

with the king's prenomen; he is 'the good god, lord of the lands, lord of achievement'. The 'strap' of the bracelet consists of four strings of beads, of gold, carnelian, lapis-lazuli and jasper, in the form of tiny *wedjat*-eyes, scarabs and spheroids. The gold scarabs are in some cases inscribed with the king's prenomen. There are eight gold spacer beads.

BRACELET WITH
WEDJAT

(CARTER 25600, J.d'E. 62372;
LENGTH 16.2 CM, HEIGHT 3.5 CM)

The central element of this flexible bracelet from the left arm of the mummy is the powerful *wedjat*-eye, associated particularly with the falcon-god Horus, and also with Osiris. Its name means 'that which is complete or healthy', a description of it when restored after it had been stolen by Seth. This *wedjat* is made of a flawless piece of carnelian, set in a gold cloison fixed to a back plate of gold. Emerging from the eye on the right side is an *uraeus* wearing the double crown of Upper and Lower Egypt.

An inscription chased on the plate reads: 'lord of the two lands, image of Re, Nebkheperure, ruler of all that is in order, given life like Re for ever and ever'. The 'strap' of the bracelet consists of nine rows of beads made of glass of several colors and thin gold granulated beads. At six places the rows are held together by long gold spacers which are made to look like thin gold granulated beads.

BANGLE WITH A BIRD

(CARTER 256UU, J.D'E. 62384; DIAMETER 5.2 CM)

What is the bird on this bangle? Many Egyptologists would identify it with the bird, apparently the swallow, used in the word for 'great', *wer*, on the basis of the shape of the tail. The position of the feet, however, is not what is expected. Carter, with his special avian knowledge, considered it to be the swift, and he supported his identification by the presence of the sun-disk on the bird's back. He noted that swifts nested in holes in the western cliffs by the Nile, and emerged at dawn, making a great noise, similarly returning at dusk to roost. Unfortunately the Egyptians were not as precise as one would like in depicting birds and other creatures, and on lexicographical grounds the *ment*-bird is the swallow. Its significance on this bangle, therefore, remains elusive, although some association might be made with Spell 86 of the Book of the Dead: 'Spell to be transformed into a swallow', which Carter mentions. The bird is made of carnelian, the beads of blue glass and quartz. This piece was found in the wrappings of the mummy, by its left elbow.

BANGLE WITH A MINIATURE SCENE

(CARTER 620(43), J.D'E. 62405; DIAMETER 8.5 CM)

There is some dispute about the nature of these objects – are they armlets or anklets? The difficulty of slipping fixed circles of some not very robust material over the foot and up to the ankle offers a strong objection to their being anklets. A number of such objects were found scattered on the floor of the Annexe, many being quite plain. This one, made of ivory, is more elaborate. It is ribbed, and has inlaid on both sides small plates made of copper or bronze.

On one side (not visible) the prenomen of Tutankhamun is inscribed in cartouche in fine gold wire. On the other side, also in gold, is a small-scale scene: the king as a lion mauls an enemy lying prone on the ground. A standing figure of a goddess, probably Isis, holds out protective wings towards the scene and to two cartouches containing the names of the king. There is a *shen*-sign of dominion between the wings.

BRACELET WITH SCARAB

(CARTER 269N, J.D'E. 62360; DIAMETER 5.4 CM)

Another piece from the cartouche-shaped box, this fixed bracelet is one of the finest and most substantial jewels from Tutankhamun's tomb. Its principal embellishment is a scarab, standing clear of its base. It is made of gold with the body of the scarab composed of pieces of lapis-lazuli, skillfully fitted together within gold cloisons. Each side is enriched with false beads of gold, lapis, quartz, turquoise and carnelian, with a border simulating granular work. On the bend of the bracelet at each end is a charming design of a central mandrake fruit flanked by poppy flowers, with gold rosettes between the stems. The mandrake fruits are made of translucent quartz, their backs painted green; the poppy flowers are of carnelian. The bracelet itself is made of solid gold, and it has a hinge on one side and a fastening device on the other, both held together by gold pins. This piece is quite small and it has been suggested that it was worn by the king when a child.

RINGS

DOUBLE RING WITH THOTH

(CARTER 4C, J.D'E. 62437; DIAMETER 2.2 CM)

In one of the repacked boxes in the Antechamber the excavators found a piece of linen wrapped around eight gold rings. Carter believed that this little bundle represented part of the intended theft on the second occasion when the tomb was broken into. This ring is of solid gold, a double ring with two bezels decorated with divine figures. The left bezel has a figure of a baboon squatting on a shrine; it wears a moon-disk on its head. The right bezel has an ibis-headed deity, carrying

LAPIS-LAZULI DOUBLE RING

(CARTER 256FF1, J.D'E. 62431; DIAMETER 2.3 CM)

In the course of unwrapping the mummy Carter uncovered two groups of finger rings, not on the king's fingers but placed near the wrists, five over the right wrist and eight by the left. These were mostly of semiprecious stones – chalcedony and turquoise – one of gold, one of resin and this one of lapis-lazuli. It is a double ring with a double bezel shaped like cartouches. In the right cartouche a figure of the king kneels offering milk or some other liquid to the deity in the

other cartouche. The king is identified by his prenomen, written a little enigmatically: at the top is the sun-disk, below a winged scarab and the royal figure, which itself could be taken as part of the written name, shown kneeling on a basket which is regularly a component of Tutankhamun's prenomen; plural strokes are missing. The god receiving the offering is Amon-Re; he is shown seated on a throne wearing his feathered headdress, and holding the *was*-scepter and *ankh*.

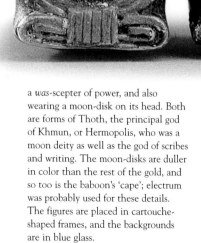

a *was*-scepter of power, and also wearing a moon-disk on its head. Both are forms of Thoth, the principal god of Khmun, or Hermopolis, who was a moon deity as well as the god of scribes and writing. The moon-disks are duller in color than the rest of the gold, and so too is the baboon's 'cape'; electrum was probably used for these details. The figures are placed in cartouche-shaped frames, and the backgrounds are in blue glass.

Ring with Amon-Re

(Carter 44f, J.d'E. 62451; diameter 2 cm)

Another of the rings found in the linen bundle in the Antechamber. Carter reconstructed the scene: one of the robbers, having helped himself to a collection of gold rings, wrapped them in a piece of linen taken from the tomb equipment. When he was caught the bundle was confiscated and tossed into the box where they were ultimately found. If this reconstruction is true, it says much for the integrity of the Necropolis guards, who might easily have slipped them into the folds of a garment. The story of their survival may not, however, have been as Carter surmised. This ring is very heavy, and of solid gold, with a bezel shaped like a cartouche. Inside, carefully chased, is a figure of god, named as Amon-Re. He is seated on a throne, the characteristic feather pattern of the side of which is rendered by small punch marks. He is shown wearing his usual cap with double feather and disk, and a streamer at the back; in his left hand he holds the *was*-scepter, and in his right, the *ankh*.

RING WITH THE SUN BARK

(CARTER 44G, J.D'E. 62450;
DIAMETER 2 CM)

The heavy gold rings found in the tomb have often been described as signets. Strictly speaking, a signet ring carries on its bezel a name or device which can be used for identificatory purposes. You seal a letter with a signet, and the recipient recognizes the impression. You seal a door or a box with a seal to give the sealing an authority. Egyptians used signets to seal letters and other documents, and the signet might well take the form of a scarab set in a ring, or a solid ring with an inscription cut into the bezel. Many of the rings found in the tomb could have been used as signets, but none seems specially designed for use as a signet. This solid gold ring, for example – one of those from the robber's bundle – would produce an impression if it were applied to a mud sealing, but it is not primarily to be considered a signet. The design on the bezel is religious/magical. It shows a bark holding a sun-disk with two baboons on either side, standing and raising their paws in adoration, greeting the sun at dawn. The background is blue glass.

TRIPLE RING WITH FIGURED BEZEL

(CARTER 265FF5, J.D'E. 62428;
DIAMETER WITH FIGURES 2.6 CM)

An intricate and carefully crafted bezel distinguishes this ring, one of those found by the right wrist of the mummy. The ring itself is not simple; it has a triple shank made of resin and covered with gold foil. Each end of the shank is made to represent a posy of flowers consisting of a central papyrus in felspar, flanked by two red poppies in carnelian. The three parts of the shank are bound around with gold wire, and the three together are bound with more wire just below the posies. The bezel itself is at its base cartouche-

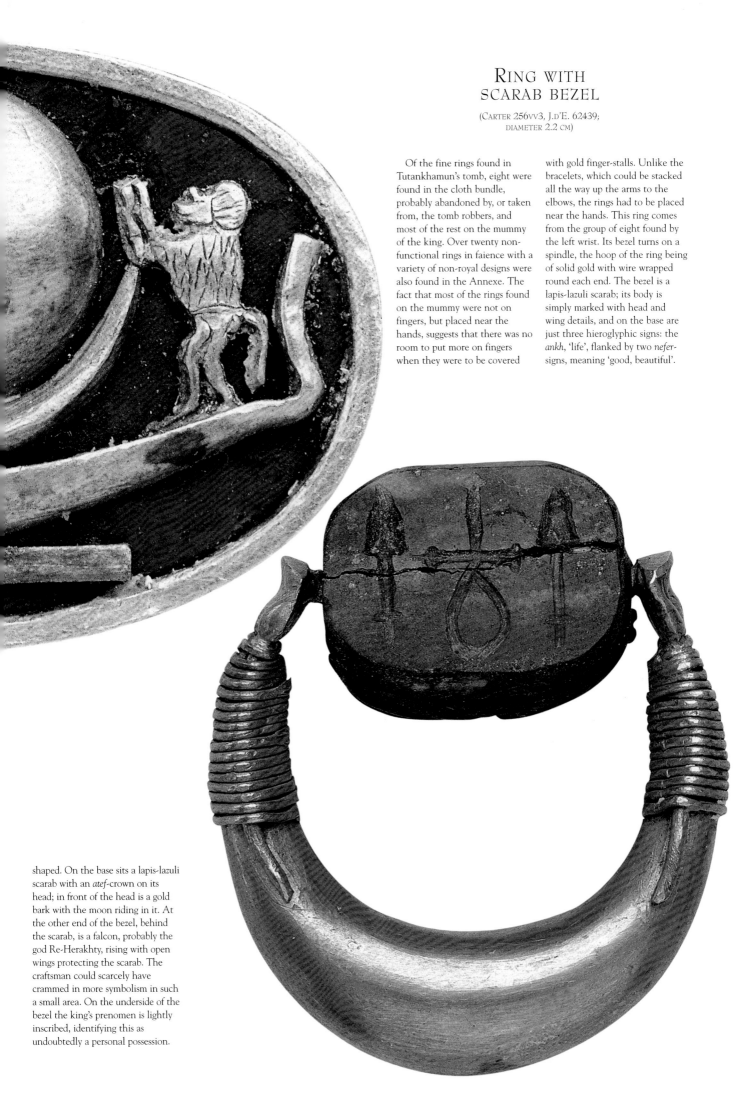

RING WITH
SCARAB BEZEL

(CARTER 256vv3, J.D'E. 62439;
DIAMETER 2.2 CM)

Of the fine rings found in Tutankhamun's tomb, eight were found in the cloth bundle, probably abandoned by, or taken from, the tomb robbers, and most of the rest on the mummy of the king. Over twenty non-functional rings in faience with a variety of non-royal designs were also found in the Annexe. The fact that most of the rings found on the mummy were not on fingers, but placed near the hands, suggests that there was no room to put more on fingers when they were to be covered with gold finger-stalls. Unlike the bracelets, which could be stacked all the way up the arms to the elbows, the rings had to be placed near the hands. This ring comes from the group of eight found by the left wrist. Its bezel turns on a spindle, the hoop of the ring being of solid gold with wire wrapped round each end. The bezel is a lapis-lazuli scarab; its body is simply marked with head and wing details, and on the base are just three hieroglyphic signs: the *ankh*, 'life', flanked by two *nefer*-signs, meaning 'good, beautiful'.

shaped. On the base sits a lapis-lazuli scarab with an *atef*-crown on its head; in front of the head is a gold bark with the moon riding in it. At the other end of the bezel, behind the scarab, is a falcon, probably the god Re-Herakhty, rising with open wings protecting the scarab. The craftsman could scarcely have crammed in more symbolism in such a small area. On the underside of the bezel the king's prenomen is lightly inscribed, identifying this as undoubtedly a personal possession.

OTHER JEWELED OBJECTS

GOLD BUCKLE OF THE KING AND QUEEN

(J.D'E. 61987; LENGTH 9 CM, HEIGHT 9 CM)

Openwork plaques of this kind are often called buckles, although there is no satisfactory evidence to show that this was their actual purpose. Not all openwork pieces look like buckles, and it might be better to think of them as attachments for belts or other items of formal dress or equipment. They are not, as has sometimes been suggested, decorative elements from chariots.

Four openwork plaques were found in a box in the Antechamber; three others come from unidentified places in the tomb, and all are illustrated here. This example is particularly elaborate in its design, which is carried out by repoussé work, with details in chasing, and in parts richly embellished with gold granulation. The gold has the reddish-purple sheen found on many other pieces from the tomb.

The central scene shows Tutankhamun and Ankhesenamun (named in cartouches) within an elaborate kiosk which has a double cornice topped by a frieze of *uraei* with disks, and above this a winged sun-disk. The king sits casually on a throne, his feet on a footstool. He wears elaborate dress and the *atef*-crown, usually associated with Osiris and the dead king. The king is not dead here; he is approached by Ankhesenamun who presents a bouquet, and gently touches the king. The scene is closely similar to one on the back of the gilded shrine. In both cases the queen wears a feathered headdress, but on the shrine the king wears the blue crown. Elaborate floral arrangements flank the royal pair. Beneath the kiosk, and symbolically under the feet of the king, are shown two prone foreign captives, an Asiatic and a Nubian. Two identical scenes occupy the ends of this piece, set at right angles to the main scene. The king is shown as a sphinx with human arms holding up in front of him a figure of Ma'at, goddess of truth and order, holding the *ankh*-sign of life, and squatting on a basket. There is a pendent *uraeus* and sun-disk above the sphinx's head, and over his back is a protective vulture holding an ostrich-feather fan.

GOLD PLAQUE WITH A BULL ATTACKED

(CARTER 44A, J.D'E. 61983; LENGTH 8.5 CM, HEIGHT 6 CM)

A number of the gold plaques, some of which look like buckles, carry scenes of hunting or of animals attacking other animals. This piece has such a scene. It is one of the four found in the Antechamber. The central depiction, disagreeable as it is, again demonstrates the Egyptian ability to convey the movement of animals in a most lively and life-like manner. The tendency to make non-human representations more fluid can be found in tomb scenes in Thebes in the mid-Eighteenth Dynasty; the Amarna tendency in art promoted it further. The theme here is of a bull attacked by wild animals – a fairly common theme in Egyptian and Western Asiatic art. The unfortunate bull is attacked by a leopard from above, and by a lion from below. Desert plants fill the open spaces. In the two end sections, ibexes graze on plants. Much of the detail is again carried out skillfully in granulation.

GOLD PLAQUE WITH HUNTING SCENE

(CARTER 50TT, J.D'E. 61985; LENGTH 8 CM, HEIGHT 3.2 CM)

This piece of gold openwork – not a buckle, but a plaque of some kind – was found in a box in the Antechamber containing a large amount of clothing and textiles. It scarcely belonged there in the first place, and may have been part of a group found elsewhere in the same room. It seems to be complete in itself, and shows a violent scene of hunting, with two dogs attacking an ibex on the left and a bull on the right. The setting seems not quite to be the desert, because elaborate and unnaturalistic plants occur within the scene. Much of the detail is marked out by granulation, and this technique is used to particularly good effect in delineating the heads of the hunting dogs. There is great movement in the depiction of the interweaving of the animals, not the static idea of Egyptian art, which is here completely confounded. The top and bottom borders are filled with rosettes. The gold is of the purplish-red kind.

PLAQUE OF THE KING IN HIS CHARIOT

(J.D'E. 87847; HEIGHT 6.7 CM, WIDTH 8.5 CM)

Where this plaque or buckle was found is not known. It probably strayed in antiquity from the group of similar pieces found in the Antechamber. The principal motif is the king in his chariot returning from campaign. Two captives run ahead of the horses, an Asiatic and a Nubian – it was a wide-ranging campaign! The king's hound runs with the horses, and the king is offered 'life' by the vulture Nekhbet above, and 'protection' by the winged uraeus Wadjyt behind him. In the space below, a variant of the common heraldic device symbolizing the union of the Two Lands includes bound figures of kneeling captives, the usual Asiatic (on the Lower Egyptian side) and Nubian (on the Upper Egyptian side). The text on a panel before the horses' heads is too worn to be read; that between the wings of the uraeus contains Tutankhamun's prenomen; and that behind the wheel of the chariot wishes 'all life and protection be behind him like Re for ever'. The gold again has the purplish-red color.

GOLD
MUMMY BAND

(CARTER 256B, J.D'E. 60673;
WIDTH 4.9 CM)

When the lid of the innermost coffin was raised, Carter, his assistants and the visitors invited to attend that most important occasion saw for the first time the mummy of a dead king, wrapped and ornamented for burial. It was an awesome sight, but also one which certainly filled the excavators with foreboding at the task that lay ahead. Everything apart from the mask had been liberally anointed with unguents which had set hard. Still much could be seen or detected of the surface trappings, and it was evident that the king's body was very richly equipped. What then seemed promising would turn out to be spectacular when removed and cleaned of the hardened unguents.

From the *ba*-bird on the royal chest, straps of gold and beads were disposed over the lower part of the body as if they were holding the linen wrappings in place. Carter noted that some of these straps had been made originally for what was expected to be a smaller body, and then later adapted to fit Tutankhamun's somewhat larger mummy. The main strap, running down the body, had two lines with texts in which Nut and Geb, the deities of sky and earth, address the body. From this central strap ran at right angles transverse straps with single lines of text in which the king is declared to be 'revered before' the four Canopic genii and Anubis, the god of embalming. The part shown here incorporates two separate transverse straps: the upper section, containing the cartouche with Tutankhamun's name, belongs to the right side of the body and comes from the text in which the king is 'revered before Amsety'.

The lower section belongs to an individual strap, in the text of which some of the epithets usually applied to Osiris are applied to Anubis: 'lord of the Holy Land, Foremost in the West'; it continues, 'may he grant that the lord of the Two Lands, Nebkheperure, should be the first [or unique] at the head of...'; the precise meaning is uncertain because some of the text is lost.

The signs in the text are inlaid with colored glass.

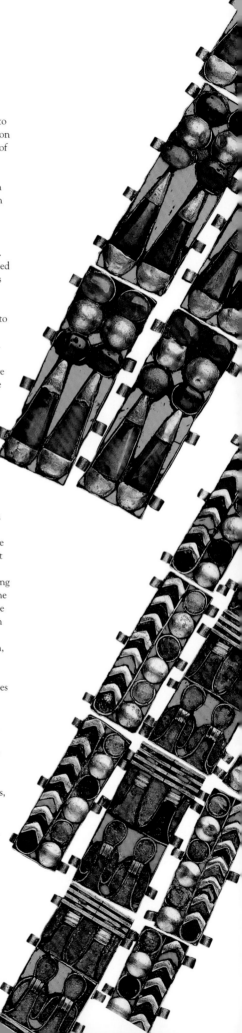

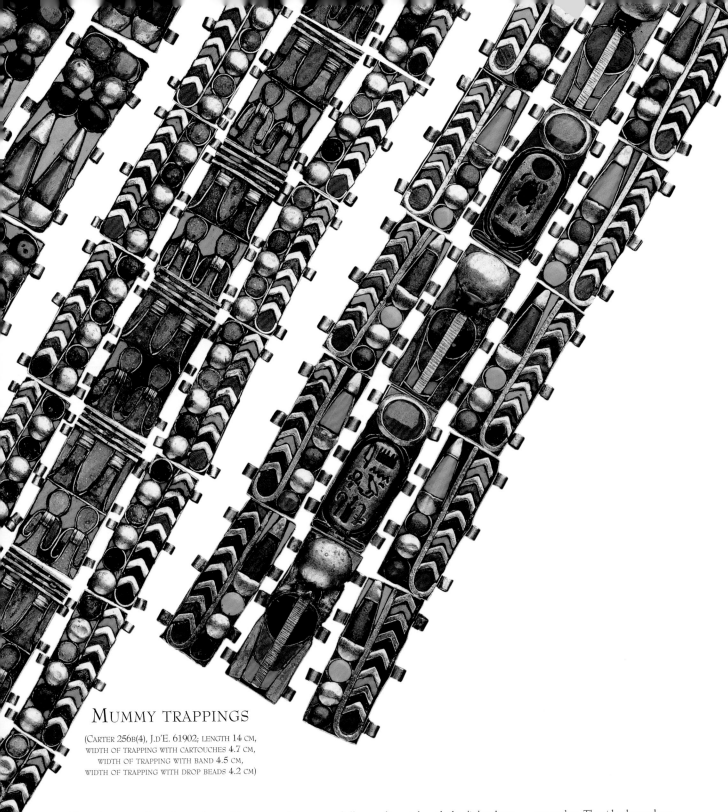

MUMMY TRAPPINGS

(CARTER 256B(4), J.D'E. 61902; LENGTH 14 CM,
WIDTH OF TRAPPING WITH CARTOUCHES 4.7 CM,
WIDTH OF TRAPPING WITH BAND 4.5 CM,
WIDTH OF TRAPPING WITH DROP BEADS 4.2 CM)

These three straps formed part of the decorative elements placed on the outside of the royal mummy in addition to the gold straps with inlaid funerary texts. Carter describes them as being placed 'along the sides of the mummy from the shoulders to the feet', arranged in festoons attached to the transverse trappings, as seen in the previously illustrated gold band. They are not, strictly speaking, jewelry, but they were made by the techniques of jewelry, and their spectacular appearance is comparable with the decorative straps of many of the pectoral necklaces from the tomb.

The structural character of all three of the illustrated pieces is similar: small gold plaques with cloisonné inlaid decoration are strung together, with beads separating and edging them. The left-hand strap consists of two rows of plaques side by side, with a simple repeated design of drop-beads and disks. The disks are not necessarily sun-disks, because some are inlaid with dark blue glass, the rest with transparent quartz set in reddish paste which gives them a pinkish tinge. Other inlays are in light blue glass and quartz.

The central strap has a single row of gold plaques decorated

alternately with the *djed* and *tyet*, amuletic signs of endurance and power. The plaques are fringed by further gold plaques on each side with patterns of disks and chevrons. The inlays are again of dark and light blue glass, transparent quartz and carnelian.

The right-hand strap has the most elaborate scheme of decoration. The central row of gold plaques has *uraei* alternating with the names of the king, both prenomen and main name, or nomen. Each *uraeus* and cartouche is topped by a sun-disk, solid gold in the case of the *uraei*, and inlaid carnelian for the

cartouches. The side plaques have inner rows of drop beads and disks, and outer rows of chevrons and disks. The inlays are of the same materials as in the other straps.

On the reverse of these straps are remains of religious texts, including the invocation of the heart from the Book of the Dead. Where royal cartouches occur, the names within, although mostly defaced, can clearly be read as those of Tutankhamun's ephemeral predecessor, Neferneferuaten. These straps therefore provide further evidence of a certain economical recycling of old funerary equipment for this burial.

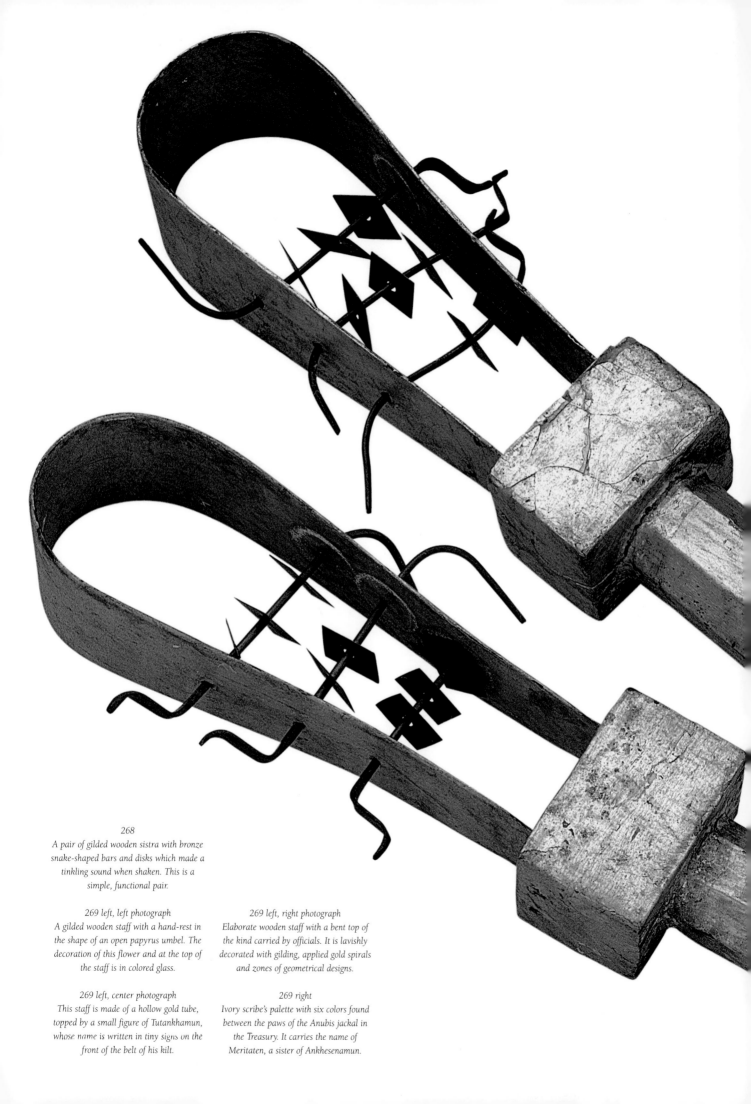

268
A pair of gilded wooden sistra with bronze
snake-shaped bars and disks which made a
tinkling sound when shaken. This is a
simple, functional pair.

269 left, left photograph
A gilded wooden staff with a hand-rest in
the shape of an open papyrus umbel. The
decoration of this flower and at the top of
the staff is in colored glass.

269 left, right photograph
Elaborate wooden staff with a bent top of
the kind carried by officials. It is lavishly
decorated with gilding, applied gold spirals
and zones of geometrical designs.

269 left, center photograph
This staff is made of a hollow gold tube,
topped by a small figure of Tutankhamun,
whose name is written in tiny signs on the
front of the belt of his kilt.

269 right
Ivory scribe's palette with six colors found
between the paws of the Anubis jackal in
the Treasury. It carries the name of
Meritaten, a sister of Ankhesenamun.

PERSONAL POSSESSIONS

Among the formal, religious and funerary objects which composed the most important part of the equipment discovered in Tutankhamun's tomb, there were other objects which belonged essentially to the private life of the king. Of those that are included in this chapter, some, by the inscriptions they carry, are converted, at least magically, into funerary objects; but they also represent some of the activities in which the king would have engaged on an informal basis during his lifetime.

How did a young king spend his time? It cannot be thought that affairs of state would have been seriously supervised by a young monarch, although he might have been required to put his name or his seal to decisions recommended by his advisers. To this end he should in theory know how to read and write; and the presence of scribal equipment in the tomb suggests that he would have been literate.

It cannot be suggested that Tutankhamun played a musical instrument, but music would have been an important element in Court and religious life, and it would be convenient to have a few instruments on hand for use in the afterlife. Similarly, board games would be needed. The playing of the game *senet* is one of the activities shown in tomb scenes as something in which the deceased could engage. The ebony gaming box on a stand is a fine example of what the king might need to while away the time in the afterlife.

Kings and officials are regularly shown carrying sticks and rods in the exercise of their authority. About 130 examples were found in the tomb, and Carter ventured the view that Tutankhamun was a collector. Some sticks are simple, some may be described as fighting staves; some were sticks of authority, wonderfully carved with figures of foreign captives; one carries an exquisite small figure of the king, the whole being in gold. Here were sticks for every occasion, and many of them showed signs of having been used before they were placed in the tomb.

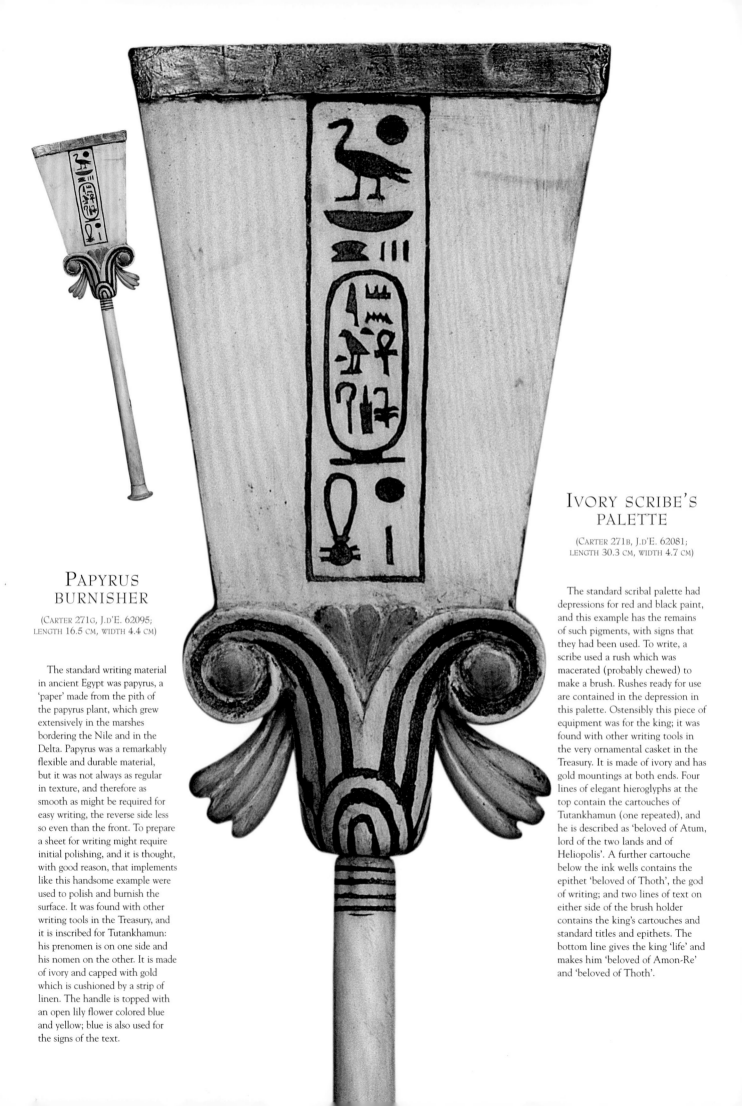

IVORY SCRIBE'S PALETTE

(CARTER 271B, J.D'E. 62081;
LENGTH 30.3 CM, WIDTH 4.7 CM)

The standard scribal palette had
depressions for red and black paint,
and this example has the remains
of such pigments, with signs that
they had been used. To write, a
scribe used a rush which was
macerated (probably chewed) to
make a brush. Rushes ready for use
are contained in the depression in
this palette. Ostensibly this piece of
equipment was for the king; it was
found with other writing tools in
the very ornamental casket in the
Treasury. It is made of ivory and has
gold mountings at both ends. Four
lines of elegant hieroglyphs at the
top contain the cartouches of
Tutankhamun (one repeated), and
he is described as 'beloved of Atum,
lord of the two lands and of
Heliopolis'. A further cartouche
below the ink wells contains the
epithet 'beloved of Thoth', the god
of writing; and two lines of text on
either side of the brush holder
contains the king's cartouches and
standard titles and epithets. The
bottom line gives the king 'life' and
makes him 'beloved of Amon-Re'
and 'beloved of Thoth'.

PAPYRUS
BURNISHER

(CARTER 271G, J.D'E. 62095;
LENGTH 16.5 CM, WIDTH 4.4 CM)

The standard writing material
in ancient Egypt was papyrus, a
'paper' made from the pith of
the papyrus plant, which grew
extensively in the marshes
bordering the Nile and in the
Delta. Papyrus was a remarkably
flexible and durable material,
but it was not always as regular
in texture, and therefore as
smooth as might be required for
easy writing, the reverse side less
so even than the front. To prepare
a sheet for writing might require
initial polishing, and it is thought,
with good reason, that implements
like this handsome example were
used to polish and burnish the
surface. It was found with other
writing tools in the Treasury, and
it is inscribed for Tutankhamun:
his prenomen is on one side and
his nomen on the other. It is made
of ivory and capped with gold
which is cushioned by a strip of
linen. The handle is topped with
an open lily flower colored blue
and yellow; blue is also used for
the signs of the text.

GILDED BRUSH HOLDER

(CARTER 271E1, J.D'E. 62094;
LENGTH 30 CM)

In the hieroglyphic script the word for 'write' and cognates used a sign which represented a scribal kit – a palette, a bag of spare ink, and a tube to hold the brushes; these components were linked with a cord or strap, and scribes were often shown with their equipment slung over their shoulders. The ordinary palette had space for rush brushes, but a specially made holder would complete a good 'desk' set. This brush holder, found with the other items of the writing kit already described, is an especially elaborate example. It is shaped like a column with a palm tree capital. The abacus forms the lid and it pivots to open. It could be kept shut by having a string wound round the two little knobs on top and side of the tube. The top knobs and little base plate are made of ivory and the tube is of gilded wood, encrusted with zones of decoration with inlays of carnelian, obsidian and glass. The king's two cartouches are included in the central zone.

GILDED SCRIBAL PALETTE

(CARTER 171E2, J.D'E. 62080;
LENGTH 30.3 CM, WIDTH 4.3 CM)

This gilded wooden palette, the same size as the last and from the same box, is especially interesting because in the formal royal titulary at the top the king's name is given as Tutankhaten, the name he bore before he moved from El-Amarna. The epithet given is 'beloved of Thoth, lord of the god's word'. Carter was of the opinion that both palettes had been used, and that this one would have been the one the king used in his early reign. The question must be raised whether Tutankhamun knew how to read and write hieroglyphics or the hieratic script. The evidence for royal literacy is very slight, and it might be thought that someone in the king's position could have got through the affairs of state relying on advisers and secretaries. On the other hand, an ability to read and write was considered such an advantage in ancient Egypt that every effort might have been made to ensure that the heir to the throne obtained at least the basic competence to deal with written documents.

A Treasure Above All Treasures

271

GAMING BOX ON A STAND

(CARTER 345 (BOX), 383 (DRAWER), 580 (STAND), J.D'E. 62058; BOX: LENGTH 44.6 CM, WIDTH 14.3 CM, HEIGHT 8.1 CM; STAND: LENGTH 55 CM, WIDTH 17.5 CM, HEIGHT 20.2 CM)

One of the most satisfying examples of the ancient cabinet-maker's craft, this piece of semi-recreational furniture was found in several pieces in the Annexe. The box is made of some ordinary wood, veneered with ebony, and marked out top and bottom with playing squares of ivory. The stand and sledge are of ebony, most tastefully embellished with gold on the 'drums' beneath the lion paws and the braces which strengthen the joints. The lion claws are ivory. Inscriptions in yellow paint along both sides, and at the end where the drawer enters the box, contain very full titularies of Tutankhamun, with many epithets, including the unusual 'beloved of all the gods, may he be healthy for ever', a significant variant of 'may he live for ever'. Board games were much played in ancient Egypt, and one in particular, *senet*, was seen to be played in the afterlife. In the preliminaries of Spell 17 of the Book of the Dead playing at *senet* is listed as an activity which would be beneficial to the deceased, and in some tombs of the New Kingdom the deceased and his wife are shown playing.

DECORATED GAMING BOX

(CARTER 593, J.d'E. 62059;
LENGTH 27.5 CM, WIDTH 9 CM,
HEIGHT 5.8 CM)

The playing pieces belonging to
the ebony gaming box described
above were not found, and Carter
deduced that they might have been
made of gold, and therefore
convenient things to be 'pocketed' by
thieves. Ivory gaming pieces were
found which may have belonged to
this less distinguished box, also found
in the Annexe. It has interesting
features, and when new was probably
a very attractive object. It is made of
an ordinary soft wood embellished
with ivory. On both sides are plaques
carrying floral designs, lightly scored
and stained in part with black and
red color. The playing surfaces are
covered with ivory, divided into

squares by a material Carter
described as stucco, then covered
with gold foil.

There are two drawers fitted with
ivory plates and little ebony bolts
which engage in gold staples. Like
the previous box, this one could be
used for two different games. One
employed the full surface marked
out with 30 squares; this is *senet*.
The other side is marked out for a
game formerly known as *tjau*; this
view is now thought to be incorrect.
At one end are three rows of four
squares each, with the central row
extended by eight more squares.
There remains much debate about
how these two games were played.

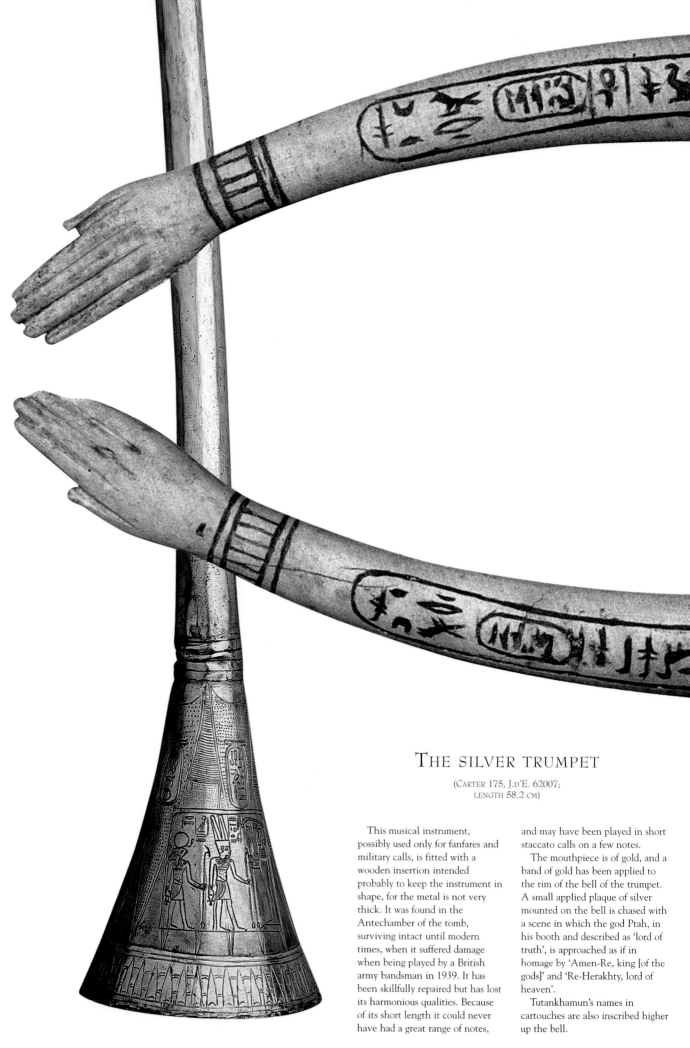

THE SILVER TRUMPET

(CARTER 175, J.D'E. 62007;
LENGTH 58.2 CM)

This musical instrument, possibly used only for fanfares and military calls, is fitted with a wooden insertion intended probably to keep the instrument in shape, for the metal is not very thick. It was found in the Antechamber of the tomb, surviving intact until modern times, when it suffered damage when being played by a British army bandsman in 1939. It has been skillfully repaired but has lost its harmonious qualities. Because of its short length it could never have had a great range of notes,

and may have been played in short staccato calls on a few notes.

The mouthpiece is of gold, and a band of gold has been applied to the rim of the bell of the trumpet. A small applied plaque of silver mounted on the bell is chased with a scene in which the god Ptah, in his booth and described as 'lord of truth', is approached as if in homage by 'Amen-Re, king [of the gods]' and 'Re-Herakhty, lord of heaven'.

Tutankhamun's names in cartouches are also inscribed higher up the bell.

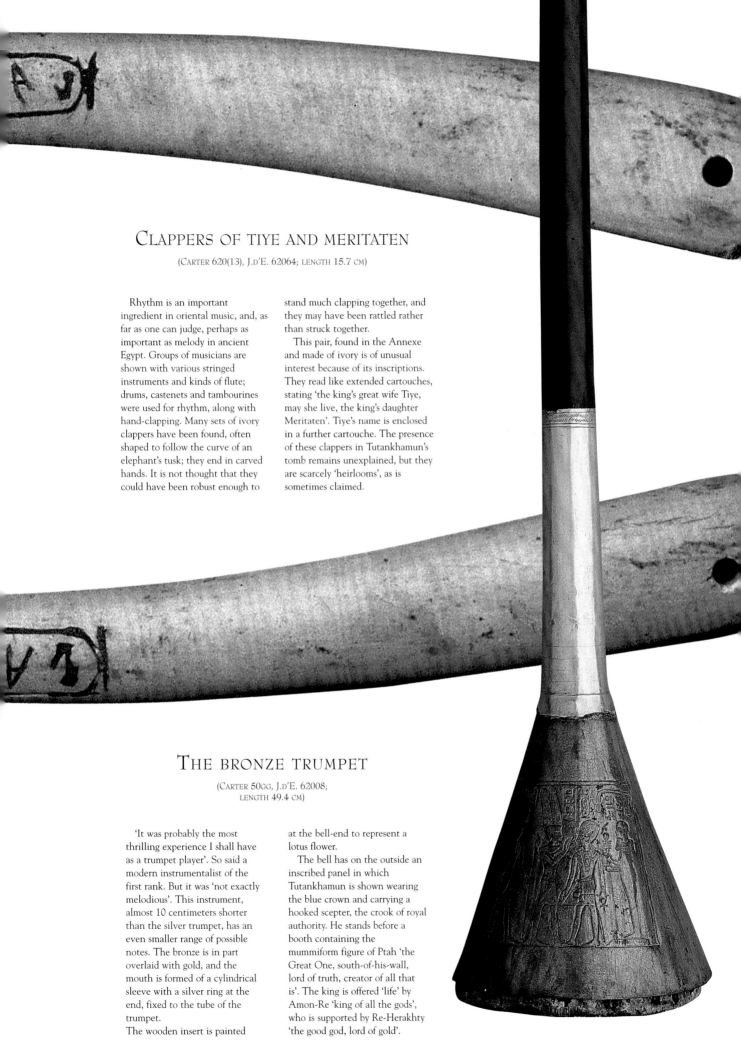

CLAPPERS OF TIYE AND MERITATEN

(CARTER 620(13), J.D'E. 62064; LENGTH 15.7 CM)

Rhythm is an important ingredient in oriental music, and, as far as one can judge, perhaps as important as melody in ancient Egypt. Groups of musicians are shown with various stringed instruments and kinds of flute; drums, castenets and tambourines were used for rhythm, along with hand-clapping. Many sets of ivory clappers have been found, often shaped to follow the curve of an elephant's tusk; they end in carved hands. It is not thought that they could have been robust enough to stand much clapping together, and they may have been rattled rather than struck together.

This pair, found in the Annexe and made of ivory is of unusual interest because of its inscriptions. They read like extended cartouches, stating 'the king's great wife Tiye, may she live, the king's daughter Meritaten'. Tiye's name is enclosed in a further cartouche. The presence of these clappers in Tutankhamun's tomb remains unexplained, but they are scarcely 'heirlooms', as is sometimes claimed.

THE BRONZE TRUMPET

(CARTER 50GG, J.D'E. 62008;
LENGTH 49.4 CM)

'It was probably the most thrilling experience I shall have as a trumpet player'. So said a modern instrumentalist of the first rank. But it was 'not exactly melodious'. This instrument, almost 10 centimeters shorter than the silver trumpet, has an even smaller range of possible notes. The bronze is in part overlaid with gold, and the mouth is formed of a cylindrical sleeve with a silver ring at the end, fixed to the tube of the trumpet.

The wooden insert is painted at the bell-end to represent a lotus flower.

The bell has on the outside an inscribed panel in which Tutankhamun is shown wearing the blue crown and carrying a hooked scepter, the crook of royal authority. He stands before a booth containing the mummiform figure of Ptah 'the Great One, south-of-his-wall, lord of truth, creator of all that is'. The king is offered 'life' by Amon-Re 'king of all the gods', who is supported by Re-Herakhty 'the good god, lord of gold'.

DECORATED STAFF

(CARTER 227A, J.D'E. 61756;
LENGTH 108 CM)

Stick contests, friendly and passionate, are still very common in Upper Egyptian villages, and there are few countrymen who do not carry a sturdy staff which may be turned to several purposes. Stick 'games' are shown occasionally in tomb scenes, and it is evident that sticks were important personal possessions. Carter thought that Tutankhamun must have collected sticks as a hobby, so many examples were found in the tomb. Many are simple, but others are of unusual shapes, embellished with figures in the round and decorated in such elaborate ways that they could scarcely be used for anything very active. This stick, for example, would stand very little rough use. It is curved at one end in a manner of sticks sometimes held by officials and even soldiers. The end is shod with a gold ferrule. The bands of decoration, of great variety and intricacy, are in addition to gold – the predictable material – made up of marquetry carried out, not in various woods but in different colored barks and even the iridescent wings of beetles.

STAFF WITH INVOCATION OF AMUN

(CARTER 204, J.D'E. 61667; LENGTH 145 CM)

This staff was found along with a large number of others in the Antechamber, many among the litter of chariot parts. Their variety is considerable, and some are most elaborately decorated with gold incrustation and inlays.

This example is relatively simple, but gorgeously simple. It is completely covered with gold foil, with just a little tasteful decoration at its top and beneath the hand-hold, in inlaid glass. There is also a text in gold against a blue glass background which states 'the good god, son of Amun, King of Upper and Lower Egypt, lord of the two lands, Nebkheperure, son of Re, of his body, his beloved, lord of diadems, Tutankhamun [ruler in] southern [Heliopolis], beloved of Amun, given life for ever and ever'.

In all cases where the name Amun occurs, it has replaced Aten. Presumably it was a stick made early in the reign, and 'corrected' for the burial.

STAFF WITH GOLD FIGURE OF KING

(CARTER 235A, J.D'E. 61665; LENGTH 131 CM
HEIGHT OF FIGURE 9 CM)

Many of the staves found in the tomb were just instruments of authority, to be carried on official occasions, or in particular ceremonies.

This great staff is such that a special role might have been assigned to it; but nothing obvious can be suggested, especially as the figure is of the king himself. It was found with an almost identical one in silver, wrapped up in linen and placed between the two outermost shrines in the Burial Chamber. In

this case the shaft is tubular, of gold and hollow throughout. At the top is the royal figure socketed into a gold plate soldered to the staff.

The figure is cast solid, with details subsequently chased. The king is shown as a young man, even a child, although no distinctly childish elements like the side-lock of hair is added. He wears the *khepresh*, the blue crown, and a kilt, and he stands with his arms slightly raised, his hands turned backwards, in a strange gesture.

STICK WITH A LIBYAN CAPTIVE

(CARTER 100A, J.D'E. 61734;
LENGTH 109 CM)

The three sticks with handles shaped in the form of bound captives were found in a long box in the Antechamber of Tutankhamun's tomb, along with bows, bow-cases and other long objects.

The sticks illustrated here all carry Tutankhamun's prenomen, and may therefore be confidently assigned to his reign. But it must be doubted that he ever saw foreign captives brought before him in triumph by a victorious general, although his commander-in-chief, Horemheb, may have started the campaign to regain those parts of the Egyptian region of influence which had been lost in the reign of Akhenaten. Libya at this time posed little threat, but that did not prevent the inclusion of a Libyan prisoner on one of the sticks. The Libyan is almost entirely gilded, apart from his feet and hands which have been added in ebony. The head, although on such a small scale, is wonderfully realized, with much significant detail. At the other end of the stick there is a blue glass ferrule.

STICK WITH A NUBIAN CAPTIVE

(CARTER 48B, J.D'E. 61735;
LENGTH 102 CM)

This stick is almost identical to the last, except that a Nubian replaces the Libyan as part of the handle.

Sticks with figures like those found in the tomb are unknown from elsewhere, and no special idea for their function can be offered. Undoubtedly they offer humiliation to Pharaoh's traditional enemies.

Nubia was the land most closely linked to Egypt; the Nile was their common river, and from the earliest times trade and warfare distinguished relations between the two. Nubia was Kush, and Kush could scarcely be mentioned without the adjective 'vile'. The Nubian depicted on this stick was distinctly black, and the blackest of woods, ebony, was used to fashion the ungilded parts – feet, hands and head. The last is very finely carved, with characteristic features of the black inhabitants of Nubia, and the tight curly hair. A blue glass ferrule ends the stick.

STICK WITH ASIATIC AND NUBIAN CAPTIVE

(CARTER 50UU, J.D'E. 61732;
LENGTH 104 CM)

Egypt in antiquity was not easily invaded, protected by the sea and the deserts. In its isolation it was a privileged land, and for many centuries it escaped the turmoil and destruction brought about by the movements of peoples which affected Asia Minor in particular. For almost a millennium historic Egypt had no serious enemies, and it did not seek to extend its rule over neighbouring countries. Yet the Nubians to the south, the Libyans to the west, and the Asiatics (not always differentiated by race) to the east were seen to

be the traditional enemies, potential if not active. Consequently in the depiction of the myth of royal power images of these peoples were used with predictable regularity, being destroyed, dragged as prisoners, or, as here on the handle of a stick, bound and crushed by the royal hand.

The stick is gilded, the figures of the Asiatic and the Nubian are carved in the round to make the handle. The exposed body areas of the Nubian are inlaid in ebony, and those of the Asiatic in ivory.

WEAPONS

One of the major royal images of the New Kingdom was the king as warrior. He was the gallant champion of his country; nobody was braver or stronger.

After the rather pacific Amarna interlude the warlike image was revived for Tutankhamun: as warrior king he is best seen in the miniature paintings of foreign campaigns and hunting on the painted box found in the Antechamber. There is, however, no reason to believe that the young king himself took part in Asiatic or Nubian campaigns, but he may well have joined in the hunt in his chariot.

Nevertheless, the king had to be properly equipped, and in his tomb were placed many weapons, some of

280–281

Part of the decoration on the inside of the body of Tutankhamun's chariot. The figures here represent bound captives, Nubians and Asiatics; they are carved on a base of gesso-plaster and then gilded.

which were of small size, some fully capable of being used effectively, some designed for hunting, not battle, and some for ceremonial purposes. Most spectacular were the chariots: two very grand and probably ceremonial, one not so grand but still highly decorated, and three of lighter construction, probably for everyday use. The king in his chariot is usually shown drawing a bow, and bows were lavishly provided. There were fourteen of the ordinary kind, known as 'self' bows, and about thirty composite bows of complicated structure; several hundreds of arrows and arrowheads were also found, as well as quivers and bow cases, one of them most elaborately decorated.

The throw sticks or boomerangs found in the tomb are mostly of ceremonial kinds, too grand for use in the hunting field. So too are the so-called openwork shields, which could scarcely have withstood a powerful blow. The *khepesh* swords, used more like clubs than cutting weapons, were of Asiatic design, as were the composite bows mentioned above. Asia contributed much to the arsenal available to the Egyptians. Asia, and most probably the Hittites, provided the iron used for one of the two daggers found on Tutankhamun's body. The iron dagger is not now seen as so wonderful a piece as the golden dagger, but the use of iron on such a scale in Egypt at this date is unique, and this dagger would have been more wonderful to the Egyptians than the gold.

STATE CHARIOT

(CARTER 120, J.D'E. 61989; WIDTH OF BODY 105 CM,
DEPTH 46 CM, DIAMETER OF WHEELS 90 CM,
LENGTH OF AXLE 216 CM, LENGTH OF POLE 250 CM)

Of the four chariots found in the Antechamber, dismantled and in disarray, were two which were designated state chariots by Carter. There has been some confusion about which he described as 'the first', and which 'the second'. A careful comparison of notes, descriptions and photographs establishes that the one illustrated here is Carter's first state chariot. It is lavishly gilded and would have made a gorgeous sight when driven about in the bright Egyptian sunlight.

The most striking part is the body, within which the king would have stood. The framework is constructed of artificially bent wood with thin wood sidings covered with gesso-plaster and gilding. The floor is of leather thong mesh originally covered with an animal skin, possibly leopard, mat and several layers of linen cloth. The decoration of the outside of the body is mostly of a running scroll pattern, with a central panel containing the prenomen, name and Horus name of the king; above, a winged sun-disk, and at the sides *uraei* with the crowns and heraldic plants of Upper and Lower Egypt; beneath, a panel with lily flower decoration.

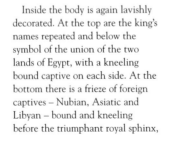

Inside the body is again lavishly decorated. At the top are the king's names repeated and below the symbol of the union of the two lands of Egypt, with a kneeling bound captive on each side. At the bottom there is a frieze of foreign captives – Nubian, Asiatic and Libyan – bound and kneeling before the triumphant royal sphinx, shown on each side and trampling further enemies. This frieze is bold and fluid in conception, and executed with great liveliness.

The six-spoked wheels are ingeniously made of artificially bent wood, the 'tires' made of leather. Gilding, lavishly applied, somewhat restricts the discovery of precise details of construction.

The pole of the chariot and the yoke which rested on the necks of the two chariot horses are also made of artificially bent wood and gilded.

The terminals of the yoke are carved in the forms of an Asiatic and a Nubian captive.

Beneath the chariot is shown the head of the domestic god Bes.

OPENWORK SHIELD
WITH SEATED KING

(CARTER 488B, J.D'E. 61578; HEIGHT 74 CM, WIDTH 50 CM)

The coronation and reign of Tutankhamun provide the theme for the openwork scene on this shield. It has suffered some damage, but the elements of the whole design can be reconstructed without much uncertainty. The gilding here is not of red gold.

The king is shown seated on an elaborate throne, the space between the legs filled with the heraldic device signifying the union of Upper and Lower Egypt, as can be seen in the so-called ecclesiastical throne from the tomb, though it is partly torn away. The king wears a ceremonial dress with 'cape' and broad collar; he holds the crook and the flail of royal authority, and on his head is a circlet of *uraeus*-serpents and the red crown with flying streamers. The tip of the crown and of its curled extension are broken away, as are the wings of the sun-disk set in the top of the curve of the shield.

Also broken away is one of two notched palm branches which closely flanked the king; the one on the right is complete, and shows at its bottom the tadpole, indicating one hundred thousand, and the *shen*-sign. These palm branches signify long reign for the king. The tadpole and *shen* are all that is left of the second palm branch. Two ostrich-feather fans form the outer limits of the scene, and between the right-hand fan and the palm branch is a panel with a text: 'His Majesty appears within Thebes, upon the platform for foretelling the wonders of the possessor of power, Nebkheperure, given life'.

The king is therefore shown at the time of coronation with all the promise of his reign lying ahead. The scene is placed on a large basket-sign here indicating 'festival', below which two plovers with trapped wings and raised hand-shaped claws offer adoration, and pray for children and a long life for the king. These are the *rekhyt*-birds, standing for the common people of Egypt, trapped but loyal.

OPENWORK SHIELD
WITH KING AS SPHINX

(CARTER 379A, J.D'E. 61577; HEIGHT 89 CM, WIDTH 54 CM)

Four functional shields were found in the Annexe of the tomb; these were solid, with animal skins covering the wood. There were also four non-functional openwork shields which Carter considered to be ceremonial. Whether this identification is correct or not – they would certainly not have served a useful purpose in battle – they have the shape of shields, and the scenes on some of them are distinctly bellicose.

This example is full of warlike symbolism, vaunting the royal power, and the text on the right confirms this purpose. Here the king is shown as a sphinx in active role, trampling two prone enemies beneath his paws. Usually one

Asiatic and one Nubian would be expected as the representatives of conquered nations; but the two here have black bodies, and seem to be Nubian, although they wear Egyptian-style kilts, which are gilded. Across the bottom of the shield runs an extended sign for 'foreign country'. The sphinx is shown very formally, with upraised tail and carefully placed paws. The royal head wears the *nemes*-headdress, and the double crown of Upper and Lower Egypt.

The panel in front of the sphinx identifies him as Tutankhamun, and describes him as 'the good god, who tramples the foreign lands and smites the great ones of all foreign lands, possessor of

power like the son of Nut, valiant like Monthu, visiting Thebes'. Monthu, the old Theban god, whose shrine was preeminent in Thebes before the advent of Amun, was seen as a war-god, and is often shown as a falcon hovering over the king in battle. Here a falcon behind the head of the sphinx holds the *shen*-sign of universal power in its talons; it is alighting on, or hovering over, an ostrich-feather fan. The falcon is not named, but it is reasonable to identify him as Monthu. In the circle of the shield at the top is the winged sun-disk, manifestation of Horus of Behdet.

The gilding on this shield is carried out in red gold, which gives the piece a somewhat angry aspect.

OPENWORK SHIELD WITH THE KING SLAYING LIONS

(CARTER 379B, J.D'E. 61576;
HEIGHT 88 CM, WIDTH 55 CM)

The scene in this openwork shield shows Tutankhamun as the destructive king in pursuit of the safety of his realm. The central feature is a figure of the king himself leaning forward to grasp two lions by their tails. In his right hand he wields aloft a *khepesh* sword with which he will smite and kill the lions, which symbolize the enemies of Egypt. A panel of text in front of the king's head expresses his prowess; 'the good god, strong of arm, powerful of heart, like Monthu visiting Thebes… who fights lions and smites wild cattle…' It is the traditional image of a warlike king, but here it is lions he smites, not Asiatics and Nubians. He is shown wearing the Nubian wig and, perhaps surprisingly, an *atef*-crown. The winged sun-disk in the curve at the top of the shield is Horus of Behdet, protective deity and one with whom the king may be identified. Behind the king's raised arm is perched the vulture goddess Nekhbet, also with wings outstretched in protection. She wears the white crown of Upper Egypt and has the royal flail emerging from her back. She is raised high on a basket on top of a clump of papyrus plants which properly stands for the North, the Delta, the realm of Nekhbet's fellow protective deity, the cobra Wadjyt.

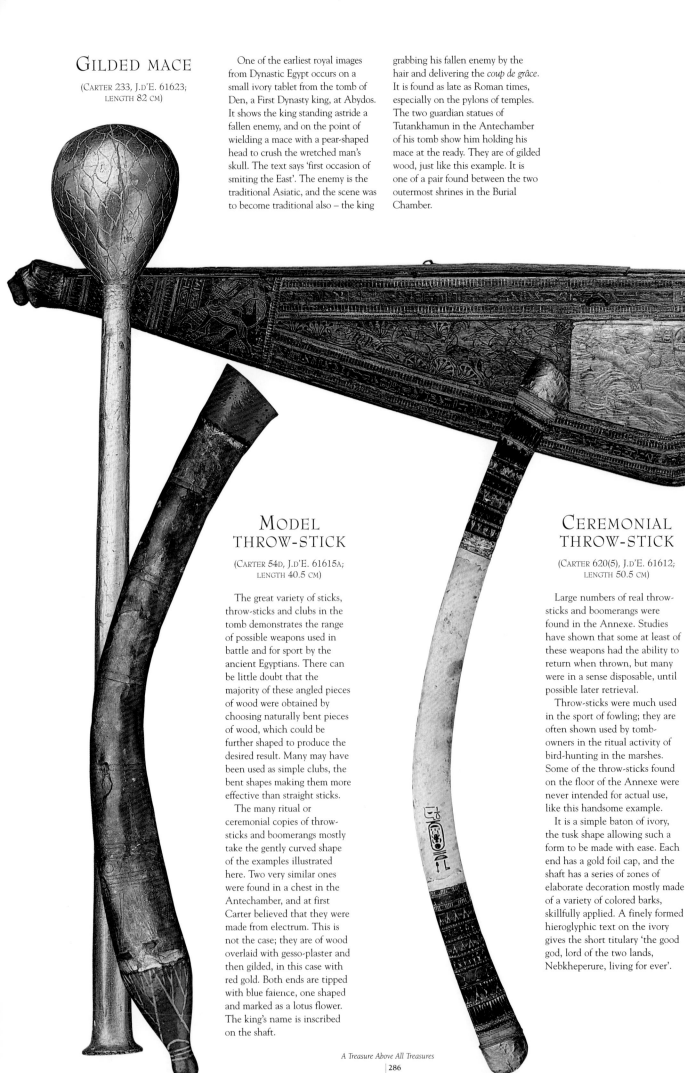

GILDED MACE

(Carter 233, J.d'E. 61623;
length 82 cm)

One of the earliest royal images from Dynastic Egypt occurs on a small ivory tablet from the tomb of Den, a First Dynasty king, at Abydos. It shows the king standing astride a fallen enemy, and on the point of wielding a mace with a pear-shaped head to crush the wretched man's skull. The text says 'first occasion of smiting the East'. The enemy is the traditional Asiatic, and the scene was to become traditional also – the king grabbing his fallen enemy by the hair and delivering the *coup de grâce*. It is found as late as Roman times, especially on the pylons of temples. The two guardian statues of Tutankhamun in the Antechamber of his tomb show him holding his mace at the ready. They are of gilded wood, just like this example. It is one of a pair found between the two outermost shrines in the Burial Chamber.

MODEL THROW-STICK

(Carter 54d, J.d'E. 61615a;
length 40.5 cm)

The great variety of sticks, throw-sticks and clubs in the tomb demonstrates the range of possible weapons used in battle and for sport by the ancient Egyptians. There can be little doubt that the majority of these angled pieces of wood were obtained by choosing naturally bent pieces of wood, which could be further shaped to produce the desired result. Many may have been used as simple clubs, the bent shapes making them more effective than straight sticks.

The many ritual or ceremonial copies of throw-sticks and boomerangs mostly take the gently curved shape of the examples illustrated here. Two very similar ones were found in a chest in the Antechamber, and at first Carter believed that they were made from electrum. This is not the case; they are of wood overlaid with gesso-plaster and then gilded, in this case with red gold. Both ends are tipped with blue faience, one shaped and marked as a lotus flower. The king's name is inscribed on the shaft.

CEREMONIAL THROW-STICK

(Carter 620(5), J.d'E. 61612;
length 50.5 cm)

Large numbers of real throw-sticks and boomerangs were found in the Annexe. Studies have shown that some at least of these weapons had the ability to return when thrown, but many were in a sense disposable, until possible later retrieval.

Throw-sticks were much used in the sport of fowling; they are often shown used by tomb-owners in the ritual activity of bird-hunting in the marshes. Some of the throw-sticks found on the floor of the Annexe were never intended for actual use, like this handsome example.

It is a simple baton of ivory, the tusk shape allowing such a form to be made with ease. Each end has a gold foil cap, and the shaft has a series of zones of elaborate decoration mostly made of a variety of colored barks, skillfully applied. A finely formed hieroglyphic text on the ivory gives the short titulary 'the good god, lord of the two lands, Nebkheperure, living for ever'.

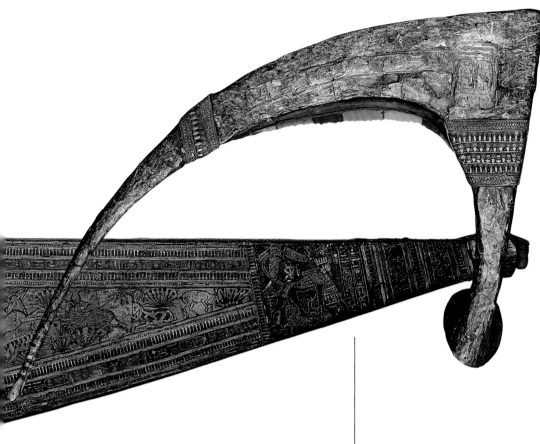

CEREMONIAL SICKLE

(CARTER 561, J.D'E. 61264;
LENGTH 27 CM)

The sickle was the implement commonly used for the cutting of barley and emmer-wheat. It was shown in vignettes in the Book of the Dead, in which the deceased works in the fields in the afterlife, and this fine example, although a model, was in the tomb presumably for posthumous use. Actual sickles have survived from antiquity, and they are very much of the shape of this piece. The handle is set eccentrically, as here, so that the tool could be manipulated more efficiently. The teeth of real sickles are serrated flints. This model, perhaps a ceremonial sickle, was found in the Annexe. It is made of wood, and has applied decoration in gold and electrum foil, with bands of varied designs of colored glass and calcite. The teeth are made of red and blue glass. An inscription on the gold foil gives Tutankhamun's titulary and calls him 'beloved of Hu', this deity being the embodiment of food.

BOW CASE

(CARTER 335, J.D'E. 61502;
LENGTH 153 CM)

Three composite bows of the kind introduced into Egypt from Asia about 250 years before the reign of Tutankhamun were found in this extraordinary box, which stood on its end in a corner of the Treasury. It is made of wood, covered with linen and plaster, and decorated all over with several series of scenes and designs in delicate marquetry of colored barks and green stained leather. Each end is in the form of a faience lion head, and there is a panel of gold on each side. These panels carry embossed scenes of the king in his chariot engaged in hunting with the bow. On both sides also are marquetry panels with scenes of dogs and animals in the chase, a great variety of wild life being depicted. Other panels show the king as a standing sphinx harassing Asiatic and Nubian captives. There are many zones of abstract decoration, and substantial inscriptions along the edges and between the various scenes, giving the king's titulary and vaunting his prowess as a king of action.

STICK WITH FINE DECORATION

(CARTER 50JJ, J.D'E. 61673;
LENGTH 116 CM)

Among the sticks found in the Antechamber there were several distinguished by exceptional decoration. This stick in particular is embellished with remarkable bands of geometrical and natural motifs, interspersed by lines of inscription carried out in very fine granulation. The motifs, in gold, include floral and insect elements and a variety of geometrical designs. The short texts encircling the stick contain conventional royal titles and the prenomen and nomen cartouches of the king.
The long text which runs down the length of the stick announces 'the appearance by the king himself to take firm action with his forces'.

STICK WITH GILDED HANDLE

(CARTER 98, J.D'E. 61730;
LENGTH 56.2 CM)

This fairly ordinary wooden throw-stick has little to distinguish it until the handle is examined closely. It is of gold plate, embellished with texts, abstract designs and small scenes, all carried out in granulation, some being of exceptional delicacy. Even the hieroglyphs and cartouches in the two bands of inscription are worked in granulation. There are two wide zones of lozenge decoration and two narrow zones of rosettes. Most remarkable are the two zones below the upper line of text, and above the lower line of text. Both contain desert scenes with animals and plants: chases involving tiny hares, ostriches, dogs and antelopes, all worked in the finest granulation. This was not a throw-away throw-stick.

IRON DAGGER AND SHEATH

(CARTER 256K, J.D'E. 61585;
LENGTH OF DAGGER 34.2 CM)

Two daggers were included among the bandages of Tutankhamun's mummy. This iron example may not be quite so striking artistically as the gold one, but culturally it has great significance. Many centuries were to pass before Egypt would enter the Iron Age, but here is a weapon of a metal that was already being used by some Asiatic peoples like the Hittites. In the tomb it was clearly as highly regarded as the gold dagger.

It was found lying along the mummy's right thigh; the metal was black, with only a few small touches of rust. The blade is not decorated, but the handle is embellished with zones of gold granulation arranged in chevron and diamond designs, separated by bands of cloisonné inlays of glass and semiprecious stones. The pommel is made of rock-crystal, carefully shaped but not turned, as Carter suggested.

The gold sheath has a feather pattern on one side with the head of a desert fox at the tip. The reverse side has a repeated design of open lily flowers contained within a rope border.

BRONZE *KHEPESH*

(CARTER 582A, J.D'E. 61588;
LENGTH 59.7 CM)

The serious involvement of the Egyptians with their Asiatic neighbors in what is called the Hyksos Period, just before the Eighteenth Dynasty, introduced them to many new weapons, methods of warfare and techniques of metal-working. Weapons of this kind were undoubtedly of Asiatic origin, but they were readily adopted by the Egyptians, and advanced processes in the production of cast bronze were employed for their manufacture.

This kind of sword was called *khepesh* in Egyptian, often translated as 'scimitar'. The scimitar, however, was a slashing, cutting weapon, while the *khepesh*, never apparently forged with a sharp edge, was used as an efficient clubbing weapon. Kings in the New Kingdom are often shown wielding the *khepesh*.

This fine example, which is cast as a single piece, is modestly decorated with sunk lines along the blade and a lily flower below the handle, which is inlaid with ebony.

GOLD DAGGER AND SHEATH

(Carter 256dd, J.d'E. 61584; length of dagger 31.9 cm)

This gold dagger was found tucked under a girdle at the mummy's waist. It is brilliant, and could be classified more as a jewel than an offensive weapon. The blade is of hardened gold, decorated simply with a palmette design and two chased lines. The handle has areas of elaborate decoration, of the standard of the finest goldsmiths. The inlays are of semiprecious stones and glass, and geometrical designs in gold granulation. The flaring pommel carries figures of falcons, and on its top is a design of lily flowers enclosing the two cartouches of Tutankhamun. The sheath is decorated on both sides differently: on one side, probably the front, a feather or *rishi*-design is carried out in repoussé work with glass and semiprecious stone inlays; at the bottom is the head of a desert fox or fennic, and there is a line of lilies at the top. The reverse side has scenes principally of the desert hunt: dogs and lions attack ibex, calves, bulls and antelope, the figures being in repoussé work.

BOATS

290–291
*A fully rigged sailing boat from the
Treasury of the tomb. It has a central
cabin and two kiosks at the stern and
prow, and two steering oars. Its sail is
lowered but not properly furled.*

In describing the many boats found in the Treasury and the Annexe of Tutankhamun's tomb, Carter made a good and reasoned attempt to describe the construction of the actual boats of which models had been found. Nothing, however, provides better evidence than the real thing, and no boat has been more informative than the great river craft found by the pyramid of Cheops in 1954. Here was a real boat, made of real cedar planks, fastened with ropes and ties, one which had been used in the lifetime of Cheops, and which could be used by him in his afterlife.

Tutankhamun and his celestial court were to have no shortage of craft for the many journeys to be undertaken after death. Egypt lived by the Nile, and most activities involving travel made use of boats. Of the thirty-five boats from the tomb, eighteen were in the Treasury, and were clearly seen to be 'wanted on voyage' to the afterlife. To that end, they were all pointing to the West – the direction in which the blessed dead were to travel.

The rest of the boats were retrieved from the Annexe, where they were jumbled up along with a great miscellany of objects, and not in the best of condition.

As model boats held little attraction for tomb robbers, none were probably taken, and it may be thought that a complete flotilla of royal craft was recovered. There were boats for all occasions in the Treasury: one papyrus skiff for recreational trips among the reed beds of the Delta; two boats with in-turned papyrus-formed prows and sterns, for night-time lunar travel; four solar barks for day-time journeys with the sun-god Re, with up-turned lotus-flower prows and sterns, a gilded throne for the king, and two steering posts; eight barges with no sails, but with steering oars, large stepped cabins with doors and windows, and small cabins or shelters fore and aft, all gaily painted. Most impressive were three sailing boats found complete with rigging and sails. These also had large central cabins with steps for loading cargo, and small open kiosks fore and aft in which the king or the captain could sit.

All the craft are made of solid wood covered with gesso-plaster and painted according to function with simple or elaborate patterns.

TRANSPORT BARGE

(CARTER 309, J.D'E. 61335;
LENGTH 110 CM)

A royal progression by river would have needed a very substantial flotilla of boats, many of which would be used by the Court officials and other staff, and for the transport of materials necessary for the comfort of all. Among the boats of Tutankhamun's fleet were seven craft usually called barges, with no sails but with double steering oars. This example, found in the Treasury, and pointing West, is characteristic of the group. Its principal feature is a double roofed central cabin with three windows on each side and a door at the back end. Both roof tops have cavetto-cornices, simply painted. The whole of the cabin is otherwise decorated with checker patterns which may represent textile hangings or the painted woven wicker superstructures of actual barges. At prow and stern there are smaller cabins or kiosks which probably served as shelters for members of the crew. The hull is also painted with checker and chevron patterns. It has been noted that some of the yellow decoration is carried out with orpiment, an arsenical natural material sometimes used in ancient Egypt.

SOLAR BARK

(CARTER 311, J.D'E. 61344;
LENGTH 155 CM)

The king's destiny in the afterlife was closely bound up with two deities, Osiris and Re. The former was the personification of the dead, and his role in the posthumous future of the king was one which post-dated that of the sun-god Re. The king's expectations were clear as far as Re was concerned, but quite distinct from what could be expected by non-royal persons. One of the principal expectations for the king was to join Re in the heavens, and to accompany him on his daily journey across the sky. The bark in which he travelled was of specific shape for the daytime; it had a raised prow and an elegantly re-curved stern. The form, like those of so many Egyptian boats, is derived from primitive craft made of papyrus for travelling about the marshes, and even on the Nile itself. This boat is one of several solar boats found in the Treasury with its bow pointing to the West. It is of wood, with some gilding at both ends, and painted decoration along its length. Texts on the bulkheads, fore and aft, give the two cartouches of Tutankhamun with standard epithets.

Solar Bark

(CARTER 307, J.D'E. 61346;
LENGTH 148 CM)

The destiny of the king in the solar bark with Re is one of the oldest royal beliefs of Egypt. An utterance in the Pyramid Texts states: 'The reed-floats of the sky are set down for Re so that he may cross on them to the horizon, to the place where the gods were born, and where he was born with them. The reed-floats of the sky are set down for this king so that he may cross on them to the horizon, to the place where the gods were born, and where he was born with them'. In an extract from the Book of the Dead inscribed on the door of the second shrine in the Burial Chamber, the Osiris Tutankhamun is said to 'go forward in peace, sailing the barge of Re'.

This solar bark – the reed-float of the Pyramid Texts – is very similar to the one illustrated on the left. Like it, it has one throne placed in the middle. Clearly the king would be on his own in the sky 'sailing the bark of Re'. On the gilded stern and prow are inscribed Tutankhamun's names with standard titles.

Like the other boats in the Treasury, it was placed facing West.

FURNITURE AND BOXES

294
A vignette from the Gilded Shrine showing Tutankhamun seated on a throne. It has a low back, a cushion, and sides decorated with a scaled or rishi pattern.

295
Gilded wooden casket placed in the Antechamber. It is richly decorated with colored faience inlays. The sloping lid could be secured with two violet faience knobs and a sealed cord.

Culturally one can come very close to the ancient Egyptians through furniture. The best products of the ancient cabinet-makers may not quite come up to the work of the French *ébénistes* of the eighteenth century, but there is nothing primitive about them. The shapes of chairs, beds, stools and chests could all bear reproduction today.

Tutankhamun's tomb contained a great quantity of furniture, some of which would only be suitable for the very great house or palace. There were six beds, low to the ground with headboards usually decorated with figures of the household deities, Thoeris and Bes; one can be folded up, and was presumably used in travelling; its hinges are of copper. With the beds go head-rests, used to raise the head up. Of the six chairs, the Golden Throne is outstanding; but scarcely less striking in an opulent way is the ecclesiastical throne, made in the form of a grand folding chair. The other chairs were all splendidly designed, and

one is of small size and possibly used by the king in childhood. For informal sitting the Egyptians used stools, and the twelve examples from the tomb cover most of the types in use in the New Kingdom, including three-legged stools, most useful on irregular surfaces. The seats of most of the stools are coved – curved in both directions – to seat a person comfortably.

The chests and boxes from the tomb range from the painted box with remarkable miniature paintings to simple chests for domestic storage. There were more than fifty found, many containing precious objects. They provide a wonderful conspectus of the skills of the Egyptian craftsman. The techniques of joinery are precise, and even modest materials could be transformed by the application of veneers of ivory and ebony, of gilding, of inlays of faience, glass and semi-precious stones, and of simple or masterful painting.

THE GOLDEN THRONE

(CARTER 91, J.D'E. 62028;
HEIGHT 104 CM, WIDTH 53 CM,
DEPTH 65 CM)

For many people this throne, along with Tutankhamun's golden mask, typifies the beauty and opulence of the tomb. And yet its presence in the tomb raises questions which have no obvious answers. For example, why was it tucked away, covered with a piece of old linen, beneath the Thoeris couch in the Antechamber? It was as if it had been slipped surreptitiously into the tomb. But many other fine pieces were similarly stuffed into odd corners, and given little honor in their placings. One special reason provides part of the answer for why it seems to have been smuggled into the tomb.

The clue lies in the great scene on the back of the throne.

What is depicted there is not something to be associated with the court in Thebes or Memphis, but something that belongs to El-Amarna and the later years of the reign of Akhenaten. The king sits on a throne within a kiosk with floral side pillars and a cornice of *uraei* and flowers; he is being anointed by his queen with perfumed ointment. He wears an elaborate form of the *atef*-crown, and she a feathered headdress with an *uraeus* circlet and lyre-shaped horns.

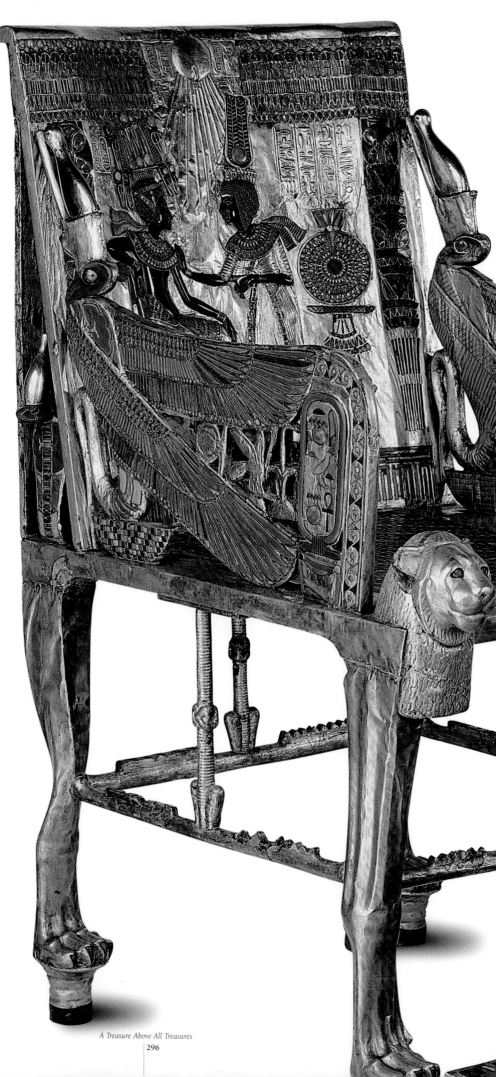

A Treasure Above All Treasures

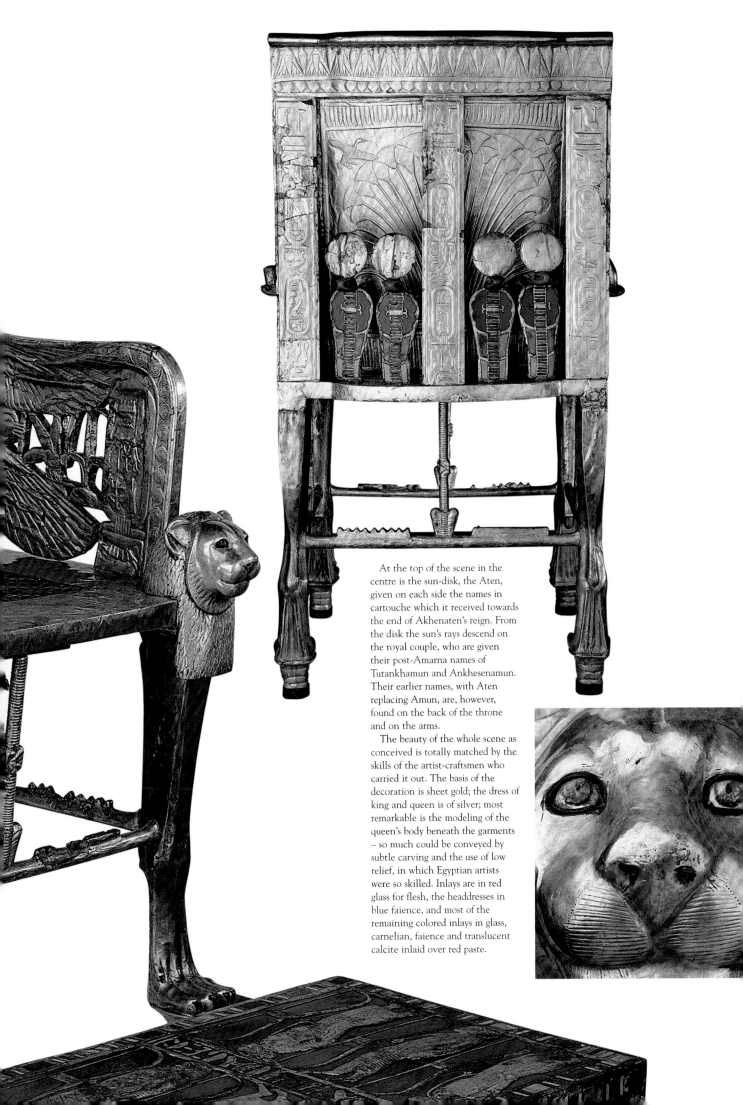

At the top of the scene in the centre is the sun-disk, the Aten, given on each side the names in cartouche which it received towards the end of Akhenaten's reign. From the disk the sun's rays descend on the royal couple, who are given their post-Amarna names of Tutankhamun and Ankhesenamun. Their earlier names, with Aten replacing Amun, are, however, found on the back of the throne and on the arms.

The beauty of the whole scene as conceived is totally matched by the skills of the artist-craftsmen who carried it out. The basis of the decoration is sheet gold; the dress of king and queen is of silver; most remarkable is the modeling of the queen's body beneath the garments – so much could be conveyed by subtle carving and the use of low relief, in which Egyptian artists were so skilled. Inlays are in red glass for flesh, the headdresses in blue faience, and most of the remaining colored inlays in glass, carnelian, faience and translucent calcite inlaid over red paste.

THE GILDED SHRINE

(CARTER 108, J.D'E, 61481; HEIGHT 50.5 CM, WIDTH 26.5 CM,
DEPTH 32 CM, LENGTH OF SLEDGE 48 CM)

In Tutankhamun's tomb there were a number of pieces each of which on its own might well have been considered a good return for the years of labour endured by Carter. This shrine easily falls into this top category. It contains a little gilded stand to hold a figure, probably of gold, and of a god. But which god? The scenes and texts on the shrine give no sure clue. It might be suggested, however, that the shrine was a private point of devotion, placed within the king's appartments; it was found in the Antechamber, not in the most holy parts of the tomb.

It is in the form of the Upper Egyptian shrine, originally of the vulture goddess Nekhbet; and suitably there are fourteen forms of the goddess with outstretched wings on the shrine's roof. All the decoration of the shrine – and the whole is covered with decoration – is carried out in gold foil fixed by gesso-plaster and linen reinforcement to the plain wooden shell of the shrine.

The scenes are wonderful examples of repoussé-work and chasing; they provide a mixture of semi-formal, ceremonial and private domestic scenes. On one side the king with Ankhesenamun hunts birds: above, in a papyrus skiff, below, seated on a folding stool with the queen handing him his next arrow. On the other side are intimate scenes of the queen offering gifts to the king and receiving a drink from him in her open cupped hand. On the back of the shrine the queen gently touches the king, bringing a cone of scented unguent; below, she presents him with jubilee festivals and millions of years of reign. Both leaves of the door, and the inside of one leaf, carry further scenes of the queen presenting various ritual objects to the king. The gold from the inner side of the left leaf has been lost, taken presumably in antiquity.

The doors are fastened with two silver bolts fitting into little gold staples, and the shrine stands on a wooden sledge covered with silver foil.

THE PAINTED BOX

(CARTER 21, J.D'E. 61467; LENGTH 61 CM,
WIDTH 43 CM, HEIGHT 44.5 CM)

One of the objects which especially caught the attention of the excavators in the Antechamber was this box, which Carter called the 'painted casket'. And this emphasis in spite of all the dazzling gold on every side! But Carter was first and foremost an artist, and it was as an artist that he looked at and appreciated the remarkable miniature paintings which embellished what was in other respects a fairly ordinary box. He could see the skill of the artist who had painted the scenes in tempera on a plaster ground, and he could appreciate the use of color and the attention to fine detail. No brushes were available to the ancient artist, apart from rushes, chewed and trimmed; and yet, as Carter wrote: 'a magnifying glass is essential to a due appreciation of the smaller details, such as the stippling of the lions' coats, or the decoration of the horses' trappings'.

The surviving contents of the box suggested that it had been used primarily to store articles of the young king's wardrobe, and it is difficult to see what relationship there was between what was in the box and what was painted on it. There are four principal scenes proclaiming the manly prowess of the king: two show him as the great conqueror in battle, and two as the fearless huntsman in the desert. On one side Tutankhamun in his chariot and with drawn bow

charges into a mêlée of Asiatics 'trampling on hundreds of thousands, putting them into confusion'; on the other side, in a parallel scene, the king launches himself into a tangled crowd of black enemies 'destroying this land of vile Kush'. In the former scene three registers of chariotmen support the king, and in the latter two of chariotmen and one of foot soldiers.

The two scenes on the lid show hunts in the desert: one is general, the quarry consisting of bubal-antelopes, gazelles, wild asses, ostriches and a lone hyena who is making its escape; the other is specifically a lion hunt of the kind known to have taken place in Syria in the New Kingdom.

The two ends of the box carry heraldic confrontations of the royal sphinx trampling on fallen enemies. Tutankhamun is 'the image of Re' and the 'son of Amun'.

TRAVELLING CANOPY

(Carter 123, J.d'E. 60705;
base 98.5 cm, height 201 cm)

In Egypt the sun is a blessing
and a curse. It brings life to the
land, and in antiquity was the
omnipotent deity Re, and in the
Amarna Period the Aten disk. It
also made life uncomfortable, and
for general living the Egyptian
house had no large windows.

FOOTSTOOL WITH ENEMIES

(Carter 378, J.d'E. 62045;
length 58.7 cm, width 31.7 cm)

Associated with, and probably
belonging to, the 'ecclesiastical
throne' was this footstool. It is
made of a very ordinary wood but
with a top surface rich in
decoration and full of significance.
There are nine figures of captives,
the conventional enemies of
Pharaoh, depicted as distinctive
racial types – but general rather
than particular. Four are of black
peoples and five of Asiatics and
Libyans. Eight wear long
garments, each with somewhat
different arrangements of folds
and pleatings. One, however,
wears what appears to be a loose
cloak which leaves some of the
body exposed. Their hands are
bound together and their necks
are linked by a cord. The text on
the dividing bar in the centre is
quite explicit: 'all lands and all
mountainous countries, and the
great ones of Retjenu (Syria) are
together as one beneath your feet,
like Re for ever'. The bodies are
gilded, and exposed flesh is of
ebony or cedar; the background is
made of plaques of blue faience.

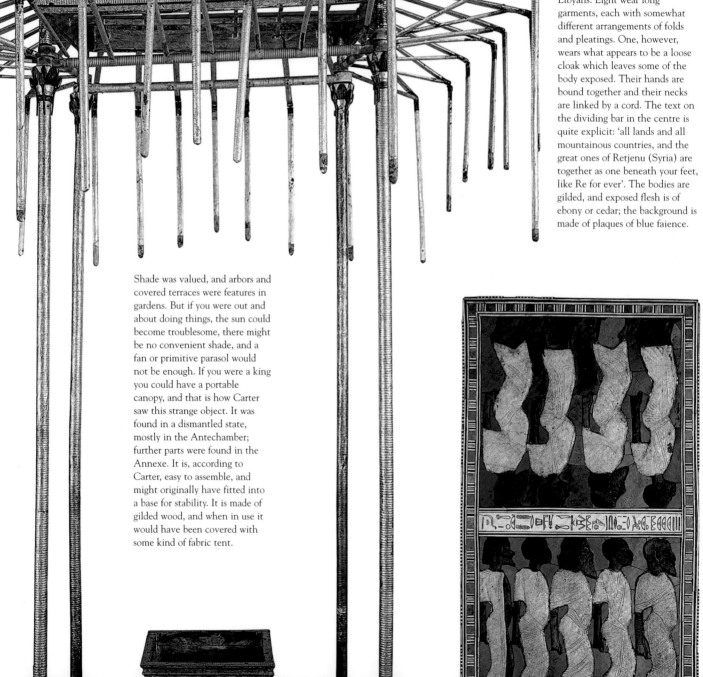

Shade was valued, and arbors and
covered terraces were features in
gardens. But if you were out and
about doing things, the sun could
become troublesome, there might
be no convenient shade, and a
fan or primitive parasol would
not be enough. If you were a king
you could have a portable
canopy, and that is how Carter
saw this strange object. It was
found in a dismantled state,
mostly in the Antechamber;
further parts were found in the
Annexe. It is, according to
Carter, easy to assemble, and
might originally have fitted into
a base for stability. It is made of
gilded wood, and when in use it
would have been covered with
some kind of fabric tent.

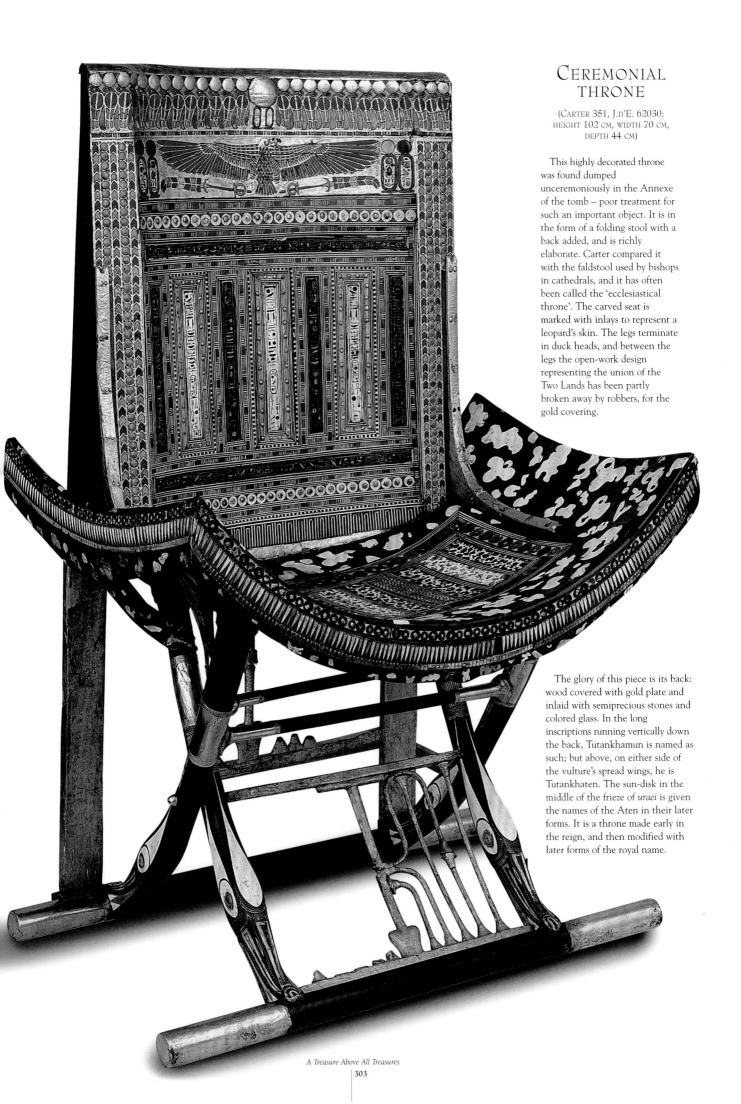

CEREMONIAL THRONE

(CARTER 351, J.D'E. 62030;
HEIGHT 102 CM, WIDTH 70 CM,
DEPTH 44 CM)

This highly decorated throne was found dumped unceremoniously in the Annexe of the tomb – poor treatment for such an important object. It is in the form of a folding stool with a back added, and is richly elaborate. Carter compared it with the faldstool used by bishops in cathedrals, and it has often been called the 'ecclesiastical throne'. The carved seat is marked with inlays to represent a leopard's skin. The legs terminate in duck heads, and between the legs the open-work design representing the union of the Two Lands has been partly broken away by robbers, for the gold covering.

The glory of this piece is its back: wood covered with gold plate and inlaid with semiprecious stones and colored glass. In the long inscriptions running vertically down the back, Tutankhamun is named as such; but above, on either side of the vulture's spread wings, he is Tutankhaten. The sun-disk in the middle of the frieze of *uraei* is given the names of the Aten in their later forms. It is a throne made early in the reign, and then modified with later forms of the royal name.

Stools were the most common seats in Egyptian houses. In the New Kingdom folding stools were much used, the tops consisting of leather or animal fur.

In typical Egyptian manner, the real was reproduced in imitation, and false folding stools were made with fixed seats decorated like animal skins.

This superior example from the Antechamber is made of ebony, and the seat, which is double coved, imitates a leopard skin, with the markings made of ivory inlays. At one side a false tail

CHAIR WITH THE GOD HEH

(CARTER 87, J.D'E. 62029;
HEIGHT 96 CM, WIDTH 47.6 CM, DEPTH 50.8 CM)

In many respects this is the most aesthetically satisfying chair from the tomb. It may lack the splendor of the Golden Throne, and the intricate decoration of the ceremonial throne, but it has elegance, style and the distinction of restrained decoration. It is a typical chair of the New Kingdom, with coved seat, sloping back and lion legs. It is made of a fine-grained hard wood, possibly cedar, and embellished tastefully with some gilding. Between the legs there was originally gilded fretted decoration in the form of the heraldic representation of the union of the Two Lands, but most of the gilded wood was torn away by thieves in antiquity. The back of the chair has a figure of the god Heh kneeling on the sign for 'gold'. He holds notched palm-branches in his hands, the usual divine indication of long reign for the ruling king. A large *ankh*-sign of 'life' hangs on his right arm. Most beautifully carved texts around Heh and on the frame of the chair contain Tutankhamun's titulary and proclaim his divine origins. It was found carelessly tumbled in the Antechamber.

hangs down with an ivory tuft.

It is also possible that at each corner a paw hung down, but that these were torn away in the robbery because the claws were of gold. The legs terminate in duck heads inlaid with ivory, their beaks with pink-stained tongues clasped on the cross bars, which are embellished with gold. The foot-stool shown here was not found with the stool. It is of simple design with some ivory inlay.

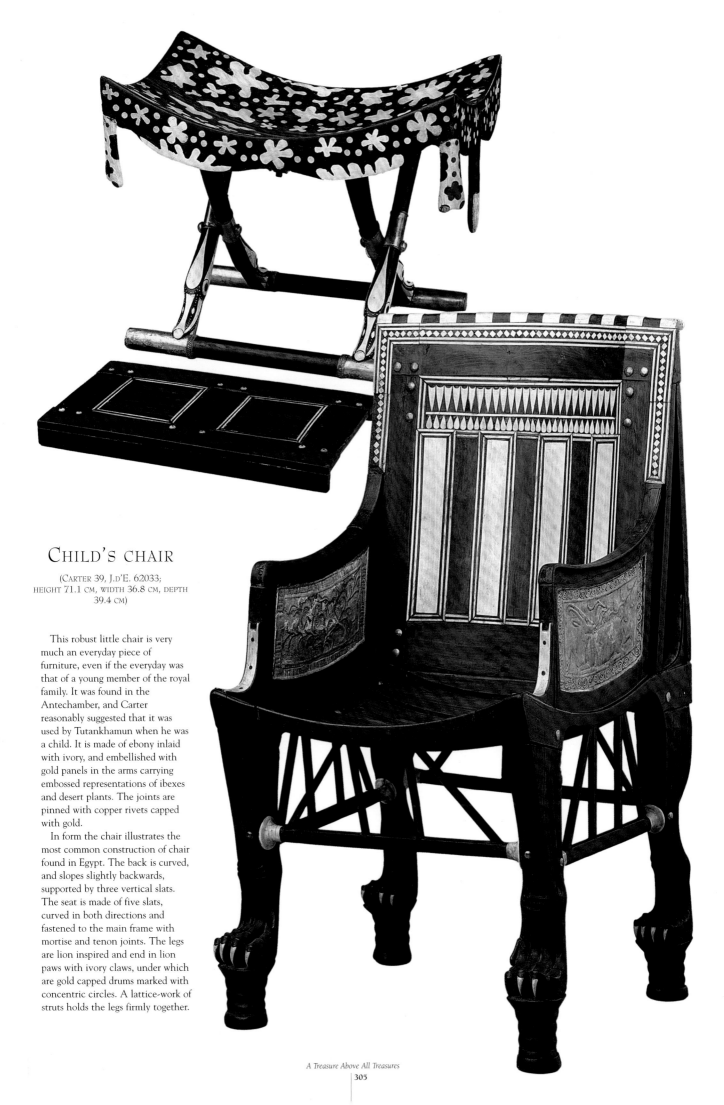

CHILD'S CHAIR

(CARTER 39, J.D'E. 62033;
HEIGHT 71.1 CM, WIDTH 36.8 CM, DEPTH
39.4 CM)

This robust little chair is very much an everyday piece of furniture, even if the everyday was that of a young member of the royal family. It was found in the Antechamber, and Carter reasonably suggested that it was used by Tutankhamun when he was a child. It is made of ebony inlaid with ivory, and embellished with gold panels in the arms carrying embossed representations of ibexes and desert plants. The joints are pinned with copper rivets capped with gold.

In form the chair illustrates the most common construction of chair found in Egypt. The back is curved, and slopes slightly backwards, supported by three vertical slats. The seat is made of five slats, curved in both directions and fastened to the main frame with mortise and tenon joints. The legs are lion inspired and end in lion paws with ivory claws, under which are gold capped drums marked with concentric circles. A lattice-work of struts holds the legs firmly together.

BED WITH LION HEADS

(CARTER 497; LENGTH 177 CM, WIDTH 103 CM, HEIGHT 37 CM)

Among the jumble in the Annexe were four beds. This one was in poor condition, and its footboard had been wrenched away from it.

The footboards of Egyptian beds are often incorrectly called headboards. In ancient times in Egypt, however, you slept with your head-rest at the open end and with your feet pointing towards the footboard.

It is characteristic of Egyptian beds that they were made with curves to hold the body in the bed, and the cross trusses underneath are bowed to take the sag of the mattress when a body is lying on it.

This bed is gessoed and gilded all over. It is low to the ground, and the legs are leonine, stumpy and thick. The two legs at the head end are continued through above the frame to show lion heads – almost finials – which would protect the sleeping occupant of the bed. The lions' eyes are inlaid with quartz and colored glass.

BED WITH FLORAL FOOTBOARD

(CARTER 466, J.D'E. 62014; LENGTH 175 CM, HEIGHT 68.6 CM)

Carter considered this bed to have the best proportions of all the non-ritual beds found in the tomb. It stands relatively high on its lion legs, and it is elegantly bowed from front to back. The so-called drums underneath the lion paws here and on much other furniture were designed to facilitate the stabilization of the bed on uneven floors.

The whole bed, including the mattress, is gilded. When in use it would have been lavishly piled with linen to soften the surface. The footboard is divided into panels of decoration embossed in the gold foil. In the centre is the conventional heraldic design of the union of the Two Lands of Upper and Lower Egypt. On either side are two panels, one showing a clump of papyrus, the other, narrower, a trophy bouquet of papyrus and lotus flowers. In these designs Carter claimed to see the influence of Amarna naturalistic art.

BED WITH OPENWORK FIGURED FOOTBOARD

(CARTER 47, J.D'E. 62016; LENGTH 185 CM,
WIDTH 90.1 CM, HEIGHT 74.9 CM)

Of the six beds found in Tutankhamun's tomb, this one may have been a truly functional piece of domestic furniture. There was also a folding bed which could have been used on travel or campaign, but not at home and certainly not in the palace. This bed, from the Antechamber, has the characteristic bowed shape, with a mattress of woven string between the main frame. It is made of ebony and has lion legs and feet. Its most notable feature is the footboard: it has three panels, each containing three figures in openwork – centrally the god Bes, a leonine dwarf with a lotus headdress, a domestic deity charged to protect the home; he is flanked by two rampant lions with similar headdresses, their front paws resting on sa-signs signifying 'protection'. These finely carved figures are embellished in part with gold leaf, and all have tongues of pink-stained ivory. Here is powerful protection for whoever slept on this bed.

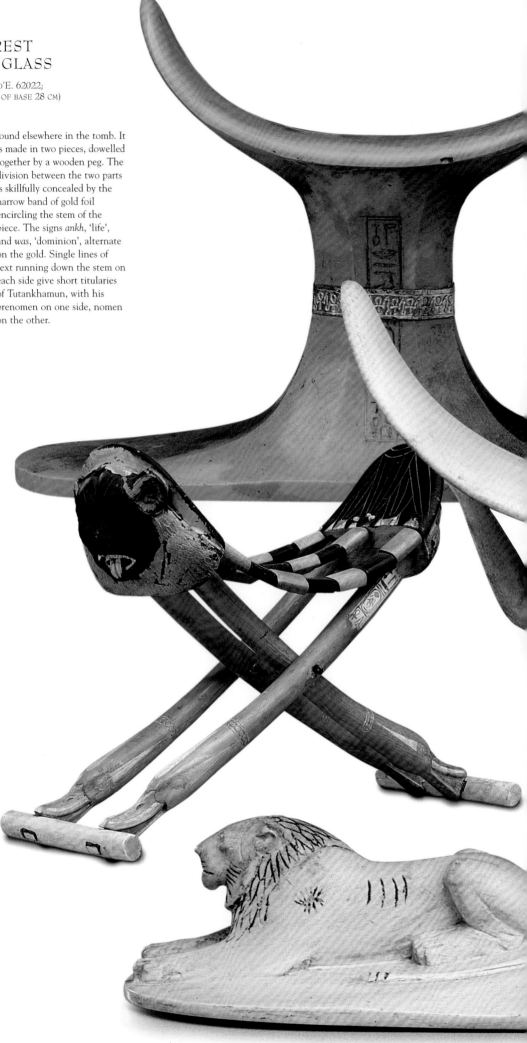

HEADREST
OF BLUE GLASS

(CARTER 403A, J.D'E. 62022;
HEIGHT 18 CM, WIDTH OF BASE 28 CM)

All four of the headrests illustrated here were found in the cabinet on tall legs. Carter did not think that they were originally intended for this cabinet, but were stored there after the robberies. They form a remarkable group, put together no doubt fortuitously by the Necropolis guards.

This example is made of turquoise-blue glass, an unusually large piece for this material, although outclassed by another headrest in violet glass found elsewhere in the tomb. It is made in two pieces, dowelled together by a wooden peg. The division between the two parts is skillfully concealed by the narrow band of gold foil encircling the stem of the piece. The signs *ankh*, 'life', and *was*, 'dominion', alternate on the gold. Single lines of text running down the stem on each side give short titularies of Tutankhamun, with his prenomen on one side, nomen on the other.

HEADREST AS A
FOLDING STOOL

(CARTER 403D, J.D'E. 62023;
HEIGHT 20 CM, WIDTH 26 CM)

This headrest is almost a joke-piece. The shape is that of the folding stool common in the Eighteenth Dynasty. It is made almost entirely of ivory, stained to great effect; it cannot be folded, but at the cross points where the legs would have folded small bronze pins are inserted. The legs terminate in duck heads, the beaks being dowelled to the white-painted wooden batons which form the stands. The object is outstanding for the two heads of Bes which ornament the ends of the actual rest. The faces are stained green, like some of the segments of the rest. Bes, as ever, sticks out his tongue – a vulgar gesture to warn off demons, snakes, scorpions and other harmful agents which could damage the sleeping person. Bes was, in spite of his grotesque appearance, a much loved domestic deity: by terror he turned terror away. The backs of the Bes heads are marked with lotus flowers. Tutankhamun's prenomen is inscribed at the top of one leg.

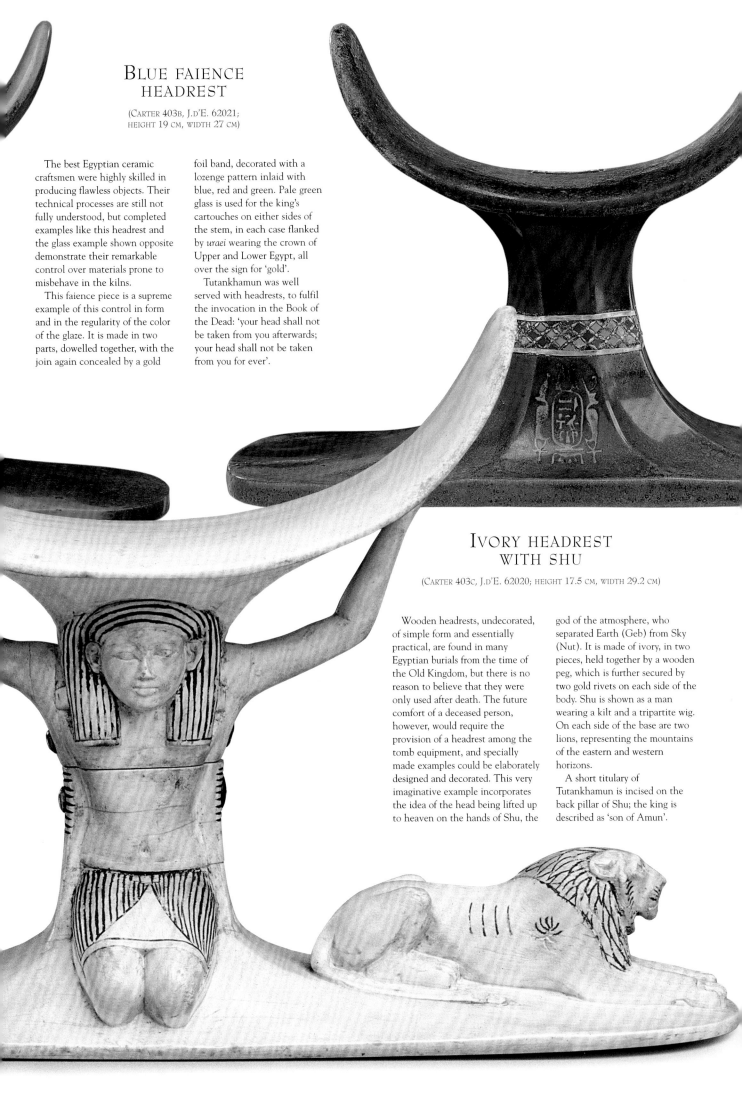

BLUE FAIENCE HEADREST

(CARTER 403B, J.D'E. 62021;
HEIGHT 19 CM, WIDTH 27 CM)

The best Egyptian ceramic craftsmen were highly skilled in producing flawless objects. Their technical processes are still not fully understood, but completed examples like this headrest and the glass example shown opposite demonstrate their remarkable control over materials prone to misbehave in the kilns.

This faience piece is a supreme example of this control in form and in the regularity of the color of the glaze. It is made in two parts, dowelled together, with the join again concealed by a gold foil band, decorated with a lozenge pattern inlaid with blue, red and green. Pale green glass is used for the king's cartouches on either sides of the stem, in each case flanked by *uraei* wearing the crown of Upper and Lower Egypt, all over the sign for 'gold'.

Tutankhamun was well served with headrests, to fulfil the invocation in the Book of the Dead: 'your head shall not be taken from you afterwards; your head shall not be taken from you for ever'.

IVORY HEADREST WITH SHU

(CARTER 403C, J.D'E. 62020; HEIGHT 17.5 CM, WIDTH 29.2 CM)

Wooden headrests, undecorated, of simple form and essentially practical, are found in many Egyptian burials from the time of the Old Kingdom, but there is no reason to believe that they were only used after death. The future comfort of a deceased person, however, would require the provision of a headrest among the tomb equipment, and specially made examples could be elaborately designed and decorated. This very imaginative example incorporates the idea of the head being lifted up to heaven on the hands of Shu, the god of the atmosphere, who separated Earth (Geb) from Sky (Nut). It is made of ivory, in two pieces, held together by a wooden peg, which is further secured by two gold rivets on each side of the body. Shu is shown as a man wearing a kilt and a tripartite wig. On each side of the base are two lions, representing the mountains of the eastern and western horizons.

A short titulary of Tutankhamun is incised on the back pillar of Shu; the king is described as 'son of Amun'.

CARTOUCHE-SHAPED BOX

(CARTER 269, J.D'E. 61490;
LENGTH 64.5 CM, WIDTH 29.8 CM, HEIGHT 31.7 CM)

This unusually shaped box, found in the Treasury, contained many pieces of jewelry, including the sets of earrings illustrated earlier. The reddish wood of which it is made is probably coniferous; there are ebony bands to embellish and strengthen the construction. The cartouche-shaped lid carries the name of Tutankhamun, executed in the most handsome hieroglyphs, made up of ebony and stained ivory. Less grand, but still elegantly formed, hieroglyphs are used for the many texts which are incised and filled with blue paint on the upper rim of the lid, surrounding the cartouche, and in three bands on the body of the box. They all include extended titularies of the king with a wealth of epithets establishing his authority at home and his power over foreign lands. The panel on the end of the box contains the king's two cartouches and his Horus name, beneath an extended sky-sign. It is thought that this box may have been used on state occasions to store changes of jewels.

CHEST WITH MARQUETRY PANELS

(CARTER 267, J.D'E. 61462;
LENGTH 44.45 CM, WIDTH 29.8 CM,
HEIGHT 27.9 CM)

A hieratic text on the lid of this box notes: 'Gold: jewelry of [or for] the funeral procession, made in the bed-chamber of Nebkheperure'. Jewels were found in it when the Treasury was cleared, but probably not those for which it was intended. But who can say? The chest, like so many in the tomb, and indeed in Egypt generally, was made of a fairly ordinary wood, and then embellished to give it a fine, finished, appearance. Good wood for joinery was not easily available in Egypt, and by this form of construction a fine external form could be made on a simple base. In this case the fine external form consists of strips of ivory veneer on the box and the domed lid, and then panels outlined in thin strips of ebony and ivory, containing bone patterned marquetry. Carter estimated that there were about 47,000 separate pieces of tiny inlay of ebony and other woods, each individually placed, stuck in position and subsequently polished. The knobs are made of pink-stained ivory.

ORNATE CHEST

(CARTER 551 (BOX), 540 (LID), J.D'E. 61477; LENGTH
72 CM, WIDTH 40.6 CM, HEIGHT 63.5 CM)

The scenes on this masterpiece of
Egyptian decorative art are focused
on the domestic life of the king and
queen, rather than the warlike
activities given such prominence in
the tomb. The chest found in the
Annexe separated from its humped
lid is made of an ordinary soft wood
veneered and embellished with
ebony and ivory, much of it stained
in muted colors; there are also
colored faience inlays and gilding on
the cornice. The principal scene on
the end of the chest shows the royal
couple seated in a garden; the king
shoots his bow at birds and, it would
seem, fish in the ornamental pool.
The whole field is packed with
flowers, some growing and others in
trophies and bouquets. The other
sides of the chest have further floral
arrangements and friezes of animals
in a hunting context, as found
elsewhere in the tomb. The domestic
theme is continued on the lid of the
box, which shows the king and
queen in a garden; she hands him
bouquets.

CHEST WITH
OPENWORK DESIGN

(CARTER 271, J.D'E. 61344; HEIGHT 42.5 CM,
LENGTH 48.2 CM, WIDTH 44.4 CM)

Like all the boxes in the tomb this
chest from the Treasury was rifled and
repacked. Inside it is divided into
sixteen compartments, thought to have
contained objects of precious metal.
On discovery it held the king's personal
writing equipment and a few other
objects not originally intended for it.

It is made of a softish plain wood,
richly embellished with ivory veneer
and gilded wood. Its most noticeable
decorative feature consists in the
repeated groups of four gilded
hieroglyphs: two *was*-scepters
flanking an *ankh*, all placed above a
basket signifying 'all', the group
meaning 'all life and dominion'. This
motif makes up the decoration on all
the sides and also the top of the box.
The feet of the box are shod with
bronze, and the knobs used to secure
the box with sealed cord are of pink-
stained ivory. The extensive texts
which fill all the available surfaces
contain the royal titulary, repeated
many times with variants of the
epithets. In a few places the name
Ankhesenamun is also included.

VESSELS AND OTHER OBJECTS OF CALCITE

The material used in Egypt from Predynastic times for the production of the majority of stone vessels has traditionally been called alabaster, but it is more correctly called calcite. It is a crystalline form of calcium carbonate, is white to yellow in color, translucent, and often very attractively banded or zoned. Up until the New Kingdom most Egyptian 'alabaster' was quarried at Hatnub, about twenty kilometers from El-Amarna.

This stone is relatively easy to work, and, as can be seen from the vessels and other objects found in Tutankhamun's tomb, it could be carved with great virtuosity. The largest and most important calcite object from the tomb is the Canopic Chest. More humble are the sixty or so vessels of traditional, simple forms, receptacles for oils, unguents and other materials for the use of the dead king in the afterlife. Some were made and inscribed in earlier reigns and had clearly been taken from storerooms for convenience.
In addition, there were about twenty others, some of which were also used for precious materials, but were carved in fantastic and extravagant shapes which displayed remarkable craftsmanship but not always a taste that can still be appreciated. A common design element is the heraldic device signifying the union of Upper and Lower Egypt; it consists of a central sign with the meaning 'unite', on each side of which are tied lilies and papyrus stems and flowers, representing the Two Lands.

Some of the vessels are lamps, and some copy forms which might otherwise be made of less durable materials, like the chest and the most attractive ointment pot with a lion on its lid. Many of these intricate pieces were carelessly strewn around the tomb, possibly by the ancient robbers, and it is remarkable that a piece like the standing lion unguent vessel has survived virtually intact. One of the most elegant of the vessels is the so-called wishing cup which carries a good-will text on its rim. Some, like the ornate boat in a tank, have no obvious purpose; they were, perhaps, simply ornamental.

312
Bulbous calcite perfume vessel flanked by clumps of papyrus plants and the notched palm branches which were used symbolically to represent the long life of the king, terminating in tadpoles and shen-signs.

313
Elaborately designed perfume vase of calcite. It is jug-shaped, with the stems and flowers of lily and papyrus on either side. The whole is supported by an unidentified male figure with a lotus chalice on its head.

PERFUME VESSEL WITH NILE GODS

(CARTER 210, J.D'E. 62114;
HEIGHT 70 CM, WIDTH 36.8 CM)

Complicated vessels like this container were among the objects from the tomb which for many years were rejected by puritanical connoisseurs and austere designers as being outrageously vulgar. It is now easier to observe something as intricate as this without condemning it out of hand, while at the same time wondering why so much effort had to be put into the making of a simple bottle for scented oil. Who could easily pour a few drops of the precious liquid from something as unwieldy as this?

Symbolism here takes precedence over functionalism. The rebus of the main design represents the union of the Two Lands, spelled out in a wealth of symbols. The body of the vessel itself represents the *sma*-sign of unity; on its left stands a plump Nile god wearing a clump of papyrus on his head and catching hold of the fret of papyrus plants tied to the *sma*-sign. This all stands for Lower Egypt, the Delta, and this point is emphasized by the *uraeus* wearing the red crown of Lower Egypt perched on a scepter set behind the papyrus plants. On the right is Upper Egypt, with another

Nile god with a lily clump on his head, and grasping lilies tied to the *sma*-sign; here the *uraeus* wears the white crown of Upper Egypt. Overseeing the whole is a vulture with outstretched protective wings perched on the lip of the vessel. It wears an *atef*-crown and should be Nekhbet. The text on the neck of the vessel proclaims of the king: 'you have united Upper and Lower Egypt under your sandals; you will be on the throne of Horus like Re for ever'. Both Tutankhamun and Ankhesenamun are named on the body of the vessel. The fretted base shows the royal prenomen supported by two figures of Horus, all resting on signs for 'gold'.

This extravagant piece is made out of four pieces of calcite cemented together. The principal elements are highlighted with gilding and inlays of colored paste or faience. A fine detail is the gilding of the bodies of the two *uraei*, which curl down the lengths of the scepters on which they perch.

This vessel stood in front of the doors of the second shrine in the Burial Chamber.

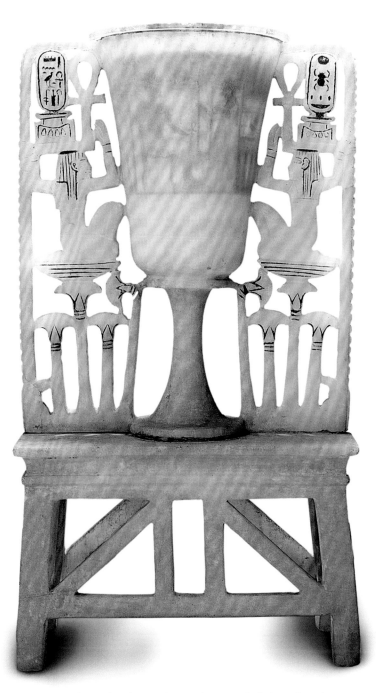

LAMP WITH PAINTED SCENE

(CARTER 173, J.D'E. 62111;
HEIGHT 51.4 CM, WIDTH 28.8 CM)

During the New Kingdom most domestic lamps were in the form of simple open pottery saucers in which oil – probably sesame or castor – was burned with a floating wick of linen. The lighting arrangements in great houses would be expected to be more elaborate, and two pieces from Tutankhamun's tomb confirm this supposition.

The triple lamp is an elegant piece, fit to grace an ancient drawing room. The lamp shown here, however, is more formal, grander, and unique in its

decoration. The lamp itself is in the shape of a lotus chalice which is flanked by fretted side pieces which incorporate figures of the god Heh, supporting cartouches with the king's name (left) and prenomen (right) placed on signs for gold, and accompanied by *ankh*-signs of life. The figures of Heh kneel on baskets supported by clumps of papyrus. The outer edges of the side pieces are formed of notched palm branches, indicating the long life offered to the king by Heh. The lamp with the side pieces

is cemented to a calcite base in the form of a low table with fretted trellis-work.

The promised long reign of Tutankhamun is the theme of the design of this lamp, and it is taken up again in the most unusual painting, which can only be seen properly when the lamp is lit. The scene is painted on the inner side of a thinly shaped calcite insert which fits closely in the bell of the lamp itself. The fit is well-nigh perfect, and this precision says much for ancient craftsmanship.

The scene which shines through the translucent calcite shows the king, wearing the blue crown, seated casually on a throne, and in front of him stands Ankhesenamun holding out two notched palm branches: she is presenting him with the symbols of a long reign. On the other side of the lamp can be seen, again through the calcite, the names of the king who is 'the good god, lord of the Two Lands, lord of achievement' and 'son of Re, his beloved, lord of diadems'.

CALCITE PERFUME VASE

(CARTER 57, J.D'E. 62116;
HEIGHT 52.9 CM)

The variant forms used by Egyptian stone-vessel designers seem to have been infinite, even when the basic theme was conventional. This perfume or unguent vase is no exception. It was found along with other fine examples in the Antechamber, leaning against the wall between two of the great ritual couches. It had been opened and its contents removed by the ancient robbers. The container for the precious material has a long neck and bulbous body, and it is enclosed by the design representing the union of the Two Lands of Upper and Lower Egypt. The container here itself stands for the sign for union, and the plants of the two parts of the country are entwined around it – the papyrus of Lower Egypt on the right and the lily of Upper Egypt on the left. On the outside on each side is the notched palm branch ending in the tadpole and *shen*-sign, standing for a royal reign of millions of years. This upper part is cemented to a base shaped like a table with struts. The inscription gives the two names of Tutankhamun in cartouches.

PERFUME VASE WITH PAPYRUS COLUMNS

(CARTER 61, J.D'E. 62117;
HEIGHT 61 CM)

This is one of the group of perfume vases which were stacked between two of the ritual couches in the Antechamber. The theme in the upper part is the union of the Two Lands. In detail, however, these vases differ from each other. For example, a more complicated knot unites the various stems around the neck of this vase. Along the base of the upper part the environments of the two plants are suggested: on the left the bases of papyrus plants springing from a marshy bed, on the right a checkered pattern, probably representing a system of irrigated plots for the growing of lilies. The lower part (not shown here) takes a novel form. The central stand, flaring out widely at the base, is flanked by papyrus-capital columns, linked to the central stand higher up by extraordinary spirals carved out of the calcite. The royal cartouches are inscribed on the body of the vase.

THE LOTUS CHALICE

(CARTER 14, J.D'E. 67465; HEIGHT 18.3 CM)

When the excavators entered the tomb they found this vessel lying on the floor. It is a stemmed cup in the form of an open lotus flower with two elaborate handles. These take the form of a lotus flower and buds, on top of which is a basket supporting a kneeling figure of Heh, the god of a million years, who holds in each hand a notched palm branch which ends at the bottom with a tadpole and the *shen*-sign – the whole group indicating an eternity of reign for the king. A text on the side, inlaid with blue paint, gives the king's two cartouches and describes him as 'beloved of Amon-Re, lord of the thrones of the two lands, lord of heaven'. One half of the text running around the rim gives the king's titulary; the other half contains a wish: 'May your *ka* live, may you pass millions of years, you who love Thebes, sitting with your face towards the north wind, your two eyes seeing happiness'. Hence it has been called the 'wishing cup'. The lotus represented in this cup is the white variety which in ancient Egypt seems especially to have been used as the model for fine drinking cups. There is a fragment of a plaque in the collection of Eton College which actually shows Tutankhamun drinking from a lotus cup.

PERFUME VASE WITH HATHOR HEAD

(CARTER 60, J.D'E. 62118; HEIGHT 50 CM)

A somewhat more elaborate variant of the idea of the union of the Two Lands forms the main design in this vase. One may speculate about the significance to be placed on the use of this design on these great vases: it may have been used just for its satisfactory appearance and its ability to be varied, rather than for any subtle political or funerary significance.

In this case, however, there is an additional religious reference in the design associating it and its contents with the cult of Hathor, a goddess of many aspects. Here her head is shown like a mask on the neck of the vessel, with a broad collar underneath; there are also two swellings below the decorated base of the neck which have been interpreted as breasts.

The base of the piece, made separately, includes two amuletic groups in which a central *ankh*-sign holds two flanking *was*-signs. The multiplicity of religious and amuletic references that may be found in the decoration of elaborate pieces like these perfume vessels suggests that there may have been no careful supervision over their designers, who were allowed to incorporate symbols almost at will.

CALCITE BOAT
IN A TANK

(CARTER 578, J.d'E. 62120;
HEIGHT 37 CM, WIDTH 58.3 CM)

Whatever its purpose, this object
remains a remarkable product of
the ancient craftsman. A pedestal
in a rectangular tank supports a
boat with ibex heads at prow and
stern. In the middle of the boat
rests what seems to be an open
sarcophagus in a kiosk
supported by four chunky
columns with double capitals
of lotus and papyrus. In the
prow kneels a nude female
holding a lotus flower; in the
stern a nude female dwarf
steers the boat. Both tank
and boat are richly decorated
with floral and geometrical
patterns, inlaid with colored
paints and embellished with
gold in a rather restrained
way. The panel of inscription
on the end of the tank gives no
clue to the purpose of the piece; it
contains cartouches with the names
of Tutankhamun and
Ankhesenamun, flanked by *uraei*
on papyrus (right) and lily (left),
named respectively Wadjyt (for
Lower Egypt) and Neith (strangely,
for Upper Egypt).

OIL JAR WITH STAND

(CARTER 520, J.D'E. 62123;
HEIGHT 58.5 CM)

Carter wrote that when this calcite jar was inspected the residue in it still showed something of the nature of the contents: 'beneath the hardened crust the oil has remained viscid to the present day'. It differs markedly from the other oil and perfume vessels found in the Annexe. It is bulbous in shape, with a flared rim and a domed top, and it stands on a separate calcite base. Lid and body are richly decorated with designs and texts inlaid with colored pastes and glass.

On the lid is a bird with outstretched wings surrounded by a frieze of checkered inlays and floral elements. Under the rim are incised papyrus flowers with green inlays in between. Checkered and floral decoration also embellish the upper part of the vase, and below is a finely inscribed text in four lines of colored hieroglyphs with the names of Tutankhamun and Ankhesenamun; they are offered power and eternal influence by the *uraeus* Wadjyt.

CALCITE CHEST

(CARTER 40, J.D'E. 61466; LENGTH 33 CM;
WIDTH 17 CM, HEIGHT 24 CM)

This stone casket leads one to think that it must have had some special purpose. It has been suggested that it may have been used to hold a magical contract between Tutankhamun and his wife made at the time of his coronation. It contained, among other rather trivial objects, small balls of mud with hair and papyrus fragments mixed in – seemingly magical material.

There is no ready answer. The text on one end is inexplicit about purpose. It contains just the

cartouches of Tutankhamun and Ankhesenamun with titles and the tags, 'given life for ever and ever' for the King, and 'may she live, may she be fruitful' for the queen. The names are post-Amarna. The chest is made of two pieces of calcite, cut with the precision of a joiner; the two fastening knobs are of obsidian (naturally occurring black glass). Formal bouquets of flowers decorate the lid, and bands of checker pattern and flower petals adorn the sides and ends of the chest.

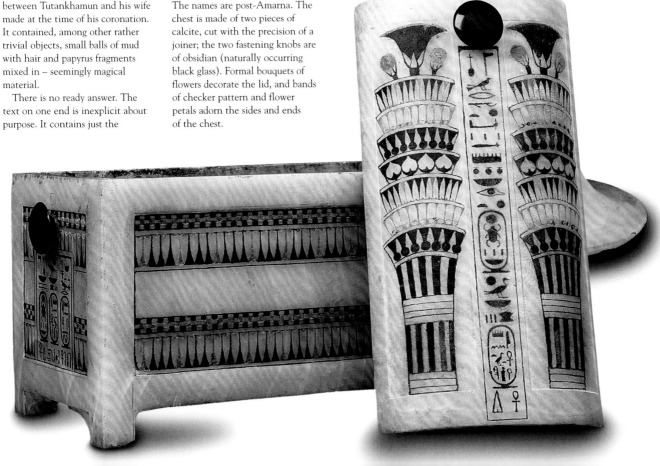

CALCITE IBEX VASE

(CARTER 584, J.D'E. 62122;
LENGTH 38.5 CM, WIDTH 18.5 CM,
HEIGHT 27.5 CM)

Throughout Egyptian history craftsmen produced imaginative objects for the dressing-tables of royalty and the highly placed in society. This unusual cosmetic container, found in the Annexe, is in fact rather large for an ordinary dressing-table, and it is a puzzle to decide how it might have been used domestically. Its shape is that of a recumbent ibex, set on an oval base. The artist who made it was a close observer of natural life – like Carter himself from childhood, his father being a notable painter of animals. The ibex is skillfully modeled, and the head in particular presents a convincing image of a bleating creature, with its mouth partly open, revealing a tongue made of pink-stained ivory. One of the real horns is missing, as is the beard and the mouth of the vase on the back. The eyes are inlaid with translucent quartz with details painted on the back, set in copper frames.

LION UNGUENT CONTAINER

(CARTER 579, J.D'E. 62114;
HEIGHT 60 CM, WIDTH 19.8 CM)

One would like to think that this charming calcite ointment jar was prepared specially for the use of Tutankhamun and Ankhesenamun. Both their names are inscribed on the creature's chest. It is a standing lion with one front paw raised as if in greeting, the other resting on the hieroglyphic sign for 'protection'. It does not represent the god Bes, who had leonine characteristics, but some association with that deity is certain. On the footboard of one of the beds illustrated earlier the openwork panels have Bes flanked by lions with their front paws on the 'protection' sign. Here the protruding tongue is of pink-stained ivory, the eyes are of gold foil, and the teeth of gold. It is likely that all the claws, removed in antiquity, were also of gold. The headdress, which is also the stopper of the vase, is in the form of an open lotus, such as is shown worn by the lions on the footboard of the bed. The fretted base has paint-filled designs of flower petals and mandrake fruits.

OINTMENT JAR WITH LION LID

(CARTER 211, J.D'E. 62119;
HEIGHT 27 CM, WIDTH OF JAR 12 CM)

This jar was found in front of the doors of the second shrine in the Burial Chamber, and by some chance it had not been opened by the robbers.

Its contents were therefore found intact – a fatty mass amounting to about 450 grams. This material was carefully analyzed at the time, the conclusion being 'it appears probable that the cosmetic consisted of about 90 per cent of a neutral animal fat, with about 10 per cent of some resin or balsam'.

No doubt modern methods would produce a more precise analysis.

The piece is very regal in character and carries the king's cartouches. It is made of two kinds of calcite. The lid, in the form of a recumbent lion with pink ivory tongue and gold eyes, is pivoted on an ivory peg, and closed by two ivory knobs. The jar proper is supported on calcite cross bars with heads of Asiatics and Nubians carved in red and black stones. Scenes of the desert hunt are carved on the sides of the jar.

324–325
Pectoral scene of the king, supported by Atum and Iusaas, is offered a long reign by Amun-Re.

RAMESSES II

CONTENTS

326
Figure of Ramesses II from one of the Hathor pillars in the hall of the Hathor temple at Abu Simbel.

327
Emile Prisse d'Avennes' drawing (1847) of Ramesses II at the battle of Qadesh.

328
Relief figure of Ramesses II as a child, seated on a cushion in the form of the horizon sign. He has the lock of youth and holds his finger to his mouth, in the characteristic attitude of a child (Louvre, N522).

PREFACE

"Who is your favorite ancient Egyptian?" I have been asked this question from time to time by curious friends and strangers. There must be, they think, someone – king, queen, commoner – with whom I must have a special sympathy. Some people fall in love with Akhenaten, or Nefertiti, or Hatshepsut; they believe they know enough about them to allow judgments to be made and affections engaged. The difficulty for the professional Egyptologist is that sentiment alone cannot be a good basis for judgment. The paucity of written evidence of a human or personal kind from ancient Egypt makes it very difficult to get close to any ancient Egyptian, and for a king it is virtually impossible. Consequently, I have never been able to say "X is my favorite ancient Egyptian." But I can say quite unequivocally that it is not Ramesses II. His reported pronouncements are many, but almost without exception they are boastful and vainglorious, and many of the physical remains of his reign are equally grand and pompous. The picture that Ramesses would have us accept as being a true representation of himself is probably that contained in the florid texts on the so-called rhetorical stelae, the long inscriptions that proclaim his greatness and achievements in the most general terms. The Ramesses of these inscriptions is not therefore particularly attractive.

Nevertheless, it cannot be denied that there is a singular engaging impressiveness to Ramesses, much of which, no doubt, he – through the agency of his high officials – set out to promote through buildings, statues, and inscriptions. And we must not forget his mummy, with a head so well preserved (for a man nearing his century) that a convincing match can be made between it and those sculptures that seem to offer the best portraits. As a result, Ramesses has been much written about over the years, and particularly so during the last half century. In a sense, people believe that they know him, and are able to deduce something about his personality. There was all the publicity surrounding the moving of the Abu Simbel temples, the conservation of the wonderful tomb of his wife Nefertari, the excavation of Piramesse, the Delta Residence, and the regal journey of the king's mummy to Paris for scientific examination. Scholarly monographs have been published on the great monuments; a spectacular exhibition of objects from his reign toured North America in the 1980s; and there have been popular biographies, and even a many-volumed novel on his life and times.

As far as this Egyptologist is concerned, the greatest boost to studies of the reign of Ramesses II has been the publication of the texts of the Nineteenth and Twentieth Dynasties, under the unassuming title *Ramesside Inscriptions*. The diligence and energy of the author, Professor Kenneth Kitchen, is almost unequaled in the history of Egyptological scholarship. Two large volumes contain all the known significant texts of Ramesses II's reign, one for the king himself and his family, and one for his contemporaries, from the highest officials to humble workmen. And there are supplementary volumes of translations and commentaries. Kitchen's own *Pharaoh Triumphant* offers in popular form the results of his scholarly compilation. The present book owes so much to Kitchen's pioneering efforts in Ramesside studies; to him I am hugely grateful.

In this general survey of Ramesses and his reign I have attempted to treat my subject without bias. I may occasionally be dismissive, but I hope never disrespectful. Ramesses may not be my favorite ancient Egyptian, but he certainly commands much of my interest and a great deal of my admiration.

330
Royal head with nemes-headdress from a granite colossus ascribed to Ramesses II in the forecourt of the temple of Luxor. It was possibly made at first for King Amenophis III.

331–334
South wall of the great hall at Abu Simbel. At the top: Ramesses II makes offerings to various deities and has the years of his reign confirmed by Thoth and Sefkhet-abu in the presence of Re-Herakhty. In the middle: scenes of triumph in the Syrian, Libyan, and Nubian wars.

336–337
A scene from the Ramesseum in which Ramesses kneels before Amun-Re, receiving the elaborate atef-crown and a plurality of jubilee (sed) festivals, which are suspended from a palm rib notched with the expected years of a long reign.

338–339
The façade of the great temple of Abu Simbel at night, the floodlighting dramatically revealing the subordinate figures of queens, princes, and princesses accompanying the four colossal figures.

RAMESSES
THE GRAT

340 and 341
Granite colossus of Ramesses II from
the temple precinct of Ptah at
Memphis, a statue later usurped by
Ramesses IV of the Twentieth
Dynasty. It now stands in Cairo,
near the main railway station.

The modern traveler, arriving in Cairo probably after dark, is introduced to ancient Egypt as the tourist coach drives into town and passes the main railway station. Here a great granite colossus of a king tries to dominate the chaotic environment of the tangle of roads at high and low level, which confuse the visitor. Here is the first view of Ramesses II, not seen as he would have wished to be seen, but seriously diminished by urban disorder. A tour guide may try to excite interest in the statue; most travelers, however, will continue to doze gently, or to mop up without commentary the strange and colorful scenes of modern Cairo life as they pass by. This great figure achieved for only a short time the attention that town planners had expected it to provide in front of the railway station; as the system of elevated throughways has developed in this busy part of Cairo, so has poor Ramesses languished in a pool of pollution, little regarded,

and seriously worrying not only lovers of the pharaonic heritage of Egypt, but also the national and civic authorities. Ramesses no longer performs a function, and, what is worse, he stands as an admonitory reminder of the dangers of unconcerned planning. He will be moved, perhaps to the relative calm of the garden in front of the Egyptian Museum, perhaps back to Memphis, perhaps to some other public position in the city, less environmentally dangerous than Ramesses Square. It will not happen too soon.

When the monumental memorial of the great king was brought into Cairo in 1955, its transfer from Memphis, not many miles to the south of Cairo on the west side of the Nile, formed part of a plan to improve and modernize the city following the revolution of 1952. Ramesses II was an outstanding symbol of native Egyptian greatness, hailing from the distant past.

He was, furthermore, in statue form being

moved to a part of the city where visitors arriving and leaving by train would encounter him, in greeting or in farewell, where he would stand dominantly and appropriately in what was already Place Ramsès, Midan Ramsis, Ramesses Square. He was, in a sense, at that time coming home in triumph, a proper object for national pride.

It might never have been so, however, for that colossus was at one time destined to travel to London. Long ago, in the early nineteenth century, it had been offered to Great Britain by Muhammad Ali Pasha (1769–1849), virtual ruler of Egypt and founder of the modern Egyptian state. It was one of many extravagant gifts offered to helpful governments by that great leader, who might have seen himself as a reincarnation of Ramesses, if the reading of ancient Egyptian names and the identification of the great historical figures of antiquity had been sufficiently advanced in the formative years of his power.

342 top
The French boat Louxor moored at Luxor in preparation for the removal of the western obelisk from the temple of Luxor, under the direction of Jean Baptiste Apollinaire Lebas.

343 right
The obelisk of Ramesses II in the Place de la Concorde, Paris. One of the pair erected in front of the great pylon of the Temple of Luxor, it was presented to France by Muhammad Ali in 1830.

342–343
Painting by François Dubois of the Place de la Concorde on 25 October 1833 at the moment when the Luxor obelisk was finally raised into an upright position.

343 top left
Inlays on the northern face of the base of the Paris obelisk illustrating the skillful methods devised by J.-B. Lebas to lower the stone shaft for transfer to the boat Louxor.

343 bottom left
Metal inlays in the southern face of the granite base of the Paris obelisk showing the processes by which the monument was raised to its present position.

Another product of mighty Ramesses' reign, the great obelisk now in the Place de la Concorde in Paris, was another presentation by Muhammad Ali, readily accepted by the French nation, which has nursed a deep and abiding interest in ancient Egypt dating back to Napoleon's Egyptian adventure in 1798. The obelisk was erected in Paris in 1836, some years after the death of Jean-François Champollion, who by then knew how to read the royal names and much of the rest of the texts which embellished the monument. Would Ramesses have approved of the recent gilding of the pyramidion at the top of the obelisk? I suspect he would have nodded assent. He would certainly have arranged for his entourage to raise a cheer, even if it had been inappropriate for the divine ruler to display such emotion himself.

In his early years of working on the decipherment of hieroglyphs, Champollion had deduced the name of Ramesses in ancient cartouches, the ovals which were used to enclose royal names in ancient Egypt. His supposition was soon confirmed by his reading – again with a degree of guesswork – of the name of the king Thothmes, or Tuthmosis, or as many now prefer, Thutmose. It is said that Champollion was so excited by his discovery that he rushed to his brother Jacques Joseph, crying out his success and collapsing in a faint for several days. And so the 'father' of Egyptology knew how to recognize the name Ramesses; and by 1836, when the Luxor obelisk was set up in Paris, there were many who could read the name, and who even knew something about the creator of that great monument.

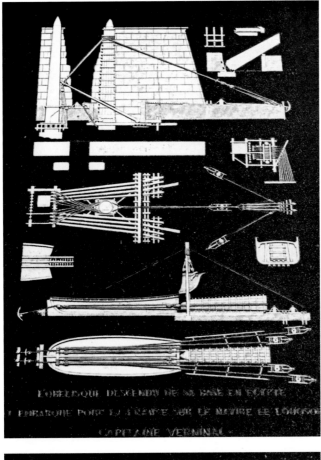

L'OBELISQUE DESCENDU DE SA BASE EN EGYPTE
L'EMBARQUE POUR LA FRANCE SUR LE NAVIRE LE LOUQSOR
CAPITAINE VERNINAC

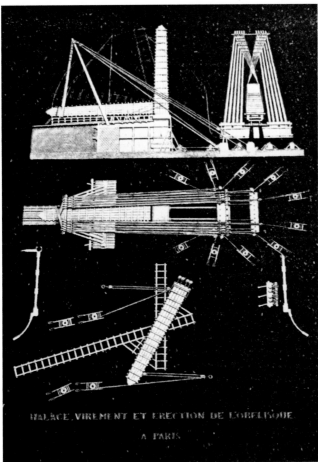

HALAGE, VIREMENT ET ERECTION DE L'OBELISQUE
A PARIS

Ramesses II

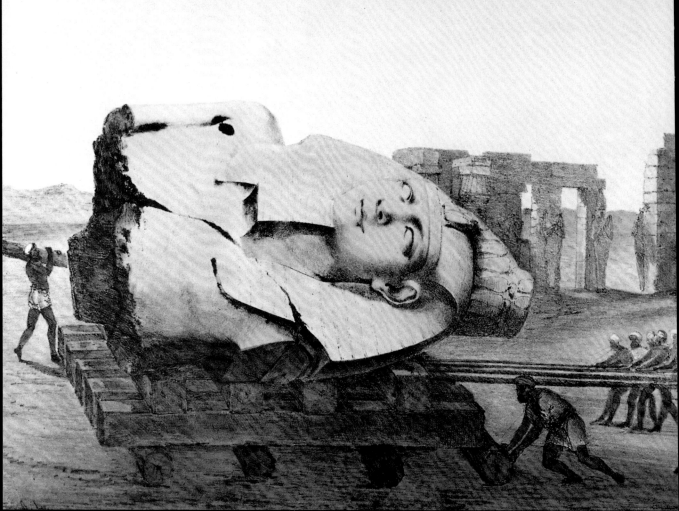

344 top left
The Egyptian Sculpture Gallery in the British Museum in about 1860, with the bust of Ramesses II on the left, and in the distance, a cast of one of the Abu Simbel colossal heads.

344 top right
A squad of Royal Artillerymen moving the bust of Ramesses II from the Townley Galleries to the new Egyptian Sculpture Gallery in the British Museum in 1834.

344–345
Giovanni-Battista Belzoni's illustration of the removal of the Younger Memnon from the Ramesseum. It took place during the heat of the summer, to utilize the waters of the flooded Nile.

345 top
The 'Young' or 'Younger' Memnon, the upper part of a granite colossus of Ramesses II from the Ramesseum, the mortuary temple of the king in Western Thebes; now in the British Museum (EA 19).

Paris then had a visible presence of Ramesses II. London was denied its own magnificent colossus of the king because, it was said, the problems of moving the great sculpture from the mounds of Memphis were at that time insurmountable for local resources on the grounds of engineering, and, probably more crucially, of expense. But London in fact already had its image of Ramesses II, one very much finer artistically than the Memphite colossus. It was not known to be a representation of the great king when it first reached London in 1817. It had been identified as "certainly the most beautiful and perfect piece of Egyptian sculpture that can be seen throughout the whole country [i.e., Egypt]" by William Hamilton, an envoy of Lord Elgin who had traveled through Egypt in 1803 and published his *Aegyptiaca* in 1809. The statue's reputation attracted the attention of Jean-Louis Burckhardt, a Swiss scholar living in Cairo who in 1816 persuaded the new British Consul-General in Egypt to join him in the enterprise of removing the royal bust from the Ramesseum in Western Thebes, and presenting it to the British Museum. With all the proper official permissions of the time in order, the work was accomplished by Giovanni-Battista Belzoni, Italian strongman turned incipient archaeologist. It was the first great piece of Egyptian art to enter the British Museum, and its arrival was much appreciated by visitors to the museum and by the museum's trustees. The latter were not at that time fully convinced that Egyptian

art could ever be compared in level terms with Greek and Roman art. Nobody was sure about the identity of the sculpture's subject. It was royal – surely; it came from a temple – certainly. But whose temple? The French scholars who accompanied Napoleon's expedition to Egypt had called the Ramesseum – now known to be the king's mortuary temple – the Memnonium, the temple of Memnon, erroneously associating it with the two massive quartzite statues known since antiquity as the Colossi of Memnon. Memnon in classical literature was an Ethiopian king; his identification with the subject of the so-called Colossi of Memnon in Western Thebes (in fact the Eighteenth Dynasty Pharaoh Amenophis III) demonstrates the ingenious desperation of classical and post-classical scholars to explain Egyptian buildings and sculptures by reference to information provided by the only ancient texts they could read.

It need hardly be stated that the Ramesseum and the colossi of Amenophis III had nothing to do with the mythical Memnon; but names persist, and even today in the British Museum the great bust of Ramesses II is affectionately known as the Young or Younger Memnon.

It would be some years after its arrival in London before the Younger Memnon would be recognized to be part of a great figure of Ramesses II, but by then that king, seemingly incognito, had already made his mark on the consciousness of the British public.

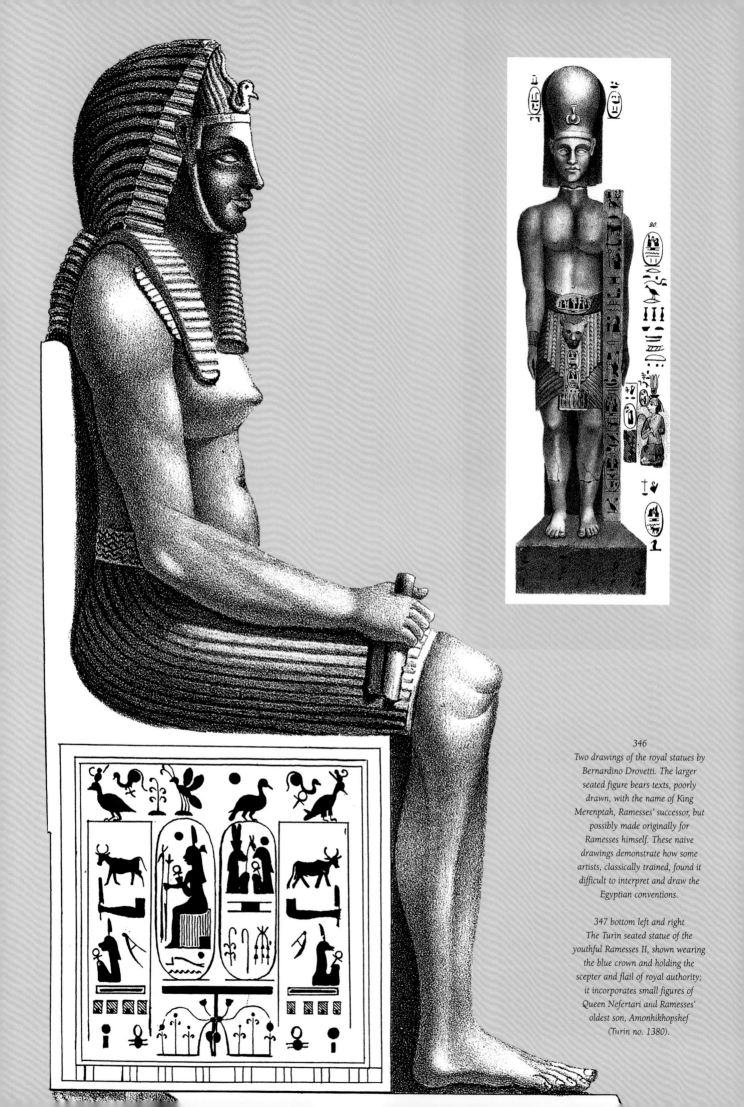

346
Two drawings of the royal statues by Bernardino Drovetti. The larger seated figure bears texts, poorly drawn, with the name of King Merenptah, Ramesses' successor, but possibly made originally for Ramesses himself. These naive drawings demonstrate how some artists, classically trained, found it difficult to interpret and draw the Egyptian conventions.

347 bottom left and right
The Turin seated statue of the youthful Ramesses II, shown wearing the blue crown and holding the scepter and flail of royal authority; it incorporates small figures of Queen Nefertari and Ramesses' oldest son, Amonhikhopshef (Turin no. 1380).

So too he had, in a less powerful but equally artistic manner, in the third important collection of Egyptian antiquities in Europe, in the Egyptian Museum in Turin. The Paris obelisk was a towering memorial to the fame of the great king. The London Memnon was wholly impressive, and distinguished further by possibly being the inspiration for the poet Shelley's sonnet "Ozymandias." The Turin black-granite, life-size seated figure was human in scale and in its sympathetic treatment; it is Ramesses as a young man, its style harking back to the refined post-Amarna artistic standard of his father Sethos I. It was found in the temple of Karnak by Jean Jacques

Rifaud, a French artist who worked for Bernardino Drovetti, French Consul-General in Egypt from 1811 to 1814 and from 1821 to 1829. Drovetti was a native of Piedmont, a highly intelligent, somewhat devious diplomat and politician who engaged in serious rivalry concerning the collection of antiquities with Belzoni, the agent of Henry Salt. It was a sad conflict between men whose aims were similar but who were unable to divide between themselves the rich collecting fields of the Theban area. Part of Drovetti's fine collection found its way to Turin in the 1820s, including the most distinguished statue of Ramesses II.

347 top center
A version of the nomen of Ramesses II which shows the versatility of the hieroglyphic script in writing Ramessu-Miamun, with the elements Ra and Amun shown as seated gods facing each other.

So, at a very early stage in the history of Egyptology, Ramesses was well placed in the centers of budding Egyptological scholarship to provide his own image as the exemplar of pharaonic power. But what was known of Ramesses at this early time, before the hieroglyphs were deciphered and the texts read? The name at least was known from the Bible, though not always clearly as the designation of a royal person: "Joseph placed his father and his brethren, and gave them a possession in the land of Egypt, in the best of the land, in the land of Rameses, as Pharaoh had commanded" (Genesis 47:11). Under a new king, unspecified, the oppression of the Children of Israel is said to have begun: "Therefore they did set over them taskmasters to afflict them with their burdens. And they built for Pharaoh treasure cities, Pithom and Raamses" (Exodus 1:11). From this place began the actual Exodus of the Israelites: "And they departed from Rameses in the first month, on the fifteenth day of the first month; on the morrow after the passover the children of Israel went out with a high hand in the sight of all the Egyptians... And the children of Israel removed from Rameses, and pitched at Succoth" (Numbers 33:3-5). Here in the biblical record Rameses and Raamses refer to places and not directly to a person, or more specifically to a king or Pharaoh. Yet a tradition had grown up that the oppression and even perhaps the Exodus of the Children of Israel had taken place in the reign of a

king called Ramesses. So any king so named was threatened with a poor reputation by those who found truth in the very words of the Bible.

We shall see toward the end of this book how the myth of Ramesses lasted in Egyptian history and in the secondary literary tradition. Some of this tradition persisted into classical times, with Ramesses appearing in various forms and under a variety of names in the classical record in-so-far as it touched on Egypt. Herodotus, that most entertaining of Greek writers, whose history was written in the fifth century B.C. and included sections on Egypt based partly on a personal visit to that land, had the closest contact with the living tradition among the late pharaonic Egyptians. Yet he talks of Rhampsinitus. The much later historian, Diodorus Siculus, writing in the first century B.C., talks of Remphis, and quite separately provides at secondhand an account of a building which he calls the tomb of Osymandyas. Other classical writers speak of Rhamsesis and of Rhamses, and there was some confusion between the king of these names and the great conqueror Sesostris, or Sesothis, who should be identified with Senwosret III of the Twelfth Dynasty. The priest Manetho, a native Egyptian historian from Sebennytos who composed in the third century B.C. an account of Egyptian history in the form of annals and based on surviving Egyptian records, was apparently the first to divide the kings of Egypt into the dynastic structure still used today. His history is preserved in

Ramesses II

minimal form in a number of later classical writers, and in his listing of the kings of the Nineteenth Dynasty there occurs a Rapsaces or Rampses, who reigned for sixty-six years – clearly Ramesses II.

In terms of reliable historical information, the classical writers, like those of the Bible, provided little useful evidence from which European scholars in the early nineteenth century could form a coherent idea of the reign and achievements of the king who was to be known as Ramesses, Rameses, or Ramses II. Egyptian names are not easily converted into modern forms. To be more precise, they can easily be converted, but different scholarly systems and traditions prefer certain forms of conversion over others. The name we give here as Ramesses, consisted in Egyptian of three parts: Ra-mes-su, 'Ra (or Re) created him.' This was the king's principal name, usually written in the second of the two cartouches in the royal titulary. It was usually given the added epithet 'beloved of Amun.' The first cartouche contained what may be called the throne name; in the case of Ramesses II, it was User-Ma'at-Re, usually abbreviated to Usimare and meaning 'one strong in *ma'at* (truth or order) is Re,' with the added epithet Setpenre, 'one chosen of Re.' The first cartouche name, now usually called the prenomen, was for the Egyptians the principal royal name. The second cartouche contained the 'family' name by which the king was known before his accession. For Ramesses II, the various forms, like Rampses, are easily explained by

textual confusion or even imperfect memory. Usimare is thought with good reason to be the origin of the Osymandyas of Diodorus, or the Ozymandias of Shelley. Shelley never saw the Ramesseum, the funerary temple of Ramesses II and almost certainly the tomb of Osymandyas of Diodorus. Shelley may never have seen the great bust from the Ramesseum in the British Museum, the Younger Memnon, thought by some to be the inspiration for Shelley's sonnet. It is certain, however, that Burckhardt and Henry Salt, who removed the bust from the Ramesseum, were quite in the dark as to its identity.

348 and 349
Cartouche containing the prenomen of
Ramesses II, 'Usimare Setpenre,'
surmounted by the sun-disk and two ostrich
feathers, and flanked by uraei, *wearing the*
white (left) and red (right) crowns, symbolic
of Upper and Lower Egypt.

It is piquant to consider the extent to which Salt became obsessed with the opening up and subsequent copying of the scenes of the great rock-cut temple of Ramesses II at Abu Simbel. In 1813 Burckhardt had been the first European to report the existence of the Abu Simbel temples, and he stimulated the interest not only of Salt but also of William John Bankes, a wealthy British traveler who first journeyed into Nubia in 1815. Salt sent Belzoni to open the great temple in 1816, but success came only at a second attempt in 1817. It is difficult now to comprehend how little was known of ancient Egypt and its history at this early time. When Salt and Bankes came to Abu Simbel in the autumn of 1818 they had no way of judging whether the temples there were contemporary with Karnak or with the great late temples of Edfu and Dendera and Philae. By the examination of a Greek text scratched on the leg of one of the great seated colossi of the main temple, Bankes deduced that this temple predated the reign of the king Psammetichus mentioned in the text. From his classical knowledge Bankes remembered that there were kings named Psammetichus in the Twenty-sixth Dynasty (Saite), which was understood to have flourished in the seventh and sixth centuries B.C. Bankes rightly concluded that Abu Simbel was much earlier than the Ptolemaic and Roman temples, and predated the Saite period by a fair number of years. In 1818, however, the hieroglyphic decipherment debate continued unresolved, conducted principally between Jean-François Champollion in France and Thomas Young in Britain. The crucial steps were still to be taken, and Champollion had not yet recognized the cartouche of Ramesses II, which would have given the workers at Abu Simbel the chance of dating the temples there to the reign of that king.

William John Bankes for a short time took a lively interest in decipherment, and even made a few small contributions of value to it. He also discovered the king-list in the Abydos temple of Ramesses II, and recognized its importance without in fact being able to read any of the royal names. Henry Salt, on the other hand, believed he

could do much more. He had built up a library of the earliest Egyptological publications and entered into correspondence with the leading scholars working on decipherment. His results were not always accepted, and he resented the gentle derision that was often shown toward his writings. Nevertheless, he provided at least one excellent service to Egyptology by taking under his wing the young John Gardner Wilkinson, who arrived in Egypt from Naples in 1821. Wilkinson had been diverted from a career in the army to one of Egyptological scholarship by Sir William Gell, who maintained an intellectual salon in Naples, acting, among other things, as an intermediary between desk-scholars in Europe and field-workers in Egypt. At the start of his long sojourn in Egypt, Wilkinson devoted his attention especially to collecting and identifying royal names in cartouches. In his travels throughout the country he noted new examples, subsequently analyzing them and developing great skill in identifying the kings so named. Salt wrote to Gell about Wilkinson's abilities: "I have not indeed seen any person here who has entered with so much spirit into the study of hieroglyphics... he works *like a horse at it.*" Champollion may have first recognized the name of Ramesses in hieroglyphs, but Wilkinson preceded him in noting that royal names could be written in more than one way. His own collections of cartouches from the monuments provided him with ample evidence of variant writings, and he became utterly familiar with what might be termed the vagaries of the hieroglyphic script in the writing of royal names. When he traveled for the first time into Nubia in 1823, accompanied by an old college friend, James Samuel Wiggett, on the occasion of their crossing the Nile at Semna in a flimsy improvised ferry boat, down to the gunwales in the water, he commented in his journal that he and Wiggett sat facing each other "like the 2 gods in the name of Ramesses." Here he is referring not to the simple writing of Ramesses' cartouche, but to one in which the gods Re and Amun confront each other in the writing of Ramesses-Meryamun.

350 top
Portrait of Giovanni-Battista Belzoni in Turkish dress. European travelers in Egypt commonly dressed à la turque, *as they called it, for reasons of comfort, convenience, and even safety.*

350–351
Belzoni's version of a scene in the first hall of the great temple at Abu Simbel showing Ramesses II smiting a Libyan captive. To the left stands Queen Nefertari. It is not a careful copy.

351 bottom left
Belzoni's illustration of the
first hall of the great temple.
He was disappointed by the
meager harvest of objects found
within the temple.

351 bottom right
Belzoni's illustration of the temple of
Abu Simbel viewed from the east
bank of the Nile. He first attempted
to enter the great temple in 1816,
but only succeeded on his second
visit in 1817.

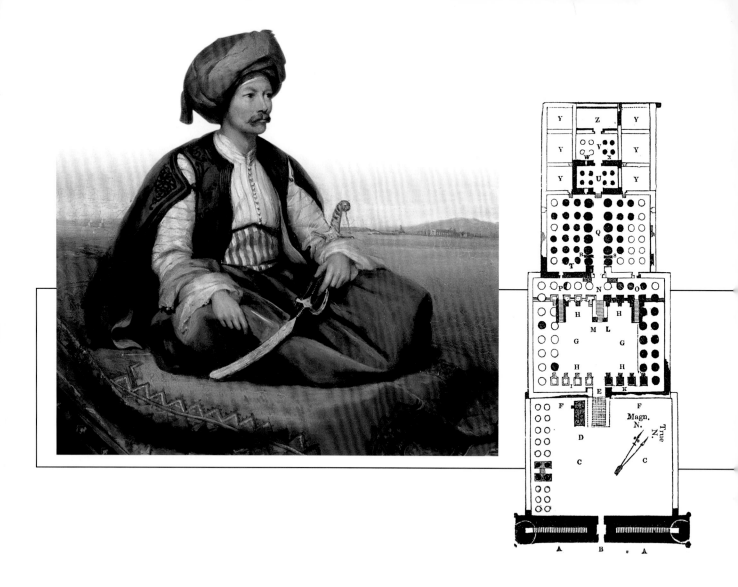

Wilkinson spent twelve years continuously in Egypt collecting inscriptional and graphic material from the monuments, acquiring in the process not only a competent grasp of the hieroglyphic script and the Egyptian language, but also an unparalleled knowledge of the culture of ancient Egypt. In 1837, after his return to Britain, he published the three-volume work for which he is best known, *The Manners and Customs of the Ancient Egyptians*. His second chapter is devoted to the history of Egypt, and it is instructive to see to what extent he was able to provide an account of the reign of Ramesses II, bearing in mind that he was writing within fifteen years of Champollion's crucial announcement of the decipherment principles in 1822. Active field-workers and serious desk-scholars were still few; many were limited in their interests, and some were not prepared to accept Champollion's system. The whole Egyptian field was open to wild theorizing and guesswork, much of which was based on slender or shaky evidence. Scholars of integrity, competent in understanding the solid advances of the respected few and acquainted firsthand with the monuments, were needed to distinguish between what was true and what was false. Such a scholar was Wilkinson.

What then did he have to say about Ramesses II? Not a great deal, although he devoted ten pages to his reign. Misled by some classical sources, he placed the king, whom he called Remeses, toward the end of a long Eighteenth Dynasty. He felt able to accept the Manethonian sixty-six years for the length of his reign, supporting this opinion by his own recording of dates on the surviving monuments up to the king's sixty-second year, and by reckoning that the vast number of monuments left by the king at places as far apart as Tanis in the Delta and Abu Simbel in Nubia "bear ample testimony to the length of time required for their execution." This last argument was somewhat fallacious, but Wilkinson may be excused for marveling at the multiplicity and magnitude of Ramesses' structures, all of which he had visited and studied himself. From his observations, particularly in the temples of Luxor, Karnak, Abu Simbel, and the Ramesseum (which he continued to call the Memnonium, because of its established usage), he drew wide and detailed conclusions on the state of the army in Remeses' reign, on its range of weaponry, and on the elaboration of its practical procedures in open battle and in sieges. He accepted the identification of Remeses with Sesostris, and in consequence, again following

classical sources, attributed to Remeses the digging of the canal from the Nile to the Red Sea. Time and more abundant evidence would in due course correct these mistaken claims. Yet in spite of his understandably inadequate knowledge, Wilkinson captured something of the flavor of the reign, although his general opinion was touched with hyperbole: "The reign of Remeses was conspicuous as the Augustine era of Egypt, when the arts attained a degree of perfection which no after age succeeded in imitating, and the armies of Egypt were extended by this prince considerably farther into the heart of Asia than during the most successful invasions of his predecessors." Already for Wilkinson he was "Remeses the Great."

The pre-eminent position Wilkinson allotted Ramesses II was based primarily on the evidence provided by the standing monuments of Egypt. As we have noted, he had himself visited and studied the great structures and the remains of great structures from Tanis to Abu Simbel, all liberally stamped with Ramesses' name. He believed that there must be many more still to be revealed "at Memphis, and other principal cities, whose sites are now unknown or concealed by mounds." To judge a king's reputation by the abundance of his monuments is, unfortunately, a risky business. It

does not allow for the quality or the morality of his rule, the state of the administration, the prosperity of his country, or the conditions under which his people lived. For ancient Egypt it is rarely possible to present a rounded picture of an individual ruler, or to provide an adequate factual account of his reign. For Ramesses II much information, unknown to Wilkinson, has been gained in the subsequent period from inscriptions, written documents, the contents of tombs, and the careful investigation of towns and settlements. Much of this information will be used in later chapters of this book, and a better position should be reached from which better judgments can be made than Wilkinson was able to achieve. And yet even today the view that Wilkinson expressed on Ramesses and his reign is one which would be recognized and endorsed by a very large part of the armies of tourists who tramp the sites of Egypt at the present time. In so many places on the usual course followed by visitors in their short holidays in Egypt, the guide will declaim: "And here we see the king, Ramesses II, offering to the gods"; or "This colossal statue is of Egypt's greatest ruler, Ramesses II"; or "This part of the temple was added by Ramesses II to the structure begun by his predecessors"; or "This building (or that statue)

was usurped by Ramesses II, who carved his name over those of King... who built the temple (or had the statue carved)."

The guide, when he has reached the point of understanding his group, may say: "And who built this temple?" or "Whose cartouche is this?" The chorus will answer: "Ramesses II."

The quintessential traveler in Egypt of the nineteenth century was Amelia Blandford Edwards, a successful novelist who with a companion abandoned a trip to Italy in 1873 because of bad weather and fled eastward to Egypt and the sun. At once she was fascinated by the country, wrote up her travels in *A Thousand Miles up the Nile* (published in 1877 and revised in 1889), and helped to found the Egypt Exploration Fund (later Society). The account of her travels makes most entertaining reading, and she took much trouble to get her facts right. But for our story here the point of interest is that she included a whole chapter on "Rameses the Great." By the time of her visit, much more was known than when Wilkinson wrote in the 1830s. The 'greatness of Ramesses' idea had been nurtured and matured. She starts the chapter in positive manner – she did not like to show hesitation, or to be contradicted – and sets out the case for her hero without equivocation: "The central figure of Egyptian history has always been, probably always will be, Rameses the Second. He holds this place partly by right, partly by accident. He was born to greatness; he achieved greatness; and he had borrowed greatness thrust upon him." She then outlines the known events of Ramesses' reign, from time to time eulogizing him, criticizing him, reflecting dogmatically on his character, but ultimately admiring him. She is not afraid of attributing intentions and emotions as a confident novelist may, but a trained historian would not:

"The evening of his life was long and splendid. It became his passion and his pride to found new cities, to raise dykes, to dig canals, to build fortresses, to multiply statues, obelisks and inscriptions, and to erect the most gorgeous and costly temples in which man ever worshipped." Then: "To estimate the cost at which these things were done is now impossible. Every temple, every palace, represented a hecatomb of human lives... We know how the Hebrews suffered.... Yet even the Hebrews were less cruelly used than some who were kidnapped beyond the frontiers." Having expressed herself freely on many of his achievements, Amelia Edwards admits that it would be in vain to try to state what manner of man Ramesses was. Yet she tries: "That he was personally valiant may be gathered, with due reservation, from the poem of Pentaur [the account of the battle of Qadesh]; and that he was not unmerciful is shown in the extradition clause of the Khetan [Hittite] treaty. His pride was evidently boundless." Finally she can conclude "that he was neither better nor worse than the general run of Oriental despots – that he was ruthless in war, prodigal in peace, rapacious of booty, and unsparing in the exercise of almost boundless power." She ends with a neat dig at what might today be thought of as Ramesses' male chauvinism: "His princes and ministers habitually addressed him in the language of worship. Even his wives, who ought to have known better, are represented in the performance of acts of religious

Ramesses II

adoration before him. What wonder then, if the man so deified believed himself a god?"

Seduced by the image of Ramesses II proclaimed by means of the great buildings and by the grandiose scenes and texts with which they were embellished, Amelia Edwards in a sense accepted the estimation of the king's achievements as they were presented by his administrative and priestly high officials. She should not be blamed too severely for this. In dealing with remote antiquity, the scholar – and, by extension, the interested member of the public – has to form judgments on the basis of the evidence available. In the case of Ramesses II the evidence is considerable, but it is dominated by the great works of his reign; it is difficult to avoid the use of words loaded with secondary, but critical, meanings. Ramesses II was from the time of Wilkinson 'the Great'; his works are mighty, magnificent, grandiose, ostentatious, even pompous; he himself is characterized as self-centered, self-glorious, bombastic, full of pride, a prime promoter of his own greatness. Even good historians have fallen into the trap of judging him by the external manifestations of his reign. James Henry Breasted, a scholar of impeccable training, wrote in the early twentieth century a *History of Egypt*, which became a standard work, retaining its authority for many decades, but never revised after 1909. It is still available, and still worth reading, but more for the flow of his narrative than for his frequent moralistic reflections, mostly no longer

sustainable in the face of new evidence and more recent interpretations.

Breasted was more restrained than Amelia Edwards in his estimation of Ramesses II, but even he could not resist the attempt to humanize him on doubtful premises and criticize him in consequence. Breasted considered the Rifaud/Drovetti statue in Turin as an outstanding sculpture: "Nothing better was ever produced by the Egyptian sculptor." It was for Breasted "a faithful portrait," judging on the basis of the features of the king in his strikingly well-preserved mummy. So: "In person he was tall and handsome, with features of dreamy and almost effeminate beauty, in no wise suggestive of the manly traits which he certainly possessed. For the incident at Kadesh [Qadesh] showed him unquestionably a man of fine courage with ability to rise to a supreme crisis." The "indomitable spirit" he showed in his subsequent Asiatic campaigns "more than redeemed the almost fatal blunder at Kadesh." Subsequently "he was quite ready to enjoy the well-earned peace," which would last for the rest of his long reign. Then comes the Protestant censure: "He was inordinately vain and made far more ostentatious display of his wars on his monuments than was ever done by Thutmose [Tuthmosis] III. He loved ease and pleasure and gave himself up without restraint to voluptuous enjoyments." To exemplify this last statement Breasted adds, "He had an enormous harem, and as the years passed his children multiplied rapidly." In later years

"Ramses lived on in magnificence even surpassing that of Amenhotep III... He had lost the vitality for aggressive rule." His realm became threatened by foreign infiltrators, but "senile decay rendered him deaf to alarms and complaints which would have brought instant retribution upon the invaders in the days of his vigorous youth." The threats "never roused him from the lethargy into which he had fallen." In the end "he passed away... none too soon for the redemption of his empire. We are able to look into the withered face of the hoary nonagenarian, evidently little changed from what he was in those last days of splendour in the city of Ramses, and the resemblance to the face of the youth in the noble Turin statue is still very marked."

In judging the man and his achievements in these terms, Breasted offered more than one hostage to fortune. The discovery in subsequent years of new and significant inscriptions and other written evidence from Egypt itself and from other sources, in particular Hittite records, requires substantial reassessments of what happened during the sixty-seven years of Ramesses II's reign. Breasted might now be obliged to modify some of

his judgments on the king himself, but it would still be unwise of him to prepare a new character reference on the basis of changed, but woefully inadequate, evidence. Those who work close to a period or a person who lived many millennia ago often believe that they achieve insights which allow them to leap beyond the available material to form assumptions, to draw conclusions on tenuous evidence supported by 'deep understanding.' Egyptologists are often so closely involved in scholarly investigations that they come to believe that they are almost tuned in to the same wavelength as their own particular fragment of antiquity. In the course of this book we shall be examining many different aspects of the reign of Ramesses II 'the Great,' but the whole story will not be told. Egyptian history is constructed from a diverse mixture of sources: many are public and official, and therefore of uncertain validity; many are private inscriptions, but couched in terms favorable to the existing regime; many are wholly private, personal, and generally more trustworthy. In the case of Ramesses II it is evident that the surviving evidence of all kinds is very unevenly spread over the whole reign, and that there are

many gaps in the record. Some evidence which one feels ought to exist just has not survived.

A significant case is that of the biblical oppression of the Israelites in Egypt, which many scholars have believed should be dated to the reign of Ramesses II, with the Exodus following in the reign of Merenptah. From Egyptian evidence alone the whole sequence of oppression and exodus could be considered as something that never happened. People who accept the biblical account find it hard to believe that such a significant episode (from the Jews' point of view) could have left no trace in Egyptian records. Egyptologists who understand the patchiness of surviving records, the nature of the Delta environment in which the Israelite sojourn is thought to have taken place, and the probable insignificance (in Egyptian eyes) of the existence of a relatively small alien group in the northeast of the country are mostly not surprised that nothing has so far been found to support the biblical account. It is not necessary to deny the general truth of the biblical account, but it is possible, and right, for scholars to question much of the detail. Wilkinson accepted the biblical account and placed it in the reign of

Tuthmosis III. Amelia Edwards considered it to be generally accepted that the oppression took place under Ramesses II, and the Exodus under Merenptah. Breasted, like the good historian he truly was, expressed caution and reasonably suggested: "There is probably little question of the correctness of the Hebrew tradition in attributing the oppression of some tribe of their ancestors to the builder of Pithom [in the eastern Delta] and Ramses; that a tribe of their forefathers should have fled the country to escape such labour is quite in accord with what we know of the time." More cannot reasonably be said. In the near century that has elapsed since Breasted wrote, no material evidence has emerged which seriously changes Breasted's opinion. Much more is known of the city Ramses, which Egyptologists identify as Piramesse; excavations in the eastern Delta have clarified the circumstances of life in Ramesside and earlier times. But a clinching text remains to be found. The Children of Israel, therefore, will not play a significant part in the chapters that follow. Ramesses will occupy the center of the stage, as he would have expected. But first we must see how it all came about that Egypt became his stage.

358–359
The face of one of the granite standing colossi in the forecourt of the Luxor temple. The serene nature of the features belies the strength of the personality represented. The eyes are angled to look down at the viewer.

POST-AMARNA EGYPT: HOREMHEB TO SETHOS I

360

A realistic portrait of Akhenaten from one of the sandstone colossi placed in the Aten temple at Karnak in the early years of the king's reign. The royal features are shown almost in caricature (Luxor Museum, J53).

361

A talatat block retrieved from the Ninth Pylon of the Karnak Temple, showing Akhenaten worshiping the Aten with his hands raised to receive its life-giving rays. Between the royal figures is a small Nefertiti (Luxor Museum, J223)

362–363

Karl Richard Lepsius's drawing of the royal family in the tomb of Ay at Amarna, with Akhenaten, Nefertiti holding one of their daughters, and two other daughters behind her. This scene is now badly damaged.

I f Ramesses II and his father Sethos I (Sety) were to return to this twenty-first-century world, or were able to view from their vantage point in the day-boat of the sun-god Re, they would surely be very vexed to observe the matters that most interest the Egyptologists who write so prolifically about the history and civilization of the "Beloved Land" of Kemet. They would be horrified to see the amount of paper devoted to the reign of Akhenaten, the great attraction generated by the heretical religious views of that king, and the attention devoted to the artistic peculiarities of the so-called Amarna period. How could it have happened that, in spite of the best efforts of royal agents following the deaths of Tutankhamun and Ay, the reputation of 'the criminal of Akhetaten' (as Akhenaten was sometimes called) stands so high, not only in the close world of the scholar, but even in the consciousness of the literate public! Not that Sethos or Ramesses would know much about

scholarship or the literate public.

The dazzling city of Akhetaten, the spiritual center of Akhenaten's regime which the king declared he would never leave, had been razed to the ground. Much of its stone was reused in the construction of buildings in Khmunu (Hermopolis) across the river in the reign of Ramesses II. The unusual temples erected at Karnak by Akhenaten and Nefertiti before the move of the court to Akhetaten had been dismantled and used to fill the pylons constructed by Horemheb. For an Egyptian visiting the centers of Akhenaten's power in the early years of the Nineteenth Dynasty, not much in the way of great buildings would have remained visible. There was then good reason to believe that the land of Egypt had been purged of the sickness that had afflicted it during the reigns of Akhenaten and of his immediate successors who could be considered in some way contaminated by the Amarna infection. What precisely was the reason for the deep hatred of the Amarna regime?

It may not just have been the Atenist cult, which had subverted the established religion of the land, incurring the deep hostility of the ancient priesthood. It may have been the disastrous effect of an inadequate foreign policy which had seriously threatened the integrity of the kingdom. It may have been a general malaise resulting from the neglect of the established social system of the country, with the bulk of the population alienated from the strange new culture of the court. It may just have been because the reign of Akhenaten, with its strange, exclusive practices affecting all aspects of life in Egypt, rendered the country almost unrecognizable for what it had been. The period was simply one to be forgotten, and the removal from the recorded national memory of Akhenaten's reign took with it also the reigns of Neferneferuaten, Tutankhamun, and Ay. These last reigns were of little consequence, but they were contaminated by their blood links with Akhenaten.

Consequently, when the list of the ancestors was drawn up to be recorded in the great temple of Sethos I at Abydos, the names of the Amarna Pharaohs were omitted. After Amenophis III, the dazzling monarch of the late Eighteenth Dynasty, the next recorded name was that of Horemheb. The young prince Ramesses is shown presenting to his father the papyrus roll bearing the names of the ancestor kings who were to participate in the offerings for the Kings of Upper and Lower Egypt. So the Amarna kings were not to be included in the distribution of offerings. But it must be noted that they were not the only ones to suffer this exclusion. Hatshepsut, the female Pharaoh of the mid-Eighteenth Dynasty, was not listed, presumably because her reign was thought to have been a usurpation of part of the rightful reign of Tuthmosis III. And no room was found for any of the kings who reigned between the Twelfth and the Eighteenth Dynasties, some of whom were monarchs of substantial achievement and worthy of memorial, particularly those who had initiated and largely carried through the expulsion of the Hyksos, the contaminators of the integrity of Egypt during the so-called Second Intermediate Period. Nevertheless, the deliberate omission of the Amarna Pharaohs, who had reigned in the

relatively recent past, can only be accounted for on the grounds that they were not thought worthy of association with the names in the noble roll-call of acceptable ancestors. To say the least, they had rocked the boat of state; they had upset the balance of the land; they had seemingly ignored Ma'at, the goddess of order, on whose influence Akhenaten had laid such stress.

Horemheb, however, was one of the chosen, in spite of his link with the rejected regime through his holding of important offices of state during the reigns of Tutankhamun and Ay. He had himself possibly no blood relationship with the Amarna royal family, although a qualification in this respect needs to be made. His second wife, Mutnodjmet, may have been a sister of Nefertiti and daughter of Ay, who was probably the senior non-royal person in Egyptian life even in the later years of Akhenaten. This identification is by no means certain, but if it is true, it would provide a slender basis for the legitimacy of Horemheb's claim to the throne after the death of Ay. On the other hand, such a link with the Amarna regime, and particularly a family relationship with Nefertiti, should not have commended him to those who were determined to eradicate the memory of 'the criminal of Akhetaten.'

364 left
Seated figure of the god Amun, protecting King Horemheb, shown standing and holding the heqa-scepter of royal authority. This remarkable group was found buried in the main court of the Luxor temple (Luxor Museum).

364 right
Massive gold ring with rectangular bezel. On one side is the prenomen cartouche of King Horemheb, Djesekheperure Setpenre; on the other, the king shown as a lion and described as "lord of power" (Louvre, N747).

365
Head of the schist statue of Tuthmosis III from the cache of sculpture found in the Karnak temple in 1904; a perfect representation of New Kingdom royalty carved with consummate skill and artistry (Luxor Museum, J2).

We may never know how it came about that Horemheb became king, but what is clear is that his reign was seen as meritorious by his successors of the Nineteenth Dynasty, who even set up, or allowed to be set up a personal cult in his memory. It was centered on the spectacular tomb he had prepared at Saqqara, built probably during the reign of Tutankhamun. Some scholars even believe that it was begun during the reign of Akhenaten, when Horemheb's rise in the ranks of the army and administration in Memphis commenced. The great Saqqara tomb, rediscovered in 1975 and fully excavated for the first time in the subsequent years, reveals in its size, quality of decoration, and the tone of its inscriptions, the standing of Horemheb in the period following the abandonment of Akhetaten. It is not clear to what extent the return to Thebes on the religious front, and the rehabilitation of Memphis as the administrative center of the north, or even the whole country,

were due to the activities of Horemheb. It must be presumed that he worked closely with Ay, perhaps already viewing the possibility of his own accession to the throne of Egypt in due course. He may also have organized, if not led, the few small expeditions of a punitive, but not necessarily acquisitive, nature in Asia Minor and Nubia.

In about 1323 B.C., King Ay died, and he was buried in a substantial tomb in what is known as the Western Valley of the Kings. It is situated near the tomb of King Amenophis III, father of Akhenaten, and it may well have been started in the reign of Tutankhamun, intended for that monarch. Ay had reigned for less than four years, scarcely time to prepare a decent traditional Eighteenth Dynasty tomb. The tomb in which Tutankhamun was interred was in all probability intended for Ay. In switching the sepulchres and supervising the burial of the young Tutankhamun, Ay by tradition established his right to the throne. And it may be

supposed that in performing a similar duty for Ay, Horemheb established his own right to succeed, although no explicit scene or text in Ay's tomb establishes the fact. There is nothing in the surviving record to suggest that Horemheb usurped the royal power against any opposition, and it seems clear from his own surviving record in the form of buildings and texts of achievement that he ruled without any uncertainty. With his record of many years of service in the army and the civil administration, he knew the problems of Egypt and understood the methods to be used to solve them. In the text on the back of a double statue in Turin, showing himself as king with his wife, Queen Mutnodjmet, the account of the royal coronation includes a reference to his having spent many years as deputy or vice-regent of the Two Lands (of Egypt). He clearly stepped into the royal role as if he had been waiting in the wings for the expected cue for his entry.

366 top left
Relief from Horemheb's Saqqara tomb showing a group of foreigners – Syrians, Nubians, and Libyans – raising their hands in greeting, possibly to Horemheb; not captives, but possibly envoys (Louvre, E11273).

366 top right and 366–367
Relief from Horemheb's Saqqara tomb showing a group of African captives squatting on the ground, being supervised by attendants with batons, and having their details noted by a scribe (Bologna, 1887).

367 center
Relief, probably from Horemheb's tomb at Saqqara. The middle register shows female mourners, the other registers, male mourners, all attending the funeral of the tomb-owner (Louvre, E11247).

367 right
Gold earring with small blue glass inlays, from the tomb of General Horemheb at Saqqara. The standing sphinx in the center, wearing the blue crown has the profile of a king of the Amarna Period (Cairo JE97864).

368 top left
Part of a scene of the Opet festival reliefs in the Luxor temple in which sacrificial animals are led in procession. The prize bull shown here, suitably fattened, wears a feathered garland between its horns.

368 bottom left
Priestly attendants bear the great weight of one of the divine barks in which the images of the gods Amun, Mut, and Khonsu travel from Karnak to Luxor for the Opet festival.

368 top right
Attendants with papyrus flowers bring geese for the Opet festivities, followed by others who lead prize bulls decked with garlands, so heavy that their hooves turn up under the weight.

368 bottom right
Music and dancing were important elements in Egyptian festivals, and groups of musicians are shown in the Opet reliefs. Here three lutenists with long-necked instruments are followed by four percussionists with hand-clappers.

Some serious consideration needs to be given to Horemheb because he was undoubtedly the progenitor of the kings of the Nineteenth Dynasty – if not physically, then politically and inspirationally. A long but, sadly, damaged inscription in Karnak sets out the extensive steps he took to wipe out corruption and the exploitation of the helpless lower ranks of society. No doubt there had been a serious deterioration in the administration of justice and the practices of day-to-day government during the Amarna and post-Amarna periods. An even less well-preserved stela set up in Memphis included much of what is found on the Turin double statue. Horemheb is declared to be the son of Amun, thereby reinforcing his royal origin by divine connection. The text also states that he rehabilitated the temples and the old cults of the land. The evidence of his work in the Theban area shows that he revivified the cults at Luxor and Karnak, and in so doing not only built afresh, but also usurped work that had been started in the reign of Amenophis III, and then taken up again during the reign of Tutankhamun. The prime example of Horemheb's conscious elimination of Tutankhamun can be seen in that part of the Luxor temple which is still usually called the colonnade of Horemheb, with the scenes and inscriptions carved on the walls of the court in which the colonnade stands. Here the work representing the celebration of the Festival of Opet, ostensibly under Horemheb, was mostly carried out in the reign of Tutankhamun, and wherever his names appeared in the texts, they have been altered to those of Horemheb. The scenes themselves, wonderfully designed and carved, have

much in common stylistically with those found in the Saqqara tomb of Horemheb, which were also designed and carried out in the reign of Tutankhamun. Many sculptures in the temples of Karnak and Luxor show the unmistakable features of the young king, but were usurped and inscribed for Horemheb. Quite clearly the decision to eliminate Tutankhamun, along with his Amarna predecessors and Ay, from the memory of the Egyptians was a deliberate act of policy, the precise reasons for which are now not easy to determine. And yet, the royal tombs of Tutankhamun and Ay were not officially desecrated in the reign of Horemheb. These kings were dead, and their tombs inaccessible; they were out of the way; their tombs were not public monuments that might serve as reminders of the past.

The case was very different with the unusual temples built by Akhenaten and Nefertiti at Karnak. They had to be dismantled, just like the temples and palaces at Akhetaten. In Karnak it is certain that the destroyer was Horemheb because the neatly shaped blocks used for their construction were reused to form the fillings of the pylons built in the great temple of Amun under Horemheb. These blocks, approximately three handspans long and known as *talatat* (from the Arabic for three), were laid neatly in layers within the outer skin-walls of the pylons. The blocks have been removed and, since World War II, studied and partially reassembled. In a sense, therefore, the elimination of the temples of Akhenaten and Nefertiti has turned out to be somewhat temporary.

Although Horemheb had a distinguished military career behind him, if one may judge from his titles, there is not much evidence of his having conducted any substantial campaigns either during the reign of Tutankhamun, or when he was king. He had been in every respect commander in chief: his titles, as presented in his Saqqara tomb, rather overemphasize his position: "Overseer of Generals of the Lord of the Two Lands, General, General of the Lord of the Two Lands, Greatest General, Greatest General of the King, Greatest General of the Lord of the Two Lands." In presenting his position with such hyperbole he was simply emphasizing the evident fact that he was number one in the military hierarchy; he undoubtedly saw himself primarily as a military man.

369 left
Relief representation of a king in the Luxor temple, named by the cartouche as Horemheb. The royal features, however, show indubitably the young Tutankhamun; the cartouche has clearly been carved over.

369 right
Painted quartzite colossal statue. Stylistically it may be dated to the reign of Tutankhamun, but it was usurped by both of his successors, Ay and Horemheb, in whose funerary temple it was found (Cairo, JE59869).

Ramesses II

In making promotions he unsurprisingly favored other military men, the most notable of whom was Pramesse. Scribal statues of this distinguished officer of state, set up by the tenth pylon at Karnak, bear texts that trace the rise to power of Pramesse. He was the son of Sety, an army officer of fairly modest rank, who hailed from the Delta. The texts may not chart with precision the steady course of Pramesse through the ranks of the military hierarchy. He had been overseer of horse, charioteer of His Majesty, king's messenger in all foreign lands, general of the lord of the Two Lands, and royal scribe of troop commanders. He also held important civil and religious positions: overseer of the treasury, overseer of the river mouths, overseer of the priests of all the gods. He eventually was made deputy of His Majesty in the South and the North and vizier. By fortune or by sheer talent, Pramesse gained Horemheb's favor and was promoted from rank to rank until he occupied the highest positions in the civil, religious, and military sections of Egyptian life.

It was a remarkable advancement, and it has been concluded, probably rightly, that at a relatively early point in his reign Horemheb decided that Pramesse was the man to succeed him on the throne of Egypt. Much emphasis has been placed by historians of the New Kingdom on the military element in this rise to great offices of state, of someone from an apparently simple Delta family. But Pramesse presumably demonstrated in his career more than a military efficiency and a capability to command. Like Horemheb himself, his abilities

became apparent through the success with which he exercised his successive offices; in the end, no doubt, his handling of administrative matters at a high level, combined probably with a loyal trust in his monarch, commended him as the possible successor to the throne of Egypt.

The question of succession and the legitimacy of the claim to royalty by Egyptian kings were always matters of concern for the ruling Pharaoh. For a king with a family including sons, the question of succession was on the whole determined by the principle of primogeniture in the first instance; there might be difficulties, however, in following this principle in some cases, especially where the claim to the throne might be

complicated by marriage – the status of the wife of the prospective heir having herself the possibility of affecting the succession through her own royal parentage. The background to succession is rarely clear, but the need for a king to ensure the 'right' succession might require the use of some constitutional device like co-regency, or simple regency. We shall see shortly what arrangement King Sethos I used to establish the smooth succession for his son Ramesses to the kingship. For Horemheb, growing old and still childless, and furthermore suffering from a constitutional impediment of his own uncertain claim to divine kingship, the matter of succession was of great, if not paramount importance.

Horemheb had but the slightest blood relationship with the Eighteenth Dynasty royal line. With no children, he could not expect to be the founder by blood of the line which would follow him. He himself had, however, acted as "Deputy of the Two Lands," according to the text on his Turin double statue; this title has usually been taken to mean that he acted as co-regent with King Ay, who himself was childless. In Horemheb's case the device worked well, and he became king in due course on the death of Ay. And so, to secure the succession for Pramesse, he appointed him "Deputy of His Majesty in the South and the North," a title perhaps more explicit than "Deputy of the Two Lands." Again the device worked, and when Horemheb died in about 1295 B.C., Pramesse succeeded him, dropping the *p* or *pa* (the definite

370
Head of King Horemheb from a scene in his tomb in the Valley of the Kings; he offers wine to Hathor, goddess of the West. The bright colors contrast strongly with the blue-gray background.

371 top
The prenomen and nomen of Horemheb, finely carved and painted in his Theban tomb. The prenomen (right cartouche) reads Djeserkheperure Setpenre; the nomen (left cartouche) Horemheb Meryamun.

371 bottom
Horemheb honors Isis four times; a scene from the king's Theban tomb. The goddess is "mother of the god, lady of heaven, mistress of all the gods." On the right stands jackal-headed Anubis.

Ramesses II

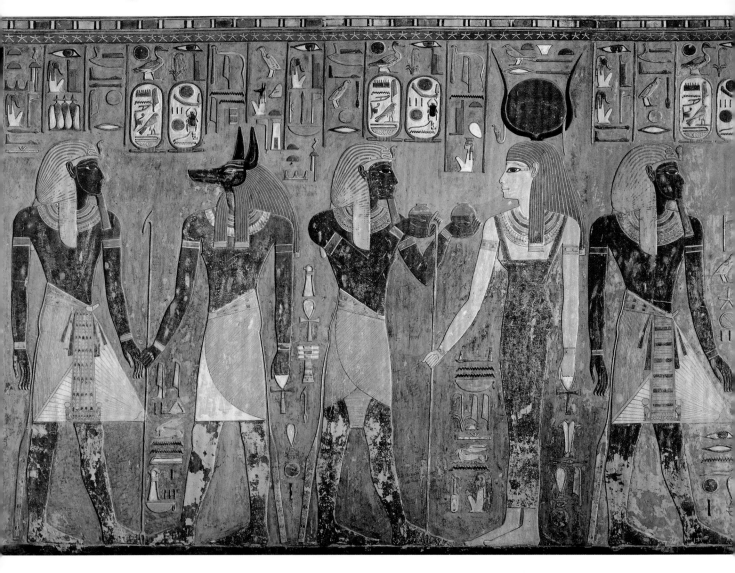

article) at the start of his name, becoming Ramesse, or Ramesses as he is now usually called, using the Greek form. He is seen to be the founder of the Nineteenth Dynasty, but some historians with very good reason prefer to consider Horemheb himself as the founder. His reign was a kind of transitional period between the final 'eliminated' rulers of the Eighteenth Dynasty and the new Delta line of the Nineteenth Dynasty. We should remember, however, that the dynastic divisions were not established as such at this period of Egyptian history, although changes in family lines were recognized. In this respect Horemheb was undoubtedly seen to belong to the succeeding kings of the line of Ramesses, and, as we noted earlier, his first tomb at Saqqara became an honored cult-center especially during the reign of Ramesses, when his sister Tia had her tomb built adjacent to that of Horemheb, the illustrious progenitor of the Ramesside Dynasty.

Pramesse, now for us Ramesses I, officiated at

the burial of Horemheb in the main Valley of the Kings, thereby reinforcing his legitimacy. The tomb is large and finely decorated with texts and representations from the compositions used for royal burials in the New Kingdom; they are set against a very distinctive blue-gray background. The whole scheme and its execution are very different from what was placed in his non-royal Saqqara tomb. There is no evidence of a cult attached to the Theban tomb, apart from the common royal funerary cult. The latter, however, was usually practiced in the royal mortuary temple built on the edge of the cultivated plain in Western Thebes. Horemheb's mortuary temple was built at the south end of the line of temples, adjacent to the site of what was to become the mortuary temple of Ramesses III at Medinet Habu. Its remote position was determined by the existence of a temple foundation for Ay, and possibly even one for Tutankhamun. Nothing of consequence can now be seen on the ground; it

has disappeared along with other Eighteenth Dynasty mortuary temples, dismantled during the Ramesside Period.

Very little has survived to suggest that Horemheb developed an aggressive foreign policy during his reign to counteract the weaknesses of the Amarna Pharaohs. He was undoubtedly fortunate that, for other reasons, the most threatening forces in the Near East were preoccupied and unable to exploit the weakened state of Egyptian imperial power, particularly during the reign of Akhenaten. A moment of real danger had occurred when the Hittite king, Suppiluliumas, sent one of his sons as a prospective husband for a widowed Egyptian queen, probably to be identified as Ankhesenamun, wife of Tutankhamun. From Hittite records it emerges that things went badly wrong, and the young prince was killed in Egypt. This tragedy happened when Ay was king; there was then a real danger of an explosive situation developing into conflict between Egypt and Hatti,

the Hittite kingdom. Nothing, however, was done
to avenge the death. Suppiluliumas died in about
1323 B.C., and his successor, Arunwandas II,
shortly afterward. His brother and successor,
Mursilis II, young and inexperienced, was more
immediately concerned with troubles brewing in
Arzawa to the west, in the lands bordering the
Black Sea to the north, and in the kingdom of
Azzi-Hayasa to the east. The re-establishment of
Hittite influence in these regions engrossed the
attention of the Hittites for many years. In the
lands formerly closely associated with Egypt,
further trouble arose in Syria involving
Carchemish, and it seems probable that Horemheb
took advantage of the Hittite involvement
elsewhere to launch a raid on the coast of
Lebanon, his forces possibly pushing as far east as
Carchemish. Details are uncertain, but it does not
appear that this small campaign represented more
than a testing of local weaknesses. A rebellion in
Nubia was also dealt with promptly and firmly.

372–373
*In the antechamber of Horemheb's
royal tomb the king makes offerings
and greeting to a series of deities;
jackal-headed Anubis, Isis the Great,
Horus-son-of-Isis, Hathor, "Lady of
Heaven," and Osiris.*

373 bottom
*Upper part of a figure of the goddess
Hathor, from Horemheb's tomb. She
receives wine from the king, and is
here described as "chief of the West,
lady of heaven, mistress of all
the gods."*

Post-Amarna Egypt

By concentrating on rebuilding the economy of Egypt, rehabilitating the cults and shrines of the gods, and restoring a degree of national confidence and pride, Horemheb prepared the way for his chosen successor. It was presumably evident that there could be trouble in Asia Minor, and in choosing Pramesse to succeed him, Horemheb based his judgment on Pramesse's military background and his tested administrative abilities. So we may conclude on the evidence of inscriptions which would hardly have been composed in contrary terms. But the evidence is positive, and in the absence of any different indications, we should accept that Horemheb chose wisely. The one possible drawback was Pramesse's age. At the time of his accession he may already have been in his mid-sixties, an advanced age for ancient Egypt, and scarcely the age at which to assume so awesome a role. But a man in his sixties with a distinguished record would be more acceptable as king and founder of a new line than someone of less tried achievement. Pramesse also had a son, Sety, who was in his forties when Horemheb died. The succession looked promising, and Horemheb's expectations were not to be disappointed.

On assuming the throne, Pramesse, now Ramesses, took as his distinctive name (after called the throne-name) Menpehtyre, which means 'one enduring of strength is Re.' It suggested positive action, and by intention or by chance it recalled the throne-name of Amosis, first king of the Eighteenth Dynasty, Nebpehtyre, 'one who is possessor of strength is Re.' Sadly, he had little chance to prove himself as a ruler of strength. His reign lasted less than a year and a half, and his son Sety found himself, far sooner than he might have expected, turned from Ramesses' deputy into his successor, King of Upper and Lower Egypt. The change might have been disastrous for the new dynasty and for Egypt, but no evidence has survived to suggest that the careful foundations of stability laid by Horemheb, and presumably consolidated by Ramesses in his short reign, were disturbed by internal discord. Egyptian official records, however, do not usually mention matters which might reflect badly on the established regime.

374–375
Scenes in the burial chamber of Ramesses I. Left: beetle-headed Khepri, the sun-god at dawn, receives offerings from the king. Right: he is led to Osiris by Horus-son-of-Isis, Atum, and Neith.

375 top
Ramesses is greeted by falcon-headed Horus-son-of-Isis, wearing the double crown, and jackal-headed Anubis, god of embalming. A blue-gray wash is used for the background color, as in Horemheb's tomb.

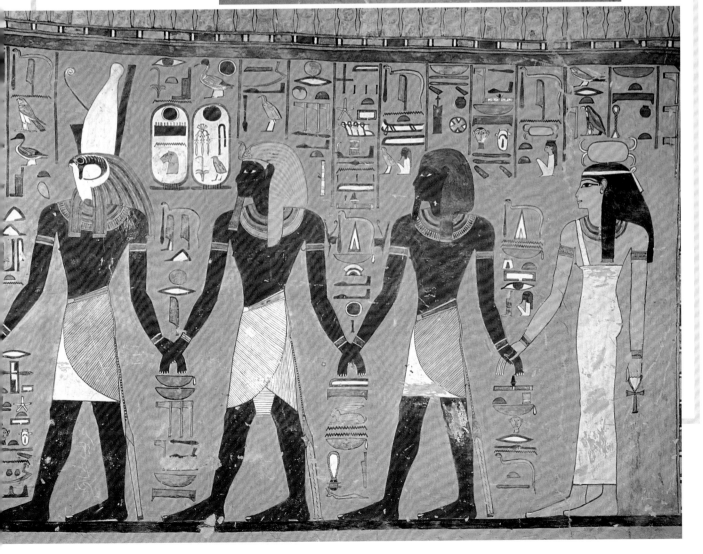

Sety became king – he is often given the Greek form Sethos – and took as his throne-name Menmare, 'one enduring in *ma'at* (truth or order) is Re.' He took over the running of the country and the prosecution of a lively foreign policy, following no doubt the plans his father had drawn up with him.

Sethos honored the memory of his father and promoted a cult in his honor by dedicating a chapel close to his own remarkable temple at Abydos, and later by including a further chapel for him in his mortuary temple in Western Thebes. Most of the very fine reliefs from the Abydos chapel are now in the Metropolitan Museum of Art, New York – but not the surviving part of the great stela of dedication, the text on which sets out what Sethos regarded as his debt to his father, and the extent to which he had put into practice the policies they had surely discussed together in his father's lifetime. Sethos reorganized the army, led a campaign against the Fenkhu (Phoenicians) in the Levant, and generally cleaned up rebellious peoples – possibly infiltrating tribesmen – in the desert. Much of this activity took place while Ramesses was still alive, and Sety, the crown prince, more than suggests in retrospect that whatever good happened in Ramesses' short reign was the result of his own skills and initiative. As King Sethos, he set out to take most of the credit without actually rubbishing his father and his achievement. He was also prepared to view the beginning of his reign as the start of a new era. In the Karnak scenes depicting his triumphs in the early part of the reign, he designates his first year as *wehem mesut*, 'repeating of births.'

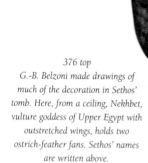

376 top
G.-B. Belzoni made drawings of much of the decoration in Sethos' tomb. Here, from a ceiling, Nekhbet, vulture goddess of Upper Egypt with outstretched wings, holds two ostrich-feather fans. Sethos' names are written above.

376 bottom
Belzoni's illustration showing Sethos being led into the presence of Osiris "first in the West and Great God," by Horus. Behind Osiris stands Hathor with the emblem of the West on her head.

377
Head of Sethos from a composite statue made in a number of pieces. The head and upper part of the body are made of alabaster (calcite), originally with eyes and eyebrows of other materials (Cairo, JE36692).

These words were used from time to time in Egypt to indicate the start of a new era – renaissance is the word often used to translate them – but nearly always as seen at the time or shortly afterward. By regarding the start of his reign as a *wehem mesut*, Sethos endowed himself with an importance which had perhaps been intended by Horemheb for Ramesses I.

Sethos in fact had some justification in making this claim, because it was he who put into effect the prospective policies of Horemheb, and in most ways prepared the ground for his son Ramesses II. Sethos achieved so much in his moderately long reign of eleven to fifteen years that had he survived a little longer, he might have confronted the Hittite challenge at Qadesh and secured a reputation which would now stand higher than that of his great successor. But that is idle speculation. Sethos had enough to do from the outset of his reign in continuing the rehabilitation of the internal condition of Egypt, and in re-establishing a strong Egyptian presence in Asia Minor. His campaigns are graphically and finely recorded on the outside of the northern wall of the great Hypostyle Hall of the Karnak temple. The foray made while he was still crown prince had introduced him to the kind of campaigning to be expected in Asia Minor. He did not delay in delivering a sharp reminder to the unruly tribes of Palestine that the Egyptian lion was once more awake and ready to pounce. In his very first year (c.1294 B.C.), an attack was launched from the border post of Sile at the northeastern edge of the Delta. His first target was the Shasu tribe, or collection of tribes, noted for their independent spirit, the ancestors of the modern Bedouin. Sethos' forces were already organized into three divisions named after the great gods Amun, Re, and Sutekh, or Seth, the last of whom had risen to prominence through the patronage of the kings of the Nineteenth Dynasty who came from the region of Seth's cult center in the Delta. These divisions would figure in the great Qadesh adventure of Ramesses II, joined with a fourth named after Ptah, the great Memphite god.

From Gaza Sethos moved north into Palestine, the land then known to the Egyptians as Canaan, and here a number of towns were captured. In the same campaign in Year 1, or a little later, Egyptian power was extended into Lebanon, and in what was probably a campaign of later years, his forces moved against Amurru, in northern Lebanon, and went east to take the town of Qadesh. By that time the Hittites were not involved in any confrontation, although in another campaign, unfortunately undated, and only partly visible on the outer wall of the Hypostyle Hall, Sethos claimed to have attacked and seriously defeated the land of 'vile Kheta,' a designation commonly applied to the Hittites. It is not always possible to confirm the details of campaigns and conquests set out in the triumphant scenes placed by Egyptian kings on temple walls. The tradition of overemphasizing the extent and success of campaigns was well

established by the time of the Nineteenth Dynasty, and it was not the practice to underestimate the outcome of foreign adventures. Scenes and inscriptions in temples within Egypt were composed as statements of intent as much as of achievement. They contained a religio-magical element designed always to vaunt the power of the reigning monarch. They were prompted not by simple braggadocio, but by the need to proclaim the greatness of the king. It should not, however, be understood from this that nothing in these temple scenes should be believed. But their claims need always to be treated with caution, and checked when possible against other evidence. In the case of Sethos' campaigns a number of inscriptions set up in the regions penetrated by his armies confirm an Egyptian presence. Two inscriptions found at Beth-Shan in northern Canaan, one dated to Year 1, the other with its

380
Ippolito Rosellini's drawing of the scene shown in the photograph on its right. A comparison illustrates the damage suffered by the temple wall since the 1820s, much of it caused by the women of Luxor scraping off sandstone dust for magical purposes.

381 top
In another Karnak relief, Sethos I
smites a foreign notable with his
mace, in front of an approving
(but noticeably smaller) Amon-Re.
The prisoners are all Asiatics.

380–381
Scene from the outer wall of the
Karnak Hypostyle Hall, showing
King Sethos smitting the collected
foreign rulers from north and south,
to the glory of Amon-Re, who
receives the presentation with
upraised scimitar.

381 top
In another Karnak relief, Sethos I
smites a foreign notable with his
mace, in front of an approving
(but noticeably smaller) Amon-Re.
The prisoners are all Asiatics.

382–383
A scene reproduced in the
Description de l'Égypte *showing*
Sethos I in his war chariot hunting
down and shooting at his Syrian
enemies, some of whom have been
struck by his arrows and have fallen
in the water to die.

date lost, record Egyptian military activities in the region. The remains of a stela of Sethos found at Tell al-Shihab, some miles to the east of the Sea of Galilee, although lacking its main text, further confirms the presence of Egyptians there during his reign. In addition, there is a suggestion from Hittite records that some form of treaty may have been concluded between Mursilis II and Sethos. No date is offered, but we should probably be right to conclude that it was in Sethos' early years; as a result the Asiatic situation was stabilized for the rest of his reign. And so Egyptian influence in Asia Minor was partially restored, with a limited Egyptian presence in the region.

The other places from which trouble might have been expected, especially at times when Egypt appeared to be vulnerable, were Libya to the west and Nubia to the south. One part of the series of scenes on the outer wall of the Hypostyle Hall does in fact deal with a Libyan campaign, unfortunately without a date and singularly unspecific in detail. There need be no doubt that such a campaign occurred. Although the northwestern boundary of Egypt had apparently been untroubled for a very long time, the absence of evidence for military activity in the region may disguise the brewing of potential trouble. Ramesses II would in due course be obliged to set up fortresses in the area, and any aggressive inroads by Libyans would take place later in the Nineteenth

382 bottom
Sethos steps down from his chariot
to accept the submission of the chiefs
of the Lebanon, some of whom are
organizing the felling of trees for the
royal bark and flag staves. From the
Description de l'Égypte.

383 bottom
Sethos in his war chariot, raising his
scimitar, charges headlong into his
Syrian enemies. A scene on the outer
north wall of the Hypostyle Hall at
Karnak. From the Description de
l'Égypte.

Dynasty. Again, in this vaguely recorded campaign Sethos may have been pre-empting an attack, or simply suggesting to the Libyans that it would not be profitable to mount hostile activity now that Egyptian power had been revivified.

In the south, in Nubia, things remained peaceful for most of Sethos' reign. A local skirmish, prompted by good intelligence information, nipped in the bud a possible revolt in Kush. It was probably a very modest campaign, not thought worthy to appear among those commemorated on the walls of the Hypostyle Hall at Karnak; it was, however, the subject of two inscriptions found on Sai Island and at Amara, both administrative centers between the second and third cataracts of the Nile. In general, Nubia was well settled, and Sethos even chose the very distant site of Nauri, near the third cataract, to carve a huge inscription dealing with the legal arrangements concerning his great Abydos temple about six hundred miles to the north in Middle Egypt. Its position there seems beyond explanation; the local inhabitants would not have been able to read it, and if they had asked its meaning from some passing Egyptian scribe, they would have been very puzzled by the detailed instructions concerning the temple's lands and the immunities of those who worked on them. Other indications suggest that Sethos may have been considering the development of Nubia beyond its simple imperial function; he may have begun the work on the great temple at Gebel Barkal (Napata), downstream from the fourth cataract, one of his son's foundations.

385 top
Sethos returns to Karnak from his campaign against the Hittites (undated), driving before his chariot two files of prisoners for presentation to Amun. The king, looking backwards, is about to mount his chariot. From Karnak.

385 right
A detail from a scene in the Karnak temple in which Sethos is shown attacking a Hittite force. Beneath the king's horses, a tangle of confused and slain enemy is ridden over by the supporting Egyptian chariots.

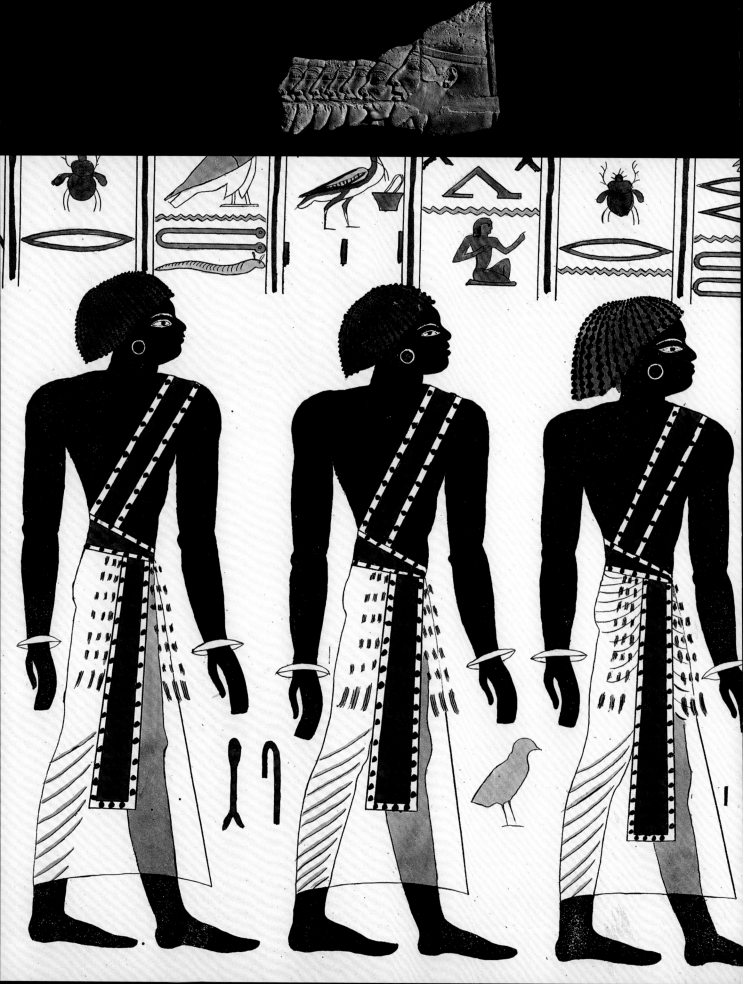

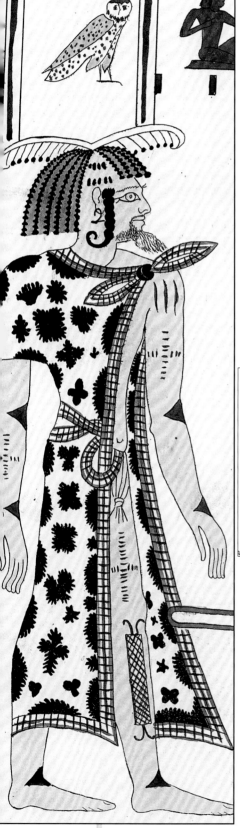

His hand may also be detected at other sites where Ramesses II left major memorials. In so many ways, the great works of the son seem to have taken up, expanded, and then surpassed what the father may have intended or even begun.

Among the most memorable structures surviving from ancient Egypt, few make such a stupendous impression as the Hypostyle Hall in the great temple of Amun at Karnak. Here is a forest of massive columns, 12 with open papyrus capitals forming the center aisle, with 122 smaller columns with closed capitals, 61 on either side of the central colonnade. Here, as in so many places in Egypt, the visitor is reminded of Ramesses II, under whom much of the decoration of the hall was carried out. But the history of the planning of the hall goes back at least to the reign of Horemheb, who put in hand the building of the Second Pylon of the temple, thereby creating a great court to the west of the Third Pylon, built by Amenophis III. Some work at

386 top
The heads of Asiatic princes about to be struck by the royal mace. From Karnak.

386–387
Belzoni's copy of the representatives of the four races of mankind, shown in the fifth hour of the Book of Gates *in Sethos I's tomb. On the right are Libyans, and on the left, Nubians.*

387 right
Karnak scene of uncertain date, copied by Wilkinson, of the attack on the Hittites by Sethos I. The king drives his chariot into the Hittite forces, firing arrows as he goes. For its time, this copy is remarkably accurate.

the entrance to this great court may be dated to the reign of Ramesses I, and much of the subsequent inner construction of the columns and the decoration of the internal and external walls was carried out in Sethos' reign.

Who can now tell what the original plan entailed: an open court with a colonnade, as at Luxor, or the majestic columned hall we know today? The work of a successor can so easily conceal the work and the intentions of his predecessor.

Greater certainty attends the foundation and building of Sethos' most splendid construction, the unusual but stupendous temple of Osiris at Abydos. Although much of the work on the building was carried out in the reign of Ramesses II, the textual record makes it clear that Sethos instigated the

project. Abydos was one of the most sacred sites in Egypt; the center of the cult of the dead king, the divine Osiris. It was almost exclusively a place of pilgrimage and never was, or ever became, an important administrative center. Earlier kings had built cenotaphs or similar structures at Abydos, but no great cult temple had been built, possibly because of the remoteness and lack of political importance of the site. Sethos' family came from the Delta, from the heartland of Seth, the brother, rival, and murderer of Osiris; Sethos' very name meant 'the one of (or belonging to) Seth,' and he may well have been advised that the still uncertain legitimacy of the new dynasty needed further strengthening by an important act of devotion to Osiris, with whom he would in due course be identified in death.

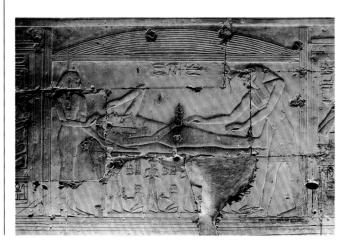

Whether the primary purpose of the foundation was religious or political, the result was exceptional, both in its originality and its decoration. Here, sadly, is not the place to examine this temple in detail, but at least it may be said that the exquisite limestone reliefs in the second hypostyle hall and in the chapels dedicated to the principal gods of Egypt, in the main Osiris chapel, and in the chapel dedicated to the king himself, represent the most perfect expression of ancient Egyptian relief carving. They have an exceptional purity where color has been lost, and stunning splendor where color has survived. The style and execution hark back to the best work produced in the reign of Amenophis III, but with a relaxing of formality, which can be ascribed to the lasting influence of the revolutionary art of the Amarna Period.

The same artistic quality can be found in the work in Sethos' mortuary temple at Thebes, but there the medium – sandstone – was less receptive of the sensitivity of line and the precision of carving which the limestone of Abydos allowed. Similarly, his tomb in the Valley of the Kings is generally recognized as containing the artistically finest versions of the standard New Kingdom royal tomb compositions, whether in painted carved

relief or just in painted outline. The tomb sadly has suffered dreadfully at the hands of man and at the depredation of Nature since it was first rediscovered by Belzoni in 1817. The standard of work set by the royal craftsmen in Sethos' reign was not to be maintained in subsequent reigns, in the case of Ramesses II presumably because the scale and quantity of what was built in his time far exceeded the capability of skilled craftsmen to decorate to the level of Sethos' reign. The works carried out under Sethos in the great northern capital of Memphis can now scarcely be determined, and little remains from the buildings set up in the new Delta Residence.

From a relatively early point in his reign, Sethos associated his young son Ramesses with his activities in the field of war and in peaceful events at home. In the Karnak scene dealing with the Libyan foray, the figure of the young Prince Ramesses was inserted into the composition, in one place just simply added, in another replacing an original figure of an official. The insertions were presumably made during Sethos' reign; if later, then more emphasis would surely have been placed on them.

Some years before his death, Sethos decided to clinch the succession by associating Ramesses with him as co-regent. The circumstances are set out in

the course of a great inscription in Sethos' Abydos temple, and dated in Ramesses Year 1. It is, as might be expected, an account full of hyperbole and quite unspecific in detail. Ramesses states that his father in principle made over Egypt to him before he was born, "while I was in the egg"; in due course "while I was a child in his arms" Sethos in the presence of the people said, "Crown him as king that I may see his beauty while I am still living."

The words make up a kind of myth: Ramesses was scarcely a child when he became co-regent. In fact he was probably in his teens, even approaching twenty. But the reality of his promotion cannot be doubted. Yet he was still not given royal titles: in the corridor of the king list in Sethos' Abydos temple, Ramesses is shown as a youth, wearing the side-lock, and described as "hereditary prince and senior king's son." His co-regency was not a full co-regency, such as was not uncommon in ancient Egypt; he did not share regnal years with his father. But he was poised to take over the kingship, as Sethos had planned. On Sethos' death in about 1279 B.C., the transition was apparently seamless. And so Year 1 of Usimare, Ramesses-mery-Amun began.

390 top
The Gallery of the Lists at Abydos. Right: Sethos and his son Prince Ramesses make presentation of offerings to various deities. Left: They present the names of the kings of Egypt to be included in the presentation.

390 center
The young Prince Ramesses stands in front of his father Sethos, holding open a papyrus roll from which he reads out the names of the ancestor kings who are to be included in the offerings.

390 bottom
Part of the king list from Ramesses II's temple at Abydos, close to his father's temple. The middle row contains the cartouches of the kings of the Eighteenth Dynasty, omitting Hatshepsut and the Amarna rulers (British Museum, EA117).

391
From the chapels in the Abydos temple: Sethos is embraced by the jackal-headed Wepwawet, the local necropolis deity; above Sethos, Nekhbet, the vulture deity, offers the king life and dominion.

RAMESSES II AND
THE EXTERNAL WORLD

392
Ramesses II grasps the hair of three representative enemies: Asiatic, Nubian and Libyan. From Memphis, on a block reused by Merenptah. This small scene recalls the grander representations of domination found on temple pylons (Cairo, JE 46189).

393
A painting by Prisse d'Avennes of the young Ramesses shown as the iunmutef-priest, with side-lock and leopard garment, offering to the deity: he holds a pellet of incense between his fingers.

Self-confidence, backed by some years of near-royal authority and experience, is thought to have characterized the reign of Ramesses II from its outset in about 1279 B.C. The great text which was set up in the temple of Sethos in Abydos, dated in Year 1 of Ramesses, dwells chiefly on the extraordinary works which the son would accomplish in the memory and honor of the father. There is no mention of what was to be done in Asia Minor, Libya, and Nubia. The tone and content are domestic, and little doubt could be left in the mind of the reader of the text that young Ramesses knew what was to be done and how it was to be done. How long would he have to complete his program? His grandfather had become king in his sixties, and reigned for less than two years; his father was probably in his mid-thirties when he succeeded, and he reigned for possibly sixteen years. Old age was not expected in ancient Egypt even for kings, and Ramesses on accession in his early twenties could not have expected a reign of more than thirty years. Was he

then starting a sprint or a middle-distance race? How could he have expected that it was to be a marathon? Bombastic inscriptions, not unexpectedly, always predicted long life for the king, and in the Abydos inscription toward its end, the deceased Sethos thanks his son for his devotion to his memory, and states that Re, the great sun god, has granted him an eternity of years: "Pass eternity for your lifetime as King of Upper and Lower Egypt." He, Sethos, had suggested to Osiris that he should double Ramesses' lifespan while again Re granted him eternity and everlastingness, and millions of jubilees. Rarely was such a prediction to be so amply fulfilled. In his exceptional reign of sixty-six years plus a few months, Ramesses would celebrate more jubilees than were ever recorded for an Egyptian king.

In about 1279 B.C., however, Ramesses had no idea that he would have plenty of time to carry through any programs that he may have considered suitable for his reign. He may have had no program, but just a wish to make his mark at home

and abroad, in building, in improving the lot of his people, in establishing good administration, in reimposing Egyptian power in lands that once were under the control of the Pharaoh. These were traditional purposes for a new Egyptian king, and in Ramesses' case, he had no serious pieces of unfinished business left over from the reign of his father. In the Abydos inscription, references are made to the structures left incomplete but completed by Ramesses, and to all the commercial and administrative arrangements made for the running of the temple of Abydos, and in the land of Egypt generally. But every Egyptian king left great works uncompleted, to be finished by his successor, and no living king would pretend in a formal text that he was simply carrying out what his predecessor had started. And we know from the provisions made in the great inscription set up by Sethos at Nauri, far to the south in Nubia, that very adequate arrangements had been made in his lifetime for the running of the temple and the temple estates.

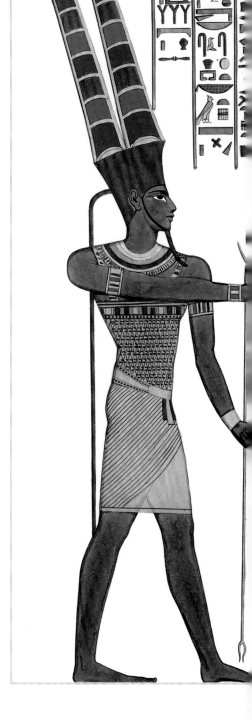

Numerous building works and other domestic activities engrossed Ramesses' attention in the early years of his reign, and it was not until Year 4 that he turned his gaze to the east and began to consider military activities in a region which had been mostly dominated by Egyptian power up to the reign of Amenophis III – the last of the 'recognized' kings of the Eighteenth Dynasty before the disintegration of influence under that 'criminal of Akhetaten.' It will be recalled that a short campaign under Sethos into Canaan had begun the process of imperial rehabilitation. The lurking presence of Hittite power to the north was now an important factor in the balance of power in Western Asia, and some kind of treaty between Sethos and Mursilis II, the Hittite king, appears to have temporarily settled relations between Egypt and Hatti. But the endemic instability of the region could only in time lead to further confrontations. In about 1295 B.C. Mursilis II died, and was succeeded by his son Muwatallis, who apparently recognized that the threat of attack by

Egypt was increased after the accession of Ramesses II. In this he was not mistaken.

The first campaign into Asia took place in Year 4 (c.1276–1275 B.C.). Details are rather sketchy: the remains of two inscriptions set up by Ramesses at Byblos and at Nahr al-Kalb (Dog River) near modern Beirut, both dated to Year 4, provide the reliable confirmatory evidence of the campaign. No specific record can be identified among the many war scenes found in the Theban temples or elsewhere in Egypt. The Egyptian forces apparently moved quickly through Canaan, up into Phoenicia, and even convinced the king of Amurru to switch allegiance from the Hittite king to the Egyptians. It may have been a trial campaign for what would follow in Year 5. Still, numerous small towns and districts were reoccupied after about fifty years of submission to other masters; their names are not recorded in the dated records of the campaign, but they may well be included in the lists of foreign dependencies carved on the walls of the Theban temples.

394
A group of New Kingdom bronze weapons including a khepesh-sword inscribed for Ramesses II. In the scene opposite, such a weapon is being offered to the king by Amon-Re as a pledge of victory.

394–395
Reproduction by Rosellini of a scene of the King Ramesses holding the topknots of Asiatics, Nubians, and Libyans, ready to be smitten by his bladed mace. The king is in the presence of Amon-Re, who is presenting him with the khepesh-sword.

396–397
Part of a scene showing prisoners
bunched together, presumably
waiting for the king's mace or sword
to descend on their heads. The faces
are finely carved with the features
of Nubians clearly distinguishable
(Cairo, JE69306).

397 top
Detail of a drawing by Lepsius
of part of a scene in the temple
at Abu Simbel of submissive
prisoners about to be destroyed by
the royal mace. The three usual
racial types are shown: Asiatic,
Nubian, and Libyan.

397 bottom
Drawing by Rosellini of a kneeling
captive, certainly of Asiatic origin as
indicated by his beard and the
meager strapping on his body. The
royal arm is shown wearing a guard
to protect it from the snapping
bowstring.

Ramesses was presumably pleased with the outcome of his first punitive strike into Asia. Opposition was slight, and one major result was the defection of the king of Amurru. While this switch of allegiance may have delighted the Egyptian king, it was not well received by the Hittite king Muwatallis.

The Hittite empire, strategically strong in its heartland, was surrounded by potentially dissident vassals to whom a firm hand was usually applied when necessary. Egypt, however, was another matter. It was sufficiently far away to be safe from a direct Hittite strike, but something could be done to counteract the results of Egyptian activities in areas now seen to be within the ambit of Hittite power. If there were to be a serious settlement of the rivalry between Egypt and Hatti (or Kheta, as the Egyptians called it), it would have to take place in Asia at a point where the rival powers would most probably seek naturally to confront each other. Such a place was Qadesh in Syria, to the east of Amurru.

The contest which took place soon afterward, in Ramesses' Year 5, was wholly predictable, and the kings on both sides made ample provision for a major confrontation. During the winter following Ramesses' 'first expedition of victory,' Muwatallis began to muster his forces, calling up support from all parts of his imperial domain. Ramesses,

undoubtedly well served by some useful intelligence of what Muwatallis was planning, understood that his second expedition of victory might not be as easy an operation as his first. Suitable arrangements were made to prepare and equip a very substantial Egyptian force; allies might have been forewarned of what might be expected of them. It was to be a classic encounter. In the spring of about 1274 B.C. the operation was launched. The army set out on the ninth day of the second month of summer (according to the Egyptian calendar, out of step with the natural year) in Year 5. What followed was to be so important for the rest of Ramesses' reign that a full treatment of the campaign will be postponed for the next chapter. For the present let us record just that after a difficult and seemingly inconclusive, battle, the forces of Egypt and Hatti disengaged; Ramesses returned to his Delta capital, to pursue activities elsewhere, and, no doubt, ponder his options. As for Muwatallis, his forces did not retire immediately to his capital, Hattusas, in the Anatolian uplands, to lick their wounds, metaphorically speaking. Muwatallis took advantage of the Egyptian withdrawal to move south, recover Amurru, and take over the part of Syria in the neighborhood of Damascus known as Upe. Threats from the east, from Assyria, diverted the Hittites and prevented progress south.

For some years Ramesses apparently considered it prudent not to renew operations in Asia Minor. He had many other things on his mind, and he would undoubtedly have wished to delay any further 'expeditions of victory' in Asia until he could be sure of some success. Egyptian power remained recognized by many vassal rulers in Canaan and adjacent lands, and it may be assumed that good information was sent regularly to the Egyptian court at Piramesse in the Delta by agents operating in these parts. An Egyptian king with pretensions to restore the power and influence of his country in regions formerly well within the sphere of Egyptian dominion could hardly remain idle for long. In the case of Ramesses II there exists much pictorial and some inscriptional evidence to show that he did campaign in the east. Unfortunately, many of the great tableaux of war carved on the walls of Luxor, Karnak, and the Ramesseum and elsewhere are undated, or have lost their dated epigraphs. Some

of the expeditions can be assigned probable dates from inference and by means of other dated monuments. In Ramesses' Year 8 (c.1272–1271 B.C.), a sharp campaign was conducted in Canaan, extending eastward into Moab, where there were strong indications of a slackening of allegiance to Egypt. Ramesses was accompanied by his oldest son, Amonhikhopshef, who was allowed to conduct a foray on his own. Apparently the opposition put up little fight, and it was not long before Egyptian forces could move north as far as Damascus, recovering parts of the territory that had defected to the Hittites after Qadesh. A list of the places retaken or captured anew was carved on the front pylon of the Ramesseum, although many of the names have been lost.

Encouraged by his relatively easy success in the south of the Levantine lands, Ramesses directed his forces north into Syria, into lands that were more directly affected by Hittite suzerainty. After reasserting his control over the seaports of

Lebanon, he turned east, driving north to Qadesh along the Orontes valley, subduing the small principalities of Dapur and Tunip. He set his mark on Dapur characteristically by having a statue of himself erected there. No trace has survived. The Egyptians were playing a dangerous game in campaigning so openly in regions which were nominally under Hittite control; but it is very probable that Ramesses engaged in such provocative action because he knew through good intelligence that Hatti was troubled not only by threats from the east, but also by internal dynastic squabbling. At about the time of the campaign of Years 8–9, the Hittite king Muwatallis died and was formally succeeded by Urhi-Teshub, his young son by a concubine, whose position was challenged by his active uncle Hattusilis. Ruling as Mursilis II, Urhi-Teshub had a short and uneasy reign, and he was eventually supplanted by Hattusilis in about 1264–1263 B.C., Year 16 of Ramesses.

398 left
Detail of a Syrian fortress attacked by Ramesses II, as shown by Rosellini. The defenders are slaughtered by the king's arrows, while, below, cattle are driven away to escape from the Egyptians.

398 right
Scene from the north wall of the great hall at Abu Simbel as drawn by Franz Chrétien Gau in the early nineteenth century. Ramesses II attacks a Syrian fortress, supported by his sons in chariots.

399
Rosellini's depiction of the three princes in chariots, supporting their father Ramesses in his attack on a Syrian fortress: Amonhikhopshef, Ramesses, and Prehiwonemef, the three oldest, but scarcely old enough to engage seriously in battle.

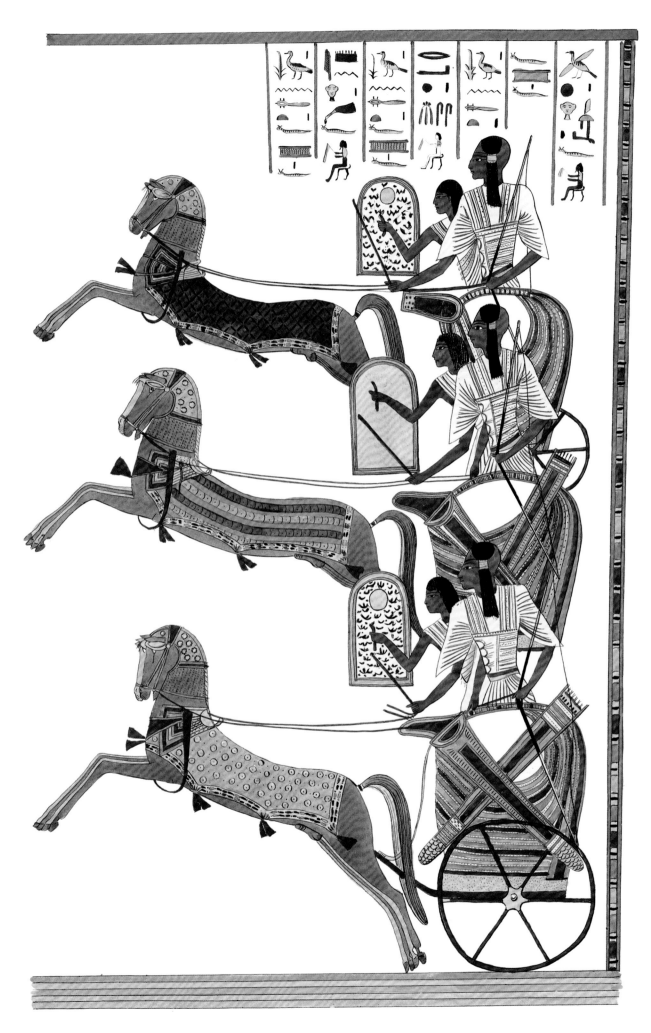

400

Detail of the relief in the Ramesseum depicting the assault on Dapur in the Orontes Valley, a Hittite stronghold. This kind of action-filled scene, not in horizontal registers, was developed in the Nineteenth Dynasty.

401

The Assault on Dapur; a drawing by Rosellini. Ramesses directs from his chariot, and his troops engage with the enemy on foot and in chariots, while others use ladders to scale the walls of the citadel.

Ramesses II and the External World

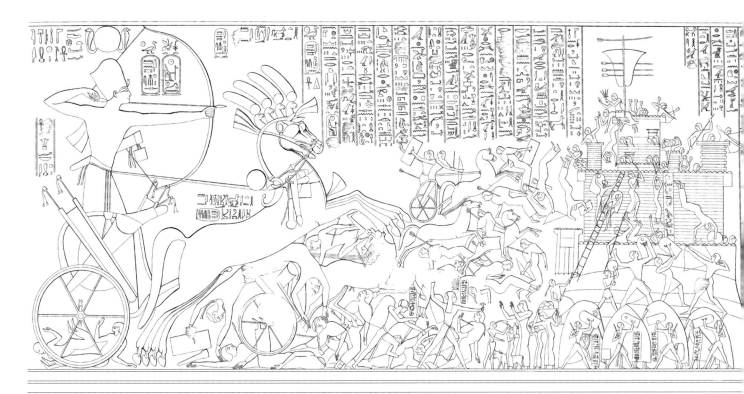

In the meanwhile not much seems to have passed between Egypt and Hatti. The last dated campaign into Asia took place in Ramesses' Year 10, commemorated by a very damaged stela at the Nahr al-Kalb in Lebanon. It may have recorded yet another small foray into Syria, perhaps to recover Dapur and Tunip. These towns may have reverted to the Hittites, and an assault to recover them seems to be depicted in reliefs in the Luxor temple and the Ramesseum. In the accompanying text Ramesses boasted that he took part in the battle without troubling to put on his body armor, and only bothering to collect it after spending two hours in the field. No further dated texts have been found referring to Asiatic activities until Year 18. In the intervening time it is quite probable that further expeditions were sent into Asia, whether led by Ramesses or by one of his sons. It seems unlikely that Ramesses would have failed to test the political temperature of the region, especially as there was much movement from Assyria to the east, and internal trouble in Hatti. Peace, on the other hand may have seemed a favorable alternative to war; campaigning was expensive, especially in Asia Minor and the Levant, if no tribute was being received from

vassal peoples. Revenues from the region were undoubtedly much reduced from what they had been in the heyday of the Egyptian Empire one hundred years earlier. But the necessity to show the flag weighed heavily on Egyptian monarchs of the New Kingdom. Minor irritations such as local defections, as well as probings into the imperial domain by peripheral states owing ultimate allegiance to Hatti (or, increasingly, to the Assyrians), could develop into serious confrontations. An unusual source of irritation between Egypt and Hattusilis, the Hittite king, developed when the usurped Urhi-Teshub, at first exiled to central Syria, fled as a political refugee to Egypt. From Hittite sources it emerges that this unexpected development contained the seeds of possible conflict. It happened in about 1262–1261 B.C. Hattusilis demanded the handing over of Urhi-Teshub, but Ramesses refused. Hittite annoyance was extreme, and a serious confrontation, that might have led to a repeat of the Qadesh campaign, was threatened. It was not, however, a good time for Hattusilis to march south. As for Ramesses, he seems to have felt that some steps should be taken to indicate his readiness to fight, even if he had no particular desire to do so in

the cause of Urhi-Teshub. A large formal inscription dated in Year 18 was set up at Beth-Shan in the north of Canaan. Its text is of the kind sometimes called 'rhetorical'; it praises the king and vaunts his achievements without stating any specific actions. Historically, therefore, it tells us very little, except that it was set up in Asiatic lands in Year 18. Whether or not Ramesses himself accompanied any army that may have moved into Canaan in that year is not stated. The text is full of eulogy and bombast. It could serve as a marker of what might happen if a new and serious war started. Nothing seems to have followed. The saber-rattling had presumably been effective. Things had at last settled down in Asia as far as Egypt was concerned. There seemed little prospect of advantage in renewing large-scale military activities. Hattusilis on the Hittite side had much to engross his attention without engaging unnecessarily in conflict with Egypt. Assyria had now become a distinct and serious threat from the east. Why, then, continue the tense relationship with Egypt when a treaty of mutual support might be negotiated? Consequently, long, drawn-out negotiations with Egypt began, which ended in about 1259–1258 B.C., Year 21 of Ramesses II.

Generally speaking, formal treaties were not commonly entered into by Egypt. The kinds of foreign policies followed by Egyptian kings scarcely ever involved adversaries who would have been considered on equal footing with Egypt. For the Hittites, however, the case was very different, and so too for other major players on the diplomatic stage of Western Asia. Formal treaties were regularly used to establish peaceful relations both with important foreign powers and also with less important, but significant, vassal states. It may be assumed, therefore, that the impetus for a treaty came from the Hittite side, and that the negotiations leading to the preparation of an acceptable text were conducted mostly in Hatti and not in Egypt. There seem to have been perhaps two treaties of earlier dates between the two countries, so that the idea of such a diplomatic agreement was not entirely novel to the Egyptians. Nevertheless the ending of hostilities could not have come as an unwelcome development to Egypt.

By exceptional but fortunate chance, the text of the treaty has survived in Egyptian and Hittite versions. Two monumental inscriptions, one in Karnak and one in the Ramesseum, give the Egyptian version. The Hittite version has survived on a clay tablet found at Hattusas, the capital of Hatti; it is written not in Hittite but in Babylonian cuneiform, which was much used for international diplomatic exchanges at that time. It may represent the agreed text, drawn up in Hattusas and sent to Piramesse, where presumably

it was translated into Egyptian. The hieroglyphic version represents a further stage of textual transmission from a hieratic rendering on papyrus. From the reading of the hieroglyphic text it is made clear that the original text was the one sent by Hattusilis, inscribed on a silver plate or tablet. It arrived in Piramesse on the twenty-first day of the first month of winter, Year 21 of Ramesses II, that is, late in about 1259 B.C. The text given in hieroglyphs follows precisely the text on the cuneiform tablet, with some changes in the order of the sections resulting probably from a misunderstanding by the Egyptian secretaries who prepared the translation. An Egyptian version was presumably sent back to Hatti to clinch the agreement.

The treaty clearly represented a very important diplomatic event. Nothing in the text suggests that either side played politics in claiming credit for the agreement. Important envoys from Hattusas brought the silver tablet with the text of the treaty, made by Hattusilis, the great ruler of Hatti, son of Mursilis II and grandson of Suppiluliumas, for Usimare-Setpenre (Ramesses II), great ruler of Egypt, son of Menmare (Sethos I) and grandson of Menpehtyre (Ramesses I) to establish peace and brotherhood between them forever. The main text begins with a short historical preamble. Then the clauses of the agreement establish that peace should remain between the two countries forever. Neither party will encroach on the lands of the other. If an enemy attacks Egypt, Hatti will come to help,

or send suitable help; and the same should happen if an enemy attack Hatti. If fugitives flee from Egypt to Hatti, they will be extradited back to Egypt; and so too for fugitives from Hatti to Egypt; in neither case should severe action be taken against the returned fugitives. The gods of Hatti and of Egypt are then called upon to witness the treaty. The Egyptian version of the agreement ends with a detailed description of the two circular seals stamped on the reverse of the silver tablet – a positive indication that the Hittite text was the basis for the Egyptian version.

Although Egyptian sources are silent about reactions to the Hittite treaty, this is not unusual. In the absence of appropriate documents nothing can be known. But from Hittite sources it becomes evident that there was relief and pleasure on both sides. Hattusilis wrote a congratulatory letter to Ramesses, and the two principal queens, Puduhepa and Nefertari, similarly exchanged enthusiastic greetings and gifts. Letters of approval were received in Hattusas from the queen mother Tuy (widow of Sethos I); from Sethhikhopshef, at that point the oldest surviving king's son, and therefore crown prince; and even from the distinguished vizier Paser. The richness of surviving documents on the Hittite side considerably enlarge our knowledge of the extent to which exchanges could be made between Near Eastern countries both on the diplomatic level and the personal. Clay tablets, the common medium for international correspondence at this time, do not easily deteriorate, and if burned

become terra cotta, which is even more durable. Papyrus documents, on the other hand, unless preserved in very dry conditions, are destroyed by damp or by insects, and would never survive fire. The Delta, unlike Thebes, was damp and not kind to organic remains. At least major documents might be set up in temples, carved in stone.

It would take some years before the Hittites and the Egyptians would achieve a reasonable *modus vivendi*. Mutual distrust could hardly be dispelled by the signing of a treaty. Again from Hittite records, it appears that Hattusilis had reason to object to a tendency on Ramesses' part to treat him as less than an equal. Similarly, there was some tension over the continued exile in Egypt of Urhi-Teshub. His flight from Hatti had taken place before the treaty was concluded, and its terms over fugitives were not to be applied retroactively. Ramesses seems to have done nothing about the ex-king's presence in Egypt, and there is no evidence to suggest that the Hittite refugee plotted against his uncle. Indeed, he probably enjoyed the small niche he had been granted in the Egyptian court, and ceased to be considered a threat at Hattusas. When negotiations began toward arranging a marriage between Ramesses and the daughter of Hattusilis and Puduhepa, the Hittite queen even suggested to Ramesses that he should consult Urhi-Teshub about the parlous state of the Hittite treasury.

In the matter of this marriage, which was concluded in Ramesses' Year 34 (c.1246–1245 B.C.), while the event itself was celebrated by

monumental texts set up in Egypt and Nubia (the best preserved in the great temple at Abu Simbel), again the accounts of preliminary negotiations have been found, in part at least, in the Hittite archives. From the formal Egyptian inscriptions the impression is gained that the event resulted ultimately from Ramesses' own victorious activities in Asia and against the Hittites. He claimed outrageously that he had conquered Hatti entirely on his own, and that the Hittites were obliged thereafter to pay annual tribute to Egypt, so draining the treasury in Hattusas. The inscription further describes attempts made by the Hittites on an annual basis to appease Ramesses, but such efforts were met with no favorable response. In the end the Hittite king consulted his army and high officials, suggesting that he should offer his eldest daughter as a wife to Ramesses, together with what treasure remained in their coffers. The Egyptian text continues with an account of the dispatch of the daughter with quantities of precious metals, slaves, and livestock, and of Ramesses' delight when he heard of her approach. It is reported as if he had no idea of what was happening, as if it were all a great surprise. So an escort was sent to accompany the bridal procession through the last stages of the journey. It arrived in Piramesse in the third month of winter, Year 34. Ramesses was very pleased with his new wife, and she was given the Egyptian name Mahor-neferure, which means something like 'she is one who sees Horus, the beauty of Re,' Horus presumably being Ramesses

himself. Sometimes the name was abbreviated to Maneferure. The reality behind the marriage may have been significantly different. Hittite records in the form of letters and other documents, rather less formal than the Egyptian grand inscriptions, suggest that the course of events began with the offer by Hattusilis of his oldest daughter as a bride, together with a bigger dowry than anything similar in recent times. Some kind of haggling followed, including the intervention by Queen Puduhepa, who pointed out that resources were not too great on the Hittite side, a fact that Ramesses could confirm by reference to Urhi-Teshub, as mentioned earlier. She chided Ramesses for claiming that he also was impoverished, and she was worried that after the marriage her daughter would be kept in isolation, and not allowed to receive visits from Hittite envoys. The exchanges between Ramesses and the Hittite royal couple probably lasted for several months or longer; in the end all difficulties

were resolved, and Puduhepa announced that it was time for envoys to come from Egypt to pour rich oil over her daughter's head, no doubt an important element in the betrothal ceremonies. So, ritually committed, or sanctified, she could travel to Egypt. There were no more difficulties, the envoys came, the oil was poured, and Puduhepa, who took a leading part in the negotiations, announced that "on that day, the two mighty countries had become one country, and you, the two mighty kings, had found true brotherhood."

The marriage seems to have been a success, both in political terms and in respect to Ramesses' regard for Mahor-neferure. No serious differences between Egypt and Hatti apparently occurred during the rest of Ramesses' reign. Also for the Hittites new, tempting opportunities were available. From the Hittite archives evidence emerges to suggest that Egypt became a fancied

place for important visits by influential Hittites. Egypt, it seems, had been discovered as a desirable tourist venue. The life and the climate of Piramesse were very different from what was experienced in the Anatolian heartland of the Hittite empire. One important visitor was the Hittite crown prince Hishmi-Sharruma, who would succeed Hattusilis in about1237 B.C., taking the name of Tudhaliyas. Ramesses also attempted to bring Hattusilis himself to Egypt. The Hittite, possibly suspecting a plot, showed no eagerness to accept the invitation, giving as an excuse his wondering what he would do in Egypt. The reason may have been more fundamental. Hittite kings were much occupied with ritual activities, and it may have been the case that Hattusilis saw nothing but danger in a long absence from Hattusas. Unfortunately Hittite records do not tell of the outcome of this exchange of courtesies, and it seems possible that the visit was finally cancelled because Hattusilis developed

problems with his feet. It is tantalizing to speculate whether a meeting between the two great kings did ever take place, if not in Egypt, then in Canaan or Syria. Further, did Egyptian doctors help to heal Hattusilis' feet? The possibility is suggested in Hittite sources, and it is known that Egyptian medicine was highly thought of in the Near East at this time. An echo of such medical help may be found in the story of the princess of Bakhtan, ostensibly dated to Ramesses' reign, but inscribed a thousand years later. We shall return to this story toward the end of this book. The mentioning of Mahor-neferure on a colossal statue found at Tanis, and on a number of small objects, indicates her ready acceptance into the court of Ramesses II, and there is no reason to doubt that Ramesses was happy with this testimony to the Hittite alliance. Nothing, sadly, is known of her later life, and it is not impossible that she died prematurely. It is known, however, that a second

Hittite princess joined Ramesses as a wife some time before the death of Hattusilis in about 1237 B.C. (Year 44). The event is commemorated on two stelae, one found at Coptos, cult-center of the god Min about forty miles north of Thebes, and the other, much damaged, at Abydos. Not so much fuss was made on this occasion, although a large dowry accompanied the princess in her progress to Egypt; no great greeting party was sent to accompany her on the last stages of her journey. It was not such a significant diplomatic occasion as the earlier marriage: peace was well established between Hatti and Egypt; it was almost a routine event. Not even the name of the princess is included in the inscriptions. In a few years Hattusilis would be dead, but the change of ruler seems to have made little difference to the good relations between the two powerful kingdoms. And so it remained for the rest of Ramesses' reign.

404–405
A relief from Fraktin, in central Turkey, showing the remarkable status of Queen Puduhepa in relation to her husband Hattusilis. She offers a libation to the great Hittite goddess Arinna, while the king separately performs a similar ceremony for the weather god.

A papyrus in the Berlin Museum contains a literary composition of the kind called a 'model letter.' It is not a real letter, but one composed as an exercise, probably for student scribes. Such letters usually contain lists of places, commodities, and equipment, and they presumably were intended to test the abilities of young scribes to deal with rare vocabulary and unusual names. The Berlin letter, written in a good Nineteenth Dynasty hand, purports to having been sent by a senior Egyptian official in Nubia, called by the common name Paser. He requests the unnamed recipient to prepare the tribute to be sent. Then comes the list of commodities to be included; some are strictly Nubian, others come from tropical Africa to the South, brought to Nubia along ancient trade routes. There are domestic cattle and wild creatures like gazelles, oryx, ostriches, monkeys, and baboons; animal products like ivory, panther skins, and ostrich feathers; plant products like ebony and special fan-shaped palm fronds; and much gold and semi-precious stones – hematite, jasper, amethyst, crystal. In addition there was human tribute, people from Irem, tall Terek people, and Nehesyu (a general name for Nubians). Paser advises his correspondent to increase the contributions every year. This list demonstrates the value of Nubia as a source of unusual and precious materials, above all gold, the greater part of the Egyptian supply of which came from Nubian mines.

In the Nubian temple of Bayt al-Wali, now re-erected just south of the new High Dam, there are exceptionally well-designed and carved low-relief scenes of warfare, with one series devoted to a campaign against Nubians in which sons of Ramesses, Amonhiwonemef, and Khaemwese took part. If this campaign took place very early in his reign, or even when Ramesses was still co-regent, as has been suggested, then these sons would have been almost infants. After the rout of the Nubians, the presentation of tribute is shown, here supervised by the Nubian viceroy Amenemope, whose father was a Paser. The splendid procession of tribute could be seen as a complete illustration of the list of products itemized in the model letter in Berlin. There are additions: a giraffe, ostrich eggs, ostrich-feather fans, and bows. No doubt the list of Nubian products was to a great extent traditional, even standardized; but there may be no doubt about the actuality of the campaign depicted. It may, however, have been quite a modest skirmish in Lower Nubia, scarcely warranting more than a mention, but used in this temple as a vehicle for a heroic scene of battle, and a highly imaginative scene of tribute. No small campaign in Lower Nubia would have yielded the tribute from tropical Africa shown at Bayt al-Wali.

406–407
Ramesses presents two files of Nubian
prisoners to Amon-Re of Thebes and
the goddess Mut, between whom sits
the deified Ramesses himself, with a
sun-disk on his head and ram's horns.
Abu Simbel; by Rosellini.

408–409
*A scene of triumph in Abu Simbel: after
an unspecified campaign against Nubia,
Ramesses returns with files of Nubian
captives. The text describes him as "the
Good God, strong of horns, who strikes
the South and tramples on the North."*

Ramesses II

410–411
Nubian captives on their knees with arms bound tight, and all roped together. From the base of the colossal figure of Ramesses II on the south side of the entrance to the great Abu Simbel temple.

410 center
Rosellini's illustration of a scene in the Nubian temple of Bayt al-Wali, in which Ramesses II srikes a Nubian chief. The king is "the Good God who subdues the nine bows and tramples on the leaders of vile Kush."

410 bottom
Rosellini's outline drawing of a Nubian and an Asiatic prisoner, arms tied and roped together, kneeling before the king. From their dress, both captives are shown to be men of importance.

411 right
Cartouche containing the nomen of Ramesses II, Ramessu-Meryamun (Ramesses-beloved-of-Amun). The sign representing Ra is here not a simple sun, but a divine figure with falcon-head wearing the sun disk.

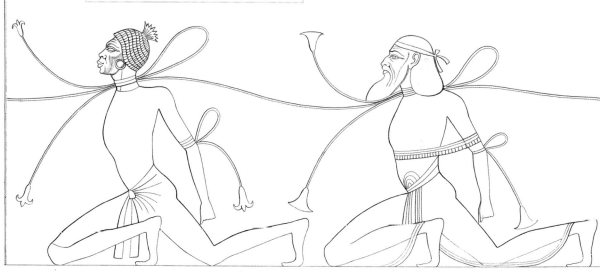

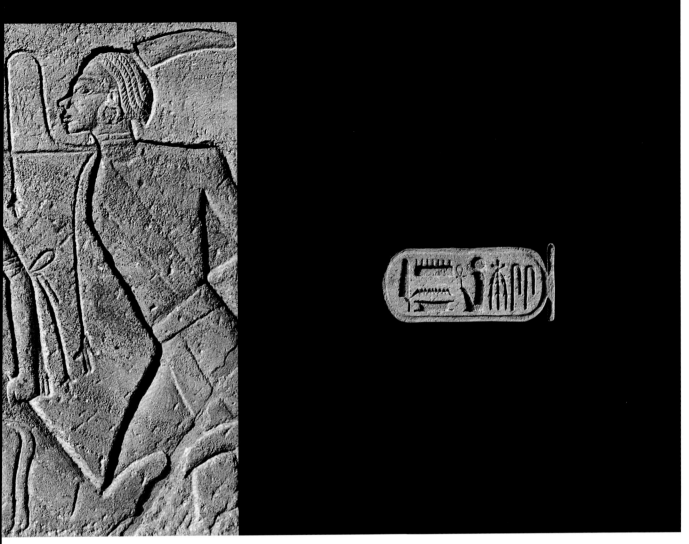

For most of Ramesses' reign, Nubia remained a peaceful land, well settled by Egyptians, but not on a permanent basis. Nubia was very different from the Asiatic territories so regularly troublesome to Egypt. Nubia was in a sense a continuation of Egypt to the south, linked to Egypt by the Nile. It was valued as a source of raw materials, and as the conduit for goods from tropical Africa. But it was never considered as part of Egypt proper. Egypt began in the south at Elephantine (Aswan); what lay beyond was territory that could be dominated, but not integrated into Egypt. It was a kind of external province to be administered by the Nubian viceroy, known formally as the 'King's Son of Kush.' The hinterland of the Nile valley in Nubia was vast, home to tribes ever ready to exploit Egyptian weaknesses, with a tradition of strong local princes, and in earlier times a powerful principality based on Kerma, south of the third cataract. During the Middle Kingdom, when Nubia was first seriously occupied by Egyptians, a series of commanding forts was constructed in the region of the second cataract. These forts were lost to Egypt in the Second Intermediate Period but reoccupied and rehabilitated in the Eighteenth Dynasty. To a great extent they had lost their strategic value by the reign of Ramesses II; they were superseded by settlements and towns constructed more for reasons of trade and administration than security. Strangely, following the establishing of temples and towns under King Amenophis III at places like Soleb, Sesebi, and Sedeinga, great interest was shown in these rather remote reaches of the Nile by Akhenaten, at least in the early years of his reign; traces of structures built at that time have even been found recently at Kerma, once the center of Nubian native power. Towns were founded in Nubia under Ramesses II, and a new administrative center was developed at Amara, between the second and third cataracts; it was given the resounding name Piramesse-Miamun, 'the house (or town) of Ramesses, beloved of Amun.' It became the principal Nubian base of the viceroy of Kush, which had formerly been at the fortress of Buhen at the second cataract, and at Miam (Aniba) farther north, opposite the rocky bluff of Qasr Ibrim. The impression is certainly gained that Nubia was no longer troublesome, an impression reinforced by the statements of achievement found in inscriptions of high officials who served in these southern lands. In particular, the viceroy of Kush Setau, who held office in the latter part of Ramesses' reign, concentrates on non-warlike activities. We shall examine his personal record later in this book. Here, however, it is worth mentioning that in his great stela set up in the temple of Wadi al-Sabua, Setau mentions a campaign against Irem, a part of Nubia that has not been located with certainty. It may lie to the west of the Nile, to the south of the third cataract, in the region once dominated by the kingdom of Kerma. A tradition of independence perhaps still persisted there, well removed as the region was from the centers of Egyptian power in Nubia. Sethos I had been obliged to deal with an uprising in Irem, in a small campaign in which the young Ramesses had taken part. Then, in Year 38 of Ramesses (c.1242 B.C.) or possibly a little later, trouble in Irem led to another punitive campaign, which yielded over seven thousand captives; it was graphically recorded on the town walls of Amara. On this occasion several sons of Ramesses had their small experience of active service, of whom the names of only two have survived: Merenptah, ultimate successor of his father, and Setemuia, his eighth son, who did not outlive Ramesses.

Perhaps the most remarkable part of Ramesses' activities in Nubia was the construction of temples. He did not inaugurate the practice of temple-building in the country – it had a history extending back in a modest manner to the Twelfth Dynasty, and more substantially to the beginning of the Eighteenth Dynasty – but he developed it to an extraordinary degree, for reasons which passed far beyond simple devotion to the great gods of Egypt. We shall return to this matter in a later chapter. One of the temples constructed late in the reign, under the supervision of the viceroy Setau at Wadi al-Sabua, was built partly with the help of captive labor. A smaller inscription also erected in that temple by Setau and dated to Year 44 (c.1236 B.C.) records the sending of a punitive expedition led by an officer named Ramose into the Tjemeh-land to acquire labor for the building of the temple. There has been much debate about the precise location of Tjemeh-land. It certainly lay to the west of the Nile valley, and contained peoples who from time to time sought to infiltrate the fertile land of Egypt. It may not be a precise geographical designation, but a vague name for 'those out there to the west.' In the later Nineteenth Dynasty, Tjemehu seems to be used more precisely for tribal groups threatening Egypt from further north, on the west side of the Delta. Other words occur for these western infiltrators, like Tjehenu and Meshwesh, who also seem mostly to inhabit the northern and coastal regions of modern Libya. The word Libya, or Libu in ancient Egyptian, occurs for the first time in a papyrus of the Nineteenth Dynasty in the British Museum containing so-called scribal exercises like the mock letter describing the products of Nubia. In a passage containing an encomium of Ramesses II, after some general account of his triumphs over foreign lands, the scribe writes: "Libu is fallen to his slaughtering, fallen to his knife."

It would appear that no great organized power existed out to the west, comparable with Hatti or the Assyrian empire in the east. But, as in Nubia, there were 'peoples,' tribes, some probably settled in or near the oases in the Western Desert, others in the more fertile coastal plains. Their movements could be checked by occasional punitive expeditions, which could also be used for the 'recruitment' of workmen for temple-building, or even for the

Egyptian army. However, the attraction of the fertile Egyptian lands exercised a strong pull on the western peoples, and later in the Nineteenth Dynasty serious campaigns had to be mounted to defeat their inroads into the Delta. It is likely that the threat of such inroads already existed in the reign of Ramesses II, but could for the time being be settled by occasional forays. The threat for the future remained, and steps were taken by Ramesses to secure the western approaches to the Delta by the construction of desert forts.

Traces of possible forts, not yet properly investigated, suggest that they were built at intervals of about two days' march, and the largest, and perhaps the last in the chain, is at Zawiyat Umm al-Rakham, over two hundred miles to the west of Alexandria, in the neighborhood of Marsa Matruh. Recent excavations have shown that it was much more than a simple fortress. The main enclosure measures about 15,000 square meters (16,500 square yards) with massive mud-brick walls more than 4 meters thick, and one great gateway flanked by towers clad in limestone. There are the remains of a small temple and a number of storage magazines containing pottery vessels from Canaan and the eastern Mediterranean lands. The fort seems to have doubled as a trading center, or at least a place for landfall for trading vessels arriving in Egyptian territory in an area where they might be attacked and plundered by Libyan tribes. At that time there were no recognized ports on the western side of the Delta – Alexandria would not be founded for nearly one thousand years. The commandant of the fort at the time when the inscribed doorframes of the magazines were installed was called Nebre. Excavation has not yet revealed whether Nebre was ever called upon to engage in punitive forays against the Tjemehu, the Tjehenu, the Meshwesh, or the Libu, or to defend the fort against direct attack. At such a distant outpost of Egyptian power, many days away from the nearest places that could be considered to be in Egypt, the garrison may well have felt isolated, but ready to kill time by engaging in modest trade well away from the sharp-eyed government officials who supervised imports and the collection of duty at the more regular ports of entry into the Delta from the Mediterranean.

412 top
Asiatic prisoner from one of the lines
of foreign captives shown at Abu
Simbel. Although the theme of captives
is much repeated, the individual
carving of their heads is noticeably
distinctive, not repetitive.

412–413
One of the most striking and well-
designed images in the great hall of
the temple at Abu Simbel, in
Rosellini's depiction. Ramesses,
dismounted, spears a Libyan
chieftain, and tramples on another.

Ramesses II and the External World
412

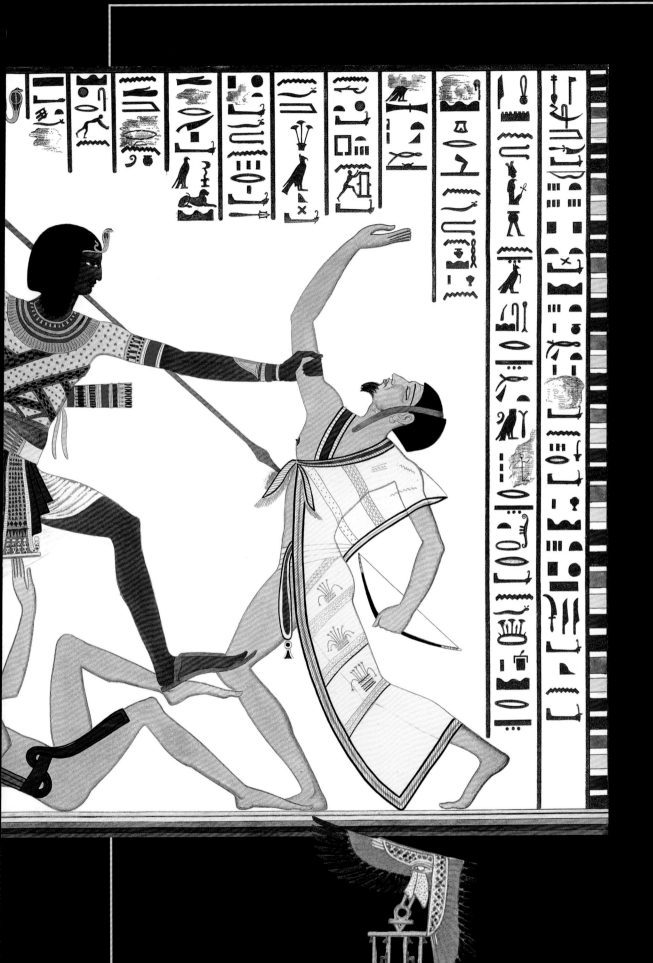

Ramesses II

414 and 415
Two details of the scene of Ramesses II slaying Libyans. Left: he treads firmly on the head of the fallen foe. Right: he grasps the upraised arm of the standing Libyan before spearing him.

416–417
Photograph of the scene depicted by Rosellini. It demonstrates vividly the energy and stark realism of the actual wall carving, unencumbered by coloring and detail.

Mention was made in the first chapter of this book of the oppression in Egypt and the Exodus of the Children of Israel. Further con-sideration needs to be made at this point. The Israelites were a foreign people in Egypt who made their escape with disastrous consequences for the forces of Egypt – so goes the biblical account. There is no evidence from Egypt to confirm the presence of Israelites in the country at any time, and none to confirm the biblical account of the Exodus. This lack of evidence has not deterred scholars from postulating what may lie behind the biblical account, and from assigning dates to the various events and stages of 'enslavement' mentioned in the Bible. Views differ widely. Some believe that the mentions of Ramesses in the Bible should not be taken at face value. For the Israelites at the time when the texts of the biblical books were established, the name Ramesses could have been invoked as the very embodiment of Egyptian power and tyranny. So the name was included anachronistically; its use was almost an irrelevance, a red herring. The oppression and Exodus should then be taken back to the beginning of the Eighteenth Dynasty, to the time when Egypt was being purged of the Hyksos (Asiatic) rulers and their peoples, who had dominated parts of Egypt for many years. Other scholars take a more literal view of the biblical narrative, maintaining that the construction of Piramesse took place near the beginning of Ramesses II's reign. Then the Exodus could be dated to the middle of his reign. A more generally accepted view is that the oppression continued during Ramesses' reign, but that the Exodus occurred under Merenptah, his successor. In the absence of better evidence than is at present available, I cannot see how the question can be resolved. The idea that foreigners might be impressed to work on royal buildings is, however, well established; the case of the carrying off by Ramose of Libyans to work on the temple at Wadi al-Sabua demonstrates conclusively that such exploitation did take place. It was surely not exceptional, and Israelites may indeed have been used to work on Piramesse and Pithom. So it is not difficult to believe that the oppression did take place during the reign of Ramesses II. The date of the Exodus is another matter; it must remain undecided until the unlikely discovery of new and clinching evidence. The last twenty or more years of Ramesses' reign passed with scarcely any recorded troubles with external powers. For more than twenty years – longer than the reigns of most Egyptian kings – peace prevailed between Egypt and those lands from which trouble traditionally came. There was peace, but trouble was brewing in the east and in the west. No surviving records from the time suggest that Egypt regretted the absence of conflict, or Ramesses the opportunity to display once again his military prowess. When he died in about 1213 B.C. it was already his Year 67. He was a very old man, a survivor from heroic times. In this way he would surely have wanted us to remember him, even if the reality at times had not been so heroic.

THE BATTLE OF QADESH

To discuss the progress of a battle fought about 3,275 years ago, the details of which are known only from texts and representations heavily slanted in favor of one side, requires a fair degree of skepticism as well as a strong dose of imagination. James Henry Breasted, writing in 1906, considered the battle to be "of special interest, being the first battle in history of which we may follow the tactics and the disposition of both armies." He had himself written a long study of the battle a few years earlier, and was confident that he had satisfactorily elucidated the story told and depicted in Egyptian temples. Others have followed, writing from the Hittite as well as the Egyptian side. Military tacticians have examined the terrain and interpreted the progress of the fighting in terms of medieval and modern practices. The language in which the commemorative texts are written has been analyzed and subjected to close scholarly attention. No ancient battle or campaign has been so meticulously studied for the periods before the well-recorded engagements of Greek and Roman history.

Ramesses II would fully approve of this attention. The encounter between Egypt and Hatti in his Year 5 (c. 1275–1274 B.C.) was, as far as the Egyptian king was concerned, the most important event of his long reign, and he seems to have decided that this was to be the case soon after the battle took place. But how was he to know that nothing else of such importance would happen in his remaining sixty-two years? Here I believe one may truly say that no lack of evidence has deprived posterity of some other major success or defeat. We may be confident that had anything approaching the importance of the battle of Qadesh occurred later in the reign, no effort would have been spared in commemorating it on the walls of Ramesses' great buildings, or on formal stelae set up at strategic points throughout Egypt and Nubia. Sir Alan Gardiner, who wrote a thoughtful account and translation of the Qadesh texts toward the end of his life, said elsewhere of Ramesses' personal feat of arms at Qadesh, "that he never tired of proclaiming to his subjects on the temple-walls built by him." In fact all the verbal and visual memorials on these temple walls were put up very soon after the battle had been fought, when most of the great buildings had been built or were in their later stages of construction; they had massive walls and monumental pylons, offering huge surfaces just waiting to receive something more specific than the usual representations of the king smiting the usual foreigners.

Qadesh then was celebrated in the major Theban temples, built or extended by Ramesses: at Luxor, where he added a great court and a massive pylon entrance, the Qadesh texts and scenes were placed on the façade of the pylons and on the outer walls of the courts; at Karnak they embellished some of the outer walls of the Hypostyle Hall; in the Ramesseum, his projected mortuary temple in Western Thebes, the huge 'canvases' of the pylons received their versions. Qadesh was also celebrated on the outer walls of the temple Ramesses had built at Abydos, and most famously (because most easily inspected) on the northern wall of the first hall in the great temple at Abu Simbel. If the battle were also depicted in the temple of Ptah at Memphis or in any other structure at Piramesse, no trace survives.

There are, however, a few papyrus copies of what Breasted called the Poem, but Gardiner more precisely termed the Literary Record. These copies may be dated late in the reign of Ramesses II or even later in the Nineteenth Dynasty, probably copied at first- or second-hand from the existing monumental versions.

No campaign was ever so variously recorded by the Egyptians, and it must be assumed that the preparation and organizing of the texts and their

carving on the great temples were carried out only after a considerable degree of central planning. The texts for the most part follow what must have been compiled as a master version. Two main compositions present the events of the campaign, not in parallel terms, but as independent statements. These two compositions Breasted called the Poem and the Official Report. The former has often be called the Poem of Pentawer, after the scribe Pentawer, who made one of the papyrus copies now in the British Museum. He was, however, only the copyist, and in no way responsible for the content of the text he copied. The third element in the memorial is the representation of the campaign pictorially in great relief scenes. These scenes contain many fascinating vignettes of significant episodes and of topographical details, all composed, as should be expected, from the Egyptian point of view; hieroglyphic label-texts accompany these vignettes. Breasted termed this pictorial element the Reliefs. It has been pointed out, however, that this traditional division into three parts does not give a fair idea of what was intended by those who drew up the scheme for the public celebration of the Qadesh battle. The Poem, which Gardiner more accurately calls the Literary Record, is an independent account

of the battle couched in florid terms after the manner of the many laudatory inscriptions set up in honor of the king's ostensible achievements; many such inscriptions were put up for Ramesses in the course of his long reign. The Literary Record in all the surviving versions follows a basic text. It is commonly carved apart from the reliefs, existing as a substantive text on its own. It is not found, for example, at Abu Simbel, where presumably a shortage of space within the temple prevented its inclusion. The composition called the Official Report belongs closely to the relief scenes; it is the text that explains the scenes, and Gardiner considered the ensemble of Report and scenes as forming one integrated whole. So he called this ensemble the Pictorial Record. In the description of the campaign that follows, details will be drawn from all the sources in the Literary Record and the Pictorial Record, and it must be remembered that all of the sources throw the best possible light on the actions of the Egyptians. Unfortunately, the Hittite records of the battle have not been preserved, or at least have not yet been found. They would undoubtedly present a very different picture of what happened, and of the outcome of the encounter. The Hittites would surely not have been seen Qadesh as a defeat for their forces.

418
Ramesses' return from campaign, as shown in Abu Simbel. He rides in triumph, his horses handsomely decked with feathers, preceded by his groom, and accompanied by his attendant lion, shown here by Rosellini as a leopard.

423
Ramesses on campaign, in a Rosellini depiction. The Pharaoh rides alone in his chariot, wearing elaborate attire more suitable for the parade ground than battle. His spirited horses also are finely decked with splendid feather headdresses.

426
Some of the large party of reinforcements, the Nearin, who had marched from the coast of Amurru, arriving at a crucial moment in the battle. The force consisted of infantry and chariotry; a phalanx of the infantry is shown here. At Abu Simbel.

427
At Abu Simbel the two main scenes of the Egyptian camp and of the battle of Qadesh are separated by a register of chariotry, both Egyptian and Hittite, riding in all directions. Rosellini's depiction.

It will be recalled that interest in western Asia was actively revived in the reign of Sethos I, and one campaign succeeded in re-establishing Egyptian influence in parts of Canaan and Lebanon. Ramesses II conducted his first campaign into Asia in his Year 4 (c.1276–1275 B.C.), achieving some limited gains but at the same time alerting the Hittite king Muwatallis to the threat offered to his southern client states which had acknowledged Hittite suzerainty. The way in which events could develop to the disadvantage of Hatti was signaled by the defection of the land of Amurru, occupying roughly the seaboard of Lebanon. This change of allegiance may have provided the crucial factor which determined the future course of action for Muwatallis. Power politics in the Near East were always complicated, and the Hittites could not risk ignoring the additional threat from distant Egypt. There was surely a fair degree of understanding between Hatti and Egypt about how things were turning. Diplomatic contacts between the two powers were well established, and it must be supposed that both sides realized that the issue could only be resolved by a passage of arms, a full-scale encounter between the armies of both sides. Skirmishing would not settle the matter. To this end, therefore,

both sides set about preparing for the expected clash. It would occur, if not by mutual arrangement, almost certainly by tacit understanding, on 'neutral' territory, that is, neither in Egypt proper nor in the heartland of Hatti in the Anatolian uplands. Lebanon and the lands to the east represented the region for a classic encounter; it may be doubted, however, that this 'away' fixture for both sides had a venue fixed in advance. Much depended for the timing and the place on the intelligence collected by both sides, with the knowledge that the campaign season usually began in the late spring when some months of good weather could reasonably be expected.

And so, following Ramesses' campaign of Year 4, during the autumn and winter months, both sides made ready for the next campaign season. On the Egyptian side, apart from his native infantry and chariotry, Ramesses had at his disposal troops called Sherden, who are described as having been captured by the king in battle. The Sherden were a people from the sea who from time to time launched piratical raids on the Delta coast, with or without the encouragement of the Libyans. They are generally thought to be the people who ultimately gave their name to the island of Sardinia, and who might have come in earlier times from the region of

the Caucasus. They were good professional fighters, distinctively armed with long swords and helmets fitted with horns and spikes ending in circular knobs. By the time of Ramesses II many may have been settled in fortresses in the Delta, prepared to fight as mercenaries in Pharaoh's army. They formed a distinct contingent in the army that Ramesses led out from the frontier fortress of Tjel (Sile) on the sixth day of the second summer month of his Year 5.

What was the opposition to be? Rather formidable! Muwatallis had not wasted his time, or spared his clients and allies in collecting a force made up of contingents from "all the foreign lands as far as the sea." So said the Egyptian account, which then lists the places which provided these contingents: Hatti itself in force; then Naharin, the most important of the Hittite allies, often in confrontation, but for the moment in alliance; it lay to the east and south. From the west support came from Arzawa, Luka, Pidasa, Masa, and Dardany, the last being undoubtedly the Homeric Dardanoi, here first mentioned in surviving records. Beyond the Hittite heartland to the north, the land of Keshkesh on the Black Sea sent a contingent, and from the east of Asia Minor, Kizzuwadna joined forces.

There were contingents listed from principalities closer to Qadesh, including that city itself, along with Carchemish, and Ugarit on the Levantine coast. Other places less easily located also joined in. It was a formidable grouping – 'coalition' is probably not the right description; Muwatallis had called in all his favors, and most places had obliged and responded to the Hittite demand. According to figures attached to scenes in the Pictorial Record, two groups of forces on the Hittite side are given as 18,000 and 19,000, and a force of 2,500 chariots is specified. There is nothing to indicate whether these figures represent the totality of the fighting troops facing the Egyptians, but it should be remembered that

warfare in those distant times was not conducted on a vast scale. There is, furthermore, little reason to accept the Egyptian figures.

On the Egyptian side, Ramesses' forces were organized into four divisions, named after the major gods, Amun, Re (or Pre, as he is called in these texts), Ptah, and Sutekh (or Seth), the tutelary deity of the Nineteenth Dynasty. Apart from the Sherden, impressed troops who marched with the main army, Ramesses also expected to be helped in due course by a force of Nearin, being mustered on the coast in Amurru. They would prove their worth at a most crucial point in the coming battle. In considering the arrangements to be made in preparation for a substantial campaign

in antiquity, we must appreciate the difficulties of communication over long distances and rough terrain, and the need to prepare well in advance orders for the movement of troops which would actually work out fairly precisely when a planned engagement took place. So many campaigns in medieval and modern times have failed to develop in accordance with initial plans, and the ability of a commander to improvise on the ground has often determined whether or not the outcome was successful. How difficult it must have been both for Ramesses and for Muwatallis in the thirteenth century B.C. to ensure that all the contingents turned up on time and in the right place, according to plan! In the case of the Qadesh campaign,

success and failure on both sides were to be determined by prompt action or improvisation, bad timing, and poor communications. The unusual amount of tactical and strategic detail contained in the various compositions and scenes has enabled students of warfare to reconstruct the battle and its preliminaries with a high degree of probability.

428–429
Among the Egyptian forces was a detachment of Sherden, ancestors of the Sardinians who were distinguished by their horned helmets and round shields. Here they are shown with Egyptian infantry in Rosellini's illustration.

And now to the campaign. Armed no doubt with the best intelligence his agents could provide, Ramesses would have known that the forces of Hatti were on the move from the various countries of the Hittite alliance, ordered to muster at some convenient place in Syria, possibly Aleppo. Timing was crucial. From previous campaigns it would have been known how long a force of a certain size would need to travel from the eastern Delta to Qadesh or thereabouts. On this occasion, however, the forces were larger than previously employed, and the support and supply arrangements correspondingly more complex. Some day-to-day supplies would certainly be expected to be provided by the friendly (or vassal) peoples through which the army would pass; but much would have to be brought along from Egypt, notably the paraphernalia required for the Pharaoh, his sons, and his senior staff, including apparently the vizier of Lower Egypt. The distance from the eastern Delta to Qadesh was about 460 miles (643 kilometers) by a very direct route. Aleppo, on the other hand, was in relatively easy reach of the main Hittite force and contingents from countries like Naharin and Kizzuwadna; troops from the Black Sea coast and central and western Asia Minor had much farther to travel, but should have timed their arrival in northern Syria accordingly. At this point we may note with what a degree of disdain the writer of the Egyptian monumental texts regarded the Hittite forces, and in particular the Hittite king. He is never mentioned by name, but usually called "the Fallen One of Hatti," or even more dismissively, "the vile Fallen One of Hatti." In public pronouncements in the ancient world, there was no room for politeness and magnanimity.

Leaving Egypt in the spring, the Egyptian army took precisely one month to travel to Djahy, a general name for Palestine/Canaan in its northern part. The journey had been without trouble, the army moving through the "narrow passes" as if it were traveling "on the roads of Egypt," and all along the route it was made welcome by the local peoples. Moving forward to the north, the army came to Shabtuna, a place seven or eight miles south of Qadesh. At this point Ramesses decided to press forward without delay, and closed up to Qadesh, where he received news that the "vile Fallen One of Qadesh" (a variant form of the insulting appellation of Muwatallis) was on the move with his mustered allies; and he was brought news of possible disaffection in the Hittite horde. Two Shosu Bedouin came to Ramesses to report that their fellow tribesmen who were serving with the Hittites were prepared to defect and come over to the Egyptian side. They also informed the Egyptians that the enemy forces were massed in the region of Aleppo. This news – false as it turned out – was much better than Ramesses could have expected, and he decided without further checking to ford the Orontes river and set up

camp to the northwest of Qadesh. He had in support his own immediate entourage and the division of Amun.

Without independent intelligence this was a rash move. Most of the Egyptian army lay far back to the rear, led by the division of Pre, followed by the divisions of Ptah and Seth, some miles further back in the woodlands to the south of Shabtuna. The country was such that it would not be easy to call up the successive divisions in support if a general battle developed. But a major engagement was not expected at that time, and Ramesses no doubt felt confident to prepare his camp within sight of Qadesh. That city itself was well protected from sudden attack.

The Orontes and a tributary flowing into it from the southwest, north of Qadesh, formed a natural moat all around the city except on the south side, and here the water protection had been completed by the cutting of a canal between the main river and the tributary. While his camp was being prepared, Ramesses had his traveling throne brought out and positioned in a kiosk, so that he could sit and observe Qadesh, the countryside around, and the activity of his troops.

430 top
First aid in Ramesses' camp before reaching Qadesh. After the long march from Egypt, the feet and legs of the infantry needed much attention. This intimate scene shows a soldier receiving some sort of treatment from a comrade.

430 bottom
In scenes of Qadesh in Theban temples, one vignette shows a tussle between Egyptian and Hittite charioteers in a corner of the Egyptian camp – a preliminary skirmish, less clearly shown at Abu Simbel.

432–433 and 433 bottom
The hieroglyphs are explicit: "Coming of
Pharaoh's scout with two scouts of the
Fallen One of Hatti, into the presence of
Pharaoh. They beat them to say where
the vile Fallen One of Hatti is."
At Abu Simbel and in Rosellini's depiction.

Then came an intelligence bombshell. His marauding scouts picked up two Hittite spies and brought them to the royal presence after their resolution had been softened by a severe beating; a vignette shows the wretched men being beaten with staves. They then readily told Ramesses that they were from the Hittite king, sent to discover the Egyptian positions. When Ramesses said that he had heard that his adversary was in the neighborhood of Aleppo, they told him that Muwatallis with all his forces was waiting in hiding to the east of Qadesh: "See," they said, "they stand armed and ready for combat behind Old Qadesh."

In fury, no doubt, and certainly in anxious anticipation of imminent trouble, Ramesses called a council of war to inform his advisers and commanders of what the Hittite spies had told him. How could this have happened when he had been assured that the Hittites were many miles away at Aleppo? His commanders threw the blame chiefly on the rulers of the vassal lands through which the Egyptians had traveled, but also on Pharaoh's advisers. Daily situation reports should have kept him fully informed of the Hittite movements. And now the positions were reversed, with Muwatallis being fully informed of the movements of the Egyptian army, while his own army was ready and waiting in concealment behind Old Qadesh. The advantage lay with Muwatallis, and he did not delay in exploiting it, sending a force of chariots and infantry across the Orontes to cut through the division of Pre, and to swing round to attack directly the unfinished camp of the Egyptians.

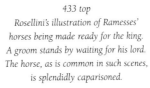

433 top
Rosellini's illustration of Ramesses'
horses being made ready for the king.
A groom stands by waiting for his lord.
The horse, as is common in such scenes,
is splendidly caparisoned.

434 top
Pharaoh's ceremonial chariot from
the Qadesh reliefs in the
Ramesseum, as depicted by Rosellini.
The chariot is fitted with an
elaborate sun shade topped by the
vulture goddess Nekhbet. The royal
bodyguard is in attendance.

There was near-panic in the Egyptian lines; hasty arrangements were made to evacuate the royal sons who had come on campaign, while Ramesses scrambled into his armor, ready for the fight. He had his chariot with his trusty horses, Victory-in-Thebes and Mut-is-contented, and somewhere about the camp was his pet lion Killer-of-his-enemies. It may not be doubted that at this critical juncture Ramesses, who was still a young man in his twenties, showed real courage and royal leadership. The official accounts of course make out that he alone was left to meet the enemy assault and bring about their defeat. The forces on the Hittite side at this moment included 2,500 chariots, by the Egyptian estimate. The battle was intense, and one may imagine that a very confused situation developed in which the troops of the division of Amun were unable to be deployed satisfactorily. In fact, Ramesses in his desperation felt that he had been deserted not just by the division of Amun but also by the great god Amun himself. He had to remind Amun of the extent of his devotion to him, and of the vast quantities of booty which had been lavished on him. Why was he deserting him? Naturally Ramesses' prayer of complaint was answered, and Amun came to his aid with unparalleled effect: he was "more efficient than millions of foot-soldiers and ten thousand of chariots." As a result Ramesses was fully reinvigorated; in his many charges he overcame the host of Hittite chariotry, securing a total victory.

434–435
Prisse d'Avennes' representation of
Ramesses II in his chariot driving
headlong into the Hittite enemy, which is
scattered and trampled down. The lion on
the arrow quiver holds a human head in
its mouth. From the Ramesseum.

The reality was rather different. Among the scenes in the Pictorial Record is one showing the arrival of a large force of reinforcements, advancing in perfect order. The accompanying text announces "the arrival of the Nearin of Pharaoh from the land of Amurru." These were the troops whom Ramesses had apparently mustered in Amurru to march to the east to join the Egyptians in the neighborhood of Qadesh. The name Nearin is a puzzle; it does not seem to refer to any particular place or tribe; it may mean 'young men,' and in military terms, perhaps 'newly raised troops.' Whatever the meaning, the Nearin arrived and, again according to the accompanying text, found the Egyptian camp surrounded and pressed by the Hittite attackers. In the camp "His Majesty sat alone without his army," hemmed in by hostile chariots. The text notes that the division of Amun had not completed the establishment of the camp, while the other divisions were still on the march, some being in the woods of Rabwy or Labwy. Then "the Nearin smashed into the host of the vile Fallen One of Hatti, just as it was on the point of entering Pharaoh's camp, and the entourage of His Majesty killed them, not allowing any to escape, for their hearts were sure in the great strength of Pharaoh, their good Lord; for he was behind them like a mountain of copper and a wall of iron for ever and ever."

So was the course of the battle turned. The intervention of the force from Amurru had come just in time, like the Prussian Blücher to the support of Wellington at Waterloo. How chancy are military matters: the Nearin are not mentioned in the Literary Record, nor in the main text accompanying the Pictorial Record. Their contribution, however, was so crucial for success that they could not reasonably be omitted from the scenes which illuminate so strikingly the course of the battle – not only animating the conflict but also providing dashes of realism. As for what happened in the Egyptian camp, the official narrative is a highly unsatisfactory source. It was composed with the intention of placing all the glory on the king: "I was like Monthu [the Theban war god], I discharged arrows to the right and took captives to my left. In their eyes I was like Seth in his time. I found the 2,500 chariots, in the middle of which I was, tumbling before my horse. None found his hand to fight, their hearts disconcerted in their bodies because of fear of me; their arms were all weak and they were unable to shoot." And there is much more in similar vein to demonstrate the power of Ramesses, so that at the end of the day "my army came to praise me, turning their faces to one side at what I had done, my senior officers coming to extol my strong arm, while my chariotry similarly boasted by my name, saying: 'What a fine warrior, who steadies the heart; you save your infantry and your chariots. You are the son of Amun, who achieves success with his two arms... . You are great in victory in the presence of your army, in the sight of the whole land.'" And then, without a tongue in the cheek, the soldiers declare that Ramesses is not speaking boastfully, that he protects Egypt and curbs the foreign lands; and that he has broken the back of Hatti forever. What more could Ramesses have said if he had spoken boastfully?

In an attempt to inject a little reality into the events of that first fateful day, we need to discount the extravagant claims made by Ramesses, without necessarily impugning his bravery in action. The brilliant attack by the Hittites had caught the Egyptians off guard; the division of Pre was scattered, and confusion descended on the division of Amun at the camp. In the mêlée that ensued, Ramesses led what might have appeared to be a last stand in the Egyptian camp. But he was never quite alone; he had his own bodyguard and enough supporting units to prevent the Hittite chariotry from overrunning the camp entirely. Then came the Nearin from Amurru, hoped for, no doubt, but scarcely expected to arrive with such good timing. In respect of this counterattack, it appears that the Hittite intelligence system, up to that point shown to be much superior to the Egyptian, slipped up. The advance of a large military force from the west, moving up the valley of the Eleutheros river toward Qadesh, could scarcely have been overlooked if spies had been operating in that direction. In fact, the relief was the one successful strategic move made by the Egyptians in the campaign, and credit must be given to them, if not to Ramesses himself, for the forethought that planned the intervention from Amurru.

436 bottom
A bare-backed horseman rides off: "The arrival of the scout to hasten the army." In other Qadesh scenes he is said to be hurrying the army of Ptah, as Pharaoh was in the battle unsupported.

437
Rosellini's illustration of the encounter between Egyptian and Hittite chariots, in which the former are shown drawn up with arrows being discharged in unison, while the latter are partly disorganized and in disarray.

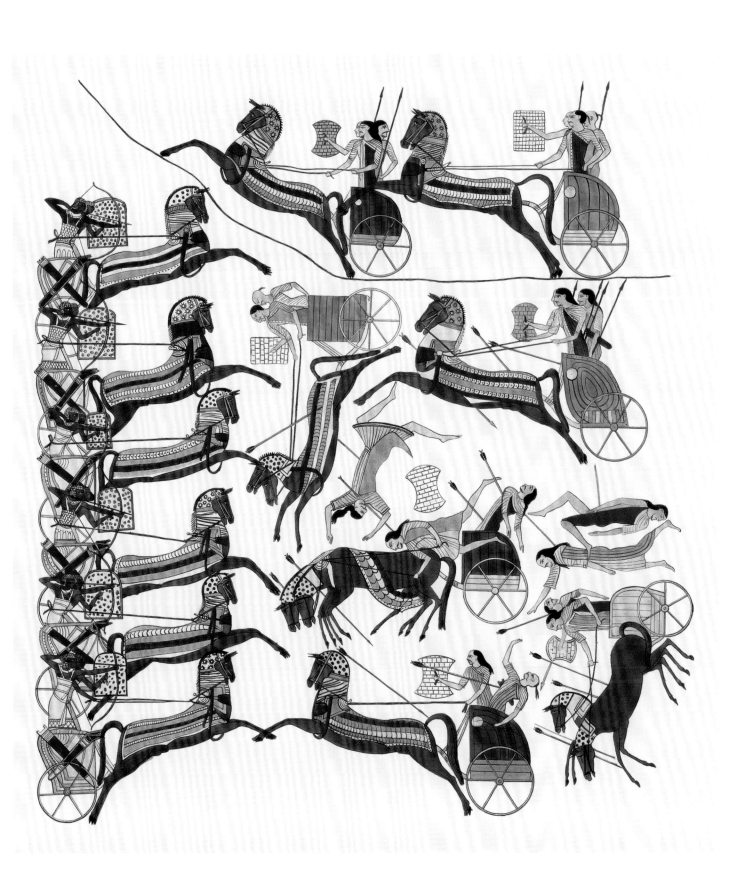

The Battle of Qadesh

From the main Literary Record supplemented by vignettes in the relief representations, it seems that after the happy arrival of the Nearin, the advantage passed to the Egyptians. Ramesses talks of having made six charges into the Hittite ranks, and slowly the enemy was forced back toward the Orontes, and obliged to retreat across the river to where the main body of Hittite troops remained waiting to be engaged. Many were drowned in the river, and some important Hittites and their allies were killed in this stage of the conflict. Lively scenes illustrate some of the calamities that befell them. For the moment, as dusk fell, danger had been averted, and the Egyptians were able to regroup and pull themselves together. What was the situation? The division of Amun had panicked, and was presumably badly mauled by the Hittite chariotry. The division of Pre was taken by surprise while still on the march, thrown into confusion, and also badly mauled. The division of Ptah, which the vizier had been sent to bring forward, had probably arrived just in time to see the final stages of the battle; it was intact. The division of Seth had so far played no part in the battle, but had by evening come up to join the rest of the Egyptian army camped northwest of Qadesh.

Ramesses was not at all satisfied with the

showing of his troops; and with very good reason: "What's the matter with you, my senior officers, my foot-soldiers, and my chariotry, who don't know how to fight?" There was he, in the middle of the turmoil with his shield-bearer and household staff, setting about the enemy while his troops were abandoning him. They should be ashamed of themselves. Perhaps they could do better on the next day. And indeed, they would need to do better, because the bulk of the Hittite army remained unbeaten. On the other hand, from details contained in the vignettes, it becomes clear that a number of important leaders on the Hittite side, including members of Muwatallis' family, had

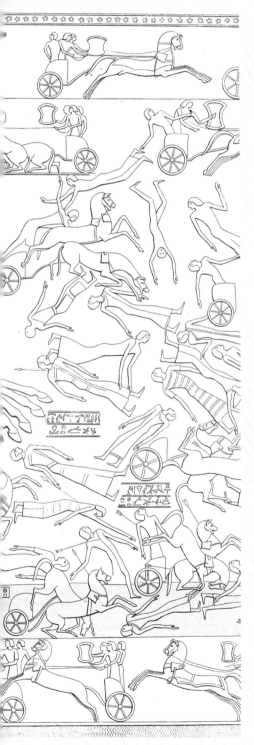

been killed on the first day of fighting; and much of the chariotry, which was used for speed and surprise in attack, had been lost.

When the next day dawned, Ramesses marshaled his divisions for immediate action. He himself was eager to repeat his noble deeds of the previous day, while his troops, at least in outward show, were prepared to support him with a better will than before. The details of this second stage of the battle of Qadesh, as recorded in the Literary Record, are very sketchy.

On this occasion the Egyptians made the first strike, crossing the Orontes by ford, and driving into the massed Hittite army.

Now the advantage in chariots lay with the Egyptians, and seemingly it was fully exploited. The Hittites were not only surprised, but terrified, according to the Official Report: "Get ready, don't go near him; the great goddess Sakhmet [a fierce lioness deity of Memphis] is with him. She rides with him on his horse, and her hand is with him. Whoever approaches him, a breath of fire will come to burn his body." So one of the enemy called out.

It may be inferred from the lack of further description of the battle that the result of the first great charge by the Egyptians was significant, but not decisive. Much more effort would be needed

to secure outright victory. And Ramesses may not have had confidence in the determination of his officers to seek victory with enthusiasm. For the Hittites also there seems to have been a realization that any victory would be a bloody victory, and such an outcome might not be acceptable to the leaders of the allied contingents. In fact a stalemate had been reached, and the Hittite king – the Vile Fallen One of Hatti – made overtures to Ramesses. The Literary Record suggests that Muwatallis groveled before Pharaoh before sending him a letter in which he accepted Ramesses' superiority and his claims over all territories, including Hatti. Too many had been killed: "Do not be hard in your actions, victorious king, peace is better than fighting! Give us time to breathe!" One would here be pleased to have the Hittite view of the negotiations.

It would be more matter-of-fact, although heavily biased in favor of the Hittite point of view. It could be conjectured that when it became evident that neither side would quickly gain the advantage, Muwatallis prudently decided to make the first move toward a settlement. So he sent a letter to Ramesses, couched in terms which would flatter the Egyptian king.

438–439
Rosellini's drawing of the scene in the Ramesseum showing the crucial attack by Ramesses in his chariot during which he routed the Hittites. Many of them, here named, died in the waters of the Orontes.

439 bottom
In the initial encounter between Egyptian and Hittite chariotry, the Egyptians, according to the Abu Simbel version, scattered the Hittites, leaving the field, as shown partly here, littered with shattered chariots and dead soldiers.

He might even have said, "You are Seth, Ba'al in person." The tactical grovel was part of the usual procedure between rival rulers in ancient times. He would not have admitted any Egyptian claims of sovereignty over Hatti lands, and he would certainly not have conceded such sovereignty for the future. The core message was surely that which the Egyptian text offered: "Peace is better than fighting." One item in the Hittite's letter seems to convey a bitter truth. The Egyptian report has Muwatallis stating that Ramesses had spent the day before "killing hundreds of thousands. You have come today, having left no heirs." In saying this he surely was referring to the death of two brothers, whose fates are recorded separately in the relief scenes. Here was good reason for calling a truce; the future of the Hittite kingship might be seriously threatened.

Ramesses then, as reported, called off the attack and summoned his military leaders and

In the course of the description of the battle given above, references were made from time to time to parts of the relief representations which form an important part of the Qadesh record. Many significant facts and details can be gleaned from them to supplement the main compositions, which concentrate on the behavior, thoughts, and exploits of the Pharaoh. Most notable is the scene recording the arrival of the relief force of Nearin from Amurru. Some other scenes should be specially mentioned, along with the hieroglyphic epigraphs accompanying them. The beating of the Hittite spies is graphically portrayed, and the accompanying text explains: "Coming of Pharaoh's scout with two scouts of the Fallen One of Hatti into the presence of Pharaoh. They beat them to say where the vile Fallen One of Hatti is." In another scene the vizier is shown hurrying back to summon forward the divisions still on the march: "Hurry forward! Pharaoh your Lord stands alone

advisers, and had Muwatallis' letter read out to them. With obvious relief, and great enthusiasm, they all agreed: "Peace is exceedingly good, O Sovereign, our Lord! There is no blame in coming to terms when you make it, for who can oppose you in the day of your fury?" Making peace from a position of strength was magnanimity. With such unanimous approval Ramesses decided to call a halt to the battle. Presumably he wrote back to Muwatallis, agreeing to the cessation of fighting, and after a suitable interval for tidying up the loose ends of battle, the Egyptian army withdrew peacefully to the south. In due course, having enjoyed a triumphant journey through the vassal states of Canaan, the king and his army arrived safely in Piramesse, the royal residence city in the Delta. So ended the passage of arms at Qadesh.

in the battle." The same message is conveyed by Pharaoh's butler to the division of Ptah, and similarly by yet another emissary of the king. Meanwhile, in a scene on much grander a scale, Ramesses is shown in his chariot shooting arrows at the enemy. Variants of this scene, accompanied by differing texts vaunting the king's activity, are found in the various temples. The Hittite king, on the other hand, is given no starring role.

He is shown in his chariot, turning away from the town of Qadesh. In some temples a long text states, "The great, vile Fallen One of Hatti stands in the middle of his infantry and chariotry, with face turned back, trembling, his heart distressed. He never came out to fight because of the fear of His Majesty, after he had seen His Majesty overcoming those of Hatti and of the chiefs of all foreign lands who had come with him, for His

Majesty overthrew them in an instant, His Majesty being like a divine falcon... ." Many of those who did engage in battle from the Hittite side are shown usually in turmoil, and the names of important Hittites among the slain, or drowned in the Orontes, are listed. One graphic vignette shows the prince of Aleppo being held upside down. The epigraph explains: "The vile Prince of

Aleppo being emptied [of water] by his soldiers, after His Majesty had cast him into the water."

A number of small incidents are illustrated, in which Egyptian or Hittite soldiers are shown on the move or engaged in battle. Such scenes persuasively provide the flavor of war – the disjunctive, almost aimless, activities of small groups of soldiers, separated from their units, and

not quite sure about what they should be doing. The carnage is highlighted by vignettes showing piles of hands cut off dead Hittites, in one of which a scribe is depicted noting down numbers, while prisoners are brought in by one of Ramesses' sons. A number of young sons had accompanied their father on campaign, and some are shown individually bringing captives to Pharaoh.

The Battle of Qadesh

The remarkable value of the various relief scenes lies not only in the richness of the information they contain about one specific, identifiable battle, but also in the dramatic visual invention of the tableaux. Extensive areas of temple walls are filled with a great number of scenes, some huge, involving the king, others intimate and small-scale. The compositions are elaborate and very dramatically designed. The execution is not of the highest quality, due possibly to the fact that they were carved in the space of a very few years after the battle had been fought. Color, now lost, would have concealed much of the deficiencies in execution, and rendered the overall effect exceptionally striking, especially in the bright Egyptian sunshine. At Abu Simbel, where the color survives within the great temple, something of the effect may be appreciated, although the representations there are not at quite so large a scale as in the Theban temples. The best carvings are at Abydos, where the medium is limestone, which allows for crisper carving than the sandstone used elsewhere. Unfortunately the Abydos reliefs on the outer walls of the Ramesses temple have lost most of

their upper courses, and many of the desirable small-scale vignettes are lost. But the various representations, in mass and variety unparalleled in Egyptian temple art, present a wonderful narrative sequence of what for Ramesses II was the most momentous event of his reign. And it was all over and visually commemorated while more than fifty years of that reign remained to come.

Who in the end won? In the last chapter it was pointed out that when Ramesses and his army returned to Egypt, full of victorious bombast, the Hittites were left at Qadesh. Unopposed they moved to recover Amurru, and to annex the part of Syria known as Upe. More might have been gained had not troubles with his allies, and in particular Assyria, obliged Muwatallis to withdraw to Anatolia. He certainly believed that he had come better out of he Qadesh contest than Ramesses. It is true that his army had been mauled and some of his allies subsequently reneged in their allegiance; but he had kept Qadesh, and regained control over regions previously lost to the Egyptians. He assuredly believed that he had won, although no record

survives to signal his satisfaction, and no steps are known to have been taken to laud the triumph in word and scene. Ramesses also assuredly believed that he had won, and he spared no effort to publicize his victory. A battle had taken place on a massive scale, and Ramesses had returned to Egypt with most of his army intact. By a stretch of the imagination he could maintain that he had won. Modern historians, on the other hand, maintain that the crown of victory should go to Muwatallis. In the long term, the Hittites certainly gained an advantage, but it would be difficult to demonstrate that they had actually beaten the Egyptians.

On balance, one might declare the Egyptians to be the winners of the battle; but for the campaign as a whole, they were the losers. One certain outcome of the battle of Qadesh was a realization on both sides that such a major confrontation should not happen again. Both sides might engage in minor expeditions and forays, but otherwise, an uneasy general peace prevailed, until the position was regularized by the treaty of Year 21.

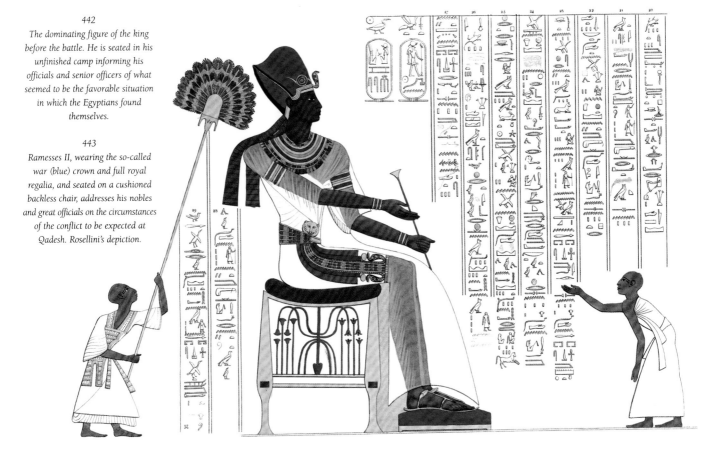

442

The dominating figure of the king before the battle. He is seated in his unfinished camp informing his officials and senior officers of what seemed to be the favorable situation in which the Egyptians found themselves.

443

Ramesses II, wearing the so-called war (blue) crown and full royal regalia, and seated on a cushioned backless chair, addresses his nobles and great officials on the circumstances of the conflict to be expected at Qadesh. Rosellini's depiction.

THE GREAT BUILDER

444
In the forecourt of the Luxor temple, a head from a colossal statue of Ramesses II confronts the visitor. Is it he, or is it usurped from Amenophis III? The answer scarcely matters: here is royalty personified.

445
The upper part of a colossal granite statue of Ramesses holding the flail and crook, the royal insignia, and wearing the double crown. It comes from the temple of Khnum on the Island of Elephantine (British Museum, EA67).

ention was already made of the extraordinary impression the surviving legacy of Ramesses II makes on the modern-day visitor to Egypt. His is the cartouche most readily recognized; his is the name most readily invoked when a site is visited or a building entered. He seems to have been everywhere, and built or fiddled with most of the great structures from antiquity, with the prime exception of the pyramids. And even with the pyramids, we shall find out in due course that his son Khaemwese on his own account fiddled with many of them, but of course ostensibly in the name of his father Ramesses. When we say that a king was a great builder, what do we really mean? Certainly not that all the great temples and other structures bearing his name were necessarily built with his agreement or under his supervision. The best that can be said is that a king may be judged a great builder if there are many buildings which can be shown to have been built in his reign, and carry meaningful inscriptions about construction and purpose, or at least examples of the king's name.

But even then, the carved word or name may be misleading; for earlier texts can be modified, names recut, and steps taken to give the impression that a piece of work was carried out under a king different from the one who was actually responsible in the first place. The intention was not always *damnatio memoriae* – the deliberate attempt to destroy the memory of a predecessor who has lost his reputation. Sometimes the change seems to have been made gratuitously, to annex a building or a part of a building, just to claim it for someone other than the original builder.

When we talk of a 'builder,' as we have said, we are not referring directly to the king himself, at least not in every case. There are, however, many buildings which were undoubtedly planned and constructed at the instigation of the king, or on his agreement with what his officials may have suggested.

Generally speaking, there is rarely any specific evidence of a king's involvement in a project, apart from those that closely affected

him personally, such as his tomb and his mortuary temple. In the case of Ramesses II, however, we gain the impression that he took more than a usual interest in many of the buildings that were erected in his name, in addition to those of most intimate concern. The inscriptions of many of his high officials responsible for major projects, as we shall see later, show that they apparently worked with the positive encouragement of the king; and some of these officials were undoubtedly responsible for those features of glorification, amounting subsequently to deification, which became such a notable element in many of the temples, especially in Nubia. It is not difficult to imagine how eager his officials would have been to present proposals to the king when he visited a place like Thebes after his accession: "May I interest Your Majesty in this proposed extension to the temple of Luxor?"; "What about completing the great plans for the Hypostyle Hall at Karnak, already so nobly continued by your revered father Sethos?"

The Temple of Sethos I at ABYDOS

When he succeeded Sethos, Ramesses in name if not in fact was already engaged in works which were started by his father, and these he felt he had a special responsibility to complete. It is not possible to put in any order of priority the various undertakings, but it is possible to note especially those that had a high priority. Top of the list comes the Osiris temple at Abydos, which, as was indicated earlier, was a sanctuary of unique plan and exquisite decoration. From the great dedicatory inscription, carved in 120 lines on the western half of the wall beneath the portico leading into the first hypostyle hall, it is recorded that Ramesses II paid a visit to Abydos toward the end of the third month of autumn in his Year 1 (c. 1279 B.C.). He had traveled north from Thebes, having taken part in the important festival of Opet, possibly following his supervision of the burial of his father Sethos. Feelings of filial piety were therefore unusually strong at that time, and his visit to Abydos during the return journey to Memphis and the Delta Residence was a positive indication of his intention to fulfill one of Sethos' cherished projects. According to the text, a wretched state of affairs existed at Abydos. Earlier royal structures were in a ruinous condition, and as for "the temple of Menmare [Sethos], its front and rear parts were being built when he went forth to Heaven [died]. There was no one to finish its monuments, no one to put up its columns upon its terrace." The statue designed for the temple was unfinished and lying on the ground, and not made according to the specifications. The affairs of the temple were in a mess. So Ramesses called upon his officials to get on with the work. As he said, "A good opportunity to make provision for those who have passed on; pity is helpful, caring is good, a son should devote himself to (the memory of) his father. My heart has driven me to make good works for Merenptah [part of Sethos' full name]." And so on and so on!

Suitably commissioned, the officials in charge of building works set about completing what had been planned in Sethos' reign. The result, a mixture of the meticulous craftsmanship of the earlier reign, and the slapdash grandeur of the later, was impressive and singularly moving. In brief, the temple consisted of two open courts with pylons and massive walls, leading the visitor from the level of the fertile valley up to the desert escarpment on which the temple proper was built.

Although the pylons are mostly destroyed and the walls reduced in height, the walk through the first and second courts, rising upward, is even now endowed with an extraordinary feeling of anticipation. The main temple building is not a towering structure; it almost seems to squat on the first desert ridge, scarcely to be seen until the visitor passes into the second court. From a portico with square pillars, the first columned hall is entered through a single central doorway (seven were originally planned). This hall runs across the main axis and its decoration is wholly of Ramesses' reign.

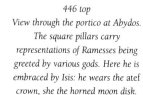

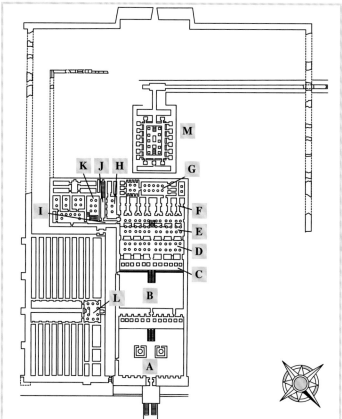

447 top left
In the first hypostyle hall at Abydos, looking through the great columns to the west wall with a scene of Ramesses, followed by the goddess Mut, adoring Ptah in a shrine who writes the king's name.

447 top right
The impressive and mysterious entry into the Abydos temple, looking west from the first hypostyle hall into the second. The decoration in the former is from Ramesses' reign, in the latter mostly from Sethos' reign.

447 bottom
View through the entrance in the Second Pylon at Abydos to the second court. Beyond can be seen the portico of the main temple. The courts were planned by Sethos, but completed under Ramesses II.

	LEGEND		
A	FIRST COURT	H	CHAPEL OF NEFERTUM
B	SECOND COURT		AND PTAH-SOKARIS
C	PORTICO	I	CORRIDOR OF THE LISTS
D	FIRST HYPOSTYLE HALL	J	CORRIDOR OF THE BULL
E	SECOND HYPOSTYLE HALL	K	HALL OF BARKS
F	CHAPELS OF THE DEITIES	L	PALACE
G	OSIRIS COMPLEX	M	OSIREION

The Great Builder

448–449
The Corridor of the Lists at Abydos, looking north. On the left the young Ramesses reads the list of royal ancestors to his father Sethos; on the right are scenes of gods and the reversion of offerings.

448 bottom
Seven chapels lead off the second hypostyle hall. Here, at the west end of the Amon-Re Chapel, is a false door, flanked by reliefs of the King offering wine to the god.

449 top left
From the small Isis chapel in the Osiris complex at Abyos, Sethos receives the jubilee elements from Isis, supported by Horus-son-of-Osiris. On the side walls, Sethos offers trays of food to Isis.

449 top right
On the south wall of the Amon-Re chapel at Abydos, the king makes multiple offerings of cloths, collars, and pectorals to the god in his living form and also as mummiform and ithyphallic.

A second hypostyle hall lies behind the first, and like the first is much wider than it is deep. Seven doors allow access to this second hall and they correspond with the entrances to seven shrines on the further side of the hall. These are dedicated to the three Osirian deities, Horus, Isis, and Osiris himself; to the three great national gods, Amon-Re, Re-Herakhty, and Ptah; and one to King Sethos himself. The Osiris shrine leads into another suite of rooms devoted to the Osirian mysteries. The second court, the complex of shrines, and some other parts of the temple lying to the south are most wonderfully decorated with painted low reliefs of Sethos' time. Adjacent rooms include the corridor in which the famous list of kings or ancestors is carved, where Ramesses apparently did not instruct his officials to ensure that the completion work and decoration should be carried out to the same standard as that achieved in his father's time. His officials or their building and decorating contractors saw no reason to expend an infinite amount of time on work which had been planned essentially for the dead Sethos.

By a happy chance the main buildings of the temple escaped the ravages of destruction found elsewhere in temples established in populous areas, and dreadfully treated by generations of squatters up until the nineteenth century. The Sethos temple became sanded up and inaccessible, apart from the stonework of the pylons and great courts, which alone provided as much building material as was needed to satisfy the demands of the relatively small local population.

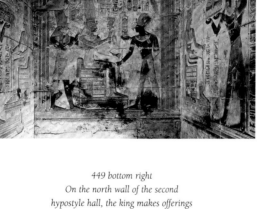

449 bottom right
On the north wall of the second hypostyle hall, the king makes offerings before a shrine containing the seated Osiris supported by Isis (behind) and Ma'at and Renpet (in front). On the right are Osiris and Horus.

449 bottom left
The hall of Nefertum and Ptah-Sokaris: the king makes offerings to the deities, here to Sokaris, shown falcon-headed. The king is Sethos I, and his identity has not been usurped by his son.

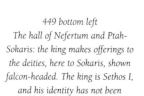

The Temple of Ramesses II at ABYDOS

Less well preserved, however, was the much smaller temple built for Ramesses II himself, to the north of the Sethos temple and just beyond the small shrine put up by Sethos in remembrance of his father Ramesses I. It is possible that Ramesses II's temple was started or planned before his accession to the throne, but most, if not all, of the decoration was executed subsequent to his accession. Some of the extended surfaces of the outer walls carry records of the battle of Qadesh. The reliefs here and within the temple, especially in the shrines dedicated to Osiris and other major Egyptian deities, are very sensitively carved in the hard, fine-quality limestone with which the temple is built; much of their brilliant color has survived. By Ramesses' standard, this temple is a modest structure, and everything about it is on a modest scale. It is as if the king, in arranging for its construction, instructed his officials to ensure that it did not compete with the nobility and grandeur of his father's temple. It was, however, probably never intended to be more than a small statement of Ramesses' devotion to Osiris and the gods of Egypt. His major statement had already been made in the completion of Sethos' temple, in which, when finished, the presence of Usimare-Setpenre Ramessu-Miamun was inescapable.

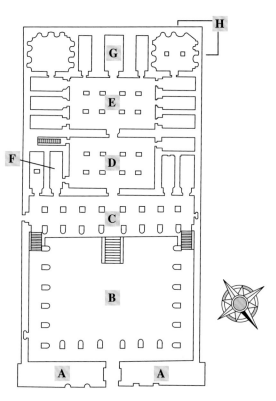

450 top
Scene on the lower jamb of the door leading into the first hall. Ibis-headed Thoth writes the texts in front; behind, holding a cup of water and the god's writing equipment, is a minor deity called "seeing."

LEGEND

A SECOND PYLON
B COURT
C HALL
D SECOND HALL
E THIRD HALL
F ROOM OF THE KING LIST
G SANCTUARY
H QADESH SCENES

450 bottom
The shattered head of a black granite colossal figure of a king, probably Ramesses II, in the court of his Abydos temple; probably from one of a pair of seated statues originally placed in front of the temple's entrance.

450–451
The door into the first hall of Ramesses' Abydos temple. The texts on the jambs state that it was made "as a monument for his father Osiris... the making of a doorway in black stone."

451 bottom
View of the remains of Ramesses II's Abydos temple. The outer walls, made of fine white limestone, were carved with sunk reliefs illustrating the great triumph of the king in the battle of Qadesh.

The Great Builder

452
One of the androgynous kneeling semi-deities representing the cities and nomes (provinces) of Egypt. They bring the produce of the land for the provisioning of the temple. Here is the representation of Hutsnofru "The Mansion of (King) Snofru."

452–453
Ramesses II wearing the afnet headpiece, makes a gesture of uncertain significance to Osiris, who is seated and holding the insignia of royal power. The colors on the reliefs in this temple are unusually well preserved.

The Temple of
KARNAK

When Ramesses had been in Thebes to bury
his father and to celebrate the Opet Festival, he
had the opportunity before traveling north to
Abydos to make a tour of the building projects
initiated during Sethos' reign, and to consider
what further might be done to enlarge the great
temples, thereby promoting his own importance
and providing substantial wall spaces for the
carving of the achievements of the new reign.

In the festival of Opet, about which more will

be said later in this book, the images of the three
deities of the Theban divine triad – Amun, Mut,
and Khons – were taken from Karnak by river
upstream about two miles to Luxor, where sacred
mysteries took place, including a symbolic
marriage between Amun and Mut. So Ramesses
in person could observe the 'facilities' in both of
the great Theban temples. Their histories were
very different. Karnak had been the cult-center of
the god Amun, closely associated with the great
god of Heliopolis, Re. So, as Amon-Re, the god
was also associated with the fertility deity Min of
Coptos. The importance of Karnak greatly
increased when the Theban kingdom was
revivified at the beginning of the Eighteenth
Dynasty; thereafter, few kings failed to leave their
mark on the temple buildings. Within its great
precinct, the temple was regularly enlarged by the
addition of new structures and by the
modification of the most sacred shrine of the
great god. Many of the buildings of the early and
middle reigns of the dynasty were dismantled in
antiquity, and as the temple stands now, the most
distinctive monumental stamp was made by
Amenophis III. His plan for the development of
the complex probably determined to a great
extent what happened subsequently after the
Amarna interlude.

LEGEND

A	FIRST PYLON	K	AVENUE OF THE RAM-
B	SECOND PYLON		HEADED SPHINXES
C	THIRD PYLON	L	FORECOURT
D	FOURTH PYLON	M	HYPOSTYLE HALL
E	FIFTH PYLON	N	RELIEFS OF SETHOS' WARS
F	SIXTH PYLON	O	RELIEFS OF RAMESSES II
G	SEVENTH PYLON	P	SANCTUARY
H	EIGHTH PYLON	Q	FESTIVAL HALL OF
I	NINTH PYLON		THUTMOSIS III
J	TENTH PYLON	R	SACRED LAKE

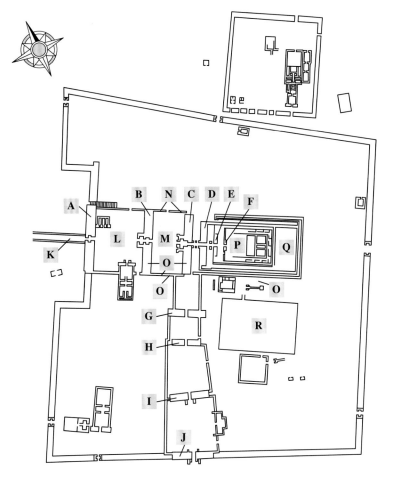

It was he who arranged for the construction of what is now called the Third Pylon, which was to act as a great formal entrance to the temple. It now serves as the rear wall of the great Hypostyle Hall.

In its building many of the dismantled earlier structures were used to pack the void between the outer skin walls of the pylon. No regard seems to have been paid to the age of the demolished buildings, or to the standing of the Pharaohs in whose times they had been built; the works of even his immediate predecessors were not spared. This clearance, however, provided the space and opportunity for further development, perhaps for the laying out of the great court in front of the Third Pylon, which began to be transformed into the Hypostyle Hall by Horemheb and Sethos.

When Ramesses II revisited Karnak at the beginning of the Opet Festival in his Year I, he would have found the Hypostyle Hall structurally complete, with much relief

decoration inside and out celebrating the warlike deeds of his father. The western entrance was formed by the Second Pylon, built under Horemheb and Ramesses I, also stuffed with blocks from dismantled earlier structures, including the temples built outside the Karnak precinct in the early years of Akhenaten. Here was not much scope for great works, but Ramesses' mark was substantially placed on the elements of the hall, particularly on the inner and outer walls on the southern side, and on the columns where his cartouches appear ubiquitously.

As is so often the case, his cartouches have in many places been recut for later Pharaohs; he was not immune from the indignity of usurpation. This is evident also in the case of the sphinxes forming the monumental avenue leading from the quay, the landing place on the canal leading down to the Nile.

456–457
*Ram-headed sphinxes with figures
of Ramesses II, originally part of
the avenue which led westward
from the Hypostyle Hall; after the
construction of the First Pylon they
were moved and "parked" in the
forecourt.*

From this quay the river processions to Luxor and the west bank of the river would start at the beginnings of festivals, and the evidence suggests that the quay itself was built or rebuilt under Ramesses, perhaps for the start of the Opet Festival of Year 1. The sphinxes in the avenue are not human-headed recumbent lions, but ram-headed lions – criosphinxes, as they are called. Beneath each ram head is a mummiform figure of the king, originally inscribed for Ramesses II, but later usurped by Pinudjem I (c. 1060 B.C.), high priest of Amon-Re in the Twenty-first Dynasty, virtual ruler of the Theban district who even assumed royal titles and used cartouches. This avenue now stops at the First Pylon (built c. 1350 B.C.), but it originally continued as far as the Second Pylon; the redundant sphinxes are now unceremoniously lined up like parked cars to the sides of great First Court, again a sorry fate for monuments of Ramesses.

Within the Karnak precinct, Ramesses undertook no further structural work on a grand scale; but a considerable amount of minor building work, and a great deal of relief carving was completed. Scenes celebrating both the warlike activities of his early years and many ritual activities may be observed on the southern outer wall of the Hypostyle Hall, where Ramesses appears to have usurped himself. Here scenes and texts of the battle of Qadesh were carved in the years following the contest; subsequently the battle scenes were recarved with new scenes of warfare and triumph, although the Literary Record was left largely untouched.

It seems almost as if Ramesses' officials had run out of space to show newly commissioned scenes, and were obliged to recycle space already occupied by scenes which were better seen at Luxor and in the Ramesseum. A suggestion that the 'cover-up' may have been a tactful act to avoid embarrassing Hittite envoys at the time of the treaty negotiations of Year 21 seems wholly unlikely. Uncontroversial in every respect was the fine series of framed tableaux carved in sensitive sunk relief on the girdle wall around the eastern parts of the main temple; here Ramesses is shown as the dutiful and pious servant of the gods, making offerings to many deities, national and local. These scenes are unusually unostentatious in content and modest in scale.

458
A view at dusk down onto the Hypostyle Hall at Karnak, showing clearly the architrave beams that carried the huge roofing slabs. Outside the great entrance can be seen the colossus of Ramesses with Bintanta.

459 top
Looking through the massive papyrus-bud columns of the Hypostyle Hall to its northern wall. These columns had not yet been decorated at the time of Ramesses' accession and so received huge cartouches in heraldic devices.

459 bottom
In this view through the Hypostyle Hall, Ramesses' names and titles can be made out on the architraves; his cartouches are clearly visible on the nearest column, with a scene of Amon-Re and Amunet receiving worship from the king.

460 top
On a column in the Hypostyle Hall,
the prenomen of Ramesses II. Above
it, gods make presentations to the
king: on the left, Amon-Re, in the
center Khonsu, mummiform and
with moon disk; on the right Isis.

460 bottom left
Ramesses makes an offering of food
to the form of Amon-Re called
Kamutef "bull of his mother," shown
in the form usually associated with
the fertility god Min. Aphrodisiac
lettuce grow behind.

460 bottom right
Ramesses II, very sensitively
portrayed, offers incense to the god
in a scene on one of the columns.
He wears the blue crown and holds
an incense burner into which he
projects a stream of incense pellets.

461
On two adjacent columns, Ramesses II
makes offerings to two different forms
of Amon-Re: on the left, to the god as
Kamutef, the fertility form; on the
right, as king of the gods, his most
common designation.

The Temple of
LUXOR

462

The device commonly found on the thrones of seated colossal figures, showing Nile deities representing Upper and Lower Egypt binding together the Two Lands with the lily of the South and the papyrus of the North. At Luxor temple.

463

The head of a colossal statue of Ramesses II (probably usurped from Amenophis II) and, in the background, a smaller seated colossus of the king. In the court of the Luxor temple.

Moving on from Karnak to Luxor at the time of Opet, Ramesses had the opportunity to assess the possibilities for development – possibilities which were lacking at the principal Theban sanctuary. The Luxor temple, also dedicated to the gods of the Theban triad, was essentially a foundation of Amenophis III. Here the relatively small but immensely graceful temple had been extended in a northerly direction by the great colonnade in which work by Amenophis III, Tutankhamun, and Horemheb was to be seen. Perhaps more had been planned, to provide the temple with a monumental entrance and grand approach. Here then were opportunities for Ramesses' architects, and they met the challenge. A great court with side colonnades was planned, to be entered through a massive pylon, the two wings of which would cry out for majestic relief scenes. Unusually, the axis of

the temple had to be turned, so that the new entrance would line up with the avenue leading from Karnak to Luxor. It is a strange, almost uncanny, experience to enter this temple as it now exists, to pass through the great court, with an intrusive mosque built into its space on the east side, and then to turn about five degrees to the left in order to walk along the old temple axis through the great colonnade to the main buildings and sanctuary of the Amenophis structure. But try to do so when the temple is not flooded with tourists.

In a text on the great entrance pylon, Ramesses takes credit for the inspiration of this building, and he declares that he took a personal interest in the work in progress. It was certainly carried forward with speed, for this inscription states that the work was completed in the king's Year 3.

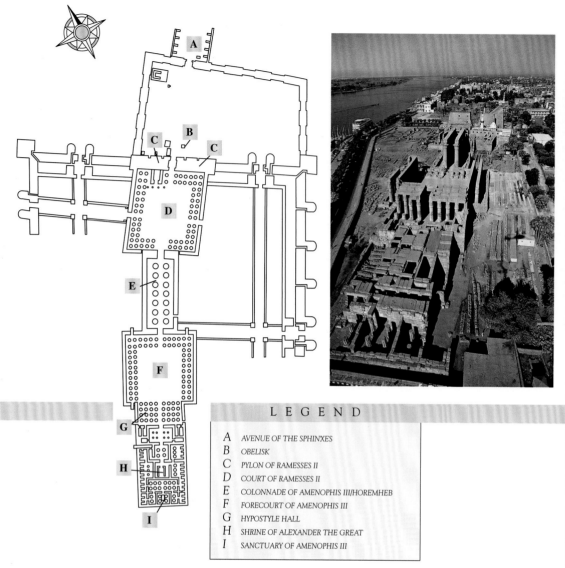

LEGEND

A AVENUE OF THE SPHINXES
B OBELISK
C PYLON OF RAMESSES II
D COURT OF RAMESSES II
E COLONNADE OF AMENOPHIS III/HOREMHEB
F FORECOURT OF AMENOPHIS III
G HYPOSTYLE HALL
H SHRINE OF ALEXANDER THE GREAT
I SANCTUARY OF AMENOPHIS III

Ramesses II

It became the first major building work in which his own hand may be detected; it bore all the hallmarks of a statement by Ramesses the Great. When it was completed, its façade presented an overwhelming sight: great flag-poles set into the niches in the pylon wings rose high with flying pennants; the entrance was flanked on each side by a colossal seated figure and two huge standing figures of the king; in front of the seated colossi were two obelisks, twenty-five meters high, only one of which remains *in situ*.

The other was presented to the French nation by Muhammad Ali Pasha; it was erected in the Place de la Concorde in Paris in 1836. A relief carved in the southern wall of the Ramesside court shows the façade as it was planned, with pylons, flagpoles, colossal statues, and obelisks. And in this form it can be viewed today, with the absence of the flagpoles and one obelisk; some of the statues are in a ruinous state. It remains an overwhelming sight. The spaces between many of the columns in the first court are occupied by colossal granite figures, ostensibly of Ramesses II, and so inscribed; but some were certainly usurped from earlier kings. One is nevertheless greatly impressed by the sheer bulk of colossal granite statuary of this king.

464 top
Aerial view of Luxor temple. The main complex extends southwards from the great colonnade, including the buildings planned and mostly constructed by Amenophis III. The Ramesses court and pylon lie beyond the colonnade.

464–465
Aerial view of Luxor looking eastward. The change of the temple's axis to the left of the colonnade, to align the Ramesside additions with the avenue leading to Karnak, is clearly visible.

465 bottom
The great pylon built under Ramesses II for the Luxor temple, approached from Karnak along the avenue of sphinxes. The obelisk missing from the right of the entrance is now in Paris.

466 top
The façade of the Luxor temple carved on the south wall of the court. It shows two seated and four standing colossal figures, two obelisks, and great flagstaves with pennants set into the pylon wings.

466 bottom
Floodlit aerial view of the pylon forming the monumental entrance commissioned by Ramesses II to the Luxor temple. Outside can be seen the top of the surviving obelisk, and within, part of earlier shrines in the court.

467
To the left of the main entrance to Luxor, a much damaged seated colossus of Ramesses II and the obelisk, set on a base with baboons raising their paws to worship the sun at dawn.

468 top left
In the court of Ramesses II in the Luxor temple, three standing royal colossi occupy the spaces between the papyrus-bud columns of the colonnade. On the columns, Ramesses offers flowers to Amon-Re Kamutef.

468 bottom left
The colossus in one of the columnar spaces of the Luxor colonnade. There can be little doubt that the statue, although inscribed for Ramesses, was made for an earlier ruler, possibly Amenophis II.

468–469
The northeast corner of the court in Luxor. Great seated statues flank the doorway leading to the Horemheb colonnade; standing colossi between the columns crowd the available space – an overpowering rather than an aesthetic effect.

How could so much be produced to such a generally high, if not inspired, standard? And for the building of the great court and the pylons, and indeed for the many buildings we have not yet considered, how were such immense quantities of sandstone quarried and dressed and transported to their destinations?

From the time of the Eighteenth Dynasty, the principal stone used for the construction of temples was sandstone. It was an even-textured, relatively soft stone, easily quarried and dressed, capable of spanning wider spaces than limestone, and easily inscribed with texts and relief scenes. The main quarries lay on both sides of the Nile at a place now called Gebel al-Silsila, 'the mountain of the chain,' so named because it was claimed that in medieval times a chain was slung across the Nile there; the intention was to restrict river traffic and extract tolls. At this point the Nile is relatively narrow and the cliffs on both sides come right down to the river; it was therefore a reasonably easy matter to move quarried blocks to the river for transport north to the temple sites.

This place was considered sacred to certain river deities, and especially Hapy, the god of the inundation; many private memorials were left there by visiting officials to testify to the special devotion shown to these gods. And there are four huge royal inscriptions containing almost parallel texts addressing praise and making offerings to Hapy. Sethos I was the first to show his devotion; then came Ramesses II, and his text is dated in his Year 1. In honoring the deity of the quarry region so early in his reign, Ramesses or his building officials must already have had in mind at least some of the great projects which would need stone from Gebel al-Silsila and,

consequently, the beneficent attention of Hapy. Rather less grand inscriptions were placed in the small rock-cut temple, or *speos*, cut in the reign of Horemheb, but mostly left undecorated by that monarch. Some of Ramesses' executive officials who visited the quarries to inspect the progress of work left their memorials in that convenient shrine.

From a scrutiny of the rock cliffs which are the walls of the open quarries, it is clear that the stone was cut from its bed with a minimum of wastage, the lines left by the removal of blocks indicating the economy of the process. The procedure was very different in the granite quarries at Aswan, about forty miles to the south of Silsila. In this desolate and rugged region, great granite boulders could be found which could be worked with painstaking skill into statues and architectural elements. Obelisks and monolithic columns, however, had to be quarried from places where unblemished rock could be extracted. Expert skills in the discovery of accessible beds of stone, and technical mastery of simple tools, were needed to obtain all that was required to embellish the great temples. These temples were otherwise constructed of sandstone with mud-brick for subsidiary buildings and for huge perimeter walls.

Once a suitable length of granite had been identified and then cut from its rocky bed, it was a relatively straightforward process for the Egyptian specialist craftsmen, skilled in working the stone, to produce an obelisk. But no one should fail to appreciate the precision of the cutting of the finished object, with its exact tapering and smoothness of the surface.

To carve a great granite colossus, standing or sitting, was another matter, requiring not only

superb stoneworking skills, but the eye of an artist. Many of the colossal figures produced in the course of Egyptian history impress more for their size than for their artistry. Immense competence in the working of hard stones according to practices, even formulas, for the production of the standard forms ensured a remarkable consistency in the representation of the human form. One may rightly admire the precision of the carving, the modeling of the limbs, the excellence of finish; all these aspects are properly addressed and achieved; but they do not as such produce real works of art. Something beyond the satisfying of rules and conventions is needed. This special factor is most usually displayed in the carving of the head, in particular the features, of the subject. It is not just a question of portraiture, for a good likeness is not *ipso facto* a good work of art. In the case of the many colossal statues of Ramesses II, look chiefly at the head, and in many you will find not just competence, but true artistry. Such is the case with the face of the great head in the British Museum, the Younger Memnon, which was discussed in the first chapter of this book. In spite of its size, it has great sensitivity, and must have been truly impressive when it topped its statue – possibly a seated colossus – in the second court of the Ramesseum. Even more impressive, if not perhaps so artistically satisfying, was the yet greater seated colossus, the remains of which lie tumbled at the west side of the first court. It has been estimated that it stood originally about fifty-seven feet (seventeen meters) tall, and weighed over one hundred tons – a very considerable problem for the haulage department of the royal workshop, which was entrusted with moving it from Aswan to Thebes.

471

The colossus to the west of the entrance to the Horemheb colonnade. By the king's right leg is a small figure of Queen Nefertari. On the base, the royal titulary is presented by priests with leopard-skin cloaks.

The Great Builder

470

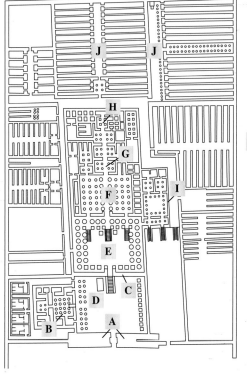

LEGEND

- A FIRST PYLON
- B PALACE
- C SECOND PYLON
- D FALLEN COLOSSUS
- E SECOND COURT
- F HYPOSTYLE HALL
- G ROOM WITH ASTRONOMICAL CEILING
- H SANCTUARY AND BARK HALL
- I TEMPLE OF TUY
- J MUD-BRICK STOREHOUSES

The Ramesseum:
the so-called Tomb of MEMNON

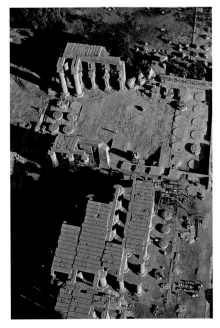

472–473
Panoramic view of the Ramesseum, showing the extent of the temple enclosure, standing now on the very edge of the cultivated plain. The temple proper is surrounded by subsidiary buildings, notably the vaulted storehouses on the left.

472 bottom
Drawing by Lepsius of the reconstructed façade of the main temple building of the Ramesseum. Osiride figures of Ramesses are engaged with the square pillars of the colonnade.

473 top
View down on the main buildings of the Ramesseum; many rooms still have their roofing slabs, neatly arranged in place. The remains of the great fallen colossus can be seen at the top in the center.

473 bottom
Lepsius's drawing of a cross section from east to west of the main buildings of the Ramesseum, with a suggested reconstruction of the great colossus in front of the second pylon on the left.

The Ramesseum, mortuary temple for the dead king, but much more than that, was planned early in the reign of the king. No convenient texts date precisely the commencement of the work, or its completion, but much of its principal structure had been completed in time for the carving of texts and reliefs commemorating the battle of Qadesh of Year 5. It was laid out on a grand scale, grander than any other royal mortuary temple in Western Thebes apart from that of Amenophis III, which lay to the south and is now marked almost only by the two massive seated statues, the Colossi of Memnon. Of all the temples built along the edge of the cultivation, this temple of Amenophis III may well have been the grandest and possibly the most beautiful in terms of statuary and relief decoration. It was still to be seen in the time of Ramesses, and it is likely that he had his own temple planned to rival, if not to outdo, the earlier structure. At least Ramesses would have one great statue to exceed in height those vast quartzite colossi which still

dominate the flood plain. Within its great mud-brick enclosure wall, measuring about 300 by 185 yards (275 by 168 meters), the Ramesseum itself occupies about one quarter of the available space. Approached from the river by a canal and a quay, the visitor arrived at a huge pylon giving entry to the second court. In front of the second pylon stood the massive seated colossus. Both pylons carry Qadesh texts and reliefs to act as a constant reminder of military glory for all who might come to conduct the services of memorial and offering for the dead king; and, before his death, for those who would come to the temple to engage in the many activities which were carried on in the other buildings in the complex. The colonnades surrounding the courts are now mostly gone, but much of the core of the main temple survives: part of a huge hypostyle hall, followed by two smaller pillared halls, the sanctuary, and side rooms for the storage of temple furniture. In front of the temple and to the south, a small palace was built, a kind of *pied-à-terre* for the king on his occasional

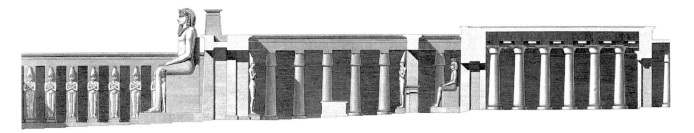

visits to Thebes. It was appropriate that it should be within the temple precinct, for this precinct was particularly his private and personal domain; here his cult ceremonies would take place after his death. Most of the remaining space around the main temple was occupied by storerooms, work rooms, living quarters for priests and temple servants, places where all manner of instruction in special activities took place. Most notable architecturally is a series of barrel-vaulted mud-brick structures of great size, storerooms which by happy chance have survived three thousand years of potential vandalism. The Ramesseum was Ramesses' major construction in Thebes, and in spite of its ruinous condition, it still retains a special atmosphere. Here the visitor may feel closer to the king than in other, more grandiose places like the Hypostyle Hall in Karnak. Or does the very ruinous condition provoke thoughts of the transient nature of greatness, here seen to have crumbled into the shattered remains of the great colossus?

474 top
Scenes on the rear wall of the second court. Ramesses is led by Monthu and Atum toward Amon-Re, Mut and Khonsu before whom he then kneels to receive jubilees, noted by Thoth, the divine scribe.

474-475
The portico on the west side of the second court of the Ramesseum, with a view into the hypostyle hall and beyond. The square pillars of the portico have engaged figures of Ramesses as Osiris.

474 bottom
Head of one of the two colossal statues of Ramesses that stood in the second court on either side of the entrance into the main temple. The king wears the nemes headdress and double crown.

475 bottom left
Seated royal statues usually show the king as if he were fully in repose, with his hands opened downward and placed on his stretched kilt. This fragment comes from a statue of this type in the Ramesseum.

Ramesses II

475 bottom right
Two rows of column bases, all that
remain of a colonnade running
between the ranges of mud-brick
storehouses behind the main temple.
The columns were polygonal,
unusual for this period.

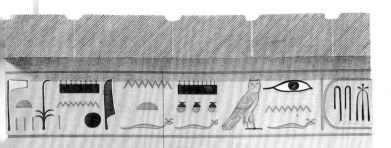

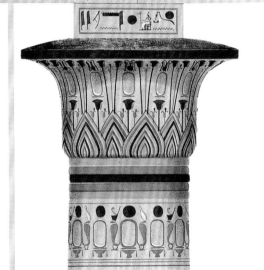

476
On the wall of the hypostyle hall, Ramesses II receives the crook and flail of royal authority from Amon-Re, as well as the khepesh-sword of strength, and the symbols of many jubilee festivals.

477 top right
View through the hypostyle hall of the Ramesseum, showing columns of two kinds: papyrus-bud capitals and open papyrus-flower capitals.

477 bottom
Lepsius's reconstruction of parts of the hypostyle hall with its color. The inset photograph of an open papyrus capital shows how rich the coloring is, but not as garish as Lepsius suggests.

478–479
Ramesses II in his chariot rushes headlong into the Amurru forces defending the city of Dapur in the Orontes Valley, part of the Syrian campain of Years 8/9, shown in the Ramesseum. The scenes include the assault on the city of Dapur, shown here on the right, with Egyptian troops using ladders to attack the fortifications.

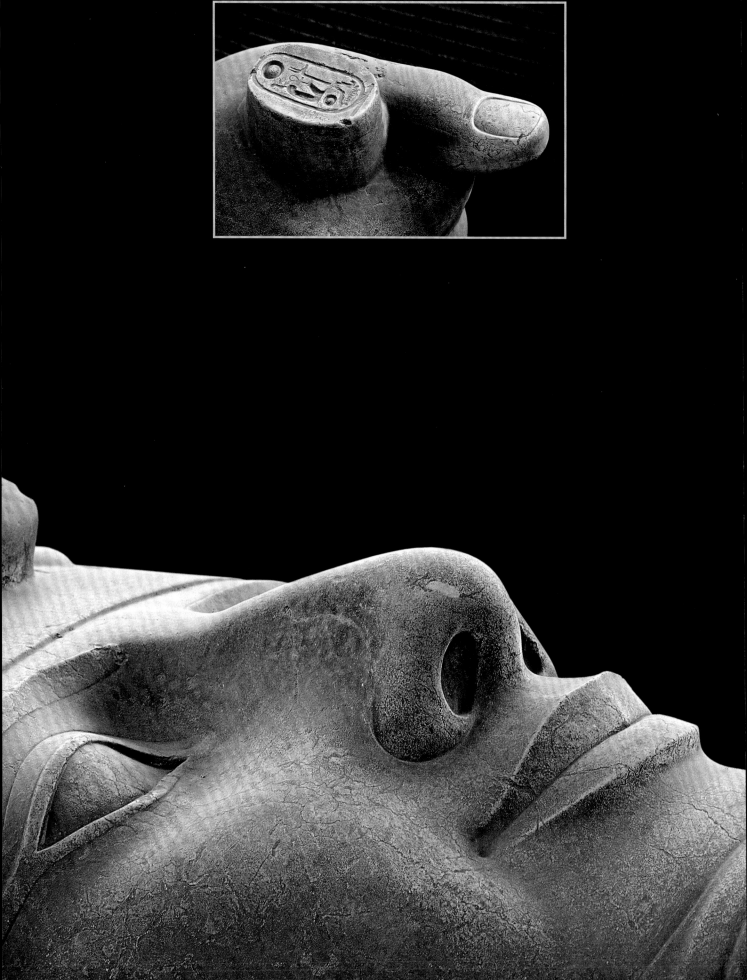

The Great City
of MEMPHIS

The survival, in varying degrees of reasonable condition, of the temples in Thebes in which Ramesses' hand may be seen to have worked gives a somewhat false idea of the importance of Thebes during his reign. The political center of gravity of Egypt in the Nineteenth Dynasty lay in the north of the land. Its great cities were Memphis and Heliopolis, both not far from modern Cairo; increasingly influential was Piramesse, the Delta Residence of Pharaoh. There were other cities in the northeast of the country, the importance of which remains to be fully discovered. Memphis had from the time of the unification of Egypt in the First Dynasty been politically very important; it was also the cult-center of Ptah, and possibly the principal home of members of the royal family, as we shall see. Ptah was throughout Egyptian history one of the most respected of Egyptian deities, a creator god, with an intellectual theology much favored by thoughtful people; his great temple in Memphis with its associated shrine of the living Apis bull, was very much honored and increased in Ramesses' reign. Sadly, little more than the city's plan, with much destroyed foundations, can now be seen in the palm trees of Mit Rahina, the modern town that occupies much of the ancient city area.

480 top
The left hand of the alabaster colossus from the Ptah temple in Memphis. The fist grasps the baton often found in one or both fists of stone sculptures; it carries the prenomen of Ramesses II.

480 bottom
The alabaster colossus of Ramesses II, still lying prone in Memphis, is considered one of the most striking of royal representations. The face, in its perfect preservation, offers a serene image of the great ruler.

481 top
Granite fist from a colossal statue of Ramesses II. It was found in the ruins of Memphis by the French during the Napoleonic expedition to Egypt; it was later surrendered to the British army at the Capitulation of Alexandria, 1801 (British Museum, EA 9).

481 bottom
This colossus is one of the many found in Memphis that can be ascribed to Ramesses II with certainty, and is not an usurpation. The carving is wonderfully sensitive and remains unusually crisp.

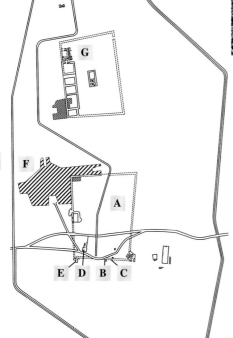

LEGEND

A ENCLOSURE OF PTAH TEMPLE
B ALABASTER COLOSSUS OF RAMESSES II
C ALABASTER SPHINX
D EMBALMING HOUSE OF APIS BULLS
E HATHOR TEMPLE OF RAMESSES II
F VILLAGE OF MIT RAHINA
G PALACE OF APRIES

482–483
The sculpture park established by the Memphis museum to exhibit sculptures and other stone monuments found in the Memphis area. The colossus shown here is another Middle Kingdom sculpture usurped for Ramesses II.

482 bottom
Aerial view of the Memphis sculpture park with the alabaster sphinx and (below, right), a granite colossus of Twelfth Dynasty date, reinscribed for Ramesses II.

483 top right
A four-faced limestone capital showing the goddess Hathor, represented as usual with cow ears. From her small Memphis chapel, in which she is described as "Eye of Re" and "Lady of the southern sycamore."

483 bottom right
Monumental alabaster sphinx from the Ptah temple, now in the Memphis sculpture park. This noble piece is not inscribed, or it has lost any text through erosion. It may be of Ramesses II, but could be earlier and usurped.

Fragments of many colossal sculptures of the king lie around the temple precinct, and two are well known, the prone alabaster masterpiece now housed in a special building on the site, and the other the forlorn giant which stands in Ramesses Square in Cairo. These statues give some idea of the magnificence of the temple and the city in its heyday. The traces of other smaller religious buildings built or modified in Ramesses' reign have been found in modern excavations, but much of the city remains to be explored and planned. It is otherwise known that Memphis was a flourishing center for trade, mostly river-borne, and much from distant lands; it was the Egyptian city above all that acted as a magnet for foreigners, and during the Ramesside Period there were many foreign

enclaves where strange gods were worshiped, and unusual languages spoken. Eulogistic texts speak of the prosperity and liveliness of Memphis, the availability of everything that one might need, and the generous provision of religious and other establishments.

482 left
Small granite colossus of Ramesses, now placed in the Memphis sculpture park. The king is shown with two divine standards, for Ptah (left) and Ptah-Thoth (right), both gods described as being "under his moringa-tree."

484 bottom right
Two sculptures of Ramesses II at
Tanis. The standing colossus was
originally made for a Twelfth Dynasty
king; the triple sculpture shows
Ramesses between Re-Herakhty and
the earth god Ptah-Tatenen.

485
Upper part of a royal statue in
Tanis, inscribed for Ramesses II, and
possibly made for him. The slight
bend in the arm suggests that the
complete piece was a seated figure
with hands on lap.

484 top
A view over part of the temple area
of Tanis, which became the
northern capital of Egypt in the
Twenty-first Dynasty, after the
abandonment of Piramesse.
In the foreground, a fallen colossus
of Ramesses II.

484 bottom left
Fragments of sculptures and obelisks
litter the temple area of Tanis. The
city was embellished with great
colossi, obelisks, and other sculptures,
many of Ramesses II, all brought
from Piramesse, with some originating
in Memphis and Heliopolis.

The Sites of
HELIOPOLIS, PIRAMESSE, TANIS AND QANTIR

Of Heliopolis even less can be said. Like Memphis it had enjoyed a priority in religious matters from the earliest historic times. It was the cult-center of the sun-god Re, the greatest of the gods, who by syncretism or union elevated other gods to primacy within the divine community; so Amun became universalized as Amon-Re. Sadly, the site of Heliopolis, now absorbed into greater Cairo, has never been fully investigated, and surviving remains can only hint at what Ramesses did to develop the great national shrine. Plundering of monuments from the site of the city in late antiquity has in a sense preserved parts of the greatness of Heliopolis. Obelisks in particular were taken as ready-made ornaments for other cities. A number of the obelisks in Rome were exported there by Augustus and other emperors; some had been installed originally in Heliopolis by Ramesses II; others of earlier date were 'improved' by texts added by the great king. The two obelisks set up in Alexandria by the Ptolemies, the so-called Cleopatra's Needles, were first placed in Heliopolis by the King Tuthmosis III of the Eighteenth Dynasty and later inscribed with additional texts by Ramesses II; one is now in London and the other in New York. The prime status of Heliopolis among Egyptian cities is indicated by the fact that its Egyptian name, Iunu, the On of the Old Testament, was often used for Thebes as the Upper Egyptian Iunu.

Heliopolis never lost its reputation or its appellation. Indeed, the Greek name by which it is most commonly known, meaning 'City of the Sun,' persists as the name of a smart district of Cairo through which pass travelers to Egypt coming from Cairo airport to the center of town. The site has never been forgotten, even if it has

never attracted sufficient archaeological attention. Ironically, its principal surviving monument is yet another obelisk, set up by King Sesostris I (c. 1950 B.C.) and still miraculously standing.

The fate of Piramesse has been even stranger than that of Heliopolis. This foundation of the Nineteenth Dynasty, and mentioned in the Old Testament, was well-known to have been the great Residence of Pharaoh in the Delta, especially from the time of Sethos I. It was brought into prominence by Ramesses II and given the name Per-Ramesse-Aa-nakhtu, 'the House of Ramesses, Great of Victories,' now usually abbreviated to Piramesse. It was for many reasons a place of new beginnings, lacking the hothouse religiosity of Thebes and the commercial bustle of Memphis. It was not just a place of retreat for the king, although it may have started as such, and retaining in texts of praise an image of restfulness, peace, and abundance. It was a city which with its suburbs spread out to cover a large area, with palaces, temples, residential districts, and business and industrial quarters; it was also a garrison city, where troops could be housed and trained in readiness for forays into Asia. It was very extensive, it was renowned in its time, and yet it

disappeared utterly from sight. Its rediscovery is one of the least-known successes of late-twentieth-century archaeology, but it will probably remain little known and rarely visited because what has been discovered lacks the visual impact of other well-known Egyptian sites.

Even now there may be a few scholars who believe that Piramesse should be identified with the huge remote mounds of Tanis in the northeast of the Delta. Tanis has the remains of a vast temple area, with fallen obelisks, statues, and other monuments bearing, among others, the names of Ramesses II. For nineteenth-century scholars, it seemed the obvious place for Ramesses' Delta Residence. We shall say more about the Ramesside monuments at Tanis later in this book, but for now let it be said that it is mostly accepted that when the branch of the Nile on which Piramesse was founded (the Pelusiac branch) began to silt up, rendering the city somewhat isolated and less effective as a place for trade and easy communications, the kings of the Twenty-first Dynasty moved the Delta capital to Tanis, transferring much of the stonework and monumental sculpture from the old to the new site. At the time this was an eminently practical step, for the Delta totally lacked building stone, and communications with the quarry districts in Upper Egypt were not simple for internal political reasons. The region that is now accepted as the site of Piramesse covers two places, Tell al-Dab'a and Qantir. The former is the ancient Hyksos capital of Avaris, the cult-center of the god Seth, and the homeland of the royal family of the Nineteenth Dynasty. In and around Qantir, a few miles from Tell al-Dab'a, excavations have revealed substantial traces of palace buildings and

487
Detail from the triple sculpture of Ramesses standing between Re-Herakhty and Ptah-Tatenen. The hand of Re-Herakhty holds Ramesses' hand in a reassuring manner as he leads the king forward along with his fellow god.

486 top left
On one of the Tanis obelisks, Ramesses II kneels and offers two bowls of wine to Atum, Lord of the Two Lands. Below is the top of the formal Horus name of the king. Probably from Heliopolis, originally.

486 bottom
Ramesses, wearing the blue crown stands making an offering of a shenes loaf to Atum, lord of Heliopolis. This scene occurs low on the shaft of an obelisk at Tanis, probably made for Heliopolis.

associated structures, stables, storerooms, and a parade yard. At both places the possibilities of significant discoveries exist in spite of the absence of surface indications and the generally wet conditions prevailing in the Delta. It will be many years before clear pictures may be obtained of the great imperial city Piramesse-Great-of-Victories. But much is already known about this city from inscriptions and from model letters and compositions of the kind we have met describing the tribute of Nubia. It was founded on the western bank of the branch of the Nile, which was locally called the Waters of Re, and a large part of its area was enclosed by a subsidiary branch or canal known as the Waters of Avaris: "His Majesty [Ramesses II] has built for himself a castle called Great-of-Victories... it is like Upper Egyptian Heliopolis [Thebes], and its extent is that of Memphis... . Everyone has abandoned his own town and come to live in its neighborhood." Four sacred sanctuaries were established there: in the west, the temple of Amun; in the south – that is in old Avaris – the temple of Seth; in the east, the temple of Astarte (a god of Syrian origin); and in the north, the temple of Wadjet (the cobra deity of Lower Egypt). A model letter written by Pabes to Amenemope, both described as scribes, presents a glorified impression of Piramesse. Pabes has just arrived in the city and found it in a wonderful state: "The surrounding countryside is full of every good thing... its pools have fishes... its meadows are flourishing... its granaries are full of barley and emmer wheat." Long lists of fruits and vegetables are given; there is "the smooth wine of Kaenkeme, sweeter than honey."

Ships come and go, unloading their cargoes; "joy resides in it... . The small [who live there] are like the great [elsewhere]." Every day was a holiday and everyone dressed accordingly. And there is much more to extol the place. It was without a doubt a city to admire, one planned and developed lovingly throughout Ramesses' long reign. Its spacious layout and grand buildings made it so much more agreeable than the ancient topsy-turvy cities of Memphis and Thebes. There is no reason to doubt that Piramesse was special, and well deserved the attention devoted to it by the king himself. Obelisks at Tanis came from here, and there may have been six or eight pairs of them set before the temples, along with many great statues. It is stated that Ramesses himself chose some of the stone to be carved into statues. An inscription of his Year 8 from the region of Heliopolis records that the king happened to be strolling about the quarry area of the Gebel Ahmar (Red Mountain) nearby. Here was a source of the tawny-brown quartzite rock much valued for sculptures in antiquity: "He discovered a great quartzite rock, such as had not been found since the time of Re, and longer even than a granite obelisk... . It was His Majesty who uncovered it... . It emerged complete in Year 4, third month of summer, day 18 – one year later." The text later records that "His Majesty found another quarry beside it, for statues... and he ordered pieces for the temple of Ptah." He declared, "I filled the temple of Re with many sphinxes, with statues of prostration, offering vases, and of kneeling, making offerings."

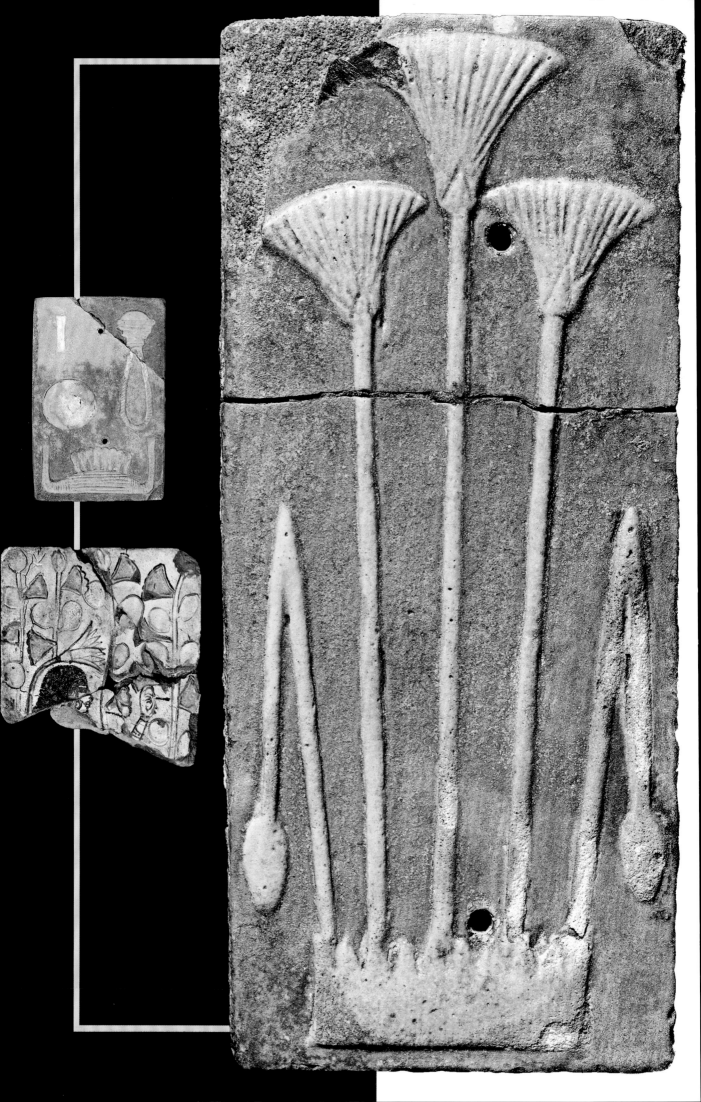

Of the palaces and public buildings in Piramesse, something of their splendor is to be found in the quantities of glazed tiles and architectural elements found at Qantir early in the twentieth century, long before regular excavations were started there. Parts of floors, dadoes, and daïses are brightly decorated in polychrome glaze with a huge variety of subjects – foreign captives, marsh and river scenes with fish and fowl, and moulded lion supports. The halls so decorated must have presented a brilliant appearance. No wonder that the king of the Hittites is said to have been overwhelmed by reports of it all; writing to a fellow Syrian prince he said: "Get ready so that we may hasten to Egypt and say, 'The will of God has happened,' and speak obsequiously to Usimare. He gives breath to whomever he wills, and every foreign land exists according to his wish. Hatti is in his sole power." As was mentioned earlier, there is no certainty that the Hittite king ever visited Piramesse, and it is doubtful if his amazement at the splendor of the Egyptian city would have induced him to surrender everything to Ramesses on the spot. It is, however, ironic that the one great monument of his reign, the magical city of Piramesse-Great-of-Victories, should have so crumbled to dust, its monuments dispersed and often usurped by others, its very site lost to view. It was the place that he, the great builder, had fostered and developed, where he had been at home for most of his long reign, and where he probably died.

488 top left
Rectangular wall tile made of glazed quartz frit, often called faience; dark blue for the background and light blue for the hieroglyphs, which read "gold, like Re." From Qantir (Louvre).

488 bottom left
Square tile of glazed quartz frit from a finely decorated building in Qantir. It is unusual in having a person included in the design; a woman with a lotus flower on her head tends plants in a garden (Cairo, JE 89483).

488 right
Rectangular wall tile of glazed quartz frit showing the holes for pegs to attach it to the wall. The motif is papyrus flowers and buds growing in a marsh, the sign for Lower Egypt (Louvre).

489 top and bottom
Parts of glazed quartz frit tiles from Qantir with aquatic scene with flowers, ducks, and fish (top; Cairo, JE 89480). The fish below is the bulti (Tilapia nilotica), now fished for food, especially in Lake Nasser (Cairo, JE 89479).

490–491
The second pillared hall of the temple
of Derr. The square pillars carry
scenes of Ramesses with various
deities: on the left in the foreground he
is embraced by Weret-hekau, on the
right by Menhit.

490 bottom
The rock-cut inner parts of the Derr
temple were preceded by a court with
two rows of built pillars and a third
row cut from the living rock and
bearing engaged figures of the king
as Osiris.

491
The east wall of the second pillared hall
at Derr. Ramesses makes presentations
to deities: here offering two bowls of
wine to Amon-Re in his fertility form of
Kamutef, "bull of his mother."

Ramesses II

Yet now in eternity, Ramesses can find a place where his monuments continue to astonish and perpetuate his name. In extra-territorial Nubia there is a whole series of temples commemorating him in divine as well as earthly splendor. It is not possible to determine whether the Nubian temple program was royally inspired or largely the result of the initiatives of successive viceroys of Kush, who exercised substantial independent authority south of the border at Aswan. There was probably no program as such. An impression is gained that in their construction these temples were designed particularly to enhance the glory of the king in

this distant land, and incidentally to boost the reputations of individual high officials. Who can now say what was the impulse for their establishment? Several of the temples are rock-cut or semi-rock-cut; the technical terms are *speos* and *hemi-speos*. They are not grandiose structures, which is not surprising considering the remoteness of their locations and the apparent absence of towns or large settlements in their vicinities. But they were temples for demonstration, not for public worship, and the conducting of temple services by small priestly staffs may have been only occasionally maintained, or minimally observed. Such in particular were the temples of Bayt al-

Wali, Garf Husayn, and Derr. The temples at Aksha, just north of the Sudanese boundary, and at Amara, to the south, were more certainly associated with towns, the latter in its day being a substantial and striking foundation. Most of the temples were founded early in Ramesses' reign, those at Garf Husayn and Wadi al-Sabua were much later when Setau was viceroy. As we learned earlier, the Wadi al-Sabua temple was built after Year 44, with the help of captured Libyans. More will be said later about the Nubian temples in the discussion of the image of Ramesses II, and of the activities of the viceroys of Kush.

492 top
The temple of Bayt al-Wali, partly rock-cut, removed and now rebuilt after the flooding following the building of the High Dam. The entrance to the forecourt has jambs with figures of Ramesses purifying the temple.

492–493 and 492 bottom
The vestibule at Bayt al-Wali showing the two multi-fluted pillars. To the right of the sanctuary door, a niche containing three images: Ramesses between two deities of the First Cataract region, Khnum and Anukis.

Ramesses II

493 top left
In the open forecourt of Bayt al-Wali, the side walls show scenes of campaigns in Nubia and Syria. Here Ramesses grasps the hair of two kneeling Syrian captives and tramples on another. He holds an axe.

493 top right
Ramesses with his khepesh-sword is about to deliver the coup de grâce to a Nubian kneeling before him. The text on the right mentions the king's oldest son Amonhiwonemef, probably not more than seven at the time.

493 bottom
The Amada temple in Nubia, built by kings of the Eighteenth Dynasty. Ramesses had no hand in its construction or decoration; but it may have inspired him or his high officials to build temples in Nubia.

The Temple of WADI AL-SABUA

The temple at Wadi al-Sabua, although a hemi-speos, was a striking structure with an avenue of sphinxes (human- and falcon-headed), pylons, and colossal sculptures. It cannot, however, be compared with the greatest of all the Ramesside Nubian temples, that at Abu Simbel, itself a speos, or, as some early Egyptologists inadequately called it, a 'grotto.' No longer can Abu Simbel be seen as it was planned; it has been raised from its original location, set back from the Nile, to a position above the waters of Lake Nasser, and approached now across a rocky forecourt, instead of, as formerly, the sloping flood plain. In moving the temple, the engineers and scholars in charge took great care to ensure that its orientation was kept precisely as it was originally, because it is believed by many scholars (and by some more vigorously than others) that the orientation was most carefully arranged in the planning of the temple.

There are natural phenomena concerning the sun and possibly other celestial bodies, which seem to be explicable only in terms which, if true, would credit the Egyptians with extraordinary care in the advanced planning and the precise engineering of the temple's inner chambers. It may be said on the cautionary side that personal observation does not confirm that the appearance of the sun at dawn on the temple façade, and in its penetration of the interior of the temple, is precisely what it was before the temple was moved. In the simplest sense, the angle with which the sun, rising above the hills on the eastern horizon across the lake, strikes the façade, is less acute than it was formerly. Nevertheless, the best care was taken in the resiting of the temple, and nothing should detract from the immensity of that operation, and the remarkable success with which it was accomplished.

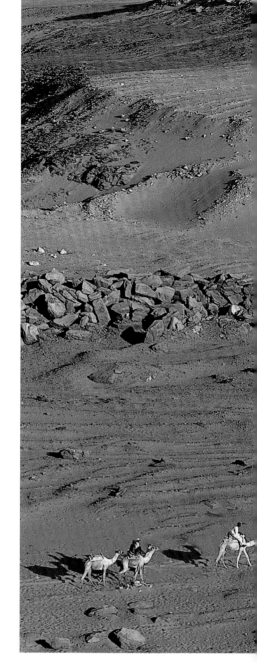

494 top
The inner court of the temple of Wadi al-Sabua. The colonnades on the north and south sides have pillars with engaged Osiris figures. The inner parts of the temple beyond were cut into the rock.

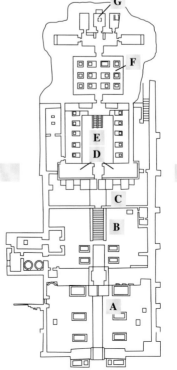

LEGEND

A   FIRST FORECOURT WITH
    LION SPHINXES
B   SECOND FORECOURT WITH
    FALCON SPHINXES
C   TERRACE WITH COLOSSUS
    OF RAMESSES II
D   STONE PYLON
E   COURT
F   PILLARED HALL WITHIN
    THE ROCK
G   SANCTUARY

494–495
Aerial view of the Wadi al-Sabua temple. The camel herd in the foreground has come from the far south of Sudan, following the routes used for southern trade since antiquity.

495 bottom
One of the six sphinxes forming the avenue in the first forecourt of Wadi al-Sabua. The royal head wears the nemes *and double crown. The provincial carving may be rather crude, but the effect is powerful.*

The Great Temple of ABU SIMBEL

Among the Nubian temples, Abu Simbel stands out as exceptional and clearly to be included among the great works of Ramesses II. Strictly speaking, it is not a building, but an excavation and monumental sculptural ensemble. From its inception early in the reign, it was a project of truly royal proportions, supervised at all stages by senior officials in the viceroy's service, but at all times pursued with the knowledge that the king himself might decide to visit the site to check on progress, and, no doubt, interfere. As is so often the case, we have no knowledge of the temple's designer; it seems likely that its unusual form, dominated outside by the four immense seated figures of the king carved from the living rock, was one approved by the king himself. In its planning, the secondary temple at Abu Simbel was probably included at the same time; here the dedication is to Hathor and Queen Nefertari, but the king is rarely out of the picture. This Nefertari temple will be considered later under the discussion of the queen herself.

The great temple at Abu Simbel, however, was to be the focus of all the religious establishment in Nubia, and the central place for royal memorials. It was, in effect, the provincial cathedral of Nubia, although it would be wrong to consider it as being liturgically so. Its primacy depended on its size, its magnificence, and its being of personal interest to the king. Its excavation from the sandstone cliff, its decoration with relief carvings, and the making of its great sculptures took a very long time due substantially, no doubt, to the difficulty of maintaining a skilled workforce in such a remote place. The work was started early in the reign – no dates have been preserved – while Iuny was the Nubian viceroy. A revealing inscription carved near the Nefertari temple and set up by an official with the resounding name Ramesse-ashahebsed ('Ramesses-rich-in-jubilees') suggests that the king had appointed one of his intimate circle to look after the work, at least in its early stages. This official, whose name may more correctly be Ramesse-ashahebu ('Ramesses-rich-in-festivals'), was chief cupbearer of the king, an honorary title no doubt, but one that does not proclaim great power. As plain Ashahebsed (or even Ashahebu), he may be the same as a court official who visited Sinai in the reign of Sethos I. With Ramesses added to his name, he seems to have advanced in the private service of the king, not just as cupbearer, or butler, but majordomo. In the Abu Simbel inscription he states that His Majesty "brought many laborers, captives of his strong arm from all foreign lands" and that he himself was "empowered to re-establish the land of Kush in the great name of His Majesty." This elevated palace official seems to have had a roving commission in Nubia, but especially to watch over progress at Abu Simbel.

496
The grandeur of Ramesses II exemplified by the head of the northern colossus at Abu Simbel. The cuts made when the temple was moved to its position above Lake Nasser are clearly visible.

497 top
The cartouches of Ramesses II from the base of one of the colossi; the prenomen faces left and the nomen, right. The former is partly written as a rebus, with a figure of Ma'at holding the user staff.

498–499
Aerial view of the two temples of
Abu Simbel, each in its artificial
modern mountain, which were built
after the temples were raised to
their new positions above the waters
of Lake Nasser in the 1960s.

498 bottom
A view across the façade of the great
temple of Abu Simbel, looking
toward the south over Lake Nasser
to the rocky hills to the southeast.
The king seems withdrawn, very
contrary to his usual disposition.

Ramesses II

499 right
*Three statues standing on the
terrace in front of the colossal
figures of Ramesses II: in the middle
is Osiris, flanked by two Horus
falcons, the divine manifestations
of the king in death and life.*

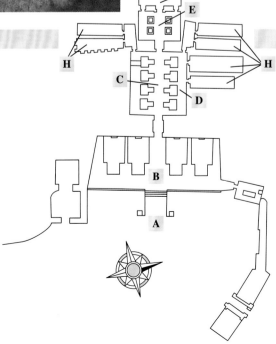

LEGEND

A FORECOURT
B TERRACE WITH COLOSSAL FIGURES
C GREAT HALL
D QADESH SCENES
E SECOND PILLARED HALL
F VESTIBULE
G SANCTUARY WITH FIGURES
    OF THE TEMPLE DEITIES
H STOREROOMS

The Great Builder

It has often been pointed out that the façade of the temple with the great statues (65 feet/20 meters high) represents what would be the entrance pylon of a standard Egyptian temple of the period. In this respect it may be compared with the Luxor temple, where the pylon built by Ramesses II is fronted by six colossal statues and two great obelisks. Behind this 'pylon' the Abu Simbel temple retains many of the characteristics of the standard Egyptian temple, with two pillared halls, a vestibule, and a sanctuary, all along the main axis, with side rooms for the storage of temple equipment, offerings, and possibly for the performance of some ritual activities. The depth of the temple from front to back is 160 feet (49 meters). The cutting of the chambers and the columns with engaged statues in the first hall shows extraordinary skill, if not

500 left
Three of the inscriptions on the rock faces near the two Abu Simbel temples. These three are to the south of the great temple; the two larger ones have scenes of the king smiting captives before Amun.

500–501
The façade of the Abu Simbel temple flooded with the light of the morning sun. The upper part of the second colossus was tumbled down by an earthquake not long after the temple was finished.

Ramesses II

total mastery of the task; some of the work is crude according to the highest Egyptian standards. Nevertheless, in its completeness, it is staggeringly impressive. The initial work of cutting out the interior of the temple was completed perhaps by Year 10. This stage would have included the carving of the reliefs on the walls: scenes of the battle of Qadesh on the north wall of the first pillared hall, with other warlike scenes, mostly unspecified, on the south and east walls; elsewhere, ritual scenes which include Ramesses among the principal deities worshiped in the temple.

In the sanctuary were statues of these deities, carved out of the living rock, Re-Herakhty, Ramesses, Amon-Re, and Ptah. On two days every year (approximately 20 February and 20 October) the sun at dawn floods directly into the temple, illuminating these statues.

502

The upper part of one of the colossal figures carved against the pillars on the south side of the great hall. Such engaged figures are usually of the king as Osiris, but here he is the living king.

It is hard to deny that the temple's designers planned this phenomenon, but it is also very difficult to believe that the Egyptian surveyors were capable of such precision. The coincidence is hard to ignore, but the intention is equally hard to accept.

Once the internal work was completed, the temple was functional, although its official inauguration would have to wait until about Year 24, when the king himself, with Queen Nefertari and a great entourage, traveled south into Nubia. By then the great façade, with its colossal figures, was completed or close to completion. It was a triumph for Ramesses as king and god; and for Nefertari, her adjacent temple, probably not seen by her previously, would be a last tribute from her devoted husband; for she was to die shortly afterward. Romantics have suggested that the visit was made in February 1255 B.C. in Year 24, so as to coincide with the spring illumination of the cult statues in the sanctuary of the great temple. No conveniently dated inscription, unfortunately, supports this precise timing.

Modern visitors to Abu Simbel, viewing the façade, often wonder why when the temple was moved to its new location, the collapsed colossus to the left of the entrance was not restored. It could have been done; but it was decided to leave the fragments in the positions in which they had lain since soon after the inauguration of the temple. In about Year 31 an earthquake struck the region, causing catastrophic damage to this colossus (there was almost certainly a fault or flaw in the rock), and also serious but repairable damage to columns in the temple. No attempt was made in antiquity by the Nubian officials in charge of works to restore the great figure, as far as can now be judged. Was Ramesses himself ever informed? Who can tell? There is, however, some satisfaction to be gained from the retention of the evidence of an ancient natural disaster. Some might interpret it as divine comment on the pretensions of the king in proclaiming his divine status.

503

The great hall, first entered by Belzoni in 1817. The four pillars on either side support figures of the king wearing the white crown (on the left) and the double crown (on the right).

504 top
Scene on one of the pillars in the great hall. Ramesses offers cloths and a libation to ram-headed Khnum, who in turn bestows on the king hundreds of thousands of years.

504–505
The painted decoration on the ceiling of the great hall: the king's short titulary alternates with a representation of the vulture goddess Nekhbet, who wears the atef crown and holds ostrich feather fans.

505
View through the pillars in the great hall across the center aisle to a royal figure on the south side, wearing the white crown. Scenes of the king making offerings to various deities can be seen on the pillars.

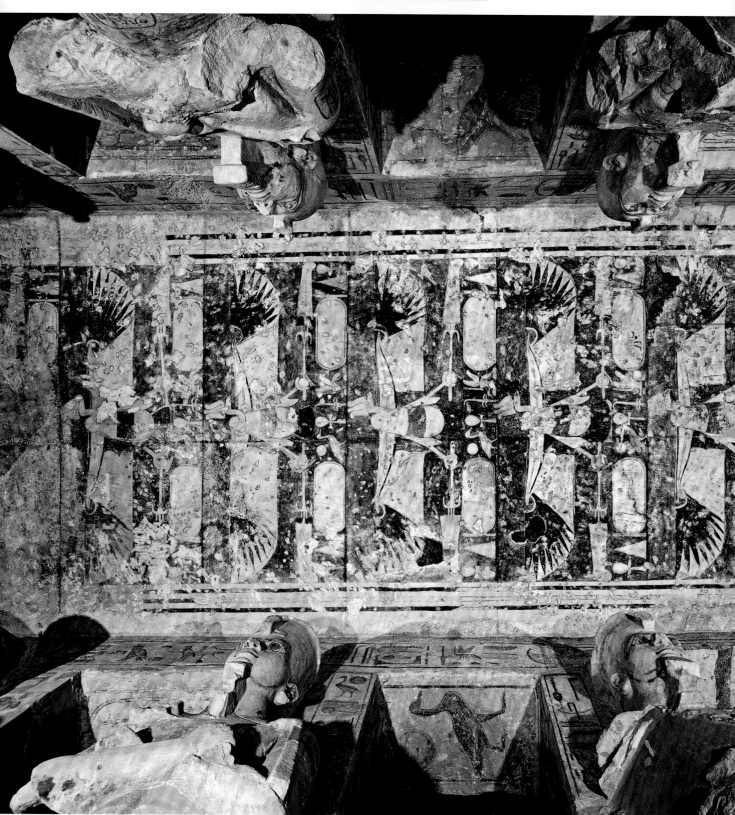

The Great Builder

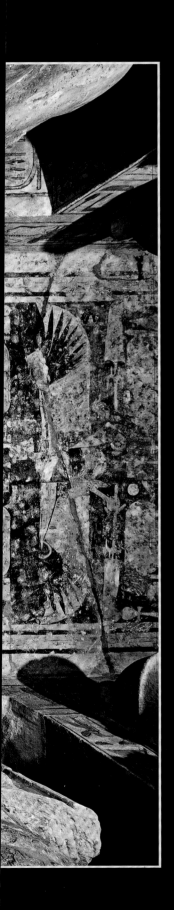

506 top
Heads of Ramesses deified and of
lion-headed Ius'as in the great court.
A change has been made here: the
figure of Ramesses has been inserted
over an earlier figure, parts of which
can still be seen.

506 bottom
Part of a scene in the great hall:
Ramesses makes a presentation of
Nubian captives to Amon-Re,
Ramesses himself deified, wearing
ram's horns, and to Mut. The gods
are seated in a kiosk.

507
Ramesses smites Syrian captives in the
presence of Re-Herakhty. Below are
princesses, starting with Bintanta on
right (not shown), then Bekmut,
Nefertari, Merytamun, Nebttawy,
Isitnofret, Henttawy, Werenro, and
Medjemmut, not entirely in order of birth.

508
*Detail from the scene in which
Ramesses II is spearing a Libyan
while trampling on another. The royal
features, while not carved in the best
Theban manner, are delineated
strongly, and are easily recognizable.*

509
*The head of Ramesses II from a
scene of presentation by him to
gods on the pillars in the great hall.
A change has been made in the
carving of the* uraeus *on his blue
crown.*

510 left
Scene on the second pillar on the left in the second pillared hall. The goddess Mut, wearing the double crown, embraces Ramesses, placing her hand behind his head in a protective gesture.

510–511
The second pillared hall of Abu Simbel. The roof is supported by four square pillars cut from the rock. The decoration shows ritual scenes and none of the warlike activities shown in the great hall.

511 top
View from the second pillared hall looking away from the sanctuary and into the great hall. In the scenes visible on the pillars, the king can be seen being embraced by various deities.

511 bottom
Scene in the second pillared hall in which Ramesses offers bouquets to Amon-Re "Lord of the Thrones of the Two Lands," and to his divine consort Mut. The king exercises his important religious function.

512–513
Ramesses offers incense and his scepter
of power while Queen Nefertari shakes
sistra before the sacred bark carrying
the image of Amon-Re. Large numbers
of priests and attendants bear the weight
of the bark.

512 bottom
The head of Queen Nefertari, from the
scene in the second pillared hall, shown
opposite. She shakes her sistra, ritual
musical instruments, and wears an
elaborate headdress, including a horned
moon-disk and tall feathers.

513 top
Four of the priestly attendants bearing
the sacred bark of Amon-Re, shown
opposite, with no apparent strain under
its great weight. They all wear the
turned-up beards usually associated with
divinity.

513 bottom
On the north wall of the second pillared
hall, Ramesses and Queen Nefertari offer
incense and shake sistra before the bark
carrying the image of the deified
Ramesses. The priests carrying the bark
have no beards.

Ramesses II

514 top
North wall of the sanctuary in Abu Simbel: right, Ramesses censes and libates before the bark of the deified Ramesses in its sanctuary; left, he stands bare-headed before his deified self.

514 bottom
South wall of the sanctuary: left, Ramesses offers incense and a libation to the bark of Amon-Re in its sanctuary; right, be annoints Amon-Re in the form of Kamutef.

514–515
The sanctuary in Abu Simbel. The three national deities, Ptah, Amon-Re, and Re-Herakhty, are joined by the deified Ramesses, wearing the blue crown, all seated and waiting to be illuminated by the sun, twice each year.

THE GREAT
IMAGE-MAKER

516
The head of one of the statues of Ramesses II attached to the pillars of the great hall in Abu Simbel.

517
Ramesses as a child (mes) squats before the Syrian god Hauron, shown as Horus. Ramesses grasps the sedge plant of Upper Egypt (su). The group forms a rebus of his name: Ra (the sun), the child, and the sedge. From Tanis (Cairo, JE 64735).

1. *The Horus:* Strong bull, beloved of Ma'at (truth, order)

2. The Two Ladies [Nekhbet and Wadjet]: Protector of Egypt, who subdues the foreign countries

3. Horus of Gold: Rich in years, great in victories

4. King of Upper and Lower Egypt: Usimare-Setpenre

5. Son of Re: Ramessu-Miamun

This resounding declaration of names was used by Ramesses II in formal inscriptions from Year 2 of his reign, long before he could with some justification call himself "Protector of Egypt, who subdues the foreign countries," or demonstrate that he was "rich in years and great in victories." There was nothing exceptional in a royal titulary of such length, and so full of arrogant claims. From the time of the Old Kingdom, Egyptian kings had used five names or appellations in their full, grandiose titulary; the name 'headings' are given in italics above, and they proclaim many of the divine

associations of the Egyptian king – any Egyptian king, not just Ramesses II. For ordinary purposes, the two names which are most commonly found on monuments are 4 and 5; the first of these, known as the prenomen, is often called the throne-name, the formal, official, name taken by the king on his accession, and by which he would have been most commonly known; in the present case it was Usimare-Setpenre, or just Usimare – the Ozymandias of Shelley. As we have already seen, name 5, known as the nomen, contained the king's name from before his accession, Ramessu, with the added epithet Miamun, 'beloved of Amun,' our Ramesses.

How divine, then, was an Egyptian king? Many scholars have considered this question, and it must be said that no solution covers all the facts that are known about Egyptian sovereignty and the ways in which the king was regarded, by himself, by his court and high officials, and by the people of Egypt in general. It has already become clear in the course of this book so far, that Ramesses II seemed

to achieve a very special position *vis-à-vis* the gods of Egypt, but it is still difficult to determine the extent to which this position was recognized as being special by Egyptians, or even by Ramesses himself.

Was it a matter of being just an outstanding case of ancient propaganda, or a true reflection of what was thought to be the case during his long lifetime? What was so special about the image of Ramesses during his reign? What changes in ordinary royal behavior or practices led to the fashioning of the royal image in divine form? Was it universal throughout the whole realm, or was it limited to certain parts of Egypt and modified for different circumstances? None of the answers which will be offered will be adequate to everyone's satisfaction, largely because of the impossibility of penetrating the true thoughts and beliefs of the Egyptians, and of the uncertainty attached to the meanings of statements in texts. How does one sieve truth from hyperbole? The attempt must be made.

All kings, from the time of the earliest dynasties, were thought of as being the embodiment of Horus, the god, and therefore as having divinity as part of their being. Horus was the living king; and in due course Osiris, the dead king, and according to one strand of Egyptian divine mythology, the father of Horus, was the god with whom the king would be identified in death. But more importantly, the ruling king was described as the son of Re (title 5), and during his lifetime this relationship with the great sun god of Heliopolis was the most important of his divine connections. So the Egyptian king was heavily invested with associated, if not actual, divinity. He was Horus, he was the son of Re; these were the formal elements of royalty, which legitimized his reign, but did not seemingly make him a god in the strictest sense. The ruling king was also called the 'good god'; but again there is much doubt about the meaning of 'good' in this appellation. It was used with the prenomen often in short citations, as on a scarab, when a full titulary would have been too long. It was almost a formality, like 'your majesty'; it probably ought not to be pressed for greater significance.

The ruling king, therefore, could be seen as being divine without quite being a god, someone above all other Egyptians who could mix on fairly familiar terms with the pantheon, who had inherited duties to fulfill in his relationship with the gods, who received from the gods everything that made him a king, and who would be protected by the gods in whatever he did for as long as he reigned. And long might he reign! Such would all kings expect, and in this and in other respects Ramesses II was at the beginning of his reign no different from his predecessors. However, he undoubtedly had very high expectations, some of which were in due course amply fulfilled. At his formal accession ceremonies, which traditionally should have been celebrated in Memphis, he was invested formally and magically with the powers that would render him godlike and imbued with the authority of his

unique position. It is not certain that Ramesses' coronation actually took place in Memphis; perhaps the Delta Residence of Piramesse was chosen; it was undoubtedly the favored place for royal ceremonies later in the reign; but it seems unlikely that at the very start of his independent rule he should formally reject the traditional Memphis, which in itself surely provided some of the mystical confirmation of the royal status of the new monarch.

In the course of the coronation ceremonies the prospective king had notionally, if not actually, to perform testing activities, which would confirm his powers and put the seal on his capabilities, for example, to run a solo race between fixed markers; he would also meet and be introduced to the gods of all the nomes, or provinces, of Egypt. He was physically crowned with the white and red crowns of Upper and Lower Egypt; he was ritually washed with the water of life, in theory by the gods Horus and Thoth, whose jugs in relief representations of the rite are shown to pour forth the precious liquid in the form of chains of *ankh*-signs, of life. He was then or in subsequent ceremonies, shown frequently on temple walls, offered long life, represented by a palm stem with an infinite number of notches cut into it to show the hundreds of thousands of years he might expect. And from this palm stem were shown suspended the signs of the *sed* festival, the *heb-sed* or jubilee, the festival, which mirrored the coronation and revivified the king for the next stage of his reign. You may remember that in the great dedication text in the temple of Osiris in Abydos, which was completed by Ramesses for his father Sethos I, the dead Sethos is reported as saying that he had personally suggested to the sun god Re that he should double the length of Ramesses' life, and that in consequence Re had generously granted the young king eternity and everlastingness and millions of jubilees. And so it was to be: perhaps not quite millions of jubilees, but certainly a very long life, and rather more jubilees than any other Egyptian king had celebrated.

518 top
Scene in Karnak: Ramesses II pouring out a libation of water to Haroeris, a form of Horus, lord of Sekhem (Letopolis, in the Delta), shown here as human, but in the text as a mummified falcon.

518–519
In the Hypostyle Hall at Karnak, Ramesses II kneels in front of the persea tree, receiving multiple jubilee festivals from Amon-Re, who is supported (but not shown here) by Mut and Khonsu.

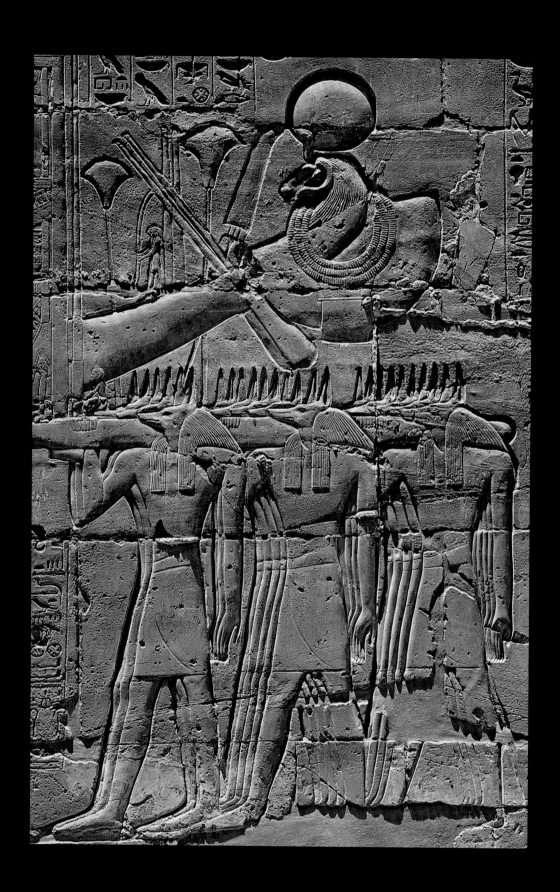

Ramesses II

responsible for Upper Egyptian celebrations, widely organized so that as many people as possible would be aware of their monarch's achievement of thirty years of rule. And yet it would seem that some people of quite modest standing took the trouble to travel north, to Memphis or to Piramesse, or to both cities, to join in the special festivities. A text on another ostracon from Thebes preserves a fragment of a letter, possibly a model, a scribal exercise, concerning a transaction involving a pair of sandals and a soldier; the meaning is rather obscure, but the writer does speak of the soldier's having gone north in the night, and comments, "For what reason should he be traveling north to the *sed* festival?" It would not have been surprising if crowds of ordinary Egyptians had flocked north for the interest and especially the fun. Great festivals have always attracted crowds, and there is much Egyptian evidence to suggest that the attendant festivities formed the attraction far more than the formal ceremonies.

Subsequent *sed* festivals, coming at three-year intervals and designed to refresh the supposedly ailing powers of the king, served to remind the Egyptians of the continuing virility of their monarch and kept the royal image in people's minds. The second *sed* of Year 33 is noted in a record of Khaemwese's proclamation carved within the same Speos of Horemheb at Gebel al-Silsila; it is also noted in a rough rock-text on the island of Suhayl south of Elephantine, almost on the Nubian border. The first three *seds* are

recorded at Biga, opposite the island of Philae, also south of Elephantine and mythologically thought of as the source of the Nile's inundation – Hapy again. Silsila preserves records of the fourth, fifth, and sixth festivals; of these the fifth seems to have been the last proclaimed by Khaemwese; thereafter the formal announcements were delegated to the vizier Khay, his successor Neferronpe, and other senior officials. Records of the eighth, ninth, tenth, and eleventh *seds* and of two others are all found on the remains of the pylon of Tuthmosis III at Armant, an ancient town a few miles to the south of Thebes and a cult-center of the god Monthu.

It is strange that all these recordings occur to the south of Thebes, but probably no special significance should be attached to this observation; it is yet a further indication of the paucity of substantial remains of buildings erected in the north during Ramesses' reign in which records might have been placed. The last of the *seds*, the thirteenth or fourteenth, was proclaimed and probably celebrated in Year 65 or 66; the record at Armant is damaged and uncertain. The magic of renewal was by now exhausted, but still the procedures had to be followed. The long series of jubilees had seemingly maintained the aging king long after his expected time; his health may have gone, but his image was well established in his people's minds. The celebration of *seds* was a kind of confirmatory process, starting from Year 30. Already by that time

Ramesses had, through his officials and agents, done much to exalt his reputation. How was a royal reputation established and maintained? Was a campaign of image-building organized from the royal residence, or separately in provincial capitals by local officials? In attempting to answer questions of this kind, one is greatly hampered by the narrow range of testimony offered by surviving records. From an examination of royal inscriptions, it does seem to appear that a principal method of proclaiming the greatness of the king was the relentless statement and restatement of his fame and glory. The extent to which this repetitive litany of greatness was heard and comprehended by the ordinary Egyptian might be questioned; the bulk of the Egyptian population was illiterate at this time, and it is unlikely that there was a general understanding of domestic and foreign politics, except in so far as lives were affected by conscription for the army and for public service, and by taxes. It would have been known, however, when the king himself might make a visitation, and crowds would have gathered for royal festivities to take advantage of anything that might be handed out as practical favors. Proclamations were made, as for the jubilees, and such information provided to apprise the populace of what was about to happen, and to praise the greatness of the king. In the case of Ramesses II, there was ample opportunity in the course of his long reign to develop and polish his image.

522

Part of a scene at Karnak in which Ramesses presents incense to the sacred bark of Amon-Re. Here are priests in the guise of the "souls of Nekhen" (the ancient southern capital), who are jackal-headed.

523 top

Lepsius's drawing of the scene in the sanctuary of the Wadi al-Sabua temple in which Ramesses offers bouquets before the sacred bark that bears the shrine with his own divine image.

In the early years, when so much temple-building took place, and in the aftermath of foreign expeditions, above all the Qadesh campaign, the visual statements carved on the pylons of temples like Luxor and the Ramesseum make clear, according to the official version of events, what wonderful deeds Ramesses had performed in the service of the great national gods and of Egypt. The huge relief scenes on the outer faces of pylons and the exterior walls of some temples, with their fresh, bright colors, could be seen and admired and talked about by anyone who passed by. Those triumphant reliefs, which decorated the inner surfaces of pylons and the inner walls of the great courts were visible only to the restricted numbers of people who were allowed access to the more public areas of temples, leading to the more private and sacred halls and chambers, where the decoration was religious and ritual in character. In all these positive illustrations of warlike activities, Ramesses was portrayed as the mighty warrior who, with the help of particular deities, protected Egypt from external attack and carried the fight into enemy territory. Some of the representations were specific, others general. This martial and protective image of the king was additionally proclaimed on a large number or free-standing stelae set up in various places throughout Egypt and particularly in Piramesse.

Some of the monuments stood almost four meters tall; at the top are small scenes of triumph and of offering to deities, below which are long texts often on both faces and the sides; in some cases the texts are so inscribed that the repeated cartouches of the king are shown in a zigzag pattern down the successive horizontal lines of the texts. They are often called rhetorical stelae because they proclaim the greatness of the king in unspecific ways, anchored only vaguely to possible events and serving principally to promote the royal reputation. To put it bluntly,

these texts do nothing except reveal the extraordinary lengths to which Ramesses, through his officials, felt he had to go to inform the Egyptian people of his achievements. And as expressed on these stelae, these achievements are fanciful and almost meaningless. A few sentences will give the flavor of the whole corpus of rhetoric:

"Victorious king, brave in battle, the powerful one who combats hundreds of thousands... like Seth at his time of fury... Nobody can oppose him in fight; all foreign lands flee before him; his face is like fire in following them... a young man, brave like Monthu, savior of the land, a husband to Egypt... who killed the inhabitants of vile Kush by the victories of his strong arm... who has destroyed the princes of Asia in their own countries and devastated the heritage of the land of Shasu... . He has seized the country of the West, turning its people into soldiers to serve him... whose power has crossed the sea, so that the islands-of-the-middle [Crete and the Greek islands?] are afraid of him... ."

And so on and so on. These extracts come from the best preserved of a large number of such rhetorical stelae found at Tanis but brought there from Piramesse in antiquity, as many as ten of them in all, most of which survive in fragments and only partially.

It seems incomprehensible that so many massive inscriptions dealing precisely with the fame and so-called achievements of a king who had been dead for about 150 years should have been transferred to a new city where their texts would have little direct relevance. In their time, set up presumably in public places in Piramesse, they acted as publicity posters for the great king and were left in position for the rest of the Nineteenth and the whole of the Twentieth Dynasties, largely because of the abiding reputation of Ramesses II; nine kings of the latter dynasty bore the name Ramesses as their nomen.

524–525
The great king in battle draws his bow to scatter his enemies with his arrows. Note the delicacy of his fingers as they draw the bow-string. The bow has been recarved. From Abu Simbel.

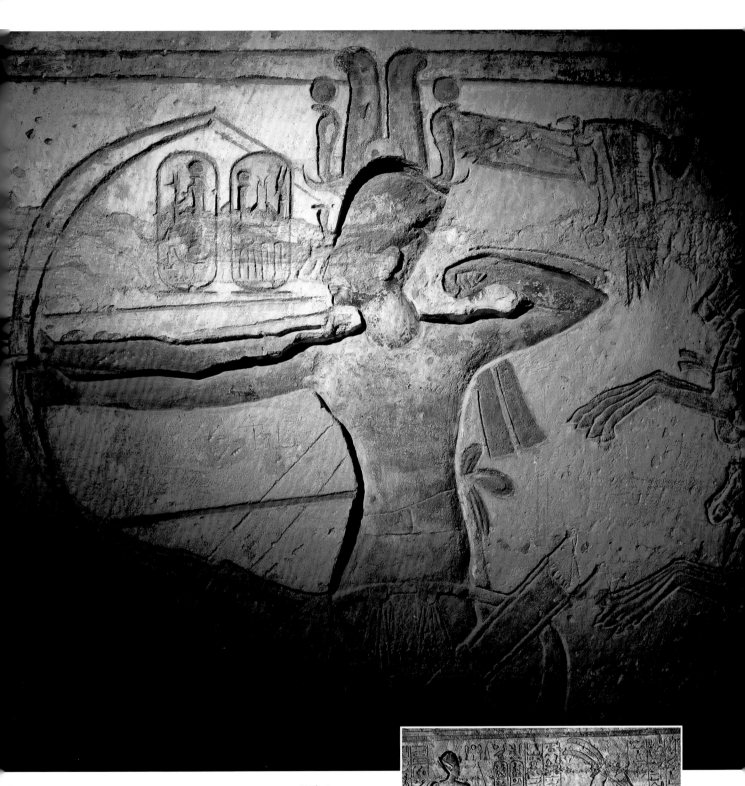

525 bottom
Ramesses displays his royal
presence, riding his chariot into
battle. The scene exalts the king in
all its details, including the figure of
his pet lion, the royal beast,
running along in expectation of
conflict. From Abu Simbel.

The Great Image-Maker

At Tanis, however, the magic of that ancest or ruler could scarcely have been so effective. Yet the greatest and most visible monuments of Piramesse, almost without exception made for and inscribed with the names of Usimare-Setpenre Ramessu-Miamun, formed the bulk of the embellishments of the great temple at Tanis. Their transference to a site more remote than that of Piramesse, and, as it happened, less affected by modern agricultural development, led to the survival of much of this monumental material. From what has been found at Tanis some ideas can be formed of how Piramesse was adorned, and how the image of the king, the long-lived Ramesses, was kept before people's sight and mind.

More striking than the rhetorical stelae were the obelisks, which were set up before the various temples in Piramesse, later to embellish the great temple at Tanis. Well over twenty obelisks, or parts of obelisks, have been identified in Tanis, all tumbled to the ground, and perhaps not all actually erected as standing monuments in that place. All bear inscriptions which contain the names, titles, and laudatory epithets of Ramesses II, and it is very evident from close inspection that not all were made during his reign, but usurped for him by the replacement of earlier royal texts, or by the addition of new texts. Attempts have been made to assign these obelisks in pairs to particular temples in Piramesse, but the evidence is as yet insufficient to identify sites on the ground, and then to distribute the obelisks with confidence to their original places. What is clear, however, is that Ramesses' temple architects enhanced the grandeur of the Piramesse temples by the placing of many soaring granite obelisks, which very definitely made visual statements about the king. One must assume that the

usurpation of earlier obelisks was due to the difficulty of obtaining suitable lengths of unblemished granite from the quarries at Aswan. It is probable therefore that some completed obelisks belonging to earlier kings were shipped downstream from places like Memphis and Heliopolis. Such recycling of old monuments must be viewed as being inspired by necessity, and not by animosity toward a particular predecessor. In places other than Piramesse, obelisks already standing might be annexed for Ramesses II by the addition of texts, without the removal of the original inscriptions. This was the case with the two obelisks known as Cleopatra's Needles. They were first made for King Tuthmosis III of the Eighteenth Dynasty (c. 1479–1425 B.C.) for the temple of Re at Heliopolis. The original inscriptions containing the names and laudatory epithets of Tuthmosis were left untouched, occupying the central column on each of the four sides, the texts running from top to bottom. While they were still in Heliopolis, additional vertical lines of text were added on each side of the Tuthmoside lines; these new texts contained the names of Ramesses II and suitable epithets, for example, "a Re whom the gods made, equipping the Two Lands," "who sets boundaries wherever he wishes," "Lord of *sed* festivals – like his father Ptah-Tatenen," "who overcomes the peoples of the South, and lays waste [?] the land of the peoples of the North," and "who despoils Retjenu and the peoples of the desert." This pair of obelisks was subsequently moved to Alexandria in Ptolemaic times, as we have previously noted. But for many centuries they remained standing in Heliopolis, offering testimony of the greatness of Ramesses and of his worthy predecessor, Tuthmosis III.

526
The façade of the Luxor temple makes the greatest statement of Ramesses' might that was visible to the populace of Thebes. Two seated and four standing colossi of the king, and two great obelisks proclaimed his majesty.

527
One of the better preserved obelisks from Piramesse, now in Tanis. The main text proclaims "all lands make obeisance through fear of him." In the scene below, the king offers a shenes loaf to Atum.

The populace could focus attention on notable monuments like obelisks, whether in Piramesse or in other great cities. Similarly, the colossal statues, which were placed before temple pylons and in the open courts behind the pylons, were even more powerful demonstrations of the ruler's might, and, more specifically, presentations of the actual image of the king himself. The demand for statues of the king to enrich the appearance of the great buildings constructed in his reign undoubtedly placed a great strain on the capabilities of the royal workshops to turn out enough pieces to satisfy the demand. Yet these statues, carved in the likeness of the king, served as the best vehicles for making his image known to the people, who otherwise might never catch a glimpse of the royal person. From certain well-attested, small-scale statues, like that in the Turin Museum, discussed earlier, it can be concluded that Ramesses was endowed with good features, a strong aquiline nose, a somewhat triangular shaped face with a firm chin, shown prominently when not masked by a beard. This is, of course, an idealized representation, but perhaps not too far from being a good portrait; those who can see beyond the drawn, thin features of the king's mummy maintain a distinct likeness between it (in the king's nineties) and, for example, the face of the Turin statue (in the king's twenties). His was a distinctly recognizable face, which could well be imprinted on the minds of his subjects. Someone traveling from Thebes to Piramesse – shall we say the soldier involved in the sandal transaction, mentioned earlier – in walking about the city might see a great sculpture and say, "Usimare himself! I know him." But would he be right? In ancient Egypt a statue represented the person whose name was inscribed on it, and, as we know, it was not unusual for a king to have statues of his predecessors inscribed or reinscribed for himself. So in Piramesse, our visiting soldier might look at one of the great colossi, later moved to Tanis, and say, "Who's that, then?" and he might ask a helpful passing scribe to read the names on the sculpture. The answer would have been, "Usimare-Setpenre Ramessu-Miamun, our noble king." Tactfully the visitor would accept the answer, but he might think, "Tell that to the marines!" or "Pull the other leg!" And he would have been right to be skeptical, for it has been shown conclusively that many of the great colossi in Tanis, moved from Piramesse, were in fact originally set up in Memphis and carved for an early Twelfth Dynasty king, Sesostris, or Senusret I (c.1965–1920 B.C.), or possibly a close successor. An embarrassing misidentification of another standing colossus as Ramesses II led to its being made the central piece in some of the showings of the Ramesses the Great exhibition in the United States in the late 1980s. The statue had been discovered in Memphis in 1962 and was visible for many years in a prone position, broken into several large pieces, among rushes in the mounds of the ancient city; it was clearly carved with the cartouches of Ramesses II. As it lay, its facial features could not be clearly seen because the nose and parts of the surrounding areas were badly damaged. When the statue was restored and shipped to America and could be seen in its magnificence for the first time, it became clear that it could not be a representation of Ramesses II; it has subsequently been closely associated with a group of early Twelfth Dynasty colossi, most of which were taken to Piramesse, and subsequently to Tanis and Bubastis, and reinscribed for Ramesses II.

Similarly, in Thebes, many of the colossal figures inscribed for Ramesses II in the great court of the Luxor temple were originally made for King Amenophis III. It is now thought that most, if not all, of these were left unfinished on the death of the great Eighteenth Dynasty king, and that they were sensibly, and economically, finished and given a new identity for Ramesses II.

It was not an inappropriate transfer of identity, for Ramesses seems to have held his great predecessor in high regard, a great builder also, the founder of the Luxor temple to which Ramesses grandly added, and the owner of the most magnificent mortuary temple in Western Thebes, a model possibly for the Ramesseum. So, as far as the Luxor statues were concerned, their reuse – scarcely usurpation – by Ramesses could have been prompted as much by esteem for an earlier king as by economy or convenience.

Colossal sculpture therefore occupied an important place in the general program of image presentation for Ramesses II, and it did not really matter very much if individual statues were made especially for the king and with his standard facial features, or usurped and adapted by inscription, and sometimes by the modification of certain facial features. There were, however, many prominent pieces, which were undoubtedly made for the king during his reign, like the colossi in the Ramesseum, including the Younger Memnon, the statue in Ramesses Square in Cairo, the wonderful alabaster colossus still at Memphis, and also the majestic figures at Abu Simbel hewn out of the living rock. Some sculptures performed an additional function, which was associated with a development in the interpretation and representing of Ramesses' image as the long reign developed.

This was the presentation of the king as divine, even as a god, more positively than just being considered as the embodiment of Horus, the living divine king.

The distinction is subtle, and was resolved in a way, which would avoid offending those Egyptians who might have scruples about worshiping the king in his actual form. Divinity in a sense was channeled through certain statues, suitably located so that they could be approached and treated as conduits for petitions and prayers.

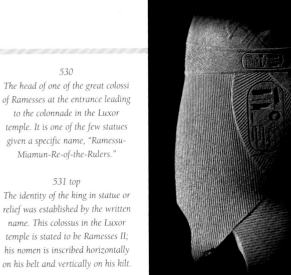

These statues were given grandiloquent titles, which identified Ramesses or associated him with particular national deities, or as a god himself. So in Piramesse there were statues of "Usimare-Setpenre-Monthu in the Two Lands," "Ramessu-Miamun, Ruler of the Rulers," "Ramessu-Miamun-Re of the Rulers," and "Ramessu-Miamun the God." In the Ramesseum the vast seated colossus was "Ramessu-Miamun-Re of the Rulers." The same name was given to the fine seated colossus in the great court of the Luxor temple placed to the right of the entrance to the great colonnade. The Abu Simbel colossi are also named, but the names do not so directly assign divinity to Ramesses, perhaps because they were made and inscribed at a time before the concept of the king's divinity had been fully developed. The divinity of the king is most clearly indicated in the temple itself, as we shall see later in this book. There may, however, be a kind of contradiction here between the inside and the outside of the temple, more significant perhaps because the statues outside were almost surely completed after the initial decoration of the temple had been planned and mostly executed. What is certain is that a huge statement about Ramesses was made by the stupendous effect of the façade with its colossi; an effect that would have done much to vaunt the greatness of the king in the eyes of anyone who visited Abu Simbel, whether in the lifetime of Ramesses II, or in a sailing *dahabiya* in the nineteenth century, or even by plane or boat after the relocation of the temple in the mid-twentieth century.

The naming of great statues was not an innovation of the reign of Ramesses II. One of the great Colossi of Memnon, set up in front of the mortuary temple of Amenophis III, is called "Nimare, Ruler of the Rulers," Nimare being that king's prenomen. The difference in respect of the named statues of Ramesses was that they were the subjects of cults, regarded as suitable recipients for personal petitions. This devotion to such statues, and probably covertly to the king himself, is demonstrated by a large group of inscriptions, said to have come from Hurbayt, a Delta town a little way to the west of Piramesse, but now thought to have been found in illicit excavations at Qantir, part of the ancient site of Piramesse. Most of these inscriptions are small and simple, and show a statue of Ramesses II receiving adoration from one or two persons. The most frequent of the named statues is of "Usimare-Setpenre-Monthu in the Two Lands." The majority of the dedicators of these stelae are unimportant people; but one stela, now in Munich, was dedicated by the vizier Rahotpe, also called Prahotpe. In the upper register it shows the king offering wine and incense to a standing statue of himself, "Ramessu-Miamun, Ruler of the Rulers, the great god, lord of heaven for ever." Behind the statue are carved four listening ears, to hear petitions. In the lower register Rahotpe is shown kneeling in adoration, with a text in which he offers praise to "your *ka*, lord of diadems, Ramessu-Miamun, Ruler of the Rulers, the great god who listens to the petitions of the whole of mankind." Rahotpe, who seems to have been the first northern vizier based administratively in Piramesse, probably in the later part of the king's reign, demonstrates in this inscription that such statue cults were not objects of devotion for simple people only. Here was the highest secular official in Piramesse making his petition to the statue of his ruler. Here indeed was recognition of the power of Ramesses, which went beyond that of an earthly ruler; here Ramesses' image in statue form had become godlike.

In his sixty-seven years of ruling Egypt, Ramesses and his advisers and close associates were able to achieve a development of the royal persona far beyond what his predecessors had been able even to attempt. His huge reputation, however, did not save him from suffering the indignity of usurpation which he had inflicted on so many of his royal ancestors. As an example of notable usurpation, consider only the huge standing quartzite royal figure now placed in the first court of the Karnak temple in front of the entrance to the Hypostyle Hall. This fine colossus shows Ramesses with his daughter Bintanta standing before his legs. On the base are added the cartouches of Ramesses IV of the Twentieth Dynasty (c.1163–1156 B.C.); the image was further usurped by Pinudjem I, high priest of Amon-Re in the early Twenty-first Dynasty (c. 1030 B.C.), who took the liberty of using royal cartouches. Perhaps Ramesses II would not have been upset by the usurpation by Ramesses IV; but he would surely have considered Pinudjem's usurpation as the impudent act of an upstart. Both probably were simply seeking a touch of greatness by associating their names with that of the Egyptian king *par excellence*. It was the image that mattered.

536
Quartzite head from Memphis, certainly of Queen Nefertiti. The sensitivity of the carving places it in the later Amarna Period. Eyes and eyebrows were inlaid, possibly with contrasting hard stone or glass (Cairo, JE 45547).

537
Head of Tutankhamun's queen, Ankhesenamun, from the back panel of his golden throne. The head is set against a background of gold sheet, and the inlays are of glass, faience, and semiprecious stones (Cairo, JE 62028).

Nefertiti, Akhenaten's wife, occupied a very special position during the period of Atenism. Some have even thought that she might have been the driving force of the revolution, which her husband ostensibly led. She figures almost as prominently as Akhenaten in the surviving visual and written records of the reign, and in consequence suffered as much as her husband from the vilification which followed the downfall of the Amarna regime. Some historians believe that she in fact survived Akhenaten, succeeding him to rule as Neferneferuaten.

By the end of the Eighteenth Dynasty it seems to have become quite normal for principal wives to take some part in politics, and even in diplomatic matters, quite prepared to take some

initiative when their own personal interests, or those of their families, were concerned. There was the extraordinary case of the Egyptian queen, almost certainly Ankhesenamun, daughter of Akhenaten and widow of the recently deceased Tutankhamun, who wrote to the Hittite king Suppiluliumas asking him to send her one of his sons to marry her. That the attempt to avoid marrying Ay, Tutankhamun's successor, failed, with the death of the Hittite prince when he arrived in Egypt in no way detracts from the extraordinary personal action of the queen. Ankhesenamun must have been desperate to take such action, but she must also have been confident that what she planned was not beyond the possibility of success.

TUY,
Ramesses' Mother

The royal ladies of the Eighteenth Dynasty showed abundant resource, and exercised notable authority in their involvement in affairs of state. It would, however, be wrong to assume that the evidence of freedom of action by particular queens implies much more than spirited individuality, except in the cases of Hatshepsut and probably Nefertiti. The independent queens otherwise showed how they could participate in the counsels of their husbands without causing constitutional problems or creating embarrassments. The Nineteenth Dynasty kings were to have some very notable queens, and few would exercise as much covert influence as Tuy, wife of Sethos I and mother of Ramesses II. She seems to have developed into a stabilizing and supporting element for the royal family in the transition to the new reign after the death of Sethos, and she remained someone on whom Ramesses could rely for good advice almost up to the middle of his long reign. It is always hazardous to draw significant conclusions from tenuous evidence, and it would be wrong to suggest that Tuy was a real power behind the throne, especially as the court at Piramesse contained several other royal ladies who were far from being ciphers. Most important, as we shall see, was Nefertari, the queen above all queens for Ramesses. At the same time there is no evidence of friction between mother-in-law and daughter-in-law. They may in fact have formed a mutually supporting alliance; Tuy and Nefertari came from non-royal parentage, and therefore may have felt slightly at a disadvantage in their relations with other court ladies, whose royal lineage was better established. But what went on in the ladies' quarter of the royal residence may

have had little significance in the more public life of the court. Tuy was a queen of experience and could therefore be a considerable ally for Nefertari, and indeed for other royal wives who may have been willing to seek her advice. She did not become a closet dowager, although it may have suited her plans from time to time to capitalize on the fact that she was the mother of Ramesses, the great conqueror of Qadesh. The degree of her acceptance as an important person within the royal family is indicated by her inclusion in sculptures, which showed her close relationship with her son. This was not common for a queen mother. The most noteworthy examples of this special treatment are to be found at Abu Simbel, where figures of Tuy are included among the other members of Ramesses' family carved as part of the great colossus groups on the façade.

Tuy, then, was part of the inner circle of the royal family, and she was even to be exploited – if that is not an unkind word – by Ramesses in the establishment of his own divine legend. The myth of the divine parentage of the reigning king had been developed during the Eighteenth Dynasty to reinforce the legitimacy of certain rulers when claims to the kingship were uncertain or shaky. Hatshepsut included a series of scenes in her mortuary temple at Dayr al-Bahri to demonstrate that Amun, the great god of Thebes, was her father. A similar series of scenes was carved for King Amenophis III in the Luxor temple. Hatshepsut had good reason to claim divine parentage in view of her irregular assumption of the kingship; Amenophis III did not labor under a similar disadvantage, but still

Ramesses II

reckoned it to be a prudent move to reinforce his undoubted legitimacy. This legitimizing of a king's right to the throne did not apparently become a matter of regular practice until a much later time in Egyptian dynastic history. The special chapels, now called *mammisi* ('birth houses'), were constructed to contain the scenes of divine birth. Nevertheless, Ramesses II or his advisers considered it to be a sensible thing to do in his own case. The evidence for such a representation of his divine birth is not as clear as it is for Hatshepsut and Amenophis III. Blocks from a dismantled building of Ramesses II were used in the construction of the mortuary temple of Ramesses III at Medinet Habu, and some of these blocks belong most probably to birth scenes showing Queen Tuy with Amun and other deities commonly involved in royal birth scenes. These blocks and many others reused at Medinet Habu came from the Ramesseum, not from the main mortuary temple of Ramesses II but from a much smaller subsidiary temple built on the north side of the hypostyle hall of the main temple. The dedicatees of this smaller temple are not wholly certain; they include Tuy and probably her husband, Sethos I, and possibly also Queen Nefertari. In this special temple Ramesses honored his mother by including her in an endowment, which would certainly have benefited from its proximity to the great mortuary temple of the king himself.

During her lifetime in the residence of her son at Piramesse, Tuy was even allowed to participate in diplomatic exchanges. At the time of the conclusion of the peace treaty with the Hittites in Year 21, as was noted earlier, she took part in the flurry of congratulatory correspondence, which passed between Piramesse and the Hittite capital, Hattusas. Her letter, we may be sure, would not have been penned personally in her boudoir on scented papyrus, unless possibly as a draft. The actual delivered letter was in Babylonian cuneiform on a clay tablet, processed in the official Egyptian chancery. It must therefore have been sent with the full knowledge and approval of high officials; it may, of course, even have been prompted by high officials as part of the diplomatic exchanges at that important time. Nevertheless, whether she wrote as directed or on her own account, the sending of the letter in itself indicates the respect in which she was held.

Within a year or two, Tuy died, and she was further honored in death by being buried in a fine tomb, specially prepared for her in what is now called the Valley of the Queens, known in antiquity as the Place of Beauty. This valley, at the south end of the Theban Necropolis, was first used during the Eighteenth Dynasty, but began to be exploited as a suitably distinct area for the burials of queens and royal children in the Nineteenth Dynasty. The finest surviving tomb, as we shall shortly see, was made for Queen Nefertari; but the one prepared for Queen Tuy may originally have been quite as splendid. It was discovered only in recent years, sadly robbed and heavily damaged; but enough traces of decoration and of tomb furniture were found to suggest that it was wonderfully decorated and richly furnished. Sometimes during her life under her son Ramesses, her name is given as Mut-Tuy ('Mother Tuy'), which apparently emphasized her position in the king's esteem. In the tomb she is just Tuy,

as she had been when wife of Sethos I. Another close female member of Ramesses' family, who has become a little better known in recent years, is his sister Tia or Tjia, who was married to a senior administrative official also named, confusingly, Tia or Tjia. The tomb of the two Tias was excavated at Saqqara in the early 1980s, on the high plateau to the south of the Step Pyramid, overlooking the plain of Memphis. It was constructed side by side with the tomb prepared by Horemheb in the reign of Tutankhamun, while he was still a general.

The Tias' tomb is not as splendid as that of Horemheb, but it is in its superstructure almost as large, with open courts and a small pyramid. There is no suggestion from the surviving reliefs and inscriptions that Princess Tia and her husband were especially honored in their lifetime; they were presumably content to live and carry out their official duties in the Memphite region. Nevertheless, the scale of their tomb and its proximity to Horemheb's tomb – already probably the object of some posthumous veneration – suggest that they were not lacking in privilege and recognition because of the close relationship with the reigning monarch.

It seems clear that this Saqqara tomb was prepared principally for the official Tia, the husband; his wife was included, as was common, and because of her royal origin was surely able to arrange that the position and size of the tomb were consonant with her status. But she did not qualify for burial in the Valley of the Queens. Such special burial would be reserved for the royal women closest to the king, his mother and his particular wives.

The Great Royal Wife
NEFERTARI

Of the wives the most important was Nefertari, without a doubt. Like so many people in antiquity, Nefertari is extremely well known, while being at the same time almost unknown. If one is asked what was her importance in the life and reign of Ramesses II, it is not easy to provide truly adequate answers. Inference and surmise must contribute substantially to the small corpus of known facts about this undoubtedly important queen. The major pieces of evidence for her fame are two structures, the secondary temple at Abu Simbel and the tomb in the Valley of the Queens, both of which have been subjected to exceptional study and conservation in recent years. It could be said that she is important because of the temple and the tomb, and there is some truth in such a claim. Early historians of ancient Egypt, such as James Henry Breasted, make only brief references to her. Amelia B. Edwards, the Victorian novelist and traveler, was convinced on the basis of the temple (the tomb had not yet been discovered) -that there was much more to her relationship with Ramesses than a straightforward formal royal alliance.

Nevertheless, Nefertari cannot be thought of as a mere cipher. Even if for people today she is known and glamorized by her spectacular temple and tomb, it cannot be questioned that in her lifetime she was the leading lady of Ramesses' court, first in the harem of the king, but perhaps second over all, respectfully, to Tuy, who occupied a special position as dowager queen. Nefertari was the great royal wife, but sadly nothing is known of her parentage and background, which might establish more certainly on what her inherited authority, if any, rested. Unless a royal wife had royal parents it was not usual for their names to be recorded. It has been suggested that she may have been a member of the family of Ay, non-royal successor of Tutankhamun, but the evidence is very slight. It is better to think of her as belonging to the family of some high official who had been spotted by King Sethos or his 'talent scouts' as being a girl of a good family who would provide the young prince with good children. In the great dedicatory inscription of Abydos, dated in Year 1, in listing the many favors he owed to his father, Ramesses expressly mentions the setting up of his own household, chosen from the royal harem, with wives selected from the whole land of Egypt, and a suitable collection of concubines. Prince Ramessu was himself probably in his mid-teens at the time, and it is not surprising that the choice of his principal bedfellows should be made by his father. He would have plenty of time later to make his own royal selection after he became king. By the time he did become king, Nefertari was already to be regarded as great royal wife. She had by then produced an heir, to be the first crown prince, Amonhikhopshef, and had therefore established her priority among the wives of the king. From the outset of the reign, Nefertari is the queen who is almost exclusively shown attending the king in his official duties, and she was to retain this position until she died.

It will never be possible to decide whether a true love-match existed between Nefertari and Ramesses. The temple at Abu Simbel and the tomb in the Valley of the Queens may indicate great and sincere regard for a wife who had fulfilled her duties in every respect throughout many years of marriage; for a wife who participated in the activities of the state without creating problems; who may even have accompanied the royal party on the Qadesh campaign; who is at least shown in temple reliefs in many places throughout Egypt, to be at her husband's side in performing ritual acts; and who stands beside him – admittedly on a much smaller scale – in many great sculptures. There is good reason to believe that she played her part to the very best conventional standards; she could be wholly relied on. Consequently, for all this devotion to duty she earned the respect and possibly also the affection of Ramesses. But 'love' in the modern sense, as the indicator of a truly happy marriage, was probably a meaningless idea in the context of the pharaonic court. A king had ample opportunities to engage in sexual activities within his well-stocked harem, whether he might be in Piramesse or in the quite separate establishment at the place called Mi-wer, probably the modern place called Gurob on the edge of the Faiyum depression in Middle Egypt. That Ramesses took advantage of these opportunities is adequately shown by the processions of his children displayed on many temple walls; these we shall consider later. No one could ever claim that he remained faithful to Nefertari; no one in antiquity would ever have thought that fidelity in the royal marriage bed was even desirable. Let us therefore put aside the idea of Ramesses as the eternal lover of Nefertari.

541 left
A small image of Nefertari, dwarfed by the legs of her husband's colossal statue. From one of the standing figures of Ramesses with his great royal wife, at Luxor temple. Here she wears a long tripartite wig, not her characteristic vulture headdress.

541 right
This graceful elegant of Nefertari is in the vestibule of the queen's Hathor temple at Abu Simbel. The image clearly displays the gracefulness of the queen's proportions.

Nefertari's Hathor Temple at
ABU SIMBEL

Respect and gratitude are different matters. Consider first what seems to be a remarkable recognition of Nefertari's worth in the partial dedication of the small temple at Abu Simbel to the queen. It may never be known whether the small temple was included from the outset in the plans for the development of the Abu Simbel site. As seen today, which is indeed much as it would have been seen in antiquity, the small temple can almost be overlooked because of the massive grandeur of the main temple. It is set in a bay of the cliffs to the north of the main temple; but it is not insignificant in size, especially if considered in relation to most of the other Nubian temples of Ramesses II. The façade presents six standing colossi, four of the king and two of the queen, all of the same height of thirty-three feet (ten meters), by no means pygmy sculptures. As a subsidiary temple it is nevertheless not a structure to outdo the major monument at Abu Simbel. In planning what was to be done in this remote place, Ramesses, possibly on the suggestion of his senior officials, decided to follow the example of his great and much-honored predecessor Amenophis III, who had dedicated a temple to his wife Tiye at Sedeinga in Nubia between the second and third cataracts – even more remote a place than Abu Simbel. Both the temples, at Sedeinga and at Abu Simbel, were planned and executed while the dedicatees were still alive. They were therefore monuments consciously recognizing the importance of the two queens as living persons; they were not to be compared with any funerary monument which might be prepared in lifetime, but in expectation of death.

Among the bold inscriptions framing the figures of the king and queen on the façade of the small temple are clear statements of what Ramesses intended: "A sanctuary of great and mighty monuments for the great royal wife Nefertari, beloved of Mut, for whom the sun god Re shines, given life, and beloved"; and "He has had a sanctuary excavated in the mountain, of everlasting craftsmanship, in Nubia, which the King of Upper and Lower Egypt, Usimare-Setpenre, has made for the great royal wife Nefertari, beloved of Mut, in Nubia, like Re for ever and ever." Nothing could be more explicit than that.

The temple was dedicated principally to a form of Hathor, linked specifically with Ibshek, a locality in the neighborhood of Abu Simbel.

542–543
The façade of the Nefertiti temple, with six colossal standing figures: two of the queen, and four of Ramesses. She wears her usual feathered headdress and both are accompanied by small figures of princes and princesses.

543 bottom
The three figures on the north side of the façade. Unusually, the queen is shown as almost equal to her husband in size – but he is allowed a little extra height, as might be expected for a man.

542 top
In the pillared hall at Abu Simbel, Nefertari offers a sistrum and a bouquet of flowers to Hathor, Lady of Ibshek, who is seated but raised on a podium so that the heads of both ladies are at the same height.

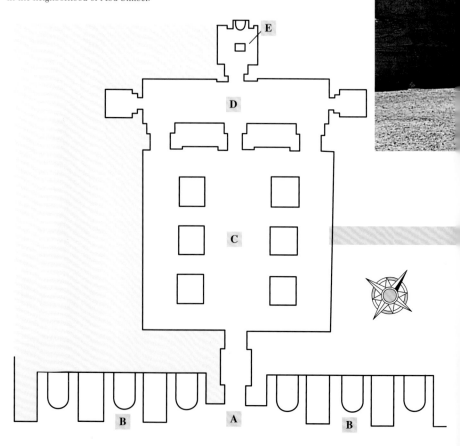

LEGEND

A   FORECOURT
B   FAÇADE WITH COLOSSAL FIGURES
C   PILLARED HALL
D   VESTIBULE
E   SANCTUARY

544–545
The pillared hall: each pillar shows on one side a form of sistrum with the head of Hathor; on the other sides, figures of the queen and deities; here Thoth and the queen are visible.

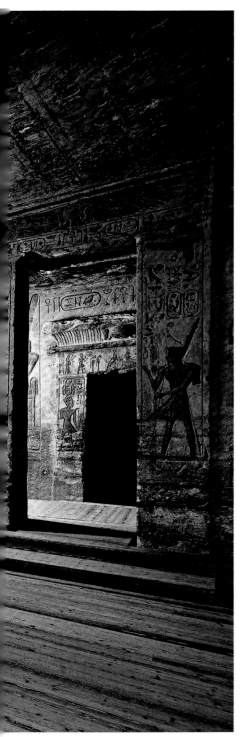

Hathor was originally a sky goddess, but she acquired many functions and aspects, often represented as a cow, as she is in some places in the Abu Simbel temple. She was also, for reasons that are far from being understood, a goddess with affinities for foreign places like Nubia, and also Sinai. Hathor, Mistress of Ibshek, is, however, mostly shown in the temple as a divine lady with a moon disk and horns as her headdress. Nefertari, the other dedicatee of the temple, is not shown as a goddess, but as a queen, engaged in ceremonies associating her with Hathor and also with many other deities, both national and specifically Nubian. She is shown in the temple as a king is usually shown in a cult temple, conducting divine ceremonies. Here in the small temple she shares the ceremonies with Ramesses, except in traditional kingly scenes such as those in which the king smites his Nubian and Asiatic enemies; in these scenes she does not actively participate, but stands in attendance on Ramesses.

What is particularly noticeable in the scenes is the manner of showing the human and divine figures.

An elongation of the usual proportions for the representation of the human body imparts a distinct and striking elegance to the figures. In this departure from the standard canon, the resulting figures of women – of Nefertari, of Hathor and of other goddesses – are unusually seductive, and seem greatly to be enhanced by the long, flowing robes which that they wear. On the other hand, the male figures are not particularly more impressive than those executed according to the standard canon elsewhere. The groupings of Nefertari with another god or goddess are mostly accompanied by identificatory texts of minimal length, and the rather simple, spare effect of figures surrounded by ample space is exceptionally striking. The elongation of the queen's figure is emphasized by the headdress which she wears on top of her wig, which is tripartite, one part falling down her back, and two side lappets hanging down to her breasts. The headdress above consists of a circlet topped by a sun disk and two long and graceful horns enclosing a pair of tall ostrich feathers.

544 bottom
Inside the entrance to the pillared hall: Ramesses, followed by Nefertari, smites a Syrian captive in the presence of falcon-headed Horus of Meha. This is one of only two warlike scenes in Nefertari's temple.

545
Each pillar of the pillared hall shows on one side a sistrum with the head of Hathor and, on the other sides, portraits of the queen and deities; here Nefertari can be seen holding a flower and a sistrum.

546

*Scenes of offerings to gods in the
pillared hall include Ramesses more
often than Nefertari, as might be
expected. Here he offers a figure of
the goddess Ma'at to Amon-Re.*

546–547

*Scenes on the north wall of the hall:
Ramesses consecrates offerings to
Ptah, then offers flowers and
libations to ram-headed Arsaphes;
Nefertari presents sistra to Hathor
of Dendera and Ramesses offers
wine to Re-Herakhty.*

Ramesses II

While the execution of the temple reliefs is
not of the highest standard, it is notably good by
Nubian standards. Ramesses is the person most
figured and honored in the temple, especially in
the innermost shrine, where he makes a
presentation to a figure of the Hathor-cow
emerging from the living rock. But Nefertari, in
her very striking scenes, leaves in the mind no
doubt that this is her temple.

The enhancement of her status is indicated
most positively by two parallel scenes. One is
conventional, showing Ramesses II being
empowered with royalty by the two gods, Seth of
Ombos and Horus, here Lord of Maha, an
unidentified Nubian locality. The two deities

hold in one hand the notched palm ribs
indicating infinity of reign; with the other hand
they touch the double crown on the head of the
king, who wears what is usually called the
Nubian wig. The second scene shows Nefertari
flanked by Hathor, Mistress of Ibshek, and Isis,
Mother of the God; they each raise one hand to
touch the queen's headdress, similarly investing
her with a power which is not stated; there are
no notched palm ribs, but Nefertari, unusually,
carries an *ankh*-sign of life, normally carried only
by deities, as here by Hathor and Isis. Nefertari
also wears the Nubian wig.

Such a scene raised the queen high in status,
at least in the Nubian context. It is unlikely that

Nefertari had ever been to Abu Simbel before
Year 24 (c.1256–1255 B.C.), when she
accompanied Ramesses and a large entourage to
attend the inauguration of the two temples. It
must be supposed that she already knew about
the temple partly dedicated to her, but it must
be hoped that the reality of the temple in its
dramatic setting would have come, if not as a
surprise, then certainly as a matter of great
satisfaction.

Her visit may have been the last major official
event that she attended, for within a year or two
she was dead, and on her way to join some of
those deities whom she was shown honoring in
her own temple.

548–549
*On the east wall of the vestibule,
Ramesses and Nefertari give floral
offerings and a sistrum to "the Great
One, who gave birth to all the gods";
this is Thoeris, known best in her
hippopotamus form.*

549 top
*In the vestibule, a scene paralleling
the coronation of the king; Nefertari
is consecrated by Hathor of Ibshek
(left) and Isis. The gracefulness of
these female figures is enhanced by
the elongation of their proportions.*

549 bottom
*Looking along the vestibule at Abu
Simbel with the entrance to the
sanctuary on the right. The offering
to Thoeris is on the left wall, and
on the right, Ramesses offers wine
to Re-Herakhty.*

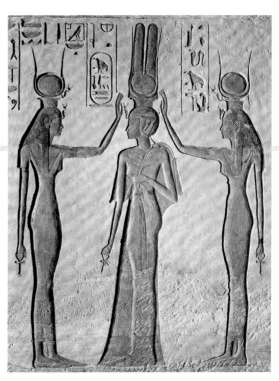

The Tomb of
NEFERTARI

The tomb prepared for Nefertari in the Valley of the Queens is now one of the best-known sepulchres in the Theban Necropolis, not only for the gorgeous quality of its reliefs, but also for the present difficulty in getting to see it. When it was discovered by Ernesto Schiaparelli in 1904, it had clearly been stripped of its funerary contents in antiquity, with scarcely a trace surviving. The state of the painted relief decoration, however, was from the first seen to be poor. The finely painted reliefs were carved into a plaster coating applied to the walls because of the poor quality of the limestone of the area. Subsequently, the action of salts in the limestone, probably activated by the humidity created by visitors, led to considerable deterioration. The tomb was closed for many years, and the reliefs in due course subjected to extensive conservation, which has seemingly stabilized them for the time being. Air-conditioning and the severe restriction of the number of visitors may delay, if not prevent, further deterioration. Sadly, therefore, it is not easy for the present-day visitor to enter the tomb and view the fine reliefs. And they are indeed very fine, of much better quality than most post-Sethos Theban tomb decoration. In death, as shown in her tomb, Nefertari is on her own to face the hazards and terrors of the journey to the afterlife. But she is not unprotected: supported by appropriate deities and friendly demons, and by the correct religious texts, she can overcome all dangers without needing the obvious support of her husband. Ramesses in no way figures in her tomb, just as in his tomb no wives are shown. The tomb is in fact very different from any prepared for private persons at this time, in which man and wife, and frequently children, participate together in the various activities represented on the walls.

550 left
One a pillar in the burial chamber: Isis takes Nefertari by the hand and offers her life (ankh). The fingers of their hands are unusually long, whereas the general proportions of the figures are conventional.

550 top right
Scene in Nefertari's tomb: Re as a mummy with ram head and sun disk, with Isis (right) and Nephthys. The texts by the mummy read: "Re is one who rests in Osiris" and "Osiris the one who rests in Re."

551
Head of Nefertari from the entrance hall. She wears her characteristic vulture headdress, topped by a circlet and a sun disk with two tall ostrich feathers. She also wears an earring in the unusal form of a cobra.

552–553
Nefertari, "great king's wife and lady of the Two Lands" presents huge quantities of food offerings to Osiris "ruler of the Holy Land," before whom are the four sons of Horus on a stand.

553 bottom left
View toward the antechamber and side chamber: deities greet Nefertari on the walls; by the entrance to the side room are beetle-headed Khepri, the sun god at dawn (left), and Re-Herakhty with Hathor (right).

Nefertari with great dignity passes through the twelve gates of the underworld; she meets and greets many deities, she engages in a game of *senet*, a board game which figures among the activities in the passage to eternity. Throughout the tomb Nefertari is shown in royal attire, mostly wearing the vulture headdress topped by the circlet, the disk, and tall ostrich feathers found in her Abu Simbel representations, and often elsewhere; but in the tomb the slender horns of the living queen are no longer included. The common Nineteenth Dynasty canon of proportions is used for the figures, which therefore lack the elongation found at Abu Simbel. Execution and coloring are superb, the painting showing much delicacy of added shading and detailing to enhance the effect. Nefertari is not the same here as the Nefertari of Nubia, but in her different form she is equally striking, and in all respects as regal as at Abu Simbel.

In death and in her tomb Nefertari was generously honored. She had, as far as one can judge, performed her queenly duties more than adequately. She had produced heirs; she may indeed have been Ramesses' favorite. There is perhaps more than formal eloquence in the way she is described in the temple of Luxor, where, at the head of a procession of children, she shakes the sistrum before the god Amun: "Rich in affection, wearing the diadem, chantress, fair of face, beautiful with the tall two feathers, chief of the harem of Horus, Lord of the Palace; whatever emerges about her is pleasing; who has only to speak and her wish is fulfilled... just to hear her voice is living, the great royal wife, his beloved, wife of the Strong Bull, Mistress of the Two Lands, Nefertari, beloved of Mut."

553 bottom right
Nefertari before ibis-headed Thoth: the text contains Chapter 94 of the Book of the Dead, *which is meant to enable the dead person to obtain a water pot and a palette for writing. The objects lie on a stand before her.*

LEGEND

A ACCESS STAIRS
B ENTRANCE HALL
C SIDE CHAMBER
D STAIRS TO BURIAL CHAMBER
E BURIAL CHAMBER
F ANNEXES
G VESTIBULE TO REALM OF OSIRIS

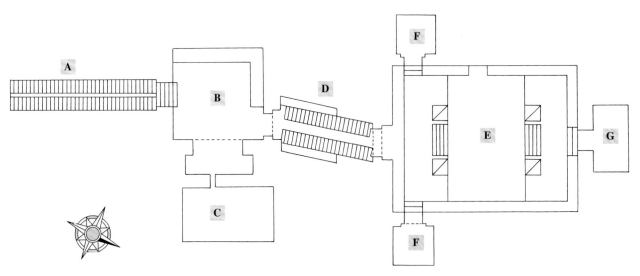

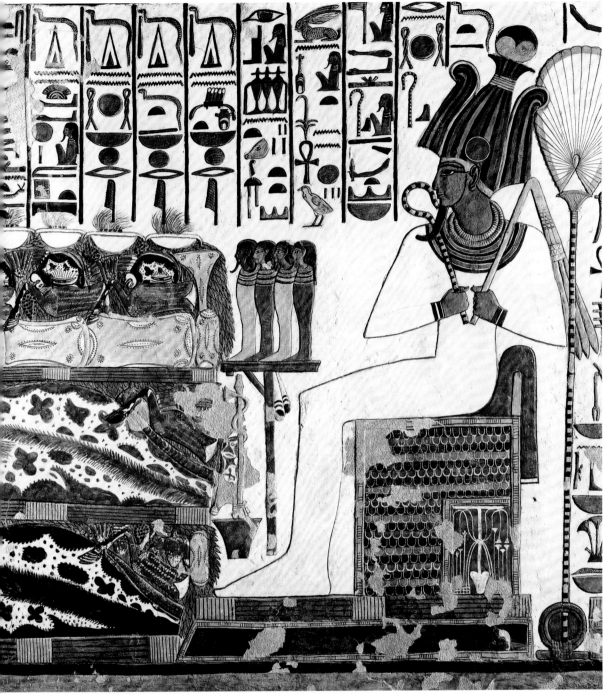

554 top left
On the left-hand wall of the stairs to the burial chamber: above, a winged serpent protects the cartouche of Nefertari; below, Anubis, the jackal god of embalming says, "I have come to you, beloved daughter...."

554 bottom
A vignette that accompanies Chapter 17 of the Book of the Dead, concerning the playing of the game senet in the afterlife. Here Queen Nefertari sits in a kiosk, competing with her destiny.

554–555
On the right wall of the stairs to the burial chamber: Nefertari offers two bowls of wine to Hathor of Thebes; to Selkis, the scorpion goddess; mistress of the holy land; and to Ma'at, daughter of Re.

555 bottom
Vignettes accompanying Chapter 17 of the Book of the Dead: Nefertari's mummy is watched over by the divine mourners, Isis and Nephthys, in the form of kites. Left, the heron (phoenix) of Re, right a Nile deity.

556–557
The burial chamber. Two pillars
show figures of two forms of Horus:
Iunmutef "pillar of his mother"
(left), and Nedjiotef "avenger of his
father," both depicted as living
priests with leopard skin, sidelock,
and, unusually, the uraeus.

557 right
In the burial chamber of Nefertari.
The walls and pillars can be seen to
have suffered badly from the effects
of salt efflorescence. The painted
reliefs in some places have
successfully responded to
conservation.

Other Royal Ladies

There may, however, have been constant tension, the threat of competition, in the royal harems, especially at Piramesse. From the outset of Ramesses' reign, and probably even earlier, the Queen Isitnofret lurked in the shadows of the royal presence. Like Nefertari her parentage is not known; presumably she too was the daughter of some worthy member of the court of Sethos I, chosen to be part of the initial 'stocking' of the harem, which Sethos arranged for his young son Prince Ramessu. She missed priority within the harem by failing to give birth to the first male child, who would become crown prince when Ramessu became king. But she did very well subsequently. She produced a second son, who significantly was named Ramessu after his father. Soon there was Khaemwese, son number four, of whom we shall learn much more in the next chapter. Another of her sons would ultimately succeed Ramesses, many years hence; this was Merenptah, son number thirteen. It cannot be deduced from the absence of Isitnofret on royal monuments and buildings in the first two decades of Ramesses' reign that she was deliberately put on one side, or denied her proper honor in the royal residence. She may not have lived usually at Piramesse, but in the harem establishment at Mi-wer by the Faiyum; but the regularity with which she produced children for Ramesses does not indicate that she was sidelined and neglected.

After Nefertari's death Isitnofret graduated to the status of Great Royal Wife, and there have survived a few monuments on which she is shown dressed like Nefertari, with a high, feathered headdress. The occasional depictions of the queen are not on any of the major monuments of the reign, the great temples, all of which were constructed in the early years, when Nefertari occupied the premier position. The most interesting record is a stela carved in the Speos of Horemheb at Gebel al-Silsila. It was set up by her son Khaemwese at the time of his announcing the second jubilee festival of his father in Year 33/34. On it are shown, in addition to the king, Khaemwese himself and two queens, Isitnofret described as Great Royal Wife, and Bintanta, her first daughter by Ramesses, described as "hereditary princess, great in favor, king's daughter and great royal wife." Already Isitnofret was seemingly being superseded; Ramesses had begun the process of concentrating the royal line by taking his own daughters as wives. Bintanta was the first. The stela also shows, in subsidiary positions, two further sons, Ramessu, who by then was crown prince, and Merenptah, who would eventually succeed.

In the early years of his reign Ramesses may have maintained a kind of hierarchy among his various wives. It was no doubt very important to make sure that status and priority of position were properly recognized, especially when the royal family in its widest sense was being established. So Nefertari came first, mother of the heir to the throne. Then came Isitnofret, whose position would have been enhanced by the deaths of Amonhikhopshef, the first crown prince, and most of the other sons born to Nefertari. By about Year 21 the succession had passed to Ramessu, Isitnofret's first male child. When Nefertari died shortly after, Isitnofret at last moved into first place, and she seems to have lived until about Year 34. By this time, however, there had been a small proliferation of great royal wives, the title being granted both to Bintanta, oldest daughter of Isitnofret, and also to Merytamun, oldest daughter of Nefertari. There is some evidence to suggest that the two great royal wives of the second generation graduated in status not long after the death of Nefertari; but the evidence is not convincing. It seems reasonable to suggest that the two daughters were taken into the royal harem according to no set order. Why should the great king be bound by any rule or custom, which would have no real validity? To become a king's wife may not have been such a change in status for a king's daughter, a young woman of royal birth who may scarcely have seen her father until she was of marriageable age. It is not for us to be censorious about the practices within a royal family of more than three thousand years ago. Presumably the most important matter was to secure a good succession, and to ensure that from a ceremonial point of view, legitimacy and status should be properly matched. Ramesses II, the Great, had no difficulty in securing his succession, as we shall see in the next chapter. Keeping his harem happy might have been a little more difficult; but as his reign advanced, formalities may have lost some of their force, and a relaxation of hierarchic principles may have been allowed in order to maintain what might be considered the happy home life of the monarch.

558 left
Painted limestone bust of a queen found in the Ramesseum. It is not inscribed, but it has been indentified as Meritamun, daughter of Nefertari. She became a wife of her father Ramesses II after the death of Nefertari (Cairo, JE 31413).

558 top right
The small figure of Bintanta standing in front of her father's colossal statue in Karnak. She was the oldest daughter of Queen Isitnofret, and became a royal wife after Nefertari's death, while her mother still lived.

559 bottom
The quartzite colossus of Ramesses II at Karnak, with the small figure of Bintanta in front of his legs. She is here described as "king's daughter, king's wife," but not yet "great royal wife."

A fair picture of the royal family as it seemed to be at the height of Ramesses' power, after two decades or more of rule, may be seen in the line-up of royalty on the façade of the great Abu Simbel temple. There above all are the four colossal seated statues of the king. Each colossus is accompanied by small figures of family members who mattered at that moment. The southern colossus has "the king's daughter of his body, Nebt-tawy," and "the king's daughter Bintanta"; second colossus, "hereditary prince, royal scribe, general, king's son Amonhikhopshef" and "queen mother and god's wife, Mut-Tuy"; third colossus, "king's wife Nefertari, beloved of Mut," and "royal scribe and first chief general of his Majesty, king's son of his body, Ramessu"; fourth (northern) colossus, "king's daughter of his body, his beloved Merytamun," "king's daughter of his body Nefertari," and "queen mother and god's wife, Mut-Tuy." Most notably represented is the queen mother, (Mut)-Tuy, twice shown. There is only one named queen, Nefertari. There are four daughters, Bintanta, Nebt-tawy, Merytamun, and Nefertari; and two sons, Amonhikhopshef and Ramessu. The most obvious omission from the line-up is Isitnofret, who was undoubtedly a royal wife at the time of the carving of the temple façade, but not yet a great royal wife. Bintanta was a daughter of Isitnofret, but still the senior female child of Ramesses; Merytamun was Nefertari's oldest daughter. These two, as we have seen, were to become great royal wives by about Year 34, and both were given the honor of having lavish tombs in the Valley of the Queens. These tombs are now in very poor condition, as is that of Nebt-tawy, who became a great royal wife later in Ramesses' reign. Of princess Nefertari nothing further is known, apart from her appearance in some of the lists of princesses, which will be discussed in the next chapter. She probably died prematurely, having been groomed for queenship.

It would be wrong to attribute to Ramesses any particular feeling or attitude toward those Great Royal Wives who were in fact his daughters, family members brought up in the hothouse environment of the harems at Piramesse and Mi-wer. Unlike Akhenaten, "that criminal of Akhetaten," Ramesses is never shown in intimate relationships with his children, dandling them on his knee, or allowing them to crawl indiscriminately over him. Of course, we know nothing of what happened when he visited the harems where his young children would be raised and educated. His sons, no doubt, would be introduced to the proper forms of training required for future state duty, if not for kingship. Daughters, however, could be considered suitable subjects for marriage to the king, for formal and dynastic reasons, if not necessarily for sexual purposes. It is not unlikely, however, that a wife taken from the harem as a suitable person to be at the king's side at times of formal ceremonies might not be as stimulating as someone brought in from elsewhere. Apart from considerations of propriety, which, as has been suggested, scarcely would have been of major concern, a young

woman, a daughter, would come to the royal presence heavily charged with the gossip and intrigue of the harem, with possibly too many personal axes to grind. For pleasure and gratification, concubines would serve the purposes very well; for someone more substantial and worthy of the royal dignity, a foreign bride might be the answer.

There is good evidence to suggest that Ramesses was delighted with the prospect of a Hittite bride. Surviving records from both sides indicate that the negotiations were carried out with enthusiasm and a determination to succeed. The texts describing the journey to and arrival at Piramesse are unstinting in their praise for the new queen; her Egyptian name, Mahor-neferure ('she is one who sees Horus, the beauty of Re'), suggests more than a simple renaming for Egyptian consumption. The king, after all, was the living Horus. She was subsequently treated with all honor, given the status of great royal wife, but she never lost her identity as a Hittite princess. A figure of the queen accompanying a colossal statue of Ramesses at Tanis has the inscription "Great Royal Wife, mistress of the Two Lands, Mahor-neferure, daughter of the great prince of Hatti." Scarcely anything is known of her life in Egypt. It is generally thought that she spent some years in the royal residence at Piramesse, and then retired to the harem at Mi-wer. A tantalizing fragment of papyrus found at Gurob, the probable location of Mi-wer, mentions linen belonging to Mahor-neferure. Hittite records reveal that she bore at least one

child to Ramesses, a daughter named Neferure, after her mother. Like most of Ramesses' family, Mahor-neferure disappears from the surviving records; if she were allowed a tomb proper for a great royal wife, it has not yet been found in the Valley of the Queens.

The second Hittite marriage undertaken by Ramesses happened about Year 44, ten years after the first. It has often been suggested that Ramesses had been so pleased with Mahor-neferure that he was only too ready to have a second Hittite wife. The circumstances are little known; even the name of the second foreign princess has not survived. The likelihood is that diplomatic reasons were uppermost in deciding the match. Ramesses by then was in his sixties, not beyond the age of sexual activity, but probably only at a reduced level. Mahor-neferure may already have died; at the best she may have been living a life of genteel retirement at Mi-wer. Meanwhile the position of great royal wife was occupied by Nebt-tawy, whose mother may have been Nefertari. There is little trace of her involvement in state occasions in the later years of Ramesses' reign, but apart from jubilees, there is no evidence of important happenings in these terminal years. Nebt-tawy had a substantial tomb prepared for herself in the Valley of the Queens, which she presumably occupied. But, as with so much of court life and activity at that time, the silence of the sources suggests a slow decline in which Nebt-tawy may have played just a role of comforting companionship for her father, the aged king.

Ramesses II

560

One of the "family" figures carved beside the legs of the great colossi at Abu Simbel. Here is his great royal wife Nefertari, wearing her usual vulture headdress, and a single uraeus on her brow.

THE ROYAL PROGENY

562

Below the scene in the Ramesseum in which Ramesses receives power and jubilees from Amon-Re and Mut, is a procession of the oldest sons of the king, starting on the right with Amonhikhopshef. Not all are named.

563

Long sidelocks are commonly the sign of childhood in ancient Egypt. But they are also worn by certain kinds of priest, such as the sem-priest of Ptah, an office that Khaemwese held for most of his life. From the base of a statue in Luxor.

"He loved ease and pleasure and gave himself up without restraint to voluptuous enjoyments. He had an enormous harem, and as the years passed his children multiplied rapidly. He left over a hundred sons and at least half as many daughters, several of whom he married. He thus left a family so numerous that they became a Ramessid class of nobles, whom we still find over four hundred years later bearing among their titles the name Ramses, not as a patronymic, but as the designation of a class or rank... Ramses took great pride in his enormous family and often ordered his sculptors to depict his sons and daughters in long rows upon the walls of his temples."

One would hope that if James Henry Breasted were alive today, he would wince at reading these extravagant words, which he wrote almost one hundred years ago. The essential facts about the children of Ramesses II have scarcely changed in the intervening time,

but there are few historians of ancient Egypt who would now adopt Breasted's rather puritanical approach and casual disregard for the facts. Sir Alan Gardiner, a friend and close colleague of Breasted who had a high regard for Breasted's ability as a historian, writing fifty years later, was more accurate and less judgmental in his brief comments on the great king's family:

"So proud was Ramesses II of his extensive progeny that it would be wrong to omit all reference to the long enumeration of his sons and daughters to be read on the walls of his temples. At Wadi al-Sabua in Lower Nubia over a hundred princes and princesses were named, but the many lacunae make it impossible to compute the exact figure."

It is very human to enjoy a little scandal about the great, even when the person concerned may have been dead for three thousand years. One out of the small number of facts that visitors to Egypt believe to have learned about Ramesses II is that he had a huge

family, and that it was probably acquired by sexual excess in the perfervid environment of his various palaces. The spirit of Breasted lives! It is a pity to disappoint the gossips, but it seems right to declare unequivocally that there is no evidence to show that Ramesses II was a sex maniac, or that his palaces were exceptionally luxurious and decadent by Egyptian royal standards. It is, however, very evident that he was somewhat vainglorious (but not especially so in Egyptian terms), rather ostentatious (but he had plenty of time to present his image in a lavish manner), and clearly philoprogenitive. The parade of his sons and daughters, carved in relief in temples from Piramesse in the north to Amara in Nubia, is quite unusual, and it remains a phenomenon of the reign, which has not yet been satisfactorily explained. Was it done as an act of pride, or one of affection, or one of magical demonstration – to present the strength of the royal line and the certainty of strong succession?

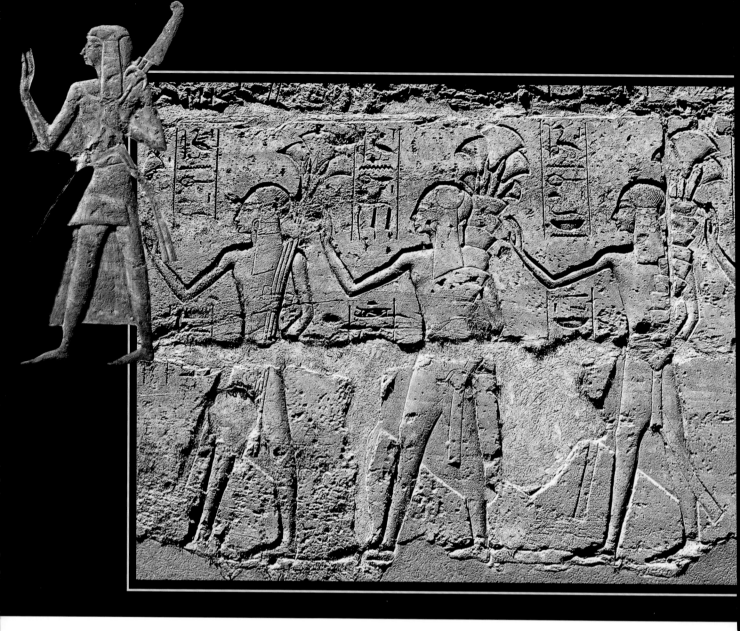

564 top left
The king's second son, Ramessu,
as shown in the Abu Simbel temple.
He had the title of "general," and
accompanied his father on
campaigns in Nubia and at Qadesh.
He was heir apparent for about
twenty years.

564–565
On the south wall of the Ramesside
court in the Luxor temple, a
procession of sons is followed by a
priest and sacrifical bull. The sons
are Nos. 15-18 in the lists: Iotamun,
Meryatum, Nebentaneb, and
Meryre II.

It is not usually possible to date with any
precision when the 'progeny' reliefs were carved.
Some of those in the great Theban temples –
Luxor, Karnak, and the Ramesseum – are
probably among the earliest. Those at Wadi al-
Sabua, carved after Year 45, were almost
certainly the latest. It has been suggested that
the presentations in the courts of the Sethos I
temple at Abydos may be of intermediate date.
Even if it is not possible to put in order the
many examples, it is yet clear that the practice
of recording the substantial family was not
confined to the early years.

One must presume that at a certain point,
relatively early in the reign, when Ramesses had
already demonstrated his ability to father
children, some palace official decided to compile
a tally of princes and princesses so that there
would be a record not only of the names of the
royal children, but also of the order of birth,

especially as far as the boys were concerned.

One could imagine that as the years passed
and the proliferation of children continued, in
the confusion of the various establishments in
Piramesse and at Mi-wer, the harem-residence
near the Faiyum, it could have been possible to
obfuscate the succession, and in other ways to
cause problems within the ranks of wives,
concubines, domestic officials, and others who
might have personal purposes to pursue. Priority
within the lists would surely have gone to the
children of the principal wives; the offspring of
lesser wives or concubines, still being king's sons
or daughters "of his body," could scarcely be
ignored, even though the prospects of a son with
an unimportant mother could at the best have
been very modest.

Of the listed princes and princesses, only a small
number have identified mothers. Careful
examination of all the lists and other

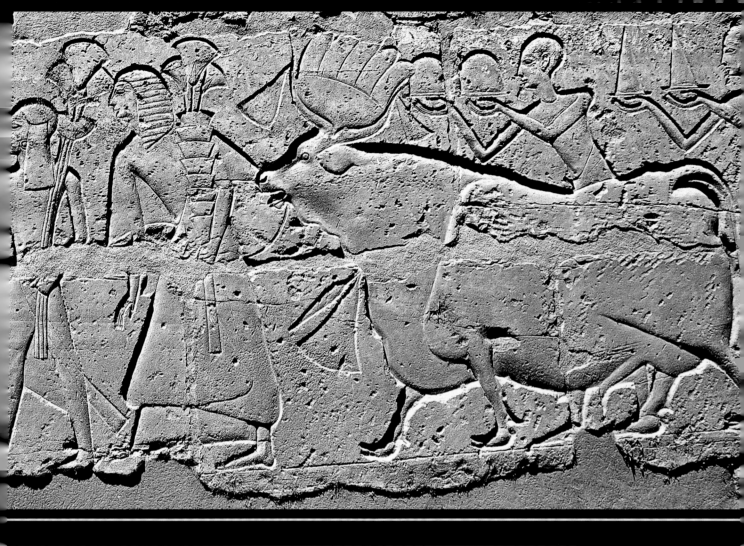

monumental sources shows that at the best computation, fifty male children can be named and perhaps about the same number of female children. It might be thought that for a king in good health with a multiplicity of wives and concubines, one hundred children over a period of perhaps forty-five years of mature activity represent rather an indifferent score – and could he not have possibly fathered children after the last temple list was carved?

It may well have been thought during Ramesses' reign that the lists established after about thirty-five or forty years were more than adequate to prove that he had produced sufficient progeny to ensure the dynastic line for a long future. It is for us, however, worth reflecting that in spite of his prolific brood, Ramesses was not in the end to sire a line to last, if not for eternity, then at least for a very long time. His successor, Merenptah, was

thirteenth in the list; he ruled about ten years. Then followed a period of about twenty-five years, a time of conflicting claims to the throne, of undistinguished squabbling, and a collapse of the legacy of Ramesses' long reign. The seeds of this collapse lay possibly in the length of Great Ramesses' time on the throne. So many of his proud, and probably capable, young sons were unable to wait for their turn to come, and their own sons equally lost any possible opportunities for succession. In a sense Ramesses by his longevity had exhausted his line. It is, if true, quite a paradox.

It is interesting to note that the lists of princes retain in the main a consistent order, established apparently by order of birth, and not by queens in a hierarchic manner. The lists of princesses, on the other hand, show some variations in order, although the damaged nature of many of the label texts impedes

identification in many cases. The lists are records of progeny, not amended from time to time as sons and daughters died. They are, one might say, statements of achievement, just as in a very different field were the repeated representations and accounts of military events like the battle of Qadesh. They should not, however, be dismissed or belittled because of their inflexibility. Apart from other considerations, they present a partial picture of the size and multiplicity of an ancient Egyptian royal family, of a kind not otherwise recorded. It may be that Ramesses sired more children than any of his predecessors, but it cannot be doubted that other long-living monarchs like Tuthmosis III and Amenophis III, to go back no farther than the Eighteenth Dynasty, surely had many sons and daughters by their various wives and concubines whose names have not survived in the records.

It would be expected that of the two sides of the royal progeny, the princes would have better expectations than the princesses; but that would be only partially true, as we shall discover. Initially, however, the princes should be scrutinized, and one of the first things to emerge is how little is known about most of them; they figure in the lists, and then no further records survive. Some undoubtedly had significant prospects, and would have known that there was a good chance that succession to the throne might come their way, if mortality intervened. Who among the first five or six sons would have conceived it possible that the throne would fall to son number thirteen (Merenptah)? To begin with, all sons would as part of their education be

can scarcely have been eight years old, while Khaemwese, son number four, may have been only five; they were the sons respectively of Nefertari and Isitnofret. They are shown taking part in the charge, each in his own chariot with attendants. Amonhiwonemef, whose name was shortly to be changed to Amonhikhopshef ('Amun is on his strong arm'), is even precociously given a speaking part: he exclaims, "I believed the sky had no limit, but the ruler [Ramesses, his father] has let us see its limit to the south. I rejoice, I am glad that my father smites his enemy; he makes his arm powerful against the Nine Bows [the traditional enemies of Pharaoh]."
The reality of any participation in battle by very

by the western side, and keep clear of the battle." Close by is shown Prehiwonemef, the third of Ramesses' sons, speeding in a chariot, and thought possibly to have been put in charge of the safety of his younger brothers in the camp. No other sons are shown in the battle scenes, or mentioned in the texts of the battle until the contest is over. Then a number of sons are represented, leading forward the most important foreign prisoners to be presented to the king: Horhiwonemef (son twelve), Meryre (son eleven), and Sety (son nine). Later, in Thebes, a further group of sons is shown taking part in the presentation of spoils of the campaign to the Theban gods: Amonhikhopshef (son one), Ramessu (son two),... (probably Prehiwonemef,

introduced to those fields of manly activity in which a prospective king would be expected to be competent, if not excel. Consequently, princes are shown as participating in military expeditions from the earliest years of Ramesses' reign, and even from before his accession. The skirmish in Nubia, which took place late in the reign of Sethos I, but is recorded in Ramesses' early rock-cut temple at Bayt al-Wali, seems to have been the first occasion for young princes to accompany their father on campaign. And young they surely were: his oldest son, there named Amonhiwonemef ('Amun is on his right hand')

young princes may be considered as presence on campaign rather than actual blooding in conflict. At the battle of Qadesh in Year 5, time had advanced and several of the royal children were by then in their teens and might have accompanied their father or other divisional commanders for further experience in a major conflict. In fact, in the documentation of the battle there is mention of the presence of members of the royal family in an episode recorded in the battle reliefs, where a messenger from the king comes to them, already installed in the royal camp, warning them "not to leave

son three), Khaemwese (son four),... (probably Monthuhikhopshef, son five),... (probably Nebenkharu, son six), Meryamun (son seven), Amonemuia (son eight),... (possibly Setpenre, son ten), Sety (son nine), Meryre (son eleven), and Merenptah (son thirteen). And so the young sons were introduced to warfare and the duties which followed a successful campaign. It is, of course, impossible to tell whether things happened as depicted, but at least indications are given of how matters should be carried forward on such occasions. So, in Year 7/8, when a quick raid into Canaan was needed to remind the local

rulers to whom they owed allegiance, one part of the force was put ostensibly under the command of Amonhikhopshef, who by now presumably was being seriously groomed as the heir to the throne in fact as well as in principle. A few years later, several princes took part in the Nubian foray against Irem; the names of Merenptah and Setemuia can be identified in the damaged record in the temple of Amara in Nubia. Setemuia may possibly be identified with Amonemuia, son number eight.

Short and inexplicit references to the princes scarcely make up a rounded picture of the developing lives and careers of Ramesses' sons. In the lists the first three are given senior military titles, which presumably they held by the time that the lists were carved. Amonhikhopshef, firstborn son and crown prince for many years, disappears from records after Year 20, to be replaced as crown prince by a son named Sethikhopshef, who does not appear in the lists as the obvious next candidate in line. It has plausibly been suggested that Sethikhopshef was in fact Amonhikhopshef renamed, the northern favored deity, Seth, replacing the southern imperial deity, Amun. This solution would therefore, not unreasonably, result in the extension of Ramesses' firstborn son as crown prince. By Year 30 the second son of the lists, Ramessu, had become crown prince, to be succeeded briefly by Khaemwese in Year 52. After a few years only Khaemwese had also died, to be followed as crown prince by Merenptah. In the lists the large brood of princes are individually called just "king's son of his body, his beloved." Where additional references to sons occur on other monuments – and there are singularly few – it emerges that some at least fulfilled functions by which they could serve the state, and presumably justify their privileged positions. Khaemwese, the great exception, we shall encounter shortly. Merenptah, who finally succeeded his father, acquired senior military rank and other administrative functions. Meryaten, who was sixteenth son, became 'chief of seers,' the high priest of Re at Heliopolis, a most important priestly office paralleling that of Khaemwese at Memphis.

566–567
Scene from the Corridor of the Bull at Abydos, completed in Ramesses' reign. The king, along with four deities, pulls tight a net trap full of birds, which he then presents to Amon-Re and Mut, accompanied by his son Amonhikhopshef.

568 bottom
On rediscovery, KV5 was
not thought to be of special interest.
Burton, who had first entered
the tomb in the 1820s, was unable to
penetrate more than a few
feet because of the rubble, as
hard as concrete, that blocked
the way.

The task facing archaeologist
Kent Weeks was formidable, but
the effort was well rewarded.
As more and more of the tomb was
cleared it became evident that it had
a most unusual plan, resulting from
its use for multiple burials.
There may yet be much more
to discover.

Mortality among the princes diminished their number as the years passed, and it seems that their father, mindful of their status and possibly of the pride he had shown in them while they still lived, chose to honor them in death by providing a communal tomb in the Valley of the Kings. For his chief wives he had arranged individual sepulchres in the Valley of the Queens, as we have seen. It was inconceivable that similar treatment might be offered to his dead sons, who had in their lifetimes fulfilled such functions in war and peace as had been required of them. There was no tradition of burial for royal children in the Valley of the Kings, but the prospect of the early deaths of many princes provided the opportunity for yet another demonstration of the king's grandiose pretensions. One should allow that a degree of paternal pride and sorrow might have entered into the plan for a multiple tomb. One might also, cynically, consider that Ramesses' own tomb, vast and of an original plan (now recently cleared, but still mostly inaccessible to the public) had probably been completed by the middle of his reign, allowing the squads of royal tomb-builders the opportunity to embark on another huge excavation in the Valley.

KV5 has, in this abbreviated designation, become one of the most interesting, if not sensational, rediscoveries in Egypt of recent years. KV stands for Kings' Valley, and 5 is the number assigned to the tomb by John Gardner Wilkinson in the 1820s. The tomb was first properly noted by James Burton, an early traveler and proto-Egyptologist, who was able to enter only part of the tomb, marking his entry with his name and the date 1825. It is not impossible that some earlier entry had taken place in the eighteenth century. These early investigations were not pursued because of the massive heaps of debris washed into the tomb by floods over the

millennia since antiquity. A new campaign to rediscover and clear the tomb was initiated some years ago by Kent Weeks, who has been for many years engaged in mapping the Theban Necropolis. What he has revealed in the subsequent years is a huge tomb with a network of corridors and chambers on several levels, thoroughly robbed, but still containing enough evidence in fragmentary reliefs and damaged tomb furniture to show that many of the sons of Ramesses II were laid to rest in it. The tomb entrance lies practically opposite that of Ramesses II's own tomb (KV7), and evidence suggests that it may have been an unfinished and unoccupied tomb of the Eighteenth Dynasty, taken over and exploited for the royal sons, prematurely deceased. From the evidence already collected it seems certain that some of the oldest and most important sons were buried in it, such as Amonhikhopshef and Ramessu. Quite possibly Amonhikhopshef was the first to be buried, and he is so named in the tomb, not as Sethikhopshef – the later name might not have been so welcome in the Theban context. This burial would have taken place by Year 30, an interment requiring special care and ceremony in view of this son's having been crown prince for almost three decades. Then perhaps was the opportunity taken to make use of the earlier unoccupied tomb, so close to the king's own prepared sepulchre, and later to develop it for multiple princely burials. The names of almost twenty princes have so far been retrieved on items of funerary equipment such as *shabti* figures, canopic jars, on wall inscriptions etc.

It may be many years before the full account of the tomb and its contents can be told, but the discoveries already made have provided unusual insights into the funerary activities of Ramesses' reign, and the apparent solicitude he extended to his sons in death as well as in life.

568–569
The tomb of Ramesses' sons (KV5), with Kent Weeks observing work on a mound of debris blocking part of the tomb. Since antiquity, great quantities of mud and rubble have been washed into the tomb by flash floods.

569 bottom
A corridor in tomb KV5 showing the entrances to some of the cell-like rooms, possibly the individual burial chambers for the sons of Ramesses II. The significance of much of the tomb plan remains to be discovered.

Two sons who were certainly not buried in KV5 were Khaemwese and Merenptah. The latter in due course qualified for his own individual royal tomb in the Valley of the Kings (KV8), and his career as king lies beyond the scope of this book. The career of Khaemwese, however, is quite another matter. He made his mark in no uncertain terms during his father's reign and achieved such a reputation that he became a figure of great wisdom and authority, about whom fantastical tales were told long after his death. There might be some justification in considering that Egypt would have fared extremely well had Ramesses not lived out his sixty-seven years of rule, but died when Khaemwese had advanced to be crown prince. All the surviving evidence points to Khaemwese's having been an exceptional person, an excellent administrator, a concerned conservator of ancient monuments, and a learned priestly official in Memphis who was undoubtedly entrusted with important responsibilities by his father.

Khaemwese was fourth son, the second born to Isitnofret. His birth predated Ramesses' accession to the throne, and in his early years Khaemwese was schooled, as were the other young sons, in the practices of warfare. As noted above, he is shown in the reliefs in the temple of Bayt al-Wali, in a chariot attending the skirmish conducted by his father in Nubia during the last years of Sethos I. He was also included among the sons shown making the presentation of offerings to the Theban deities after the battle of Qadesh. But the military life was not for him. In the listings of sons he receives no military titles; in fact, like most of the later sons, he is mostly described as "king's son of his body, his beloved"; only in the later list in the temple of Wadi al-Sabua (after Year 44) is he described also as "*sem*-priest of Ptah," a title he had held since he was about twenty years old. We shall never know how Khaemwese managed to extricate himself from a predictable military career. Was he no good in the arts of warfare, and in the handling of troops in battle? Was he simply more interested in intellectual matters? It would be good to think that some

570 bottom left
Mask of sheet gold found on a
mummy, possibly that of
Khaemwese, in the Serapeum at
Saqqara. Other objects associated
with this mummy and with the
burial of Apis bulls are inscribed for
Khaemwese (Louvre, 536).

570 bottom right
An amulet of falcon-headed Horus,
of lapis lazuli set in gold, inscribed
with Khaemwese's name. Found
on the body that is possibly
Khaemwese in the Serapeum
(Louvre, N.744).

570–571
Pectoral found on the masked
mummy in the Serapeum. Within a
pylon shape, the primary motif
consists of the vulture and uraeus
together with wings, with the
prenomen of Ramesses II above. Gold
with glass inlays (Louvre, N.767).

perspicacious palace official recognized his interest in religious and domestic matters and aversion to the military life, and recommended that he serve a kind of apprenticeship among the priesthood of Ptah at Memphis, under the tutelage of Huy, high priest of the god. In whatever way it happened, it turned out to be a good move, for Khaemwese remained in the service of the god throughout the remainder of his life.

The cult of Ptah at Memphis was one of the oldest and most respected of Egyptian religious institutions. Heliopolis (Re), Thebes (Amun), to a lesser extent Hermopolis (Thoth), and Memphis were in the New Kingdom the distinguished centers of religious influence, and of these Heliopolis and Memphis could claim the priority. Ptah was a creator god, an earth god, a god of intellectual status, always honored from at least the time of the unification of the two lands of Upper and Lower Egypt under Menes at the beginning of dynastic Egypt. His cult was highly respected, his influence essentially non-political, his authority awesome. Because of him, as much as for the location of the city, Memphis retained a position of pre-eminence among Egyptian cities, always a major center of administration and trade, well established long before upstart Thebes rose to a kind of prominence in the New Kingdom. Ramesses II, as we have seen, saw in Memphis and in its primal cult of Ptah a vital hinge on which his power could turn. The temple of Ptah was greatly extended in his reign, massively embellished with colossal sculptures. It is no surprise, therefore, that he saw the importance of maintaining the distinction of the city, and the need to ensure that its governance and administration should be overseen by officials who could be trusted. Who better, then, to establish in Memphis as his principal representative than his fourth son, whose inclination lay apparently in the direction of non-military activities?

As *sem*-priest of Ptah, Khaemwese was subordinate to the high priest of the god, but as time passed he became someone upon whom many of the principal duties of the priesthood devolved, and he seems to have acquired a position of very considerable authority in Memphis, which was not confined to religious matters. For example, there was the supervision of the subsidiary cult of the Apis bull, which was maintained within the complex of the Ptah temple. The Apis, the living animal of part of the essence of the god Ptah, was selected according to certain specified markings, and throughout its life lived in a special compound, pampered and worshiped. At death its body was mummified and taken for burial to the royal necropolis of Saqqara just to the west of Memphis. Up to the reign of Ramesses II, the mummified Apis bulls were buried individually at Saqqara. Khaemwese, however, introduced a new arrangement according to which the mummified bulls were buried in a catacomb of chambers served by a single chapel in which rituals could be celebrated. In the Late Period further catacombs were developed, and it is these that are now open to tourists and are known, erroneously, as the Serapeum. It is not impossible that Khaemwese himself was buried in or close to the bull catacomb which he initiated, but the evidence is very confusing. It is certain that he was buried at Saqqara and not in tomb KV5 in the Valley of the Kings. Unfortunately, the remains of a mummy and a coffin, which probably came from his Saqqara burial, do not appear to have survived after their discovery by Auguste Mariette in the mid-nineteenth century. The circumstances of their finding seem to have been unusual – not in a regular tomb – but there can be little doubt that he was buried in or near the bull burials at Saqqara. He had himself supervised the burials of dead Apis bulls in Years 16 and 30, and initiated the new catacomb with a burial in, possibly, Year 42/43. Burials in Years 55 and, again possibly, 65/66, were conducted by Merenptah. Khaemwese remained at Memphis for the rest of his life, undertaking many duties in addition to his priestly function. He established a remarkable reputation during his lifetime, laying the basis for a posthumous renown for sage wisdom. He has sometimes been described in modern times as an archaeologist, even the first Egyptologist, a title which he probably would have found very puzzling. The appellation has arisen out of the activities he undertook to examine and rehabilitate some of the older monuments in the Memphite Necropolis, particularly pyramids. The extent of his 'antiquarian' activities are not fully understood because the memorial texts he arranged to have carved into the facing stones of the rehabilitated pyramids have in many

cases been lost along with the stripping of the outer skins of fine limestone from the structures in medieval and modern times.

From the fragments of surviving texts it is clear that although the work on the pyramids was carried out in the name of Ramesses II, the credit for its implementation, and probably its inspiration, must go to Khaemwese: "Very greatly did the *sem*-priest, the king's son Khaemwese desire to renew the monuments of the kings of Upper and Lower Egypt, because of what they had done, and of their solidity, which was falling into decay." Such work was carried out at North and South Saqqara, at the sun temple of Neuserre at Abu Gurob, and possibly elsewhere. We may allow Khaemwese the credit. Concern for the monuments of past ages was something that the Egyptians liked to claim as the inspiration for such works. There is no doubt that when it suited their purpose, Egyptian kings and also provincial officials were pleased to look after what had been erected by their great predecessors. But they were equally ready to change or destroy the works of their ancestors if they wished to make use of sites occupied by older structures. It is perhaps a little excessive to consider what Khaemwese did with the pyramids as being antiquarian or archaeological as we would understand these words; the inscriptions he had carved on these monuments with their somewhat vainglorious claims, can hardly be thought of as early 'museum labels,' as they have sometimes been described. Nevertheless, there was merit to be gained from looking after the works of the past. In the general standard text of restoration, quoted above, Khaemwese could indeed claim credit for what had been done: for him the glory, for the dead, the honor.

Khaemwese remained ostensibly in the service of Ptah, the god of Memphis, until he died in Year 55 of Ramesses' reign. For a year or two only, at the very end, he became high priest of the god, but for the many years preceding, forty or more, he was content with the rather modest office of *sem*-priest. We must admire his order of priorities in that he did not require the highest Memphite priestly office until the very last years of his life. He was, after all, one of the senior sons of the king, although he did not achieve the position of crown prince until about Year 50. Nevertheless, his power only partially derived from his priestly position, and he

certainly acted in administrative matters as if the royal authority was there to support him. Memphis remained an important place, probably second only to Piramesse at that time, the place where coronations should be celebrated, and where jubilees should be proclaimed. As we have seen, the many jubilees celebrated by Ramesses II were acted out at Piramesse, but it also seems clear that Memphis remained the key place from which these notable events should be initiated. To that end Khaemwese served as the principal agent in proclaiming each jubilee throughout the land, and was initially involved in the proclamations of the first five jubilees, up to Year 42. He traveled the length of the country in making his proclamations; at least that is the impression gained from a consideration of the places where inscriptions record the proclamations. It must be thought possible, however, that in some of the more remote places where records have been found, like the island of Biga in the First Cataract, the task of proclaiming the jubilees may have been done in his name and not personally, as the records suggest.

572 top
Alabaster canopic jar made to contain the mummified entrails of an Apis bull buried in Year 16 or 30 of Ramesses II: "A monument made by the sem-priest and king's son Khaemwese." From Saqqara. (Louvre).

572 bottom
An amulet of Khaemwese found with the burial in the Serapeum. This tyet, *the "knot of Isis," could be used according to the* Book of the Dead *to invoke the power of Isis (Louvre, N.753).*

573
Sandstone kneeling statue of Khaemwese, found in the Karnak cachette in 1904. He is shown holding before him a shrine containing a figure of the god Ptah-Tatenen, usually associated with Memphis. (Cairo, JE 367220).

When Khaemwese died in Year 55
(c. 1225–1224 B.C.), he was succeeded
as crown prince by his younger brother
Merenptah, a son, like Khaemwese, of
Isitnofret, and originally number thirteen
in the tally of royal sons. Not a great deal
is known about his career up to that point.
He held senior military titles, and certainly
participated in some of the punitive
expeditions of the earlier years of Ramesses'
reign. He may have been too young to have
attended the Qadesh campaign, but he
subsequently made sure that his name was
included among those sons who made
presentations to the Theban gods after the
campaign. It is thought likely that even
before he became crown prince, Merenptah
had become Ramesses' right-hand man at
Piramesse, and that after Khaemwese's death
he moved easily into the position of prince-
regent for the remaining years of the reign.
He also took over some of his brother's
Memphite duties, including, as was
mentioned earlier, conducting the obsequies
for dead Apis bulls in Khaemwese's new bull
catacomb. Merenptah was probably in his
mid-fifties when he became crown prince,
and happily he had enough stamina to
survive until he could succeed his father.
By then he had ample experience of
government, and could move easily to
become the new living Horus, King of
Upper and Lower Egypt.

574 left
Shabti *figure for "the king's son, sem-*
priest Khaemwese." Here as usual he
is shown wearing the side-lock mostly
associated with childhood, but also
worn by the sem-priest and the
Iunmutef form of Horus.
(Louvre, N.461).

574 right
Sandstone shabti figure of Khaemwese
from the Serapeum at Saqqara. These
figures, whose duty was to work in
place of the named deceased in the
afterlife, usually carry agricultural
tools. This figure holds tyet *and* djed
symbols (Louvre, SH74).

575
Granite bust of King Merenptah
from his funerary temple at Thebes.
Thirteenth son of Ramesses II, he
became king when he was over 50.
On his shoulder can be seen his
prenomen as Pharaoh, Baenre-
Merenamun. (Cairo, JE 31414).

Generally speaking, daughters were not as well regarded in ancient Egypt as sons. Nevertheless, there is plenty of evidence to show that women were not without respect even in the families of unimportant persons. Women had their own particular spheres of activity in Egyptian life, and they were not thought to be of small importance, to be ignored. Daughters are usually included in representations of families on funerary stelae, and in the tombs of private officials. Their domestic functions were important, and their matrimonial prospects of considerable potential value. Within the royal family, women might play very important roles, as was seen in the last chapter: daughters could become the wives of kings, and could be given as wives to foreign rulers or princes as elements in the political game. None of these considerations were applicable to Egypt alone in the ancient world, but an impression is gained that in Egypt, women, especially princesses, were far more highly regarded than elsewhere. In the reign of Ramesses II his daughters did very well.

The lists of the daughters represented in the temples of Egypt and Nubia, parallel to those of the sons of Ramesses II, show that the recorded female progeny was about the same in number as the male progeny. As has been pointed out, there is not such strict consistency in the order of daughters as there is for the sons. But many of the lists are badly preserved, and the names of many princesses are lost or indecipherable. However, the order of the earliest born is

reasonably well established. The harem establishment of Mi-wer has been mentioned before as having been a place where a large part of Ramesses' collection of wives and concubines lived in relative domestic isolation, many miles away from the Delta Residence of Piramesse. No records have survived which give information about the division of wives and children between the two establishments, but it may be thought likely that at least one of Ramesses' great royal wives kept him company in Piramesse, and that within her entourage there might be secondary wives, concubines, and even some children, particularly boys. Most of the girl children would surely have been nurtured and educated at Mi-wer. But as they grew to maturity their royal mothers might consider bringing them to the attention of their father, if only for the self-interested reason of retaining influence. In this way the daughters of Nefertari, the first and most influential of the great royal wives, were promoted, and also those of Queen Isitnofret, whose own status apparently remained inferior to that of Nefertari until the latter's death.

Four daughters at least became royal wives, and were eventually honored with burials in the Valley of the Queens. The two most senior daughters – the firstborn girls of Isitnofret and Nefertari – were Bintanta and Merytamun. It is not certain which of these was first to become a great royal wife, but they were both described as such after Nefertari died, but before the death of Isitnofret. It is not possible to tell

which of them had precedence, but the recent discovery of colossal statues of Ramesses II and Merytamun at Akhmim, an important provincial capital, provides the suggestion that this queen might have acquired the priority which had certainly been possessed by her mother. Unexpected discoveries, however, are always open to extravagant interpretations, especially when evidence is exiguous. Two further princesses at least became great royal wives later in the reign, Nebt-tawy, who was fifth in the lists, and Hentmire, who does not occur in the lists, but is now thought certainly to be a daughter of Ramesses II, and not, perhaps, of his father King Sethos I. Nothing substantial is known about these two great royal wives, but both qualified for burial in the Valley of the Queens. A fifth daughter, Hent-tawy, number seven in the lists, presents a problem: she is nowhere recorded as a consort of her father, yet she was allowed a tomb in the Valley of the Queens. There clearly remains much to learn about the lives and fates of the daughters of Ramesses II. Those who were not married to their father, to a brother, or to a foreign prince were destined for the sheltered life of the harem. They could not expect personal tombs in the Valley of the Queens, or even the kind of communal tomb provided for Ramesses' sons, unless one such is still to be discovered. In life, however, they were condemned to a kind of benevolent incarceration; their royal genes could not be wasted on non-royal husbands.

576 left
Rosellini's strongly colored illustration of Bintanta offering a bouquet and a sistrum to the goddess Anukis (not shown); on one of the pillars in the great hall of Ramesses' temple at Abu Simbel.

576 right
Figure of Merytamun, daughter and wife of Ramesses II, from the first hall of her tomb in the Valley of the Queens. In this scene she stands in front of the djed pillar, symbol of stability. Illustration by Rosellini.

577
Figure of Nebt-tawy by Prisse d'Avennes, from her tomb in the Queens' Valley. In the tomb she is rightly described as "great royal wife," but here she is shown wearing a headdress associated with royal concubines.

THE KING'S REALM

Continuity in administration and confidence in its efficiency are the secure bases upon which good governance is founded. The politics of rulers and the intrigues within palaces might be unsettling or eccentric, but all will be well if there is a good civil service to keep the course of the ship of state steady. In ancient Egypt, long periods of untroubled government led to remarkable administrative confidence and regularity.

A highly efficient system of internal bureaucracy was developed during the Eighteenth Dynasty, which provided the Pharaoh with a settled base upon which he could develop his particular policies, especially in regard to foreign affairs. The divine ruler was unquestionably the fount of authority, and the indisputable master of the fates of his people; but the management of affairs lay under the control of those officials who were appointed expressly to carry out the will of the ruler. There is much evidence to show that in ancient Egypt the tentacles of administration embraced every activity in the land, and that few

ordinary Egyptians could live lives free from the interference of officials. Up until the Middle Kingdom (c. 1800 B.C.), local affairs were in the hands of noble provincial families, – nomarchs – who were mostly hereditary and ruled the provinces, or nomes, like minor princelings. Their power was greatest in the nomes far from the royal residence and capital, which was usually in the region of Memphis. The fairly independent administrations of the nomarchs were abolished during the Twelfth Dynasty, and a more centralized regime developed, in which the highest official in the land, usually called the vizier, acted as the king's representative in most internal matters. The power of the vizier, established at that time, formed the core around which was constructed the highly developed system of officers and senior officials, which evolved during the Eighteenth Dynasty.

It was possibly the existence of this powerful, well-established administration, which prevented the country from falling utterly apart during the reign of Akhenaten – the Amarna Period. Some senior officials migrated from Thebes to Amarna

and maintained some general control over the country. In the north of the land, administration based in Memphis seems to have been less affected, being untainted in the eyes of the Atenist regime by the dire influence of the Theban deities and their priesthoods. Senior officials like Horemheb were well placed in Memphis to avoid the greatest and most damaging effects of the rule of the Aten, and were able to appreciate the possibility of a return to what could be called 'normality' when Akhenaten might die. And so it seems to have happened. After the demise of Akhenaten and his immediate successors, it remained for Horemheb as king to rebuild the Egyptian administration and restore the kind of internal bureaucracy that had proved so successful before Akhenaten's brief revolution. One may conjecture that the essential framework had survived the intervening period, and that with the help of senior officials, Horemheb, and later Sethos I, were able to re-establish the excellent system, which had made Egypt such an efficiently run country.

By the time of Ramesses' accession, the machine of state was running smoothly, and it appears to have been the case that for the whole of his long reign there were no serious problems in the system. It is, of course, hazardous to make such a claim, because it was not in the nature of official Egyptian inscriptions to draw attention to the failings of the system. It was usually left to a succeeding regime to point out the weaknesses of a preceding period in order to demonstrate the efficiency and success of what was achieved under new management. In the case of Ramesses II, however, the emphasis in the great Abydos dedicatory text is on completion, on carrying to a successful conclusion the works and projects initiated in his father's relatively short reign. To this end there is an emphasis on continuity, and no suggestion of substantial change. As was to be expected, the administration would be supervised from the top by the two viziers, of South and North – Theban and Memphite, the latter to become based subsequently at Piramesse. The southern viziers are better documented than those of the north, and in particular Paser, who had received his appointment under Sethos, serving him for about

five years before the new king ascended the throne. Paser then continued in office for perhaps another twenty-five years. He seems to have been an exemplary chief of staff for his sovereign, and apparently viewed his role in the tradition of the great viziers of the Eighteenth Dynasty, like Rekhmire and Ramose. A strong indication of his conservative approach to the exercise of his office may be found in the tomb he constructed in the Theban Necropolis, begun under Sethos and completed under Ramesses.

Paser's family was well established in Thebes, although in origin it probably came from the north. His father, Nebnetjeru, was high priest of Amun, and his mother, Merytre, was head of the harem of Amun. He belonged therefore to the highest level of Theban officialdom, and his elevation to the position of vizier bears the stamp of strong family tradition, if not of nepotism. He did not disappoint; and his tomb, richly decorated with painted reliefs now greatly damaged, testifies to his importance and to his attachment to the status quo. Among the texts in the great columned transverse hall of the tomb chapel, completed and probably decorated during

the reign of Sethos, are the sad remains of a composition outlining the duties of the vizier. It is an ancient text; scholars still argue about the date of its composition. It occurs in a number of Eighteenth- Dynasty vizier tombs, and it is now thought that it was most probably composed early in that dynasty. There are, however, good grounds for considering it of earlier date, possibly of the late Middle Kingdom (c. 1750 B.C.), when successive viziers were exceptionally powerful, maintaining some stability for a royal regime of very uncertain power. This debate over composition need not concern us in considering the importance of this text to the mind of Paser. For him it clearly represented the traditional statement of the vizier's duties, written down a long time ago; it scarcely would have mattered if it were three hundred or five hundred years earlier. It was the text found in the tombs of the great Eighteenth Dynasty viziers, and that fact would have been enough to set the seal of authority on it.

All aspects of administration were placed under the control of the vizier, and a few extracts from the text may give the flavor of the whole.

Although the Paser version is only very partially preserved, it appears to have followed closely the version found in, for example, the tomb of Rekhmire, the great vizier of King Tuthmosis III. It is an impersonal document, not aimed specifically at any named vizier. The composition starts with instructions on how the vizier should dress and present himself in his hall:

"The sealing of the strong-rooms... should be reported to him... . The condition of fortresses of the Delta and the North should be reported to him... . He should greet the lord [the king]... every day when the affairs of the Two Lands have been reported to him... . If any agent whom the vizier may send on a mission to any official... let him not be enticed, and let him not be bullied by an official... . Anybody who petitions him about lands, the vizier should order him to appear before him... . All conveyances [of property] should be brought to him, and it is he who shall seal them... . It is he who dispatches any courier and any expedition of the king's house. It is he who appoints from the magistrates those who are to be the administrators of the North, the South, the Head of the South [Southern Upper Egypt]... . It is he who should arrange the mobilization of troops and their movement in the suite of the Lord when he travels downstream and upstream [i.e., within Egypt]... . It is he who should dispatch regional officers to construct dykes throughout the whole land... . Every plea should be reported to him... . Nome records should be lodged in his office for the hearing of cases concerning any land... . It is he who should make every public proclamation and hear every complaint... . It is he who should hear all pleas... ."

This poorly organized but very comprehensive document provides a kind of blueprint of the vizier's role in Egyptian administration. It is by no means an accurate outline of the program of any particular vizier, but perhaps a reminder of the all-embracing nature of his responsibilities. It was the kind of reminder, which an earnest official might keep on his desk, but not necessarily follow or even read from time to time. Having it in one's tomb was just an indication of being committed in principle to the best practices of the past. Nevertheless, it would not be wrong to see in this document and in its placement in Paser's tomb the idea that he accepted the blanket responsibility for Egypt's internal administration in all its complexities. The full text is amazingly detailed in its specification of the vizier's duties, of which the extracts given above provide just a flavor, and it may be properly deduced that most of the duties were carried out by subordinates in the vizier's office in Thebes or Memphis and by local officials in the provincial capitals. But the vizier was in the end responsible and answerable to the king alone.

It must be supposed that the vizier's office was daily bombarded with reports, pleas, complaints, and every kind of document. Egyptians were much given to putting things 'on paper,' but it is only occasionally that some glimpses may be obtained into the complexity and abundance of official documentation. A letter, a copy of which is preserved on a limestone flake from Thebes, sent by a scribe called Mose – a person of no real importance – to Paser, declares that he (Mose) is fulfilling all the duties assigned to him, mentioning in particular certain agricultural matters of a very local nature. Another ostracon copy of a letter was written by the scribe Nebre to Paser reporting the condition of the workmen's village at Dayr al-Madina: "Everything is in order, all the walls are in good shape, and all the workmen are receiving everything that is owed to them." Such trivialities no doubt made up the bulk of the incoming submissions to the vizier. There is little to suggest that Egypt was anything other than well administered during Paser's long tenure of the viziership.

Ramesses II

582 top
Gold kiosk-shaped pectoral with faience and stone inlays, from the Serapeum. The lapis lazuli heart scarab has a text invoking the heart of Paser to help him. The scarab is supported by Isis and Nephthys (Louvre, N762).

583 top
The lapis lazuli reverse of the gold pendant. The texts are from the Book of the Dead, that on the scarab being the special text to invoke his heart to act for him in judgment. From an Apis burial in the Serapeum.

583 bottom
Gold-faced pendant inscribed with the name and title of the vizier Paser. It is pylon-shaped and has figures of the goddesses Isis and Neith worshiping a large lapis lazuli scarab (Louvre, N762).

Paser was succeeded as vizier by Khay before Year 30, possibly as early as Year 25. He inherited an administration, which seems to have remained highly efficient throughout Paser's term, and there is little evidence to suggest that matters deteriorated subsequently. One area in which Khay acquired additional responsibilities was that of organizing the royal jubilees. Up until the fifth jubilee, in Year 42/43, Khay was commissioned to proclaim the celebrations along with Khaemwese, and for the sixth jubilee he seems to have been the sole proclaimer. It may further be assumed that his jubilee duties were not restricted to proclamation. It is interesting to note that in all cases Khay is charged to carry out the duty of proclamation in the South and in the North, and one must speculate whether he therefore was for a time acting as vizier for the whole country. One small fragment, possibly from his Theban tomb, describes him as "mayor and vizier of the South and the North." It could be the case, however, that the authority of the Theban vizier subsumed that of the northern vizier as well. It would have been very surprising if the northern vizier had no part to play in successive *sed* festivals (jubilees).

The names of a number of northern viziers during the reign of Ramesses II are known, but unfortunately exact dates for their tenures of office cannot be established with any certainty. Two had the same name, Prahotpe or Rahotpe, of whom the second may have been the last to serve Ramesses in his long reign. One stemmed from Abydos and the other from Heracleopolis in Middle Egypt, and they may have been distantly related. There remains much confusion in the discrimination between these two senior officials, largely because the surviving documentation is not sufficiently detailed to solve the problems of identification. One man was buried at Sedment, near Heracleopolis, the other possibly at Saqqara. The earlier in office was serving Ramesses II in Year 42; the second, as stated above, served later, but probably not directly after the first. A great granite stela found at Saqqara shows a vizier named Rahotpe making adoration to Osiris and the Apis on one side, and Anubis and Ptah on the other. The texts are primarily eulogistic in respect of the vizier, but

some sentences give an idea of how he considered his duties. Among other titles and epithets, he describes himself as "judge of the Two Lands, shield of the sovereign... greatest steward of the Lord in the Hall of Jubilees, who issues orders to everyone, chief of works, overseer of crafts, supervisor of the laws of the Good God in the Hall of Justice, spokesman of the King of Upper Egypt, herald of the King of Lower Egypt... who works out all the revenues in the whole land." These claims are no doubt excessive, and there is much more, Rahotpe asserting that he holds most of the senior religious appointments in the land. Overstating the case was not uncommon for Egyptian officials at all levels in the civil and religious fields. Presumably, if you were as grand as Rahotpe (Prahotpe), you could claim to be almost anything, provided that it was done in the name of the king.

While the stability of the king's realm depended to a great extent on the efficiency of the administration of the country, the continuation of stability was substantially secured by the prosperity of the country and the successful

system of taxation by which the financing of the whole could be maintained. The wealth of Egypt derived not so much from foreign tribute or the plunder acquired by warfare as from agriculture. A prosperous Egypt was an Egypt in which the progression of the seasons through the year was successfully exploited by good land management and by the complex system of taxation – by no means fully understood – which maximized the return of wealth to central treasuries. The good exploitation of the land was in turn dependent on the regular behavior of the river Nile, and on the widespread system of canals and dykes which controlled flooding and conserved water after the annual Nile flood. By the time of Ramesses' reign, the Egyptian state bureaucracy had many hundreds of years' experience in managing the land, and a clear appreciation of the importance of river and land management. Well-trained officials could estimate the effects of the annual flood, predict with some accuracy the outcome of harvests, and in consequence make fairly reliable assessments of what should be paid in taxes. It need not be supposed that the system was free

from abuse; there would always be officials who would take personal advantage of their privileged positions. A scribal exercise paints a miserable picture of the vulnerable peasant, whose crops have been devastated by snakes, hippopotamuses, mice, locusts, even cattle. Sparrows have assisted, and thieves have stolen cattle: "Then the scribe has landed at the riverbank, and sets about assessing the harvest tax; his assistants carry staves and palm rods. They say, 'Give corn,' although there isn't any. He is beaten severely, tied up and thrown into the well. His wife is bound and his children put in manacles."

As this is part of a scribal exercise, it ends with a professional encouragement: "A scribe, on the other hand, is the controller of everything.

He who writes is not taxed; he has nothing to pay." This, no doubt, was a common experience for the defenseless peasant, but it should not have been so, and would most surely have been deplored by the vizier had he known about such abuse.

Blind eyes may well have been turned, for the general good of the economy of the country.

584–585
The timeless activities of Egyptian agriculture are best shown in Eighteenth Dynasty tombs. Here, episodes in the barley harvest: treading the grain, winnowing, and recording the results. From the Theban tomb of Menna.

585 top right
Stela of the vizier Rahotpe, who may have been buried at Saqqara. He is shown, above, worshiping Osiris and the living Apis. The text below includes a self-justification. On the reverse, a text about the viziership (Cairo, JE 48845).

Closer to the system were the senior treasury officials, who supervised at the highest level the operation of the system, although they too may have been somewhat distant from what happened in the remote corners of the land. In the absence of general texts specifying the duties and outlining the activities of these and other officials, one can only deduce from occasional documents the magnitude of the responsibilities they carried. Equally, only rarely can one catch a glimpse of the extent of the wealth of the land, and of the immensely rich estates belonging to the great religious establishments throughout Egypt. A rare, but very extensive document of the Twentieth Dynasty provides astounding details of temple holdings in the reign of Ramesses III. Nothing of this kind has survived from Ramesses II's reign, but one copy of a letter on a Theban limestone ostracon gives some indication of the position in the earlier reign. It is a letter from the chief treasury official, the overseer of treasuries, Panehsy, addressed to Hori, a priest of Amun in the Southern City (Thebes). Panehsy writes from the north, giving a situation report on the land and other holdings of the great Theban temple situated in the Delta, and particularly specifying the people employed on the estates of Amun, along with their families. He states that he is submitting a list "of every man according to his occupation, together with their wives and children." Unfortunately only fragmentary pieces of information can be extracted from the central text, which includes a summary of the information collected. There are, for example,

8,760 farmers, 13,080 goatherds, 22,530 men in charge of fowl, 3,920 donkey-men, and so on. Even without precise details, it is still possible to comprehend the scale to which the land of Egypt was closely administered at the time. In a sense Egypt was easy to control; all the land that mattered agriculturally – and therefore fiscally – was flat, for the most part easily accessible from the Nile or the major waterways in the Delta. Farmers could not disappear into mountain valleys to hide from prying officials; they could not easily escape the long arm of the scribe and his bailiffs, who probably took some pleasure in enforcing the law and extracting at the same time something for themselves to pocket.

A striking feature of Egyptian administration in general is the theoretical ease with which quite humble petitioners were able to gain access to high authority when they needed to pursue matters of personal concern. The approach of the humble to the great has, it seems, always been an attractive characteristic of civil life in the Near East. While the law and its exercise by petty officials has rarely seemed to be on the side of the small individual, there always appeared to be the possibility of personal petition, even to an official as high as the vizier. So it would seem to be from a reading of the duties of the vizier, and so it would seem to have been from the few documents, which concern complaints addressed directly to high officials. No text throws such light on the workings of the Egyptian legal administration in the New Kingdom as that written up in his tomb by the treasury scribe in

the temple of Ptah, called Mose.

The text contains the details of a case involving Mose's family and the ownership of a piece of land; the matter had its origins as early as the reign of King Amosis, first of the Eighteenth Dynasty rulers, approximately three hundred years before the reign of Ramesses II. A ship's captain, Neshi, was granted land in the region of Memphis by King Amosis as a reward for services rendered during the war of liberation, which saw the expulsion of the upstart Hyksos from Egypt and the establishment of the Eighteenth Dynasty and what is now called the New Kingdom. The piece of land was to be kept as a unit and not divided by inheritance, and it seems that no problems arose to disturb this arrangement until the reign of Horemheb at the end of the Eighteenth Dynasty. After the death of the contemporary administrator of the estate, the lady Sheritre, legal proceedings allowed a division of the land between a daughter, Werenro, and her brothers and sisters. For the time being, Werenro was to administer the estate, still as a unit, on behalf of her siblings. This decision was challenged by a younger sister, who succeeded in having a declaration made so that each child should have its own share. This decision in turn was challenged by Werenro and her son Huy, and it seems that without the matter being properly settled, Huy continued to cultivate the land as a unit until he died. His widow, Nubnofret, was then evicted from the land by an individual named Khay, whose position seems to have been to act as an agent for other members of the family. In Year 18 of Ramesses II, Nubnofret returned to the

courts, bringing her case before the vizier in Heliopolis and calling for an examination of Treasury records to prove that she was indeed a descendant of Neshi and that her husband had regularly paid his taxes on the land and its produce. The appropriate documents were collected from central archives in Piramesse and produced in court for scrutiny. They did not, however, substantiate Nubnofret's claims, and she lost the case. It was shown that Huy's tax payments were not recorded, and that Nubnofret was not mentioned in the documents. So she remained evicted, and the land was parceled out to the so-called legitimate descendants of Neshi. The matter did not end there. In due course Mose, the son of Huy and Nubnofret, grew up and reopened the case, claiming that Khay had managed to have the documents from Piramesse falsified, in collusion no doubt with the officials who had collected them from the archives. These officials, probably at the suggestion of Khay, could see something to their own advantage in organizing this deception. Mose changed the direction of his and his mother's defense, relying now on the evidence of witnesses who established beyond argument that Huy had cultivated the land, paid his taxes, and was a legitimate descendant of Neshi. At last, judgment was made in favor of Huy's widow and son, and Khay was declared to be in the wrong. From Mose's point of view justice at last had been done, and the inclusion of the account of the extended affair, along with copies of some supporting documents, in the texts in his tomb serves to record his triumph and perhaps his excessively self-satisfied attitude.

In this tangled and long drawn-out matter, it is the side of Mose and his mother that is presented in the tomb. One may wonder whether it all stopped there. Perhaps other descendants of Neshi returned to the courts at a later date; they too would have had reason to feel aggrieved at having been denied part of Neshi's inheritance. As is so often the case, one's sympathies naturally lie on the side of the one who is the last to present the matter, namely Mose. There is now no way of discovering the ultimate outcome; but there is no reason to believe implicitly in Mose's statement of the case. Nevertheless, the contents of the texts in Mose's tomb throw light on many aspects of Egyptian law and administration during the New Kingdom. It can be seen that resort to law, even to the court of the vizier, was something within the capability of fairly ordinary people. In law, Egyptian women were treated equally with men in matters of land tenure and inheritance. It was possible to reopen a case if new evidence could be produced. Records existed and were preserved in central archives, in this case at Piramesse, the Delta capital of Ramesses II. The court, presided over apparently by the vizier himself, was prepared to take time over reaching a decision, and very ready to summon documentation for inspection. Nothing was arbitrary. The impression is gained of a system, which worked not just to the advantage of the bureaucracy and the administration, but even for the interests of the individual. It would be good to believe that the impression is close to the truth.

587
Kneeling statue of Panehsy, royal scribe and chief of the treasury under Ramesses II; he holds a shrine with Osiris, Isis, and Horus. He was the official responsible for the success of the Egyptian economy (British Museum, EA 1377).

The secret of the success of the ancient Egyptian system of administration was to a great extent the efficiency of the scribal class. "Be a scribe!" was surely the call that most Egyptian mothers with pretensions for improvement would repeat again and again to their sons. To be a scribe was to be in effect a civil servant; it was a safe and steady calling, and one that brought with it all kinds of advantages. It was, moreover, highly respectable as a profession, to such an extent that no great person in the land objected to being called a scribe. Among other things, being a scribe implied being literate, being able to write, whether in hieroglyphs or in the cursive hieratic script, the form used for most writing on papyrus. It also involved the ability to read, and that meant not just knowing how to interpret the great inscriptions on the mighty buildings and monuments throughout the land, but also the capacity to scrutinize documents, read letters, and comprehend calculations. Literacy was a very valuable tool. A scribe could control the papers, interpret the documents, check the accounts, or simply act as an intermediary between individuals who were not literate. It was a serious matter to be a scribe, and while the texts emphasize his responsibilities and praise his impartiality, there is no reason to believe that some scribes might find it convenient on occasion to bend the rules, or engage in a little falsification.

Some of the student exercises contain the elements of accepted practice and the outlines of the scribal ethic. Such texts were written out by student scribes and were written wholly from the scribal point of view. Nevertheless, it is possible to consider them as proper statements of how the profession and practices of scribes were estimated in the Nineteenth Dynasty. On training:

"I have placed you in the room of instruction together with the children of magistrates, to inform and teach you about that promising profession. Let me tell you how the scribe goes on, saying, 'Jump to your place! Write in front of your fellows! Tidy your clothes and see to your sandals!' You should bring your book every day with good intent; do not be idle... . Do your sums quietly, without noise from your mouth being heard. Write with your hand, read with your mouth, and seek advice. Don't be tired, don't waste time idly, or look out for your limbs! Follow the ways of your teacher, and listen to what he has to say. Be a scribe!"

So if the student paid attention and became a good scribe, his future would be good. If he came from a scribal family, he would almost certainly find a good position, possibly even following precisely in his father's footsteps. Otherwise patronage or nepotism might help. In such matters the ancient Egyptian would have seen no impropriety. And the advantages of being a scribe were not insignificant: "It saves you from hard work and protects you from all kinds of manual labor. You don't have to carry the hoe and the mattock, and therefore, no basket. It separates you from having to pull on the oar, and spares you afflictions, for you are not subject to many lords and many masters." The writer then lists a great many professions and trades which are essentially disagreeable: the child put to be a soldier, the old man, a farmer, the cripple, a doorkeeper, the blind man to look after cattle. Even the priest has a tough time, endlessly engaged in religious services and soaking himself in water three times a day, in winter and summer, in rain or shine. The baker is endlessly baking bread, his head right in the oven, while his son hangs onto his feet – and if the son lets go, he falls right into the oven. And so the writer comes to the obvious conclusion: "But the scribe, he is way ahead of every kind of labor in this world."

In addition to escaping hard work and avoiding paying taxes, the scribe had the real possibility of position and wealth in Egyptian society. He could become the trusted official of the king, with power to open treasuries and granaries, to issue the necessary offerings on days of festival, "dressed in fine clothes, accompanied by horses, and with [his] own boat on the Nile." He might have assistants, a splendid house, a powerful position, and all the king's gifts. Who would be a soldier? All the evidence points to scribal advantages, but, as we noted, all the evidence comes from texts written and probably composed by scribes. What was the other side of the coin? Were scribes regarded with respect by illiterate Egyptians? Were they seen to be the officers of a repressive, centralized state who could exploit the system to their own advantage? We shall probably never know, but it is hard to believe that scribes – that is, civil servants – were always objects of affection and respect in ancient Egypt. They were certainly not greeted with enthusiasm in the countryside, as we have seen; and the likelihood is that those who were in a position to do favors, or even just be helpful, would expect reciprocal favors. There is nothing to suggest that the official was not as venal in antiquity as he may be today in certain societies.

589 top
This Fifth Dynasty unnamed sculpture perfectly expresses the qualities expected in the Egyptian scribe. Holding his papyrus on his tightened kilt, he radiates confidence, but avoids the smugness of his Ramesside successors (Cairo, JE 30273).

589 bottom
Two New Kingdom scribes bend earnestly over their open papyrus sheets, writing accounts for their superiors. Scribes formed the backbone of the ancient Egyptian civil service, and enjoyed great privileges as a result.

The king's realm, strictly speaking, was just the land of Egypt, the Nile Valley from Elephantine (Aswan) in the south to the Mediterranean Sea in the north. It was Upper and Lower Egypt, each part organized into provinces, or nomes. Throughout dynastic history no serious attempt was made to change these limits, to extend the land area of Egypt, to incorporate, for example, the territories in Asia, which became subservient to the Egyptian king from time to time, and often for long periods. Such lands were not Egypt as it was conceived by the ancient Egyptians themselves; the inhabitants of these lands could never be Egyptians. One region, however, was specially regarded, and during the New Kingdom closely administered, and treated almost as if it were part of the mother territory of Egypt.

This was Nubia, the land of Kush, the extension of Egypt southward along the course of the river Nile, the river which provided a thread of unity to the relationship. Nubia was a source of mineral wealth, a home to tribes, which could be hostile, and the conduit for exotic products brought by caravan from equatorial Africa, an account of which was given earlier in this book. Nubia had always been a land of concern and interest to the Egyptians. It was deeply penetrated by the kings of the Twelfth Dynasty, and strong fortresses were constructed along the Nile, especially in the region of the Second Cataract. Nubia was lost to Egypt in the troubled time called the Second Intermediate Period (c.1750–1650 B.C.), but reoccupied by the forces of the kings of the Eighteenth Dynasty. As formerly, no move was made to incorporate the region into the land of Egypt proper, the king's realm; but it was seen to have a much closer relationship to Egypt than any of the other occupied lands in the Near East. It was seen to belong within the ambit of the Egyptian crown, and was consequently more closely administered than other subject countries. The head of the Nubian bureaucracy was called the 'king's son of Kush,' and often 'overseer of the southern deserts,' 'fan-bearer on the right of the king,' and 'king's envoy to every foreign land.' He was not of royal blood, and the title of king's son was honorific. This high dignitary, virtual ruler of Nubia, is now usually called the viceroy of Kush, and during the reign of Ramesses II a series of apparently very active and efficient viceroys served the king's interests in this extension of his realm.

Apart from the day-to-day administration of Nubia, the supervision of the collection of tribute, the maintenance of security, and the development of Egyptian settlements throughout the region, the viceroys were deeply involved in the promotion of the royal image, especially through the construction of the Nubian temples, in which, as we have seen, the divine aspect of the king was promoted. The first viceroy of the reign was Iuny; he had been appointed toward the end of the reign of Sethos I, when Ramesses was already effectively co-regent. He was responsible for the commencement of the work at Abu Simbel, no doubt on the instruction of the king, but he did not remain in office to see the completion of the work. This responsibility fell to his successor, Hekanakhte, who supervised the arrangements for the visit to Nubia by Ramesses and Queen Nefertari in about Year 24. Not long afterward Hekanakhte was followed by a new viceroy named Paser, in no way related to the vizier Paser, whose career was outlined earlier in this chapter. The viceroy Paser had the misfortune of being in office when the disastrous earthquake struck Abu Simbel in Year 31 or 32, inflicting huge damage, some of the results of which may still be observed today in the fallen colossal head and the ancient repairs to statues and pillars within and outside the great temple. As mentioned earlier in this volume, it is not known whether Ramesses ever heard about this disaster, although it is hard to believe that Paser could have successfully hushed it up. He did retain his office until about Year 34, a few years after the earthquake, using the time to repair at least some of the damage. It is not impossible,

591
Lid of the granite sarcophagus of Setau,
Viceroy of Kush, with a distinctive,
but strangely naive, head. Probably from his
Theban tomb. The inscription invokes the
goddess Nut as protectress
(British Museum, EA 78).

however, that the Abu Simbel disaster prompted his replacement. Among the inscriptions set up by Paser at Abu Simbel, one placed between the two temples, contains a 'dialogue' with the king, which could be considered rather piquant in the context of the great temple and the earthquake. Ramesses II greets his viceroy "You are a wholly trustworthy person, useful to his lord." Paser obsequiously answers, "One does everything as you have stated, O Horus, beloved of Ma'at!" He might have added, "It wasn't my fault that your statue fell down."

By Year 34 Paser had been replaced by Huy, a senior military officer who had been part of the company charged with escorting the Hittite princess from her homeland to Piramesse and marriage to Ramesses. It must be presumed that the successful outcome of the journey and the subsequent marriage commended Huy to Ramesses. It was surely so, and Huy's elevation to the high status of viceroy of Kush represented his reward. Paser, it seems, was just relieved of his office. Sadly we rarely know how careers finished, or what were the subsequent fates of displaced officials. It is not surprising that a copy of the great marriage inscription celebrating the Hittite-Egyptian matrimonial alliance was placed in the great temple at Abu Simbel. It was a text which served as a kind of testimonial for Huy. His tenure of office did not last long.

By Year 38 he was followed by Setau, a man of great energy who remained viceroy almost until the end of Ramesses' reign – perhaps a term of twenty-five years – and was then buried in a large, but now badly damaged, tomb in the Theban Necropolis. He may or may not have died in office. Setau was generous in leaving ample records of his activities in Nubia during his tenure, and the most informative of these memorials is a large stela which was set up in the temple of Wadi al-Sabua – one of more than a dozen inscriptions and statues – a temple for the construction of which he was largely responsible. If we can pick out details of his career, which

seem to be trustworthy, it emerges that he rose from relatively modest beginnings and owed his rise to mighty office to his own abilities and diligence. He makes no mention of his parentage (known, however, to have been Siwadjyt and Nefertmut), but claims to have been brought up as a ward in the royal household. He distinguished himself as a young scribe and was in due course appointed chief scribe of the vizier. In this position he was responsible for assessing taxes throughout the land, and he performed this task so well that all the national granaries were bursting with grain. He was then appointed by the king to be chief steward of the god Amun, in which position he again did so well that his abilities were recognized by the King, and he was made viceroy of Kush. As such, he claimed, "I collected all the revenues of this land of Kush twice over.

I made the tribute of this land of Kush like the sand of the shore; no other viceroy of Kush has ever achieved so much since the time of the God." He was successful as a military commander, organized the building of the temple at Wadi al-Sabua, and restored all the temples in Nubia which had fallen into ruin, "in the great name of His Majesty, his name carved on them for ever." By his own estimation, Setau had been a good choice for viceroy. Much of what he says about his career may be accepted, and it suggests that merit and hard work, and probably close attention to those matters which would be noted especially by the king, would secure preferment. His initial piece of luck was to have been brought up at court, where he would have been but one of many who enjoyed such a privileged beginning. His career certainly bears out the view that talent could bring success in the bureaucracy of ancient Egypt. It also bears out the frequently maintained assertion that to be a scribe could be the making of a man. On such principles was the administration of Egypt based, and in their execution was the success of the King's realm established during the reign of Ramesses II.

Ramesses II

THE KING AND THE GODS
IN LIFE AND DEATH

Ancient Egypt is generally thought of as having a culture dominated by religion, and the land of Egypt as being a place of temples and tombs. For many people the attraction of Egypt lies in these temples and tombs, and a visit to the country tends to emphasize this religious obsession. Even when an opportunity occurs to visit some ostensibly non-religious site, the visitor's attention is commonly diverted from secular considerations to religious reflections. A prime case is Amarna in Middle Egypt, the site of Akhenaten's 'new city,' Akhetaten. There is more to see at Amarna than a brief visit may reveal, but it is perhaps inevitable that the remains of Akhenaten's religious foundations, the unfinished tombs of his great officials, and the remote and evocative tomb of the king himself, should monopolize attention. And the talk and chat will mostly be about Akhenaten's religious revolution and the significance of the place in this respect. Someone may even read out parts of the great hymn to the Aten, and everyone will stand around solemnly, as if at a burial or important memorial

occasion. There then will rarely be time for a wander about the city, to contemplate the remains of houses, important villas, industrial areas. For people lived in Amarna and spent their days mostly ignoring the religious aspects of life at the highest level. The case is rather less clear when a visit is made to the workmen's village – 'the Place of Truth' – at Dayr al-Madina, where for four hundred years the craftsmen, scribes, and artisans who worked on the royal tombs lived, and for whom a mass of documentation has survived. It is even more evocative to walk through the well-marked lanes of the village, to enter the stone houses, the names of whose owners are in some cases known. Here, as we shall hear later, lived people whose careers in some cases are better known than those of the great officials of Ramesses' reign. But the visitor today is rarely told about the village and its ways of living; generally some of the small but well-preserved tombs of the workmen are shown and a visit made to the small temple near the village, which has nothing much to do with the village. Then it will be off to

another group of tombs in the Theban Necropolis, or to a temple, perhaps the splendidly preserved mortuary temple of Ramesses III at Medinet Habu, or the Ramesseum, the great mortuary foundation of Ramesses II, not as well preserved as the Medinet Habu temple, but full of interest for the visitor for very particular reasons connected with the life, achievements, and legends of Ramesses the Great. The Ramesseum was without a doubt the most important religious building constructed in Ramesses' reign, although this claim must be tempered by the fact that not nearly enough is known about the temple of Ptah at Memphis, greatly enlarged (if not a new foundation) by him, or the lost sacred establishments in the Delta Residence of Piramesse. The certainty that the king would be buried in the Valley of the Kings, and the knowledge of the large and splendid individual royal mortuary temples already existing in Western Thebes, rendered the Theban area particularly important in the course of the king's life from accession to death.

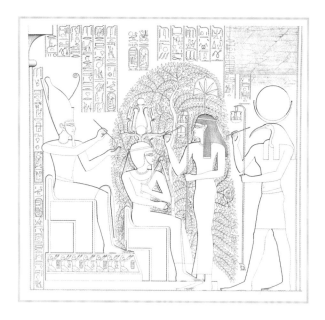

This progress was in Egyptian terms essentially a religious one in which the king at his coronation became the living form of the god Horus, in his oldest form of a sun god, shown as a falcon. His life thereafter was a steady progress toward death, when he would join the pre-eminent sun-god Re in the heavens, and also become assimilated with Osiris, the divine but dead king, whose martyrdom in life (mythologically) provided him with his justification to exist after death as the monarch of the afterlife – the Chief of the Westerners.

The three great temples of ancient Thebes, which provide evidence for the involvement of Ramesses II with the worship of the gods and the various rituals and ceremonies connected with them, are the Luxor and Karnak cult foundations and the Ramesseum. It is in these temples that the presence of the king is dominant, in such a way that modern-day visitors become persuaded of his power and even religiosity. The scenes of warfare and triumph are mostly placed on the parts of the temple buildings, which might be seen by Egyptians allowed to enter the sacred enclosures. Within the temples, where access was strictly limited and increasingly linked in the approach to the innermost sanctuaries, the scenes are almost wholly ritualistic in character. The king is shown in close association with the gods, making offerings to them corporately and individually, receiving reciprocal favors from them, participating in ceremonies connected with the temple and the cult, and involved in the periodic festivals in which the gods take part. The pervasive presence of the king in these temple scenes is neither a mark of his overweening pride nor an indication that he spent his whole time engaged in religious activities. It was the king's duty, even his justification, to act as the

go-between for the gods and the people of Egypt, not to be just the representative of the gods on earth, but in a sense the conduit for their powers. In the earlier chapter on Ramesses the great image-maker, something has already been said about the Egyptian king and his relationship with the gods, and particularly with those gods who embodied the ideas of royalty and majesty, investing the ruling king with his special powers, spiritual and terrestrial. Ramesses was no exception in accepting the gifts of the gods, especially those of divinely granted authority, of long life and many *sed* festivals. A fine and explicit scene in the Ramesseum portrays the rite by which the sun god of creation, Atum, supported by ibis-headed Thoth and Sefkhet-abu (a form of Seshat, goddess of writing), inscribes the name of Ramesses on the leaves of the *ished* tree (possibly the persea), thereby granting the king a multiplicity of jubilees. Ramesses sits on a block throne in front of the tree, wearing the horned *atef* crown. From the branches of the tree hangs the sign for *sed*, with the symbol for 'million' below.

Such scenes demonstrate the king's dependence on the gods, and the advantages he obtains from his inheritance of royal power and from his carrying out of the many ceremonies by which the gods in turn are honored and serviced in daily and periodic ritual activities. In theory, these services for the gods in all the temples of Egypt were carried out by the reigning king. Quite evidently, such a fulfillment of ritual obligations was quite beyond the capacity of a single person; even if he were to attempt to carry out all the ceremonies in one place only, for example, Piramesse, Memphis, or Thebes, the task would be impossible. But by delegation to the priestly officials in every temple and sanctuary,

the king could theoretically fulfill his ritual obligations, and in this way be seen to be involved. And so by representations and texts, the sacred duties could be seen to be accepted and by magic carried out according to the calendars of festivals and ceremonies. Such a theoretical arrangement was undoubtedly a great convenience, inasmuch as it gave the king complete freedom to carry out his ritual role whenever and wherever he wished, and to ignore it if attendance at a particular shrine was not convenient.

A king who chose to be unobservant of his religious duties might then not feel that he was being particularly undutiful; but lack of attendance to duty would not pass unnoticed, and a wise king would realize that proper performance by him was truly expected. He would therefore feel the need from time to time to proceed to a particular temple to assume his proper duties and carry out the appropriate ceremonies. It is unlikely that he would act in this way without giving ample notice of his intention to attend. The nature of religious observance in ancient Egypt was altogether different from what is now seen to be proper practice. For a Pharaoh to visit a temple for a ritual purpose was not the same as a visit by a modern king or head of state to church on a Sunday for the celebration of the Eucharist, or to a mosque for the participation in Friday prayers. Regular services in which the generality of the populace might join in formed no part of the religious life of the ancient Egyptians. The daily rituals, which served as the basis of the religious activity in a great temple, were conducted in private, and, if the king were present, he would be the principal actor in the sacred performance.

594
Wearing the atef crown, Ramesses
sits in front of the persea tree. Atum,
behind, and Sefkhet-abu and Thoth
in front, write his name on the
leaves of the tree. From the
Ramesseum, drawn by Lepsius.

595
Ramesses II, kneeling on a basket
and in front of the persea tree,
receives the jubilee symbols from the
hand of Re-Herakhty, while Thoth
writes his name on the leaves of the
tree. From Abu Simbel.

The King and the Gods in Life and Death

There is no way by which we can now discover whether Ramesses, or any other New Kingdom Pharaoh apart from Akhenaten, was particularly diligent in the exercise of his pontifical duties. Mentions of actual attendances at temples or at particular festivals are not common, and when they occur it is not always certain that the reports are factually true. The presence of the king in a temple is proclaimed perpetually by the scenes and inscriptions on the temple walls. Ramesses need not have felt guilty if he rarely made personal appearances at the great shrines of the land. Nevertheless, it may rightly be assumed that whenever he made progress from Piramesse southward to Thebes and even farther, for example to Abu Simbel, he would have taken the opportunity to visit the principal temples on his way. If the visit could be timed to coincide with a particular festival, so much the better. It would have been good for the Pharaoh, the Good God, Lord of the Two Lands, to be seen at festivals like that of Sokaris at Memphis, or the Osiris mysteries at Abydos.

The most important and spectacular divine celebrations about which much is known were the Opet Festival and the Valley Festival, both at Thebes, and both concerned with the cult of the imperial god Amun and his divine family, the goddess Mut and their child, the moon god Khonsu. Such celebrations were important not only for the temples and the services they

maintained, but also for the ordinary people of Egypt. From the religious point of view, they provided opportunities for everyone to see the deity, in the form of its cult statue, brought out from the innermost shrine in the temple and paraded about with suitable pomp. From the political point of view, it might provide opportunities for everyone to see the great officials who controlled their lives, and even Pharaoh, who could intervene on their behalf with the gods. And most particularly, for most people, from the point of view of entertainment, the festivals were occasions for all kinds of festivities, both connected directly with the sacred performances and organized separately, apart from the official activities. There was, for example, a huge provision of food and drink, made generally available from the massive slaughtering of animals and the copious brewing of beer. Accounts of what went on at festivals elsewhere and at other periods make it clear that in Egypt a good festival was a time of plenty and a time of license, when controls were relaxed and a blind eye turned to excess.

The pattern of royal progresses on the Nile and the paying of visits to temples is in rare, specific cases made clear, as in the great dedicatory inscription of Ramesses II in the Osiris temple of Sethos I at Abydos. It happened in his first year of reign. The text describes the king leaving Thebes and traveling north, back to

Piramesse. When the river flotilla reached the Thinite nome, Ramesses made a detour "to inaugurate offerings to Unennefer [an epithet of Osiris], the good things that his *ka* loves, and to greet Onuris, his brother [the god of the Thinite nome]." Here it seems certain that in doing this, in performing the other ceremonies in the temple of Sethos at Abydos, and in seeing to the various building activities, which he had himself initiated in that sacred place, Ramesses was in his own person performing acts which might usually be carried out by others in his name. And these activities at Abydos came only a very few days after he had been in Thebes, celebrating his coronation and supervising the ceremonies of the Opet Festival. Again there is no reason to doubt that Ramesses himself took part in the celebrations, an act of conspicuous and auspicious importance at the very beginning of his reign. Would he ever do the same again during his long reign? It might be expected that he would from time to time, but certainly not on an annual basis.

In the calendar of Theban festivals, the Opet represented the most important festival event in the year. It began during the second month of *akhet*, the season of inundation, on the evening of day 18, and continued for about three weeks, ending on day 12 of the third month of *akhet*. During Ramesses' reign this period would have been in the month of September in the modern

calendar. The festival gave its name to the month, Opet, in which it took place, and the name gains additional significance in that its core event was a journey from Ipetsut (Opet-sut) 'most favored of places,' the Karnak temple, to Ipet-resyt (Opet-resyt) 'the southern hidden place' or 'southern harem', the Luxor temple. Egyptian gods lived a busy social life and were much given to visiting each other in their respective shrines. Sometimes long distances might be involved, as in the case of the annual trip made by the goddess Hathor from her temple at Dendera to the temple of Edfu, 108 miles (174 kilometers) by river to the south, where her sacred marriage to the local deity Horus was celebrated. This is perhaps the best described of regular divine travel, the relevant texts at Edfu, of Ptolemaic date, providing a wealth of evidence about the official ceremonies and of the wild participation in the festivities by the general population. There can be no doubt, however, that the Opet Festival was in all respects more important in significance and greater in scale; it is just less well documented than the Edfu festival.

There are, however, splendid and extensive visual representations of the major public events of the festival on the walls of the Theban temples. Those most artistically composed and informative in detail are in the processional colonnade in the Luxor temple; they were possibly begun in the reign of Amenophis III,

completed under Tutankhamun, and usurped by Horemheb. There are further scenes added by Ramesses II in the first court of the same temple. The "Beautiful Festival of Opet," as it was called, began in Ipetsut, Karnak, when Amun, the principal deity, was brought out of the temple, his effigy in a divine bark, which was placed in a riverboat to be conveyed upstream to Ipet-resyt, the Luxor temple. He was accompanied by his divine consort Mut and their child Khonsu, each of whom was similarly conveyed in a separate boat. The journey was conducted with great ceremony, with many boats on the river and huge crowds on land. After a journey of about two miles, the divine barks were brought to the quay of the Luxor temple and taken into the innermost, secret (hidden) rooms of the shrine. There various ceremonies and rituals were performed in private; and then, after about three weeks, the gods were conducted back to Karnak and deposited in their shrines.

The second great Theban festival in which the king might have been expected to participate, if he were in the south at the right time, was the Valley Festival, the "Beautiful Festival of the Valley." It took place in the second month of the season *shomu* ('summer'), at the time of the new moon. In early days it was associated with the royal mortuary temples in the valley of Western Thebes leading up to Dayr al-Bahri.

Ramesses II

596–597
Scenes on the granite shrine of Philip Arrhidaeus at Karnak showing the sacred barks ready to take part in the Valley Festival. Two rest on stands, and two are carried by priests, preceded by the king with a censer.

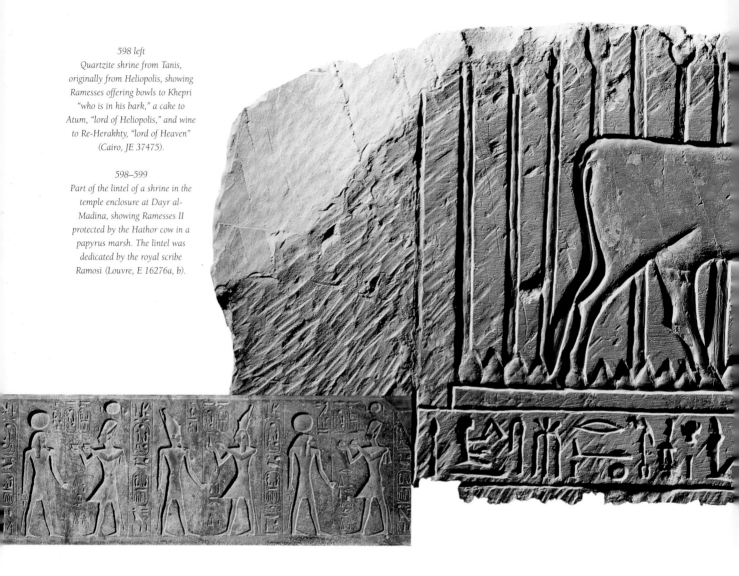

In the Nineteenth Dynasty, the three gods of the Theban triad, Amun, Mut, and Khonsu, were involved in a sacred progress which began with a river-crossing from Karnak to the west bank of the Nile, followed by a water progress along canals to the desert edge, to the land of the Theban Necropolis and the royal mortuary temples. On coming to land, the procession formed up and proceeded to visit the temples in the eponymous valley, and then to other temples along the desert edge. It did not, apparently, go to the Valley of the Kings, where there were no shrines to visit and no suitably equipped priestly establishments to welcome the visitors and entertain them. It was again a spectacular occasion, offering at the superior level of the celebrations opportunities for the great and the good to meet the deities and receive favors from them, and at the lower level of the event, the chance for the populace to view the gods and indulge in a degree of license not commonly granted them.

In the tomb of Paser, the distinguished vizier whom we have already met, there is a significant mention of the Valley Festival in an inscription on one of the pillars in the tomb's broad hall. The text is phrased like a spell from the *Book of the Dead*, empowering Paser to come forth from his tomb so that he may greet and adore Amun "when you arrive at the western desert of Kheft-hir-nebes [a name of Thebes as a whole, in all probability], I shall be first of those who follow you in your beautiful Festival of the Valley." In his lifetime Paser, as vizier and governor of Thebes, had an important role to play in the conduct of the festival, especially in the absence of his Pharaoh, and he might expect that in his afterlife he could enjoy the privilege of participating in the festival by having his image included among those which joined the Theban triad in the procession. The same text includes the words "O my lord, my city god, Amun, Lord of the Thrones of the Two Lands, grant that I may be among the ancestors, the excellent honored ones." The practice of including images of previous kings in the procession developed during the Nineteenth Dynasty, and it would seem that the privilege of joining the festivities posthumously was later extended to notable officers of state. Apparently the Valley Festival attained special importance during the reign of Ramesses II, and the Ramesseum was used as the overnight stop for the Theban deities. This was in no way inappropriate, for the temple was then best equipped to offer comfortable lodging to the gods, who would already have found themselves the subjects of regular daily rituals in that temple. There is further evidence from the early Ptolemaic granite shrine in the Karnak temple, which carries scenes of the celebration of the Valley Festival, that this use of the Ramesseum as a kind of grand way-station, or overnight billet, was still observed one thousand years after Ramesses' reign.

The presence of the king at the Valley Festival, as at the Opet Festival, was assumed but rarely expected. There are no certain records

that Ramesses II ever traveled to Thebes specially to preside at any of the great festivals after his initial attendance at the Opet in Year 1. And yet there must have been many occasions when he came south: to make presentations of tribute, booty, and prisoners after the campaigns of his early years, to inspect progress on his mortuary temple and tomb, to inaugurate the temples at Abu Simbel, and even just in periodic progress up the Nile. As part of the Ramesseum complex, a special palace for the king was built abutting the western side of the first court. It is now a complete ruin, but much of its plan can be traced. In size it was large (about fifty by fifty meters or 160 by 160 feet), but not excessively large, providing accommodation for the king and a small party of family members and attendants for short stays. Other royal mortuary temples in Thebes also provided relatively modest accommodation for the visiting monarch. It seems unlikely that such provision would have been made unless it was expected that it would be

occupied from time to time. But the existence of a grandiose rest-house does not imply that it was frequently occupied by its intended visitor. It may well have been used by privileged officials and even representative members of the royal family, and particularly on occasions like the celebration of the Valley Festival. It was probably an occasion looked forward to and therefore enjoyed occasionally by royal 'deputies.' It was an especially joyful event, much mentioned in private as well as official texts, and great celebrations involving the populace took place on the night following the main progress of the gods around the temples in Western Thebes – a change, no doubt, from life at Piramesse.

The absence of specific mentions and descriptions of the king's taking part not just in the periodic festivals in the great religious centers in Egypt, but also in the general, regular religious activities, such as the daily rituals, prevents our making a proper assessment of his practical relationship with the gods. It has been pointed

out already that a complete fulfillment of his ritual obligations was impossible, and could be made valid only by the magical force of representations of the sacred activities on temple walls. The fact that some of the scenes of the regular and important ceremonies showing Ramesses II engaged in his necessary activities with the gods have not survived does not mean that such scenes never existed, or that Ramesses did not perform the particular rituals. Massive destruction in the principal temples, at Karnak and the Ramesseum in Thebes, and in the northern cities, accounts for the absence of much of the original visual record. Nevertheless, in all those temples in which work was initiated during Ramesses' reign, there are many scenes of his conducting minor ceremonies and engaging in close relationships with the gods. He may be seen as being on very familiar terms with all the great deities of Egypt, and with many who fulfilled minor divine functions or represented provincial cults.

600–601
The Theban triad consecrates
Ramesses' reign, endowing him with
many jubilees. The king, wearing
the atef crown and holding the flail,
kneels and receives the sed symbols
from Amon-Re, Mut, and Khonsu.
In the Ramesseum.

600 bottom
Gold and lapis lazuli bracelets,
inscribed with Ramesses' name and
decorated with duck heads and fine
granulation. Found in Bubastis
in the Delta in 1906 and thought
to be part of a temple treasure
(Cairo, JE 39873).

The King and the Gods in Life and Death

A very good idea of the range of these activities and contacts can be found at Karnak on the girdle wall enclosing the principal shrine, the Central Court, and Tuthmosis III's Festival Temple. The wall dates to the reign of Tuthmosis III, but it carries on its outer face a great series of scenes in which Ramesses II engages with a great many deities. A selection of 'episodes' gives a fair idea of their range: Ramesses presents bread to Re-Herakhty; he consecrates offerings to Amun; he presents flowers to Neith; he offers incense and a libation to Amun of the Saite nome; he runs with *sed*-festival symbols toward Bastet; he offers a haunch of meat to Horus; he presents a miniature Sokar-bark to Ptah-Sokar-Osiris; he anoints the lioness-headed Mehyt; he holds up the heavens before Onuris-Shu; he measures up the temple with scribal deity Sefkhet-abu; he raises the pillar of Heliopolis before Atum; he raises two obelisks and offers incense before Re; he makes purification before Horus of Letopolis, a city in the southern Delta; he stands before Queen Ahmes-Nefertari, wife of Amosis and mother of Amenophis I of the early Eighteenth Dynasty, who was especially revered with her son in the Theban Necropolis; he pours a libation to Sakhmet; in the company of

Khonsu-Neferhotep he receives the symbol of jubilee from Amun. All these scenes – and they are but a selection from the whole series – occur on the outer south side of the girdle wall. There was no limit to his divine relationships, and a great many of them are excellently recorded on this wall in very well-designed and executed sunk relief. Further scenes are carved on the east and north sides of the same wall, and there are many similar depictions elsewhere at Karnak and in the Luxor temple and the Ramesseum. They would not have been absent from other temples throughout Egypt built by Ramesses or added to or embellished by him. A rather more limited range of activities is to be found in the Nubian temples, in which, as we have seen, Ramesses had a somewhat elevated position vis-à-vis the imperial gods and the particular gods of the cataract region and Nubia.

Whether or not Ramesses II conducted his life according to the best Egyptian ethic, we can never know. All the outward signs of piety were in place to remind him of his divine being and divine duties. Certainly in the surviving record of his reign there is much to suggest that the royal obligations were regularly fulfilled, even if the agent was not regularly the king himself. There

601 bottom right
A remarkable silver vessel with gold mounting and a gold handle in the from of a goat, from the Bubastite Treasure. The decoration contains Asiatic elements, but its dedication is by the royal butler Atumemtaneb (Cairo, JE 39867).

were plenty of deputies or representatives to act on behalf of the king, and it was surely the case that it was the carrying out of a ritual activity that mattered, not who carried it out, provided that he was properly authorized. Nevertheless, the proper service of the gods throughout life was the proper preparation for death and a proper burial. From the moment of birth every Egyptian would have had his or her eye on the ultimate goal, although it is unlikely that the prospect of death and burial would have become a matter for serious concern until an individual had reached a position in life when anything more than the simplest of burials would have been contemplated. For the Pharaoh the position was rather different. From the moment of coronation, his destiny became a matter of high concern. Up to that point the prospective king was an ordinary, if specially privileged, Egyptian. At accession he became the living Horus, and so he would remain until his death, when he would move into a different state of divinity and by the appropriate rituals, including the provision of the appropriate texts, pass from his terrestrial existence to a posthumous celestial state and also to his identification with Osiris in the underworld realm.

In considering his death and burial, a newly crowned Pharaoh would necessarily instruct his officials to arrange for the cutting of his tomb. It might be thought that the subject would be on the agenda of the first 'Privy Council' meeting of the new reign. There is some evidence from the work on other royal tombs of the New Kingdom that traces parts of the course of construction in particular cases. If a king began his reign at an advanced age, then it was imperative that work should begin as soon as possible and pursued with the utmost vigor. If the king was young on accession, then it might be thought unnecessary to start work on his tomb for some years. Whatever the circumstances at the start of a reign, there was always the chance that things might go wrong. Such seems to have been the case with Tutankhamun. He was very young on accession, and scarcely out of his teens when he died. His planned tomb, probably no. 23 in the Western Valley of the Kings, was by no means ready, and his successor, Ay, arranged for him to be buried in a small tomb prepared, no doubt, for some important official like Ay himself or for some member of the royal family. So Tutankhamun missed his proper interment by dying young and probably unexpectedly. Ay, on the other hand, becoming king at an advanced age with a small expectation of life, took over Tomb 23 and had it completed and prepared for himself within the three or four years of his reign.

602
In his relationship with the gods, Ramesses is regularly shown making offerings to, or receiving gifts from the gods, especially Amon-Re in Karnak. Here he offers the god a tray of incense pots.

603
Ramesses II, wearing the cap crown bends forward with a tray of varied offerings to the god in Karnak. He is "presenting things to his father Amon-Re," a very general designation of his offering.

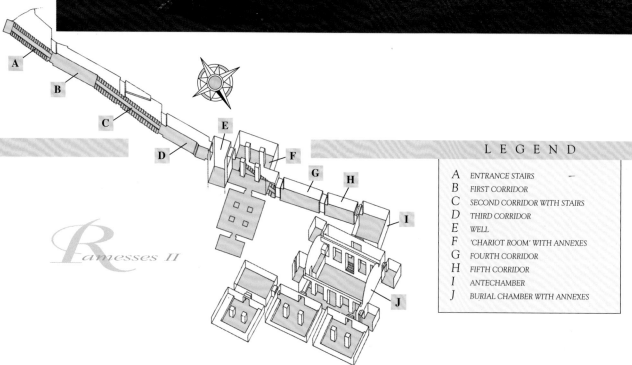

LEGEND

A   ENTRANCE STAIRS
B   FIRST CORRIDOR
C   SECOND CORRIDOR WITH STAIRS
D   THIRD CORRIDOR
E   WELL
F   'CHARIOT ROOM' WITH ANNEXES
G   FOURTH CORRIDOR
H   FIFTH CORRIDOR
I   ANTECHAMBER
J   BURIAL CHAMBER WITH ANNEXES

Ramesses II

In Ramesses II's case the arrangements worked well. Firstly, he became Pharaoh when he was young; secondly, he lived to a ripe old age. Never, presumably, did it seem that work on his tomb should be accelerated. It may therefore be assumed that his tomb was finished in form and decoration well before he was ready to occupy it. In many royal tombs of the Eighteenth and Nineteenth Dynasties there is good evidence that the work was uncompleted at the time when they had to be closed, after the funerals of the dead monarchs. Of Ramesses II's immediate predecessors, his grandfather Ramesses I (one or two years' reign) had a relatively small tomb without much decoration, while his father Sethos I (fifteen or sixteen years' reign), had a tomb with much uncompleted decoration, although in sum it is all of exceptional quality. Of his immediate successor, Merenptah (ten or eleven years' reign), unfortunately the present condition of his tomb is such that the completeness of its decoration at the time of the king's death cannot be adequately assessed. The same should be said of Ramesses II's tomb. It has been open in part since late antiquity; it has suffered flooding on a number of occasions; it has only in recent years been systematically cleared, cleaned, conserved, and recorded. The damage it has suffered over the millennia has left much of its decoration in a sorry state, but as far as one can gather from recently published reports, the tomb was finished and ready to receive the royal burial many years before Ramesses found it necessary to take the long and hazardous path to his divine destiny.

The position of Ramesses II's tomb and the character of the rock and shale through which it was cut provide good reasons for its unfortunate fate, structurally, in subsequent times. It is not known how the position for a royal tomb in the Valley of the Kings was chosen. Presumably, high officials – possibly including the vizier, the mayor of Thebes, and the high priest of Amun – inspected likely positions, advised by local officials who knew the nature of the Valley and the hazards that might endanger a badly sited tomb. The king himself may have been shown the selected site and even visited it on occasion when he came to Thebes. It could have been included in his itinerary along with the Ramesseum, which would probably have been of greater interest to him. The two places, tomb and mortuary temple, formed a complex for the care and protection of the royal body after death and for the nurturing of the royal spirit by services and offerings. In earlier periods, tomb and temple were physically joined. At Thebes, however, once the Valley had been

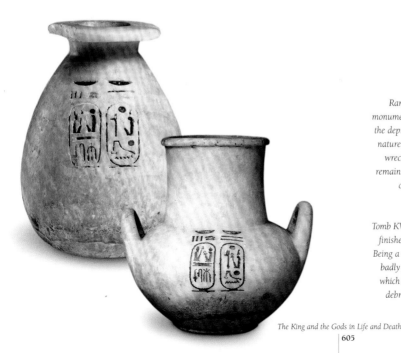

604–605
Ramesses II's tomb was once a monument of great magnificence. Sadly, the depredations of man, but mostly of nature have reduced it to a profound wreck. But much clearance work remains to be done. Here is the burial chamber after clearance.

605 top
Tomb KV7, prepared for Ramesses II and finished relatively early in his reign. Being a deeply cut tomb, it has suffered badly from the effects of flash floods which have washed huge amounts of debris into it over the millennia.

605 bottom
Two alabster vessels inscribed with the names of Ramesses II. Such vessels were commonly placed in royal burials, and many fragments of similar pieces have been found during the clearance of KV7 (left: Cairo, JE 46712; right: Louvre, N.440).

The King and the Gods in Life and Death

chosen as the resting place for the royal bodies, the temples had to be constructed elsewhere within the necropolis. In the tomb in the Valley, appropriate inscriptions and scenes ensured the safe progress of the dead king through the dangers of the underworld until he was born again into the celestial company of Re, the sun god, at dawn every day. In the mortuary temple, in the company of the Theban gods and of the other great gods of Egypt, the king could continue his relationship with these deities, so long as the services and offerings for his spirit were maintained.

In area, Ramesses' tomb is the largest in the Valley, although possibly exceeded by KV5, the tomb constructed for the king's sons, across the road into the Valley, which is not yet fully cleared. When the two tombs were cut, they were the first to be met on entering the Valley by the principal path. The king's tomb consists of a long descending corridor with two sets of stairs leading to the well or sump designed for protection and the collection of flood water; a pillared hall interrupts the continuing progress of the corridor, and at the end of the corridor a large suite of rooms, including the burial chamber, lies at approximately right angles to the corridor. The royal funerary texts inscribed on the walls of the corridor and the various chambers include *The Litany of Re*, *The Book of What is in the Underworld*, *The Book of Gates*, *The Book of the Divine Cow*, and parts of *The Book of the Dead*. On the upper walls of the well and on the many pillars in the larger halls, the king is shown with various deities in familiar meetings; they seem to recall the

scenes of similar intimacy found in the temples, where the living king could consort with the gods. In the tomb scenes it is almost as if the gods are bidding farewell to one of their number, passing from life to death and then to reunion with the pantheon in his afterlife.

When Ramesses died in his Year 67, the end could scarcely have been considered unexpected. One may wonder how often in the last decades of his reign there had been crises in his health and warnings of imminent death. One may also surmise that on such occasions, word would be sent to Thebes to prepare the tomb for occupation and to make preparations for the royal funeral. Although no king had been buried in the Valley since the death of Sethos I, there would have been in the long interim plenty of activity, with the construction of the new royal tomb, the subsequent cutting of the tomb intended for the royal sons, and the periodic funerals of many of the sons. Merenptah, who eventually succeeded his father, was the thirteenth son, and many others younger than he would have died before his accession. Whether the sons' tomb continued to be used after Ramesses' death is not yet apparent, and it may never be decided when it received its last burial. So from time to time there would have been burial ceremonies in the valley in KV5, opposite the royal tomb-in-waiting. Presumably, this tomb, KV7, was inspected regularly, and not just closed up until the day when it would receive Ramesses, and he would pass from the kingdom of the living to the realm of the gods.

606 bottom
Four blue faience vessels, made possibly for Ramesses' burial, but rescued from destruction when his body was moved in antiquity. His names are supplemented with texts invoking forms of Amon-Re and Mut.

607 top
A low relief of a clump of lilies from the tomb of Ramesses II. The lily, an alternative to the lotus, symbolized Upper Egypt.

607 bottom
Relief carving from Ramesses' tomb showing the goddess Ma'at with outstretched wings kneeling on a basket. She is "daughter of Re" and announces her intention to protect the king. She holds the shen sign of universality.

608
Cedar coffin that contained the
mummy of Ramesses II on discove...
in 1881. It was probably for a
predecessor, possibly Ramesses I.
An inked text on the front has an
account of the vicissitudes suffere...
by the body in antiquity
(Cairo, JE 26214).

609 top
Pendant of gold and semiprecious
stones in the form of a ram-heade...
falcon, the kind of jewel to have bee...
placed on Ramesses' mummy. Non...
of his actual funerary jewelry has
survived. Found in the Serapeum
(Louvre, N.764).

609 bottom
Upper part of the mummy
of Ramesses II as he may be seen i...
the Cairo Museum: a remarkable
triumph for the uncertain art of
mummification in ancient Egypt
(Cairo, JE 61078).

No account has survived of Ramesses' death and burial. From evidence obtained when his mummy was examined in Paris in 1975, it seems that the body was prepared for burial in the north of Egypt, not in the Theban area. It could properly be expected that he died in Piramesse, and that the process of mummification would necessarily have been carried out there. Long travel south would have led to rapid putrefaction of an unembalmed body, and the impossibility of successful subsequent preservation. And so, after the prescribed time required for embalming, the seventy days of the records, the royal body was conducted south by river, brought to Thebes, conveyed to the Ramesseum for a period of rest and final rites, and then taken to the tomb where the interment took place. The proceedings at all stages were accompanied by suitable pomp and extravagant scenes of mourning, and the whole series of events supervised by the new king, the new Horus, Merenptah. After the placing of the royal mummy in the burial chamber and the introduction of a great quantity of funerary equipment, the tomb was closed up and sealed. It became Ramesses' 'house of eternity.' But that was not to be.

By a strange irony, almost more is known of Ramesses' movements after death than for much of his lifetime. His tomb was to be his dwelling place forever, but it became the subject of a number of intrusions and robberies, which greatly disturbed the continuity of his posthumous existence. In Year 29 of Ramesses III (c. 1155 B.C.), scarcely fifty years after the burial of his illustrious predecessor, an attempt, or possibly two separate attempts, were made to enter the tomb, although it does not appear that any serious damage was done at that time. During the later Twentieth Dynasty, evidence came before the Theban authorities that the royal tombs in the valley had been or were being robbed. While Herihor was high priest of Amun at Thebes and the virtual ruler in that region, the legitimate Pharaoh in Piramesse being Ramesses XI (c. 1099–1069 B.C.), the mummy of Ramesses II was rescued and rewrapped and temporarily placed in the tomb of his father Sethos I, whose body was also rewrapped. Clearly both tombs had been seriously violated by this time. Further moves took place in later years: in Year 10 of Siamun of the Twenty-first Dynasty (c. 968 B.C.), a number of royal mummies, including that of Ramesses II, were deposited in a remote tomb in the hills of Dayr al-Bahri, originally made for Queen Inhapy, wife of Seqenenre-Taa II of the Seventeenth Dynasty (c. 1570 B.C.); and then, finally in or shortly after Year 11 of Osorkon I of the Twenty-second Dynasty (c. 924–889 B.C.), Ramesses' mummy, along with many other royal mummies, was placed in another tomb at Dayr al-Bahri, originally made for the burials of the high priests of Amun of the Twenty-first Dynasty. And so, three hundred years after he was conducted to meet his fellow gods in the afterlife, Ramesses found a secure resting place in which he remained undisturbed for about 2,780 years; and then in about 1870 the secret cache was discovered by Egyptians from the nearby village. In 1881 the coffin containing Ramesses' mummy was removed by the Antiquities Service to the Cairo Museum. And there it has remained ever since, apart from two excursions. For a short period in the 1930s all the royal mummies were transferred from the Cairo Museum and put on display in the mausoleum of Saʻd Zaghlul, the greatly esteemed Egyptian nationalist politician of the early twentieth century. In 1975 Ramesses made a visit to Paris, where he was met and treated like a visiting head of state; his body was subjected to extensive scientific examinations and carefully conserved.

The complicated history of the wanderings of Ramesses II and of other Egyptian kings has been pieced together mostly from dockets written on their coffins and bandages. Ramesses, confusingly, was not in his original coffin when he was placed in the Dayr al-Bahri cache. It is thought on stylistic grounds that the cedar coffin in which he was placed, now scraped clean of all original decoration, was originally made possibly for his grandfather, Ramesses I. The lid is inscribed in ink with the later king's two cartouches and a long hieratic text outlining some of the history of the royal peregrinations. Hieratic texts on his bandaging confirm his identity and some of his movements. It is sad to contemplate what survives of the great king's mortal remains. He no longer has the trappings to help him secure his continuing posthumous existence in the company of the gods with whom he was destined to spend eternity. And yet he has in a sense achieved a greater posthumous existence, and certainly a greater fame than most of his fellow Egyptian kings. His body may be deprived of its amuletic protection, but his face retains a magnificent dignity, providing striking confirmation of his terrestrial power. And indeed, his name lives. His gods have not wholly deserted him.

RAMESSES' PEOPLE

610

The workmen's village at Dayr al-Madina, established within walls from about 1500 B.C. until its ending in about 1070 B.C. Extensions beyond the walls can be seen, and at the top is the temple enclosure containing some building commissioned by Ramesses II.

611

Scenes of agriculture from the tomb of Sennedjem: above, with his wife Iyneferti, he plows; below, he harvests barley with sickles, and flax by pulling. Such was actual life on the land in Ramesses' reign.

"Pendua: First month of *akhet* [inundation], day 14: drinking with Khonsu."

A black mark (in fact a red note) therefore against the workman Pendua, who failed to turn up for work on that day in Year 40 of Ramesses II (c. 1239 B.C.). On day 16 of the third month of *akhet*, Siwadjet was away because his daughter was ill. For the same reason, Wadjmose was absent from duty on day 23 of the fourth month of *peret* (sowing), and he was away again on day 6 of the fourth month of *shomu* (summer) because he was building his house. Horemuia absented himself on the eighth day of the second month of *peret* to brew beer. Aapehty signed himself off duty for a run of days in the third and fourth months of *akhet* because he was ill, and on the same days Pehery-pedjet was absent, the reason noted "with Aapehty." Pehery-pedjet is also marked down as being away from duty "with Khonsu, dispensing remedies" and "dispensing remedies for the scribe's wife"; he clearly had secondary, medical duties, probably officially arranged. Other reasons for

absence are given as "eye trouble," "offering to his god," and "wrapping his mother"(that is, preparing her body for burial).

These details are extracted from a register of the workmen who formed part of the élite corps employed on the making and decorating of the royal tomb and the tombs of other privileged persons in the Theban Necropolis; they lived in the village community at the place now called Dayr al-Madina. The corps and its village were established in the early Eighteenth Dynasty (c. 1500 B.C.), and the corps remained active and the village inhabited until the end of the Twentieth Dynasty (c. 1070 B.C.). The members of this workmen's corps were not only privileged in being favored protégés of the Pharaoh, but unusually literate. Their company included scribes, and there is some evidence that the ability to read and write was possessed by many who were not classified specifically as scribes. A huge quantity of written material has been discovered in the area of the workmen's village, the greatest part of it written on smooth limestone

flakes, for which the term ostraca is used. Many of these ostraca carry simple texts dealing with the everyday affairs of the workmen and their families, and in aggregate they make up a formidable dossier of information about a small, but special, community, of humble status, the lives of whose members were far divorced in all respects from those of the royal family, the high officials of the land, and even of the lesser officials in a place like Thebes. But because of the survival of so many written texts concerning the daily activities of the villagers, more is known about them and their way of life, their personal habits, and the manner in which they conducted their affairs than about the members of any other stratum of Egyptian society.

The register of workmen is written on an unusually large ostracon (41 by 35.5 centimeters or 104 by 90 inches), with the text extending over both sides. The names of forty workmen are listed, practically the whole of the gang as it was constituted in the middle of the reign of Ramesses II.

612 bottom
Laborers make mud bricks: water is drawn from a pool to mix with earth; molded bricks are set out to dry; a wall is built and dried bricks carried away. From the tomb of Rekhmire (c. 1450 B.C.), drawn by Prisse d'Avennes.

By Year 40 it is most probable that the royal tomb in the Valley of the Kings was completed, and also the greater part of the sons' tomb (KV5), so that the workforce had been scaled down or reduced by natural wastage (old age or death). Pressure on the gang, therefore, could not have been as great as it would have been when major works were being undertaken, and the apparently casual attitude of individual workmen to their regular attendance was seemingly tolerated as long as clear abuse was not extensive. There is nothing in the register to indicate the imposition of any penalties. Apart from the existence of this register (and of others of later date), in itself a remarkable example of ancient Egyptian bureaucratic practice, what is so striking about it is the range of reasons listed for absence, which were apparently seen to be acceptable. Today they might add "going to a football match" or "spending the day fishing," but "recovering from a hangover," "attending a funeral," "looking after a sick wife," "tending the vines," or "taking part in wine making" are excuses as appropriate for today as for antiquity. Few documents demonstrate in so clear a manner the perennial concerns of the working man and the wonderful continuity of the ordinary human anxieties.

There are in fact many thousands of ostraca surviving from the occupation of the workmen's village. There was no shortage of limestone chips that could be used for casual documentation. Every tomb excavation in the better areas of the Theban Necropolis, and particularly in the Valley of the Kings, yielded these flakes, and they could presumably be picked up and used in a very informal way. Yet it is hard to believe that there would not have been some person delegated by the leaders of the gang to select and put on one side those pieces, which could be best employed for official purposes. But anyone with the intention to write a short note or memorandum would have had no difficulty in acquiring suitable chips of limestone as he walked about the whole district of Western Thebes. The contents of many of the notes that can be dated to the mid-Nineteenth Dynasty, even specifically to the reign of Ramesses II, are relatively trivial; a piece from which the names of the writer and the recipient are lost refers to the sending of cakes and incense by the hand of a policeman named Pesaro: an additional five measures of incense were sent "on the day of the offering that you made to Amun during the Festival of the Valley." The writer adds, "They are not taken from anything that you sent me," presumably meaning that the commodities sent were a new consignment. From this brief note it can be seen how a simple workman of the royal-tomb gang could involve himself in the festivities connected with the Valley Festival, one of the two most important annual Theban celebrations, discussed in the last chapter.

Much matter of personal concern is included in these informal communications; the outline-scribe (draftsman) Prahotpe writes to his boss, the well-known scribe Qenhikhopshef:

"Why are you behaving toward me in this wretched way? As far as you are concerned I am a donkey. If there's work – bring the donkey; if there is food – bring the ox; if there is beer – I am not included. But when there is work, then I am sought. Indeed, if I am badly behaved because of beer, don't call for me. Listen to this in the House of Amon-Re, King of the Gods, life, prosperity, and health.

P.S. I am someone with no beer in his house. I look for satisfaction in writing to you."

Simple transactions seem often to have been conducted in writing, especially when workmen were on duty in the Valley of the Kings and away from the village. Letters were sent on what seem to have been trivial matters. But such letters provide vivid evidence of the system of barter by which most transactions in Egypt were conducted before the introduction of coinage, many centuries later. Paser writes to a woman named Tutuia:

"What's the meaning of your reproach to me? When your mother was still alive, you sent for me and I came, and I gave you a garment. And I gave you the... [?], and I told you, 'take possession of these,' and they became yours. You brought three bunches of vegetables and I asked 'Where from?' and you replied, 'I didn't get them from my mother, Sitamun.' I came again after your mother had died, and I gave you a *takhbes* basket, asking you to buy a goat with it, and you said, 'One *takhbes* basket is not enough.' So I said, 'Add on a bunch of vegetables to it and buy the goat.' But

Ramesses II

now you write to say, 'I have bought you a... [?] goat, the price being one *takhbes* basket and vegetables, and another *takhbes* basket to complete the purchase. I have bought it.' And look, I gave you... [?], saying, 'Buy oil with it. Make use of it [for the transaction]. Don't use the bunch of vegetables; use that to buy oil.' I am your good brother who cares for you, my sister."

Some transactions were concerned with burial preparations, which no doubt were regularly in train in what was essentially a lower-class, but not quite peasant, society. The outline-scribe Pay writes to his son Pra-emheb, also an outline-scribe:

"Please see about acquiring the two faience hearts [amulets] that I spoke to you about [saying], 'I will pay their owner whatever price he asks.' And you should set about finding this fresh incense, which I told you about, needed for varnishing your mother's coffin. I shall pay the owner for it. And you should get hold of that wreck of a kilt and wreck of a loincloth, to have the kilt made into a sash [?], and the loincloth into an apron [?]. Don't neglect anything I've told you, watch it!"

Sickness and death were constant concerns, and many letters deal with problems of health. Again the outline-scribe Pay writes to his son Pra-emheb:

"Don't abandon me; I am not well. Don't hold back your tears for me, for I am afflicted with eye trouble [?], and my lord Amun has turned his back [?] on me. Please bring me some honey for my eyes, and also ochre newly made into sticks and genuine eye-paint. See to it properly! Surely I am your

father, but now I am out of action, straining for my sight, but [my eyes] are not well."

A great many of the ostraca carry texts dealing with very mundane activities – the provision of rations, the arrangements for laundry in the village, the completion of all kinds of petty transactions which involved the inhabitants of the village and their families. A few deal with the primary activities of the workmen; such is the large ostracon with the register for Year 40 of Ramesses II. The majority, however, deal with small personal matters. The scribe Pabaki writes to his father Maaninakhtef:

"I have paid attention to what you said: 'Let Ib work with you.' Now see, he takes all day long bringing the water jug, no other duty having been given him all day long. He has paid no attention to what you advised: 'What have you done today?' [or, perhaps, 'What will you do today?']. See, the sun has already gone down and he is still away with the water jug."

Occasionally the writer of a begging letter seems to draw excessively on divine support for his request. The outline-scribe Khay writes to a colleague whose name is lost:

"In life, prosperity and health, and in the favor of Amon-Re, King of the Gods, your good lord, daily. See, I invoke [Amon-Re, Mut, Lady of Asheru and Khonsu in Thebes] and all the gods of Karnak, that you may be healthy, and continue in life, and be held in the favor of Amun, King [of the Gods], and of the King of Upper and Lower Egypt, Lord of the Two Lands, Usimare-Setpenre

[Ramesses II], may he live, be prosperous and healthy, your good lord, that you will prosper in the service of the city [Thebes]. Please pay attention, and obtain some ink for me, and some rush brushes ['pens'], and some sheets of papyrus, very urgently."

A further paragraph, badly damaged, gives a reason for this peremptory request: Khay is lying at home sick, and is without fresh food or anyone to bring him provisions.

Trivial such documents may be, but they bring to life quite vividly the humdrum daily round of the inhabitants of one small, although superior, working community. Here in Dayr al-Madina is a distinctive group of Ramesses' people, exposed in great detail because a high proportion of them could read and write and found it convenient to correspond with one another by means of ostraca; also recording lists of objects and small commercial transactions, while at the same time exposing their thoughts, wishes, and anxieties to sympathetic (and sometimes unsympathetic) family members and colleagues. One wonders, for example, what trouble might have prompted the note sent by the woman Werel to the scribe Huynefer:

"In life, prosperity, and health, and in the favor of Amon-Re, King of the Gods: Look! Every day I speak to every god and every goddess who is in Western Thebes, that you may be healthy, may live, and be in the favor of Pharaoh, life, prosperity, and health, your good lord. Also, take care for your brother; don't neglect him. And again, for Neferkhay – take care for your brother Khay; don't neglect him."

613 top
The building of a structure with a ramp: laborers bring materials and a master mason sees to surfacing the ramp with stone slabs. The ramp itself is of stone with matting for reinforcement. From the tomb of Rekhmire, drawn by Prisse d'Avennes.

It is not surprising to see how frequently the major Theban gods are invoked in these brief communications, especially Amon-Re, the great imperial god of Karnak. Such divine invocations are undoubtedly routine; a proper letter would invariably start with the naming of the great local gods, but in communications from the workmen's village, it is very common to have other, less important deities mentioned. For example, in this last note the woman Werel calls on "every god and every goddess who is in Western Thebes" (the text actually has "in the district of the west"). Indeed, there were a great many gods and goddesses who claimed allegiance from the inhabitants of the village. Perhaps the most commonly invoked divine personage was the early Eighteenth Dynasty king Amenophis I (c.1525–1504 B.C.) together with his mother, Queen Ahmes-Nefertari; they were regarded as the patrons of the workmen. It remains uncertain why precisely these two historical figures achieved such local divine status; by the time of Ramesses II, at

least, no indication is given in surviving texts of an appreciation of why the king and his mother were such objects of devotion. It is now generally thought that the veneration arose from the possible founding of the élite corps of workmen by Amenophis I, although it seems that the village, as the corps' base and home, was not established until the reign of Tuthmosis I, the successor of Amenophis. The royal mother Ahmes-Nefertari was in her lifetime a person of great consequence in state affairs, and, again for unknown reasons, was frequently associated closely with her son Amenophis. Perhaps because of their former human status, both were thought to be more approachable than the gods of Karnak. Additionally, in the local cult, Amenophis could be consulted as an oracle for the solving of local problems, just as Amon-Re could be at a much higher level.

Hathor, as a goddess of the West, was, not surprisingly, venerated by the workmen; and of the other national deities, Ptah of Memphis, 'Lord of Truth,' as patron of craftsmen, had a special place in the devotions of the villagers. A particularly local goddess, associated with the rocky peak of al-Qurn, which overlooks the Valley of the Kings, was Meresger. Her name means 'she who loves silence,' and she was shown usually as a cobra with a female human head. Ramose, in a letter to a priest Amenhotpe in the Ramesseum, invokes Meresger in particular as:

"Mistress of the West, to keep you healthy and living, to allow you to achieve a long life and a prosperous old age, and to pursue the office of your father, and to allow your children to succeed you after an infinity of time, while you remain in the favor of Amun of the temple 'United-with-Thebes' [the Ramesseum], your good lord."

The lesser domestic deities, like the female hippopotamus Thoeris and the leonine dwarf Bes, were very popular within the village, and certain foreign deities were worshiped, probably introduced by Asiatic craftsmen, and stamped

with the attraction of exoticism. Among them were Astarte, Anat, Qudshu, and, strangely, Reshep, essentially a war god. In the village itself, cults in which the family ancestors were revered formed a significant part of the most intimate, domestic worship conducted within individual houses. The piety of these people of Ramesses is abundantly shown in the personal devotional objects found during the excavation of the village, in the textual evidence of the ostraca, and particularly in many small limestone stelae. These stelae carry carved inscriptions with representations of revered deities; many were placed in shrines in the precinct of the village, in rough shrines established in the heights of the hills, along the paths leading to the Valley of the Kings, and in the tombs prepared for the burials of the workmen and their families. Because of the wealth of talent available among members of the corps, these stelae are in many cases very well carved. The same is the case with many of the tombs, in which superior skills in painting provided unexpectedly well-decorated chambers for the not-very-important people who were to benefit from them in their afterlives.

It would be wrong to deduce from the way of life and the special advantages enjoyed by the villagers of Dayr al-Madina that the same conditions would have been found in other less-favored communities in Egypt. The privileged status of the villagers derived from their particular involvement in the making of the royal tombs in the Valley of the Kings, and in their employment in similar work for members of the royal family, for high officials, and others who might be granted special funerary favors. The workmen of Dayr al-Madina formed a protected species out of the genus 'Ramesses' people,' trapped in a closed environment, but spared most of the problems of life in the countryside, especially in the remote nomes of Middle Egypt and the distant reaches of the Delta. These 'servants in the Place of Truth,' as the royal-tomb workmen were called from the

Ramesses II

time of the mid-Eighteenth Dynasty, are the best-known ancient Egyptians of any period before Ptolemaic times. They are exceptional in having their lives exposed by texts, by the physical remains of their houses, and by their devotional stelae, and in some cases their tombs. Even their disputes have been recorded on ostraca, with details of local court cases, some of which were heard and settled in the special tribunal established for the villagers – another mark of their unusual status. A case concerning donkeys, which can with great probability be dated to the reign of Ramesses II, provides a good example of the practice of the law for such people. The beginning of the ostracon text is lost, and with it the names of some of the litigants, one of whom declares, "Return the female donkey which I delivered to you, because it belongs to the chief of police Sobkhotpe." I said to him, "Send someone for the handover. Then return my donkey and the garment which I paid for the she-donkey that you sold." The local court questioned what was said by

the water-carrier Tjay: "Were you given the donkey and the garment?" He said, "Indeed, I have them, and on this day I gave the she-donkey for the chief of police Sobkhotpe." The local court declared, "The workman Nefersenut is in the right, and the water-carrier Tjay is in the wrong." The matter was not settled by this judgment, and it was three years before Tjay had a she-donkey brought back to him. Still the affair was not settled; further items, including fields in Armant (to the south of Thebes) were thrown into the negotiation, which now included a woman litigant. The text ends, "I shall not accept the fields, but only return the she-donkey itself."

No doubt the case involving Sobkhotpe's she-donkey would be more understandable if the whole of the background and the full course of the proceedings were known. But it scarcely matters. What is of interest in a case of this kind is to observe the form of the proceedings and to be able to determine how simple disputes might be handled, how local affairs could drag on for years,

and how accessible a certain level of legal support could be secured by workmen in the village. We saw in an earlier chapter how the case over land and inheritance, reported in the texts in the tomb of Mose in Saqqara, could drag on for many centuries. One may hope that the existence of the local court or tribunal ensured that local disputes, not serious enough for the vizier's court, could be heard and settled in reasonable time. Justice, however, was not easy to obtain, especially as modern rules of evidence do not seem to have been recognized. There was apparently always the possibility of reopening a case and overturning, temporarily at least, a judgment. From the great many texts, which refer to legal disputes or give apparent transcripts of parts of trials, it is clear that the inhabitants of the village were a litigious lot, much given to wrangles over small matters and inclined to take an opponent to law, possibly because the facility of the local court was there and prepared to hear evidence and make judgment.

615 left
Decoration on the child's chair of Princess Sitamun (c. 1400 B.C.). The hippopotamus Thoeris, and leonine Bes, with knives and tambourine, were used as protective deities on beds and other personal objects (Cairo, CG 51113).

615 right
Stela of the necropolis workman Bay, who worships the hearing ears of Amon-Re, shown above as a ram and described as "the good ram." Such stelae expressing personal cults are common at Dayr al-Madina (Cairo, JE 43566).

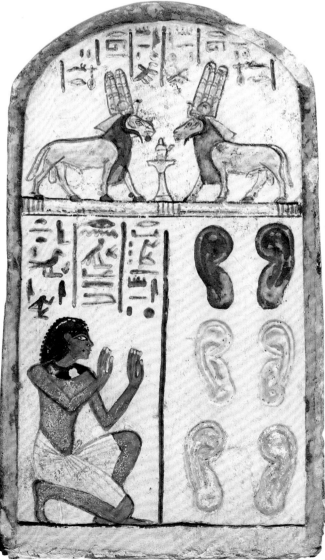

In many respects the necropolis workmen were different from the workmen and peasants who formed the bulk of the population of Egypt during the reign of Ramesses II, perhaps most notably in the matter of burial and provision for the afterlife. Unlike the majority of what may be called the 'common folk,' the necropolis workmen carried their privileged status beyond the life on earth. Many were able to be buried in the neighborhood of the village itself, some tombs even being linked closely to houses and maintained as family sepulchres over several generations. A very good representative tomb of this kind was that established by the workman Sennedjem and used for the interment of family members over three generations at least. In the numbering of the private tombs in the Theban Necropolis, it has been assigned the number one (TT1) on geographical grounds, in that the systematic identification and numbering of the Theban tombs began at Dayr al-Madina in the early years of the twentieth century, and the first ten tombs were numbered at Dayr al-Madina. Tomb 1 was discovered in 1886, and by a most unusual chance was in a virtually intact condition. It has, therefore, served as an invaluable example of what a workman's burial might contain. Above all there were the bodies.

Sennedjem himself had a large rectangular sarcophagus of wood containing a mummiform coffin and a mummy-case containing the embalmed corpse. This ensemble was remarkably fine for someone whose formal title was simply 'servant in the Place of Truth,' that is, just 'workman' or 'member of the gang.' The forms and decoration on these intimate pieces in general follows those of the kinds of coffins provided for much more important burials. Sennedjem clearly knew the current practice for a high-class burial, and he was able, through his own technical abilities and those of his sons (also workmen) and of fellow members of the gang, to prepare an equipment far better than he could have expected if he had lived and worked elsewhere in Egypt. His tomb is situated very close to the southwest corner of the village, where his own house has been identified.

There is a great temptation to surmise that Sennedjem and perhaps many of his colleagues were able to exploit their positions and professional abilities by engaging in lucrative extramural activities connected with tomb-preparation. In this way they could greatly improve the way of life of themselves and their families, and also, very importantly, make good provision for a handsome burial.

616 top left
Outer face of the door to Sennedjem's tomb at Dayr al-Madina. Sennedjem, a workman in the Place of Truth, with his wife Iyneferti, plays senet *against destiny. The texts are from the Book of the Dead.*

616 top right
Inner face of Sennedjem's door showing the locking device. Upper scene: Sennedjem, Iyneferti, and their daughter Irunefer worship Osiris and Ma'at; below: seven named sons worship Ptah-Seker-Osiris, a funerary god, and Isis (Cairo, JE 27303).

617
Head of Sennedjem's outer coffin. Necropolis workmen of Dayr al-Madina were of modest status, but highly talented, and able to obtain funerary equipment far beyond what they might otherwise have expected (Cairo, JE 27308).

618–619
Burial chamber of Sennedjem's
tomb, looking north to a wall
covered with scenes of his life with
his wife in the Field of Reeds after
death and judgment. Ritual scenes
cover the other walls.

One may also wonder whether burials of the kind enjoyed by Sennedjem would have been considered suitable by the majority of superior Theban officials. The relative remoteness of the village, tucked away in a fold in the Theban hills out of sight of the main Theban Necropolis, together with the protected status of the villagers, enabled them to get away with behavior and activities that would have been considered unforgivably presumptuous elsewhere.

In addition to Sennedjem's burial, the tomb also contained the burials of eight family members, including his wife Iyneferti, their son Khonsu, and his wife Tamaket, and of Isis, wife of their elder son Khabekhnet (whose own tomb was close by). Some of Khabekhnet's funerary furniture, including *shabti* boxes, were there also. A number of more simply prepared burials were found in the tomb – possibly of lesser members of the family. Among items of funerary equipment included in the burial chamber were pieces of furniture, pottery (some painted to represent rare

stone and glass vessels), and copies of tools of the kind used by Sennedjem in his work on earth: a cubit rod for measuring, a right-angle with plumb-bob for leveling, and a vertical level with plumb-bob for establishing the correct vertical line of a wall. Sennedjem presumably hoped to pursue his professional activities in the afterlife. Such activities, however, would be undertaken only when he and his wife were relieved from the necessary duties of plowing, sowing, and reaping in the fields of Iaru – duties brilliantly portrayed in paintings on the east wall of the burial chamber. Most of the other well-preserved, brightly painted scenes in the burial chamber depict Sennedjem and Iyneferti engaged in acts of worship and ritual acts, which in a simple way reflect contemporary paintings in royal and very senior official tombs, and particularly the tombs of the royal wives like Nefertari. There are no scenes of daily life, which were common in Theban tombs of the Eighteenth and early Nineteenth Dynasties.

618 bottom
Most private tombs of the New Kingdom at Thebes have ceilings decorated with attractive patterns. Sennedjem's vaulted ceiling has a series of scenes in which he and his wife adore funerary deities.

619 top
Figurine of Sennedjem, not truly a shabti figure as it lacks the tools carried by a true shabti. Its text speaks speaks of "all that comes forth from the offering table of Amun in Karnak for the ka of Sennedjem justified" (Cairo).

619 bottom
View looking south in Sennedjem's tomb. Many workmen's tombs were dug near the village enclosure of Dayr al-Madina. Their decoration is wholly funerary, with no scenes of daily life, probably considered inappropriate for such humble people.

The conditions enjoyed by Sennedjem and his family and colleagues in life and, by expectation and proper provision, in death, were not to be expected by the vast majority of Ramesses' people. Those who lived and worked on estates belonging to the great religious foundations throughout the land enjoyed various privileges, which to some extent would have changed from place to place. The great inscription inscribed on a rock face at Nauri in Nubia during the reign of Sethos I, Ramesses' father, deals with the affairs of the Osiris temple at Abydos, which was completed during Ramesses' reign. Among the provisions are quite stringent regulations concerning the conditions under which the large temple staff and workers on the temple estates should operate, including many exemptions from activities, which usually involved most of the unprivileged population of Egypt, like military service, the annual corvée, taxation, and the general exploitation by superiors. Such special ordinances were almost certainly made for other temples at other times, and it may reasonably be assumed that the servants and laborers on the lands of foundations like the temple of Ptah in Memphis, of Re at Heliopolis, and of the many new temples in Piramesse were accorded similar protections and exemptions. The appropriate decrees of Ramesses II have not, unfortunately, been found, and their actual promulgation can only be postulated. Nevertheless, it would probably be a mistake to assume that workers in these and other temples and on the extensive temple estates throughout Egypt would have had particularly easy lives in spite of being spared military service and the harassment of local officials.

No ordinary Egyptian peasant or workman would have been able to read and write in the manner of the élite inhabitants of Dayr al-Madina.

In the northern part of the country, where the papyrus plant was most common, the paper made from it was subject to monopoly control and difficult to come by even for trained scribes not employed in governmental or temple administrations. Furthermore, the conditions for the preservation and survival of papyrus documents in the wetlands of the Delta were far inferior to those of the drier environment of the Theban district. Consequently, very few papyrus documents have survived from Lower Egypt, dating to the reign of Ramesses II, and of these the ones that deal with commerce and agricultural matters throw very little light on the lives and conditions of the ordinary inhabitants of Egypt. The term, which seems generally to describe such people is *rekheyet*; it is written, significantly, with the hieroglyph of a lapwing with its wings locked together – pinioned and unable to fly away. So was

620 left
The regular form of transport on land in ancient Egypt was the donkey. Expeditions were equipped with large numbers for carrying equipment, and they were the common working farm animal. From Dayr al-Bahri temple, drawing by Prisse d'Avennes.

620 right
Egyptians enjoyed hunting in the desert, a sport reserved for the highest ranks of society. In this Theban tomb scene, a servant brings back the results – an oryx and a hare – accompanied by a tired hound. Drawing by Prisse d'Avennes.

621
The marshy lands on the Delta and the Faiyum are still fine hunting grounds for wildfowl. In antiquity Egyptian peasants used clap-nets to trap wild birds, as shown here by Rosellini.

the bulk of the population in a sense pinioned and certainly not able to fly away.

Some indication of the servile, depressed condition of ordinary people, Ramesses' people, may be obtained from those passages composed for scribal training, in the collections called Miscellanies. One striking piece deals with the peasant, the writer being eager to point out how much better the life of the scribe was. Parts of this piece have already been quoted in dealing with the bureaucracy of the country, in Chapter 8, where the peasant's misery at the hands of the tax assessors and collectors is vividly described. Farmers have never been slow to complain of their misfortunes, but in Egypt their lot was in general rather favorable, when they were not being harassed by petty officials. Living conditions were more comfortable than in countries where winters were cold and where rain could make working

conditions miserable; famine was not common, and cultivation was very much easier, and therefore more profitable, than in most of the other countries of the Mediterranean and the Near East. Egyptian peasant farmers should have been able to extract a reasonable living from the land, even if their tenancies were vulnerable, or even non-existent. But they were open to gross abuse by officialdom. Apart from taxes, there was the business of the corvée, in which men were conscripted for long or short periods to work on state projects, and especially on the annual rehabilitation of the country following the Nile flood. The maintenance of canals, ditches, and dykes and the re-establishment of marked boundaries were crucial for the continuance of successful land management and good agriculture. The annual call-up for these necessary tasks was undoubtedly to the advantage of everyone who

worked on the land, but that did not make it welcome to those whose names came out of the corvée-master's hat. It is more than suspected that the process was open to abuse and corruption, and that those peasants at the bottom of the human heap would suffer greatest exploitation. The distaste aroused by the corvée and the fear that its application might extend into the afterlife were serious considerations for Egyptians at all levels of society, and account in part for the existence in burials, even of kings, of *shabti*-figures which were designed to rescue the great and the good from having to dirty their hands in annual ditch-clearing and dyke-mending. The *shabti* could by magic act for a named individual if the name came up in the corvée-list of the fields of Iaru. Such a way of escape was certainly not available for the humblest in the land, whether in life or in death.

Service in the army was similarly a fate which peasants would have found hard to escape. Precise details of how Egyptian forces were recruited are quite unknown. What is clear, however, from surviving records is that a large part of the army was made up of mercenary troops, recruited possibly under duress from Nubians, Libyans, and other foreign settlers, and also from the ranks of foreign prisoners of war, who would have had little option but to serve a new master. Soldiers in all such categories might have had some training or experience of the battlefield, and in consequence were of immediate use for active service. Untrained native Egyptians were also recruited, probably by a form of corvée, no doubt administered with great unfairness by low-rank officials. There may have been volunteers, possibly including young men dissatisfied with the life on the land and the absence of prospects for the future, and even

renegades escaping from justice. The romance of life in the army was undoubtedly an attraction, but it was not an attraction that could last. As ever, the scribe could sneer at the fate of the soldier, not to be compared with the comfortable, privileged life of the petty bureaucrat. The scribe Amenemope writes to the scribe Pabes, pointing out the superiority of their profession:

"Let me tell you of the position of the soldier – he who is tormented. He is carried off as a child, 2 cubits tall [about 1 meter, or 3.25 feet], and shut up in barracks. His body is thrashed, his eye is smashed, his brow cracked, his hand split with a wound. He is floored and pounded like papyrus... . And what about his going to Palestine and marching through the hills? He carries his bread and his water like a donkey, his neck ridged like that of a donkey. His backbone is distorted; he drinks foul water and stops marching only to go on guard duty. When he comes to battle, he is

already like a plucked bird, drained of all strength. When he returns to Egypt, he is like a worm-eaten stick; he is ill, utterly exhausted, riding on a donkey, his clothes stolen, abandoned by his attendant."

I do not think that Amenemope the scribe would have been used as a recruiting agent for the Egyptian army. And yet what he wrote was probably not very far from the actuality of military service. Throughout the ages, the life of the soldier may have been thought to be romantic, but in reality has been hard and dangerous, especially for the humble infantryman. The Qadesh reliefs do not conceal the misery of battle.

The lack of evidence of the kind that illuminates the lives of the inhabitants of the workmen's village at Dayr al-Madina for the rest of Egypt prevents reliable assessments from being made about the existence of the members of the

lowest strata of Egyptian society in Ramesses' reign. While the physical conditions of life may have been reasonably tolerable, the town dwellers – those engaged in the most unpleasant industries and in the back-breaking activities of commerce – undoubtedly suffered from squalor and neglect, unregarded by the great, exploited by junior officials and uncaring masters, exposed to disease, and with a very modest life-expectancy. No matter what you were or what you did, there were particular hazards. Another scribal essay, written in the north of the country, possibly in the region of Memphis, points out starkly the reality of life for most ordinary people:

"Man issues from his mother's womb and runs [at once] to his master; the child serves the soldier, the youth is a marauder. The old man is obliged to be a farm-hand, and the grown man to be a soldier. The cripple becomes a doorkeeper, and the blind man a fattener of cattle. The bird-catcher takes

position on the threshing floor; the fisherman is submerged. The god's servant is also a farmer; the priest carries out his duties, and spends much of his time immersing himself in the river, for his duties recur three times a day; it is the same, winter and summer, wind and rain.

If the stable manager relaxes his work, his team becomes abandoned in the field, his wife is put to measuring barley, his daughter is working on the dykes, his maidservant is conscripted [?] to the gang, and his assistant is [sent] to the quarries. The baker is always baking, putting bread on the fire, with his head right in the oven, his son hanging on-to his feet; if he slips from his son's grasp, he falls down into the oven."

That is the kind of thing you must expect if you are out in the rough, unkind world. As ever, how much better to be a scribe!

The one aspect of life in which tension might be relieved and some entertainment enjoyed, was,

as has been pointed out in an earlier chapter, the celebration of the periodic religious festivals and the grander occasions of the jubilee festivals during Ramesses' long reign. It is perhaps just as well that we do not have written records of the excesses, which undoubtedly accompanied such festivities. If there were registers of absentees from work drawn up throughout the land, there would surely be very many entries on the days following festivals in which the reason for absence would be 'illness,' or more specifically, 'recovering from the festival.' One would hope that even the strictest overseer would appreciate the compelling need to observe a festival with full participation. Festivals were among the few things in life to which the *rekheyet*, the ordinary Egyptians could look forward, and happily, in Ramesses' long reign there were many festivals, and they could be enjoyed without the problems of external threats or internal disturbances upsetting their proper observance.

622 top
Rosellini's drawing of a troop of Egyptian bowmen returning to Thebes after another victorious campaign. Some carry objects that appear to be booty, but texts do not speak of such benefits for the ordinary soldier.

622–623
Soldiers preparing for battle. An Egyptian with a shield and battle axe is followed by eager Nubian bowmen, stringing their bows and flourishing their arrows. In the New Kingdom, Nubian mercenaries were used for warfare and civil security. By Rosellini.

623 top
Young men engage in wrestling, in preparation, no doubt, of having to take part in hunting and warfare when their time came. From the tombs of Beni Hasan, drawn by Rosellini.

THE LEGEND
OF RAMESSES II

If a sovereign reigns for a great many years, there is a good chance that he may be remembered in later times partly because the name is one that has become indelibly printed on the tablets of people's minds. The name may even be used to characterize a whole period. Today one can think in particular of Victoria, who was the British queen from 1837 until 1901 and whose name conjures up the culture of the greater part of the nineteenth century and is used in this respect not only in Britain itself, but commonly in America, and even in some European countries. 'Victorian' is not always used in a complimentary way; in moral matters, it suggests a very old-fashioned approach to the conduct of life; in artistic matters, it has often a pejorative force; in industrial and business matters, it regularly invokes scientific invention and commercial enterprise. 'Victorian' can be good and bad; it can represent a virtuous way of life, or one unutterably dreary and outdated.

What about Ramesses II? Egyptologists have often characterized his reign as being one of special qualities, to be considered almost an era in itself. He is commonly called Ramesses the Great, and his reign, taken with those of his successors to the end of the Twentieth Dynasty, is called the Ramesside Period. It can be given this sobriquet quite simply because most of the kings who reigned during this time carried the nomen Ramesses. But it was not a coherent period in which the characteristics of the reign of Ramesses II continued to be evident for the next 150 years. The name Ramesses served as the link, but scarcely as the model for most of the kings of the later Twentieth Dynasty, similarily named. The only king Ramesses who bears in any way comparison with the great predecessor was Ramesses III, second king of the Twentieth Dynasty (c. 1184–1153 B.C.). He was the first Egyptian ruler to carry the name Ramesses after his illustrious namesake, and he also took the

prenomen Usimare, by which Ramesses II was particularly known in much later times in the Greek form Osymandyas. Ramesses III undoubtedly saw himself as a worthy successor and endeavored during his reasonably long reign of thirty years to pursue policies in foreign and in domestic affairs which were aimed certainly at trying to restore the successes of the earlier reign. That he achieved only partial success in his purposes was not entirely his fault. The pattern of external pressures on Egypt from Asia, Libya, and the Mediterranean world had radically changed, while within Egypt the even tenor of life was seriously disturbed by tensions within society and unfavorable harvests. Still, he was Usimare Ramesses, and in a sense he must have hoped that the magic of the names would bring him success. To emphasize his close following of his illustrious (but not quite direct) ancestor, he even built at Medinet Habu a great mortuary temple roughly on the same plan as the Ramesseum, which at the

624
*Limestone slab from a structure
in the Apis complex at Saqqara,
built by or associated with Prince
Khaemwese; his head is shown
wearing the sidelock commonly
worn by the* sem-*priest of Ptah.*

time was probably the best preserved and certainly the most impressive of the surviving mortuary temples. Ramesses III also included in his temple a special chapel for the cult of Ramesses II's image in its divine bark.

Although no kings later than the Twentieth Dynasty carried the nomen Ramesses, a significant number during the Twenty-second and Twenty-third Dynasties took as part of their prenomen the significant Usimare, the name by which the original Ramesses II should, in Egyptian tradition, be better known. While the names of Ramesses II still resonated to a certain degree at the highest level of Egyptian society, a fading memory of his greatness and importance remained in the memories of Egyptians generally. An educated scribe of the latest Pharaonic times, skilled in the demotic script, might not have been able to recognize Ramesses' cartouches if he had walked past the great but probably ruined temples in the Delta cities, or in Memphis or in Thebes, but he could be well acquainted with the stories told about the great Pharaoh Usimare and his son Khaemwese.

Tales written on papyrus in the demotic script, the very cursive successor to the hieratic script (the form used on the ostraca of the Theban workmen), have as their principal character a priestly prince called Setne Khamuas. Setne is a corruption of an old priestly title, *setem* or *sem*, used in the case of Khamuas (Khaemwese) as if it were a first name. The stories are preserved on papyri in the Cairo Museum and the British Museum and are ostensibly set in the time of the great Pharaoh Usimare. The principal figure is Setne Khamuas, who retains something of his historical character of wise man or magician, although in the stories he is made to appear less than worldly-wise, or even noble.

The most entertaining episode involves magic, seduction, retribution, and a happy ending. Setne Khamuas learns of a magical book in the keeping of the spirit of a priest called Naneferkaptah in his tomb in Saqqara. By trickery, Setne Khamuas steals the book from the tomb and carries it off in triumph, although warned by Naneferkaptah that terrible things would happen to him. Setne's father, the Pharaoh Usimare, advises him to return the book, protecting himself with powerful charms. He ignores this advice and falls into an adventure which threatens to destroy him. Walking one day in the precinct of the temple of Ptah, he notices an attractive lady whom he attempts to woo. She turns out to be a priestess of Bastet, the cat goddess of Bubastis, who, having at first rejected Khamuas' advances, then arranges an assignation in her house in Bubastis. In due course Khamuas travels to Bubastis and seeks out the house of the priestess, whose name is Tabubu. He is eager to achieve her seduction, but she teases him and then persuades him to make a will in her favor. She pursues her advantage and gets Khamuas to summon his children and have them sign away their rights to any inheritance. Finally, in order to secure his purpose with Tabubu, he agrees to have his children killed, and while he and the priestess settle down to the consummation of their passion, they can hear the noise of dogs and cats tearing at the children's corpses in the court below. Even then Khamuas is denied his hard-won reward; as he stretches out his hand to touch Tabubu, she lets out a great cry and he wakes up in a state of sexual excitement, with no clothes on, in the open country. At that moment he sees a company approach with a great man carried in a litter; he turns out to be Pharaoh, his father. Embarrassed because he is in the nude, Khamuas finds it difficult to get up; but Pharaoh spots him: "Setne why are you in this state?"

"It is Naneferkaptah who is responsible," says Khamuas. Pharaoh tells him to go to Memphis, where he will find his children waiting for him. "How can I go to Memphis with no clothes?"

Usimare orders a servant to bring him clothes. Back in Memphis, he is asked by Pharaoh whether he had been drunk. He then tells of his adventure with Tabubu, and his father advises him to take the magic book back to Naneferkaptah. Protected by a forked stick and with a lighted brazier on his head, Setne Khamuas takes the book back to the tomb in Saqqara and hands it over to the spirit of Naneferkaptah.

"It is the great god Ptah who has brought you back in safety," says the spirit's wife Ahwerre.

"I told you so!" says the spirit itself. And they parted on friendly terms.

This wholly fanciful story is a product of literary invention, but peopled with identifiable characters placed in an identifiable setting. Setne Khamuas was one thousand years earlier, Khaemwese, favored son of Ramesses II and the high priest of Ptah in Memphis. In this city he was at home, and in the adjacent necropolis of Saqqara he would be buried. Of Tabubu nothing is known, but it is known that there was a small temple dedicated to the goddess Bastet in a district of Memphis called Ankhtawy, which is mentioned in the story. Bubastis lay about one hundred kilometers (sixty-two miles) to the northwest of Memphis, and was easily accessible by water. Nothing else in the story corresponds with the reality of the times of Ramesses II, the Usimare of the narrative. It is a romance, and part of a series of romances based on the imaginary happenings involving a person of historical reality who might still have been remembered in a shadowy form, along with his father, the great Ramesses II, whose sculptures were still to be seen in the city of Memphis.

Ramesses II

A rather different kind of remembered event, and involving a more clearly defined royal person, is recorded on a fine stone stela over 7 feet tall (2.22 meters), discovered in 1829 in Karnak near the temple of Khonsu, within the precinct of the great temple of Amon-Re, and now in the Louvre Museum in Paris. It is carved and set out as if it were an inscription of the time of Ramesses II, but it was undoubtedly made toward the end of the Pharaonic Period, possibly in the Twenty-seventh Dynasty (Persian) in the sixth century B.C., but before the arrival of Alexander the Great in 332 B.C. It is an unusual creation for this time, and there has been much debate about why it should have been made. Every effort seems to have been employed to produce a convincing pastiche of a Nineteenth Dynasty royal inscription. Even the language is a reasonable copy of the grammar, syntax, and spelling of an authentic text of Ramesses' time. Some kind of propaganda purpose may be suggested as the reason for its making, possibly political, possibly religious, involving the cults connected with the Khonsu temple. It is clear, however, that it was considered necessary to invoke the memory of the great Ramesses, a real presence at Karnak, the site where he could still be recalled by those who could read the multifarious inscriptions set up in his name. But who could, or would, read this stela with the story of Bentresh, Princess of Bakhtan? It is altogether an enigma. The scene at the top of the stela is in two parts: on the right, Ramesses II makes offering to the bark of Khonsu in his form 'Contriver in Thebes'; on the left, a priest named Khonsuemhet-netjerneb carries

out a similar presentation. This double scene establishes the relevance of the monument to the cults of Khonsu in Karnak, which, as emerges from the text, include that of Khonsu-Neferhotep. The text begins with a full royal titulary, including the names Usimare-Setpenre and Ramessu-Miamun, prenomen and nomen of Ramesses II, quite correctly, but with other royal names, which refer specifically to King Tuthmosis IV of the Eighteenth Dynasty (c. 1400–1390 B.C.). After a florid royal encomium, the main text begins with a retrospective preamble telling of Ramesses' annual visit to the land of Naharin (northern Syria), where he receives tribute from many foreign princes, including a special gift from the Prince of Bakhtan, is eldest daughter. Ramesses is delighted and makes her a great royal wife with the name Neferure and brings her back to Egypt, where "she did everything appropriate for a queen." Now follows the account of events, which closely involve the cults of Khonsu. A precise date establishes the time of a visit by an envoy from the Prince of Bakhtan: Year 23, second month of summer, day 22 (supposedly c. 1257 B.C. in the real reign of Ramesses). At this time Ramesses is in Thebes celebrating the Opet Festival. The envoy presents gifts, and then reveals the real purpose of his visit: Neferure's younger sister Bentresh is seriously ill – can an Egyptian doctor be sent to help? The royal scribe Djehuty-emheb is recommended and duly sent; he diagnoses an evil spirit in possession of Bentresh's body, and the Prince of Bakhtan writes to Ramesses requesting a visit from an appropriate

god to wrestle with the evil spirit. This is in Year 26. Being again in Thebes, Ramesses consults Khonsu-Neferhotep, the principal form of the god, and he suggests Khonsu-the-Contriver, "the great god who drives out sickness demons." Fortified with extra magic, Khonsu-the-Contriver (that is, his cult-image) is sent with great ceremony and an impressive retinue to Bakhtan, which he reaches after a journey of one year and five months.

As soon as Khonsu-the-Contriver has been welcomed in Bakhtan, he is taken to the sick princess, and in no time drives out the evil spirit, who submits without a struggle, saying, "Be welcome, great god who drives out evil spirits. Bakhtan is now your city, its inhabitants are your servants, and I too am your servant. Now I shall return to the place from where I came, so as to satisfy your wish in the matter for which you came to this city. May your divine majesty order the celebration of a festival in which I and the Prince of Bakhtan can take part." While these private exchanges are being made in the princess's chamber, the Prince of Bakhtan and his entourage remain outside in terror at the terrible noises coming from within. When the cure is revealed, the prince arranges the great festival as the spirit suggested, but secretly plans to keep the image of Khonsu-the-Contriver for a little more time; in fact it turns out to be for three years and nine months. Then the prince has a dream in which he sees the god leave its shrine as a golden falcon and fly away in the direction of Egypt. Ashamed at what he has done in delaying its return, he

calls the god's priest, saying, "It seems that your god is still here in Bakhtan with us. It is high time that he went back to Egypt. Get his chariot ready." And so the god leaves Bakhtan, greatly honored and weighed down with many rich gifts. The whole population of Bakhtan turns out to send him on his way. When he is back in Thebes, Khonsu-the-Contriver goes to report to the shrine of Khonsu-Neferhotep, and gives him all the gifts from Bakhtan. By then it is Year 33, second month of winter, day 19 of the King of Upper and Lower Egypt, Usimare-Setpenre. The episode has lasted ten years.

This extraordinary inscription, which is of its kind not unique among ancient Egyptian monumental texts, is a fantasy, almost a romantic fiction, and could be classified as such were it not to be seen as having connections with the cult of Khonsu-Neferhotep in Thebes and having a purpose other than fictional. It is significant that the events should be placed in the reign of Ramesses II, who had perhaps as much as seven hundred years before the text was carved, ruled over the land of Egypt. The main intent seems to be the boosting of the prestige of Khonsu by invoking long-past events, which can be linked only tenuously to the reign of Ramesses. The king's marriage to a foreign princess took place in his Year 34 (c. 1246–1245 B.C.), not Year 23, as the Late Period text has it. The foreign wife was given the name Mahor-neferure, while in the later texts she is just Neferure. The historical foreign wife was Hittite; the later has always been taken to be a princess of Bakhtan. This country is

otherwise not known, and Egyptologists in the past have usually thought the name to be a version of the Egyptian word for Bactria, a country in the farthest reaches of Central Asia. Recently, however, it has been suggested that there was a misinterpretation of a crucial hieroglyph in the writing of the place name, and that what the composer of the text had intended was Hatti, the land of the Hittites. Such a solution would greatly help to equate the 'legend' on the stela with the historic events surrounding Ramesses' Hittite marriage. The idea of having medical exchanges between countries in the ancient world is well founded. In even earlier times, the king of Babylon sent the cult-image of Ishtar of Nineveh to assist the ailing King Amenophis III of the Eighteenth Dynasty. Hittite sources record that medical help was sought from Egypt during Ramesses' reign. In general, Egyptian physicians were famous in antiquity, practicing specialization and often traveling to other countries when required. The possibility of a request for help from the Hittites is therefore by no means out of the question, and even the sending of a divine image not contrary to ancient practice. It would be possible to point to a number of apparent errors in the account of the whole episode, but these would not amount to a significant weakness in the account. For us now, it is significant to observe the persistence of the memory of Ramesses II, and the use of his name and some events of his reign to support the cult of Khonsu-Neferhotep at a time of strain in Egyptian affairs, when Persians dominated the land.

627
Heraldic device of a kind found on columns in buildings of the reign of Ramesses II. The nomen and prenomen of Ramesses are set over the sign for "gold," topped with sun disks, and flanked by uraei, *also with sun disks.*

The memory of Ramesses II continued to resonate in the writings of Greek authors, who knew nothing first-hand of the great king but relied on the faded recollections and stories of native Egyptians. Herodotus, the Greek historian, traveled in Egypt in the mid-fifth century B.C., and in Book II of his *History*, he includes his findings on the history, culture, religion, and other aspects of ancient Egypt at a time when Egypt was under Persian domination (the Twenty-seventh Dynasty, in the reckoning of Manetho). Although there had been a Greek-assisted revolution in the Delta not long before his visit, and the Persians generally were still more than suspicious of Greek, particularly Athenian, intentions, Herodotus seems to have had little difficulty in entering Egypt and traveling throughout the country for several months. There had been a considerable Greek presence in Egypt since the seventh century B.C., and not all Greek communities were necessarily anti-Persian, or particularly pro-Athenian. Herodotus picked up his information in an apparently casual manner, and does not describe or comment on the monuments of antiquity in a regular or geographically systematic manner. He does, however, talk of the king named Rhampsinitus, and of his particular monument, which was the western gateway to the temple of Vulcan, that is, the Ptah temple in Memphis, which had two colossal figures standing before it. These, according to the comments of the priests, were called Summer and Winter, the former being an object of devotion to ordinary Egyptians and the latter, the opposite. The name Rhampsinitus is now generally thought to be a corruption of Ramesses

with the added epithet sa-Neith, 'son of Neith' (the goddess of the Delta city Sais). This epithet was never part of the formal titulary of Ramesses II, but was a common royal epithet for kings of the Twenty-sixth Dynasty and later. Scholars are not at all sure that Rhampsinitus is Ramesses II, or even a conflation of Ramesses II and Ramesses III; and there is no reason to think that Herodotus had any particular Egyptian king in mind. He was purveying priestly information, and it is not clear whether he himself had been to Memphis and seen the Ptah temple and the colossal statues in that city. Herodotus also seems not to have visited the great funerary temples of the Ramesseum and Medinet Habu (Ramesses III), in the first of which he would have seen colossal statues greater than those in Memphis and on which he could hardly have failed to comment. In fact he gives no general account of Thebes and its monuments, and some scholars have doubted, probably erroneously, that he ever traveled in Upper Egypt. He says more about Rhampsinitus, however, in presenting at length a story concerning him which might contain vague recollections of the prosperity of the years when Ramesses II was king, and even of his great mortuary temple, the Ramesseum. According to the story, Rhampsinitus was immensely rich, with a vast store of precious objects, for which he built an apparently impregnable treasure-house. The builder, knowing the reason for the structure, incorporated in it a loose stone, by the removal of which he might be able to enter and steal treasure from time to time. He himself never took advantage of the loose stone, but he passed on the knowledge of it to his two sons on his deathbed.

They immediately began to exploit the possibility of wealth, and continued to do so until the king, aware that thefts were taking place regularly, set traps. One of the sons got caught, and he persuaded his brother to cut off his head so that his body might remain unidentified. The king, astonished at finding the headless body, there still being no sign of obvious entry into the treasure-house, had the body displayed publicly in the hope of discovering its identity by the appearance of a weeping mother. She, in great distress had her surviving son retrieve the body by tricking the guards and making them drunk. Again the king was angered and more determined than before to catch the other thief; he used one of his daughters as bait, installing her in a brothel and requiring her to ask any client what had been the cleverest and most wicked thing he had ever done. Once again the thief saw through the trick, visited the brothel, duped the daughter, and escaped, leaving her holding on to the arm of a newly dead man. The king then gave up, offered the thief a rich reward, and when he surrendered, he was offered the king's daughter as his wife., and Rhampsinitus declared: "The Egyptians are wiser than the rest of the world, and this man is wisest of them all." One may assume that if Rhampsinitus were indeed Ramesses II, he could easily have spared one of his large number of daughters, especially as the one in question had become what might be called 'soiled goods,' for whom he might not easily find a respectable husband.

Some scholars have thought that the whole story refers to Ramesses III, and that the treasure-house was the temple of Medinet Habu, or one of

its subsidiary buildings. It is much more likely, however, that the Ramesseum, the mortuary temple of Ramesses II, is the intended site. There is good evidence to suggest that in the late Pharaonic Period, the Ramesseum was the more striking complex of buildings, in spite of the fact that the Medinet Habu temple was in a far better state of preservation. But Medinet Habu had by then already become a busy township in itself, the main temple being almost engulfed by domestic and other buildings. It remained so, and became even more cluttered with mud-brick structures until it was extricated from its engulfment in mud-brick by excavators in the early decades of the twentieth century. It was never visited in modern times by early travelers and archaeologists to the same extent as the Ramesseum, where an uncluttered precinct offered more open access to the structures of its founder. Furthermore, within the precinct at the back of the temple, there is an impressive range of vaulted mud-brick buildings, storerooms for temple goods, and possibly seen in late antiquity as the positive evidence for the treasure-house of Ramesses II; and these storerooms were only a few hundred meters from the small palace built within the precinct for the king's occasional visits to Thebes.

It will never be possible to determine satisfactorily who Rhampsinitus was, or to confirm the details of the story recounted by Herodotus. The amiable Greek historian ends his account of the Egyptian king by reporting the priestly opinion that up to the time of his death, Egypt was well governed and prospered greatly. These judgments would apply better to the long and generally successful reign of Ramesses II than to that of Ramesses III, when the country suffered from internal as well as external problems. It would, however, be quite a mistake to place too much reliance on all that Herodotus recounts. He follows the reign of Rhampsinitus with that of Cheops, the builder of the Great Pyramid, who in fact reigned about thirteen hundred years before Ramesses II. Nevertheless, there remain in the account of Rhampsinitus' reign faint suggestions, which can quite properly be traced to memories of the great king.

Even more positive resonance may be found in the work of the later Greek writer Diodorus the Sicilian, who composed his *History* in the first century B.C. Although he never traveled in Egypt as far south as Thebes, he includes descriptions of Theban monuments, including what he calls "the tomb of Osymandyas." This "tomb," as described, bears a close resemblance to the Ramesseum, especially in respect of the colossi of the great king which littered the precinct, and were clearly to be observed in the first century B.C. Diodorus writes in particular of one vast seated colossus of the king carved from a single piece of the black stone of Syene, that is, the so-called black granite (more properly described as granodiorite) from the quarries at Aswan. He gives a summary description of the statue, which he calls the biggest in Egypt, and he paraphrases the inscription on it: "King of kings, Osymandyas am I. If anyone wishes to know how great I am and where I lie, let him surpass my works." Osymandyas has very reasonably been identified as a Greek corruption of Usimare, Ramesses II's prenomen. The Ramesseum is described as the "sacred precinct of Memnon" by the Greek geographer Strabo, who was a contemporary of Diodorus. The use of Memnon to describe the maker of the Ramesseum (whether tomb or temple) clearly suggests that Strabo, and other classical authors who use the name (probably following Strabo), were ignorant of the historical Ramesses and employed the name of the mythical Greek hero as being a suitable candidate for the ownership of this great structure. For much the same reason, the two great statues of King Amenophis III, which dominate the flood plain not far from the Ramesseum, were called the Colossi of Memnon – and still are, erroneously but affectionately, to this day. Confusion over identification reveals the ignorance of these Greek writers about the Ramesseum and its builder, and the use of the name Memnon makes it evident that they were floundering in a morass of part information, part legend, part romantic invention. If they visited Egypt they had to rely on what they were told by Egyptians or by Greek inhabitants of Egypt, or what they may have read in the writings of earlier Greek authors. They could not read hieroglyphs, and if they had been able to do so, they would still have had difficulty in extracting information that they could properly comprehend. What they gleaned surely came to a great extent from what the local folk-memories purveyed, and we all know how unreliable such memories can be. If Diodorus was close to the truth in calling the Ramesseum the tomb of Osymandyas, his fellow writers like Strabo were well off the mark in bringing Memnon into the story.

629

Marble bust of Herodotus of Halicarnassus, Greek historian of the fifth century B.C., whose account of Egypt, in the second book of his History, *contains the story of Rhampsinitus, apparently Ramesses the Great.*

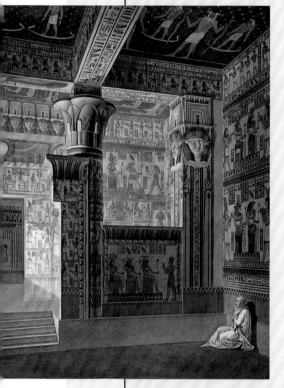

But it was Memnon who stuck in later tradition, so that when the engraved scenes of the Ramesseum were published in the massive French *Description de l'Égypte*, one of the most important products of the Napoleonic invasion of Egypt (1798–1801), the great mortuary temple of Ramesses II is described as the tomb of Memnon, the Memnonium. The connection with Ramesses II was not made, and even if the name of Osymandyas was also sometimes used, it could not have been understood that it concealed the true prenomen of the great king, Usimare. It would be some years before the name Ramesses in hieroglyphs would be identified by Jean-François Champollion, to whom must go the greatest credit for the decipherment of the Egyptian script.

At the beginning of the nineteenth century, scholars were about to step from the ignorance of the past into the knowledge and clarity of the future, as far as Egypt was concerned. At that point, the name Ramesses was known from the chronicle of Manetho as having been a long-lived king of the Eighteenth-Nineteenth Dynasties. The name was also known from the Old Testament as that of an Egyptian town (in fact, probably Piramesse) on which the Children of Israel had toiled. The name could not yet be recognized in its hieroglyphic form, and buildings that carried the name could not be dated. When Henry Salt and William John Bankes came to Ramesses' great temple at Abu Simbel in 1818, one year after it had been opened for Salt by Giovanni-Battista Belzoni, they had no idea when the temple had been carved out of the rock or who was represented by the great seated colossi on the façade. Bankes, standing on the sand-drift in front of the entrance, noted a Greek inscription high on the leg of one of the colossi referring to a campaign in Nubia during the reign of a king named Psammetichus. From classical sources Bankes knew that there were kings named Psammetichus in the Twenty-sixth Dynasty. They ruled in the seventh and sixth centuries B.C., and Bankes deduced that the builder of Abu Simbel must have lived many years earlier. The carver of the Greek text must have stood on a sand-drift high above the pavement leading to the temple entrance in order to reach the point on the leg that he had chosen for his inscription. The name of the temple owner would be known within ten years of the Salt-Bankes visit, but before the decipherment of hieroglyphics, scholars and travelers could only guess at the identity of kings.

It is not surprising, therefore, that Memnon was accepted in the early nineteenth century, but it is surprising that the name may still be used even today. Diodorus wrote about the great seated colossus in the Ramesseum. In 1801 William Hamilton, an envoy of Lord Elgin, traveled through Egypt, and in the Ramesseum noted the bust of a colossal statue: "It is certainly the most beautiful and perfect piece of Egyptian sculpture that can be seen throughout the whole country. We were struck by its extraordinary delicacy; the very uncommon expression visible in its features." He goes on to say, "The place in which it is to be found exactly answers to the sacred precinct of Memnon [Hamilton uses the Greek of Strabo here]." A little over fifteen years later, this bust

630
A reconstructed view in full color of the inside of the small Ptolemaic temple at Dayr al-Madina, as envisaged by the artists of the Description de l'Égypte. *It is probable that Egyptian temples were even more brightly painted.*

was removed from the Ramesseum by Belzoni on behalf of Henry Salt and the Swiss orientalist Jean-Louis Burckhardt, who together presented it to the British Museum. In London it was known as the Memnon, or the Younger Memnon, being smaller than the great Colossi of Memnon (a different king) or the shattered granodiorite monster in the Ramesseum. Even now the bust in London is sometimes affectionately called the Younger Memnon, although its true identity has been well known for almost two hundred years.

The Young Memnon arrived in London in 1817 and was soon included in the display of Egyptian and other ancient sculptures, although not, as one unsympathetic trustee pointed out to Salt some years later, "among the works of Fine Art... . Whether any statue that has been found in Egypt can be brought into competition with the grand works of the Townley Gallery [that is, Greek sculpture] remains to be proved." Nevertheless, the bust made its mark in London and received much favorable publicity. At about the time of its arrival, the poet Percy Bysshe Shelley was writing his sonnet "Ozymandias," and it has often been claimed that its inspiration was this bust from the Ramesseum. Few scholars, whether of ancient Egypt or of English literature, now believe this attribution is correct in spite of the temporal coincidence of the bust's arrival and the sonnet's composition. The king represented in the bust was never identified with the Osymandyas of Diodorus, and it is now supposed that the source for Shelley's sonnet, apart from Diodorus (for Shelley was a good classical scholar), was William Hamilton. He had written

about the Ramesseum and the Memnon, and may have even talked to Shelley about the great fallen colossus in the temple. Hamilton indeed may be the person involved in the opening lines of the poem:

> I met a traveller from an antique land
> Who said: "Two vast and trunkless legs of stone
> Stand in the desert. Near them, on the sand,
> Half sunk, a shattered visage lies... ."

Diodorus is undoubtedly the source for the lines:

> And on the pedestal these words appear:
> "My name is Ozymandias, King of kings:
> Look on my works, ye Mighty, and despair!"

And so was Ozymandias (Osymandyas), Usimare, introduced by way of a poem to the British public, and at the same time the noble features of the great Ramesses were revealed in the British Museum under the alias of 'Memnon.' There is nothing to connect the two 'revelations,' nothing to suggest that that at that time (1817), Ozymandias and the Younger Memnon were one and the same person, although not the same sculpture. But it would be only a few years before the hieroglyphic cartouches of Ramesses II were identified. In no time would the extent of his building works throughout Egypt be appreciated, and his presence identified in the impressive battle scenes of Qadesh in the temples of Thebes and at Abu Simbel. John Gardner Wilkinson, in his *Manners and Customs of the Ancient Egyptians*

(1837), compares at length Diodorus' description of the Memnonium with the actual surviving features of the Ramesseum, and concludes very properly that Ramesses II was its builder. He notes, further, that the long reign ascribed to this king by Manetho (sixty-six years) is practically confirmed by the dates in Year 62 already discovered on his surviving monuments. In France, Champollion had identified the name Ramesses among the first royal cartouches he deciphered, and he was soon to reveal the extent and importance of his monuments, including the great obelisk from Luxor, which he recommended for removal to Paris. It was, after many delays, taken down and transported to the French capital, where it was re-erected in the Place de la Concorde in October 1833. In Italy, by about the same date, the fine seated statue of the young Ramesses II from Karnak was established in the Egyptian Museum in Turin. At the same time, many monuments of that king and of his reign were entering the great collections of Europe and bringing the myth of the great Ramesses to practical view. The legend of Ramesses II was thus being renewed with knowledge drawn from ancient sources that could provide a new age with a profile very different from the one that survived to the late Pharaonic Period; Ramesses would soon be invested with a new glamour. No matter what the scholars may say about the impossibility of getting close to the great kings and queens of ancient Egypt, there are many people who see the monuments of Ramesses II, especially the resited temples of the king and of his wife Nefertari at Abu Simbel, and feel that they know him more than a little.

GLOSSARY

afnet Tight-fitting cap crown with a short "tail," and on the brow, the *uraeus*.

ankh Egyptian word for "life;" written with a sign similar to a cross with a loop at the top; carried by gods and offfered to kings.

Apis Sacred bull, incarnation of Ptah, the god of Memphis. Kept in the temple precinct of Ptah in Memphis and buried in Saqqara, in a place called now the Serapeum.

atef A crown incorporating ram's horns, the sun-disk and ostrich feathers, worn by Osiris, and sometimes by the king.

blue crown Crown with *uraeus*, shaped something like bishop's miter, usually colored blue, and worn by the king in battle.

canopic jars Four containers placed in a burial, containing the embalmed entrails of the deceased.

cap-crown A tight-fitting crown, sometimes thought erroneously to be a form of the blue crown; worn by the king in carrying out certain functions.

cartouche Oval rope-shape with tie, used to enclose the prenomen and nomen of the king.

djed Pillar-like sign, sometimes described as Osiris' backbone; often used amuletically with the sense of

"endurance," and decoratively with the *tyet*-sign.

faience Glazed quart frit, a material much used in ancient Egypt for moulded vessels, small figures and colored inlays.

flail One of the two signs of power regularly held by the king; its origin is uncertain, but may be agricultural.

hemi-speos Temple of which part (e.g. the sanctuary) is cut into the rock, and part built free-standing.

heqa Crook-shaped scepter, one of the two signs of royal power.

hypostyle Hall in a temple, the roof of which is supported by many pillars.

Iunmutef "Pillar of his mother," a form of Horus, and also of a priest representing him, and associated with the *sem*-priest.

Iusa'as Heliopolitan goddess, 'She who becomes great as she comes,' a divine expression of the female principle.

ka The element of a person's being, often, but inaccurately, equated with the "soul." Its function was specially important after death, in representing the deceased.

Kamutef "Bull of his mother;" the name of Amon-Re in that of the god Min, mummiform and ithyphallic.

khepesh Curved scimitar-like sword, symbol of royal power, often shown being presented to the king by a god.

Ma'at Egyptian word for "truth, order," and personified as the goddess Ma'at, shown with the feather of "truth;" often presented as a small figure with the feather on the squatting goddess's knee.

mammisi Birth-house; a room or separate building in a temple in which the divine birth of the king is shown and celebrated.

Memnon Classical here incorrectly identified with the Egyptian king of the Colossi of Memnon (Amenophis III and of the Ramesseum (Ramesses II).

Memnonium Tomb of Memnon, erroneously applied by early travellers and scholars to the Ramesseum.

Menhit Protective goddess, in origin possibly the cobra, but later often shown as a lioness-headed woman.

moringa Tree with oil-yielding fruit, associated with certain deities, who are described as being "under" or "in his moringa tree."

nemes The most common royal headdress, made possibly of cloth, pleated, with "wings" and lappets, with the *uraeus* on the brow.

nome Term used for the provinces of ancient Egypt, of which there were 22 in Upper Egypt and 20 in Lower Egypt.

nomen Names contained in the second cartouche of a king's titulary; his birth name.

Opet The greatest annual Theban festival, when the gods of Karnak, the Theban triad, Amon-Re, Mut and Khonsu, traveled by river to Luxor to celebrate a sacred marriage.

Osiride pillar Square pillar in a temple with an attached figure of Osiris, mummiform, usually with the identity of the appropriate king.

ostracon Sherd of pottery or sliver of limestone, used for casual writings.

persea The tree *Mimusops schimperi*, on the leaves of which the gods traditionally wrote the name of reigning monarch.

prenomen Name contained in the first cartouche of the king's titulary. His throne name.

Renpet Goddess, the personification of the year, especially in connection with the years of the king's reign.

sed The royal jubilee, the festival of renewal, celebrated after thirty years of rule, every three years following.

sem-priest Priest especially in the service

of Ptah in Memphis, shown wearing a leopard skin and with a long sidelock.

Serapeum Name given to the part of the Saqqara necropolis where the embalmed Apis bulls were interred.

shabti Funerary figurine placed in a burial to act as the deputy of the deceased when called upon for certain menial tasks in the afterlife. Often called *ushabti* or *shawabty*.

speos Rock-cut temple, such as Abu Simbel.

stela Inscription, usually in the form of a freestanding monument, with funerary, historical or celebratory texts.

tyet Object in the form of a knot, used amuletically and associated with Isis; sometimes called "blood of Isis;" often used decoratively in alternation with the *djed*-pillar.

uraeus The cobra placed on the brow of a king, representing the protective goddess Wadjet of Buto in the Delta.

user-staff Staff with the top often in the form of an animal's head, representing "power;" usually carried by gods.

Weret-hekau Goddess often in serpent form, "Great one of magic," closely associated with Isis and the protective power of the king.

AUTHOR

T. G. Henry James was born in 1923 in Neath, South Wales and passed away in 2009. Educated at Oxford University, he spent his whole professional life in the British Museum, where he was keeper of Egyptian Antiquites from 1974 to 1988. He worked in Egypt on excavations and the United States. He specialized in the publication of texts on stone and on papyrus, and in writing history; he also wrote many books on aspects of Egypt-ian life, the country, its monuments, and its art. His most famous books are: *Howard Carter: The Path to Tutankhamun* (1992), *A Short History of Ancient Egypt* (1995), *Egypt Revealed* (1997) and *Tutankhamun: The Splendor of the Boy Pharaoh* (2000).

For White Star he published *Tutankhamun* and *Ramesses II* (2000 and 2001) and he was one of the contributors to *The Valley of the Kings* (2001).

INDEX

BIBLIOGRAPHY

Alfred, C., *Akhenaten and Nefertiti*. London, New York, 1973.

Alfred, C., *Akhenaten, King of Egypt*. London, New York, 1988.

Alfred, C., *Jewels of the Pharaohs*. London, 1971.

Alfred, C., *Tutankhamun: Craftsmanship in Gold in the reign of the king*. New York, 1979.

Baines, J., and J. Malek, *Atlas of Ancient Egypt*. Oxford, New York, 1980.

Baker, H.S., *Furniture in the Ancient World. Origins and evolution, 3100-475 B.C*. London, 1966.

Beinlich, H. and M. Saleh, *Corpus der hieroglyphischen Inschriften aus dem Grab des Tutankhamun*. Oxford, 1989.

Bierbrier, M.L., *Tomb Builders of the Pharaohs*. London, 1982; Cairo, 1989.

Bietak, M., *Avaris: Capital of the Hyksos. Recent Excavations*. London, 1996.

Bleiberg, E., & Freed, R., eds., *Fragments of a shattered visage. Proceedings of the International Symposium on Ramesses the Great*. Memphis, TN, 1991.

Breasted, C., *Pioneer to the Past*. London, 1947.

Carnarvon, the Earl of, and H. Carter, *Five Years' Explorations at Thebes; a record of work done, 1907-1911*. Oxford, 1912.

Carter, H., *The Tomb of Tut.ankh.amen*. 3 Vols. (Vol. 1 with A. Mace). London, 1923-33.

Carter, H. and A.H. Gardiner, "The Tomb of Ramesses VI and the Turin plan of a royal tomb" in *Journal of Egyptian Archaeology*, 4, pp. 130-158. London, 1917.

Černý, J., *Hieratic Inscriptions from the tomb of Tut'ankhamūn*. Oxford, 1965.

Davies, Nina M., and A.H. Gardiner, *Tutankhamun's Painted Box*. Oxford, 1962.

Davies, N. de G., *The Rock Tombs of El Amarna*. 6 Vol., London, 1903-08.

Davis, T.M., and others, *The Tomb of Harmhabi and Touatankhamanou*. London, 1912.

Davis, T.M., *The Tomb of Iouiya and Touiyou*. London, 1907.

Desroches-Noblecourt, C., Kuentz, C., *Le Petit temple d'Abou Simbel*. Cairo, 1968.

Desroches-Noblecourt, C., *Tutankhamen. Life and Death of a Pharaoh*. London, 1963.

Eaton-Krauss, M., *The Sarcophagus in the Tomb of Tutankhamun*. Oxford, 1993.

Eaton-Krauss, M. and E. Graefe, *The small golden shrine from the Tomb of Tutankhamun*. Oxford, 1985.

Edwards, I.E.S., *Treasures of Tutankhamun*. London, 1972.

Edwards, I.E.S., *Treasures of Tutankhamun*. New York, 1976.

Edwards, I.E.S., *Tutankhamun: his tomb and its treasures*. New York, 1976.

Edwards, I.E.S., *Tutankhamun's Jewelry*. New York, 1976.

El-Khouli, Ali A.R.H. and others, *Stone Vessels, Pottery and Sealings from the tomb of Tut'ankhamūn*. Oxford, 1993.

Faulkner, R.O., *The Ancient Egyptian Book of the Dead*. London, 1985.

Faulkner, R.O., *The Ancient Egyptian Pyramid Texts*. 2Vol. Oxford, 1969.

Fox, P., *Tutankhamun's Treasures*. London, 1951.

Freed, R.E., *Ramesses the Great. His Life and Works*. Exhibition Catalogue. Menphis, TN, 1987.

Gardiner, A.H., *Egypt of the Pharaohs*. Oxford, 1961.

Gardiner, A.H., *My Working Years*. Privately published, 1962.

Gardiner, A.H., *The Kadesh Inscriptions of Ramesses II*. Oxford, 1960.

Gurney, O.R., *The Hittites*. London, 1952 (latest revision, 1999).

Habachi, L., *Features of the deification of Ramesses II*. Glückstadts, 1969.

Hornung, E., *Conceptions of God, in Ancient Egypt*. London, 1983.

James, T.G.H., *Howard Carter. The Path to Tutankhamun*. London, 1992.

James, T.G.H., "Howard Carter and Mrs Kingsmill Marrs", in *Studies in Honor of William Kelly Simpson*. Boston, 1996.

Jones, D., *Model boats from the Tomb of Tut'ankhamūn*. Oxford, 1990.

Kitchen, K.A., *Pharaoh Triumphant. The Life and times of Ramesses II*. Warminster, 1982.

Kitchen, K.A., *Ramesside Inscriptions*. Vol. I *Ramesses I Sethos I and Contemporaries*: Texts, Oxford, 1968-9; Translation, Oxford 1993; Annotations, Oxford, 1993.

Kitchen, K.A., Vol. II, *Ramesses II, Royal Inscriptions*: Texts, Oxford, 1969-1979; Translation, Oxford, 1996; Annotations, Oxford, 1999.

Kitchen, K.A., Vol. III, *Ramesses II. His Contemporaries*: Texts, Oxford, 1978-80; Translations, Oxford 2000; Annotations, forthcoming.

Leek, F.F., *The Human remains from the Tomb of Tut'ankhamūn*. Oxford, 1977.

Littauer, M.A. and J.H. Crowel, *Chariots and related equipment from the Tomb of Tut'ankhamūn*. Oxford, 1985.

Lucas, A. and J.R. Harris, *Ancient Egyptian Materials and Industries*. 4th ed. London, 1962.

Manniche, L., *Musical instruments from the Tomb of Tut'ankhamūn*. Oxford, 1976.

Martin, G.T., *The Amarna Period and its aftermath. A Check-list of publications*. London, 1987.

Martin, G.T., *The Menphite Tomb of Horemheb*, London, 1990.

Martin, G.T., *The Royal Tomb at El-Amarna*. 2 Vols. London, 1974, 1989.

McLeod, W., *Composite bows from the Tomb of Tut'ankhamūn*. Oxford, 1970.

McLeod, W., *Self bows and others archery tackle from the Tomb of Tut'ankhamūn*. Oxford, 1982.

Menu, B., *Ramesses the Great. Warrior and Builder*. London and New York, 1999.

Murnane, W.J., *Ancient Egyptian coregencies*. Chicago, 1977.

Murnane, W.J., *The Road to Kadesh*. Chicago, 1985.

Murray, H. and M. Nuttall, *A Handlist of Howard Carter's catalogue of objects in Tut'ankhamūn's Tomb*. Oxford, 1963.

Naville, E. and others, *The Temple of Deir el Bahari*. 6 Vols. London, 1895-1908.

Piankoff, A., *The Shrines of Tut-ankh-Amon*. New York, 1955.

Reeves, (C) N., *The Complete Tutankhamun*. London, 1990.

Reeves, N., *The Valley of the Kings. The decline of a royal necropolis*. London, 1990.

Reeves, N. and J.H. Taylor, *Howard Carter before Tutankhamun*. London, 1992.

Reeves, N. and R.H. Wilkinson, *The Complete Valley of the Kings*. London, 1996.

Tait, W.J., *Game-box and accessories from the Tomb of Tut'ankhamūn*. Oxford, 1982.

Tanis, *L'Or des pharaons*. Exhibition Catalogue. Paris, 1987.

Tyldesley, J., *Ramesses. Egypt's greatest Pharaoh*. London, 2000.

Weeks, K.R. *The Lost tomb. The greatest discovery at the Valley of the Kings since Tutankhamen*. London, 1998.

Weeks, K.R., ed., *Valley of the Kings. The Tombs and Funeral Temples of Thebes West*. Vercelli, 2001.

Wilkinson, A., *Ancient Egyptian Jewellery*. London, 1971.

Winlock, H.E., *Materials used at the embalming of King Tût-'ankh-Amūn*. New York, 1941.

Winstone, H.V.F., *Howard Carter and the discovery of the tomb of Tutankhamun*. London, 1991.

PHOTOGRAPHIC CREDITS

Drawing by Angelo Colombo/Archivio White Star: page 1.
Araldo De Luca/Archivio White Star: page 2.
Marcello Bertinetti/Archivio White Star: page 3.
Araldo De Luca/Archivio White Star: page 4.
Alfio Garozzo/Archivio White Star: page 5.
Araldo De Luca/Archivio White Star: pages 6, 7.
Giulio Veggi/Archivio White Star: page 8.
Araldo De Luca/Archivio White Star: pages 10-11, 12-13, 14, 15, 16-17, 18, 19, 20, 21, 22, 23, 24, 25, 26, 27, 28, 29, 30, 31, 32, 33, 34, 35, 36, 37, 38, 39, 40, 41, 42, 43, 44, 45.
Suzanne Held: page 46 top left.
Photobank: page 46 top right.
Alberto Siliotti: pages 46 left, 46-47, 47 top, 48, 49.
Giovanni Dagli Orti: page 47 bottom.
Araldo De Luca/ Archivio White Star: pages 48, 49, 50.
Museum Oxford: page 51.
The British Museum: page 52.
Museum Oxford: pages 53, 54, 55, 56, 57, 58-59.
Araldo De Luca/Archivio White Star: pages 56, 57, 58, 59, 60, 61, 62, 63.
Museum Oxford: pages 64, 65, 66, 67, 68, 69, 70, 71, 72, 73, 74, 75.
News International Associated Services: page 76 left top and center.
Griffith Institute, Ashmolean Museum Oxford: pages 76 left bottom, 76 right, 76-77, 77, 78, 79, 80, 81.
Araldo De Luca/Archivio White Star: pages 82, 83, 84, 85, 86, 87, 88, 89, 90, 91, 92 top.
Andrea Jemolo: page 92 bottom.
Araldo De Luca/Archivio

White Star: pages 93, 94, 95.
Henri Stierlin: pages 96-97.
Araldo De Luca/Archivio White Star: pages 98, 99, 100, 101, 102, 103, 104, 105.
Antonio Attini/Archivio White Star: pages 106-107.
Araldo De Luca/Archivio White Star: pages 108, 109, 110, 111, 112, 113, 114, 115, 116, 117, 118, 119, 120, 121, 122, 123, 124, 125, 126, 127, 128, 129, 130, 131, 132, 133, 134, 135, 136, 137,138, 139, 140, 141, 142, 142, 143, 144, 145, 146, 147, 148, 149, 150, 151, 152, 153, 154, 155, 156, 157, 158, 159, 160, 161, 162, 163, 164, 165, 166, 167, 168, 169, 170, 171, 172, 173, 174, 175, 176, 177, 178, 179, 180, 181, 182, 183, 184, 185, 186, 187, 188, 189, 190, 191, 192, 193, 194, 195, 196, 197, 198, 199, 200, 201, 202, 203, 204, 205, 206 left.
Henri Stierlin: pages 206 right.
Araldo De Luca/Archivio White Star: pages 207, 208, 209, 210, 211, 212, 213, 214, 215, 216, 217, 218, 219, 220, 221, 222, 223, 224, 225, 226, 227, 228, 229, 230, 231, 232, 233, 234, 235, 236, 237, 238, 239, 240, 241, 242, 243, 244, 245, 246, 247, 248, 249, 250, 251, 252, 253, 254, 255, 256, 257, 258, 259, 260, 261, 262, 263, 264, 265, 266, 267, 268, 269, 270, 271, 272, 273, 274, 275, 276, 277, 278, 279, 280, 281, 282, 283, 284, 285, 286, 287, 288, 289, 290, 291, 292, 293, 294, 295, 296, 297, 298, 299, 300, 301, 302, 303, 304, 305, 306, 307, 308, 309, 310, 311, 312, 313, 314, 315, 316, 317, 318, 319, 320, 321, 322, 323, 324-325, 326-327.

Hervè Lewandowski/ Photo RMN: page 328.
Araldo De Luca/ Archivio White Star: page 329.
Alfio Garozzo/Archivio White Star: page 330, 331.
Araldo De Luca/Archivio White Star: pages 332-335.
Alfio Garozzo/Archivio White Star: pages 336-337.
Araldo De Luca/Archivio White Star: pages 338-339.
Alfio Garozzo/Archivio White Star: pages 340, 341.
R.& V./Contrasto: pages 342 top, 342-343 center.
Photos12: pages 343 top left, 343 bottom left.
Giulio Veggi/Archivio White Star: page 343 right.
T.G.H. James: pages 344 top right, 344 top left.
Archivio Images Service: pages 344-345.
British Museum: page 345 top.
Archivio White Star: pages 346 top, 346 bottom, 347 left.
Antonio Attini/Archivio White Star: page 347 right.
Alfio Garozzo/Archivio White Star: pages 348, 349.
Archivio White Star: pages 350, 351, 352.
Alberto Siliotti/Archivio Geodia: page 353 top left.
Archivio White Star: page 353 top right.
T.G.H. James: page 354.
Alfio Garozzo/Archivio White Star: pages 358-359.
Araldo De Luca/Archivio White Star: pages 360, 361.
Archivio White Star: pages 362-363.
Araldo De Luca/Archivio White Star: page 364 left.

Hervè Lewandowski/ Photo RMN: pages 364 top right, 364 bottom right.
Araldo De Luca/Archivio White Star: pages 365, 366 top left.
Chuzeville/Photo RMN: page 366 top right.
Archivio Scala: pages 366-367.
B. Hatala/Photo RMN: page 367 left.
Araldo De Luca/Archivio White Star: page 367 right.
Alfio Garozzo/Archivio White Star: page 368.
Antonio Attini/Archivio White Star: page 369 left.
Araldo De Luca/Archivio White Star: pages 369 right, 370, 371, 372-373, 374, 375.
Archivio White Star: page 376.
Araldo De Luca/Archivio White Star: page 377.
Alfio Garozzo/Archivio White Star: page 378 left.
Antonio Attini/Archivio White Star: pages 378 top right, 378 center right.
Archivio White Star: pages 378-379.
Hervè Lewandowski/ Photo RMN: page 379 bottom.
Archivio White Star: page 380 bottom.
Alfio Garozzo/Archivio White Star: pages 380-381, 381.
Archivio White Star: pages 382, 382-383, 383 bottom.
Alfio Garozzo/Archivio White Star: pages 384-385, 385 top.
Antonio Attini/Archivio White Star: pages 385 right, 386 top.
Archivio White Star: pages 386-387, 387.
Antonio Attini/ Archivio White Star: pages 388, 389, 390 top, 390 center.

British Museum: page 390 bottom.
Antonio Attini/Archivio White Star: page 391.
Araldo De Luca/Archivio White Star: page 392.
Archivio White Star: page 393.
Hervè Lewandowski /RMN: page 394 bottom.
Archivio White Star: pages 394-395.
Araldo De Luca/Archivio White Star: pages 396-397.
Archivio White Star: pages 397, 398, 399.
Antonio Attini/Archivio White Star: page 400.
Archivio White Star: page 401.
Hadiye Cangokce-Cem Cetin: pages 402, 403, 404 top, 404 center.
Ekrem Akurgal: pages 404-405.
Archivio White Star: pages 406, 407.
Araldo De Luca/Archivio White Star: pages 408-409.
Alfio Garozzo/Archivio White Star: pages 410-411.
Archivio White Star: pages 410 center, 410 bottom.
Alfio Garozzo/Archivio White Star: page 412.
Archivio White Star: pages 412-413, 413 bottom.
Araldo De Luca/Archivio White Star: pages 414, 415, 416-417.
Archivio White Star: page 418.
Araldo De Luca/Archivio White Star: pages 419-422.
Archivio White Star: pages 423, 424-425.
Araldo De Luca/Archivio White Star: pages 425 top, 425 bottom, 426.
Archivio White Star: pages 427, 428-429.
Araldo De Luca/Archivio White Star: pages 430, 431, 432-433.

Archivio White Star: pages 433 top, 433 bottom, 434-435.

Araldo De Luca/Archivio White Star: page 436.

Archivio White Star: pages 437, 438-439.

Araldo De Luca/Archivio White Star: page 440 top.

Antonio Attini/Archivio White Star: page 440 bottom.

Araldo De Luca/Archivio White Star: pages 440-441, 442.

Archivio White Star: page 443.

Antonio Attini/Archivio White Star: page 444.

British Museum: page 445.

Alfio Garozzo/Archivio White Star: page 446.

Drawing by Angelo Colombo/Archivio White Star: page 446 bottom.

Alfio Garozzo/Archivio White Star: pages 446-447, 447, 448-449, 448.

Antonio Attini/Archivio White Star: pages 449 center left, 449 center right, 449 bottom right, 449 bottom left.

Drawing by Angelo Colombo/Archivio White Star: page 450 top right.

Alfio Garozzo/Archivio White Star: pages 450 center, 450 bottom, 450-451.

Giulio Veggi/Archivio White Star: page 451 bottom.

Alfio Garozzo/Archivio White Star: pages 452, 453.

Marcello Bertinetti/Archivio White Star: pages 454-455.

Alfio Garozzo/Archivio White Star: page 454 bottom.

Drawing by Angelo Colombo/Archivio White Star: page 454 bottom.

Marcello Bertinetti/Archivio White Star: page 455.

Giulio Veggi/Archivio White Star: pages 456 top, 456 center.

Marcello Bertinetti/Archivio White Star: page 456 bottom.

Giulio Veggi/Archivio White Star: pages 456-457.

Marcello Bertinetti/Archivio White Star: page 458.

Alfio Garozzo/Archivio White Star: page 459 top.

Antonio Attini/Archivio White Star: page 459 bottom.

Marcello Bertinetti/Archivio White Star: page 460 top.

Alfio Garozzo/Archivio White Star: page 460 left.

Antonio Attini/Archivio White Star: page 460 right.

Alfio Garozzo/Archivio White Star: pages 461, 462.

Giulio Veggi/Archivio White Star: page 463.

Marcello Bertinetti/Archivio White Star: page 464.

Drawing by Angelo Colombo/Archivio White Star: page 464 top.

Marcello Bertinetti/Archivio White Star: pages 464-465.

Giulio Veggi/Archivio White Star: page 465 bottom.

Antonio Attini/Archivio White Star: page 466 top.

Marcello Bertinetti/Archivio White Star: pages 466 bottom, 467.

Alfio Garozzo/Archivio White Star: page 468 top.

Marcello Bertinetti/Archivio White Star: page 468 bottom.

Alfio Garozzo/Archivio White Star: pages 468-469, 471.

Marcello Bertinetti/Archivio White Star: pages 472-473.

Archivio White Star: page 472 bottom.

Drawing by Angelo Colombo/Archivio White Star: page 472 bottom left.

Marcello Bertinetti/Archivio White Star: page 473 top.

Archivio White Star: page 473 bottom.

Antonio Attini/Archivio White Star: page 474 top.

Marcello Bertinetti/Archivio White Star: page 474 bottom right.

Alfio Garozzo/Archivio White Star: pages 474-475.

Marcello Bertinetti/Archivio White Star: page 475 bottom left.

Alfio Garozzo/Archivio White Star: page 475 bottom right.

Antonio Attini/Archivio White Star: pages 476, 477 top, 477 center.

Archivio White Star: page 477 left and right.

Antonio Attini/Archivio White Star: pages 478-479.

Alfio Garozzo/Archivio White Star: page 480.

British Museum: page 481 top.

Antonio Attini/Archivio White Star: page 481 bottom.

Alfio Garozzo/Archivio White Star: pages 482 left, 482-483.

Marcello Bertinetti/Archivio White Star: page 482 bottom.

Drawing by Angelo Colombo/Archivio White Star: page 482 bottom left.

Alfio Garozzo/Archivio White Star: pages 483, 484, 485, 486, 487.

Hervè Lewandowski/Photo RMN: page 488 right.

Gerard Blot/Photo RMN: page 488 left.

Araldo De Luca/Archivio White Star: pages 488 bottom left, 489.

Alfio Garozzo/Archivio White Star: pages 490, 491, 492 top, 492-493, 492 bottom, 493 right, 493 left, 493 center.

Antonio Attini/Archivio White Star: page 493 top.

Drawing by Angelo Colombo/Archivio White Star: page 494 bottom.

Marcello Bertinetti/Archivio White Star: pages 494-495.

Antonio Attini/Archivio White Star: page 495 bottom.

Giulio Veggi/Archivio White Star: page 496.

Araldo De Luca/Archivio White Star: page 497.

Marcello Bertinetti/Archivio White Star: pages 498-499.

Antonio Attini/Archivio White Star: page 498 bottom.

Alfio Garozzo/Archivio White Star: page 499 right.

Drawing by Angelo Colombo/Archivio White Star: page 499 bottom.

Araldo De Luca/Archivio White Star: page 500.

Antonio Attini/Archivio White Star: pages 500-501.

Araldo De Luca/Archivio White Star: pages 502, 503, 504, 505, 506, 507, 508, 509, 510, 511, 512, 513, 514.

Antonio Attini/Archivio White Star: page 515.

Araldo De Luca/Archivio White Star: pages 516, 517.

Marcello Bertinetti/Archivio White Star: page 518 top.

Alfio Garozzo/Archivio White Star: pages 518-519.

Antonio Attini/Archivio White Star: pages 520, 521.

Alfio Garozzo/Archivio White Star: page 522.

Archivio White Star: page 523.

Araldo De Luca/Archivio White Star: pages 524-525, 525.

Alfio Garozzo/Archivio White Star: pages 526, 527.

Marcello Bertinetti/Archivio White Star: pages 528, 529.

Giulio Veggi/Archivio White Star: page 530.

Marcello Bertinetti/Archivio White Star: page 531.

Antonio Attini/Archivio White Star: pages 532-533.

Araldo De Luca/Archivio White Star: pages 534, 535, 536, 537.

Marcello Bertinetti/Archivio White Star: page 538.

Antonio Attini/Archivio White Star: page 539.

Araldo De Luca/Archivio White Star: page 541 right.

Antonio Attini/Archivio White Star: page 541 left.

Araldo De Luca/Archivio White Star: page 542.

Drawing by Angelo Colombo/Archivio White Star: page 542 bottom.

Marcello Bertinetti/Archivio White Star: pages 542-543, 543 bottom.

Araldo De Luca/Archivio White Star: pages 544, 545, 546, 547, 548, 549, 550, 551.

Drawing by Elena Tagliabò/Archivio White Star: page 552 bottom.

Araldo De Luca/Archivio White Star: pages 552-553, 553, 554, 555, 556, 557, 558 left.

Marcello Bertinetti/Archivio White Star: pages 558 right, 559 bottom.

Giulio Veggi/Archivio White Star: page 560.

Marcello Bertinetti/Archivio White Star: page 562.

Antonio Attini/Archivio White Star: page 563.

Araldo De Luca/Archivio White Star: page 564 left.

Alfio Garozzo/Archivio White Star: pages 564-565.

Antonio Attini/Archivio White Star: pages 566-567.

Drawing by Theban Mapping Project: page 568 bottom.

Kenneth Garrett: pages 568-569.

Francis Dzikowski and the Theban Mapping Project: page 569.

Louvre/Photo RMN: page 570 right.

Hervè Lewandowski/ Photo RMN: page 570 left.

Chuzeville/Photo RMN: pages 570-571, 572 top.

Hervè Lewandowski/ Photo RMN: page 572 bottom.

Araldo De Luca/ Archivio White Star: page 573.

Hervè Lewandowski/ Photo RMN: pages 574 left, 574 right.

Araldo De Luca/Archivio White Star: pages 574-575.

Archivio White Star: pages 576, 577.

Antonio Attini/Archivio White Star: page 578.

Araldo De Luca/Archivio White Star: pages 579, 580 left.

Chuzeville/Photo RMN: page 580 right.

Louvre/Photo RMN: page 581.

Ch. Larrieu/Photo RMN: page 582 top.

Chuzeville/Photo RMN: page 582 bottom.

Hervè Lewandowski/ Photo RMN: pages 583.

Araldo De Luca/ Archivio White Star: pages 584, 585.

British Museum: page 587.

Araldo De Luca/Archivio White Star: page 589.

Hervè Lewandowski/ Photo RMN: page 590.

British Museum: page 591.

Archivio White Star: page 592.

Antonio Attini/Archivio White Star: page 593.

Archivio White Star: page 594.

Araldo De Luca/Archivio White Star: page 595.

Marcello Bertinetti/ Archivio White Star: pages 596-597.

B. Datala/Photo RMN: pages 598-599.

Araldo De Luca/Archivio White Star: page 599.

Antonio Attini/Archivio White Star: pages 600-601.

Araldo De Luca/Archivio White Star: pages 600 bottom, 601.

Alfio Garozzo/Archivio White Star: page 602.

Antonio Attini/Archivio White Star: page 603.

Drawing by Paola Furbatto/ Archivio White Star: page 604 bottom.

Araldo De Luca/Archivio White Star: pages 604-605.

Francis Dzikowski and the Theban Mapping Project: page 605 top.

Araldo De Luca/Archivio White Star: page 605 bottom left.

Francis Dzikowski and the Theban Mapping Project: page 605 bottom right.

Araldo De Luca/Archivio White Star: page 606.

Francis Dzikowski and the Theban Mapping Project: page 607.

Yann Rantier-CNRS: page 608.

Chuzeville/Photo RMN: page 609 top.

Archivio Scala: page 609 bottom.

Marcello Bertinetti/ Archivio White Star: page 610.

Araldo De Luca/Archivio White Star: page 611 top.

Araldo De Luca/Archivio White Star: page 611 bottom.

Archivio White Star: pages 612, 613.

Araldo De Luca/Archivio White Star: pages 614, 615, 616, 617, 618, 619.

Archivio White Star: pages 620, 621, 622, 623.

B. Hatala/Photo RMN: page 624.

Antonio Attini/Archivio White Star: page 627.

Archivio Scala: page 629.

Archivio White Star: page 630.

Cover: *left* - The broken head of a colossal statue of Ramesses II in Luxor. © *Marcello Bertinetti/Archivio White Star*
right - Funerary mask belonging to Tutankhamun. © *Araldo de Luca/Archivio White Star*

Backcover: Detail of the statue of Ramesses II in front of the Cairo railway station, showing an arm with an armlet made up of royal cartouches with protective cobras. © *Alfio Garozzo/ Archivio White Star*

ACKNOWLEDGMENTS

The publishers would like to thank:

H.E. Farouk Hosny, The Egyptian Minister of Culture;
Zahi Hawass, Secretary General of the Supreme Council for Antiquities;
Sabry Abd El Aziz Khater, General Director of Antiquities of Luxor and Upper Egypt;
Mohamed A. El-Bialy, General Director of Antiquities of Thebes West;
Kent Weeks;
Mohamed Saleh – Former Director of the Egyptian Museum in Cairo;
Mohammed Shimi – Director of the Egyptian Museum in Cairo;
Dr Taha Abd Elaleem – President of the Egyptian Information Center;
Apya Shakran – Director General of the Cairo Press Center;
Gamal Shafik of the Cairo Press Center for the organization of the photographic assignment;
The staff and the curators of the Egyptian Museum in Cairo;

Dr Jaromir Malek, Dr Diana Magee and Elizabeth Miles of the Griffith Institute, Oxford;
Christian Leblanc;
Ashmolean Museum;
Bodleian Library, Department of Western Manuscript, Oxford;
Tanya Watkins of the British Museum, Dept. of Egyptian Antiquities, London;
CNRS Phototeque, Paris;
Robert Partridge of the Egypt Picture Library;
Rebecca Akhan of the Metropolitan Museum of Art, New York;
Musèe du Louvre, Dpt. des Antiquites Orientales, Paris;
Cristiana Morigi Govi of the Museo Civico, Bologna;
Matilde Borla of the Museo Egizio, Turin;
Hikmet Denizli of the Museum of Anatolian Civilization, Ankara;
Carla Hosein of the Oriental Institute, Chicago University;
Patricia Spencer of the The Egypt Exploration Society;
Steven Snape of the University of Liverpool;
Abbas Ataman;
Ersu Pekin;
Alessandro Cocconi and Guido Paradisi - photography assistant.